Property Rites

ELIZABETH M. SMITH-PRYOR

Property Rites

THE RHINELANDER TRIAL, PASSING,

AND THE PROTECTION OF WHITENESS

THE UNIVERSITY OF NORTH CAROLINA PRESS : CHAPEL HILL

© 2009
Elizabeth M. Smith-Pryor
All rights reserved

*Manufactured in the United
States of America*

Designed by Courtney Leigh Baker
Set in Whitman by Keystone Typesetting, Inc.

The paper in this book meets the guidelines for permanence and durability of the Committee on Production Guidelines for Book Longevity of the Council on Library Resources.

The University of North Carolina Press has been a member of the Green Press Initiative since 2003.

Library of Congress Cataloging-in-Publication Data
Smith-Pryor, Elizabeth M.
Property rites : the Rhinelander trial, passing, and the protection of whiteness / Elizabeth M. Smith-Pryor.
　p. cm.
Includes bibliographical references and index.
978-0-8078-3268-4 (cloth: alk. paper)
978-0-8078-5939-1 (pbk.: alk. paper)
　1. Rhinelander, Leonard Kip—Trials, litigation, etc.
　2. Jones, Alice Beatrice—Trials, litigation, etc.
　3. Trials (Divorce)—New York (State)—Westchester County. 4. Marriage—Annulment—New York (State)—Westchester County. 5. Interracial marriage—New York (State)—Westchester County.
　6. Scandals—New York (State)—Westchester County. I. Title.
KF228.R486S65　2009
346.747′770166—dc22
2008047143

CLOTH　13 12 11 10 09　5 4 3 2 1
PAPER　13 12 11 10 09　5 4 3 2 1

THIS BOOK WAS DIGITALLY PRINTED

to Richard

Contents

Acknowledgments xi

Introduction 1

ONE : Curious Acts 11

TWO : "All Mixed Up" in New York 40

THREE : The Trial Begins 59

FOUR : Passing and the "Seemingly Absurd Question" of Race 89

FIVE : Defending the Citadel of Whiteness from the "Awful Stain" 112

SIX : The Trial Continues: Degeneracy, Modern Love, and "Filthy Letters" 133

SEVEN : "Poor Little Cupid" and the
Marriage Contract 157

EIGHT : Blind Love and the Visibility of Race 184

NINE : The Trial Ends 213

Conclusion 239

Notes 253

Bibliography 341

Index 373

Illustrations

"His Colored Bride" 30

Courtroom scene 60

Leonard Kip Rhinelander and his attorneys 64

Lee Parsons Davis 74

"Marriage and the Color Line" 126

Leonard Rhinelander on the
witness stand 139

Alice Jones Rhinelander and her sisters 188

Composograph: "Alice Disrobes in Court
to Keep Her Husband" 205

Alice Jones Rhinelander and her parents 230

Alice Jones Rhinelander 232

Acknowledgments

THIS BOOK has taken a much longer time to write than I expected—thank goodness I continued to find the story of Leonard and Alice Rhinelander fascinating. During the years I have worked on this project I have accumulated a number of debts and I am grateful to have this opportunity to appreciate the many people who have helped me along the way. At Rutgers University, my research benefited from the insightful comments of Deborah Gray White, David Levering Lewis, and Joan Wallach Scott. Nell Irvin Painter, Alice Kessler-Harris, and Jennifer Jones also provided very helpful suggestions at an earlier stage of this project. During my time in New Jersey, my work benefited from the financial support of the Ford Foundation.

While at Kent State University, my work on this study has benefited from the support of my colleagues in the history department. I also received a one-semester research leave from Kent State's Research and Graduate Studies, which helped facilitate the writing of this manuscript. I have greatly benefited from the helpful staffs at a variety of libraries. I especially thank the staffs at Alexander Library at Rutgers University, the New York Public Library, the National Archives, and the Kent State University Library. I also thank my friend Rebecca Pressman, lawyer and librarian, for conducting additional research for me in New York courthouses.

I have also learned a great deal from the many people who have read bits and pieces of what became this book over the years, including my former colleague Nikki Brown and my current colleague Richard Steigmann-Gall.

Kevin Boyle read the entire manuscript and provided helpful comments. I thank him for taking the time out of his busy life to help out someone whom he has never met. In addition, I thank Hendrik Hartog for his comments on an earlier version of the book manuscript. Thank you to my Kent State colleague Ann Heiss for reading an early version of the manuscript and providing me with very productive feedback. I also thank Rebekah Cotton and Daniel Boomhower for reading the manuscript and providing valuable comments. In addition, the insightful comments and questions of Peggy Pascoe and Jane Dailey for UNC Press have greatly improved this manuscript and helped me clarify my arguments.

During the years I have worked on the story of the Rhinelander trial, I have had two children: Richard and Grace. This book could never have been completed without the help of the many people who have taken care of my children at times when I have needed to work. When we lived in New Jersey, my mother, Patricia Einbond, took wonderful care of my son Richard. While at Kent State, I have been able to teach, research, and write knowing my children are well taken care of at the university's Child Development Center. I truly thank the wonderful and caring teachers my children have had at the CDC over the years: Felicia Black, Nancy Condit, Jodi Monaco, and Carolyn Galizio, in addition to the many wonderful student teachers who work at the CDC. I also thank the many college students at Rutgers University and at Kent State who also took care of Richard and Grace. I thank my two children for putting up with their mother working on a book that she won't let them read until they're grownups!

Thank you to the many friends, especially in Kent, who have made my time here a happy one: Lisa and Richard Steigmann-Gall, Bekah and Chris Cotton, Elizabeth Culotta and Hans Thewissen, Keely and Dan Boomhower, and Abbe and Anderson Turner.

I also thank my family, particularly my mother, Patricia Einbond, and her husband, Jeffrey Einbond, for their support over the years. I also thank my mother for agreeing to drive to Long Island to locate documents from the Nassau County Surrogate's Court. My father, David Smith, will likely never read this, but I thank him for the many interesting discussions about the meaning of race in America. I am sorry that my in-laws, Richard and Mary Pryor, are no longer alive to read this. Both Dick and Mary proved very supportive of my decision to attend graduate school in history, and they were always interested in hearing about the progress of my book.

Most especially, I thank my husband, Richard, for the tremendous amount of support he has given me over the years. When I left the practice of law to return to graduate school, he supported me and made it possible for us to give up a lawyer's income. He has listened to me talk about the Rhinelanders for more than a decade, and he has never told me to stop. More importantly, he has helped me think through my ideas and arguments. Richard is also a superb editor, and this book is much the better for his wise suggestions and comments. He has also done some of the more tedious work related to producing a book, such as tracking down the copyright holders of images. This book and my life would not be the same without him.

Property Rites

Introduction

It is obvious . . . that the Rhinelander case is of great social significance in America for several reasons, some of which are related to the swiftly changing status of the Negro in the American nation. The past ten years have wrought something like a racial revolution in the United States. The rapid industrialisation of the South, coupled with the steady northward migration of the Negro, in response for the demand for labour in the great cities consequent upon the limiting of immigration from Europe, is causing a transformation of the economic map. Of the twelve million Negroes in the country a great part are earning the wages of white men. They are buying land and property in every city. . . . In the great cities of the North . . . the Negro community has become a social and political unit to be seriously reckoned with. . . . Along with this remarkable economic advance there goes, of course, an intensified racial consciousness. And it is in relation to that consciousness, of social position and racial inferiority, that the Rhinelander case would seem to possess an historic importance.—"Black and White in New York," *New Statesman*, 5 December 1925

SOCIETY DAZED AT RHINELANDER NUPTIAL NEWS
—*New York Daily News*, 14 November 1924

BRIDE OF RHINELANDER ONCE CALLED MULATTO
—*New York Daily News*, 15 November 1924

RHINELANDER SUES TO ANNUL MARRIAGE; ALLEGES RACE DECEIT
—*New York Times*, 27 November 1924

RHINELANDER COLORED BRIDE SUIT BEGINS

—*New York Evening Journal*, 9 November 1925

LOVE LETTERS READ IN COURT

—*New York Amsterdam News*, 11 November 1925

ALICE BARES BODY, LETTERS READ; WOMEN OUSTED

—*New York Daily News*, 24 November 1925

DEATH BETTER FOR KIP MILLS'S COLOR TRIAL PLEA

—*New York Daily News*, 3 December 1925

ON A COLD, SUNNY DAY in early November of 1925, a young husband and wife separately entered a courthouse in Westchester County, New York, accompanied by their lawyers. They had traveled to downtown White Plains to learn whether their yearlong marriage would be ended. The husband, twenty-two-year-old Leonard Kip Rhinelander, had first brought suit to annul the marriage one year earlier, only one month after his civil wedding to Alice Beatrice Jones in October of 1924. In the legal documents that started his lawsuit, Leonard Rhinelander, the youngest son of a wealthy New York family, complained that Alice Jones had lied to lure him into marriage. Leonard claimed that before their marriage, Alice told him she was white and not "colored," although, according to Leonard's legal papers, she possessed "colored blood in her veins." In Alice's response to Leonard's charges, the twenty-five-year-old former domestic servant denied all of her husband's allegations and fought strenuously to keep her husband from dissolving their marriage in a court of law.[1]

Leonard Rhinelander's accusations about his wife's color spurred a massive public interest in the couple that began in 1924 and extended beyond their annulment trial in 1925. Public fascination with the couple, their marriage, their separations, and the trial reflected, in part, a contemporary interest in the subject of racial passing expressed in an outburst of literary and nonfiction treatments of the topic. Some interest in the story surely only came from a prurient fascination with the problems of the rich. Yet the issues at stake in the Rhinelander annulment trial spoke to much broader concerns.

This book is a narrative history of the Rhinelander annulment trial.[2] In the following chapters, I tell how Leonard Rhinelander and Alice Jones met, courted, married, and separated. I also tell the story of the dramatic twists and turns of the ensuing legal battle initiated after the newspapers publicized the marriage of a New York "aristocrat" and a maid. While this book describes the making of an intimate relationship and its subsequent destruction in a crowded courtroom, it also recounts simultaneously the history of a particular place in time, the American North of the 1920s. Making sense of the Rhinelanders' story requires making sense of the convergence of historically specific factors closely linked to their narratives. For this reason, the account that follows connects to a number of important themes in early-twentieth-century history: the impact of the Great Migration of African Americans on northern states, American responses to immigration, class conflict, the rise of mass consumption, anxiety over the state of "modern marriage," and the growth of racial consciousness.

Contemporaries recognized the larger social significance of *Rhinelander v. Rhinelander* in a way they did not regarding most other popular trials of the era. Many other scandalous cases in the 1920s involved the steamy marital difficulties of the famous, the rich, and the wealthy. To a historian's eyes, however, the Rhinelander trial bears comparison with the best-known trial of the 1920s, the infamous Scopes "monkey trial." Both trials took place in 1925, and each ended up as a top-ten news story of the year.[3] Merely generating a flood of printer's ink, however, does not make a trial or any news story historically significant, no matter how dramatic or gripping it seems at the time. If that were the case, we would all know a great deal about the story of "super-criminal" Gerald Chapman's 1925 murder trial. My review of the substantial amount of newsprint devoted to the Rhinelanders in the 1920s suggests that this trial, like the *Scopes* case, and unlike the trial of Gerald Chapman, revolved around issues that spoke deeply to Americans in the 1920s. A thorough analysis of the Rhinelander trial offers us the opportunity to closely examine and understand the way that Americans responded to change in the 1920s.[4]

Yet newspaper accounts of the Rhinelander trial can provide only part of the story. Any effort to extricate the multiple meanings of the Rhinelander trial requires examining its legal issues. And as a former practicing lawyer, my analysis of the voluminous trial transcript, the legal pleadings, and the legal briefs filed on appeal of the *Rhinelander* case led me to the realization that focusing on the law and legal procedure generates a host of key questions. I kept returning to one question in particular, a question that lacked an obvious answer. How could a case like this have taken place in New York? New York had never had a law to prohibit interracial marriages. Indeed, my own parents, a mixed-race couple, had been married in New York in 1962—a good five years before the U.S. Supreme Court declared in *Loving v. Virginia* such laws (then still in effect in sixteen states including Virginia) unconstitutional.[5] Although my parents had experienced some familial and community disapproval of their marriage, they could still legally marry even before the *Loving* decision. So, how could Leonard Rhinelander try to end his marriage to his wife Alice on the grounds that she lied about her race?

In addition to the absence of any New York law that restricted marriages between the races, public policy in New York supported the preservation, not the dissolution, of marriages. Up until the 1960s, New York State possessed strict rules on ending a marriage; courts granted divorces only in instances of adultery. Unlike the laws of many other states, nothing in New York's laws on marriage (including provisions for divorce and annulment) said anything about race. It would be understandable if a claim like Leonard's had appeared in a court in South Carolina or Mississippi or Virginia. But New York?[6]

The very fact that Leonard Rhinelander filed a lawsuit to end his marriage on the grounds of fraudulent misrepresentation of race and color suggested that race did matter for marriage in New York in the 1920s, both in the realm of public and familial opinion and in New York State's legal system. Nothing in the Rhinelander trial transcript indicates that any person, lawyers and presiding judges included, ever asked how this case could make its way through New York's court system.[7] No member of the New York legal system ever said, "So what if Alice Rhinelander is really colored and not white? That's not a good enough reason to annul a marriage. We live in a state that doesn't prohibit marriage between the races." In New York, a court would throw out, probably before trial, a claim for an annulment based on the grounds that a person had lied about whether he or she loved his or her spouse. If a lie about love, seemingly the basis for a happy marriage, according to most observers, did not merit a trial to annul a marriage, how could a lie about whether someone was black or white do so?[8]

Yet Leonard Rhinelander's lawyers argued that if Leonard had known Alice was colored he would never have married her. They insisted that because (as they claimed) Alice had lied about being colored, Leonard was entitled to end the marriage. New York law allowed an annulment when a spouse had lied about a material fact, that is, a fact that, if it were known, would have prevented the marriage. A court's annulment of a marriage, would, moreover, create a legal fiction that the marriage had never existed. Therefore, to the court's way of thinking, if Alice lied about her racial identity before she married Leonard, Leonard was entitled to the legal dissolution of his marriage.[9] Not even Alice Rhinelander's attorney, who acted as her staunch defender, ever contested the grounds on which the case had been brought. Instead, much of the conflict between the lawyers revolved around the question of whether any fraud had taken place at all, whether Alice Jones was colored or white and, if she were colored whether Leonard had noticed.

Very early in the newspaper coverage of the Rhinelander marriage, however, an editorial writer questioned the assumption that people who belonged to different races should not marry underlying Leonard's claims. In his syndicated "Today" column, published in William Randolph Hearst's newspapers, Arthur Brisbane, one of the best-known American columnists of the early twentieth century, asked the same question I found myself asking: How could a case like this be brought in New York? Could a person of English ancestry try to end his marriage to his spouse on the grounds that she lied to him by claiming to be English but her ancestors were really Irish? No, for such a case would seem absurd on its face. So Brisbane wondered how the courts would deal with Leonard Rhinelander's claim, especially since New York did not prohibit marriage between the races.[10]

In this book, I argue that Leonard Rhinelander's case against his wife made its way through New York's judicial system and became a cause célèbre because the assumptions underlying his lawsuit dovetailed with the understandings of race and the racial ideologies that permeated 1920s America in general and New York in particular. During the 1920s, many Americans feared the advent of a "mongrelized" America and in response engaged in strenuous efforts to shore up the boundaries of race. Membership in the Ku Klux Klan rose, racial scientists searched for a sure method of distinguishing races, white restrictionists sought to limit immigration, and white homeowners sought to prevent the "invasion" of other races into "their" neighborhoods. Alice Jones Rhinelander, accused by her husband of being "colored" while pretending to be white, symbolized the chaotic future that awaited Americans if racial lines could not be clearly drawn.

In addition, Leonard's claim that Alice lied about her race suggested that she was, through marriage, attempting fraudulently to gain access to the property rights that belonged to the Rhinelanders.[11] In no small measure, the responses to the relationship between Leonard Rhinelander and Alice Jones evoke questions about the intersections of property, class, and race. The bitter court battle over their marriage can be seen as an attempt on Leonard's part, whether at the behest of his family or not, to defend the Rhinelander family's property (in forms both tangible and intangible): *their* land, *their* money, and *their* status as upper-class New Yorkers. Closely aligned with their defense of these forms of property was the Rhinelanders' efforts to protect the universal understanding that they were a white family, an identity rooted in their relationship to property (as owners), and an identity at risk if Leonard married a colored woman who could reproduce colored Rhinelander heirs.[12]

During the 1920s, the status of being white could be perceived as akin to a property interest. Indeed, in his essay "The Souls of White Folk," W. E. B. DuBois acknowledged the close connections between race and property when he observed that whites "always, somehow, some way, silently but clearly" instruct others that "whiteness is the ownership of the earth forever and ever, Amen!" Still drawing on concepts of property, he observed that race hatred followed "when the black man begins to dispute the white man's title to certain bequests of the Fathers in wage and position, authority and training." Viewing the Rhinelander trial through the lens of "whiteness as property" provides an entry point to recover the meanings of the trial and to understand why the Rhinelanders went to such efforts to separate Leonard from Alice.[13] Simultaneously, thinking about whiteness as a form of property illuminates other conflicts in the 1920s North over who could have access to real estate and public accommodations.

Writing a narrative that draws on the language of race requires paying attention to the historical specificity of race.[14] Many historians agree that American ideas about race evolved to serve a particular purpose during the era of slavery to maintain a specific form of labor system. These ideas about race supported the "property regime of slavery," that is, a system in which racial identity could categorize a person as property.[15] Once this system of forced labor ended with the South's defeat in the Civil War, the concepts of race that structured slavery could have faded away. Yet ideas about race evolved to serve a different purpose. Thus, sixty years after the end of the Civil War, when Leonard Rhinelander tried to end his marriage, the meaning of race and the links between race and property could not be, and were not, the same as in earlier historical periods.[16]

This book, then, is more than merely a narrative history of an American scandal from the 1920s. Looking closely at the Rhinelander trial allows us to examine the ways in which Americans reinvented ideas about race and racism in the American North during the era of the Great Migration. It is critical to understand the ways in which ideas about race have structured economic, political, and social life in the North throughout American history: the restriction of opportunities, the maintenance of inequalities. It is my intent for this book to contribute to and elaborate on a growing body of historical scholarship that moves the study of race and acts of racism out of its traditional American habitat—the South—and asks necessary questions about the North. In addition, the newer literature on the civil rights movement in the North, which takes as a starting point the early 1930s, confirms the need to delineate the ways northerners during and after the first Great Migration actively created and enforced racial divisions that generations of northern activists struggled against and still struggle to overcome.[17] Finally, I also hope that through the story of two people in a particular time and place, readers will also grapple with conventional contemporary understandings of race and think about what we think race is, and how we decide who belongs to what race, and the impact of those decisions. Does race still matter to Americans today in matters of love and property?[18]

In thinking about Leonard Kip Rhinelander and Alice Beatrice Jones Rhinelander, I have come to the not-surprising conclusion that it is always difficult for anyone to really have a sense of another person; what drives they have, what fears, what hopes, and what weaknesses. This is particularly true for historians, given that the people we write about are often long gone. Writers of fiction have it easier in some ways; they can describe the thoughts and emotions of their protagonists as they construct their characters. In telling the story of Leonard and Alice Rhinelander, my task has been made somewhat easier by the fact that thousands of words were written to describe them. I have read and thought about the newspaper stories, the trial transcript, and some of their courtship letters. But each of these sources on the Rhinelanders and the annulment trial possess flaws.

Newspaper accounts are obviously filtered through the perceptions and concerns of the writers and editors of the newspapers who competed for readership. In the middle of the 1920s, New York's newspaper industry was divided into two major camps: the established dailies (for example, the *New York Times* and the *New York Herald Tribune*) and the upstart tabloids (for example, the *New York Daily News* and the *New York Daily Mirror*). A heated battle took place both between and within each camp to attract readers. In addition to the tabloids and the regular newspapers, African American newspapers such as the *New York Amsterdam News* appeared weekly in New York

City and appealed to African American readers, many of whom had already read the regular dailies.[19]

Trial transcripts and the legal documents generated before and after the trial also tell the story of the Rhinelanders. But these, too, have their limitations. The trial transcript obviously only recorded what was said in court and was therefore under the control and direction of the two main lawyers for the parties, each of whom attempted to construct a narrative to put their client in the best possible light while making the opposition look as bad as possible. Throughout every stage of the legal process, from writing the initial papers to begin a lawsuit through an appeal to a higher court, all those different narratives are presented, edited, argued, contradicted, and ultimately combined into a master narrative that is nominally accepted by the courts and society as the "true" version of events.[20] Consequently, a trial transcript is composed of many, often contradictory stories. Moreover, since the transcript of the trial only includes the words taken down by the court stenographer, no complete extant record of the lawyers', the judge's, or the parties' physical performance during the trial exists. The record of the Rhinelander trial, like that of most trials in the era before television cameras began to be allowed in some courtrooms, is ultimately incomplete.

Like the newspaper accounts and the legal records of the case, Alice and Leonard's letters, while as close to revealing the unguarded thoughts of the two as any available source, were still written at least in part with ulterior motives. During their courtship, which lasted from the fall of 1921 to the fall of 1924, both Leonard and Alice wanted something from the other and each told the tales they chose in order to influence (consciously or not) the other's response. In addition, only 108 out of more than 400 letters and telegrams exchanged by the two were included as evidence during the trial. Notwithstanding these limitations, a reader of the letters can still form some basic conclusions about Leonard and Alice. No conclusion, however, can ever completely reflect the richer and more complicated reality of their inner lives.[21]

Nevertheless, I have certain ideas about Leonard and Alice based on the evidence that exists about each, including the trial testimony, newspaper reports, photographs, family history, and their letters to each other. In reading about each of these two individuals it is difficult not to feel a certain amount of pity. Leonard Rhinelander seems almost the embodiment of the clichéd "poor little rich boy." Born in 1903, he was too young, unlike his two older brothers, to serve in the Great War, where one brother died. By 1921, when he met Alice, he had also lost his mother, who had died in a freak accident in

1915. Leonard stuttered and wore glasses. He was apparently educated at home by tutors and then sent to a boarding school. And just before he turned eighteen, his father dropped him off at a Connecticut institute for nervous and mental disorders and never visited him. It says something about Leonard's social development that while in Connecticut he met Alice for the first time after taking a drive in his new car with his new friend Carl, an electrician who worked at the institute, and one of Carl's friends. It is unlikely that Leonard's father, a wealthy New York City clubman, intended Leonard to befriend electricians and maids when he sent him to Connecticut.

When Alice Jones met Leonard in 1921, she had none of Leonard's economic advantages; she worked in a series of low-paid menial jobs to earn a living. She also lacked the educational opportunities that a Rhinelander, even a girl, would have. Her letters to Leonard demonstrate her struggles with writing. Alice began working when she was still an adolescent in a variety of service jobs, such as laundress and maidservant, all of which shared the common characteristics of being low in status, paying low wages, and providing little opportunity for advancement. Nothing in the court testimony, newspaper stories, or her letters suggests that Alice was anything other than a hardworking woman stuck in a servant's job with a modest taste for excitement and, until Leonard's appearance in her life, not much of a future.

And notwithstanding the tone in some newspaper articles suggesting that Leonard and Alice had an innocent fairy-tale romance, it is clear from Alice's letters to Leonard that she was well aware that he came from money (a fact Leonard never hid from her and even boasted about in his letters). Alice's hopes expressed in her letters certainly included having access to that kind of wealth. In one letter, Alice recounted a dream in which she and Leonard kissed while he gave her "*piles* and piles, brand new ten dollar's bills. But you could not give me enough of them, and everyone of them were *brand new*. I wished it had been true." In another letter, Alice described reading the *Saturday Evening Post* and coming "across the sweet dainty house and auto, this is the style of a house Len, we must have and also the car."[22] Who could blame her for wanting a house and a car? In the 1920s, consumption of mass-produced goods like the automobile seemed to have become an American birthright. Movies that Alice may have seen, since she liked to go to the pictures, depicted upper-class lives and the surrounding trappings of wealth. Given her background of little money and a life filled with hard work, it is not surprising that Alice desired a better and more comfortable life.[23]

Alice may have taken whatever steps necessary to achieve her goal. Certainly, she hoped to make Leonard jealous. She often exaggerated other men's interest in her; she implied other men gave her gifts like rings and platinum watches. In addition, after she and Leonard had engaged in premarital sex, she claimed to have been impregnated by him and to have obtained an abortion.[24] Notwithstanding Alice's efforts to bind Leonard to her, there is no evidence that she was not fond of Leonard. Alice seems to have cared for Leonard, perhaps even loved him, as he cared for and perhaps loved her. Interestingly, while their letters to each other reveal their growing regard for each other, they do not reveal any evidence that the couple discussed, at least in writing, whether race mattered to either of them.

Leonard and Alice's seemingly real affection for each other makes all the more tragic the circumstances of the story of their marriage and its subsequent implosion. From all accounts, Leonard and Alice shared a grand total of about twelve to fifteen happy months together, interspersed over a period of three years, beginning with the time they met in September 1921 through their separation in November 1924. After that November, when newspapers revealed their previously secret marriage, Alice and Leonard's lives rapidly became very public and very miserable. By December of 1925 and the end of the annulment trial, Alice and Leonard's private letters had been ripped apart in court and denounced as pornography, members of their families had been stigmatized, Alice and Leonard's personal lives and secrets had been opened to all sorts of calumnies and public humor, and their marriage itself had been held up as a monstrosity. How and why this happened is the story told in this book.

ONE :

Curious Acts

The discovery of personal whiteness among the world's peoples is a very modern thing—a nineteenth and twentieth century matter, indeed. The ancient world would have laughed at such a distinction. The Middle Age regarded skin color with mild curiosity; and even up into the eighteenth century we were hammering our national manikins into one, great, Universal Man, with fine frenzy which ignored color and race even more than birth. Today we have changed all that, and the world in a sudden, emotional conversion has discovered that it is white and by that token, wonderful! This assumption that of all the hues of God whiteness alone is inherently and obviously better than brownness or tan leads to curious acts.
—W. E. B. DUBOIS, "The Souls of White Folk" (1920)

DRESSED ONLY IN UNDERWEAR and a long coat, a twenty-six-year-old woman entered the jury room of a New York courthouse a few days before Thanksgiving in 1925. Once inside, the young woman faced eighteen men and dropped her coat to her waist so that the men could look at her back and breasts. After the twelve jurors, the judge, the attorneys, and the court stenographer had concluded their inspection, the young woman covered herself once more. A lawyer then directed her to bare her legs from the ankles to the knees. After this second fleshy display, the men filed back into the courtroom. The young woman, weeping, wrapped again in her long coat, and supported by a matronly English woman, her mother, joined them. She took a seat at the defense table next to her lawyer, the man who had suggested and supervised the exhibition of her body. Her lawyer then questioned the young man on the witness stand who had started the lawsuit that brought them all to the courthouse that November day. The lawyer asked the man whether the woman's body appeared the same color in the jury room as it did in a hotel room a few years earlier, and the woman's husband opened his mouth to answer.[1]

The husband's reply to the question raised by the bared body of his estranged wife transformed the proceedings in the case of *Rhinelander v. Rhinelander*. The *Rhinelander* case had begun one year earlier, when Leonard Kip Rhinelander asked the New York State courts to annul his marriage to his wife, Alice Jones Rhinelander. By the time Alice Rhinelander's lawyer made her undress in the jury room of the Westchester County Supreme Court building, Americans knew that Leonard Rhinelander had accused his wife of telling him she was white. He claimed she was not. Leonard also declared that he would never have married Alice if he had known she was colored. Leonard and his lawyers argued that Alice's deception about her identity required a legal dissolution of their marriage.[2]

Only a few questions remained open at this point in the trial to determine whether a judge would annul the Rhinelander marriage: Would Leonard Rhinelander, under the persistent questioning of his wife's attorney, insist that Alice looked white and that was why he did not know she was colored before they wed? Would the jurors see Alice Rhinelander as white, or would they discern evidence of color on the body parts revealed that November day? Did the all-white male jury believe that the bodies of nonwhite women were different from white women's? The fact that Alice was subjected to this test in court in the first place, however, raises additional questions for the historian: Why did Alice's lawyer insist that his client submit to a procedure that the newspapers called "extraordinary," an "ordeal," and Alice's "Gethsemane"?[3] How did *Rhinelander v. Rhinelander* get to the point at which stripping the defendant became an acceptable tactic to keep Leonard from winning his lawsuit? What kind of marriage and relationship was at the center of this case? To begin to answer these questions, the stories of the two people in this marriage, how they met, courted, married, and separated need to be pieced together.

By the time Leonard Kip Rhinelander viewed his half-naked wife in that jury room, he was twenty-two years old. Although not particularly handsome, Leonard dressed expensively, wore spats, and sported pince-nez. He parted his light brown hair in the middle and slicked it down in the manner of Rudolph Valentino. With his fashionable hair and clothes, Leonard resembled a weak-chinned version of the "sheiks" and college men pictured in cartoons of 1920s "flaming youth." Young girls flocked to the courtroom to catch a glimpse of him. If the flappers were lucky, they might get a chance to watch Leonard smoking cigarettes during breaks.[4]

As the youngest son of Philip Rhinelander and the late Adelaide Kip Rhinelander of Manhattan, Leonard belonged to one of New York City's oldest and wealthiest families. The Rhinelanders traced their lineage to a Huguenot ancestor who came to New York in the seventeenth century, settled in New Rochelle, and bought land. Descendants of this Huguenot moved to the island of Manhattan and invested wisely in real estate. By the nineteenth century, the Rhinelander family had made a great deal of money buying and developing Manhattan properties.[5] When Leonard's great-grandfather William Christopher Rhinelander died in 1878, the family resided in a handsome home in Washington Square, a location made famous a few years later by the novels of Henry James. When William Christopher Rhinelander died, the *New York Times* reported that the value of his estate ranged between $50 to $75 million (including land, bonds, mortgages, and securities), which he bequeathed to his heirs in a special trust in which his four children (Serena, Julia, Mary, and William) each owned an equal number of shares.[6]

William Christopher's only son, Leonard's grandfather, another William, helped start New York City's Metropolitan Opera House in the 1880s. Philip Rhinelander, Leonard's father, graduated from Columbia College in 1882 and worked for the Rhinelander family's real estate interests. By 1902, the Rhinelander heirs to William's 1878 estate shifted the estate's properties to a newly created corporation: the Rhinelander Real Estate Company, with shares divided among the heirs. Only a partial listing of the vast landholdings owned by the Rhinelander Real Estate Company covered properties near Wall Street, large portions of Greenwich Village, and parts of the Upper East Side.[7]

Leonard's mother, the former Adelaide Kip, also claimed an illustrious heritage in New York's old families. Her father, Dr. Isaac Leonard Kip, came from a family that landed in Dutch New Amsterdam in 1635 and gave New York City's Kips Bay its name. Adelaide Kip's maternal grandfather had served as mayor of New York City in the mid-nineteenth century. When Leonard's grandmother, Cornelia, the daughter of the former mayor, died in 1912, she left an estate valued at over two million dollars, which included a great deal of real estate. Despite the Rhinelanders' wealth and status, tragedy befell Leonard's family during his youth. Adelaide died suddenly after suffering burns when an alcohol spirit lamp that she used to fix her hair exploded. She left behind her husband, Philip, and their four children: Philip Kip, T. J. Oakley, Adelaide, and the twelve-year-old Leonard.[8] Death revisited the Rhinelanders only three years later when one of Leonard's older brothers, T. J. Oakley, a Harvard student, died while serving in the Great War in an elite regiment of wealthy New Yorkers.[9] Life, however, started to improve for the Rhinelanders after the war. Leonard's oldest brother, Philip Kip, a 1918 Harvard graduate, survived the war, started a family, and joined his father in the family firm. Leonard's sister, Adelaide, married a banker in a lavish society wedding in the fall of 1921; a distant Rhinelander relative, an Episcopal bishop, helped officiate.[10]

Despite Leonard's family background, he did not follow the usual path set out for the men of his family and class. His two older brothers had joined the Knickerbocker Greys, a quasi-military organization for wealthy boys. Leonard, however, does not seem to have belonged.[11] A family tutor found him difficult to teach as a child, and he stuttered. In 1921, when Leonard was almost eighteen, instead of enrolling him at Harvard or Columbia, his father packed him off to a Connecticut institute for the study and treatment of nervous and mental diseases run by a prominent New York neurologist. The physicians and staff at The Orchards treated Leonard for a speech impediment and what its founder, Dr. L. Pierce Clark, diagnosed as Leonard's "great sense of inferiority." The Orchards records describe Leonard as "retiring," "timid," and having a "lack of knowledge of everyday affairs."[12] Clark's diagnosis may have reflected the state of mind of a young man who had lost both his mother and older brother at an impressionable age. Leonard's surviving parent was distant; Philip Rhinelander never visited Leonard after taking him to The Orchards. The elder Rhinelander's decision to send Leonard to Connecticut for treatment, however, would have fateful consequences for the Rhinelanders. While a resident at The Orchards in the fall of 1921, Leonard, the son of wealth and privilege, met and began to court his future wife, Alice Jones, the daughter of immigrants.[13]

Unlike the long-settled Kips and Rhinelanders, Alice Jones's family did not arrive on American shores until the end of the nineteenth century, as part of a second great wave of European immigration. In contrast to the majority of immigrants arriving in the United States at this time who hailed from Southern and Eastern Europe, Alice's father, George, and her mother, Elizabeth, came to the United States in 1891 from England. In England, George Jones had worked as a coachman on a West Yorkshire estate; Elizabeth Jones cooked for the same family. Four years after settling in Westchester, Elizabeth Jones gave birth to Alice's older sister, Emily. Alice followed in 1899. Alice's birth certificate identified her father as a "laborer." By the time Elizabeth Jones gave birth to Alice's younger sister, Grace, in 1903, George Jones had changed his occupation to "coachman and gardener."[14]

At the time of the Rhinelander trial in 1925, Alice Jones Rhinelander was twenty-six years old, almost four years older than her husband. Like Leonard, Alice was not conventionally attractive, although she had dark eyes and wore her dark brown hair in a fashionable bob parted down the middle. Alice also possessed elegantly shaped hands with long tapered fingers. Unlike the children of the Rhinelanders, Alice was not destined for either higher education or a society wedding. Instead, once Alice finished school, she followed the path of her sister Emily, working as a servant in the homes of wealthy families in Westchester. During World War I, she washed laundry at the clubhouse of the New York Athletic Club on nearby Travers Island, a physically demanding job. After the war, she continued to work as a servant for a number of different households, sometimes living in and at other times doing day work.[15]

Despite the vastly different circumstances of birth and family, Leonard Rhinelander and Alice Jones embarked on an intimate relationship that began with the switch of a ring from one girl's finger to another's in 1921.[16] In September of that year, the eighteen-year-old Leonard met Alice during the same month he bought his first automobile. One Saturday evening, Leonard, with his new friend Carl, an electrician who worked at The Orchards, and one of Carl's friends, motored south from Connecticut over the border into Westchester County. Leonard's choice of companions that evening probably would not have pleased his father. Philip Rhinelander most likely would not be happy to hear that an electrician who had managed to get Leonard to invest $600 in a business venture in which his son lost all his money had convinced Leonard to drive him around in Leonard's shiny new car.[17]

During their travels, Leonard's automobile developed minor trouble in the city of New Rochelle, in Westchester County, a residential suburb of New York City made up of small cities, towns, and villages connected to the metropolis by commuter trains and paved roads.[18] As Leonard's car slowed down, the three young men hailed a pretty young woman walking on the side of Pelham Road. They invited her to join them for a ride. At first she declined, then she changed her mind. Despite the car trouble, the four young people drove to Port Chester, about ten miles away, and then back to New Rochelle. At one point, Carl took the wheel and dropped off his friend and Leonard and took the young woman for a ride before taking her to her home. The young woman was Alice Jones's eighteen-year-old sister, Grace.[19]

The next day after this meeting, Leonard drove his roadster back to New York to find Grace Jones. He came upon her walking with her twenty-two-year-old sister, Alice, on Pelham Road. Recognizing Leonard from the day before, Grace suggested that they go to a movie and find another person to make a foursome. Grace and Alice chanced upon another young man, and the four headed in Leonard's car to a movie theater in nearby Mount Vernon. Since they could not find four seats together, Grace and Leonard paired off. Alice and the other man sat on the other side of the theater. Once seated in the dark, Leonard placed his hand on Grace's leg. She pushed it off. Despite the rebuff, Leonard asked Grace for a date the next day. He also gave Grace a star sapphire ring when he drove the two sisters back to their small, wood-framed home on an alley behind the Pelham Road.[20]

Only two days later, Leonard returned to New Rochelle with Carl to see Grace. He found Grace at home with her mother and Alice. For most of Leonard and Carl's visit, the young people sang popular songs with Alice accompanying on the piano in the small front parlor. Toward the end of the evening, Mrs. Jones instructed her youngest daughter to return Leonard's ring. After Grace did so, Leonard turned around and placed the ring on Alice's finger. Grace took the switch poorly and later complained, "That is a fine thing to do to a girl—take the ring off one and give it to the other." Despite Leonard's casual substitution of one Jones daughter for another, over the following three years he and Alice forged a complicated relationship: neither a storybook romance about a wealthy young man marrying a maid nor a "Jazz Age" tale of a wealthy young man ensnared by a "golddigger."[21]

Once Leonard turned his attention away from Grace to Alice Jones, he often drove his new car the twenty-one miles down the coast of Connecticut to New Rochelle in the evenings. On the days he did not drive, he took the train.[22] If Leonard had any interest in his family's history, he would have known about the Rhinelander family's ancestral links to New Rochelle, a thriving town of New York City commuters on the Long Island Sound.

New Rochelle was settled in the late seventeenth century by Huguenot refugees, one of whom was Philip Jacob Rhinelander, the first Rhinelander in America. By 1920, New Rochelle had grown to include about 36,000 residents. In the twenties, city boosters declared New Rochelle the "Queen City of the Sound." From the maple- and elm-lined suburban streets of New Rochelle commuters to New York City could reach Grand Central Station by train in half an hour on the thirty-four trains that headed there daily.[23]

Although the local Chamber of Commerce touted the city's "congenial neighborhoods" and its "increasing number of handsome homes," they failed to mention the outskirts of New Rochelle where the Joneses made their home. The Joneses lived in a house much more modest than those of the commuters who rushed to their jobs in New York City. Despite the obviously lowly circumstances of the Jones family in comparison to the Rhinelanders, Leonard continued to call on Alice Jones throughout the fall of 1921.[24]

Some evenings the couple headed to the Loew's Theater in New Rochelle to watch a movie. In 1921, Leonard and Alice could have seen Rudolph Valentino in *The Sheik* or Charlie Chaplin in *The Kid*. Sometimes they stayed in at the Jones's home and played records on Alice's Victrola. According to Leonard, Alice liked the hit song "Love Will Find A Way" from Eubie Blake and Noble Sissle's popular 1921 all-black Broadway musical *Shuffle Along*.[25] On evenings at home with the Joneses, Leonard and Alice might enjoy tea and toast with her parents before he headed back to Stamford. Occasionally they were joined by Alice's sister, Emily, her husband Robert Brooks, and their young daughter, who lived with her grandparents while her parents worked as servants in separate households. Perhaps those evenings spent with Alice's family in their small kitchen gave Leonard the sense of belonging that he did not get from his own family or at The Orchards. When Leonard needed to head to the train station, Emily and Robert sometimes drove him to catch the midnight train. In between Leonard and Alice's frequent visits, they wrote each other affectionate and flirtatious notes and letters. They occasionally talked on the telephone, although Alice left her house to use it, since the Joneses, like most Americans at the time, did not have one.[26]

On some fall nights, Leonard and Alice drove around in Leonard's car and necked, as did many young people in the 1920s when out from under parental supervision. Like other young men let loose in an automobile in this decade, Leonard viewed his car as a tool to seduce women. In early October of 1921, Leonard wrote Alice that he would like to "take some long rides and maybe if you are real nice to me once in a while, I will let you drive. I bet I know you are wondering what I mean by being real nice. Well, I will leave that to your imagination." Leonard also expressed his disappointment about trying to visit Alice, only to find her out. Yet he still gave her a pin to wear along with his ring.[27]

In case the novelty of driving his car might prove too weak to attract Alice at the beginning of their relationship, Leonard also stressed his family's social status. In one letter written at the end of October in 1921, about five or six weeks after they first met, Leonard bragged about his shopping trips in New

York City to prepare for his sister's upcoming wedding. "I wishes that you had been along and seen the attention I received in all the stores," he wrote. "It's 'horrible' to be so prominent, isn't it, dear?" Since Alice worked as a maid, it is unlikely that she encountered that problem in the shops, though she wrote back wistfully that he must have "had some sport." Despite their class differences, Leonard urged Alice to attend his sister's wedding in November at New York society's "smart bridal church" St. Thomas Episcopal, where the bride wore a gown of "point lace, worn by her own and the bridegroom's ancestors for several generations."[28]

Although it is difficult to measure the success of Leonard's strategies, Leonard and Alice's relationship did grow more physically intimate during the fall. Toward the end of October, Leonard referred again to his car when he asked Alice, "How did you enjoy our little ride last evening? To my mind it was short but sweet." In her letters, Alice reminded Leonard of their "wild excitement" and let him know that "I have had some sweet hearts, but I have not loved them, like I have taken to you so. I have never let a fellow love and caress me, the way you do Leonard."[29] She also tried to make Leonard jealous when she told him about her plans to attend dances without him and then later told him she was only kidding. Yet at other times Alice described spending quiet evenings sewing at home when they could not be together.[30]

By the beginning of December, Leonard let Alice know how happy she had made him a few nights earlier, adding, "I hope and pray sweetheart, that you will always continue to do so." In the same letter, however, Leonard fretted about Alice's active social life without him. He asked Alice to give up her "many numerable sophisticated friends." In other letters that month, Leonard teased Alice about his showing up unexpectedly at her house. He wondered if he would find out "that my little Alice was out on a rampage?" To reassure him, Alice let Leonard know that she would not see a film "because I did not have the heart to go without you dear." Leonard addressed Alice affectionately as "dearest" and "sweetness" in his letters. They called each other "sweetheart" and "Honey Bunch."[31]

Three days before Christmas in 1921, Leonard and Alice ventured out of Westchester down to New York City, with plans to eat dinner and see a Broadway show. On the trip there in Philip Rhinelander's chauffeured car, Leonard and Alice engaged in heavy petting and Leonard invited her to stay overnight with him in the city.[32] When the car arrived in Manhattan, Leonard registered the couple at the Hotel Marie-Antoinette on 68th Street and Broadway under the names "Mr. and Mrs. Smith" while Alice waited in the car.

After leaving the hotel, the two headed downtown to the bright lights and marquees of Times Square, where they were likely dazzled by the "massed effect of tremendous jazz interpreted in light" embodied by Times Square and Broadway in the twenties. After a Broadway show, Leonard and Alice dined out and then returned to their hotel room around midnight to begin their sexual relationship. Leonard left on Christmas Day to eat dinner with his family and then rejoined Alice. They stayed in the hotel for almost a week.[33]

After Alice headed home to her parents in New Rochelle and Leonard returned to The Orchards, tensions arose between the two. In the early days of the new year of 1922, Alice reconsidered their relationship. She informed Leonard that she was not sure she should return a ring to another suitor. "But Lenard," she wrote, "if you want me to keep steady company with you, I love you enough to be true to you dear. But you will after give me a ring. . . . And if you do, you will never hear any more about any man." "I am very found of you Lenard," she continued, "But I have not told you, I really adore you dearie, But I do not want to get so crazy for you, if there is nothing in it." Alice also expressed doubts about their December hotel stay, when she felt she had agreed foolishly to stay overnight.[34]

In a move perhaps calculated to bind Leonard to her after they had engaged in premarital sex, Alice implied that she had become pregnant. In veiled language contained in three separate letters written in January 1922, she suggested that she needed to have and then did have an abortion. Alice blamed Leonard: "I think I bared the pain and you should afford to bare the expence, Because the whole fault was on you. But it will never happen again. Because you will after be prepared hear after." Alice informed Leonard that an unnamed "operation," which was required because Leonard was not "prepared," cost twenty-three dollars (equivalent to $281 in 2007), a substantial amount of money for a domestic servant in 1922.[35] Yet Alice probably never paid the money to an abortionist. Given the timing of their hotel stay, and the then-current state of medical technology (that is, before pregnancy tests), it is unlikely that Alice could have known she was pregnant and had an abortion by mid-January 1922, when she penned those words. Instead, Alice may have claimed to have had an abortion to emphasize both the way she had suffered for loving him and her demand that he make a commitment. Alice also let him know that she was unhappy at home and she might have to settle down with another man if Leonard's only interest in her was to pass the time.[36]

At the same time Alice wrote about an abortion, Leonard suggested that they find an apartment in Manhattan. Although Leonard professed his love and told Alice that she made him happy, he did not offer to marry her. Yet he still wanted to make sure that Alice did not see any other men and that their physical intimacy would continue. Consequently, at the end of January, Leonard and Alice returned to the Hotel Marie-Antoinette, this time prepared with condoms to avoid pregnancy. They stayed together for two weeks and photographed each other in bed. But their time together ended when an unwanted intruder—a lawyer—interrupted their hotel idyll with a knock on the door.[37]

A member of a firm of longtime Rhinelander family retainers, Spotswood Bowers, separated the young couple. Alice headed home, alone, to Westchester. Bowers did not take Leonard to the Rhinelanders' Manhattan home or send him back to The Orchards in Connecticut. Instead, he booked Leonard into the Hotel Belmont in New York and then packed him off to a wintry Atlantic City for two weeks with a male companion. Despite the forced separation, the lovers stayed in touch. Leonard even managed to elude his companion and visit New Rochelle when Alice came down with the flu. To ensure that Leonard stayed away from Alice, Leonard's father arranged for Leonard and a chaperone to travel to Bermuda. Despite his companion, Leonard wrote to Alice. Ensconced in an expensive Bermuda hotel, he contrasted Alice to the New York society girls in the same hotel who appealed to his companion. Leonard disliked their drinking and smoking, but more importantly, he wrote, "they all lack the quality and the living fire which you and only you possess." In Alice's letters to Leonard, she pleaded with him to hurry back: "Please try and coax your father, not to send you away again, because you get terrible lonesome, because I really do not, no how I am going to do without you." As an incentive for his return, Alice promised Leonard that she had given up all other men.[38]

Despite Alice's pleas that Leonard come back, Leonard's stay in Bermuda during February and March 1922 began a long voyage that kept the couple apart for two years and tested their bond. While Leonard traveled to Washington, D.C., Havana, Panama, and California, he and Alice exchanged numerous letters. At times, their letters reflected the sometimes unreasonable expectations each seemed to have of the other. Leonard seemed to forget that Alice was not a rich society girl but a working woman, a fact made perfectly clear in her letters. In March 1922, Alice wrote Leonard to tell him that she would start a new job in the neighboring suburb of Pelham Manor and she planned to live out and not work as a live-in servant. Only a few months later, Alice's letters included the return address of a different employer. Her comments about her new job indicated she had joined a large household staff and would live in her employer's residence. Yet she also described to Leonard shopping trips to Manhattan, where she bought a "new Polo coat" for Easter.[39]

In his letters Leonard never referred to Alice's employment. In May of 1922, when his chaperone became ill, Leonard sent Alice a telegram in which he asked her to visit him in California. Leonard suggested that Alice board an express train to San Francisco.[40] Alice refused. "I suppose dear heart you are surprised at me, in not coming out to you," she wrote. "Well dear heart supposing if I had come I would not have known where I was going to stay, and hated the trip alone, but did not no how much the trip would cost. Just when I started to get a nice bank book started I suppose you wanted me to draw it out as that I would after do. I work hard enough for it, Leonard, without spending it foolish." She suggested to Leonard that if he really wanted her company, he could send a ticket.[41]

On the other hand, Alice wanted Leonard to forget that his father controlled the purse strings of an underage son who had to wait for his inheritance. She blamed Philip Rhinelander for their separation: "I no Leonard I will make you happy if I had my own way with you, But you father as it yet being the boss."[42] During their first year apart, Alice spent the summer working for an employer who had rented a cottage in the Adirondacks at an exclusive resort. Over the summer Alice constantly told Leonard about the many eligible men she met in the mountains. "All of the boys seems to like me," she boasted. "I could have a date every night of the week. But I do not wait, because I have dear Leonard."[43] While she worked on his jealousy, Alice continued to give Leonard a hard time about his father: "I will help you to fight this battle. But I wished you was more independent like me. If you only had a good trade, and you would not after look forward, for your father's help." Despite her belief that Leonard might be more independent if he followed a trade, Alice dreamed about their future together funded by his family's wealth. She sent him clippings of pictures from the *Saturday Evening Post* of a house and a car and told him that they were the ones they must have. Alice also tried to convince Leonard to come to the Adirondacks instead of going to Hawaii. "I suppose when you go to Honolua," she complained, "you will fall for one of those wild queens down there. You like something rocky dono't you Len."[44]

By early September of 1922, almost one year after they had met, their relationship turned acrimonious. Alice lost her temper when Leonard told her he could not return East that fall but instead would head to Arizona. She felt "terrible about, this new plan of your's what's the idea, Len in going out to Arizona now." Alice reminded Leonard that she had remained loyal to him over the summer and turned down other men. Now she told him to forget her "as you do after do the right thing, for your father." Yet Alice also declared they should have married before he left. She complained, "Your money came first before me, or we could of kepted it a died secret." If they had secretly married, he could have supported her and she would not have to work. "And you away having a gret time," she wrote bitterly, "what you spend in going around, it would keep me, nicely."[45]

Angry that Leonard would not return, Alice wrote again the same day, "Get off your mind about me coming out to Arizona, or any other place, as I will never, will." Then she gave him one last chance: if he wanted to keep her, he had to come back and marry her. If he did not, she threatened, she would never write again. "And hope you have a happy future life, the one your dad's wants you to have and be happy," she added.[46] In response, Leonard begged Alice to not leave him: "Are you going to turn me down simply because I said I am not coming home this winter or are you going to make a fool out of me and cause me to live my future life alone, because I am not good enough for you?"[47]

In October 1922, Philip Rhinelander enrolled his son in an Arizona ranch school for the sons of wealthy families. When Leonard sent Alice a picture of him at school, Alice expressed dismay at the rustic surroundings: "I never thought you would be in, such a low, and lonesome looking. I feel very much disappointed with you, and also your father sending you at such a place." The rough environment, however, was designed to toughen up the sons of the eastern elite. Alice also took the opportunity to tell Leonard not to stay out West but instead declare his independence from his father. While Alice doubted his ability to do so, she continued to hope he would return, at least for Christmas, suggesting a secret visit to her family. The visit never occurred.[48]

For almost two more years Leonard stayed out West while Alice worked in Westchester. During their time apart, the two continued to write despite Alice's frequent threats to stop. Unfortunately, the available correspondence from these two years consists mainly of Alice's letters; few of Leonard's letters were introduced as evidence during the trial. In her letters, Alice told Leonard repeatedly about the different men she had turned down while she waited for him. In other letters, she recalled their hotel stay in New York and hinted at their sexual conduct. At other times, Alice expressed her anger about his absence and the reasons behind it. "I do not want, to hear no more about age, and be coming your own boss, because," she wrote in one letter, "if you do not return we will put things right off, and forget about everything whats happened between the both of us." She felt that Leonard could not stand up to his family: "If I had loved you and had trouble like that with my family I would of told them something long ago. But you are too easy with your father, and you want me to be easy with you, but I cant be that way."[49]

By January 1924, as Leonard's twenty-first birthday approached, Leonard and Alice's letters reflected anxiety about what would happen at that point: would Leonard challenge his father? Early in the year, Alice prayed for his return in the spring, "because," as she put it, "my love, is burning for you nobody, but you. I have fought it almost two years, and I can fight it for another few months." She reminded him that at the Hotel Marie-Antoinette she had acted as his wife, but she wanted to really assume that position: "That will be my happy day, if it ever comes."[50] In March, Alice addressed directly Leonard reaching the age of majority: "But dear am I right or wrong, arent' you at age this birthday coming May." She insisted that she deserved to be his wife and she hoped to take his dead mother's place in his life. But Alice fretted that problems might arise even this close to her goal of marrying Leonard when he turned twenty-one. "My poor heart is just acking for you day, and night," she complained, "but I am very much afraid when your return to me, I feel I shall be taken from you easy as a top, because I am really terrible broken up, over you the way the things, what as been done to you, I would call it cruel."[51]

Despite Alice's fears, when Leonard turned twenty-one he returned to New York. He stayed in Manhattan with his father during the week and spent the weekends and some evenings with the Joneses in New Rochelle; he and Alice renewed their sexual relationship. During the summer of 1924, Leonard and Alice took an unaccompanied trip to New England after telling Alice's mother that they would be chaperoned.[52] In August, the *New York Times* reported that Leonard had inherited from his grandfather's estate $40,000 in cash, almost $300,000 in securities, jewelry, and shares in an oil company and a mortgage company. Leonard's cash bequest would be worth today about $470,000 and $300,000 of securities would be the equivalent of $3.5 million. During the same month that he received his inheritance, Leonard, now independently wealthy, placed a deposit on bedroom furniture at a Westchester store. Two months later, on 14 October, Leonard and Alice made their way to the New Rochelle city hall, obtained a marriage license, and were married by Mayor Harry Scott. Although the couple rented an apartment in New Rochelle, they stayed with Alice's parents while they set up their new household. Leonard did not tell his father about his marriage, and he continued to stay in Manhattan during the week.[53]

The newlyweds lived together on weekends in the Joneses' cramped home for almost one month. They purchased additional furniture and contemplated hiring an interior decorator for their new apartment. On 13 November, however, their world changed forever. The local paper, the *Standard Star*, published a report that Leonard, the son of a well-known New York family, had married the daughter of a Westchester "colored" man. Once this news broke, Alice and Leonard's lives would never be the same.[54]

Within hours of the appearance of the *Standard Star* report, newspaper reporters from New York City leapt on the story. Journalists raced to New Rochelle and pursued interviews with the young couple. Given the geographical proximity, any major story in Westchester that featured the son of a wealthy Manhattanite made good copy for New York City journalists. Railroad commuters picked up city papers at newsstands at Grand Central Station and throughout the city. The story seemed tailor-made for the age of "jazz journalism," characterized by the popular and cheap small-format tabloid with big headlines and even bigger photographs.[55] News of the secret Rhinelander wedding appeared at a fortuitous time for the city's tabloids, and competition heated up. The first New York City paper to run the story, the *New York Daily News*, founded in 1919 and considered the first twentieth-century tabloid, had already achieved fame for its sensationalized stories and extensive use of photographs. By 1924, the paper had a daily circulation of 750,000,[56] and its success inspired new competitors: William Randolph Hearst's *Daily Mirror* and Bernarr McFadden's *Evening Graphic* (soon nicknamed the *Porno-Graphic*).[57]

Working to upstage its rivals, the *Daily News* rushed the story of the Rhinelander wedding into print by seven P.M. on 13 November in its "pink edition" (an edition that always carried the next day's date). The paper blared the story of Leonard and Alice's marriage under the front-page headline "RHINELANDER BRIDE STUNS 400." The six-paragraph inside article brandished a no less sensational heading, "SOCIETY DAZED AT RHINELANDER NUPTIAL NEWS." Although the headlines focused on high society's response to Leonard and Alice's wedding, the text of the piece revealed a more complicated story.[58]

The *Daily News* introduced Leonard and Alice Rhinelander with the report that a "bombshell was tossed into the aristocratic ranks of blue-blooded New York and Newport society yesterday." "The amazing information," it continued, "leaked out that young Leonard Kip Rhinelander was secretly married on Oct. 14 to Miss Alice Beatrice Jones, daughter of a West Indian."[59] The revelation that the bride's father might be West Indian appeared to be what made the news of the wedding a "bombshell" for "aristocratic" white New Yorkers. As many readers of New York's papers were well aware, New York City had seen a large influx of immigrants from the Caribbean in the first part of the twentieth century. Most of these migrants were of African descent, like the Jamaican Marcus Garvey, the controversial leader of the Universal Negro Improvement Association (UNIA) headquartered in New York City who had been convicted of mail fraud one year earlier.[60]

The next few paragraphs of the *Daily News* report, however, blurred the emerging portrait of the bride and her family. The paper identified Alice's mother as "a white woman of English birth." In contrast, Alice's father possessed a "swarthy complexion" and had driven "a stagecoach for members of the New York Athletic club." The combination of "swarthy" skin and working-class occupation in the body of the father implied that he might be West Indian of African descent. This conclusion seemed further buttressed by the additional apparently uncontradicted information that the bride's sister had married a "colored butler." Moreover, the brother-in-law's employer informed the *Daily News* that the butler's wife had always been "regarded" as "colored."[61] If the bride's own sister had been "regarded" as "colored" by white employers of domestic servants, what was the bride "regarded" as and by whom?

In marked contrast to its description of the social status of Alice Jones's family, peopled with stagecoach drivers and butlers, the *Daily News* distinguished the groom as "the son of Philip Rhinelander, millionaire New York society man. His mother was Adelaide Kip of the ultra-exclusive New York Kips." But the newspaper also recounted how Adelaide's son failed to follow the exclusionary traditions of his ancestors because he and Alice Jones maintained a "close" friendship for at least three years before they married. Perhaps more shocking, Leonard reportedly had even introduced Alice into elite white society when Alice "spent six weeks in the company of the fashionable at Newport," a claim that apparently had no basis in reality. In the same way that New Yorkers would have understood the subtext of a term like "West Indian," readers of the *Daily News* would have recognized Newport as a well-known summer playground for America's richest white families.[62]

By this point in the *Daily News*'s narrative, readers may have wondered how this unusual marriage between a "blue-blood" and the daughter of a "swarthy" West Indian could have occurred. At the very end of the article, the *Daily News* hinted at one possible answer: on "the marriage license the girl gave her color as white. She is of light complexion."[63] The report that Alice Jones "*gave*" her color as "white" on her marriage license, coupled with the information about her father and older sister, assumed that Alice presented herself as white to the county clerk when she and Leonard obtained their license. Once readers made their way through the *Daily News*'s first article on the Rhinelanders, they would have learned that this recently discovered marriage took place between a young white aristocrat and a young woman of at least a questionable racial background who, nevertheless, described herself as white when she married. Although the *Daily News* did not characterize Alice's actions as passing for white when she identified herself to the county clerk, readers may have recognized them as such.

One day after the *Standard Star* and the *Daily News* published their stories, the rest of New York City's papers weighed in with contradictory reports on Alice Rhinelander's ancestry. On the morning of 14 November, the conservative *New York Times* greeted its readers with the news that "SOCIETY YOUTH WEDS CABMAN'S DAUGHTER," thereby immediately defining the bride and the groom by the occupational and social positions of their families. Like the *Daily News*, the *Times* emphasized the groom's status as the son of Philip Rhinelander, a member of one of Manhattan's oldest families. Unlike the *Daily News*, the *Times* did not focus on high society's response to the marriage.[64]

Yet, like the *Daily News*, the *Times* article hinted at the potential complications posed by the marriage, with its report about the bride's sister's marriage to a "negro" butler. The *Times*, however, left the question of Alice's ancestry unresolved when it revealed: "In giving the necessary data to the Westchester County Clerk, the bride said that she was 23 years of age, white, born in Pelham and the daughter of George Jones and the former Elizabeth Brown. The record disclosed that Jones said he was born in Leicestshire, England, and that his wife was a native of Lincolnshire. They were married in England thirty years ago, and have lived in New Rochelle for twenty-nine years. Jones's ancestors at one time lived in the West Indies." Although the *Times* reported that both of the bride's parents claimed they were born in England (which suggested that they possessed white European ancestry), the paper still referred to Alice's sister's marriage and the father's West Indian ancestry. But, again, according to the *Times*, the bride reportedly "*said*" that she was white (that is, Alice self-identified as white when she applied for her marriage license).[65]

The *Times*'s article on the Rhinelanders went on to describe the condition of the Jones family home, "one of three small frame dwellings on the outskirts of New Rochelle," in an unspoken comparison to the family home of the Rhinelanders. The comparison also served to reinforce the Jones family's lower social status. At the end of the article, the *Times* returned to the Rhinelander family with the information that Leonard's mother had died "in 1916 from burns received when a lamp exploded in the family's country home at Tuxedo Park." Readers of the *Times* would have known that Tuxedo Park was an exclusive, all-white suburb of New York City. The *Times* also observed that Leonard's father belonged to prominent organizations, including "several historical societies, membership in which is confined to descendants of those who settled America," presumably all white, thereby emphasizing the exalted social position of the Rhinelanders.[66]

The *Times* was issued only once daily, but the *Daily News* churned out a number of editions each day from the "pink" to the "final." During the course of Friday, 14 November, it ran off multiple editions with updated information and continued speculation about Leonard and Alice Rhinelander.[67] With the appearance of Friday's "home edition," the story of race or "color" became central once the front-page headline announced "RHINELANDER'S COLORED BRIDE." Thus the editors of the *Daily News* proclaimed to their readers and anyone who merely glanced at the front page on newsstands that Alice Rhinelander was "colored." The article on page three (a greatly expanded version of the earlier "pink" article), now captioned "BLUEBLOOD WEDS COLORED GIRL," painted the marriage as interracial. In this revised report, the *Daily News* equated social status with color as it described Leonard Rhinelander as the "heir to a fortune of $100,000,000 in Manhattan real estate and a member of one of New York's most exclusive families [who] has taken unto himself the daughter of a colored man for wife." The article claimed that Alice Rhinelander, "the daughter of a colored coachman," worked as a "nurse girl" before her marriage. This identification of Alice as a servant implied that she, too, as well as her father and brother-in-law, must be colored.[68] The description of Leonard as an "heir to a fortune" presumed his status as white.

The same edition, on the other hand, described the Rhinelanders as a "Loving Pair": "happy in their love, supremely happy; her skin may be dark, but her eyes are filled to their depths with worship of him." The "dark skin" of Alice in this article, however, seemed at odds with her "light complexion" in the earlier "pink edition," suggesting that once the paper identified Alice as "colored," the perception of her complexion changed. The report also appeared to positively portray a consensual interracial union, which could make a troubling picture in the mid-1920s North.[69]

While the *Daily News* darkened Alice Rhinelander and categorized her as "colored," the paper played up the exclusive nature of the Rhinelander family and the society to which it belonged. Like the earlier pink edition, the home edition returned to New York society's reaction to the marriage. Indeed, a *Daily News* reporter imagined New York's elite discussing the "sensational" Rhinelander alliance "wherever the 400 gathered last night, whether at the dinner table, the opera, the theatre or in the ultra-exclusive 5th ave. millionaires' clubs." The reporter described the Rhinelanders as "play[ing] for 200 years a part in the history of the country of their adoption, which is hardly equaled by that of any other of the older families in America." He also stressed that the Rhinelander family carefully restricted its lineage. Indeed, Leonard Rhinelander's grandfather disinherited one of his sons when he married without the family's approval.[70]

Perhaps the most surprising aspect of the home edition report on the Rhinelanders was its new implication that a colored Alice did not pass as white when she married Leonard. According to this updated account, Leonard "went into this marriage compact with his eyes wide open. He knew his bride's father and mother. He knew that his wife's sister, Emily, is married to Robert Brooks, colored butler." This information again contradicted the earlier pink edition, but the pink edition did not have the benefit of an interview with one of the Rhinelanders. The home edition included an excerpt from an interview with Leonard that seemed to confirm that no passing had taken place.[71]

Barbara Reynolds, the first reporter to catch up with Leonard, worked for New Rochelle's *Standard Star* and was a contributor to a New York wire service. She had waited outside the Jones's home on Thursday, 13 November, and when she spotted Leonard, she asked whether he realized that his marriage to Alice Jones would generate publicity. Leonard replied that he had not. Once Leonard realized Reynolds's occupation, he asked whether he could avoid the press's interest. Reynolds told him it was already too late and showed him that day's *Standard Star*, with its report on his marriage.[72] Portions of the rest of Reynolds's conversation with Leonard appeared in the next day's *Daily News*: "He spoke frankly, but briefly, to reporters who greeted him as he stepped out of a big limousine to enter his father-in-law's humble home, at 763 Pelham road, New Rochelle, yesterday. 'Is it true that you married the daughter of a colored man?' he was asked. 'Yes,' was his prompt reply, 'and we are very happy.' 'Does your father know you are married?' 'No, he does not. I was in town today and went to his office but I missed him.'" In her published interview, Reynolds observed that Leonard "appeared worried" about his father's reaction to his secret marriage.[73] Leonard's fear of Philip Rhinelander's response may have been well-founded.

Despite Leonard's straightforward admission, the *Daily News* still alluded to the ambiguous nature of Alice's ancestry. The paper reported that witnesses at the wedding "had not the slightest suspicion that Miss Jones was not a white woman." This information suggested that the officials involved in the wedding did not deliberately sanction an interracial marriage, though, as we have seen, nothing in New York would have forbidden such a union. The observation that the officials did not suspect her "color" also implied that even if Leonard knew, Alice may still have passed as white when she married.[74]

When the *Daily News*'s "afternoon edition" arrived on newsstands, New Yorkers received their first glimpse of the new Mrs. Rhinelander. Under a banner headline, "HIS COLORED BRIDE," the paper again scooped its competitors, printing a full-page portrait of Alice on the front page.[75] Readers could now make their own judgments about Alice, constrained, however, by the large print text, "COLORED." The same edition also reported that the couple had fled their apartment and retreated to the Jones's family home.[76]

By this point, the *Daily News* realized that the marriage warranted enough attention to assign primary responsibility to cover the story to Grace Robinson, their new "front-page girl," or "sob sister," the pejorative nickname for female reporters. The paper expected front-page girls to, as one female contemporary of Robinson's remarked, "put more emotion, more color, more animation into their work." The paper may have chosen Robinson to write about the Rhinelanders because of her earlier involvement with its society column; they knew she could write colorful articles that would increase circulation.[77]

In Robinson's first article she purported to give readers of the *Daily News* the inside story on the Rhinelanders' relationship and Alice's color. Robinson told her readers about Alice's statements in an interview conducted by New York reporters. According to Robinson, Alice denied any "West Indian blood in our veins." Despite Alice's disclaimer, Robinson reported the existence of some "mystery" about the Jones family in New Rochelle but also said that the Joneses "are well known as a respectable, industrious family, never associated with the colored elements." Robinson also told her readers that during the

The public's first view of Alice Jones Rhinelander on the front page of the afternoon edition of the *New York Daily News*, 14 November 1924. © *New York Daily News*.

interview Alice declared she would file a lawsuit for libel against the newspapers for calling her father "colored."[78]

Although Robinson noted that Alice refused to allow reporters to see her under a bright light, she still provided a lengthy description of the bride. Robinson's language, however, raised more questions about Alice than it answered. She reported, "Mrs. Rhinelander is of the type generally described as 'extremely dark.' Her features are strong and distinctly European in conformation. Her lips are full and red, her nose is not flat and her heavy bobbed hair, although slightly curly, is jet black, resembling the hair of many Spanish or half-Spanish women. In fact, Mrs. Rhinelander might pass for a Latin beauty in Newport society." Robinson's characterization of Alice as a "Latin beauty in Newport society" hinted at racial passing (since some of those who passed as white purportedly identified themselves as Spanish) and the blurring lines of class status.[79]

Alice's disavowal of West Indian ancestry also made the front page of Hearst's afternoon paper, the *Evening Journal*, which featured the front-page headline "Young Rhinelander's Bride Denies Taint," on Friday, 14 November.[80] A small photo of Alice, captioned "Society Youth's Bride Who Denies Mixed Blood," accompanied the headline. According to the paper, Alice denied possessing any "West Indian blood" and emphasized that her parents were "of English stock for generations back." Alice also declared, "I can't help it that dad is dark and he can't help it. But there is no reason for anyone to say he is colored just on that account."[81]

The avalanche of publicity about the Rhinelanders set off a chain reaction.[82] On Friday, 14 November, Philip Rhinelander issued a statement to the press through his attorney, Spotswood Bowers, the same lawyer who had separated Alice and Leonard two years earlier. Leonard's father confirmed "that his son, Leonard Kip Rhinelander, who is over twenty-one years of age, was married on October 14 without his knowledge." He added that he had "never met the young lady, but is informed that she is of English parentage."[83] Despite this communication, or perhaps spurred on by Rhinelander's obviously tepid support for his son, the press kept working the story. While reporters hounded the Rhinelanders in Manhattan for more information, Leonard and his in-laws in New Rochelle tried to protect themselves from intrusions. Leonard nailed up heavy curtains in the Joneses' dining room to prevent reporters and curious onlookers from peering in the windows. Despite these precautions, someone threw rocks and broke the windows on the house next door, owned by Alice's sister Grace and her husband. Rumors spread that the Ku Klux Klan, newly revitalized in the 1920s, had targeted the Joneses.[84]

Day after day through the rest of November, the New York press stayed on the story of the Rhinelander marriage. Desperate for scoops, reporters started to dig into Alice's background, for, as the *Daily News* phrased it, "everybody in society knows the bridegroom, the son of Philip Rhinelander. But nobody in society, until Thursday evening when the DAILY NEWS came out with the story, knew there was such a person as Alice Jones."[85] The press revealed that Alice was two years older than her stated age on her marriage license. Reporters tracked down Alice's school records and interviewed former teachers and classmates. The *Daily News* reported that some of Alice's former schoolmates believed she was Spanish, that the principal of her school thought Alice was white, and that a former teacher "considered her a colored child, but said she 'was a nice little girl.'" In addition, Grace Robinson announced "the surprising fact" that the Jones family attended an exclusive Episcopal church in Pelham Manor, a small Westchester village. Since George and Elizabeth Jones had immigrated from England, their attendance at an Episcopal church, the American branch of the Anglican Church, should not have been such a surprise.[86]

The pink edition of the *Daily News* on Saturday, 15 November, called Alice a "mulatto" and observed, "Mr. and Mrs. Leonard Kip Rhinelander could not be found yesterday by reporters. It was said they had left town. But some interesting details of the romance between the heir to $100,000,000 and the colored girl who once worked in a laundry were unearthed." The paper then provided for its readers a lengthy discussion of color and Alice Jones's family: "Alice is the daughter of Mr. and Mrs. George Jones of New Rochelle. George is colored. There is little doubt of that." This emphatic statement about Alice's father suggested that perhaps doubt still existed about the "color" of other members of George Jones's family. Yet the same article quoted a former coworker of Alice's who recalled that Alice wept when a workplace inspection classified Alice as a "mulatto."[87]

Despite this designation of Alice as a "mulatto," the *Daily News* reported uncertainty over Alice's background: "Alice got good marks in school. Some thought her colored. Some did not. She seldom mingled with colored people. She never went to a colored church or to a club or lodge where colored folk are found."[88] The final edition of the *Daily News* on Saturday returned to the angle of romance with Grace Robinson's article about how such an unlikely couple met. She emphasized the improbable nature of their relationship and the social gap between the two families. To illustrate the point, her article featured photographs of a Rhinelander family member's home and the Jones's family home side by side. Robinson also returned to the question of race with the comment that "Mrs. Rhinelander was popular with young white men in New Rochelle and she was seen dancing in inns in that vicinity countless times."[89]

Like the *Daily News*, the *Times* also reported that a former coworker of Alice's during the war remembered that an official enumeration of aliens identified Alice as "mulatto." Alice's coworker recalled that the inspectors asked a "number of Italians of swarthy complexion" whether they were white or black. But the inspectors simply put Alice on their forms as a "mulatto." In the same report, however, the *Times* quoted Alice's younger sister, Grace, who asserted that "this whole thing about our being negroes is just jealousy. My father isn't colored but is of West Indian descent."[90]

Despite Grace's statement, the *Evening Journal* pointed out that "it had seemed pretty well understood around New Rochelle that Alice Beatrice Jones Rhinelander was not to be accepted in society. She had worked as a waitress and as a laundress in various homes and in places where she had worked the mistresses made a point of using only 'colored' help." Apparently, at least in one sector of New Rochelle's citizenry (those who could afford domestic servants), Alice's employment confirmed her identity as "colored." In fact, during the late 1910s and 1920s, African Americans increasingly filled domestic service positions in the North, replacing the Irish "Bridget" of an earlier generation.[91] Yet the *Evening Journal* also reported that the 1915 New York State Census identified the Jones family as "white," which contradicted the "reports that the secret marriage of a month ago [was] inter-racial." Moreover, a black "chauffeur's apprentice" claimed that he dated Alice until she ended their relationship and informed him she was "white."[92]

Not only New York's daily papers weighed in on Alice and Leonard's marriage. Through the wire services, the story of the Rhinelanders turned up in papers like the *Emporia Gazette* in Kansas City and southern newspapers like the *Atlanta Constitution*. Marcus Garvey's newspaper, the *Negro World* (the organ of the UNIA), also took notice of the Rhinelander wedding, coming to its own conclusion about the Joneses' race. The *Negro World* reported that although Alice and her family claimed to be English and not colored, "pictures published in the New York newspapers indicated that she is of mixed African and European origin." Given Alice's possibly "mixed" ancestry, the article reiterated the UNIA's opposition to race mixture, but it also "commended"

Leonard for marrying Alice rather than keeping her as his mistress. Nevertheless, the paper concluded, "it would have been better for him to have married in his own social set and racial connections." While journalists continued to dig into the conflicting reports about Alice Rhinelander, the Jones family and their new son-in-law continued to seclude themselves inside the Joneses' small home.[93]

If it weren't for the intense publicity of the Rhinelander marriage, Leonard and Alice Rhinelander might never have seen the inside of a courtroom. But only a few days after the first press reports appeared, on Sunday, 16 November, Leon Jacobs, a Manhattan lawyer identifying himself as Leonard's attorney, arrived in Westchester to see the young couple with his own eyes. The papers that Sunday contained new disclosures about Alice's background. Both the *Daily News* and the *Times* reported that Alice's father's naturalization papers designated George Jones a "colored man." In addition, the *Times* wrote that the 1915 marriage license of Alice's older sister, Emily, and her husband described both as "colored." The Sunday *New York American* made clear the significance of these official documents: "In view of the records made available yesterday, speculation became keener as to the future attitude of the bridegroom's family and the future position of the flashing-eyed Mrs. Rhinelander."[94]

Despite the unhappy results of Alice and Leonard's earlier encounter with a Rhinelander lawyer at the Hotel Marie-Antoinette, the Joneses allowed Leon Jacobs into their home.[95] After this first meeting, Jacobs returned on Tuesday accompanied by another lawyer, Joseph Strong. Strong later testified in court that Jacobs had told him that he needed to meet Leonard and Alice to identify them before a lawsuit was started. During this visit, Strong also notarized assignments of mortgages that Jacobs had Leonard sign that transferred the legal rights from Leonard to Jacobs.[96] Two days later, on Thursday, 20 November, Jacobs drove alone to New Rochelle. He convinced Leonard and Alice that they could not be kept safe from the reporters or the Ku Klux Klan if they remained with the Joneses. For their own protection, Leonard should leave with him while Alice stayed with friends. Once it was safe, the couple would be reunited. Leonard fled with Jacobs in an automobile with curtained windows to an unknown destination. Alice went to the home of nearby friends to wait until the couple could be together again.[97]

Once Leonard left Westchester, Jacobs shuttled him around the East Coast for a few days, with stops in Washington, D.C., and Newark, New Jersey. During this time, Leonard spent his waking hours with his lawyer. With rumors flying that unknown parties had whisked Leonard away from his in-laws' house, the press intimated that Leonard might try to annul his marriage after being summoned to meet with his father. After four days in the company of Leon Jacobs, with no signs of his father, Leonard agreed to end his marriage to Alice. On Monday, 24 November, while standing with Joseph Strong in the unlikely location of the Ninth Street station of the Hudson Tubes in Manhattan (the subway that linked New Jersey and New York), Leonard signed legal papers asking the courts to annul his marriage.[98]

Two days later, on the Wednesday before Thanksgiving, almost two weeks after the first news of the Rhinelander wedding broke, Leon Jacobs and Joseph Strong returned to the Joneses' home in New Rochelle. In the presence of Alice's mother and her sister Grace, Strong handed to Alice Leonard's complaint, the legal document that started his annulment lawsuit. Before leaving, Jacobs read out loud a note from Leonard in which Leonard urged Alice to fight the case. Jacobs also warned Mrs. Jones that the Ku Klux Klan might try to burn down her house.[99] Like the Jones family, Leonard faced a bleak Thanksgiving. Accompanied by Joseph Strong, Leonard traveled to Long Island to begin an almost two-month stay at Strong's summer home. During this stay, perhaps more accurately a form of house arrest, Strong spent nearly eight hours a day with Leonard.[100]

In the document handed to Alice before Thanksgiving, Leonard accused Alice of using fraud to obtain his consent to marry. "Prior to said marriage," the document read, "the defendant [Alice] represented to and told the plaintiff [Leonard] that she was white and not colored, and had no colored blood, which representations the plaintiff believed to be true, and was induced thereby to consent to said marriage, and entered into said marriage relying upon such representations, which representations plaintiff after said marriage discovered to be wholly untrue." The document also included the charge that when Alice misrepresented herself as "white and not colored" she did so "with [the] intent to deceive and defraud this plaintiff." Once Alice received Leonard's complaint, she had twenty days to hire a lawyer and respond.[101]

The revelation that Leonard had initiated legal action against Alice galvanized New York's newspapers, whose coverage of the Rhinelanders had started to wane absent new sensations. Once it became known that Leonard's attorney had served Alice with legal papers, even the relatively staid *Times* gave the news of Leonard's lawsuit major coverage in its Thanksgiving Day issue. The *Times* considered the story so newsworthy that it reprinted the entire legal document. It also included Alice's statement to the press: "I will never give him up. I love him dearly and he loves me dearly. All the Rhinelander millions cannot take him from me."[102]

Like the *Times*, the *New York American* felt that its readers deserved to see the complete text of Leonard's complaint. But the *American*'s Thanksgiving Day coverage hinted that although Leonard claimed Alice "hid" her color from him, a messier story might emerge. The *American* observed, "The bride and her parents have consistently maintained that they were white, without a drop of colored blood in their ancestry, until yesterday when Mrs. Jones uttered her cryptic comment concerning the bridegroom's ability to see with his eyes." According to the *American*, the "cryptic comment" was elicited when Alice's mother was asked about Leonard's assertion that Alice deceived him. "'That's a lie,'" she reportedly said. "'He has eyes just as I have, and he could see just as well as I can see. He loves her, I tell you!'" Thus, the paper asserted that Mrs. Jones admitted that the family was not white and that Alice's appearance was proof.[103]

Once Leonard filed his annulment papers and charged that Alice committed racial fraud, the press increased its focus on definitions of race and the legal system. On the day after Thanksgiving, the *Evening Journal* reported that Alice planned to contest Leonard's suit because she believed it was his family's idea.[104] The *Evening Journal*'s reporter remarked that Alice's lawyer, New Rochelle city judge Samuel F. Swinburne, had started to investigate the Jones family's ancestry. Swinburne asserted that George Jones's ancestors came from India and not the West Indies. "In this event," the reporter continued, "it is pointed out, they would be members of the Aryan race, which is collateral with the Caucasian." But this would not necessarily mean that the Jones family was white. Indeed, by 1923 the U.S. Supreme Court had ruled that for purposes of eligibility for American citizenship, "Aryans" from India were not "white."[105]

At the same time that discussions of race took on a greater significance in reports on the Rhinelander marriage, news about the lawyers' legal strategies and their conceptions of race started to play a bigger role too. The newspapers, especially the tabloids shifted their narrative gears to a storyline about a legal battle. Well aware of the press's interest in the case, the lawyers cooperated with the papers, giving interviews and providing reporters with copies of the legal documents. On Saturday, 29 November, the day's reports on the Rhinelanders exposed the lawyers' legal maneuvers and public relations efforts.

At first, Swinburne took the offensive, telling the press that "his client's main objective would be to prove that she was white." Indeed, Swinburne declared that his legal response to Leonard's claims would "'emphatically refute the last three paragraphs of the complaint, which allege, in substance, that Alice Beatrice Jones practiced fraud to bring about the marriage by misrepresenting facts.'" Swinburne also told the press that he would "'prove, too, that George Jones, the bride's father, is not a colored man.'" Judge Swinburne denied reports that George Jones had identified himself as "colored" when he filled out his naturalization papers. Instead, Swinburne suggested that a court clerk completed Jones's forms incorrectly when the clerk "'saw his dusky complexion and put down "colored man."'" Consequently, Alice's attorney argued that "color" and "race" were not equivalent and that official documents could be wrong.[106]

Yet when reporters asked Judge Swinburne about the accuracy of the description of Emily Jones as "colored" on her marriage license, he argued that Alice's sister's actions did not affect his case; only the parents' race mattered. In fact, Swinburne meant that only the "white" parent mattered. Swinburne argued that "under the laws of the State of New York Mrs. Rhinelander is white because her mother is white."[107] Swinburne's reliance on Alice's mother's color as a way to determine Alice's legal identity, however, contradicted his earlier claim that Alice's father was not "colored." And despite Alice's lawyer's confident statement about the relationship between Alice's mother's identity and Alice's color, it was impossible to state definitively Alice's racial identity as defined by law; New York did not legally define "Negro," "colored," or "white." Unlike many other jurisdictions in the United States, no statutory law in New York defined race.[108]

Although Swinburne asserted that his client and her family were white, his statements to the press only sowed confusion. Yet in presenting his client in the best possible light, Swinburne offered some insight into his planned courtroom strategy if Leonard's case made it to trial. Swinburne indicated that he might introduce into evidence Leonard's letters to Alice, which he implied would demonstrate that the couple had discussed the "question of 'color,'" although he gave no hint about the contents of these discussions. He also would contend that Alice's father had tried to persuade Leonard not to marry his daughter because "'he and his family were English working people and that there was a social gulf between his daughter and Rhinelander which could not be bridged.'"[109]

By the end of November, the *Times* reported that Alice believed Leonard was being kept from her but that he had sent a note to encourage her to contest his lawsuit. Swinburne continued to show the defense's readiness to respond to Leonard's case when he alluded to a legal distinction he would make to counter Leonard's allegations of fraud. "'In our defense,'" he asserted, "'we will neither affirm nor deny that Mrs. Rhinelander is of negro blood. They have made that charge and they will have to prove it. That has nothing to do with our end of the case. We are concerned with their charge of fraud and we shall concentrate on that.'" Swinburne explained, "'Young Rhinelander knew this girl and her family for some time before the marriage. He paid attention to her sister before he courted Alice. He knew the entire situation.'"[110] With these words, however, Swinburne raised the question of what exactly it meant if Leonard "knew the entire situation." Swinburne also contradicted earlier reports that his main objective would be to prove Alice white. On Sunday, 30 November, the *American* quoted Swinburne: "'The issue is not color. She could be as black as coal and that fact would have nothing to do with the case.'"[111]

Swinburne's new line of argument hinted that Alice might not be pure white, and the issue surfaced again the following Tuesday, 2 December, in a *Times* interview with the attorney. The lawyer backed away from his earlier defense of his client's claim to whiteness, stating that the fact that the couple lived "'together after knowledge of her parentage is the only important thing that we must prove in the trial.'" But he didn't say what exactly this "knowledge of her parentage" might be. On the same day, the *American* reported Swinburne's claim that he could produce eight witnesses who would testify that Leonard knew everything about Alice Jones before their marriage.[112]

On 5 December, the *Times* announced that Alice's lawyer had prepared for her signature her formal response to Leonard's complaint. Alice's attorney noted that her answer would be made public and released to the newspapers as soon as it was served on Leonard and his attorney. The press predicted that Alice would deny all of Leonard's claims, but no one knew whether she would maintain that she was "of white parentage or not."[113] By Tuesday, 9 December, the newspapers announced that Alice's answer had been delivered to Leonard's attorney. In her response to Leonard's legal claims for an annulment, she denied all deceit. But Alice's emphatic denials failed to resolve the questions about her racial identity. Nevertheless, according to the *Times*, Alice's attorney still argued that "'since they do not openly charge that Mrs. Rhinelander is a negro or has negro blood in her veins, there is nothing there that needs to be disproved.'"[114]

Only days after Alice Rhinelander replied to her husband's lawsuit, Leonard and his lawyer rewrote the original complaint. The amended complaint addressed Alice's lawyer's statements that the original lacked a specific claim about Alice's "color." Leonard's new complaint contained two brand-new paragraphs. First, Leonard alleged "on information and belief" that Alice was "colored" and "with colored blood." In a separate paragraph, Leonard alleged "on information and belief" that Alice had "colored blood in her veins."[115] Thus, Leonard accused Alice of being "colored" and put the burden on her to prove that she was not.

In Leonard's amended complaint, he swore that he married Alice in the "full belief" that she was white and "without colored blood." Moreover, Leonard maintained that he and Alice did not cohabit as man and wife once he knew she did not have "entirely white blood and ancestry." Leonard's revised legal papers clearly accused Alice of being colored and passing for white.[116]

At some point before Alice responded to Leonard's new charges, her lawyer demanded that his lawyer specify when and how Alice misrepresented her color. Right after Christmas, Leonard's lawyer served Alice with a bill of particulars that declared that Alice lied about her color to Leonard a number of times between May and October 1924 in her parents' home. Leonard claimed that in 1924 he had learned about her older sister's marriage to a "colored man," which led him to ask Alice about her "parentage and blood." His questions, according to Leonard, led Alice to deceive him repeatedly. When Alice responded to Leonard's amended complaint, she did not directly deny the accusation of passing. Rather, Alice denied any "knowledge or information" about Leonard's claim that she was colored.[117] In effect, Alice's rejoinder to Leonard's revised complaint stated that she did not know her own racial ancestry. Alice's lack of knowledge suggested that if she indeed possessed any African ancestry her ignorance led her to act as if she were white—a lack of knowledge that posed a problem in an era when knowledge about race was deemed critical.

TWO :

"All Mixed Up" in New York

New York has gone almost completely native and soon we'll all be mixed up.
—CARL VAN VECHTEN to GERTRUDE STEIN, 10 December 1926

The case is attracting world-wide attention. The Nordics pretend to believe that the purity of their race has been outraged. For this reason, the case transcends in importance the fate of Mr. and Mrs. Kip Rhinelander.
—EDITORIAL, "The Rhinelander Case," *Messenger*, December 1925

NEWCOMERS TO NEW YORK CITY in the 1920s would have been struck by two different features of the country's largest metropolis: its soaring skyscrapers and its heterogeneous people. Whether the visitors arrived by train in Grand Central Station or by boat on the West Side docks, their eyes would have been drawn upward to the city's tall buildings. Then their eyes and ears would have turned slowly earthward to fasten on the different skin colors, languages, and nationalities of the people thronging the streets of New York. The city's skyscrapers, its "futuristic pinnacles," identified New York as the polestar of modern twentieth-century America—a symbol of the "spirited promise of a new civilization."[1] As visitors wandered through New York, they might head downtown to Wall Street, the center of the nation's financial industry, and then take the subway to midtown and locate Times Square, in whose "every nook and cranny, blossom and dance the electric advertising signs," a sight Leonard and Alice beheld when they rushed to the theater before heading to the Hotel Marie-Antoinette in December 1921. By 1924, sightseers strolling by newspaper stands throughout the city would see the latest headlines and photographs of Alice Rhinelander on the front pages of tabloids like the *Daily News* or the *Daily Mirror*, which could be purchased for only two cents.[2]

Like the city's tall buildings, subways, tabloids, and bright lights, New York's jumbled crowds represented something new about modern America. As cultural historian Ann Douglas put it, the city by the twenties had become "racially and ethnically mixed," a "mongrel Manhattan." In New York, tourists might discover Syrians in Little Syria, Chinese in Chinatown, Italians in Little Italy, "Negroes" in Harlem, and "Nordics" all around the town. One visitor to New York in the twenties described the city as a "greedy, spraddling monster," a "noisy Thunder Lizard of a town," which he found "peopled by an alien and an alienated swarm."[3] Not all New Yorkers were pleased by the variety of New York life either; many felt threatened by this explosion of difference. In the late teens, a white New York lawyer and socialite named Madison Grant gave voice to those anxieties when he penned *The Passing of the Great Race*, a jeremiad against demographic change in America. Inspired by alarms that white "native Americans" of the superior "Nordic" stock would be swamped by the tide of immigrants from "inferior" races, Grant prophesied a terrible destiny for New York and the nation. A cursed New York would become "a *cloaca gentium* which will produce many amazing racial hybrids and some ethnic horrors that will be beyond the powers of future anthropologists to unravel."[4] Alice Jones Rhinelander, a daughter of immigrants who claimed ignorance of her own background, might be a harbinger of such a terrible future.

The mixed ancestry of New Yorkers like Alice pointed to a "mongrelized" American future—a future many feared and despised. The growth in this population also pointed to a time to come when the privileges attached to particular European ancestries would feel increasingly under attack. In response, many white Americans launched preemptive strikes to protect and maintain the entitlements associated with their whiteness.[5] In the twenties, white Americans sought membership in the Ku Klux Klan, resorted to eugenics and science, pushed for immigration restrictions, and led a drive for segregation to uphold white supremacy. White supremacist Lothrop Stoddard articulated the fear that propelled these reactions: "Once the principle of the color-line is abandoned," he warned, "White America is doomed, and a mulatto America stands on the threshold." Yet, paradoxically, during the same decade many white Americans were attracted to the other side of their constructed color line as they tanned, listened to jazz, and danced black-inspired dances.[6] The contradictions generated by these competing impulses stimulated a growing interest in the study of "mixed races" and helped generate a great deal of attention both in and out of New York on the Rhinelander marriage and annulment trial.

New York's mixed character in the twenties was the result of the flood of newcomers to the city generated by two large streams of migration: foreign immigration and internal migration from other parts of the United States. In the late nineteenth and early twentieth centuries, European immigration drove population growth in New York City. In the 1890s, Alice Rhinelander's parents joined this migratory stream when they set sail to America from England on the SS *Majestic*. They chose to settle in Westchester, a county adjacent to but an integral part of the greater New York metropolitan region.[7]

By the beginning of the early twentieth century, Russians, Austro-Hungarians, and Italians dominated the stream of foreign migrants into the United States. In 1920, New York City's foreign-born white population exceeded 2,000,000 people out of a total population of 5,620,048, while Westchester's foreign-born white population exceeded 80,000. Between 1920 and 1930, despite the imposition of immigration restrictions in 1921 and 1924, over 600,000 new European immigrants arrived in New York City. The foreign-born white population increased substantially statewide as well.[8]

New York City's population of persons of African descent also surged in the early twentieth century, as did the black populations of nearby Westchester and Nassau counties. The community of persons of African descent in the city doubled in size from 1900 to 1920, and doubled again during the twenties, growing from a little over 60,000 people in 1900 to over 300,000 in 1930. Statewide, the number grew from 134,000 in 1910 to 413,000 in 1930. Westchester's population of persons of African descent grew from 8,986 in 1910 to 11,066 in 1920. The growth in the population of New Yorkers of African descent rested on both internal migration and immigration. This combination created what Charles Johnson, editor of the National Urban League's journal, *Opportunity*, termed a "Negro New Yorker," who was made up of "one part native, one part West Indian and about three parts Southern."[9]

The tremendous growth in the population of "Negro New Yorkers" in the first few decades of the twentieth century reflected in great part the Great Migration of African Americans from the South to the North. During the Great War, when European immigration declined and industrial jobs became available, hundreds of thousands of native-born persons of African descent abandoned the southern states to seek employment in the North.[10] Migrants from the Caribbean islands, a group collectively known as "West Indians," moved in large numbers to the city in the early twentieth century as well in search of economic opportunity. In 1910, over 11,000 foreign-born blacks lived in New York, and by 1930 that number had increased to over 54,000. In their coverage of the Rhinelander marriage, most New York newspapers referred to Alice's father, George Jones, as either a West Indian or a descendant of West Indians. Alice's lawyer, however, claimed at one point that her father's ancestry was *Indian* (from the subcontinent of India) not West Indian, to deny that George Jones was colored.[11]

African Americans also moved north in search of greater political and social opportunities than those available to them in the Jim Crow South. Urged on by newspapers like the *Chicago Defender* and advocates like W. E. B. DuBois, the black migration continued into the twenties. Indeed, DuBois told southerners why moving north made sense: "We can vote in the North. We can hold office in the North. As workers in northern establishments, we are getting good wages, decent treatment, healthful homes and schools for our children. Can we hesitate? COME NORTH!"[12]

Although New York did not possess the industrial opportunities available in Detroit or Cleveland, New York City attracted black migrants. According to Eugene Kinkle Jones, executive secretary of the National Urban League, migrants headed to New York because "the heterogeneity of the population has generated an atmosphere of freedom and democracy." Kinkle observed, "It seems to be a general impression among Negroes throughout the country that in this State they have a better chance for advancement, more rights as citizens and better prospects for the future than in other States of the Union."[13] For southern blacks New York offered a promising future.

During the early twentieth century, New York became the headquarters for organizations like the National Association for the Advancement of Colored People (NAACP), the National Urban League, and Marcus Garvey's Universal Negro Improvement Association, and the city emerged as "the dynamo for generating the social energies propelling the Negro masses towards what they hope will be a better day."[14] But not all New Yorkers hoped such a day would come for the city's growing black population.

The changing demographics of the city, the state, and, indeed the nation as a whole provoked a series of reactions in those white Americans who, like Madison Grant, foresaw a coming catastrophe. Many like Grant and Lothrop Stoddard also identified the moment as a time of growing competition between races. In 1920, Stoddard offered a vision of a forthcoming worldwide racial battle in *The Rising Tide of Color Against White-World Supremacy*. He ranted that the United States had been "invaded by hordes of immigrant Alpines and Mediterraneans, not to mention Asiatic elements like Levantines and Jews." "As a result," he maintained, "the Nordic native American has been crowded out with amazing rapidity by these swarming, prolific aliens, and after two short generations he has in many of our urban areas become almost extinct."[15] Those who agreed with Grant and Stoddard feared that without active resistance to these changes, the white race would perish.

Americans in the 1920s created and contested (both physically and intellectually) a nation centered around what one historian calls a modern "racial regime" supported by a growing emphasis on shoring up "the unchangeable fact of race difference."[16] A revived Ku Klux Klan aimed its sights outside of the South to focus its animus on immigrants, Catholics, Jews, African Americans, and Bolsheviks. Indeed, the Klan flexed its muscles by bringing the 1924 Democratic National Convention to a virtual standstill in New York, that, "un-American" city, as delegates debated whether or not to condemn the group. During the same year, white law students at Columbia University dressed as Klansmen burned a cross on campus to force an African American student out of the dormitories. The Klan also threatened a black Staten Island family who planned to move into a white neighborhood. One year later, the Klan continued to assert its presence when it marched in force down Pennsylvania Avenue in Washington, D.C.[17]

Increased race consciousness lay beneath the efforts by the Klan and others made anxious by the changes wrought by population movement. To the NAACP's Robert Bagnall, the rise of the Klan could be blamed on "a desire to bolster up a waning sense of superiority." Bagnall suggested that the ideas of the Klan and thinkers like Lothrop Stoddard emanated from "minds dwelling amidst shadows, creating imaginary hob-goblins, and striking in hysterical and maniacal fury at innocent victims."[18] In 1925 anthropologist Franz Boas, a "liberal" thinker on race, also noted the existence of a "world-wide 'complex' of race consciousness that has grown up during the past century." To support his observation, Boas pointed to writings by the Count de Gobineau in the nineteenth century and more recently Madison Grant. Boas blamed the burgeoning interest in race on "the more intimate interracial contact which has accompanied the extension of modern commerce and the exploitation of foreign continents." Two years later, Kelly Miller, a Howard University professor, also took notice of white Americans' "growing racial consciousness," which he saw leading to the desire to segregate blacks in the North.[19] Race consciousness flourished in a variety of ways during the twenties, much of it expressed through the language of science.

Interest in the scientific study of race was high, especially in the field of eugenics, which promoted a "new vision of a race of better men." This "new vision" emphasized the importance of heredity and racial purity. Although the eugenics movement had started in the late nineteenth century, the years between 1905 and 1930 constituted the highpoint of its dominance in American science and culture.[20] Popular magazines like the *Saturday Evening Post* (which Alice read), in addition to academic journals, disseminated eugenics theory. Many Americans imbibed eugenics at a young age as the subject filtered into the high school curriculum through biology textbooks.[21]

Most eugenicists abhorred the polyglot nature of American cities in the 1920s and saw urbanization as a sign of national degeneration. The results of the 1920 census revealed that the American population had become more urban than rural. Albert E. Wiggam, who helped make the precepts of eugenics accessible to Americans, bemoaned the flow of people from the countryside into the cities. In "The Rising Tide of Degeneracy: What Everybody Ought to Know About Eugenics," Wiggam pointed to urbanization as an element leading to the nation's "downfall." Those Americans drawn to the overcivilized city from rural areas, "man's natural habitat and breeding ground," no longer reproduced enough of the best kinds of Americans.[22]

As a consequence of this failure to adequately reproduce, Madison Grant found New York a particularly threatening site of race-mingling, where the "native American" would be overtaken by "a polyglot mass of aliens of every kind and description," which would lead to the "establishment of colonies of foreigners in our midst." In a 1925 article on the perils of immigration, Grant railed against "unchecked" immigration and complained about the inefficiencies of local city governments, which he blamed on the "mixed character of our city populations." Yet in the same year, in sharp contrast to Grant and Wiggam, the NAACP's Walter White found positive aspects to "mongrel" Manhattan. He observed, "New York's polyglot population, which causes such distress to the Lothrop Stoddards and the Madison Grants . . . has created more nearly than any other section that democracy which is the proud boast but rarely practised accomplishment of these United States." Indeed, New Yorkers of African descent began to acquire a greater political presence in New York in the teens and twenties.[23]

Despite Walter White's celebration of a diverse and mixed New York, fears of race-mingling haunted eugenics circles and shaped responses to interracial marriage and immigration. When the American Museum of Natural History in New York hosted the Second International Conference on Eugenics in September 1921 (the same month Leonard met Alice), more than half of the over one hundred papers presented discussed the problem of marriages between persons of different races and ethnic backgrounds. As one paper presented at the conference described the eugenics perspective, "Intermarriages between whites and blacks, just as much as wrongful sexual relations without marriage, are essentially anti-social tendencies and therefore opposed to the teachings of sound eugenics." Not surprisingly, the eugenics movement concerned itself with maintaining "racial purity."[24]

Since eugenicists categorized races as either "superior" or "inferior," many adherents believed the amalgamation of such races could only produce lower-quality people. To avoid this result, some eugenics proponents promoted the reproduction of those deemed "fit" and the sterilization of the "unfit." Eugenicists who favored such "negative" eugenics often supported legal restrictions on marriages, including interracial unions, and immigration restriction.[25] Eugenicists justified prohibitions on marriage and limits on immigration by pointing to the dismaying results of army intelligence tests undertaken during World War I. The tests demonstrated to the eugenicists that immigrants from southern and eastern Europe and African Americans were mentally inferior to white Americans.[26] Consequently, "cross-breeding" could only harm white America.

Concerns over racial purity also surfaced in the widespread admiration of the so-called Nordic race in the 1920s. Worship of Nordicism by many white Americans took off when a New York publishing house reissued Madison Grant's 1916 book *The Passing of the Great Race* in three revised editions in 1918, 1920, and 1921. The term "Nordic," along with the belief that the Nordic race surpassed all other races, passed into common usage in this decade. F. Scott Fitzgerald's *Great Gatsby* featured a disagreeable character who rants about "Nordic" superiority without any explanation of the word. Fitzgerald's contemporary readers did not need one.[27]

Readers of *The Great Gatsby* and Madison Grant's *Passing of the Great Race* would have known that Grant classified humankind into three groups: the

"Caucasians," the "Negroids," and the "Mongoloids." In his book, however, Grant obsessed about the "Caucasian," or "European," race. Grant subdivided the European race into three separate and unequal branches or "subspecies": the "Nordic," the "Mediterranean," and the "Alpine." He proclaimed the "Nordic" race the "white man par excellence" and a race of "rulers, organizers and aristocrats." Grant feared that the numbers of Nordics had decreased in Europe because the best types of men were killed during World War I.[28]

Not only Europe suffered from a deficit of Nordics. According to Grant, while a pure Nordic race had founded the United States, it declined as immigration from the other, lesser European groups grew at the end of the nineteenth century. Consequently, America's Nordics needed to become more racially aware or else face a "racial abyss." "Native Americans" might disappear from those places where they would be overtaken by inferior types. According to Grant, himself a "native" of New York, one location where the "native Americans" could vanish would be New York. Given these views, Grant joined with other eugenicists to promote immigration restriction to preserve America's Nordic racial purity before it was too late.[29]

In the twenties, eugenicists like Grant and Wiggam joined with other anti-immigrationists to push Congress to limit immigration from "racially undesirable" countries. Indeed, the 1924 immigration restriction act, the Johnson-Reed Act, took its name from Congressman Albert Johnson, who served as president of the Eugenics Research Association from 1923 to 1924. Eugenicists like Albert Wiggam worried openly that the country was "replacing the noble strains" with "weaker, slower and lower strains of immigrant blood." The campaign to curtail immigration based on eugenic ideas about race and fears of "mongrelization" proved successful. In 1921, and again in 1924, Congress reduced immigration from southern and eastern Europe, the places whose peoples, the so-called Mediterranean and Alpine races, eugenicists deemed inferior to "native stock" white Americans. As historian Mae Ngai points out, Congress created a quota board that narrowly defined the term "native stock" to encompass only those descended from whites in the United States as of 1790. By the time Congress enacted its permanent immigration restriction act in 1924, legislators completely prohibited immigration from south and east Asia and established quotas for other nations.[30]

Although the 1924 immigration law appeared to allow for unrestricted immigration from countries in the Western Hemisphere, it reduced immigration from many of the islands in the Caribbean. The law provided that immigration from colonial possessions like the British West Indies would need to come under the quota of the colonizing country. Only a few months after the law went into effect, W. A. Domingo, a Jamaican living in New York, complained in the pages of *Opportunity* that this provision constituted "a deliberate discrimination against those countries of the New World from which Negroes had been coming to any extent, while exempting those from which Caucasians are still coming without limit." Since Canada could still continue to send immigrants to the United States without limits, Domingo charged that Congress designed the 1924 law to make sure fewer people with African ancestry entered the United States. One historian of Caribbean migration to New York confirms that the law had the effect that Domingo believed Congress intended. The number of persons of African descent from the Caribbean migrating to the United States after 1924 fell dramatically. Despite the harshness of the 1924 immigration law, eugenicists still did not feel completely satisfied. In 1925, Madison Grant complained that West Indian immigration needed to be further restricted to keep out "peoples of so-called colored blood." By 1930, Lothrop Stoddard still feared that Americans needed to "guard[ing] our gates" to keep undesirables out.[31]

Although immigration restriction limited the number of the "wrong" Europeans entering the United States, completely excluded Asians, and reduced the numbers of West Indians, it could not stanch the flow of African Americans into the North. By 1931 the *Literary Digest* observed, "Broader grow the black belts in northern cities—in New York, Philadelphia, Detroit, Pittsburgh, and Chicago. Northward and cityward the Southern Negro is wending his way." The migration of black people out of the South in the teens and twenties accelerated a growing movement in the North toward racial separation that had started at the beginning of the twentieth century.[32]

In the early years of the century, while some African Americans felt that race prejudice was "not the ruling sentiment" in the North, outbreaks of tension did occur. The century opened with a race riot in New York City in August 1900. Progressive Era reformers organized the NAACP in 1910 in the wake of a northern race riot and lynching in Springfield, Illinois. Over the course of the teens, violence continued to erupt in places affected by the Great Migration, such as East St. Louis in 1917 and Chicago during the Red Summer of 1919.[33] The rise in race-based violence appeared to be the "unhappy manifestations of a spirit that the North did not realize it possessed." This new spirit in the North rested on white northerners' fears that an influx of African Americans would lead to increased political, economic, and social power for blacks at the expense of whites. As African American men returned from fighting in the Great War and black women participated in the war effort, white Americans worried that African Americans would no longer accept a subordinate place in American society. Many white Americans worked to assert their supremacy over blacks in all fields of existence. And northern African Americans resisted.[34]

In the teens and twenties, white northerners tried to separate themselves from their neighbors of African descent. Unlike southern Jim Crow, northern segregation generally took on a de facto, not de jure, form. Some northern states, like New York, for example, had laws on the books that prohibited discrimination in public places. New York's civil rights laws provided that "all persons within the jurisdiction of this state shall be entitled to the full and equal accommodations, advantages and privileges of any place of public accommodation, resort or amusement." Nevertheless, African Americans were often denied access to commercial establishments in New York. Consequently, many African Americans countered with lawsuits under the Civil Rights Law.[35]

The stories behind the legal actions brought by New York's black citizens highlight the ordinariness of the places and amenities that whites tried to deny to African Americans. These conflicts over access to places like theaters, resorts, and restaurants also suggest that the realm of consumption became a contested field where maintaining the color line was considered supreme. In New York, for example, when two boys, Harold Robinson and William Jackson, went to a candy store to buy ice cream, the waitress refused to serve them because they were "colored" and "those are my orders." On a sunny June day, Carroll Johnson and three female friends rode a trolley to a park operated by the trolley company. When the four tried to purchase buttons to join the other dancers on the park's dancing pavilion, no one would sell them the required buttons. In the middle of a hot July, Conrad Norman, a teacher, accompanied his white students to a bathing beach. When the students and their teacher attempted to buy tickets to use the bathhouses to change into their swimming suits, the cashier, Mrs. Shaefer, refused to sell them. When Norman asked whether it was because of his color, she responded, "Well, yes." Susan Joyner hoped to see a matinee at a theater and bought a ticket to sit in the orchestra section. When she walked over to her seat, someone approached her and told her to go to the box office. Theater employees then told Miss Joyner that she would have to sit in the balcony.[36]

Although some African Americans won their cases, these kinds of lawsuits proved insufficient to counter growing efforts to segregate. New York's courts interpreted the civil rights law narrowly; judges only applied it to the specific establishments listed in the statute. And sometimes the desire to subordinate blackness bordered on the absurd. In 1924, the *New York Times* reported that a beauty contest in New York City had been cancelled when it appeared an African American girl might win. Although the promoters of the contest "declined to admit they had drawn the color line in the beauty contest . . . they made a mystery of their reasons." These mysterious reasons, however, most likely rested on the fact that the victory of an African American girl over white girls might call into question the inherent superiority and beauty of whiteness. Not surprisingly, as early as 1919 the *Crisis* warned African Americans in northern cities to "be on the alert lest [their] rights be curtailed by those white people whose superiority consists in making other people uncomfortable."[37] This warning proved prescient especially as whites tried to limit legally or extralegally blacks' ability to own property and live in neighborhoods of their choosing.

Recent historical scholarship on residential segregation in the North examines the rise of conflict in the early twentieth century that developed when African Americans moved into neighborhoods perceived by whites as "theirs." Many whites felt the movement of African Americans into "their" residential districts constituted an "invasion" that required repulsion. Some cities, especially in border states, complied with the demands of their white citizens. In Baltimore, Maryland, and Louisville, Kentucky, local governments enacted laws to keep blacks from living in certain parts of the city. White residents of Harlem tried unsuccessfully to get New York City to do the same. African Americans and the NAACP fought against these kinds of laws, and by 1917, the U.S. Supreme Court ruled these municipal statutes unconstitutional in *Buchanan v. Warley*.[38]

White Americans, however, still resisted the movement of African Americans into "their" neighborhoods, perhaps spurred on by the likes of Madison Grant, who observed that if whites wanted to maintain racial purity, "they cannot continue to live side by side" with "Negroes." It is not surprising, then, that in the aftermath of a riot in Johnstown, Pennsylvania, in 1923, the mayor of that city tried to throw out of town *all* recent African American arrivals. Not only such extreme measures were tried. After the Supreme Court decided *Buchanan*, Many white homeowners in northern communities chose to incorporate private residential covenants into the deeds to their homes. The covenants prevented owners of real estate from selling their properties to certain buyers, primarily African Americans and Jews.[39] Although the NAACP took up a legal battle against this strategy to limit blacks' residential choices, the Supreme Court accepted in 1926 the argument that residential covenants constituted private agreements even though they required the action of a court for enforcement. The decision in *Corrigan v. Buckley*, would not be overturned until 1948, in *Shelley v. Kraemer*.[40]

When residential covenants did not exist or were ignored, white northerners used violence to maintain the racial purity of their residential districts. The best-known outbreak of violence over housing in the twenties took place in Detroit, only a few months before the Rhinelander trial opened, in 1925. In the twenties, Detroit experienced a large in-migration of black southerners. At the same time, membership in the local chapter of the Ku Klux Klan rose. This combination intensified tensions in Detroit. When an African American doctor, Ossian Sweet, and his wife, Gladys, purchased and moved into a home in a white neighborhood, an angry white mob threatened the Sweets and their guests. Shots fired from the house into the crowd killed one white man. The police arrested the Sweets and others in the house and charged them with murder.[41]

The NAACP hired celebrated lawyer Clarence Darrow to defend the Sweets, and the defendants were ultimately acquitted. Yet many American whites refused to acknowledge any responsibility for fomenting violent clashes. A white commentator in the popular weekly magazine *Outlook* suggested the *Sweet* case was really about the "race problem," that "two races were on trial; two races forced by fate to live together, but making a sorry, disorderly, and often bloody mess of it all." In a further circumlocution, the author concluded, "The Sweet case is simply another illustration of the difficult race problem which, almost overnight, the North has had thrust on it." This kind of interpretation of the case, however, shifted the responsibility for the violence in Detroit, and implicitly in other locations in the North, away from white northerners to an abstract "race problem."[42]

Many African American commentators in the 1920s noted the rise in hostilities. As early as 1922 the editors of the *Messenger* suggested that "the spirit of Dixie holds the nation in its grip." One year later, W. E. B. DuBois observed a growing northern " 'Jim Crow' movement." In the same year, the *Messenger* acknowledged the links between the movement of African Americans out of the South and increasing conflict in the North: "While the hegira of Negroes north will work certain vital, far-reaching and beneficent economic, social and political changes . . . it will also produce new social and economic problems which the Negroes will be compelled to grapple with in the North." In particular, the *Messenger* pointed to jobs and housing as the new battlefields in the North as economic competition between white immigrants and black New Yorkers would only continue to grow. Indeed, even before World War I, most New York labor unions refused to admit African Americans into their ranks. The *Literary Digest* reported in 1927 that the worst racial confrontations were taking place in the North, not the South, as a consequence of the migration.[43]

Yet at the same time that racial consciousness rose and new racial distinctions were being drawn in the North white Americans' fascination with "Negroes" reached a peak, especially during the Harlem Renaissance. NAACP executive secretary James Weldon Johnson's 1930 history of black Manhattan recalled Harlem's image in the twenties as "exotic, colourful, and sensuous; a place of laughing, singing, and dancing; a place where life wakes up at night." This image of Harlem, which ignored many of the day-to-day realities of the neighborhood, drew many whites uptown.[44]

William Pickens, a field secretary for the NAACP, tried to explain the paradox of white fascination with blackness in the twenties by resorting to the new language of Freudian psychology. He argued that white Americans' unconscious minds contained "forbidden desires and repressed emotions" about color. These unconscious desires could invade the conscious mind if the "Censor," which guarded the unconscious, let them. In a society that worked hard to subordinate blacks, the "Censor" needed to work especially hard to repress any positive feelings about blacks. Consequently, Pickens suggested, the "Censor" sometimes broke down and allowed "repressed desires and feelings respecting people of color" to escape.[45]

White Americans' attraction to African American locations like Harlem and the appeal of color accentuated their contradictory desire to establish inflexible lines between races. Writing for the *Messenger* in February 1925, Eulalia Proctor declared the twenties the "Bronze Age," pointing out that in addition to flocking to Harlem and Chicago's South Side, white Americans were drawn to dissolve differences by becoming, at least for a while, a facsimile of the "other." As an example, Proctor pointed to the "brown beauty" chorus line of *Shuffle Along* and its appeal to white men. "Sheba, bronzed and artful," she wrote, "became the popular synonym for all that is attractive and chic in femininity!" Proctor suggested that white women sought to tan themselves in response. Another author, writing about race in the 1920s, contended, "It is impossible now to tell a light [colored] girl from a white one when she is made up fine with cheeks like rose leaves in the summer. This trick has been favorable to white girls along the color line. The white girl now passes for colored whenever she wishes." In 1929, a poem in the *Crisis* described a "downtown girl" (that is, white) who craved an "Afro-tan" to be "dark and chic!"[46] Such changes, however, only seemed to raise the possibility of mistaken racial identifications.

Not only white women sought to darken their skin. Eulalia Proctor observed that for white American men, "the desirable thing in masculinity" was to possess "engagingly dark and sleek hair, insolently glancing dark eyes, . . . a tawny glow" and to resemble the main character in the film *The Sheik*, played by the Italian actor Rudolph Valentino. As an Italian immigrant, Valentino belonged to a group perceived by some historians as occupying an uneasy position between black and white in the early twentieth century.[47] Despite the successful movement to restrict immigrants from Italy, white moviegoers responded to Valentino's allure. So-called mulattos had a similar allure. In an article in the *Crisis*, a college student who self-identified as "mulatto" described his interactions with white "co-eds" and their fascination with him: "To them you are an unknown quantity. Neither black nor white. They wished they dared know you more intimately."[48]

Toward the end of the decade, H. L. Mencken, the white editor of the *American Mercury*, acknowledged the growing appeal of African Americans to white Americans and the increasingly amalgamated nature of American culture. Mencken declared that the United States had entered what he crudely called a "Coon Age." Given the incorporation of African American culture (jazz, dancing, "Aframerican" food) into white America, Mencken observed, "the proud Nordic Blond, pushing always, has pushed at last into colored society." Consequently, white and black social interactions had increased in the "new cosmopolitanism." "As everyone knows," Mencken wrote, "the old social barriers are rapidly disappearing in the larger cities of the land, and especially in New York. There is no longer any aristocracy there, in the old American sense; anyone is free of society who has suitable clothes and agreeable manners."[49] Mencken linked the assimilation of African American culture by whites to a breakdown in class and racial barriers.

Mencken did not view this "culturally pigmented" transformation as necessarily positive. White America's attraction to African Americans could become a problem, he asserted, for this blurring of color and social lines inevitably led to "somewhat disconcerting fruits in the tender sphere." The "fruits" to which Mencken referred included the "scion of the princely Rhinelanders [who] took to wife a worthy colored girl" and the recent marriage of the New

York City heiress Ellen Mackay to the Jewish song writer Irving Berlin.[50] That Mencken's discussion turned from blurred cultural color lines to the problem of "mixed marriages" attests to an intense societal interest in "miscegenation" that extended beyond the circles of eugenics advocates. One disturbing fruit of marital race mixing would be racially mixed offspring, "a walking chaos," who might not easily fit a single category and would stand as living proof of the mongrelization that Madison Grant predicted for New York and America.[51] Alice Jones Rhinelander, depicted as the daughter of a white English mother and a father with an unknown but possibly African ancestry, perhaps embodied the confusing fruit of race mixture.

In the early days of the newspaper coverage of the Rhinelander marriage, reporters struggled with the problem of how to characterize Alice. At times, both the *Daily News* and the *Times* identified Alice as a "mulatto," though neither newspaper defined the term. Apparently, it was assumed that readers knew what the term meant. Yet the word "mulatto" possessed no clear and fixed definition during the 1920s.

Four years before Leonard and Alice married, the 1920 federal census offered one definition of "mulatto" that drew on a conceptual framework of "blood": Those who would be counted as "'black' (B)," according to census officials, included "all persons who are evidently full blooded negroes, while the term 'mulatto' (Mu) includes all other persons having some proportion or perceptible trace of negro blood." This definition left it to census enumerators to determine "proportions" or perceive "traces" of blood. By the end of the decade, however, the Census Bureau eliminated the category "mulatto" from the list of colors and races to be counted in 1930. Instead, census enumerators received instructions to code those "of mixed white and Negro blood" as "Negro" because "both black and mulatto persons are to be returned as Negroes without distinction."[52]

The census category "mulatto" made six appearances between 1850 and 1920. The term first appeared in the census of 1850, but it wasn't defined. Only in the first census after the Civil War, in 1870, did "mulatto" get defined broadly as a "generic [term], [which] includes quadroons, octoroons, and all persons having any perceptible trace of African blood." By the 1890 census, however, Congress called for an exact breakdown of "the number of negroes, mulattoes, quadroons, and octoroons." The instructions for the enumerators precisely spelled out the definition of each category, which ranged from the "mulatto," those "persons who have from three-eighths to five-eighths black blood," to the "octoroon," those "persons who have one-eighth or any trace of black blood." The 1900 census eliminated any categories distinct from "black" and "white," while the term "mulatto" reappeared again for the 1910 and 1920 censuses.[53] Over the years, then, those Americans identified as "mulatto" in one census might fall into a different category in another. No wonder New York's press chose not to proffer their own definitions.

If definitions of mulatto seesawed over time, so too did the perceptions of mulattoes. In the early twentieth century, the mulatto was referred to as degenerate, a "mongrel . . . the quintessence of deterioration," and inferior to both whites and blacks. In the 1920s when eugenicist Charles Davenport examined the mixed personage of the "browns," he concluded that racial mixing produced disharmonious results. According to Davenport, the "browns" proved inferior to both "blacks" and "whites," for they "were muddled and wuzzle-headed." Yet Davenport and others who studied mulattoes, such as Edward Reuter, at times also argued that the "mulattoes of North America" proved intellectually superior to blacks.[54]

When whites deemed mulattoes superior to blacks, they usually worried that mulattoes posed a threat to society.[55] In an article titled "Dangers of Race Mixture," *Current History* magazine in 1927 posited that "mulattoes" possessed some of the "intelligence and ambition" from their white ancestry as well as an "insufficient intelligence" from their other ancestry. Consequently, mulattoes were unlikely to realize their goals, which turned them into problems. Often, the desire to be white constituted the mulatto's main problem. As a Virginia advocate of racial purity concluded, "The highest ambition of many of these [mulattoes and near-whites] is to be classed as white and to marry white." Madison Grant, however, made it clear that such people could never "transform[ed] . . . in any way into white men." Endorsing this line of reasoning, a 1924 essay in *Current History* suggested that mulattoes should emigrate and thus "eliminate that unfortunate no-man's land . . . where black is not black and white is not white."[56]

While the mulatto male could never become white, the mulatto female appeared as a "Jezebel" who seduced white men. In her discussion of the "Bronze Age," Eulalia Proctor commented on the sex appeal of brown-skinned chorus girls. According to another author, the "primitive sex-appeal of the octoroon girl is highly potent with the average young white male." Although the author referred to the "octoroon girl," no hard and fast lines separated the "octoroon" in the popular mind from the "mulatto."[57] Even if mulattoes did not want to become white or seduce white men, they might perceive themselves as better than darker-skinned people. A 1924 popular magazine identified the "mulatto" as *the* source of the nation's "negro problem" and argued that their superiority to "the pure negro" made them "disliked by both whites and blacks." Walter White even argued that Marcus Garvey's race-first propaganda promoted antagonism between "Negroes" and "mulattoes."[58]

While the definitions of mulatto and images associated with the mulatto lacked coherence, the 1920s experienced an increased scientific interest in mulattoes, or "mixed-race" people.[59] This interest in the "mixed-race" person reflected the era's increased interest in understanding and delineating race. One strand of this interest, exemplified by the studies of Charles Davenport, strove to prove mulatto inferiority. Some of the renewed interest in the mulatto in the 1920s, however, pointed to different perceptions of the term, which did not necessarily highlight concepts of racial hierarchy but still continued to differentiate between races. The research project undertaken by anthropologist Melville Herskovits, a student of Franz Boas, for example, still assumed the naturalness of the idea of race itself while he argued that terms like "mulatto" or "quadroon" proved too clumsy to accurately represent the realities of race.[60]

Despite Herskovits's more "liberal" approach to race, in a preliminary report on his project in *Opportunity*, he accepted the division of "mankind" into three distinct races: "White," "Negro," and "Mongol." He proposed to examine "race crossing," and he argued that "the best way . . . is to work with groups which are of known racial mixture." Herskovits planned to focus on "Negro-white crossing" because he suggested the physical differences between whites and Negroes were more distinct than the differences between any other racial groups. As he proceeded to study "Negro-white crossing," Herskovits began to construct the concept of the "American Negro," a "new physical type."[61]

During the course of his research, Herskovits argued that this new American Negro constituted a physically "mixed type," unlike the white race. Despite its mixed nature, Herskovits proposed that the American Negro was a "homogeneous" group. In fact, Herskovits contended that fewer than one-quarter of those he classified as American Negro had no white ancestry. That is to say, that although the American Negro comprised a predominantly mixed group, all of its members were essentially the same. Accordingly, classifications like "mulatto" or "quadroon" were no longer necessary.[62]

Herskovits also addressed white Americans' fear of race mixing. According to Herskovits, most American Negroes were not the product of recent race mixing. In an article in the popular magazine *Current History*, Herskovits rushed to reassure the white reading public of this fact: "I myself have observed that there is a pressure within the Negro community against associating with Whites which parallels that in the White group with regard to Negroes." Herskovits argued that although the American Negro did not exist as a "pure" race, most of the impurities dated from the distant past. Moreover, since all or most American Negroes were the result of some race mixture, no one needed to distinguish between "Negroes" and mulattoes. All "Negroes" were mulattoes and all mulattoes were "Negroes." But whatever one chose to call them, the American Negro could be distinguished from white Americans. Although Herskovits didn't specifically address what it meant to be white, his conclusions on the American Negro left the impression that while the American Negro was mixed, the American white was pure.[63]

Despite Herskovits's reassurances that the American Negro could be differentiated from white Americans, the possibility of transgressing racial lines became more threatening, in part because the very behavior of white Americans, for example in tanning, eroded the lines between the races and made it more difficult to tell who was what. To illustrate this point, journalist George Schuyler described an incident at the end of the twenties that would have persuaded the likes of Madison Grant or Lothrop Stoddard that white Americans had not done enough to protect their race and that their failure only produced confusion. Schuyler described a mix-up in racial identification when the employees of a Washington, D.C., hotel dining room would not seat a group of suntanned whites. A fight broke out and punches flew until the manager realized the groups' membership in the "Nordic" race despite their tanned skins. He issued an apology. Given the misidentification, ensuing confusion, and violence, Schuyler concluded slyly that "if this tanned vogue becomes as prevalent as did the bobbed-hair mania a few years back, there is no telling what strange things may happen."[64]

The presence of greater numbers of people of African descent in northern cities, combined with the presence of immigrants from southern and eastern Europe, worked to blur the lines between races. Cities like New York seemed to be, in Carl Van Vechten's phrase, "all mixed up." Despite immigration restrictions and the strenuous efforts to segregate the North, a strong potential for confusion existed. The stories of Leonard and Alice Rhinelander's marriage and of Leonard's claim that Alice lied to him about her race, hit the pages of New York City's press only a few months after Congress passed the 1924 immigration law. By the time the stories appeared on newspapers' front pages, readers both in and outside of New York had heard plenty about desirable and undesirable races and the dangers that mongrelization posed to the country. At the same time, many white Americans contributed to the sense of confusion through their growing interest in "Aframerican" culture and their pursuit of tanned skin.

Popular interest in the story of the Rhinelander marriage suggested that white Americans remained uncertain about how to draw exact lines between the races despite the Klan's, eugenicists', racial separatists', and scientists' efforts to point them out. In addition, Leonard's claim that Alice "passed" as white suggested that being considered white was something valuable that could be fraudulently obtained. Given this combination, the pretrial publicity about the Rhinelanders, with the press alternately disputing and confirming different identities for Alice and her family, grabbed the public's attention. Perhaps the upcoming trial would resolve the confusion.

THREE :

The Trial Begins

It is all a petty, silly matter of no real importance which another generation will comprehend with great difficulty. But today, and in the minds of most white Americans, it is a matter of tremendous moral import. One may deceive as to killing, stealing and adultery, but you must tell your "friend" that you're "colored," or suffer a very material hell fire in this world, if not in the next.—W. E. B. DUBOIS, from review of Nella Larsen's *Passing* (1929)

JUST BEFORE TEN O'CLOCK on a crisp autumn morning in early November 1925, the White Plains, New York, courtroom doors swung open to admit those members of the public who awaited the upcoming Rhinelander annulment trial.[1] Once the doors opened, scores of people, including wealthy matrons, chambermaids, porters, and flappers pushed in and tried to secure seats. When the courtroom filled, eight deputy sheriffs struggled to control the overflow crowd that spilled into the corridors. Despite the chilly air, hundreds of disappointed spectators who failed to squeeze in to the packed courtroom lingered in the street outside Westchester County's Supreme Court.[2]

Justice Joseph Morschauser of the New York Supreme Court would preside over the trial that Monday morning, 9 November. But the crowd did not come

The crowd attending the Rhinelander annulment trial in White Plains, New York. Alice's sister, Grace Miller; her brother-in-law, Robert Brooks; and Robert's wife, Emily Brooks, are seated in the foreground. Elizabeth and George Jones are seated in the row in front of their daughters. © Bettmann/Corbis.

to see the bespectacled judge who had been sitting on the bench since 1906, even though he had been the judge in the divorce case of well-known actor Lionel Barrymore two years earlier.[3] Instead, the spectators waited to get their first glimpse of the parties to this unusual case, who up until this point they had only seen pictured in the press. Not long after the crowd packed the courtroom, three lawyers appeared and took their seats at the plaintiff's table: lead counsel for Leonard Rhinelander, the gray-haired, seventy-four-year-old retired New York Supreme Court justice Isaac N. Mills; Mills's son, LeRoy Mills; and New York City attorney Leon R. Jacobs, the lawyer who separated Leonard and Alice one year earlier. Three defense lawyers filed into the courtroom and took their seats: lead counsel for Alice Jones Rhinelander, Lee

Parsons Davis, a forty-three-year-old former Westchester County district attorney; his junior colleague Richard E. Keough; and Alice's initial attorney, New Rochelle City Court judge Samuel F. Swinburne. Both Mills and Davis had been selected to act as trial counsel by Leonard's and Alice's attorneys (Jacobs and Swinburne, respectively). Jacobs needed local counsel in Westchester to avoid any prejudice of the jury against city lawyers. Swinburne may have hired Davis because of Davis's growing reputation as a litigator in Westchester courtrooms.[4]

The crowd expected a fierce battle between the two lead attorneys, who were well-known and respected members of the Westchester bar. Considered a formidable opponent in Westchester's courts, Isaac Mills had been practicing law since 1876, when he graduated from the Columbia College School of Law after attending Amherst College. In 1883, the citizens of Westchester elected him to the judiciary; he served for twelve years as county judge. In 1896, he helped found the Westchester County Bar Association. Ten years after stepping down as a county judge, Mills was elected to sit as a New York Supreme Court justice on the same court he was currently appearing before (the same year Justice Morschauser took his seat). Once Mills returned to private practice after retiring from the bench (again), he took on high-profile cases in Westchester.[5]

Somewhat hard of hearing, Mills (still referred to by everyone as "Judge" Mills) periodically used an old-fashioned ear trumpet to catch everything going on in the courtroom. Although the press sometimes described his speaking voice as bland, Mills used a slow and dramatic speaking style to make his arguments and drew on biblical analogies to emphasize his points. Like his ear trumpet, Mills often comes across in the trial transcript and the press as rather old-fashioned; his rhetorical techniques and grandiloquent gestures were reminiscent of his youth in the late nineteenth century and the stage melodramas of that time. Reporters described his courtroom style as "Warfieldian," a reference to a contemporary actor who specialized in melodrama. Notwithstanding Mills's eccentric traits, he had been hired by a very well-to-do and well-connected family who could easily afford the best legal representation.[6]

Mills's much younger opponent, Lee Parsons Davis, like Mills, received his legal training at Columbia, graduating in 1903. Davis practiced law in New York City for a few years, first with Coudert Brothers, a law firm founded in 1854 by three French brothers, and then as a trial lawyer for the New York City Railways Company. A few years later, he moved to the Westchester suburbs and served as an assistant district attorney before joining a local law firm. In 1916, Westchester County voters elected the thirty-four-year-old Davis to the office of district attorney, where he was renowned for winning more than thirty first-degree murder convictions. When he returned to private practice in 1922, Davis brought with him a reputation as a skilled courtroom attorney, with a deep, dramatic voice prone to sarcasm and a talent for courtroom tactics that often convinced juries of the validity of his clients' claims.[7] Despite their differences in style, Davis and Mills were both skilled and experienced litigators, each with a strong desire to win his client's case and willing to go to great lengths to do so. They knew each other, and they would have had some knowledge of each other's style and strengths in the courtroom.[8]

Right after the lawyers entered the court, Alice Jones Rhinelander, dressed in a tight-fitting cloche felt hat and a fur-trimmed coat, joined her legal team at the defense table, accompanied by a female clerk from Samuel Swinburne's law office. To the dismay of the crowd, Alice's husband, Leonard Rhinelander, failed to put in an appearance that morning. The defendant's family, however, appeared in court to lend moral support. The crowd stared at Alice's parents, Elizabeth and George Jones, and her older sister and brother-in-law, Emily and Robert Brooks, as they took their seats in the courtroom. The elder Joneses dressed conservatively; Mrs. Jones wore a bulky, old-fashioned hat in contrast to her daughter Alice's. The long-faced Mr. Jones sported a trim and snowy mustache and looked "like a picture of an old Spanish hidalgo," although he bore a remarkable resemblance to white supremacist and eugenics propagandist Madison Grant. No members of the Rhinelander family appeared in court that morning, or indeed at any other point during the trial, despite published suggestions that they engineered Leonard's legal case.[9]

The first order of business was jury selection, which took up most of the morning. Although American women had recently gained the right to vote, they did not sit on New York juries until 1937, so only men would hear the case. The lawyers posed few questions to the potential jurors. Significantly, the press reported two different versions of one of Isaac Mills's questions. According to the *New York Times*, Mills asked each potential juror "is it not apparent that there is a visible trace of Negro blood in this defendant?" The *New York Evening Journal*, however, reported that Mills declared, "One can look at the defendant and see that the presence of Negro blood is not very apparent."[10] The conflicting reports reflected lingering uncertainty about Alice Jones's ancestry.

Mills and Davis selected twelve married white men for the jury who came from different towns and cities in Westchester. Mills was pleased with the composition of the jury; he predicted that white, married men would sympathize with Leonard's predicament of finding himself married to a "colored" woman. Once the jurors were assembled, court broke for lunch. No one had yet seen Leonard Rhinelander in the courtroom.[11]

After lunch Davis refused to allow Mills to begin his opening address to the jury until Leonard arrived in court. Davis wanted to make sure none of the jurors knew Leonard and would be biased in his favor. Around half past two, Leonard, accompanied by a bodyguard, walked into the courtroom and, with all eyes upon him, joined his attorneys at the plaintiff's table. Everyone looked to see if Leonard would glance at his wife, Alice, since he had not seen her in almost one year. He never looked her way. Once Leonard took his seat, Isaac Mills stood up and faced the jury.[12]

Before Mills began, he tried to offset any negative impression Leonard's late entrance might have made on the jurors. He apologized for his client's delay and blamed it on advice given to Leonard by Leon Jacobs. (Leonard had spent the previous evening in a Westchester hotel room with Jacobs and a bodyguard.) According to Mills, Jacobs assumed jury selection would take as long in Westchester as it did in New York City, "but," Mills said, "we don't do things that way." After apologizing, Mills summarized his version of the applicable law. He explained to the jury that according to New York's marriage law, "any material misrepresentation or concealment of a material fact—material to the matrimonial relation, such that if known to the other party it would naturally have prevented the marriage—is sufficient ground for such an action of annulment."[13]

The law, Mills continued, also provided that when two people decided to marry, they had "an affirmative duty" to tell one another "all facts material to their contemplated marriage." This duty would be violated by a "false representation, an actual false statement—in this particular instance the statement by the young woman or others—her father in her presence—and the statement being adopted by her acquiescence—that she is entirely of white blood." Indeed, Mills remarked, the "same situation of law may arise if such a fact as that were simply concealed from the other side."[14] Thus, according to Mills, Alice had two duties: to not falsely represent her racial identity and to not conceal her race—she could not pass as white and marry Leonard.

Once Mills established his legal view of the case, he turned the jurors' attention to the questions they would answer at the end of the trial: Was Alice "colored?" Did Alice before the marriage represent herself to Leonard as

Leonard Kip Rhinelander and his attorneys, Isaac Mills (left) and Leon Jacobs (middle), in court. © Bettmann/Corbis.

"white and not colored and had no colored blood?" Did Alice represent herself as white to Leonard because she wanted to deceive him and convince him to marry her? Was Leonard persuaded to marry Alice because she represented herself as white? Did Leonard enter into the marriage with the "full belief" that Alice was "white and without colored blood"? Did Leonard continue to live with Alice knowing that she committed fraud or knowing she was not white? Mills then sketched out the evidence and witnesses he would use to support Leonard's claims. He turned quickly to the question of race and how to determine who is white and who is black.[15]

Although the annulment trial revolved around the question of whether Alice had misrepresented herself as white, Mills briefly addressed Leonard's ancestry. "The first fact which we shall establish, as to which I suppose there is no possible question, as it is sustained by presumption, is this: we shall prove that this plaintiff is of pure white stock and a descendant of one of the original

French Huguenot settlers of New Rochelle."¹⁶ Since New York law did not define "pure white stock," Mills's representation of Leonard as a "descendant" of Huguenots functioned to verify Leonard's claim to pure whiteness.

Although Mills declared he could demonstrate the purity of Leonard's claims to whiteness, he did not claim Alice was pure black. Instead, Mills argued to the jury that Alice possessed a "substantial strain of black blood and that it has come to her through her father."¹⁷ Mills planned to offer public documents to prove George Jones's "color," and he enumerated the ones he would bring into court. Alice's father's applications for naturalization as an American citizen identified him as "colored." Mills also discussed the three Jones daughters' birth certificates. New York law required that birth certificates indicate the child's color. The birth certificate for Emily, Alice's older sister, classified her as "mulatto"; Alice's birth certificate listed her color as "black"; and Alice's younger sister, Grace, was designated "black, negro, mixed." Mills told the jurors he would also introduce marriage licenses into evidence. Emily Jones's 1915 marriage license labeled both the bride and groom "black." In contrast, Alice and Leonard's 1924 marriage license registered both parties "white."¹⁸

Mills's proof of the Jones family's "color," however, would not be built solely on documents. Mills also proposed to question witnesses on the subject of color. He announced he had subpoenaed Alice's brother-in-law, Robert Brooks, "an out-and-out colored man," to appear in court. Then, in a surprising move, Mills brought up the subject of a six-year-old white girl who had come to America in 1891 with George and Elizabeth Jones—Mrs. Jones's first child born before her marriage to George Jones. Mills claimed the Joneses had sent the girl out of their home when she was twelve to work in domestic service, two years before Alice's birth. He told the jury the now-grown woman would be in court the next day and that they could compare her appearance with those of her three half-sisters. Davis interrupted Mills and questioned the relevance of Mills's revelation of Alice's older half-sister. Justice Morschauser, however, allowed Mills to resume this line of thought after first asking whether Davis still planned to dispute "that there is a strain of colored blood in your client." Since Davis did not admit to changing the defense's strategy of denying that Alice was colored, Morschauser ruled that Mills could continue to address the question of Alice's color.¹⁹

After bringing up the half-sister, Mills insinuated that his investigations uncovered no evidence of George and Elizabeth Jones's marriage in England. Moreover, he described a fruitless search in England for information about

George Jones's ancestry. He had learned, however, that Mr. Jones had been "known" as a "colored man" and his children were "known" as "mulattos" in Westchester. Given the evidence, Mills concluded, "it will not be in doubt for a second that the allegation in our complaint that she [Alice] is of substantial colored blood is true, and I challenge any proof to the contrary."[20]

Once Mills dealt with Leonard's and Alice's racial identity, he turned to the evidence he would introduce on the subject of whether Alice had lied to Leonard about her race and whether Leonard had been deceived. Leonard would be his own star witness on these issues. Although placing Leonard on the witness stand and subjecting him to Lee Parsons Davis's expected grilling on cross-examination posed a risk, Mills needed to persuade the jurors that the white son of wealthy New Yorkers could be deceived by the "colored" daughter of immigrants. A Westchester jury might also simply dislike a wealthy New Yorker—even one with ancestral links to the county. Leonard might also betray some lingering feelings for his wife in his testimony, and a jury might hesitate to sever their marital tie. Nevertheless, Leonard was the only person who knew all of the facts that might lead to an annulment, and his testimony would be vital. Mills was preparing the jurors to sympathize with his client and not his client's rejected wife.

To that end, Mills began by stressing Leonard's tender age when he met Alice in 1921—only seventeen. At seventeen, according to Mills, Leonard had a slight build, although he had built up his physique over time. Mills played up the tragic circumstances of Leonard's mother's death in 1915, followed by the death of his older brother, who was "killed in the war over there." The lawyer did not stop with recitations of Rhinelander family history to paint a sympathetic portrait of Leonard. To the surprise of the courtroom spectators and the defense attorneys, Mills advanced an unexpected representation of Leonard: "We shall show you, as you will see when you hear him, that he is suffering, and has suffered, from a physical infirmity which affects his speech, which tongue-ties him; as it is spasmodically at times, you can hardly get a word out of him. I shall be obliged to examine him with great patience and care and I shall ask you to exercise the same patience in listening to him."[21]

After astonishing the crowd with this unflattering depiction of his own client, Mills startled them again when he linked Leonard Rhinelander's "physical infirmity" to a claim that Leonard suffered from "mental backwardness." By making these connections, Mills hoped the jury would find that a scheming Alice could easily deceive his client. This tactic could work, because Mills's portrayal of Leonard resonated with fears of bodily degeneration and "the menace of the feebleminded" that circulated in popular culture and eugenics literature in this era.[22] Yet drawing on the discourse of feeblemindedness and degeneracy to explain how Alice had deceived Leonard raised some pitfalls for Mills. Identifying Leonard as feebleminded would reflect poorly on the Rhinelanders, even if the tactic successfully freed him from a marriage that "tainted" the whole family. While the language of feeblemindedness frequently referred to immigrants and the poor, popular eugenics author Albert Wiggam claimed that many "imbeciles" and "morons" came from wealthy families. Wiggam also equated feeblemindedness and a lower intelligence with an immoral character. To combat this hereditary menace to the white race, Wiggam proposed that all "imbeciles" and "morons," regardless of family status, be segregated in "special institutions" and sterilized.[23] If they could not reproduce, then their harmful effect would be limited to the present generation and not passed down through the ages. Despite the potentially negative effects of this characterization of Leonard, Mills pursued it over the repeated objections of the defense.[24]

Once Mills detailed Leonard's mental deficiencies, he proceeded to recount Leonard's version of his romance with Alice and the methods used by the Joneses to persuade Leonard that they were a white family. Mills depicted the two younger Jones sisters (Grace and Alice) as aggressive women who initiated a relationship with Leonard. Grace "accosted" Leonard and his friends on the street the first time Leonard drove from Connecticut to Westchester in September 1921. Once Leonard met Alice a few days later, "this defendant took the plaintiff. We will show you how she took him." Mills claimed that Alice's subsequent letters to Leonard would demonstrate how Alice seduced Leonard—a mere "boy, upon whom no woman ever smiled before, as we shall show you, tongue-tied, diffident, as the evidence will show you."[25]

With these phrases, Mills foreshadowed a central element of Leonard's case: Leonard was the hapless dupe of the sophisticated "gold-digging" Alice. Over Davis's objections, Mills disclosed to the jury that Alice had been the mistress of another man before she met Leonard. He told the jurors about Leonard's and Alice's week-long stay at the Hotel Marie-Antoinette in Manhattan—the product of an act of seduction by an experienced woman preying on an innocent boy. And Mills accused Alice of deceiving Leonard with tales of an abortion. Mills told the jury that Alice used her letters to weave a web to ensnare Leonard and to get him to marry her after Leonard's father separated the couple. After reading one letter and focusing on the erotic undertones, or, as Mills put it, "these lascivious expressions," he declared, "That is typical. That is what the boy was fed on. We shall show you that he became utterly infatuated with her. He reached the condition where he did not know black from white or anything." In Mills's version of their courtship, Alice's sexual allure blinded Leonard to her race.[26]

Leonard's susceptibility to Alice and her letters recalled the storyline of the 1915 film *A Fool There Was*, which starred Theda Bara as a "vampire," or one of those "women who used their bodies as lures to attract able-bodied and financially secure males." In the film, earlier a novel and a play, the female vampire with an ambiguous racial background preyed on upper-class white men from good families. According to literary scholar Bram Dijkstra's reading of this narrative, the depiction of men who succumbed to the vampire "provided a dramatic warning to the ruling class of early-twentieth-century America that it must not give in to the enticements of the flesh." Seduction by a vampire inevitably led to degeneracy and destruction. Since this image of the vampire still resonated, even ten years after the film's release, the *New York Evening Journal* recognized that Mills sought to "brand her [Alice] as a black vampire." Indeed, Mills even claimed that Alice's "lascivious" letters reduced Leonard to the condition of "an utter slave in her hands" and led to Alice's successful "assault" on Leonard.[27]

According to Mills, Alice convinced Leonard to marry her after she persuaded him that she was white. Mills recounted for the jury how Leonard returned to Alice from Arizona in 1924 when he turned twenty-one in spite of his father's wishes. But only one issue kept them from marrying immediately: the "subject of the sister's marriage to a Negro came up. He had never seen the Negro."[28] It was at this moment, Mills contended, that Alice and her family committed fraud. The Jones family told Leonard that Emily's marriage had disgraced their pure white English ancestry. Leonard believed them and married Alice. Mills insisted that Leonard "was ready to accept her inferior social position, her less [sic] wealth, her poverty, her inferior social position[;] he knew those things, he was ready to take them; but this ancient and proud lineage, he would not inflict upon it the undying disgrace of an alliance with colored blood. That is where he drew the line." Leonard would never have married Alice if he had known she was "colored."[29]

Despite the fact that he had introduced salacious details about the Rhinelanders, Mills finished his opening with an effort to show that he was not scandalmongering. "I hope you will understand, gentlemen, every one of you," he said, "that I have not made this revelation, revealing on the one hand the character of this defendant and revealing upon the other the weakness of my client wantonly, I have not made it wantonly. I would not do that. I try this case, gentlemen, as I told them, only upon the condition which it demands, that the truth and the whole truth shall be revealed, let it cut where it may. That will be our case, gentlemen. On that can any man hesitate or doubt the result?"[30]

After Mills's lengthy opening, Justice Morschauser and the attorneys agreed that the defense would make its opening statement the next morning. The judge told the jury to not form any opinion about the case from the press since the men had only heard from one side. He also warned the jurors to refrain from discussing the case with their wives. It would have been difficult to ignore the widespread press coverage of the trial. Many of the articles in New York's papers highlighted Isaac Mills's portrait of Leonard as a defective white man and his simultaneous emphasis on the Rhinelanders' exclusive social status.[31]

The *Herald Tribune* pointed out that Mills described Leonard Rhinelander, or "Kip," as the papers began to familiarly call him, as the "weakling descendant of the French Huguenots" and a "weak, utterly unsophisticated young man." Perhaps not surprisingly, the *Herald Tribune* painted a similar portrait of Leonard for its readers. It described him as a "slender young man of markedly nervous type, dressed in a blue double-breasted suit, tan shoes and white spats, and wearing horn-rimmed glasses." According to the principles of eugenics, Leonard's physical appearance reflected his purported mental deficiencies. Grace Robinson in the *Daily News* also focused on Mills's characterization of Leonard as a "mental incompetent, a poor motherless boy" faced with "a designing woman of many love affairs."[32]

Yet at least one reporter questioned Mills's charge that Alice deceived Leonard into marriage. In the *New York Evening Journal*, Margery Rex skeptically described the day's events: "A white aristocrat enslaved by a black girl! That was the picture—a sketch in 'sepia' drawn yesterday by Isaac Mills. . . . In describing how his young and not over bright Caucasian client was drawn into a love tangle with Alice Beatrice Jones of New Rochelle, and finally into marriage, Mills shocked court-hardened ears as he reviewed the relations of the pair." Rex offered readers another theory for how the relationship between Alice and Leonard reached the altar: "How could this backward youth, left motherless at fifteen, the blushing diffident boy who has such an impediment in his speech that he flees rather than seeks the society of women, how could a youth with such a sense of pesronal [sic] inferiority help but succumb to and be delighted in the company of an adoring attractive girl—whose social inferiority was, in a way, a charm?" Although Rex adopted Mills's language of backwardness in talking about Leonard, she felt that Leonard consented to the relationship. Perhaps Leonard's attraction to Alice demonstrated his attraction to the comforts of family life available at the Jones home.[33]

Finally, the press accounts that day showed that despite his impressive listing of the documents he would use to prove Alice and her family were "colored," Mills had not yet established any reliable method to differentiate white from black. The papers appeared still confused over the question of color. In the *Daily Mirror*, for example, reporters described Mrs. Jones as "one splash of white in a sea of black, . . . even though Jones himself is not particularly black, nor are his daughters." The *Daily Mirror* reported mistakenly that the Jones family's Italian son-in-law was "black," asserting that he looked like a "composite picture of the 'Roaring Forties' and Broadway in Harlem on a Saturday night." Margery Rex reported that Alice Jones Rhinelander looked like a "nice-looking, well-bred mulatta [sic], a casual glance would deceive you."[34] Although Rex's comment on Alice's appearance suggested that racial difference was not necessarily evident, it also implied that a closer look would show Alice was not white. Rex's observation raised the question of why Leonard did not or could not take that closer look, a question that also occupied the minds of the defense.

At ten o'clock the next morning, Tuesday, 10 November, Lee Parsons Davis requested a meeting with the judge and Isaac Mills in Justice Morschauser's chambers. After a brief conference, the three stepped back into the courtroom and Davis opened Alice Rhinelander's case to the jury in a room packed with spectators. Both Alice and Leonard appeared that morning, with Alice clutching a white handkerchief, an accessory that the press observed was in frequent use during the long day.[35]

To defend Alice from Leonard's charge of fraud, Davis prepared to prove two points: first, that Alice never represented herself as white to Leonard; and second, that Leonard did not marry her because of any representations about race. As he faced the jury, Davis chose to begin with Alice Jones's ambiguous racial identity. Davis remarked that at the beginning of the lawsuit, Alice, advised by Samuel Swinburne, had made a "technical legal denial" about her "blood." To the surprise of the crowd, Davis announced that "in the interest of shortening this trial, the defendant's counsel withdraws the denial as to the blood of this defendant and for the purposes of this trial admits that she has some colored blood in her veins." At this admission, Isaac Mills leapt in to comment that he considered Davis's action "manly and appropriate." Davis then requested that Justice Morschauser instruct the jury to disregard Mills's description of Leonard as mentally unfit and of Alice as "unchaste." Morschauser denied both motions.[36]

Once Davis dealt with these "legal technicalities," he confessed to the jury, "I feel a tremendous responsibility in the face of most astute counsel." He continued, "I am a bit worried and a bit nervous for fear that within my limitations I may fail in offsetting an impression which may have been made upon you overnight." Davis admitted his anxiety came from a strong feeling of anger that had "swept" over him after Mills's opening. Davis accused Mills of confusing the issues, arguing, "Now, here they are in a nutshell, stripped of all legal phraseology. The first one is, has little Alice Rhinelander colored blood in her veins? Well, it is not her fault if she has." To create sympathy for his client and counter Mills's depiction of Alice as a gold-digging vampire, Davis often referred to Alice Rhinelander as a "girl" or a "little girl." Davis told the jury that given his admission about Alice's "blood," the question of Alice's racial identity no longer remained in the case. Instead, "Alice Rhinelander must go through this prejudiced world, unfortunate as it is, branded openly now—if it is a disgrace in your eyes, it is in the eyes of some white people— with the admission that there is colored blood, to what extent we really do not know, coursing through her veins." Indeed, Davis's "branding" of Alice had very real consequences outside the courtroom; some restaurants even refused to serve her during lunch breaks throughout the trial.[37]

Once Davis declared the issue of racial identity resolved, he instructed the jury that the second issue was whether "Alice Rhinelander represent[ed] to Leonard Rhinelander before her marriage on October 14, 1924, that she was pure white." Then Davis moved swiftly to the defense's major theme: If Alice told Leonard she was white, did Leonard *believe* her and rely on her representations in making his decision to marry? "You see," he asserted, "that is an essential thing, because if I make a representation to you—suppose I told you that a clear Chinaman was an American Indian or of pure white American blood, I represented that to you; well, that would be false, but you would not believe it. Of course, you would have to be blind, you see, to believe that."[38] Thus, Davis argued, even if Alice Rhinelander represented herself to Leonard as white, even if she tried to pass, Leonard should not have believed her. In 1925, only one year after the United States had enacted a strict, racially based immigration restriction law, Americans knew one could not make a "Chinaman" into a "white American." Therefore, a now admittedly "colored" woman could not become "white." Davis implied that even though Isaac Mills argued that Leonard was "blinded" by Alice's sexual lures, it would be impossible not to know Alice Jones looked colored and not white. Consequently, Leonard could not have been led to marry Alice by any representations she made that she was white.

After Davis outlined the defense's case, he attacked Mills for presenting a "vicious," "uselessly cruel," and "un-American" opening. Davis argued that Mills took this approach only because "the Rhinelander millions—not young Rhinelander's but Philip Rhinelander's millions—are back of this, to crush a concededly humble family, to save what they consider to be an ancient name, trailing back to the original Huguenots of New Rochelle. But they are not going to do it if it is within my power to prevent them." Thus, Davis accused Leonard's family of resorting to underhanded tactics to protect their "ancient name." Davis connected their wealth with unfair behavior and painted the old New York family as "un-American."[39]

In order to prove that Alice could not have deceived Leonard, Davis also needed to rebut Mills's depiction of Leonard as easily influenced. Davis tore into Mills's claim that Leonard suffered from mental backwardness. "Here is Judge Mills' case: Why, this poor son, this dear boy, descended from this long line, was—may I use the slang expression?—bughouse: his mental machinery wasn't going around according to his years. He was braintied poor fellow." Sarcastically, Davis mocked Mills for trying to show that Alice initiated her and Leonard's "intimate association" through her letters. "So you see, gentlemen, that is one ground for annulling this marriage," he said. "This descendant of a long and ancient line stuttered and went to a stammering school and was so braintied that he didn't know what that letter meant." To Mills's claim that "this little girl has seduced father's boy," Davis bluntly declared, "That is the first time, although I have prosecuted much in the way of crime, that I have ever heard a girl charged with raping a man."[40]

Davis returned again and again to the Rhinelander family's superior social status and what he described as their attempt to crush the Jones family. This repetition emphasized the social and racial differences between the families. He told the jury that it was "not enough that this son of wealth comes into this humble home and takes this girl, but because Papa gets cross about it afterwards, he has to drag her in the slime to get rid of her. That is what they want you to do." Contrary to Mills's claim that Alice "took" Leonard, Davis portrayed Leonard, a New York aristocrat, taking Alice out of her "humble home." Davis, however, saved the full strength of his vehemence for what he thought of as the Rhinelanders' attack on the entire Jones family through Mills's disclosure of Mrs. Jones's "white" older daughter. "What has this to do with this trial, I ask you?"[41]

Once Davis branded Mills's opening as an attack on the character of the humble Jones family, he switched gears and outlined the facts that the defense expected to prove. Like Mills, Davis started with ancestry and race, even though he had already argued the issue no longer remained in the case. Davis discussed his client's family background and emphasized that Alice's mother "well, you can see it in her face—comes from the purest kind of old English stock." Then Davis addressed Mr. Jones's uncertain ancestry and introduced an unsettling line of thought. Davis told the jury that George Jones remembered his mother, but not his father, who had died when George was a small child. According to Davis, George Jones's mother (an English woman assumed by all to be white) told her son that his father was a West Indian. Davis observed, "It is true of all of us that we get our lineage and our ancestors a great deal by what the law calls hearsay." By equating knowledge about ancestry with hearsay (a form of secondhand evidence generally kept out of court due to its presumed unreliability), Davis raised the disconcerting possibility that no one really knew his or her racial background.[42]

Despite the uncertainty of hearsay, Davis went ahead and categorized George Jones as a "colored" man. Davis told the jurors that George Jones had been "regarded" as a "mulatto in England, and the viewpoint in England and the Continent and France, as you know, is entirely different towards a dark skin than it is here." Since only seven years had passed since the end of World War I, some of the jurors may have remembered hearing how America's black soldiers experienced better treatment abroad than at home. According to Davis, then, the different treatment of colored people abroad and at home meant that George Jones "didn't really know what negroes were or the viewpoint towards them that, unfortunately, some of us Americans adopt, until he came to this country, and that was thirty-five years ago. And here he found himself regarded as a Negro."[43]

After Davis concluded that George Jones was a "Negro" based on his mother's recollection of his paternal ancestry and American racial ideology, he turned to other methods to demonstrate the color of the other members of the Jones family. Davis asked the jury implicitly to use their own power of observation to classify the Joneses. First, Davis asked Alice's older sister Emily to stand up. He told the jury that Emily had married a "colored" butler ten years earlier, which, Davis pointed out, preceded by a number of years Leonard's

Lee Parsons Davis, Alice's attorney, speaking to the jurors during the Rhinelander trial. © Bettmann/Corbis.

romance with Alice. He mentioned Alice's younger sister Grace Miller and her marriage to an Italian, which showed that interracial unions were not unusual in the Jones family. Indeed, Davis's categorization of George Jones as a "Negro" and his earlier appeal to the jury to see Mrs. Jones's whiteness made it clear that their marriage was interracial, too.[44]

In order to hammer home his argument that Leonard could not have been deceived by Alice, Davis circled back to the differences in social status between the couple. He described the Joneses' small, cramped home in New Rochelle: "I have been there. It is humble, but it is as clean as the finest mansion in Fifth Avenue."[45] This comparison of the humble home and a Fifth Avenue mansion helped Davis reverse Mills's version of Alice's courtship with Leonard and placed Leonard, not Alice, as the initiator of the relationship. Indeed, Davis continued, Alice "was a member of a happy family in this humble abode and working to help support herself and the family by doing what? Now, this will be important. We will prove it as dealing with the question of whether or not this son of the long line was deceived. She was working as a maid servant, a perfectly honest, decent employment, but working as a maid servant in a private family when Rhinelander came into her life." In addition to pointing out that Alice's presence in a "humble abode" should have raised some questions for Leonard, Davis suggested that Leonard must have known that any woman who worked as a "maid servant" was "colored."[46]

Davis again countered Mills's argument that Leonard was mentally backward, pointing out that when Alice met Leonard, he was not, as Mills portrayed, residing in an "insane asylum" but rather attending a special school to help with his stuttering. Although Leonard may have stuttered, Davis asserted, he was not insane or feebleminded. Indeed, Davis maintained, Leonard's behavior was merely that of a man in love. Consequently, Davis proclaimed, "I think the issue that Judge Mills should have presented to you was not mental unsoundness but blindness. Blindness."[47]

Davis concluded his opening arguments with the assertion that Leonard, not Alice, wanted to keep their marriage secret because he feared his father. Davis pointed out that once the press publicized the Rhinelander marriage and proclaimed Alice part "Negro," Leonard still lived with her. "He was happy. He would go around the house in his pajamas and a fine pair of moccasins he had brought from the West and a bathrobe. He did not care, and continued in the face of this, this is evidence that he was not fooled, in the face of all these newspapers branding this family as negroes, and he had his own eyesight before."[48]

Finally, Davis reminded the jury that their job would be to determine whether Alice told Leonard before their marriage that she was white and whether or not that fooled him, "whether or not he could see with his own eyes that he was marrying into a colored family." Davis concluded, "I will try not to unnecessarily throw any filth in this case, but I say now that if that is attempted by the other side, I will wear no kid gloves. . . . I came here originally to try this case on those issues that you have heard outlined. Judge Mills has taken the lid off and now, if it is to be a real fight, let the fight go on and you be square from now on."[49]

The newspaper reports on Davis's opening statement lacked the drama of those that had followed Judge Mills's address the day before, but the *Daily News's* front-page banner headline, "YES, SHE'S COLORED," made up for the lack. The *Herald Tribune* found Davis's admission a "dramatic moment" and determined that Davis's strategy would be to "picture Alice Jones, not as a sort of dusky vampire who imposed her will upon a weakling in order to attach herself to the Rhinelander name and fortune" but instead to show her as a "girl who made a love match and whose name is now being dragged in the slime by the lawyers hired by the Rhinelander millions."[50]

The different styles of each opening statement illuminate the character of the two lawyers, as well as that of their respective clients. Each lawyer wanted to present a compelling story about Alice and Leonard's relationship, a narrative that would help explain to the jury how and why their clients married, and what happened after the marriage. Each lawyer also constructed his competing narrative in a manner calculated to elide some of the more inconvenient facts in his client's case. Although the lawyers directed the narrative flow in court, their clients had been the source of the two tales, and Leonard and Alice were, at least theoretically, in charge of what their lawyers could and could not say.

In his opening statement, Mills proved quite willing to misrepresent facts when they didn't suit the narrative he had constructed to explain Leonard's actions. Leonard, for example, was not seventeen but eighteen when he met Alice. Similarly, despite Mills's claim that Leonard had never met Robert Brooks, Emily's husband (the "colored butler") until 1924, later testimony demonstrated that Leonard had met him numerous times as early as 1921. Mills also claimed that he would call Mrs. Jones's first daughter, Alice, Emily, and Grace's half-sister, to testify in order to demonstrate that Mr. Jones was colored. But he never followed through on this threat.

An outside observer might be tempted to feel sorry for Mills's predicament.

His client was not particularly impressive and may not have told his lawyer all the facts, and Mills himself, who appeared to be stuck in a previous age, seemed ill-suited to argue the case. His choice of words (for example, his description of Mr. Davis's admission during his opening argument as "manly and appropriate" and his mispronunciation of the colloquialism "gee" with a hard G), his ear trumpet, his skull cap, and even his apparent attitudes about young women and how they should behave all seem to have come straight from the late nineteenth century. On the other hand, Mills proved more than willing to use calculatingly questionable tactics to portray Alice and her family as the guilty parties. At various times during the trial, Mills portrayed the Joneses as lying, sexually promiscuous, greedy souls with nothing redeeming whatsoever in their characters.[51]

Lee Davis, in contrast, seemed to have played the bluff man of the people, with his encomiums to the Jones family's happy, humble, little home and its salt-of-the-earth inhabitants. Davis also made it clear that he intended to attack Leonard and Leonard's wealthy family during the trial to challenge Mills's version of the courtship story. Yet Davis's argument and client had some problems as well. After all, many Americans and northerners generally viewed interracial marriage, as well as any other mixing of the races, with disfavor and contempt during this time. And Alice herself, as would become clearer during the trial, was not exactly pure in either her motives or her behavior. Davis may very well have been worried about whether his case was winnable.

After the two opening arguments, Mills presented the first of his twenty-one witnesses. Although the defense had conceded Alice's color, Mills nevertheless introduced documentary evidence about the Jones family's ancestry. Consequently, the first two witnesses testified to the authenticity of official records such as birth certificates, marriage licenses, and George Jones's naturalization papers. The testimony related to documents, however, showed that written evidence was not necessarily completely trustworthy on the question of race. When a representative from the Metropolitan Life Insurance Company testified about Elizabeth Jones's application for a life insurance policy for Alice, he revealed that a 1900 application described Alice's color as white and a second application dated eight years later labeled Alice's color black. Under Davis's cross-examination, the agent admitted that the company's agents filled out the forms and based their responses on the applicant's appearance. Agents did not ask the applicant for their race.[52]

After setting out the proof on race, Mills switched his attention to the next element of his case: Leonard's "mental backwardness," the factor that made Leonard susceptible to Alice's deceptions. He called Dr. L. Pierce Clark, a New York physician and founder of The Orchards who specialized in the treatment of nervous and mental disorders, to the stand. Dr. Clark described Leonard's eleven months in residence at The Orchards.[53]

As he had during Mills's opening statement, Davis objected to this line of questioning; and Justice Morschauser once again overruled him. Mills asked the doctor for his general impressions about Leonard's physical and mental condition during his time under Clark's care. The doctor offered that Leonard's "primary, main difficulty was a speech one—a stammering—chronic stammering speech disorder; stuttering. In addition to that, we found that it was based upon a great sense of inferiority, of incompleteness of development in his judgment and his memory and his power of attention." Since Mills hoped to stress Leonard's backwardness, he asked, "Isn't stammering often accompanied with some mental weakness, as well as nervousness?" Dr. Clark replied, "Always."[54]

Although Dr. Clark confirmed Mills's argument that Leonard was mentally deficient, Leonard's treatment files, which were introduced into evidence, told a somewhat different story. According to these records, upon Leonard's arrival with his father he "appears rather retiring and makes no effort to talk unless directly addressed. His main difficulty appears to be in getting started[,] for once he begins a sentence he is able to go on with it. There is, however, a tendency to hurry with his speech and there is present a sense of fear." Leonard's chart also revealed that he possessed a "general physical condition below par" and "a meagre and superficial knowledge of many simple facts." As the clinicians set up a plan of treatment, they worked to reduce Leonard's stammering. Over time, Leonard's speech improved. His physical condition improved after the clinic started to administer three daily doses of "Hormotone." By September 1921, Leonard's chart indicated that he had bought a car and that "he is greatly pleased with it, has taken some of the club members out and shows a general feeling of being decidedly more superior." A few weeks after meeting Grace and Alice Jones in September, Leonard was "becoming a changed man." The records noted that "he has recently made the acquaintance of some young girls. He calls on these friends, is looking for phone calls, talks well over the phone."[55] It appears that by the time Leonard met Alice and throughout the early period of their courtship, Leonard showed no signs of mental or vocal deficiencies.

Notwithstanding this contradictory evidence, Mills continued with his strategy to depict Leonard as mentally deficient. He returned to this topic the next day with three new witnesses: Julie Despres, the governess who worked for the Rhinelander family from 1908 to 1913; Sidney Ussher, the family clergyman who had officiated at Leonard's mother's funeral; and J. Provost Stout, a former tutor. When Mills examined Julie Despres, an elderly women in a black veil, about Leonard's condition, he frankly admitted that his point was to "simply claim that he [Leonard] was backward in his mental development at this time, when he was eighteen years of age, when he first came in connection, contact, meeting, with this defendant . . . And that as [sic] bearing upon the probability of the practice of fraud." Both Despres and Ussher provided testimony that fit with Mills's strategy. Each claimed that Leonard had serious learning disabilities and often forgot parts of his French drills or Sunday school lessons.[56]

Mills also tried to get the Reverend Ussher to testify about the Rhinelander family's origins. Davis objected and argued that the defense never claimed that Leonard Rhinelander was anything other than white. Mills also wanted to use the clergyman's testimony to get the information in front of the jury that Leonard's older brother, T. J. Oakley, had been killed in France during the war. When Davis objected to this line of questioning, Mills admitted that he wanted this information on the record because it spoke to the family's "blood." Justice Morschauser sustained Davis's objection.[57]

Mills could not completely control this discussion about Leonard's mental abilities, for the former family tutor, J. Provost Stout, claimed that Leonard had been "slow and diffident" but not "deficient." This distinction implied that Leonard's "slowness" did not rise to the level of a serious defect that would make Leonard easily deceived. Indeed, on cross-examination, Lee Davis asked Stout whether he had ever "observe[d] a boy who was slow in mathematics but awfully fast at baseball?" Stout responded, "Decidedly." Davis followed up, "Did you ever observe a boy that was a little slow in spelling but worked fast when he made love? Did you ever observe such a boy?" Stout replied, "I have."[58] With these two questions and Stout's responses, Davis undercut Mill's portrait of Leonard as a degenerate, feeble-minded boy who succumbed to Alice's deceptions. Instead, Davis used Stout's testimony to support his argument that Leonard pursued Alice even though he knew she was colored.

In the early afternoon on Armistice Day, Wednesday, the eleventh of November, Leonard Rhinelander took his seat in the witness chair, prepared to testify on his own behalf. He would be in for a grueling eight days. During much of his testimony, the press reported, his face showed little emotion. Leonard appeared on the stand dressed in a well-made blue suit with gray spats. As usual, his hair was parted neatly in the middle and slicked back, and he wore a pair of "academic looking" pince-nez. While Leonard swore to tell the truth, the crowd outside the courtroom complained about not being admitted. The possibility of hearing sensational facts had drawn many to the Westchester County Courthouse. The *Daily News* described the crowd as a "buzz of angry voices. It was the mob of sensation seekers outside, pleading for admittance to seats long since fought for and filled. Sweet young flappers, denied admittance reportedly by orders of Justice Morschauser appealed in vain to hard-hearted attendants." The lucky spectators in the courtroom again included most of Alice's family; still no Rhinelanders attended.

Seated in the witness chair, Leonard crossed his legs, and placed his hands in his lap, clasping and unclasping them nervously over his knees. He drank often from a glass of water.[59] Over the course of the next few days, Mills hoped to get Leonard to testify about Alice's deceptions. With Leonard on the stand, Mills planned to prove the elements of Leonard's fraud action by showing how Alice controlled Leonard sexually, how she maneuvered him into an engagement, and finally how she misled him about her race before they wed. Before turning to the issue of how Alice deceived Leonard, Mills first wanted to focus on Alice as a Jezebel, a lascivious colored woman, who gained sexual control over Leonard. By doing so, Mills moved outside of the actual legal issues at stake to try to gain the jury's sympathy.

Mills began his characterization of Alice Jones as a temptress by introducing Leonard to the jury with a series of questions about his client's premarital relationship with Alice Jones. These questions were designed to contrast Mills's youthful client and the more mature, sexually experienced Alice. Mills asked whether Leonard had "ever had any experience with a woman, I mean any sexual experience, or anything of that sort" before he met Alice.[60] Leonard replied that he had not.

While gently leading his client, Mills elicited Leonard's version of his initial encounters with the Jones family in 1921. Mills intended to show that the Jones family plotted to marry their daughters to white men. Consequently, the sexual behavior of at least two of their daughters, Alice and Grace, was devised to bring about miscegenation. Stuttering frequently, Leonard described for the jury a youthful excursion in his new motor car with some male friends in the fall of 1921. Leonard and his friends stopped the car after they developed car trouble, and at that point they were "picked up" by Grace Jones,

Alice's younger sister, who was walking on the sidewalk.[61] Leonard's tale of his first meeting with Grace Jones implied that Grace and Leonard's friend drove off together to have sex.

Mills's questions about Leonard's first contact with the Jones family suggests that Mills believed that Grace's "pick up" of Leonard and his friends on the street reflected her sexual availability. In the early twentieth century, working-class women or "women adrift" (a term that entered popular usage in the 1910s after it appeared in a federal report on working women) might pick up strangers to partake of new forms of urban entertainment, like watching movies or dancing at cabarets and dance halls, in return for sexual favors. This practice, also known as "treating," reflected working-class adolescent girls' pursuit of "a romantic and erotic identity, an identity reified by the movies, song, fashions, and dance steps of urban America." These behaviors, however, were perceived by some as a "girl problem" that required regulation. Indeed, New York passed a law that gave the parents and legal guardians of "problem" girls the right to have their daughters placed in reformatories. Mills must have hoped his depiction of Grace Jones (and by implication her sister Alice) as an immoral and loose woman would illustrate for the jury the dangers posed by the Jones sisters to men like Leonard.[62]

Continuing with his use of leading questions over Davis's repeated objections, Mills tightly shaped Leonard's testimony about his relationship with the Jones family.[63] Leonard claimed that three days after his car stopped for the first time in New Rochelle, he drove back only after he received Alice's written invitation. When Isaac Mills started to question Leonard about Alice's postcard, Lee Parsons Davis objected, arguing that the card itself should serve as evidence of its contents. Mills admitted that he did not have it but that he had a number of Alice's other postcards and letters. Mills maintained that Alice's card would have showed that Leonard went back to New Rochelle only because of Alice's invitation. Davis, however, maintained that the postcard never existed because Leonard returned on his own.[64]

By crafting Leonard's testimony to represent Alice as the pursuer of an intimate relationship, Mills shaped a picture of her as a "problem girl," but he also tapped into a long-standing image of the African American woman as an "oversexed-black-Jezebel" who was not only sexually available but also initiated sex. This Jezebel was often depicted as a "yellow girl," a female mulatto, a term that could be easily applied to Alice, since the press had already identified her as a mulatto.[65] This sexualized image of the black or mulatto woman predated the 1920s, and during the era of slavery served to justify white men's sexual control of slave women. But at the beginning of the twentieth century, these images lived on, particularly in the South, where some white women publicly expressed the belief that all black women were immoral.[66]

Yet the belief that black women were sexually promiscuous may have taken on a more intense meaning in the North during the Great Migration, as more African American women moved to northern states. Indeed, scholar Hazel Carby argues that the migration sparked a "moral panic" about black female migrants who were considered "sexually degenerate and therefore, socially dangerous." During the same decade, light-skinned African American chorus girls in Broadway shows like *Shuffle Along* and "octoroon girls" were credited with a "primitive sex-appeal."[67]

Yet Mills's strategy to use Alice's own words in her letters to Leonard to cast her as the promiscuous black woman who lured Leonard into a sexual relationship, and then "enslaved" him as part of her scheme to marry him was sometimes rewritten by the press. One reporter indicated that Alice's behavior in winning "her man" did not necessarily stem from her race. Margery Rex, for example, suggested that Alice's letters simply revealed the "ancient formula of all Alice Jones's sex regardless of color, creed and previous condition of servitude . . . of honeyed words and clinging persistence." In other words, Alice's conduct could be attributed to any woman. Indeed, a female doctor's article about marriage and women published in the mid-1920s suggests that if Alice pursued Leonard, she was not unusual. In *Harper's Magazine*, Dr. Beatrice M. Hinkle bemoaned the dismal state of marriage in America in the 1920s. "Owing to the timidity and fear on the part of men," Hinkle wrote, "they [women] are more openly in pursuit of husbands than ever before but with this difference—they want to make their own terms."[68]

After Leonard described the beginning of his relationship with Alice, Mills read excerpts from Alice's letters to show how she led Leonard on. During the remainder of Mills's examination of Leonard, Leonard spoke only to identify Alice's letters or to answer brief questions about their correspondence. In placing almost one hundred of Alice's letters into evidence and reading them aloud, Mills added Alice's voice to the trial to condemn her as a fraud. Significantly, Mills read only those letters, or parts of them, that he felt fit best with the particular story he intended to tell. Lee Davis often responded to Mills's readings by insisting that the entire letter be read to the jury so that the excerpts could be placed in their larger context. In particular, Davis emphasized the affectionate expressions that Alice sprinkled throughout her letters in order to construct a countertale: one of love, not deceitful seduction. Davis also pointed out to the jury that Alice made numerous spelling and grammatical mistakes in her letters in order to contrast Alice's social status with Leonard's.[69]

During Mills's examination of Leonard, it emerged in passing exactly how all of Alice's letters ended up in the hands of Leonard's attorneys. Under Mills's questioning, Leonard perhaps inadvertently revealed that Leon Jacobs, his lawyer, had gone into Leonard's room in his father's house and taken them, without either asking Leonard or receiving his permission to do so. In an amusing colloquy that arose during the attorneys' wrangling over the existence of the postcard that Alice supposedly used to invite Leonard back to New Rochelle, Mills kept asking Leonard whether Leonard had "delivered" all of Alice's letters to his lawyers. To Mills's consternation, Leonard kept saying that he had not done so. Finally, Mills admitted in a conference at the bench with Davis that Jacobs had "taken" the letters after the suit was originally filed. Jacobs had also returned to New Rochelle and taken Leonard's wedding gifts to Alice, including the furniture for the apartment they never shared. Davis later used these details to portray Leonard as the pawn of his family.[70]

The reading of Alice's intimate letters in open court energized the city's daily newspapers. New York's papers reprinted as many of Alice's letters as they could for their readers' delectation; sections deemed too graphic were only hinted at. To some extent, Mills's strategy of using Alice's letters to link her actual writing to the behavior she described in the letters worked. For example, the *New York Times* declared that Alice's writing was "illiterate and crude" and the *New Yorker* described her letters as "violent and half-savage."[71] When Mills read one of Alice's early letters in which she described a night of wild excitement, he asked Leonard to explain what took place. According to Leonard, he went with Alice and her friend Kitty to a cabaret for drinks where they began to feel "rather frisky." Mills's questions about this letter also elicited the information that Kitty, Alice's "intimate friend," was white.[72] Mills's question implied that no white woman would knowingly be an intimate friend of a colored woman, and thus Alice had to have passed as white during the time she knew Leonard.

Mills's questioning of the twenty-two-year-old Leonard about the couple's relationship revealed the generation gap between the elderly lawyer and his client. To some extent, Leonard's responses to Mills's inquiries offered a counternarrative to Mills's motif of Alice the temptress. Leonard's pictures of his relationship with Alice resembled the new style of courtship known as "dating," a form of courtship that became significant in the 1920s. In fact,

Leonard's testimony about his premarital relationship with Alice described numerous activities that could be characterized as dates. Alice's description of their "wild evening" could be read simply as one where two couples went out on a date to a cabaret. Leonard and Alice drove around in his automobile and went to the movies; Alice's letters mention dancing. Someone of Isaac Mills's generation might perceive these activities as dangerous. The practice of dating had originated with white upper-class and working-class youths from varied backgrounds, especially in places like New York City before its adoption by white middle-class youths. So dating might be understood as an activity that blurred the lines of social status. At the same time, since some of the particulars of dating included dancing and listening to jazz (activities linked to African Americans), their adoption by white youth eroded rigid lines between the races.[73]

Mills referred repeatedly to Alice's description of the physical intimacies that she and Leonard had shared. In one letter, possibly written in early December 1921, for example, Alice let Leonard know she was alone at home and thinking of him: "Just think of me, this evening being hear alone, Mother and father, and sister Emily, and hear husband, as gone to the Westchester to see Buddies—And I am hear alone, thinking of you, dear heart. . . . I only wished Lenard, was coming down this evening. How I could carress, you dear, Because you no, you love for me, to carress you dear. But my heart, feels very lonesome, this Eve. But what, can I do dear, because you are so, far from me sweet heart." After using Alice's letters to bolster the claim she initiated their relationship, Mills shifted to the next stage of his argument about Alice as the Jezebel who seduced Leonard into premarital sex.[74] He asked Leonard:

> Q. There was a time, was there, when you went to the Hotel Marie Antoinette with the defendant?
> A. Yes.
> Q. Now, you have in mind the first time? Can you tell me what the date of that was, the first time—or about?
> A. That was December 23 [1921].
> Q. After these letters that I have been reading in evidence?
> A. Yes.
> Q. Now, up to that time had you had any sexual intercourse with Alice?
> A. No.
> Q. Had you made any attempt to have any up to that time?
> A. No.

Davis objected to Mills's questions, arguing that they fell outside the scope of the case. The press recognized that Mills hoped to score points with the jury, and the *Daily News* observed that Mills read Alice's letters "with an eye to the psychological effect upon the jury." Leonard's testimony about the hotel seemed designed for the same effect.[75]

After Judge Morschauser overruled Davis and advised Mills to continue, Mills asked Leonard to inform the jurors how he and Alice ended up in the same hotel room. Leonard recalled that he and Alice drove together in his car to New York City after he invited her to attend the theater in December of 1921. Once in the car, Alice let him know that she intended to spend the night in a hotel. Leonard then asked whether he could "accompany her." At first she refused, but after twenty minutes of Leonard's "persuasion" (methods unspecified), Alice agreed.[76]

After showing that Alice engaged in sex with Leonard after knowing him for only three months, Mills moved on to demonstrate Alice's brazen nature. Mills introduced a January 1922 letter that mentioned two issues Mills believed confirmed Alice as sexually immoral. The first was her search for an apartment in New York for them to share—as an unmarried couple. The second was her apparent abortion. In her letter to Leonard, Alice remarked she was "alright now only I have to take that medicine. I will not after go to him anymore, Only if something turns up, for instance if I feel pain, or queer feeling inside of me, but up to now I feel fine."[77] By reading this letter to the jury, Mills demonstrated that Alice knew enough about sex to take care of an unintended pregnancy.

Describing Alice as a seductive Jezebel who constantly reminded Leonard of their hotel stay, Mills argued that she sexually enslaved Leonard and manipulated him into an engagement. Mills ascertained from Leonard that he and Alice had never discussed marriage prior to their time spent in the Hotel Marie-Antoinette in late 1921 and early 1922.[78] Mills used the letters Alice wrote after Philip Rhinelander separated the couple to show how she gained control over Leonard by making him jealous of the other men who tried to court her and reminding him of their previous sexual encounters. The press noted that "the excerpts [of Alice's letters] selected by Mr. Mills to read to the jury" often contained "unprintable" sections. For example, in a letter dated 19 May 1922, a few months into Leonard's enforced travels, Alice informed Leonard that she had made a new female friend. Alice's friend introduced her to lots of other young women and men, "but," she wrote, "none appeals, to me like my dear Leonard, I was just thinking of you the other evening, how you have carressed And held me. And wanted me badly at time, Now dear all of those things come in my mind. I only wished you was hear now to do it to me."[79] In the same letter Alice let Leonard know that she had taken to rereading his letters while undressed in bed, "which you can see me in bed like the Antoinette." This last point most likely referred to a photograph Leonard had taken of her at the hotel. In response to reading one of Leonard's letters, Alice declared, "You made me feel very passionate for the want of you, telling me how happy my little hand as often made you feel, and several other things, but cant help to tell you." After Mills read this letter, Davis declared, "I am still desirous of keeping the filth out of this case." Mills replied, "Well, that is impossible."[80]

Reading the letters in which Alice reminded Leonard of their sexual experiences served another purpose. Mills wanted to portray Alice using her sex appeal to push Leonard to enter into an engagement. In February 1923, Alice declared she could not wait for Leonard forever.[81] Mills introduced a few letters from one month later in 1923 to show that Alice had succeeded with her constant reminders of their physical pleasures in convincing Leonard to get engaged. In March 1923, for example, Alice wrote she was sorry that she was not a virgin when she first met Leonard. She said she revealed this so that he would trust her around other men. In the same letter, she thanked Leonard for telling her that she would get a car as a wedding present. In April 1923, Alice thanked Leonard for a ring and told him she had the ring engraved from him to her with the date of 23 March 1923, "So I can never forget it, when you had given it to me."[82]

At least one newspaper did not seem to find Alice's behavior particularly guileful. The *New York Evening Journal* commented that women's pursuit of men was neither new nor unusual, except perhaps, in Westchester. Thus, the *Journal* offered to provide for its readers "this little reminder of VAMPS HISTORICAL," especially to enlighten the "happily married men of Westchester County, who in so many cases are innocent as new-born lambs of the fact that their wives proposed." It went on to compare Alice to famous "vamps" like Venus, Cleopatra, and Madame de Pompadour.[83] The *Journal's* discussion poked fun at the Westchester suburbs, making the idea of the "vamp" seem less threatening since she could be embodied in a suburban matron.

Having established the fact that Alice had succeeded in getting engaged to Leonard, Mills still felt it necessary to show that Alice pressured Leonard to return from ranch school out West and marry. Mills read a letter from January of 1924 in which Alice asked Leonard to return, "so then I will not after give you up." One month later, Alice dwelt again on their earlier sexual experiences: "*Please please* think of me, and pretend I have you in my arms, petting your soft face, and getting ready to love you like you no I just love to carress you and bring you into dreamland." In the same letter she told Leonard that she would never forget their stay at the hotel and registering as Mrs. Smith but, she added, "My wouldant I rather be called Mrs. R. That will be my happy day, if it ever comes."[84]

Despite Mills's efforts to portray Alice as the pursuer in her letters, on 12 November, the main story in the *Daily News* was "HOW RHINELANDER WOOED HER." Indeed, Grace Robinson reported that Leonard's story about his romance with Alice revealed only a "commonplace little love affair." Instead of denouncing Alice for chasing after Leonard, Robinson suggested in one article that Leonard "tumbled for the hospitality and charm of an uncultured colored girl" because he had so little in his life. In another piece, Robinson informed her readers that "before it [the reading of Alice's letters] was over, women spectators in the court room were sobbing, Alice was applying her handkerchief freely, and Leonard looked as though he were about to fly from his high perch near Justice Morschauser and gather his broken girl bride into his arms." She suggested Alice's letters led one to "pity the simple girl who put [her thoughts] on paper rather than to censure her." In addition, although the *Daily Mirror* appealed to more prurient readers with its front-page headline, "KIP WITHOUT SIN TILL HE MET COLORED BRIDE, HE SWEARS," the theme of love as the primary motive behind Leonard and Alice's marriage instead of seduction appeared to play a part in that newspaper's account of the trial. Indeed, the *Daily Mirror*'s reporter observed, "Just how much good the reading of the missives is doing young Rhinelander's case is open to question. About the court room, it was apparent that they were arousing a great deal of sympathy among the auditors for the wife."[85] The *New York Times* apparently concurred. It described Alice's correspondence as "fervid, illiterate letters of a woman to whom Rhinelander was a Prince Charming" but also that "they conveyed the impression that she was very much in love with him."[86]

The press's sympathy for Alice went only so far, however. Its coverage did not imply acceptance of an interracial marriage, loving or not. Indeed, Margery Rex of the *Evening Journal* wondered if Alice regretted that she "wed outside her race. . . . Does she feel more keenly than ever the evils of racial intermarriage? Those evils which, but for her white mother's choice of a colored mate, would not blight her own life?" After Rex labeled such marriages

THE TRIAL BEGINS : 87

"evil," she then spoke to the main problem that she perceived with interracial marriage and speculated whether Alice would choose to have children "bearing the unwieldy burden of a double inheritance—black and white?"[87]

In Leonard's first days on the stand, Mills used Alice's letters to construct a narrative of Alice's sexual control over Leonard that eventually led to the couple's marriage. But Mills had not yet demonstrated to the jury how Alice and her family deceived Leonard about her race. That alleged deception, and what it reveals about notions of passing and the meaning(s) of race, formed the heart of Leonard's suit, and cannot be discussed without exploring what race and passing meant in 1920s New York.

FOUR :

Passing and the "Seemingly Absurd Question" of Race

I had not been long engaged in the study of the race problem when I found myself
face to face with a curious and seemingly absurd question: "What is a Negro?"
—RAY STANNARD BAKER, *Following the Color Line* (1908)

In New York, where only one person out of thirty-four is an acknowledged Negro,
it is a matter of common repute among the colored folks of Harlem that more
than ten thousand of their numbers have "passed" and are now accepted as white
in their new relations many of them married to white folks, all unsuspected.
—CALEB JOHNSON, "Crossing the Color Line" (1931)

AS THE JURY SAT through the daily reading of Alice's love letters to Leonard, Isaac Mills used Alice's words to picture a scheming colored woman who would lie about her race to marry a man like Leonard. Back in November of 1924, when Leonard Rhinelander and his attorneys first declared that Alice Jones had falsely represented herself as white, they accused her of being colored and passing. Contemporary readers of New York's newspapers, who were fascinated by the story of the Rhinelander marriage and Leonard's attempt to dissolve it, would have been familiar with the concept of passing for white. The idea of passing resonated with New Yorkers in the 1920s because it evoked a number of fears about change in New York in the early twentieth century. According to a 1925 article in the mainstream *Century Magazine*, "literally thousands" passed as white in New York City, where, the anonymous author pointed out, "it is the easiest thing imaginable to 'get by' " and to pass as "one of French or Spanish or Italian or Jewish blood." Not surprisingly, in a city transformed by foreign immigration and internal migration, stories of passing held a certain fascination.[1]

The extensive press accounts of Leonard and Alice's marriage and their annulment trial produced and reproduced several sometimes confusing and competing narratives that echoed the era's anxieties about race. Passing as white challenged the belief in the existence of race by pointing out both the permeability of the boundary between the black and white races, and the likelihood that there was no such thing as a black or white race. A great deal of the early press coverage of the Rhinelanders tried to make sense of Alice's and her family's ancestry and thereby fit them into an American racial template. Were the Joneses English and therefore white? Was George Jones a West Indian and therefore colored? Was Alice a mulatto? To attempt to answer these questions for their readers, newspapers both described Alice's physical appearance and printed her photograph. In addition, they printed stories about the various ways in which official documents, including census returns, birth certificates, and marriage licenses, categorized the Joneses.[2]

Up until the second day of the trial, no one seemed sure about how best to identify the Joneses. Although New York State asked for data on race and color on some official forms, no statute in New York provided a ready answer to the question of which category people belonged in. And even when Lee Davis announced in his opening statement that Alice possessed some "colored blood, to what extent we really do not know, coursing through her veins," doubts still existed in the courtroom about how to fix racial categories, an uncertainty that mimicked the larger uncertainty about the issue in American society at large. Davis implied that Leonard should have known Alice was colored because she worked as a maid. And, despite the difficulty in pinning down race, Isaac Mills plunged ahead to prove that Alice passed as white. Leonard's allegations and the responses to them thus reveal how American ideologies of race and racism operated at a specific historical moment.[3]

Any discussion of passing in America needs to address its definition.[4] I define passing as the process by which a person who is *believed* (either by him- or herself or others) to be a member of one race identifies him- or herself or is identified by others as a member of another race. My definition of passing stresses the historically contingent nature of race and therefore that what people think passing is or what it means changes over time too.[5] Understanding the role played by *belief* in the process of creating the notion of "passing" is key. In the early twentieth century, journalist George Schuyler called Americans' belief in race and the differences between races a "racial superstition" and a "mysterious voodooistic force."[6] This superstition, however, renders race *real* for the believer. Once race becomes real and a classification that can be negotiated, then race must exist as a fixed essence *that does not have to be visible*. In other words, people can "belong" to a race even if they don't look like they do; or, as Werner Sollors puts it, "certain descent characteristics, even invisible ones, [are] viewed as essential and more deeply defining than physical appearance, individual volition, and self-deception, or social acceptance and economic success."[7]

Since to believe in passing requires that one believe in the reality of race and simultaneously believe that people might try to move from one racial category to another, there needs to be some way to designate or assign people to a particular racial category. In many ways, people's belief in the existence of passing is generated by the way a society defines race. Passing cannot exist unless race is defined; otherwise what would someone pass between? But if a society's definitions of race prove too loose, this very looseness might generate passing. To make this even more complicated, definitions of race constantly change over time.[8]

Therefore, the truth of Leonard's allegation that Alice passed as white and the resolution of his lawsuit depended on specific historical understandings of, and beliefs about, race in the 1920s. But we must also recognize that Americans' belief in race and passing in the 1920s was shaped by earlier understandings of both concepts.[9] Indeed, accounts of people of African descent self-identifying as white and thereby passing stretched back into the era of slavery. Historian Winthrop Jordan's classic study of American ideas about race links passing to the creation by white Americans of a rigid color line in the seventeenth and eighteenth centuries. According to Jordan, "some accommodation had to be made for those persons with so little Negro blood that they appeared to be white, for one simply could not go around calling apparently white persons Negroes." The "silent mechanism of 'passing' " could then serve as the means by which some slaves liberated themselves from their bonds in the eighteenth and nineteenth centuries.[10]

Perhaps the best-known story of a slave who passed as white and therefore free is the antebellum narrative of Ellen Craft, a slave who dressed as a white man on her way to freedom. Accompanied by her husband, who played the part of her slave, Ellen Craft escaped from Georgia to Boston in 1848. Southern slaveowners found similar actions a serious problem. Legal historian Ariela Gross has documented lawsuits in which slaveholders sued railroad companies for conveying passing slaves to freedom. According to Gross, many slaveholders perceived passing for white as "the most disturbing deceit by a slave," more so than faking a physical or mental disability that might affect a slave's ability to work. Consequently, slaveholders found some slaves, as Walter Johnson points out, "too white" to keep.[11]

Sometimes those "too white" slaves ended up in a courtroom where judges attempted to determine whether they were indeed free. Such cases proved to be a common enough occurrence that southern states enacted "presumption laws" to provide guidance for determining a slave's status. Some states resolved these questions by checking the person's reputation and making a visual determination of his or her race; other states applied a more "scientific" approach by estimating a person's "black blood." However courts determined the boundaries of race, the judicial assignment of a specific racial category upheld the difference between free and slave status and helped to maintain the antebellum South's labor system in which "racial and labor regimes were mutually dependent."[12]

With the end of slavery, passing and race took on new meanings. A 1929 commentary on passing compared the meaning of passing in the era of slavery and in the author's own time: "The purpose is different mainly in that instead of being used as a means to escape from chattel slavery, it is used to effect an escape from an industrial, commercial, political and social bondage, in which Negroes are now living, quite as drastic as was the chattel slavery, in which their forefathers lived." So, by the twentieth century, passing might serve as a way to achieve success in an increasingly industrialized—but still racialized—society.[13]

One way to analyze this transformation in the meaning of passing and race and the continued value of categories of race in America is the concept of whiteness being a form of property, which would be passed down to one's children. Many American whites understood, at least subconsciously, that they received benefits from the mere state of being "white." Because these privileges and benefits had, by the start of the twentieth century, become associated with being white, preserving a distinction between blacks and whites remained crucial to protecting and expanding those privileges. As Eva Saks argues, after the Civil War, "the value of white skin dropped when black skin ceased to signify slave status" but "racial devaluation could be reversed if white blood could internalize the prewar status of white over black."[14]

African Americans certainly recognized the benefits and privileges attached to the status of being white. They had to live each day of their lives facing the reality of those privileges, and the reality of how the lack of those privileges affected them and their friends, families, and children. In the absence of such privileges, there would have been no reason to pass. NAACP field secretary Williams Pickens, writing in a 1927 essay in *Opportunity*, could not have made the point any clearer: "Colored Americans are often accused of 'wanting to be white,' when a better analysis would show that what they really want is the freedom and privileges of white persons."[15]

The "freedom and privileges" that accrued to a person legally recognized as white were both societal and financial. They included the right to vote in the South, the ability to travel and live wherever one wished, the opportunity to attend a good school, and the potential to get a good job. Even in the North, African Americans were banned from certain kinds of employment and prohibited from joining more than a few unions.[16] Throughout the country African Americans were barred from less obvious privileges, such as the ability to easily borrow money from banks, the ability to celebrate in public without being arrested, and as, the Rhinelander case was attempting to address, the right to marry whomever one wanted. As Progressive Era journalist Ray Stannard Baker pointed out in 1908 in a discussion of the "color line," the "ideal is whiteness: for whiteness stands for opportunity, power, progress."[17] It is no wonder that, given just how powerful and all-encompassing these privileges were, the category of whiteness needed to be carefully and diligently bounded.

Whites in the 1920s most likely did not conceive of these benefits and privileges as a property right as such. Most Americans conceive of "property" as tangible. Notwithstanding that conception of property, in many ways white Americans acted as though their status as white was something they owned and had to strenuously defend. This chapter, as does this book as a whole, recounts repeated acts in the name of such defense: fervent calls to defend the white race against passing and impassioned outcries against "race mixing." Passing could now be perceived as an attempt to steal, by lying about one's true race, the status and benefits of whiteness, the rights of first-class citizenship. Production of mixed-race children who were legally acknowledged as heirs of their parents and families also threatened that status in two different ways. First, of course, was the obvious threat: that the children would be light-skinned enough to pass and thus steal white peoples' benefits. Second, mixed-race children somehow threatened the greater status of whiteness by their mere existence. Contemporary writers and pundits often warned that both white families and the white race would become contaminated, or "tainted" by marriages and reproduction across racial lines.

Isaac Mills relied upon these fears throughout the Rhinelander trial. In his opening statement, he proclaimed that Leonard would not allow his family to suffer the "undying disgrace of an alliance with colored blood," and in the final sentences of his closing statement, he begged the jurors to allow Leonard to "redeem" his family's name, which he had "besmirched" by his marriage to Alice.[18]

At first, the concept of whiteness as a property right might seem to stretch a rhetorical point beyond its valid application. But much of the rhetoric inside and outside the courtroom during this trial argues in favor of its usefulness as a metaphor. The quote from Picken's essay in *Opportunity* could just as easily have read: ". . . what they really want is the freedom and privileges *belonging to* white persons." Certainly early-twentieth-century history is replete with examples of behaviors hard to comprehend except in the context of people acting to prevent a theft of their property. And the treatment and transfer of actual property (real estate in particular) during that era is thoroughly intertwined with attempts to limit access to African Americans. Given the ferocity of this defense of whiteness, equating whiteness with property feels intuitively, if not legally, valid.

The legal system played an integral role in assigning racial categories for purposes of allocating these rights and privileges. But, as Virginia Dominguez observes in her study of racial classification in Louisiana, the arbitrariness of the ways in which the law categorizes race becomes clear once legal categories are examined over time. Indeed, legal treatises on race from the early twentieth century make it clear that while the law can be a "powerful" method of defining a society, the often contradictory definitions of race across state lines and even within a state call into question the entire enterprise of trying to define race.[19]

In the late nineteenth century, segregation laws and antimiscegenation statutes, especially in the South, were designed to map out physical boundaries between black and white and thus prevent the mingling of the races. Antimiscegenation laws also indirectly restricted the legal transmission of property through legally joined black-white families.[20] In order to prevent racial mixing, however, legislatures needed to define race. Ironically, the profusion of legislative efforts to block interracial contact may have increased the numbers of people passing. Historians Joel Williamson and Willard Gatewood suggest that the heyday of passing occurred during the 1880s through the 1920s, in part as a reaction to the strict enforcement of legal segregation in the South.[21]

Most of the legal definitions of a "colored" person or a "Negro" appeared in the context of legislation that prohibited marriages between the races. Yet no consistent definition appeared from state to state. A 1927 survey of state laws banning racial intermarriage reported the wide variety of definitions for "Negro." Marriages were prohibited

> between white persons and persons of African descent (Georgia, Oklahoma, Texas), or between white persons and persons of negro blood to the third generation (Alabama, Maryland, North Carolina, Tennessee), or between white persons and persons of more than one-fourth (Oregon, West Virginia), or one-eighth (Florida, Indiana, Mississippi, Nebraska, North Dakota), or one-sixteenth (Virginia) negro blood; other statutes in more general terms prohibit marriages between white persons and Negroes or mulattoes (Arkansas, Colorado, Delaware, Idaho, Kentucky, Louisiana, Missouri, Montana, Nevada, South Carolina, South Dakota, Utah, Wyoming).[22]

Most states relied on the popular notion that "blood" or "fractions of blood," specifically Negro blood, could define race, although the proportions of Negro blood that made one a Negro varied from jurisdiction to jurisdiction.

In the nineteenth century, the idea that one's race could be determined by the fraction of black blood one possessed took hold as one way to conceive of race. This concept took on a life of its own when American state legislatures enshrined the metaphor of blood in laws that prohibited miscegenation. The great interest in eugenics, heredity, and genealogy in the late nineteenth and early twentieth centuries only emphasized the importance of conceiving of blood as race. This metaphor of blood as race has proved remarkably persistent and widespread. It was used by a significant percentage of people who wrote about race in this time period (including W. E. B. DuBois), whether they saw themselves as white or colored.[23]

Applying the metaphor of blood to real people can, however, prove problematic. As Eva Saks observed in her discussion of race and miscegenation law in the nineteenth century, the concepts of " 'black blood' and 'white blood' . . . were mutually constitutive, and equally fictitious." Not surprisingly, trying to prove quantities of blood to determine race could be difficult, and courts in miscegenation cases were often forced to appeal to appearance or other outside factors to resolve the question of blood.[24]

If the concept that race was determined by blood in antimiscegenation statutes proved confusing, southern state legislators often compounded the confusion when they defined race differently for laws segregating schools. Given this, the incongruous result of such legislation could be that one person might be considered white for marriage and colored for school.[25] Such an absurd result, which only highlighted the arbitrariness of legal definitions of race, nevertheless had the sanction of the nation's highest court. In 1896, the U.S. Supreme Court observed in *Plessy v. Ferguson*, "It is true that the question of the proportion of colored blood necessary to constitute a colored person as distinguished from a white person, is one upon which there is a difference of opinion in the different States, some holding that any visible admixture of black blood stamps the person as belonging to the colored race . . . and still others that the predominance of white blood must only be in the proportion of three fourths." Although the Supreme Court recognized that what made a "colored person" varied from state to state (and could vary within a state), the question of how to distinguish a "colored person" from a "white person" should "be determined under the laws of each State."[26] Consequently, uncertainty over how one could precisely determine whether someone was a Negro or colored was integral to the American legal system.

Many early-twentieth-century discussions of passing acknowledged a link between contradictory and inexact definitions of race and the ability of people to pass in between those arbitrary racial categories. The male protagonist in Charles W. Chestnutt's novel *The House Behind the Cedars* (1900), for example, learned that he could leave his home state, where he was considered black, and pass as white in another because the laws in each state defined race differently. A few years later, journalist Ray Stannard Baker addressed the subject in his collection of articles on race, *Following the Color Line*, where he observed that "legislatures have repeatedly attempted to define where black leaves off and white begins."[27] Baker's reference to repeated attempts to define race suggests that legislatures needed to keep trying because they could not get it right.

In his essay on the mulatto titled "The Problem of Race Mixture," Baker opened with what he called the "seemingly absurd" question "What is a Negro?," a question Baker observed numerous statutes and court cases had tried to answer. To answer this question for his readers, Baker observed that he had come into contact with people "as white as I am, whose assertion that they were really Negroes I accepted in defiance of the evidence of my own senses." "I have seen blue-eyed Negroes and golden-haired Negroes," he continued; "one Negro girl I met had an abundance of soft straight red hair. I have seen Negroes I could not easily distinguish from the Jewish or French types; I once talked with a man I took at first to be a Chinaman but who told me he was a Negro. And I have met several people, passing everywhere for white, who, I knew, had Negro blood."[28] Moreover, Baker admitted he knew of those who "'crossed the line' by declaring that they are Mexican, Brazilians, Spanish or French." In the face of the chameleonlike nature of race, Baker found himself forced to admit that "nothing, indeed, is more difficult to define than this curious physical colour line in the individual human being." Despite Baker's acknowledgment of the absurdity and curious nature of race, his discussion of race still assumed the existence of an actual color line.[29]

Once Baker unsettled his white readers with his report on the porousness of the color line, he introduced a few examples of individuals who "cross over to white." However, he also made sure to emphasize that many light-skinned mulattoes chose to stay on their side of the color line because, as he quoted an African American who changed his mind about passing, "white people don't begin to have the good times that Negroes do." Notwithstanding Baker's attempt to allay the anxieties of white Americans who read his book, Baker concluded his discussion with the disconcerting remark that "no one, of course, can estimate the number of men and women with Negro blood who have thus 'gone over to white'; but it must be large."[30] Baker's discussion of the absurdity of race and the inability of legislators to get it right suggests that these failures helped produce the large numbers of those going over to white.

By the 1910s and 1920s, discussions of passing proliferated. White southerners experienced anxiety over "invisible blackness" in the early twentieth century. Such anxiety existed on a national level and became a frequent topic in fiction and nonfiction in the 1920s and early 1930s. The twenties opened with the rumor that President Warren Harding had passed for white.[31] Only a few years earlier, in 1918, Ellis Porter had signed up to serve in the armed forces even though he was a "Negro." He served for three years with a group of white soldiers before he was arrested for "fraudulent enlistment in the army." A year later newspapers reported that a colored man passed as white to serve as an officer in the navy. In 1923, the *Nation* published an article that described three colored people, at least one of whom lived in the North, who tried to pass as white. The author described one man "tall, white, with brown hair and brown eyes, and with Caucasian—or should I write Nordic?—features . . . who did not identify himself as 'colored' when he took a job in Philadelphia. He lost his job, however, when an old acquaintance informed his employer that the 'Nordic' looking man was 'colored.' " A historian of Washington, D.C., has suggested that passing occurred so frequently during the 1920s that theaters hired doormen of known African descent to keep passers out. Even the first full-length play written by an African American and presented on Broadway, *Appearances*, contained a minor subplot about passing.[32]

In the mid-1920s, commentators pointed to results of the 1920 federal census as proof of an acceleration in the rate of passing. As early as 1922, *Current Opinion* suggested that census statistics underreported mulattoes and that the nation's black population was undergoing a process of "internal 'whitening.' " In 1925, an editorial in *Opportunity* compared the 1910 and 1920 census statistics on mulattoes and concluded that the large decline in the number of mulattoes had to be the result of passing, when mulattoes "fade into the great white multitude." A few years later, the National Urban League's Charles Johnson estimated that about 10,000 people or more passed each year based on "an analysis of United States census figures and on the personal knowledge of members of his race." Though the notion that some black Americans were melting into whiteness received a good deal of press, questions were raised about the accuracy of the data.[33]

Anxiety over passing in the twenties appeared linked to black migration to the North.[34] Inklings of this change had started to appear as early as the beginning years of the century. In 1902, Cyrus Fields Adams wrote in *The Colored American Magazine*, "Thousands of persons of mixed blood have immigrated to the North, where they have intermarried with Caucasians, and are known as such. I think there are millions of people in the United States who have a strain of African blood of which they themselves are not aware." During the Great Migration, when scores of southern blacks crossed the geographic boundary of the Mason-Dixon line, such movement propelled a rise in the popular fascination with passing—which can, after all, be conceived of as the crossing of another socially constructed line or boundary between the races.[35]

By the twenties, the North seemed to be the new location where passing had taken hold. In 1921, William Pickens declared, "White-colored people a re in high places in almost every large city of the Union, especially in the North and West." One year earlier, a pamphlet called *The Amalgamation of America*, which sold for one dollar, raised the connection between migration and passing. Its author, Sylvester Russell, described the United States as a "gradual mixing country" and proclaimed that a great deal of "racial assimilation" took place in northern cities. According to Russell, the problem of the "pure white colored who knowingly pass for white" that alarmed the white South was beginning to affect the North as "white coloreds" began to migrate from the South to the North. To make his point, Russell recounted numerous anecdotes about passers, including "lily white colored men" and the "thousands of colored girls" who "are lily white" and "proud of it because they are living in a day when they can fool the white man just as he fooled their ancestors."[36]

In a 1926 article in *Opportunity* focused on white Americans' anxieties over the movement of African Americans, the National Urban League's Elmer A. Carter wrote of the "synchronous but more subtle migration" of passing. He described the Great Migration as an "Ethiopian excursion [which] fills the North with apprehension and the South with dismay." But he observed that "a more formidable migration" constituted the "most ambitious offensive ever launched by the lowly sons of Ham." "What is this subtle migration?" he mused. "In what form does this new offensive take shape? It is nothing less than the crossing over of thousands of Negroes from their own race to the dominant white race; it is the deliberate annihilation of ethnic affiliation when physical appearance does not proclaim it." By using this language of a military engagement to describe the act of passing, Carter likely evoked the militant image of African American soldiers returning from the war and the concurrent rise of the New Negro. But Carter also explained why African Americans passed. "The color line, invisible but ever present," he declared, "is a constant reminder of [their] inferior status. . . . To escape then, the color line, countless Negroes sometimes known as mulattoes, quadroons, quintaroons, octoroons and other more or less accurate designations of race infiltration have voluntarily exiled themselves from the Negro race and cast their lot with the irreproachable Nordic Blond."[37]

Not only authors in African American publications connected racial and geographic migrations. In 1922, a letter from a "Southerner" (presumably white) appeared in the *New York World* in response to a call from reporter Heywood Broun to desegregate Broadway theaters. The "Southerner's" response focused on passing instead of desegregation and repeated a story about "two Negro girls" he knew "who couldn't be identified as Negroes in the little Southern town where they lived except for the fact that everybody knew them." "Southerner" claimed both girls had been sent up North for their education and never returned home. "They are up here somewhere passing as white girls." In a 1931 article in the mainstream journal *Outlook and Indepen-*

dent, Caleb Johnson discussed "crossing the colored line" and argued that the "social problems involved in the mingling of white and black . . . formerly concerned only the South; now, with the influx of Negroes into the North until cities like New York, Chicago and Philadelphia have colonies numbering hundreds of thousands, they are a matter of national concern." Johnson warned his readers that passing was not difficult in the United States because it was easy to move. Such a warning would have resonated after a decade of demographic change.[38]

In 1927, sociologist Edward B. Reuter advanced the theory that one might pass successfully if one crossed geographic boundaries to a new region where one's history and family were not known. In *The American Race Problem*, Reuter addressed population movements and the way they disrupted traditional systems of knowledge and thereby increased the ability to pass. Reuter observed, "Each year the mulatto group loses a larger or smaller number of its members through their disappearance into the white population. Many individuals whose percentage of Negro blood is only one-eighth or less are to all appearances white persons. In any region where the person and his ancestry are not known he may pass as a person of pure white ancestry."[39] Mass migration like that taking place in the late 1910s and 1920s could only help migrants "disappear" into whiteness.

The belief that the rate of passing accelerated in the twenties was not only a function of the physical ability to relocate. Job discrimination in the North may also have led to passing. Even before the 1920s, African Americans faced growing difficulties in gaining employment in the North. Numerous articles in both the African American and the white press asserted that economic imperatives helped to drive up the pace of passing. A 1911 study in Chicago on black women and employment found that if African American women were "so nearly white that they can be mistaken for white girls" they might obtain decent-paying jobs such as a sales clerk in a department store. If they did not pass as white, the stores would refuse to hire them. *The Nation*'s 1923 comment on passing depicted the unmasking of a passer at work.[40]

Passing for economic opportunities might serve as the first step to passing to avoid social limitations. Although Louis Fremont Baldwin's 1929 pamphlet *From Negro to Caucasian; or, How the Ethiopian Is Changing His Skin* (which discussed the Rhinelander trial) pointed to access to employment as a motive for passing, it also suggested a relationship between passing for a job and passing in social relations. Indeed, Baldwin offered to publicly explain "the manner in which many Negroes in America . . . have abandoned their one-time affiliation with Negroes . . . by mingling at first commercially or industrially, then socially with Caucasians, [and] have ultimately been absorbed by the latter." Baldwin pointed out the difficulty for people to know for sure whether they were "Negro" or white and he hinted that at least five thousand passed as white every year. Baldwin's pamphlet contained an endorsement by "A. E. Shadd, Bishop of the United Holy Church of America, Western & Pacific Coast District," who admitted that members of his own family had "Crossed Over." Shadd "felt it his duty to give the author permission to add his personal testimony as to the prevalence of the practice alleged to be in vogue."[41]

Commentators in this era also observed that changing social relations between blacks and whites in the North promoted passing. In 1923, an editorial in *Opportunity* discussed a recent controversy over Harvard University's attempt to segregate its black and white students. The editor concluded that Harvard's move might convince mulattoes to "avoid embarrassment by concealing their identity entirely. Instead of keeping them apart[,] the tendency would be to fuse them beyond any hope of separation." In the *Messenger*, editor Chandler Owens argued that passing could not be stopped, and he emphasized that white Americans' mistreatment of African Americans led to passing. Owens contended that passing meant that "you can go any place if you have the money to pay your way. . . . In other words, 'passing for white' is passing for what the Negro is not, because better opportunities are given to what he *is not* than to what *he is*."[42] Thus one effect of the Great Migration, residential, occupational, and social segregation in the North, may have had unintended consequences for white northerners.

Because New York was a desirable destination for southern migrants and foreigners it made a logical setting for easy passing. In 1916, a *New York Age* theater critic reviewed a play in which the main character, a New Yorker and a wealthy Yale graduate, learned the "truth" about his racial ancestry when he became engaged to a white woman. Lester Walton's review of "Pride of Race" observed, "There are hundreds of men and women in New York City who, although fully aware of their racial affiliations have gone over on 'the other side' and feel highly elated over being able to practise deception." Fifteen years later, Caleb Johnson's article in *Outlook* also pointed to New York as one place where a great deal of passing occurred.[43]

Other commentators reflected on the ease of passing in New York. An anonymous author in the *Century Magazine*, probably Walter White, described his life in New York as a "white Negro" in 1925. He talked about the experiences of others like him who could pass and observed that many New Yorkers did so because they were "tired of facing . . . barriers and [were] choosing instead to cast their lot where race will not keep them from the opportunities they seek." "It is the easiest thing imaginable to 'get by' in places like New York," he added, "where there is so great an admixture of southern European blood." Indeed, a Howard University scientist's 1931 study of color suggested that "those with facial features and hair which permit, will very often identify themselves with any foreign nationality in order to cross the color line if for no better reason than to attend a segregated theater." Leonard Rhinelander even testified that he attributed Spanish ancestry to Alice's father, George Jones.[44]

If the existence of "mongrel" New York facilitated passing, it thereby made New York even more of a "mongrel" city. In his 1928 study of mulattoes, Edward Reuter addressed the issue of passing, the physical appearances of both the black and white races, and the ways they were becoming more like each other. Reuter contended that the "Negro group" was becoming more "mulatto" and therefore more "white." At the same time, he maintained that the physical characteristics of white Americans were being transformed in such a way as to eliminate distinctions between whites and Negroes. This transformation of whiteness came about through an increase in the percentage of people who could pass: "Each year a few individuals are able to conceal the fact of Negro ancestry and escape the racial classification. A certain small percentage of octoroons show few obvious external negroid characters and are able to pass as white men." Somewhat contradictorily, Reuter suggested that the existence (and appearance) of those who passed made it easier for others to do the same while the actual number of people who passed remained small.[45]

Not only the "incorporation," as Reuter put it, into white America of those who passed modified the appearance of white Americans. The introduction into the United States of certain European immigrants also altered the physical characteristics of whiteness. Reuter proposed that immigration from Southern and Eastern Europe transformed the "physical type of the white race." According to Reuter, these new immigrants constituted a more "negroid" type with dark skin. In Reuter's view, the arrival of these nationalities further eroded distinctions between black and white. Given this blurring of the color line, Reuter warned of the repercussions:

> There is thus in process a movement tending to modify the Negro type in the direction of the white and the white in the direction of the negroid. In the present day there is no clear division between the Negroes and the

mixed bloods; a continuation of the present population movements will erase the line separating the white group from the mixtures. Every blurring of the line will increase contact on the racial borders and further the racial blending. The mulattoes will presently displace the Negroes and ultimately the mulattoes, because of further bleaching and because of continued contamination of the lower orders of the whites, will merge with the general white population.

Thus, the combined assaults on whiteness of those blacks who could pass and inferior immigrants would ultimately yield a thoroughly mixed-up population unable to be separated by clear lines of race, just as racial extremists like Madison Grant had predicted.[46]

This sense that the North, and particularly New York, had become the center for passing also surfaced in the fictional accounts of passing that flourished in the 1920s, especially but not only in African American magazines. In 1920, *Crisis* literary editor Jessie Fauset published a novelette, *The Sleeper Wakes*, that chronicles the life of a young woman raised by colored foster parents despite her possession of a "pearl and pink whiteness." When she turns seventeen, she runs away to New York City and passes for white. Fauset's 1928 novel, *Plum Bun*, also contains a plot about passing in New York. Another passing narrative set in New York appeared in *Half-Century Magazine* in early 1925 and involved a romance between a Wall Street financier who passed as white and a stenographer who passed, too. Strangely enough, the *Half-Century* had published an almost identical story seven years earlier under a different title and with a different author's name.[47] In 1926, Walter White published the novel *Flight*, in which a "creole" woman from the South passes as white and marries a millionaire. The better-known Harlem Renaissance novelist Nella Larsen, who sometimes self-identified as "mulatto," set her novel, *Passing*, mainly in New York City, although she also described incidents of passing in Chicago. Even before the twenties, authors set passing stories in New York. In 1915, the novel *Redder Blood* depicted the New York marriage of a wealthy white man and a woman who passed as white.[48]

White authors of fiction in the twenties also drew on the theme of passing. The novelist, critic, and photographer Carl Van Vechten placed a passing character in his controversial 1926 Harlem Renaissance novel *Nigger Heaven*. Edna Ferber's *Show Boat*, one of the nation's best-selling novels in 1926, incorporated the motif of passing. One year later, Jerome Kern and Oscar Hammerstein turned Ferber's novel into the popular Broadway musical *Show*

Boat, which featured a "mixed-race" cast. Another Broadway play from 1926, *Black Boy*, which starred Paul Robeson as a Jack Johnson–like fighter, also included the actress Freddie Washington as a woman who passed as white. (Freddie Washington later starred as the better-known passing character Peola in the 1934 film *Imitation of Life*, which was based on Fannie Hurst's 1933 novel on passing). The pervasiveness of the theme of passing in American life and literature and New York is also echoed in a novel that did not directly address passing. In F. Scott Fitzgerald's *The Great Gatsby*, the character of Jay Gatsby is revealed to really be James Gatz, the son of a Midwestern farmer. As literary critics have observed, Gatz passes as Gatsby amidst the luxury estates of Long Island, although he does not pass from black to white though possibly from Jewish to Gentile.[49]

One response to the perceived rise in passing was to try to tighten existing definitions of race. During the 1920s, in addition to working to restrict immigration, eugenicists participated in a movement primarily in the South to toughen laws that defined race.[50] Southern legislators worked to protect the white race and prevent passing by enacting "racial purity laws" that redefined existing racial categories. Well-known proponents of eugenics and racial purity like Madison Grant and Lothrop Stoddard endorsed such legislation in Virginia. The African American press recognized that Virginia whites feared that "Virginia blacks are getting white, not by intermarriage, but by the so-called 'back door method.' The Bureau of Vital Statistics estimates that there are 20,000 people in the State who may be either 'white or colored,' whichever they please."[51]

In March 1924, the Virginia state legislature passed a law to draw an impermeable line around the category of "white" after intensive lobbying by members of the Anglo-Saxon Clubs of America and W. A. Plecker, the Virginia state registrar of vital statistics. The Anglo-Saxon Clubs of America and State Registrar Plecker were alarmed by census statistics that revealed a rise in the rate of passing. Plecker went as far as to describe passing as more dangerous to the public welfare than a rise in mortality rates from disease. But Plecker felt state racial purity laws constituted merely a first step to stop the problem. In a letter to *The Nation* in response to an editorial mocking Virginia's new law, Plecker declared, "Our law preventing these near-white people securing marriage licenses is about the best that we are able to do at this time, until the country as a whole realizes the seriousness of the situation."[52]

Virginia's new Racial Integrity Act defined a "white person" (a category not previously defined) as someone without any "trace whatsoever of any blood other than Caucasian." The same statute also provided that any resident born before the date Virginia established its Bureau of Vital Statistics (which tracked race on birth certificates) could "file a certificate of racial composition." In this way, Virginia hoped to administratively implement a one-drop rule for Negroes because everyone's ancestry would be known and recorded. Such a strategy might work in the South, especially if people remained in the communities in which their families had resided for generations.[53]

Yet tighter definitions of racial categories did not necessarily end passing. Virginia's Racial Integrity Act of 1924 only defined a "white" person. A 1910 statute had defined "colored person" as someone who possessed at least "one-sixteenth Negro blood," which of course meant that someone with less than "one-sixteenth Negro blood" could have been considered legally white. In other words, Virginian race law contradicted itself.[54] Despite the loopholes in Virginia law, W. A. Plecker and the Bureau of Vital Statistics strove to keep "mongrels" from passing as white. By the end of the twenties, Plecker observed, "There is nothing better known to us in the Virginia Bureau of Vital Statistics, than the aggressiveness of many of these near-whites in their intense desire to cross the line." Drawing on government documents such as tax records, marriage records, and antebellum lists of "free Negroes," the bureau tried to ensure that "near-whites" could not be designated white. By 1930 Virginia tried to close any remaining gaps by redefining "colored person" in an amendment to the 1924 law.[55]

Virginia's statutory efforts to prevent passing, however, only highlighted the difficulties in doing so. Writing in New York's *Amsterdam News* in 1925 about laws like Virginia's, William Pickens argued that such efforts were a "little late" to save white racial purity. Pickens pointed out that the South possessed two to three million mulattoes, plus "the other 'lost tribe' of one million or more of mulattoes who have become blood parts of the white race in order to escape being oppressed by the white race."[56] Comments like Pickens raised doubts about whether any new legal definition of "white" or reworked definitions of "colored" or "Negro" would prevent passing. Nevertheless, Georgia and Alabama enacted similar laws in 1927.[57]

In the 1920s not only individual states tried to stop passing. During that decade, as federal census statistics were invoked to prove higher rates of passing, changes were proposed and made to census categories. Over time, as the growing desire to fix racial boundaries grew and as racial categories in the census shifted back and forth from year to year, the potential for contradictory results in categorizing by race had become a problem.[58] Despite earlier beliefs held by officials such as Carroll D. Wright, commissioner of the Department of Labor, that there would be no "difficulty in ascertaining the statistics relating to mulattoes, quadroons, and octoroons which are obtained for all other classes of population," hopes for the 1890 enumeration belied the actual results.[59] A subsequent report on the 1890 census concluded that the figures obtained from these multiple categories held little value, and therefore the 1900 census instructed enumerators to distinguish only between "black" and "white." The 1910 and 1920 censuses, however, again distinguished between the "black" and "mulatto" categories. But by 1930, the census no longer included any intermediate racial categories between "black" and "white," and the "mulatto" disappeared. While many historians are aware of the elimination of the "mulatto" category, most have not recognized how the perceived problem with passing in the 1920s played a critical role in this change.[60]

In the years between the 1910 and 1920 censuses, census statisticians admitted that intermediate racial categories produced only confusing and inconsistent results. Indeed, they asserted, "the classification of the Negro population as 'black' and 'mulatto' does not correspond accurately to any physiological characteristic, although it is a classification which measures with some uncertain degree of accuracy the admixture of white blood in the population classified as Negro."[61] There seemed to be little reason to distinguish between mulatto and black since the recognition of categories beyond black and white seemed to produce only confusion.

One aspect of this confusion centered on the varying numbers of mulattoes counted in the censuses when the category appeared. The results of the 1920 census reported a significant decline from 1910 in the number of mulattoes counted; this decline presented a problem for the Census Bureau.[62] In a December 1928 meeting of the Census Advisory Committee, the Census Bureau proposed eliminating the distinction between "black" and "mulatto." The staff reasoned that "it seems quite evident that the returns for this distinction are not even approximately accurate; and the drop in the percentage shown as mulatto from 20.9 in 1910 to 15.9 in 1920 would seem to provide the final argument against retaining this item for 1930." The Advisory Committee approved a resolution that omitted the distinction between "black" and "mulatto" in the population questions for the 1930 census. The resolution acknowledged that "the principal reason for giving up the attempt to separate blacks and mulattoes was the fact that the results of the attempt in past censuses had been very imperfect."[63]

An even clear link between the removal of the category "mulatto" from the census and the problem of passing emerged a few years later in a 1932 report on "race and nativity" statistics drafted by Joseph Hill, the Census Bureau's chief statistician. Hill's report, "Population Classified by Race and Nativity" reflected the growing concern over eliminating racial uncertainty in the 1920s. In this report, Hill discussed the 1920 census results and remarked that "a certain number of persons who according to this definition [of Negro, that is, a person with any proportion of Negro blood] strictly applied should be classed as Negroes are probably returned as white because they are not distinguishable in appearance from the white and pass as whites in the community in which they live." Definitions of race in the census could not be written in a way that would preclude enumerators from identifying the wrong people as white. Hill, like many other white authors who discussed passing, felt it necessary to observe that the actual numbers of those who passed must be small.[64]

Despite Hill's claim that few passed as white, the remainder of his report suggested that whatever the numbers, passing posed a problem that needed to be resolved. Hill acknowledged that previous "attempts to distinguish mulattoes in the enumeration of the Negro population have not been very successful," and he argued that the "very nature of things makes it impossible in a census to distinguish accurately between black and mulatto. The enumerator must either judge by appearances—which are often deceitful, and he does not by any means meet or see all the persons whom he enumerates—or he must accept the answer he gets to the question if he takes the trouble to ask it. In most cases the question probably is not asked at all, and, if it is asked and answered, it is not at all certain that the informant knows or will give the correct answer." The Bureau of the Census eliminated the problem of "deceit" or lack of knowledge by no longer counting mulattoes. No longer collecting this information also meant that no one could use census data to estimate the numbers of persons who passed.[65]

The confusion about racial classification can be tracked through the way the Jones family was categorized in the federal censuses from 1900 to 1930. In 1900, when census instructions provided for only two racial categories, "black" and "white," the census enumerator listed the family as George, Elizabeth, Emily, and Alice and classified each member of the family as white. By 1910, when the family had grown to include Grace, the enumerator again identified the entire family as white, although the census for that year included the designation "mulatto." When only George, Elizabeth, and Grace lived at home (Emily had already married by 1920 and Alice may have been working away from home as a live-in servant), the family still appeared as "white" in the 1920 census. In 1930, when the federal census eliminated the category of mulatto, only three people remained at the Jones's home in New Rochelle: George, Elizabeth, and Alice Rhinelander. For the purposes of this census, George was identified as Negro and Elizabeth was identified as white. The enumerator first wrote the designation "W," meaning white, for Alice Rhinelander; at some point, however, someone crossed out the "W" and replaced it with the designation "neg" for "Negro." Yet in the same census, Alice's younger sister Grace, who lived next door to the Joneses with her husband, Albert Miller, is identified as white, despite the tremendous publicity given to the Jones family during the 1925 trial, including references to Grace as Alice's sister.[66] Apparently, despite all of the tinkering with the census, "mistakes" could still be made.

By the end of the twenties, the subject of passing still resonated with concerns over fixing racial identity. W. E. B. DuBois in a July 1929 review of Nella Larsen's novel, *Passing*, noted the significance of passing, "this intriguing and ticklish subject of a person's right to conceal the fact that he had a grandparent of Negro descent," to white Americans. DuBois suggested that white Americans considered passing a "matter of tremendous moral import" because, "of course, . . . so many white people in America either know or fear that they have Negro blood."[67] As DuBois made clear, "passing" might seem "silly" but it could have serious consequences because it touched on potent fears about not knowing how to tell who was who. The fear that large numbers of those who should be "Negroes" were "crossing over" to become white tapped into the growing concern in early-twentieth-century America with demarcating exact boundary lines between the races.

WHEN ISAAC MILLS placed his client on the stand to testify to Alice's deceit, he wanted the white jury to feel the "tremendous moral import" of Leonard's claims that she passed. To do so, Mills took Leonard step-by-step through the story of how Alice lied. First, Leonard described how in the months between his return to New York in May and September of 1924, Alice's mother told him, in the presence of Alice and George Jones, that "they had done everything in their power to prevent Emily from marrying Brooks." In addition, when Emily defied her parents by marrying Brooks, the Joneses refused to let the couple enter their home for two years. According to Leonard, Elizabeth Jones declared the family "English" not "colored." Indeed, he claimed that in another conversation Elizabeth Jones informed him, "The first time we ever saw a colored person was on our arrival in America, while walking on Sixth Avenue. We were surprised and didn't know what they were." At this point, according to Leonard, Alice interjected, "Of course, we are not colored. We never associate with colored people and never will." Under Mills's questioning, Leonard declared he believed both Alice and her mother.[68]

Although Leonard's testimony appeared to show that Alice and her family concealed their "true" ancestry, Mills was not done yet with trying to show the jury how Alice deceived Leonard. He inquired about Alice's statements about her ancestry: "Was anything said to you at any time by Alice in regard to their being of Spanish extraction in any way?" Leonard replied, "In one of her letters she told me that she had become acquainted with a Harvard man in the Adirondacks, and he asked Alice, 'What are you,' and Alice replied, 'I am of Spanish extraction.'" Leonard said he believed Alice's claim because he had traveled to Havana and seen, as Mills phrased it, "Spanish people of Caucasian blood" with a "dark complexion."[69]

Continuing to build up the evidence that Alice lied, Mills next questioned Leonard about Alice's statements to the newspapers in 1924:

> [Mills:] Was anything said at that time by her as to whether she was of colored blood or white?
> [Leonard]: Yes.
> [Mills:] What did she say on that subject?
> [Leonard]: I told Alice, what the newspapers said, she said "This is terrible, it is not true."[70]

Mills pushed Leonard further and asked if Alice made other similar statements. Leonard replied that she denied she was colored not just to him but also to the reporters. According to Leonard, Alice declared to the press, "I am white, and I shall sue the newspapers through my attorney, Judge Swinburne." Leonard told Mills he believed Alice when she told reporters she was white.[71]

Mills then took Leonard through the tale of how his lawyer Leon Jacobs arrived on the scene shortly after the papers printed the news. Leonard described how Alice told Jacobs she was white. Leonard informed Jacobs that the Joneses were preparing to sue the press. When Jacobs returned a few days later, he asked why the Joneses had not yet filed suit. Leonard told Mills he left New Rochelle with Jacobs that day because "there was doubt in my mind." Leonard testified that he was finally persuaded that Alice was colored in

March of 1925 when Jacobs showed him her birth certificate four months after he left Alice (of course, this was more than 100 days *after* he filed suit to annul the marriage).[72]

Sensing that he had obtained from Leonard the most he could to demonstrate Alice's deceptions, Mills circled in:

> [Mills:] If you had known what is now conceded to be true before you married Alice, that she is of colored blood, would you have married her?
> [Leonard:] Absolutely not, no.
> [Mills:] When you married her did you believe her statement that she was white?
> [Leonard:] I did. I always believed her.[73]

To bolster Leonard's claims that Alice lied, Mills quickly introduced a new witness: William Lawby. Lawby, a reporter from the *New York American*, testified about his interview with Leonard and Alice on the day the Westchester press publicized their marriage. According to Lawby, he told Alice about the press accounts and let her know that she could counter the reports about her ancestry by making a statement and having her photograph taken. When Alice declined, Lawby claimed, he showed her his copy of that day's *Standard Star*. Immediately Alice warned that any paper that printed such a story would have to pay for it. She then told Lawby, " 'Well, we are not colored. There is no colored blood in us.' " After Lawby asked Alice about her sister's marriage to a "colored butler," she told him that her family disapproved and she " 'had never associated with colored persons.' "[74]

On cross-examination, Davis tried hard to undermine Lawby's testimony. After carefully setting up Lawby to describe the care he took in reporting important stories, Davis forced Lawby to admit he had cleaned up Alice's language in his published account. Davis also made Lawby acknowledge he did not take verbatim notes during the interview. Davis hoped these questions about Lawby's techniques would cast doubt in the jury's mind about the accuracy of Lawby's interview and his recollections on the stand.

Although Lawby's testimony damaged the defense, Davis asked an unexpected question, inquiring of Lawby whether he had discussed anything with Leonard outside of Alice's presence. Once Lawby admitted he had, Davis asked: "Don't you know that young Rhinelander said to you, in the absence of his wife, that he understood that her parents came from the West Indies? You will be frank, won't you?" Lawby replied, "He did make such a statement."

After getting Lawby to repeat this information twice, Davis took a gamble and asked, "Didn't he tell you that he didn't care whether she was white or black—that he loved her?" "He did not," Lawby replied. After the failed attempt to get Lawby to further aid Alice's case, the best Davis could do to salvage his line of questioning was to get Lawby to repeat that Leonard told him that Mr. Jones came from the West Indies. When Davis later cross-examined Leonard he asked why Leonard told Lawby that George Jones was West Indian. Leonard replied, "I cannot affirm or deny that statement." Under Davis's relentless grilling, Leonard finally admitted, "I might have."[75] Davis's questions to Lawby and Leonard implied that if Leonard Rhinelander knowingly wed a woman of West Indian ancestry, then he knew Alice was colored.

Leonard Rhinelander had willingly married outside of his own social group, an action that his family, and the social group to which his family belonged, would not take kindly to. Such a marriage had the potential to undermine not only the authority of New York's white upper class but also the value of that class's status and prestige. A response of some kind seemed required.

FIVE :

Defending the Citadel of Whiteness from the "Awful Stain"

Social distinction in America, at present, is a citadel set upon an eminence which can be scaled by any one of three routes,—birth, wealth, or less frequently, achievement.—MRS. JOHN KING VAN RENSSELAER, *The Social Ladder* (1924)

If anything more humiliating to the prestige of white America than the Rhinelander case has occurred recently it has escaped our attention.
—W. E. B. DUBOIS, "Rhinelander," *Crisis* (January 1926)

ONCE UPON A TIME, an heir to a New York fortune married a maid of immigrant origins. Trying to break up the marriage, his parents sent a lawyer to convince the young man to leave his wife and offered to pay her to leave the country. When the son refused to abandon his bride, his parents disinherited him and gave him only a small stipend to live on. Eight years after his marriage, the not-so-young former heir embarrassed his family again. Convinced that the family lawyer had first restricted his income and then attempted to seduce his wife and turn her against him, the eldest son met the lawyer in a downtown Manhattan office where he regularly picked up his remittance, took out a pistol, and shot him. After the shooting and his subsequent arrest, the family hired more lawyers to have their eldest son, described by the *New*

York Times as "a weak-minded member of a wealthy family," declared insane and institutionalized.[1]

In June 1884, long before Leonard and Alice were born, Leonard's uncle, William Copeland Rhinelander, shot his father's personal lawyer. His family maneuvered to have him found insane to avoid a public trial for felonious assault and instead have him committed to an insane asylum, preferably for life. The attorney hired to defend William in the sanity proceedings asserted that William's parents hoped to have his marriage annulled once the courts declared their son insane. Such a tactic might work: New York law provided that a relative could bring an action to annul the marriage of an insane person.[2]

Eight years before William Rhinelander aimed his pistol at a lawyer, he married a young Irish woman named Margueretta McGuiness. His parents didn't approve. Like many Irish female immigrants, Margueretta worked as a domestic servant, most likely in the Rhinelander home. To avoid embarrassing his family after his marriage, William changed the spelling of his name to "Rynlander." William and Margueretta even moved away from New York City, traveled to Canada, Baltimore, and Westchester, and ended up in Brooklyn in 1883.[3] By the time of William's 1884 arrest, William and Margueretta's relationship may have been strained by the peripatetic life they led with their two children. Sometime before the shooting, William was living in a Brooklyn boardinghouse without his wife and children.[4]

Despite the separation, William's filial disobedience had already set off a series of responses from his family that culminated in the obliteration of his very name from the family tree. According to a Rhinelander family genealogy compiled about twenty years after William wed Margueretta, William's father begat only two sons: William's younger brothers, Thomas Jackson Oakley and Philip, Leonard's father. William no longer existed for the Rhinelanders, except perhaps in the memory of his much younger brother, Philip. Philip Rhinelander would have been only eleven in 1876 when his brother William married and his parents' disapproval changed their lives. Philip must have remembered the events of 1876 and the public spectacle involving his brother's indictment for felonious assault in 1884 when the news reached him in November 1924 that Philip's own son had followed in his uncle's footsteps.[5]

In the proceedings to determine William's sanity, William recalled that when he first told his mother the name of his wife, Matilda Rhinelander cried, "May God in His mercy take the woman. I wish that you may never have a child." When asked what his mother meant, William replied, "That my wife should die—to absolve the family from the awful stain." His father, also William, ordered him out of the family home and rewrote his will to disinherit his oldest son. Not only immediate family reacted to his marriage. William testified that his aunt Julia Rhinelander "could forgive him any thing, even possible embezzlement and larceny, but the last, the crowning act of infamy, the marriage beneath him, was one that could not be absolved, was one that could not be condoned." Indeed, when Julia died unmarried and without children in 1890, she left money to her other nieces and nephews, including William's two younger brothers. She left nothing to William.[6]

When William's young nephew Leonard married a maid forty-eight years after his uncle's marriage, why did his family react the way they did? The widowed Philip Rhinelander may have considered Leonard's marriage a "crowning act of infamy." In response to a reporter's question in November 1924 about whether his father knew about his marriage to Alice, Leonard said he did not. When asked if it would make a difference, Leonard replied, "Oh yes, it would mean my wife's happiness and mine." By March 1925, four months after Leonard left Alice and began annulment proceedings, the press reported Leonard had been disinherited. Although William's and Leonard's weddings took place more than forty years apart, each time the Rhinelander family mobilized lawyers and the power of disinheritance to try to sunder the transgressive marriage. The familial responses to Leonard's and William's marriages demonstrates that something important must have been at stake.[7]

To understand why these marriages mattered, we need to examine the formation of New York's white upper class in the late nineteenth and early twentieth centuries. If William and Leonard had married women from their own social group, no objections would have been made. William, however, married an Irish domestic servant, a member of the "Celtic" race, and most likely a Roman Catholic. Novelist Edith Wharton, a member of New York's upper class, a distant relative of William and Leonard Rhinelander, and an adolescent at the time of William's marriage observed that "the New York of my youth was distinctively Episcopalian." And although Leonard's bride Alice worshiped in the Episcopal Church, her claims to pure Anglo-Saxonism were tenuous. Each man's choice of a working-class wife with an immigrant background had the potential to wreck the Rhinelanders' position in New York society, and consequently, William's and Leonard's marital choices had to be explained by claims of lunacy or fraud. Why else would a Rhinelander marry " 'outside of the charmed circle,' " as William called it?[8]

Examining the familial responses to William's and Leonard's marriages helps us understand the ways in which ideas about gender, race, and marriage played a critical role in the forging of a white upper class in New York. During the decades between William's marriage and Leonard's, New York's white upper class exerted a great deal of economic, political, and social power in America. While doing so, New York's elites constituted and reconstituted themselves as a self-conscious class, and the reactions to William's and Leonard's marriages expose this process of class formation. Consequently, analyzing the way New York's upper class dealt with a misalliance, a seemingly minor challenge to their power, may help us better understand how the white upper class wielded their influence and worked to defend their citadels from attack.[9]

In the late nineteenth century and the early decades of the twentieth century, elites in New York City had to weather the challenges of the dramatic social changes taking place in New York and the nation. During both eras, immigration changed the very face of the city. Only five years before the marriage of a Rhinelander to a McGuiness, Irish Protestants (the "Orangemen") and Irish Catholics battled in New York's "Orange Riot"; sixty-two people, mainly working-class Irish Catholics, died. Not only a religious conflict, the Orange Riot contained significant components of class warfare. Upper-class white New Yorkers (generally Protestants) supported the Orangemen. Members of the Seventh Regiment of New York's National Guard (many of whom were upper-class New Yorkers) participated in the action to put down the Catholic rioters. Urban violence involving the Irish in the nineteenth century fueled anti-Irish feelings among the Protestant elite, who perceived the Irish as "uniquely violent."[10]

The years in between William's and Leonard's respective marriages also saw the triumph of corporate capitalism over competitive capitalism and the transformation of the United States into a consumer culture. These transformations created much turbulence. In the 1870s, when William and Margueretta married, wealthy New Yorkers feared the social upheavals generated by clashes between labor and capital during a decade of depression. Class conflict still existed fifty years later, and the 1920s, the decade when Leonard and Alice met, began with an explosion on Wall Street. Only one year earlier in the aftermath of the Great War, violent labor strikes broke out throughout the country as the economy entered a postwar recession.[11]

When William Copeland Rhinelander married his Irish maid, the nation was celebrating its centennial, as well as its growing technological and industrial might. His marriage to a woman outside of his family's social circle in

1876, however, breached the boundaries of a class still in the process of formation, and inherently unstable. Americans were still three years away from the end of a depression set off by a Wall Street panic in 1873. The depression of the 1870s pushed wealthy New Yorkers to continue forging "a collective identity" based on "a theory of (often racial) hierarchy, a recast relationship between state and economy, and ambivalence about democracy." As New York's bourgeoisie developed a more coherent sense of themselves as a group in the 1870s, it also developed a class-centered ideology based on "the unfettered rights of property."[12] The Rhinelanders as members of New York's economic elite participated in this process of class consolidation, and the historical record reveals multiple traces of their presence.

According to those few historians who study New York's nineteenth century upper class, the composition of that group changed over the course of the century.[13] In the decades before the Civil War, the so-called Knickerbockers, primarily merchants, owners of real estate, and some bankers, whose names and money dated from the time of the Revolution, dominated New York's economy. The Rhinelanders belonged to the Knickerbocker social group; the family bought Manhattan real estate at the end of the eighteenth and during the early nineteenth centuries. Edith Wharton, related to the Rhinelanders through her mother, Lucretia Rhinelander Jones, described this group as one "composed of families to whom a middling prosperity had come, usually by the rapid rise in value of inherited real estate." As industrialization played a more prominent role in the American economy in the 1850s, manufacturers assumed greater importance in New York's economy and posed a potential challenge to the social status of the Knickerbockers.[14]

The Civil War, however, marked the beginning of a change in the status of New York's elites. Tensions between wealthy New Yorkers and the working class erupted in events like the 1863 Draft Riot. Over the course of a few days in July 1863, working-class rioters drawn from New York's Irish and German immigrant communities struck out at wealthy New Yorkers and New York's African American population. Wealthy white New Yorkers found their homes broken into and property destroyed, while rioters lynched black New Yorkers. Not surprisingly, the Draft Riots persuaded "many merchants, manufacturers, bankers, and professionals that they were being confronted by the 'dangerous classes.'" Elite New Yorkers began to recognize their common interests in the face of a class-based foe.[15]

By the 1880s, when William's sanity came into question, the upper class had literally taken up arms against the working class, in response to the waves of strikes that rippled through the American economy in the 1870s and 1880s and the sharpening of class consciousness. The elite Seventh Regiment of the New York National Guard had built itself a new armory prepared to repel the working class, by force if necessary. William's relatives contributed to the costs of building this new citadel of New York's upper class.[16] In 1872, about 100,000 New York workers struck for an eight-hour work day. After New York employers drew on the power of the city's police force, the strikes ended.[17] In 1874, almost 100,000 New Yorkers were unemployed. Two years later, New York's city government ended its previous provision of outdoor relief to the poor who desperately needed assistance. In 1877, an antidemocratic proposal to restrict to property owners the ability to vote for the members of a powerful new city agency, the Board of Finance, was almost adopted. During the same year, a national railroad strike struck fear in the hearts of wealthy New Yorkers, many of whom owned significant interests in the country's railroad companies and worried that the accompanying violence would afflict New York.[18]

Since membership in New York's bourgeoisie did not rest only on birth and connections, the group's boundaries became more permeable after the Civil War as manufacturers, merchants, and rentiers found common ground. Looking back on her youth in the 1860s and 1870s Edith Wharton commented, "It used to seem to me that the group in which I grew up was like an empty vessel into which no new wine would ever again be poured," but in fact these were the decades when new wine, but only of certain vintages, began to be decanted into New York society. New money derived from manufacturing and other new sources began to be assimilated into the culture established by older money. The Rhinelander family helped incorporate new money into old. Despite their membership in the prewar Knickerbocker elite, members of the family created new Gilded Age organizations in association with representatives of the new money. In the 1880s, for example, Leonard's grandfather William Rhinelander joined with a group of new money men led by William Vanderbilt, J. P. Morgan, Jay Gould, and William Rockefeller to establish the Metropolitan Opera House.[19]

New York elites developed a stronger sense of themselves as a unitary class through cultural pursuits at the end of the nineteenth century. According to historian Sven Beckert, "Manners, networks, and institutions showed a new degree of 'classness' in general and an overcoming of the divide between merchants and industrialists in particular." The social ascendancy of one New York family, the Astors, symbolized the assimilation of new money into old and the role played by culture. The term "Four Hundred," was coined during this period to refer to the number of people who would fit in the Astor ballroom.[20] Mrs. Astor and her acolytes set the criteria for membership in New York's new social elite, which included "lineage, bank accounts, sources of income, manners, looks, taste, reputation, and to a moderate degree, education."[21] Whether they belonged to old or new money, every member of the Four Hundred also shared certain essential characteristics—their presumed white racial identity and their Protestant Christian religious background.[22]

Most depictions of the Four Hundred focus on its extravagant and expensive lifestyle. Certain behaviors demonstrated who belonged and who did not. Fancy dances and balls served the important social function of creating spaces that obviously demarcated class lines. Women often created and maintained the social rituals and dealt with the etiquette that helped to define the proper boundaries of society. When Thorstein Veblen critiqued America's elite at the end of the nineteenth century, he pointed to the way in which clothing, "the insignia of leisure," bounded the limits of society. Upper-class women played a key role in maintaining status through their appearance and their activities, which made it clear that they did not have to work. Leonard's mother (Mrs. Philip Rhinelander) and aunt (Mrs. T. J. Oakley Rhinelander) often appeared as society matrons in press accounts of society's "conspicuous leisure" at the end of the nineteenth century.[23]

In the 1880s and 1890s, new societies based on colonial ancestry appeared in New York that also helped delineate the contours of New York's upper class. Men established and joined exclusive clubs and societies based on ancestry that served to support their elite status. In 1891, the New York Genealogical Society elected William Copeland's father, Leonard's grandfather, William, as a member. His wife, Matilda, helped found the Colonial Dames of the State of New York. Both Leonard's uncle (T. J. Oakley) and his father belonged to a number of exclusive clubs and societies, such as the Union Club (one of New York's most exclusive men's' clubs), the St. Nicholas Society, the Huguenot Society, and the Sons of the Revolution.[24]

The Rhinelanders also appeared in the *Social Register*, a national directory of the upper class listing names, addresses, telephone numbers, college affiliations, club memberships, and summer residences, first published in 1887. The first New York edition was published one year later, and it became one method to keep track of those who mattered in bourgeois New York.[25]

Wealthy New Yorkers were also researching their genealogies at the end of the nineteenth century. The Rhinelanders commissioned a genealogist to create a Rhinelander family tree, which started with the first ancestor to land in America in 1686 and settle in New Rochelle. The family tree also described the original location of the Rhinelander family in Europe. The genealogist B. D. Hassell noted that Leonard's father and his uncle, T. J. Oakley, had purchased "the ancient Castle of Schonberg on the Rhine" to mark the location where their family had originally owned land. The two younger Rhinelander brothers purchased the castle in 1884, the same year William shot their father's lawyer, and subsequently spent a great deal of money to restore it. By owning a European castle and commissioning a genealogical chart, the Rhinelanders claimed an aristocratic and pure white ancestry.[26]

The existence of a "pure" upper class, as distinct from a lower and a middle class, depends on the ability of the upper class to exclude those who do not belong. As historians of New York's upper class have observed, the need to exclude conflicted with the rise of new money and the need to incorporate new money into the old elite. Only some new money could be properly assimilated into late-nineteenth-century New York society. If Margueretta Rhinelander was a poor Irish Catholic, she could not assimilate into New York society because by the late nineteenth century, New York's elite defined itself by what it was not: not Catholic, not black, not Jewish, and certainly not poor.[27]

The concept of assimilation—the other side of exclusion—proves significant in understanding how an upper class is formed and why William's marriage to Margueretta disturbed the workings of society. If women played a critical role in exclusion by acting as social arbiters, that is as party givers and organizers of social events, women's bodies could serve as the actual site of social assimilation. Many narratives (both fictional and otherwise) on the rise and fall of white elites in New York comment on the role played by women from established families who married the men of new wealth and thereby raised their husband's social status. Given the social function played by women, strict control over the institution of marriage proved essential to create, reproduce, and maintain an elite.[28]

Not surprisingly, the strict regulation of nuptials played a fundamental role in sustaining the status of New York's elite. The very idea of "lineage," so crucial to determining who belonged to society, depended on proper "breeding" and the reproduction of an elite white stock. The practice of chaperoning to protect upper-class unmarried women from association with the wrong men came into being during the 1880s and continued at least until the 1920s.[29] Simultaneously, during the late nineteenth century, many members of New York's Four Hundred wed their daughters to European nobility in order to bolster their claims to high social status. (Such marriages continued into the early twentieth century. In 1909, a member of the larger Rhinelander family, Anita Stewart, the daughter of William Rhinelander Stewart, married Prince Miguel of Braganza, grandson of the former king of Portugal.)[30] Given the emphasis on marriage and reproduction to maintain social status, no wonder William's mother, Matilda Rhinelander, hoped her new and unwanted Irish daughter-in-law would die without bearing a Rhinelander child.

In sharp contrast to society's close regulation of upper-class women's behavior, upper-class white men entered into sexual liaisons with women from lower stations of life without much difficulty. They were not, however, expected to marry them. It was William's *marriage*, rather than his relationship with Margueretta, that was inappropriate, a point noted by the press. When the *New York Times* reported on William's arrest, it observed, "When he married an ignorant servant girl it proved the last straw, and though his father has since supported him he has had very little to do with him personally." Indeed, the *Times* made William's marriage seem the outcome of a serious character defect that originally appeared under the guise of incorrect "habits."[31]

The *Times* also weighed in on the problems of misalliances. The editors observed that some Americans denied the existence of social classes in America. Though the United States did not possess a caste system, "there is a division between the rich and the poor, between the educated and the ignorant, between the well-mannered and the boorish." In a class-based society, "the marriage of an educated son of a rich family to a servant in his father's family has become the occasion of a tragedy." The *Times* agreed that such a marriage could be objected to on the rational grounds that such a union constituted a "misalliance, in the European sense." Although the editors disagreed with the "steps which the [Rhinelander] family took to enforce that dislike," they believed "such marriages may turn out happily, but generally do not." Therefore, "a judicious parent may be not only pardoned but praised for using every honest endeavor to prevent [such a union]."[32] Such marriages not only diminished the exclusive status of the upper class; they also acted to reduce the value of that status. Consequently, William's action led to his removal from the family. Such a response was not unusual. In Edith Wharton's memoirs, she reminisced about a male cousin who "vanished" during her childhood because of the cousin's involvement with an inappropriate woman. "Vanished," she wrote, "that is, out of society, out of respectability, out of the safe daylight world of 'nice people' and reputable doings."[33] Such a banishment and the concomitant elimination of a violator of societal rules from the family could limit the damage to a family's status in society.

Thus the story of William's marriage and his arrest in 1884 appeared in an era where class consciousness and class conflict reigned. Not surprisingly, the Rhinelanders' attempts to have William found insane garnered attention not only in papers like the *New York Times* but also in the more down-market pages of *The National Police Gazette*. The press followed William's incarceration in New York's notorious prison, the Tombs, where he received visitors, including his grandmother, his wife, and a number of doctors. Only one day after William's arrest, he gave a statement to the *Times*, observing that one newspaper "says I was considered the scape-goat of my family. If marrying against the wishes of one's family makes a scape-goat, then I am one."[34]

William also defended his wife to reporters when he described her as "a beautiful Irish girl when I married her, and she has lost none of the purity, virtue, and sterling womanly qualities for which I married her. Her character is blameless and her one great fault jealousy." In the 1870s and 1880s, Irish Americans and descendants of Anglo-Saxons were perceived as members of different races. In 1876, *Harper's Weekly* cartoonist Thomas Nast drew on racialized stereotypes of the Irish and Negroes to depict both as similarly apelike. A cartoon published in *Puck* two years later depicted an Irish maid as "muscular." William's assertions about his Irish wife's beauty and virtue inverted the assumptions about the Irish highlighted in those cartoons. William's pronouncement, "I believe all are created free and equal, and I do not reckon good standing by birth alone," would not have been greeted happily by those who adhered to those assumptions.[35]

In light of William's statements, it is perhaps not surprising that his family worked behind the scenes to have a lunacy commission appointed to assess William's sanity. William hired lawyers to contest the appointment. To support her husband, Margueretta swore in writing that years earlier the Rhinelander family's lawyer, John Drake, had told her that the family would commit William to an insane asylum unless she left him and went to Europe.[36] Despite such evidence, the courts dismissed William's efforts. Instead, it appointed three commissioners to hear testimony about William's mental condition. Most of the witnesses in the crowded courtroom were doctors who labeled as delusions William's fear of familial persecution. William's parents and his brothers did not appear in front of the commission. One of William's uncles, however, testified about William's "freakish behavior."[37]

Although most of the witnesses spoke about William's mental condition, one witness for William gave credence to his so-called delusions. A schoolteacher told the commissioners about a train ride she had taken in the 1870s when John Drake and another man told her they were headed to Canada to see "a young gentleman who had married beneath him. Mr. Drake remarked that a young man who married beneath him 'should be considered insane and sent out of the country.'" William himself testified that his family had hoped to annul his marriage.[38]

On 2 September 1884, William's lawyer, George M. Curtis, suggested that the statute under which William's sanity was being considered was really "an act to permit the criminal rich and powerful, to escape justice." Despite Curtis's arguments, two of the three commissioners found him insane. On appeal, however, a court agreed with the lone dissenting commissioner and released William from jail on a ten-thousand-dollar bond. The *National Police Gazette* reported on William's joyous reunion with his wife. In March 1885, John Drake died of pneumonia. William never went to trial on the charge of felonious assault.[39]

William continued to embarrass his family with various escapades; he committed bigamy, and his first wife apparently entered an insane asylum. At one point, he was discovered living in a barn. After his arrest and subsequent release for vagrancy, the authorities told him that one more arrest would lead him to the county poorhouse. When his mother died four years later, she bequeathed William only one thousand dollars. She left her two other sons, T. J. Oakley and Philip an estate valued at two million dollars. Clearly, William's violation of his family's and society's rules meant a lifelong estrangement from their presence and the loss of family money.[40]

Despite William's flouting of the conventions of New York's upper class, the rest of his family continued to play an active role in asserting the cultural superiority of New York's bourgeoisie. Proper Rhinelander weddings were publicized in the society pages. In April 1888, the twenty-three-year-old Philip married Adelaide Kip at her parents' home on Fifth Avenue, where she wore an elaborate gown of "silver brocade," with a lace veil "held in place by a tiara of diamonds," along with a diamond necklace. Guests at the wedding reception included Mr. and Mrs. Elliott Roosevelt (Elliott Roosevelt was Theodore's younger brother and the same age as Philip).[41] Philip's marriage to a Kip brought together two old New York families in a wedding surely approved of by family, friends, and the rest of New York's society. In 1894, T. J. Oakley Rhinelander married Edith Cruger Sands, also from an old New York family, at a "large and fashionable" wedding. Numerous references to the Rhinelanders traveling to exclusive resorts, heading to Europe, and hosting dinner parties appeared in society news at the end of the nineteenth and into the twentieth century.[42]

The Rhinelanders even attended one of the most notorious society events of the late nineteenth century: the Bradley Martin Ball held at New York's Waldorf Hotel in 1897. The Bradley Martin Ball took place during a depression year when many objected to the lavish expenditure on costumes and other accouterments for the ball. Recent newcomers to New York society, Bradley and Cornelia Martin had already achieved social success when they married off their teenage daughter to the British aristocracy in 1893. The invitations to their February 1897 costume ball requested that their 1,200 guests wear court dress from the age of Louis XV. Photographs of Adelaide and Philip Rhinelander dressed as Marie Antoinette and Louis XV appeared in the March 1897 issue of *Arthur's Home Magazine*.[43]

Given Philip Rhinelander's experiences with a wayward older brother and his role in upper-class culture, he most likely raised his children to respect the boundaries of elite society. The family spent part of each summer at Spring Lake, New Jersey, where each day "Mrs. Rhinelander drives in a linen topped pony cart and refuses to countenance motor cars."[44] Philip's two oldest sons appeared to follow the family's and society's rules. Both Philip Kip (the oldest son) and T. J. Oakley (the second son) belonged as youths to New York City's Knickerbocker Greys, an institution designed to inculcate in their elite charges upper-class ideals of masculinity through the wearing of uniforms and military drilling. In June 1918, Philip's oldest son married a suitable young woman at St. Thomas Church in New York. The press reported that the marriage date had been moved up, since Lieutenant Philip Kip Rhinelander, a recent graduate of Harvard (where his younger brother T. J. Oakley Rhinelander was still enrolled), would serve in the European war that the United States had recently entered. T. J. Oakley also enlisted, went to France, and died there. New York's society pages also took notice of Adelaide, the only Rhinelander girl. In 1920, the *Times* society reporter reported that Adelaide served as the queen of a benefit Mardi Gras dance at the Ritz-Carlton. One year later, Adelaide married a banker at St. Thomas Church, where two bishops, including relative Philip Mercer Rhinelander, officiated. Adelaide's wedding party included six bridesmaids and eight ushers (including Leonard). A large reception at the Plaza Hotel followed the ceremony.[45]

By the time Leonard Rhinelander married a woman of uncertain ancestry in 1924, New York's upper class, so recently unified at the end of the nineteenth century, once again appeared in a state of flux and subject to invasion.[46] Commentators such as May King Van Rensselaer (a self-described member of New York's upper class) charted the shifts in the meaning of "society" during the late nineteenth and early twentieth centuries in New York that resulted in a certain ambiguity about who belonged. Writing in 1924, Van Rensselaer claimed that "to-day, no one can tell whether a person is socially prominent or not, because no one can be sure exactly what social prominence is."[47] This confusion over social status in the 1920s contained fears about racial passing and ambiguous racial identification, since whiteness was taken to be both a prerequisite for and proof of membership in the elite. Like William's marriage in 1876, Leonard's marriage in 1924 could be seen as threatening to destabilize an already shaky upper class.

The class tensions that ran high at the end of the nineteenth century still existed in the twentieth. After the Great War, fears of radicals prompted by the Russian Revolution led to the Red Scare and a hysterical search for radicals, especially foreigners, who could be thrown out of the country. In 1919, a strike wave rippled through the country. May Day riots broke out in many cities, including New York. The country suffered through an economic recession from 1920 until 1922, with almost five million Americans unemployed. Strikes threatened to cripple the country in the early years of the decade. Despite the sinking economy, President Warren G. Harding's secretary of the treasury, Andrew Mellon, a multimillionaire, worked to reduce taxes on the wealthy, and the income gap between the rich and poor grew.[48]

While class tensions rose after the Great War, race tensions exacerbated by the Great Migration during the war years continued to soar. The summer of 1919 saw an outbreak of violence between whites and blacks; James Weldon Johnson aptly named those months the "Red Summer." Although the summer violence took place in cities like Chicago and Washington, D.C., New York also experienced tensions brought about by the migration and the emergence of a more assertive "New Negro" who wanted access to full citizenship rights. Nationally, President Warren Harding helped further tensions when he denounced "racial amalgamation" in an October 1921 speech given in Birmingham, Alabama.[49]

The early newspaper reports on Leonard and Alice Rhinelander's marriage from the fall of 1924 focused on social status, class, and color. The press described Alice Rhinelander's father as a stagecoach driver, identified her brother-in-law as a butler, and claimed that Alice worked as a nurse or a laundress. These occupations demonstrated the Jones family's status as colored, since such working-class jobs were understood to be of low status and therefore filled primarily by Negroes in the North in the twentieth century, unlike the nineteenth when many domestic service jobs were held by Irish women like Margueretta McGuiness. In contrast to depictions of the Joneses, the press depicted Leonard's family as wealthy and noted that Leonard's father belonged to many exclusive clubs, signaling that the Rhinelanders belonged to New York City's white upper class.[50]

In light of the tentative identification of Alice Jones as colored and the undisputed categorization of Leonard Rhinelander as white and upper class, many of the papers speculated about the reaction of high society, the so-called Four Hundred, to the potentially interracial and cross-class marriage of Alice and Leonard Rhinelander. Some of the curiosity over the alliance between Leonard Rhinelander and Alice Jones was not unusual for the press of the day. New York's tabloids liked stories about marriages between partners from different social stations. At least three accounts of such unions appeared in the press during the same period that the Rhinelander marriage surfaced.[51] Public concern with these couples, like the interest in the Rhinelander marriage, might be explained by the appeal of the Cinderella factor—the possibility that a poor, working girl might marry a rich swell. Not every poor girl's marriage to a rich swell, however, earned public approbation.[52]

At the end of 1924, the *Chicago Defender* published an editorial cartoon that pointed to the fears that distinguished reactions to different Cinderella-like marriages. The cartoon illustrated a white man and woman in evening dress seated in opposing chairs. The man is reading aloud excerpts from the daily paper. First, he tells the woman, presumably his wife, about a wedding between a millionaire and a scrub woman with an Eastern European surname. She responds, "I just love to hear of those kinds of marriages—They're so thrilling!" Next, the husband mentions the union of a wealthy society girl with an Italian scissors grinder. The wife declares, "Isn't that romantic?" Finally, the man appears apoplectic as he reads a report that a wealthy jeweler married a Negro maid. His wife cries, "Disgraceful! What is Society Coming to?—Why that's an *outrage!!*"[53] The *Chicago Defender*'s cartoon spoke to the fact that distinctions among different white racial categories had started to dissolve into a larger sense of whiteness but that at the same time the line between black and white remained heavily defended. Consequently, Italians and Eastern Europeans might be marriageable but never the "Negro maid"— there could be no "dusky Cinderella."[54] Moreover, as the *Messenger*'s J. A.

"Marriage and the Color Line." *Chicago Defender* cartoon published on 6 December 1924. Used with the permission of the *Chicago Defender*.

Rogers pointed out about the Rhinelanders, "in America a white man marries a girl with Negro strain and he loses caste." Therefore, a consensual interracial marriage between Alice and Leonard undermined the "exclusive" whiteness of the upper class at a moment when it was not clear who belonged to the upper class and who was white.[55]

In early 1925, the *Social Register* contributed to the confusion over who counted as upper class. The *New York Times* reported that the recent supplement to the *Social Register* published "the name of Mrs. Alice Beatrice Jones Rhinelander, now being sued by her husband Leonard Kip Rhinelander, for annulment of their marriage on the ground that she deceived him about her race, . . . in this assemblage of the city's socially elect." The newspaper laid bare the significance of the *Social Register*'s action: "By her marriage the former laundress and nursemaid, who is alleged in the annulment action to be of negro descent, thus *passes* over hundreds of persons on the fringes of society and makes her debut therein."[56] The admission of Alice Jones Rhinelander's name to the ostensibly lily-white and exclusive pages of the *Social Register* provoked a heated discussion in New York society that spoke to concerns about how to determine social status and racial identity in the mid-1920s.

The reaction of New York's elite to the inclusion of Alice Jones's name in the *Social Register* demonstrated the need of the white upper class to keep their identity "unadulterated, exclusive, and rare" in order to maintain class privileges.[57] When Leonard Kip Rhinelander, the son of an established white New York family, married a woman with a lower social status and an indeterminate racial background, the marriage threatened the very body of New York's white upper class. Leonard's marriage might elevate his wife's social status in the same way that American heiresses hoped to elevate their status through marriage to European nobility. Alice Jones Rhinelander, through her ability to bear Leonard's children, also embodied a potential challenge to the racial purity of the upper class.[58] One commentator on the white upper class's reaction to the Rhinelander marriage and the possibility of children asked the question: If the marriage was a "'union of blue blood and black blood,'" then "will the young Rhinelander have blue-black blood?" In light of such a possibility, the white upper class struck back.[59]

The publication of Alice's name in the *Social Register* and the subsequent publicity touched a nerve among members of New York's white elite. Less than a week after the appearance of Alice Jones's name in the *Social Register*, the *New York Times* reported that the publication had received numerous complaints and would omit Alice from future issues. Sources at the *Social Register* claimed that Alice's name appeared merely to serve notice of Leonard Rhinelander's marriage.[60] The vehement reaction to the notice of the Rhinelander marriage in the pages of the *Social Register* demonstrated the role the publication played in helping to set the boundaries of "acceptable" society.

In writing about "society" in 1937, historian Dixon Wecter observed that for the *Social Register*, "*mésalliances* are almost always grounds for exclusion, but just what constitutes a socially impossible marriage is debatable." Wecter then listed various marriages the publication deemed unacceptable. Wecter pointed out that not all marriages involving lower-class women such as showgirls or actresses resulted in the offending parties' exclusion, so that there appeared to be no firm policy that defined acceptability. He also observed that "not infrequently" members of the elite who were excluded after unsuitable marriages were readmitted to the *Social Register* after they divorced and married someone more acceptable to society.[61]

From society's reaction, it was clear Alice was not acceptable. More than ten years after the Rhinelander annulment trial, Wecter still recalled the previous decade's scandal over the marriage, pointing to it as a primary example of a *mésalliance*: "Mrs. Post, author of *Etiquette*, wrote to the Social Register Association in 1925 at the time it recorded the marriage of Leonard Kip Rhinelander to the Negress Alice Jones, preparatory to dropping Mr. Rhinelander forever from its pages: 'I happen to know that you announce all the *mésalliances* of those on your list; that ends them, and unsuitable behavior ostracizes—a stand which I greatly admire, and one which in certain prominent cases has shown no little courage of principle on your part.'" In Wecter's comments he identified Alice solely by racial category and not class. Perhaps not surprisingly, another couple that Wecter listed as still excluded from the *Social Register* were Anne and James Stillman, parties to a scandalous 1920s divorce case in which the husband (a former head of National City Bank) alleged that their son had been sired by an Indian.[62]

Both of these unforgivable marriages, from the perspective of the *Social Register*, involved relationships, alleged or otherwise, across racial lines. The fact that marriage to a showgirl might be deemed acceptable, unlike marriage to a "Negress," indicates that the latter union constituted a serious violation of society's rules. Consequently, New York society ostracized Leonard. By 1926, Leonard Rhinelander's name vanished from the pages of the *Social Register*. Unlike the examples Wecter used to demonstrate the publication's willingness to forgive and forget, Leonard was never allowed to return. Leonard's disappearance from the *Social Register* stood as a clear symbol of his ejection from one of the citadels of upper-class whiteness.[63]

The ways in which the white upper class articulated their elite status did not pass without comment by African Americans. In March 1925, the *Amsterdam News* declared that "Mrs. Rhinelander Scares 400" and questioned the value of "society." The newspaper reported an interview with Alice during which she declared, "'I don't want to be one of the 400. I want my man—my man!'" Furthermore, she cried, "'I didn't marry Leonard to get into any book; I married him because I loved him. If the Social Register were to continue my name year after year, would that add to my happiness?'"[64] This part of Alice's interview substituted a romantic narrative for one concerned with social status, an individual love story for a story about the collective concerns of a social group.

The collective concerns of the white upper class, however, were particularly attuned to threats to its members because the 1920s were, like the 1870s and 1880s, a period when the boundaries of society appeared to be in flux. By the twenties the definition of "high society" wavered as the boundaries of the Four Hundred expanded to accommodate a celebrity-driven "Café Society."[65] Since the heyday of the Four Hundred at the end of the nineteenth century, New York society had fragmented, resulting in a period fraught with anxiety over social status. Moreover, the rise of mass production beginning at the end of the nineteenth century and continuing into the twentieth started to put more consumer goods into the hands of members of social groups other than the elite. As a result, it became more difficult to distinguish social status.[66]

Given the blurring of previously obvious markers of status, it was possible that someone might try to pass as upper class. In a 1925 article published in the *New Yorker*, Ellin Mackay, the daughter of millionaire Clarence Mackay, and a contemporary of Leonard, touched on the topic of someone's passing as a member of the upper class to explain why white upper-class youth preferred cabarets to society's "exclusive parties."[67] Contrary to the ideas of their society "Elders," society youth did not go to cabarets to "rub elbows with all sorts and kinds of people." Instead, Mackay declared, they went to cabarets and practiced their "fastidiousness" by choosing their own companions and not mingling with others outside of their social group. The need to go to cabarets was occasioned, according to Mackay, by the growing lack of exclusivity at society parties.[68]

Mackay claimed that society parties no longer provided an exclusive space where upper-class young men and women could socialize with their social and racial peers. Instead, she complained about the presence of "the young man who is well-read in the Social Register who talks glibly of the Racquet Club, while he prays that you won't suspect that he lives far up on the West Side." She worried that such men came from "the same dim corners of town" and then disappeared to unknown destinations after the parties ended.[69] Mackay objected to the presence of persons of unknown origins at society events.

In addition, those who tried to pass for upper class also may have been passing for white. An early-1930s essay on passing made such a claim with an anecdote about a light-skinned "Negress" who passed for white. A young white man spotted a woman whom he recognized as his mother's former maid "at a dinner dance at a fashionable New York hotel, at which most of the guests were in or near the Social Register." According to the author, "she [had] married a wealthy young man," presumably white and perhaps listed in the *Social Register*.[70]

With the erosion of barriers to New York society, observers forecast a rise in mixed marriages. In an article in the *American Mercury*, editor H. L. Mencken gave as examples Leonard Rhinelander's marriage to Alice Jones, the preference of white society girls for "chauffeurs, young lawyers, [and] automobile salesmen," and the surprising marriage of Ellin Mackay, the author of the *New Yorker* article on cabarets, to the popular Jewish songwriter Irving Berlin. Such marriages disrupted the carefully tended link between racial categories and social status that defined the white elite.[71]

One sharp criticism of this link had been published in early January 1925 by J. A. Rogers in the *Messenger*. Rogers, a Jamaican who moved to New York, discussed the published reactions to the Rhinelander marriage and focused on the idea that blood determines race and the relation of blood to status. Rogers observed, "Some months ago Eugene O'Neill wrote a play in which a humble white woman was married to a humble Negro. There was a hurricane of words and a tidal wave of angry ink. Now comes along, Life [sic] with a marriage between a 'colored' waitress and a man whose blood is so 'blue' and so 'aristocratic' that that of the Vanderbilts, Goulds, Rockefellers and many others of 'the best people' is deemed dishwater beside it and the white editorial writers are stricken speechless." Rogers suggested that white editorial writers did not touch the story because they could not comprehend a marital union across such a wide social gap. In comparing the Rhinelanders to the Vanderbilts, Goulds, and Rockefellers, Rogers acknowledged that the white upper class created hierarchies among its members as embodied in distinctions between Knickerbockers and the Four Hundred.[72]

Rogers, however, indicated that such internal distinctions within "society," as well as those between "white" and "black," had no real basis. When Rogers remarked that "steps are being taken to annul the marriage but the people of this nation had better become accustomed to such and save their indignation for less barren causes. We are just 300 years late," he alluded to the fears at the heart of reactions to Leonard and Alice's marriage. These fears centered on anxiety about "miscegenation" and ambiguous racial identities. Moreover, Rogers pointed out that racial mixing was endemic to America and referring to blood as "white," "black," or "blue" was completely nonsensical.[73]

In addition to Leonard's loss of social status by marrying Alice, Leonard Rhinelander lost money and his family position when his father disinherited him.[74] Some newspapers, however, saw the marriage in another way. In marked contrast to other New York papers, which fixated on Leonard Rhinelander as the "scion" of an old family, the *Amsterdam News* depicted a Leonard who enjoyed the fact that the Jones family did not belong to society. The story of the Rhinelander marriage offered by the *Amsterdam News* inverted the narrative of the superiority of elite white society, portraying Leonard as a man who liked home cooking and who dried the dishes after Alice and her mother washed them. In fact, Alice claimed that she and Leonard did not "want to be listed among the Rockefellers and Vanderbilts and the rest of that ilk. What is society, anyway? The women smoke and drink and lie. Their men take each other's wives. There isn't a single wholesome thing in the life of the so-called Four Hundred, as far as I can see."[75] In this way the *Amsterdam News* provided a very different portrait of the Four Hundred, one that depicted elite white society as depraved and unworthy of emulation.

Not only the African American press articulated the idea that elite white society was debased. At the turn of the twentieth century, the white upper class had been criticized for its conspicuous consumption and extravagant lifestyles. Critics of the white upper classes argued in the late nineteenth century that the white elite had become over-civilized and self-indulgent.[76] Any affront to the "civilization" of the white upper class affected their identity as superior. Even Theodore Roosevelt, a member of New York's white upper class whose younger brother Elliott attended Leonard's parents wedding reception, accused members of the Four Hundred at the turn of the twentieth century of behaving in ways that ranged from the frivolous to vice-ridden. Roosevelt urged white American men to turn away from "overcivilized decadence" and embrace virile white manhood.[77]

Depicting white society as depraved in the 1920s tapped into the remnants of a strain of thought on degeneracy that focused on the upper classes and their inherited "blood." Proponents of eugenics in the United States worried that the country would degenerate through the combined assaults of a decline in the birthrate of the fit (race suicide) and an increase in the numbers of feebleminded.[78] When the author Harlan Read called for the abolition of inheritance in 1919 because it created an aristocracy of "the idle rich," he contended that "the moral character of the idle rich is below that of workers. . . . One is insane, another degenerate, another a fool, and many a combination of all three, with idleness to increase their folly and heighten their degeneracy." In 1926 Albert Wiggam blamed "civilization with its luxury, comfort and ease" for making "eugenics a superlative necessity." Too much wealth and luxury reduced the birthrate of the "finest and most beautiful."[79]

With his marriage to Alice, Leonard undermined the exclusivity of New York's white upper class. The taint of degeneracy could easily be attached to the upper class and undercut its claims to privilege. In an age when the boundaries of whiteness and New York "society" seemed weak, such a marriage struck at the very heart of what it meant to be white and upper class and the connections between both concepts. In an attempt to counteract this trend, the *Social Register* banished Leonard and Alice from its pages and Isaac Mills depicted Leonard as a feebleminded man who could not wittingly consent to marry a woman of color and thereby taint his exclusive white ancestry. Ironically, Mills's depiction of Leonard as feebleminded reinforced the belief that the white upper classes were degenerate and worth little. Although Lee Parsons Davis disagreed with the characterization of Leonard as feebleminded, during the next segment of the trial, Davis would try to show that Leonard knew exactly what he was doing when he pursued Alice and, moreover, that Leonard's actions revealed a completely different form of degeneracy.

SIX :

The Trial Continues

DEGENERACY, MODERN LOVE, AND "FILTHY LETTERS"

Shocking, disgusting, but pitiable! That was my humble verdict yesterday as I sat through the most shocking section of the Rhinelander trial. It was so shocking to realize that centuries of blue blood, years of luxury and tutors and governesses and travel should fail to instill innate refinement in 22-year-old Leonard Kip Rhinelander.—GRACE ROBINSON, "Vile Pen in Blueblood's Hand Pitiable, Says Woman Writer," *New York Daily News*, 24 November 1925

AFTER ISAAC MILLS PAINTED Alice Jones Rhinelander as a seductive, deceptive woman of loose morals, it was Lee Davis's turn to offer a different narrative. As Davis had suggested in his opening statement when he mapped out his strategy, the defense would insist that a "son of wealth" entered the Joneses' "humble home" to "take this girl." Davis planned to present Leonard to the twelve jurors as an aristocratic young man who sought sexual pleasure with women from a lower social class.[1] Moreover, Davis planned to point out that throughout the process of Leonard's seduction of Alice, he knew the Joneses' "humble" social station and their color but chose not to "see" it.

Davis's characterization of Leonard as an aristocratic rake was calculated to capture the popular imagination. As one historian of domestic service has observed, "the sexual exploitation of servants by masters—the initiation of boys and young men into sexual relations—was an important theme of Victorian literature." This exploitation, however, also existed beyond the pages of fiction. In many instances, female servants were seduced by their employers, or another male in the household, and then abandoned. Although Alice Jones (unlike Margueretta McGuiness) never worked for the Rhinelanders, Davis still tapped into this theme to explain Leonard's pursuit of her and refute the claim that she seduced him. One reporter noted that Davis wanted to show Leonard as "a wealthy man's son in search of pleasure among the servant class—with a servant girl he at that time was not in love with."[2]

To successfully portray Leonard as a sexual exploiter of servants, Davis had to establish that Leonard pursued Alice even though he knew that she worked as a maid. At the beginning of Leonard's cross-examination, Davis asked, "When you started out to accomplish this purpose and you were holding yourself out as a prominent New York man—this purpose of having her fall—you knew that she was a maid?" Leonard admitted knowing that Alice worked as an "upstairs girl" who made beds in private homes for a monthly wage. Every address to which he sent Alice a letter, other than her family's home, was a place of employment. Given the link between domestic service and African Americans, Davis implied Leonard's knowledge of Alice's occupational status proved that he possessed the information to question her background.[3]

During this cross-examination, Davis also wanted to reverse any positive connotations of Leonard as a "scion" of the white elite, and his questions worked to dissociate Leonard from certain ideals of manhood. Thus, Davis inquired whether Leonard considered his actions to make a "maid-servant" fall for a wealthy man those of a "man" and a "gentleman." At first, Leonard replied that he did. Davis, however, rephrased the question: "To start out after a maid-servant that you didn't love, to have her fall for your lures and have intercourse with you? You considered that the acts of a gentleman did you? Yes or no?" Leonard protested he could not answer with a yes or a no.[4]

Leonard's inability to give a direct answer to Davis's question may have reflected the instability of concepts like manhood and gentlemanliness in the early twentieth century. Davis's query about gentlemanliness was imbued with white Victorian notions of manliness, which stressed "all the worthy, moral attributes which the Victorian middle class admired in a man . . . sexual self-restraint, a powerful will, a strong character." These ideals had taken hold in the market economy of the early and mid-nineteenth centuries where restraint and good character could produce positive results in a society geared around small-scale capitalism. Seeking sexual pleasure outside of marriage would have been viewed as unmanly and a sign of a lustful and weak character.[5]

During the late nineteenth century through about 1930, however, white middle-class ideas about manhood shifted from valuing manliness to prizing masculinity, a concept that encompassed "aggressiveness, physical force, and male sexuality."[6] With the rise of corporate capitalism and large bureaucracies by the late nineteenth century, self-restraint seemed less likely to produce positive economic results.

White middle-class ideals of manliness also faltered in the face of the new allure of commercial leisure. White middle-class men also found themselves facing increased economic and political competition from working-class men, immigrants, and women. As a result, they searched for new ways to bolster their identity by drawing on working-class activities like boxing and ideals of "primitive" masculinity. For them, physical force and sexual virility now became important attributes of masculinity. This redefinition of white middle-class ideals about manhood did not take place overnight, thus both concepts of middle-class manhood uneasily co-existed for a time.[7]

In the twenties, Leonard's pursuit of Alice could reflect Leonard's sexually aggressive masculinity. This may explain why the press reported that many of the young white women who tried to see the trial claimed that they came to see Leonard; women even sent him flirtatious "mash" notes.[8] The forty-three-year-old Davis did not seem attuned to this transition from manliness to masculinity, and he therefore relied on older notions of manliness to criticize Leonard.

As part of the defense's strategy to cast Leonard and not Alice as the seducer, Davis retold Leonard's story about his original introduction to the Joneses. To do this, Davis elicited from Leonard additional details and also put Grace Miller on the witness stand to rebut Leonard's story. On cross-examination, Leonard admitted that one of his companions on the night that he met Grace Jones was a married man. Leonard also conceded that he did not try to stop his married friend Carl from picking up Grace Jones, in Leonard's car—a fact that Davis hoped would suggest Leonard's own dissolute behavior. Leonard, however, claimed that this was the first time he had ever seen a girl get picked up.[9]

Following his script to reveal that at each stage of Leonard's seduction he had the opportunity to see the Jones family's color, Davis tried to ascertain whether Leonard had seen Grace Jones clearly when they first met. At first,

Leonard denied that he looked closely. Davis had Grace stand up. Finally, Leonard admitted that he did get a good look at Grace that evening; she looked the same in 1925 as in 1921. Davis then asked, "Nothing in her appearance to excite any suspicion in your mind that there is colored blood?" Leonard replied, "No." Davis followed up, "Now that you know there is colored blood in the Jones family, can you see a trace of it that would indicate to you that that is so." Leonard again responded that he could not see it. Davis then inquired, "And your eyesight's good?" Leonard could at least come back with a "yes."[10]

At this point, Davis's version of Leonard's meeting with the Joneses veered sharply from Leonard's original story. Mills had tried to show that the Jones girls ensnared Leonard in a miscegenist plot, but after prodding by Davis, Leonard testified that he gave Grace Jones a ring a few days after they met. He insisted, however, that she asked for it. Perhaps not surprisingly, Leonard's gift never emerged during Mills's questioning. Leonard still insisted that he accompanied Grace, Alice, and another man to the theater the second time he saw Grace. Although Leonard could not remember whom he sat with, he acknowledged that he saw both women under the theater lights. After the show, Leonard recounted, he asked Grace on a date for the following afternoon despite his initial "shock" that she allowed herself to be picked up by strange men. Leonard admitted that he went to Grace's house, took her for a ride in his automobile, and tried to hold her hand. Again, Davis asked whether Leonard had been suspicious at the time that Grace was not "pure white." Leonard replied that he did not.[11]

Both Leonard's credibility and Isaac Mills's argument that his client was the victim further eroded once Grace testified that Leonard asked her for a date the day they met. She also recounted the story of how she, her sister, and a male acquaintance accompanied Leonard to a show so crowded that she sat in one part of the theater with Leonard while her sister sat with the friend. In the theater, according to Grace, Leonard put his hand on her knee and she removed it. She recalled that he also suggested that they drop off Alice and the other man and drive alone in his car and that she told Leonard that she had to go home with her sister.[12]

Grace Miller's testimony about Leonard's untoward attentions bolstered Davis's argument that Leonard wanted sexual favors from women of a different social status. After determining that Leonard first tried to get intimate with Grace and then set his sights on Alice, Davis turned his attention to demonstrating how Leonard misrepresented his emotions to gain Alice's consent to sex. Simultaneously, Davis pressed the point that Leonard flaunted his social status as part of the same design. Davis had Leonard tell the jury when he fell in love with Alice; Leonard conceded that he did so soon after they met. Given Mills's argument that Alice had initiated the relationship, Davis pointed out that the time between their meeting and Leonard falling in love did not leave much time for Alice to seduce him. In fact, Davis asked, "You pursued Alice, as a matter of fact, didn't you, frankly?" Leonard agreed. When Davis inquired whether Leonard courted Alice with marriage in mind, Leonard conceded he had not. Davis then asked Leonard why he was "making love" to Alice. Leonard retorted, "because I liked her." Leonard's admission that he pursued Alice with no thought of marriage provoked one newspaper to remark that "Kip was casual in his intent and he did not look" at Alice's color and to connect Leonard's efforts to seduce Alice with his failure to care about her background.[13]

Leonard's confession that he went after Alice but did not plan to marry her fell neatly into the narrative that Davis continued to build of Leonard, the aristocratic seducer. Davis easily took apart Mills's description of an innocent Leonard. Step-by-step, Davis got Leonard to talk about the process of making "decent" love to Alice when he kissed her and held her hand. Leonard admitted that he drove around in his car with Alice, put his arms around her, kissed her, and felt a "thrill."[14]

Although Davis meant to show that Leonard's knowledge of how to make "decent love" reflected prior sexual experience, movies in the twenties often instructed men that kisses brought "thrills." Indeed, Robert Lynd and Helen Merrell Lynd's well-known sociological study of 1920s "Middletown" described young people attending films like *Flaming Youth* that showed " 'neckers, petters, white kisses, [and] red kisses.' " In addition to highlighting the physical acts of courtship, the movies featured male stars like Douglas Fairbanks and Rudolph Valentino, who embodied "sex appeal." Leonard may have seen a number of movies and modeled his behavior on the actions he saw on the screen.[15] Davis may not have succeeded in depicting Leonard as a skilled lover, but he did establish the fact that Leonard took the initiative with Alice and was the first in their relationship to declare his love.

In focusing on Leonard's actions to seduce Alice, Davis took the opportunity to challenge Mills's portrayal of Alice as deceitful. Davis depicted Leonard as a fraud who used words of love to convince Alice to engage in sex.

"What do you call it," Davis asked Leonard, "when a man writes to a girl that he loves her and puts the seeds of passion into her mind for the purpose of accomplishing this intimate relationship, when he does not love her, but simply wants to satisfy his animal desires—what do you call that but deception?" Leonard refused to accept that his behavior constituted deception. Which was worse, Davis then asked, "to lead a girl to love you and believe that you are going to marry her, and to take that from her which is most precious to a woman—Is that worse deception than for a girl to say, 'I am white and have no colored blood?' Which is the worst?" Leonard replied, "the latter," and indicated that Alice's lies were the worst kind.[16]

Davis's questions emphasized the generation gap between Leonard and Davis. Changing codes of morality and new dating practices in the 1920s and 1930s encouraged "rapid sentiment formation" through early expressions of love. It could be argued that by expressing his affection in his early letters to Alice, Leonard was not deceiving Alice but merely engaging in the appropriate steps of dating. The press supported this interpretation of Leonard's letters, frequently reporting on "Kip's Litany of Love" and never suggesting that his letters were deceptive.[17]

Davis's characterization of Leonard's behavior as deceptive, however, mirrored the themes of male fraud and misrepresentation in seduction and breach of promise to marry lawsuits. In the nineteenth century, state courts ruled on breach of promise to marry lawsuits that compensated jilted brides. During the same era, claims of seduction ended up in American courtrooms and centered on men who deceived women into consenting to sexual relations without marriage.[18] Originally, it was fathers who brought these common law actions to recover for the loss of their daughter's household labor or loss of outside wages (in cases of pregnancy) or a daughter's inability to marry. By the early twentieth century, nineteen states allowed for monetary damages in proven cases of seduction, and many of these statutes allowed the seduced woman to bring the lawsuit on her own behalf. These sorts of cases rested on the assumptions that women were weaker than men, more sexually innocent, and therefore likely to be deceived by sexually aggressive men.[19]

Changes in beliefs about sexuality in the early twentieth century made seduction and breach of promise to marry lawsuits controversial. In an era of shifting ideas about sex, new fears arose that unscrupulous and sexually active women would deploy these claims to blackmail men.[20] A number of historians of sexuality in twentieth-century America have observed that while in the popular imagination the 1920s was *the* decade of significant change in

Leonard Rhinelander on the witness stand. © Bettmann/Corbis.

sexual mores, most of these developments date back to the turn of the century. New sexual morality and behaviors had already emerged by the 1910s. Many of these behaviors emerged out of working-class culture and among elite radical women in New York City. These changes included new ideas about sexuality that favored sexual expressiveness and a move away from a focus on the procreative functions of sex. In addition, female sexuality became more acceptable, although a double standard still existed. At the same time, access to birth control expanded.[21]

Yet, the twenties were still a period of uncertainty about sexuality; the rules may have started to change earlier but many seemed unsure about the boundaries of "appropriate behavior."[22] Indeed, the redefinition of manhood as masculinity raised questions about what a man could be, as well as what role sex played in creating a man. According to Kevin White, "if the early twentieth century was marked by growing sexual choice as new alternatives developed and older taboos declined, it was also characterized by greater complexity and uncertainty around sexuality for men even more than for women." Despite the uncertainties, by the 1930s states began to repeal seduction laws and the courts rarely heard breach of promise to marry cases.[23]

Leonard's behavior with Alice and Grace and his attempts at physical intimacy might have reflected his attempts to act on his masculinity when the bounds of such actions were not clearly defined. Thus, Leonard's response to Davis that Alice's deception about race was worse than his attempt to seduce her may have more accurately reflected popular opinion and also underscored the generational gap between Leonard and Davis. In a period when anxiety over passing and miscegenation abounded, deception about race in courtship and marriage might have more serious consequences than misrepresentations about love and sex.

Since Davis did not seem attuned to changes in sexual codes among young people, he still referred to Leonard's letters as evidence of his dishonesty. Davis found it significant that in one letter, written barely one week after Leonard met Alice in September 1921, Leonard addressed her as "dear" and closed with "Much love." Leonard asked Alice to call him on the telephone and suggested that he could take the train to meet her that Friday or Saturday.[24] After Davis read this letter aloud, he asked how Leonard could claim he did not love Alice in September 1921 when he sent her "much love." Leonard conceded that he was only "fond" of her then. But when Davis suggested that one reason the affectionate words appeared in Leonard's letter was because he "had sex in mind," Leonard agreed.[25]

Reading the excerpts from Leonard's courtship letters allowed Davis to press Leonard on the state of his intimate relations at the time the letters were written and to zero in on Leonard's techniques to gain Alice's consent to sex. In another early letter to Alice, Leonard first complained, "Do you think it's quite fair when I take all the trouble to come down to see you and then find you out? I wonder if you still care for me, or, as a matter of fact, ever did? Don't think, dear, that I am angry with you but just a little upset. You cant blame me can you?" But then he changed his tone, writing, "Maybe if you are real nice to me once in a while, I will let you drive. I bet I know you are wondering what I mean by being real nice. Well, I will leave that to your imagination." Davis asked what Leonard meant when he suggested that Alice act "nice." Leonard explained that he had hoped to caress Alice, but under persistent questioning he confessed that he "meant to have intercourse with her."[26] Davis then pointed out that while Mills claimed Alice went after Leonard, it was Leonard who tried "to get into her mind and imagination having intercourse" only weeks after they met.

To show the jury that Leonard's conduct constituted those of an upper-class seducer, Davis produced letters in which Leonard not only tempted Alice with words of love but also emphasized his elite social status. In one letter, Leonard recalled their physical intimacies on a train ride and also demanded that Alice attend his older sister's society wedding in New York. "Alice you must simply come to the wedding," he wrote. "That's all there is about it. I know very well if you will like me you will do this favor for me." When Davis grilled Leonard about this letter, Leonard again agreed that he pursued his sexual goals without any thought of marriage. Davis also suggested that the letter showed that Leonard deliberately held himself out as a "big man" to seduce Alice.[27]

Although Leonard maintained that he had no ulterior motive when he told Alice about his social prominence, Davis and the newspapers disagreed. The *Daily News* found Davis's presentation of Leonard's letters persuasive, for Grace Robinson reported that "an ancient family's code of honor—that a liaison with a housemaid is the privilege of a gentleman—was written into the record yesterday at White Plains, when Leonard Kip Rhinelander admitted an affair of a rich man and a servant." Robinson told her readers about Leonard's missive to Alice in which he invited her to his sister's wedding and "almost succeeded in introducing her to the cream of New York society." The *Herald Tribune* concluded that Davis's strategy to expose how Leonard "played to the mind and emotions of Alice Jones as a Prince Charming to a dark Cinderella who worked as an 'upstairs girl' in households" undercut Isaac Mills's narrative of the case.[28]

In addition to establishing that Leonard pursued Alice, deceived her about his love, and stressed his membership in New York's white aristocracy, Davis turned to what he called the "filthy" aspects of the case. Since Isaac Mills had sought to fix Alice as the initiator of the sexual aspects of Leonard and Alice's relationship, drawing on existing stereotypes about African American women's sexuality, Davis hoped to show that Leonard instead pursued sexual intimacy with Alice. Consequently, Davis queried, "When were your acts towards Alice Rhinelander anything but the act of a gentleman?" he asked. Leonard replied that he behaved like a gentleman until he and Alice went to the Hotel Marie-Antoinette in December 1921. He agreed with Davis that prior to that hotel stay, Alice had acted in a "ladylike" fashion.[29]

Davis then pushed Leonard further, forcing him to admit that he had never acted in a gentlemanly fashion. Davis asked Leonard about his attempts to be intimate with Alice before the hotel stay. When Leonard replied that he had not had "intercourse" with Alice before their visit to the Hotel Marie-Antoinette, Davis persisted:

> [Davis:] What had you done looking to that end before going to the Marie Antoinette?
> [Leonard:] I was fairly intimate with her.
> [Davis:] I hate to ask you these questions, but you understand the manner in which your case has been handled makes it necessary, do you not?
> [Leonard:] Yes.
> [Davis:] And you know in your own heart, as you sit there, don't you, that these questions wouldn't have been asked of you if you hadn't dragged your wife in the gutter? You know that, don't you? You feel that, don't you?
> [Leonard:] No. I don't know.

Although Davis tried to get Leonard to accept responsibility for the line of questioning Davis was pursuing, the lawyer himself apparently felt it necessary to "drag" his client through the "gutter" to defend her.[30]

After this examination, Davis asked Leonard to specify which activities preceded their hotel stay. Had Leonard felt a "sex urge" with Alice? Did he know that "normal" males and females had sex urges?[31] Leonard admitted that he knew about sexual desire, and he disclosed that he "played with [his] hands" to act on Alice's sex urges:

[Davis:] Where? You recognize, Mr. Rhinelander, there is no more room for modesty in this case, don't you?
[Leonard:] Yes.
[Davis:] After what you put this girl through. Where did you play with her with your hands?
[Leonard:] I don't know the legal word for it.
[Davis:] You use your own. There is no necessity for legal terminology.
[Leonard:] The vagina or something of that sort.

According to Leonard, he planned to excite Alice to persuade her to engage in sexual intercourse. He also admitted that he wanted to satisfy his desires with Alice but he did not necessarily love her.[32]

Davis turned next to their hotel visit and tried to discover how Leonard persuaded Alice to join him. First, Davis asked about the family chauffeur who drove Leonard and Alice to New York in a "closely curtained" car when they spent their first night together at the Hotel Marie-Antoinette. Then, Davis abruptly confronted Leonard, "What is the color of your wife's body? Take your time." Leonard replied that it was "dark" but "not any darker than the arms of women that I have seen in Havana." Davis also asked whether Leonard ever saw Mr. Jones's color and whether it resembled Alice's complexion. When Leonard responded that it did not, Davis told Alice to hold up her hands.[33] The jury viewed Alice's hands, and Davis asked Leonard whether they were as dark as her body. Leonard said her hands and body were the same color. The *New York Times* reported that "at a short distance" Alice's hands and arms appeared to be an "ash brown"; the *Evening Journal* agreed. The *Herald Tribune*, on the other hand, thought she appeared "chocolate brown."[34]

Under Davis's merciless questioning, Leonard admitted that during the drive to New York he convinced Alice to stay in the hotel by playing with her. Leonard conceded, "I might have put my hand under her dress, I don't know, really." Leonard also indicated that he "insisted," to which Davis responded that Leonard was not as "dumb" or "innocent" as Mills had portrayed him. Leonard claimed that he was only "infatuated" with Alice at that time, but he allowed that he might have told her that he loved her. Davis's questioning continued: "Q. You had an animal lust, didn't you? A. Yes. Q. Which you were attempting to satisfy. A. Frankly, I wanted to be with her. A. And you accomplished it, didn't you? A. Yes, sir." Thus Davis forced Leonard to admit again that he lied to gain Alice's consent to sex.[35]

And as Davis often did during his cross-examination of Leonard, he juxtaposed a question about Alice's color with one about Leonard's sexual pursuit. Leonard conceded that he first saw Alice's body in December 1921 when they spent all day and night in bed. Nevertheless, Leonard denied that he had any suspicions that Alice was not white. Not convinced, Davis repeated, "It did not surprise you, after meeting Alice, to meet her father with his color? It did not surprise you?" Even though Leonard had already stated that Alice's color differed from her father's, he still responded no.[36] Davis continued with this line of questioning:

> [Davis:] How is your eyesight? Are you colorblind?
> [Leonard:] I am not, no.
> [Davis:] See all right?
> [Leonard:] Yes.
> [Davis:] You can distinguish black from white?
> [Leonard:] Yes.
> [Davis:] Brown from white?
> [Leonard:] Yes.

In addition to emphasizing that Leonard could distinguish between black and white but that he apparently chose not to when he seduced Alice, Davis stressed Leonard's lack of innocence in making plans for the hotel. Moreover, noting that when Leonard registered at the hotel, he left Alice in the car, Davis asked, "You didn't have in mind that the management of that hotel might see you going through the corridors with a girl who apparently on her face, possessed colored blood?"[37] Leonard responded in the negative.

In continuing his efforts to position Leonard as the initiator of Leonard and Alice's sexual relationship, Davis suggested that Leonard had brought along "those rubber affairs" in his baggage. Leonard claimed that he did not pack condoms for this trip, although he confirmed that he knew about them. He admitted that his knowledge of condoms dated back to boarding school in 1918, three years before he met Alice. Davis commented, "So you were not so innocent in 1918, were you?" Leonard refused to agree and claimed he was "morally" innocent. Despite Leonard's protestations of innocence, Davis reinforced his characterization of Leonard as the aristocratic seducer. He pointed out that Leonard had learned about sex in boarding school, a bastion of the white upper class, and so linked Leonard's sexual knowledge to his social status.[38]

Davis also tried to get Leonard to admit that he was sexually experienced before his hotel stays with Alice, but Leonard claimed that his actions came from "human instinct."³⁹ Davis then followed up with a series of questions that mystified the courtroom spectators: "And you went about it naturally?" "Yes." "Nothing unnatural about it?" "No." Davis pressed, "You did nothing that was indecent save that natural intercourse, under such circumstances might be termed indecent, did you?" Leonard again answered in the negative. Davis then introduced into evidence yet another document and handed a letter to Leonard for identification. After the court stenographer marked the letter Defendant's Exhibit N-1, Davis suggested that Leonard read it to himself. Then Davis requested a recess.⁴⁰

This presentation of Exhibit N-1 was not the first time during Leonard's cross-examination that Davis had started to introduce evidence only to withhold it after Leonard identified it. Earlier in the proceedings, Davis produced another letter Exhibit S-1, and put to Leonard a series of questions. First, Davis asked whether Leonard was a "free agent" in his own case and not under the control of his lawyers. Then Davis inquired, "Do you still want to proceed with this lawsuit?" Once Leonard replied that he did, Davis put away the letter.⁴¹ Both letters remained a mystery.

Once Davis established that Leonard achieved his goal of sexual intercourse with Alice through misrepresentations and sexual play, he turned to demonstrating that Leonard asked Alice to marry him. Mills had highlighted Alice's actions in pushing for an engagement with Leonard. He contended that Alice made Leonard jealous to convince him to marry. Davis rebutted this assertion with Leonard's letters, which chronicled his eagerness for an engagement. Indeed, Leonard testified that he considered himself engaged by March 1923 when he told Alice to purchase a ring. Davis asked Leonard the exact date of his proposal, but Leonard could not remember it.⁴²

Given Leonard's inability to recall the date, Davis brought out a letter from September 1922. In this letter, Leonard responded to two of Alice's letters that he found waiting for him in Utah. Davis read, "Are you going to turn me down simply because I said I am not coming home this winter or are you going to make a fool out of me and cause me to live my future life alone, because I am not good enough for you?" After hearing this, Leonard allowed that he had made up his mind to marry Alice either in July or August 1922 (over six months before he gave Alice the money for a ring). When Alice replied to his earlier letter, she let him know that her friends told her a wealthy man would never marry a servant.⁴³

Leonard's letter revealed that at this point in his relationship with Alice, his behavior deviated from that of the upper-class seducer that Davis portrayed (a point not lost on reporter Margery Rex, who noted it in her article on this aspect of the trial). Rather than abandoning Alice after he seduced her, Leonard decided to marry her. Leonard even pleaded with Alice to continue their relationship: "Alice, sweet girl," Davis read from one letter, "I beg of you to spare me from going into the gutter and having to face a life of misery and loneliness. Yes, dear, loneliness, because I can no longer face another girl if you give me up. Why? Because, darling, you are the only one that rightfully belongs to me and you only can I have for my own. I dare not ask another girl for her hand if you fail me, because if I did, darling, my good name would be lost, I would no longer be considered a gentleman." Davis then asked Leonard if this meant that they were engaged; Leonard said they were.[44] This excerpt suggested that Leonard felt that his premarital sexual experiences with Alice had to end in marriage or he could no longer consider himself a "gentleman." Perhaps like some members of his generation, Leonard felt that only engaged couples should have sex.

In light of the defense's argument that Leonard knew Alice's ancestry before they wed, once Leonard admitted that he wanted to marry Alice, Davis had to face the problems raised by Leonard's decision. The story Davis had begun to sketch of Leonard revealed a man who knowingly entered an interracial marriage. In an era when many white northerners strove to demarcate sharp boundaries between black and white, Leonard may have ignored their very presence. Leonard's actions might lead a jury of white men to dissolve his marriage despite the evidence. The fact that the Rhinelander marriage might turn out to be a consensual interracial union even spurred letter writers to send threatening missives to the lawyers. Some of these letters likely warned of dire consequences if the court failed to annul Leonard and Alice's marriage.[45]

Up until this point in the trial, Leonard's conduct with Alice, as Davis described it, was reminiscent of southern white men's assertion of sexual power over African American women. In the early twentieth century, many white southern men expected to have their initial sexual experience with African American women, whom they could not marry.[46] African Americans knew that black women in the South were vulnerable to sexual exploitation. The very existence of laws that prohibited blacks and whites from marrying encouraged this exploitation. Not surprisingly, advocates of civil rights opposed similar laws in the North. As the *Crisis* observed, "anti-intermarriage" laws placed "the colored girl at the mercy of any white libertine."[47] Since no such laws existed in New York, in deciding to marry Alice after having sex with her, Leonard went further than most southerners could and generated a troubling result for white northerners—a marriage across the color line.

To win his case, Davis had to do more than demonstrate that Leonard pursued Alice for sex and then marriage despite knowing her race. He needed to make sure that Leonard's marriage across the color line was an anomaly and that everyone and the twelve white men on the jury saw this case as exceptional and not a harbinger of an interracial future. Thus, Davis proceeded to attack Leonard's character to distinguish him from other white men. Davis had already started to do this when he linked Leonard's attempts to seduce Alice with his elite social status and then characterized Leonard's actions as "unmanly." Now, Davis painted Leonard as deceptive not only with Alice. Indeed, Leonard admitted that he deceived his own father about his relationship with Alice.[48]

Davis also reinforced the image of Leonard as the deceiver when he drew out from Leonard that he had lied to Alice's mother, Elizabeth (a woman everyone agreed was white), "a nice little motherly woman" who, according to Leonard, had been present when Alice deceived him about her race. Determined to show that Leonard's behavior stood outside the norm, and continuing to draw on older notions of manhood, Davis criticized Leonard for failing to act in a "manly" way when he mailed postcards to his future in-laws during a trip with Alice through New England. Leonard had told Mrs. Jones that he and Alice would be accompanied by a married couple who would act as chaperones; no married couple existed. Davis faulted Leonard for taking Alice away from her mother on false pretenses and again connected Leonard's behavior to his unmanliness.[49]

In calling attention to Leonard's deception of Mrs. Jones, Davis depicted Leonard as deceitful and unmanly since such behavior indicated Leonard's lack of sexual self-restraint. But since the concepts of manliness that Davis relied on to characterize Leonard were in the process of being redefined, Davis's strategy would not necessarily work. The press offered a different interpretation of Leonard's actions with Alice. Grace Robinson even foretold that "when the great lovers of the world are compiled on judgment day, Leonard Kip Rhinelander will be conspicuous on the list." She based her observation on her reading of the response of the, according to her, predominantly female crowd in the courtroom.[50] Robinson contended that "Rhinelander proved to be a master in the manipulation of affectionate words. Far from being a stupid, backward boy, as his counsel has presented him, he displayed genius in the management of an intricate love affair. He was a past master at 'kidding the old folks' and in the ancient art of winning a woman's love."[51] Neither an imbecile nor a deceptive seducer, Leonard was just an expert in the modern ways of love, and an example of modern ideals of white masculinity.

Despite these more positive interpretations of Leonard's behavior, Leonard tried to defend himself and explain that he only deceived Mrs. Jones with Alice's consent. Davis, however, used Leonard's response to undermine Leonard's credibility. Davis asked, "Then if the circumstances are right and someone advised you to tell a lie to this jury, why, you would do it, would you?" Davis continued, making sure to connect Leonard's actions to his social status: "You, as a gentleman, who was brought up in refined surroundings, did you consider it fair to tell this little woman that you would take care of her daughter, and the very same night take her daughter into a bedroom with you?" Leonard replied that he could not answer that question but repeated that it was all right for him to deceive Mrs. Jones since Alice agreed. Davis hammered him, "Is it a fair thing, even if a young girl consents, to deceive her mother, her natural guardian of her purity?" Again, Leonard said that if Alice agreed, his actions were fair. Finally, Davis asked whether it was worse to deceive a "mother who is trying to protect her daughter's morals, in order to take her for purposes of intercourse" or "having this little girl say, as you say she did, 'I am white,' when you had your eyesight." Leonard replied that it was his deception, "from the moral point of it," that was worse.[52]

Throughout Davis's cross-examination, he kept trying to pin Leonard down on his perception of the Jones family. At one point, Leonard claimed that if he had known George Jones's "true" color he would not have pursued his "friendship" with Alice. Yet when Davis sprung the next question, "You did not care whether he was black or white?," Leonard replied that he couldn't answer. Davis rephrased the question, asking whether, given Leonard's pursuit of a "lustful purpose," he did not care about Mr. Jones's color. Davis implied that Leonard recognized the Jones family's color but it did not matter because his "lustful" intent mattered more. Leonard agreed that while he cared about color, he gave it no thought. With Davis's repeated questions about Leonard's thoughts, Leonard continued to maintain that he did not know Jones's color and never thought about it.[53] In New York in the 1920s it seemed improbable that anyone could have been ignorant of what was at stake in not drawing firm lines between the races. Leonard's explanation that he never thought about color seemed to support Davis's contention that Leonard knew it but did not care.

After a day where Davis spent the bulk of his cross-examination on what Leonard knew about the Jones family, court ended early on Thursday, 19 November. The press wondered whether the two unread mystery letters had led to the early adjournment. On Friday, 20 November, the deputy sheriffs opened the courtroom doors at nine o'clock to get the large crowd settled. The room filled and the sheriffs barred the doors to additional spectators.[54] One hour later, a conference in Justice Morschauser's chambers attended by the lawyers delayed the normal start of the session. Then the morning in court began on an unusual note. Isaac Mills asked the judge for an adjournment because "an emergency in this case arose of which personally I hadn't before the slightest intimation."[55] Justice Morschauser granted his request.

The sudden and unexpected second adjournment on Friday morning sent the press into a speculative frenzy. On Saturday, the *Times* reported the theory that Leonard's suit would come to an end "so that the mysterious letter would never become part of the court record." Others suspected that Leonard's legal team had split over the course of the case. The press questioned Mills about whether Leonard's father had been consulted about this turning point, reporting that "Mills declared that he knew nothing of the elder Rhinelander's action and in fact had never met him." For over three weeks, Philip Rhinelander had not been seen in his Manhattan home. Nevertheless, the *Daily Mirror* imagined a Saturday meeting with Leonard's father to discuss the case. Such a meeting, according to the paper, would be a "hopeless conference" given the likely contents of the mystery letters.[56]

The *Daily Mirror* even suggested that the "adroit questions of Attorney Lee Parsons Davis . . . give an inkling of a correspondence that the aristocratic Rhinelanders would sacrifice their millions to see destroyed unread." The *Daily News* posed the question of which action the Rhinelander family would find more damaging to its social status—the continuation of their son's marriage to a colored woman (with the possibility of mixed-race Rhinelander progeny) or the revelation of Leonard's sexual behavior.[57] The *Daily Mirror* contended that by this point the trial had already seriously damaged the Rhinelander family's social status, the "bar sinister that already cuts the face of the escutcheon of the last of the Rhinelander blood is like the slashing of a gaping wound—a wound that may heal but will leave a livid scar forever."[58]

After the weekend adjournment, the trial resumed on Monday, 23 November in a tension-filled atmosphere. The large crowd spilled out of the courtroom. Over two hundred people were forced to wait outside.[59] Once the session began, Isaac Mills started to speak, "If your Honor please, I crave leave to make a statement of explanation." Lee Davis interjected that first he wanted to know the subject of Mills's statement, but Mills retorted, "I decline to inform him of the contents any more than he allowed me to read the letters when he had them marked for identification." Justice Morschauser allowed Mills to proceed.[60]

Mills said that he needed to explain his request for an adjournment on Friday. First, he complained about the two times Davis handed Leonard letters to read for identification when Davis did not read them to the jury but instead asked Leonard whether he wanted to continue his case. "That, your Honor," Mills declared, "was a deliberate threat to that witness that unless he discontinued this action those letters, which would besmirch him, would be spread upon the record of this court and made public." Davis jumped to his feet and objected, "This is the most improper statement I have ever heard from a lawyer in a lawsuit made for just one purpose."[61]

Mills told the judge and jury that after he read the letters he "thought it my duty to give to the persons who are interested in this young man, or who by nature ought to be, an opportunity. . . ." Davis interrupted, "Is there any evidence before this Court as to that? I do not care what the Judge states." Mills retorted, "I wish this man would not interrupt me. He has been ruled against." Justice Morschauser intervened to inform Mills that he hoped that he would keep his comments "within bounds so that there shall be no mistrial." Mills remarked that when Morschauser adjourned the trial on Friday the question arose as to whether it would continue. He raised his arms, clenched his fists, and declared, "My answer to his threat, your Honor, is that I defy him and dare him to do his worst. We proceed with this trial. Mr. Rhinelander take the stand."[62]

By this point in the trial, Davis planned to use the two mystery letters as a final salvo against Leonard's character. The contents of Leonard's letters, previously unknown to his lawyers, had touched a nerve, and his attorneys seemed to believe that they threatened his case. Since Davis had not spared any detail in eliciting from Leonard how he persuaded Alice to enter into a sexual relationship, these letters most likely offered more damaging evidence.

When Leonard made his way back to the witness stand, Davis handed Leonard a photograph of himself in bed at the Hotel Marie-Antoinette that apparently Leonard had given to Alice. Davis demanded, "Is there some part of your anatomy showing in that photograph down close to your waistline?" After Leonard replied that he did not think so, Davis handed him a magnifying glass and suggested that Leonard look again. Bluntly, Davis asked, "Aren't your private organs showing there?" Leonard said no. Davis passed the photo with the magnifying glass to the jury.[63]

Davis's explicit questions about Leonard's photograph signaled that this day in court would be the most scandalous so far. Consequently, Justice Morschauser asked if Davis intended to read the mystery letters. Davis indicated that he would do so but that he would provide ample warning. Morschauser then announced to the courtroom, "I want to give every woman a fair chance to leave this room. I am familiar with the contents of the letters. I would not want to stay if I were a woman." Morschauser suggested that given the momentary "lull" in the proceedings, those who wanted to leave should since the letters could be read at any time. Morschauser repeated, "If I were a woman I would not want to stay in the court room if I had not any business here except as a spectator."[64] Justice Morschauser also added that he would have any "young persons" removed if they refused to leave.

At this point, Davis made ready to present the evidence that he hoped would demonstrate Leonard's upper-class degeneracy and assure the jury that a favorable verdict for Alice would not send a positive message about intermarriage. Davis asked Leonard, "Did you tell this jury, before we took an adjournment, that your relations with Alice Rhinelander were always natural?" Leonard replied that he had. Davis then offered Defendant's Exhibit S into evidence and handed copies to Mills and Morschauser. When Davis announced that he would read the first letter, Morschauser interjected, "This letter ought not to be heard by women. Everybody that hasn't any business in this courtroom will leave, in the shape of women." After he announced a ten-minute recess, Morschauser declared, "When I come back, no women will be allowed in the room." As the courtroom cleared Alice Rhinelander and her parents absented themselves. So many women were compelled to leave, except the two or three female reporters, that the hallways became overcrowded; guards used clubs to force the crowd down the stairs.[65]

After the recess, Davis took out a letter from Leonard to Alice from July 1922 and read:

> Last night, sweetheart, after writing three full pages to you, I undressed and scrambled into my bed, but not to go to sleep. No, baby, do you know what I did? Something that you do when my letters arrive at night. Yes, love one, I took everyone of your notes which I received at General de-

livery and read them while lying on the bed . . . when you mentioned the time we were in bed together at the "Marie Antoinette," *something* that belonged to me acted the way it usual did whenever I am with you darling, and *it* just longed for the touch of your passionate little fingers, which have so often made me very, very happy. You know, don't you, old scout, what that "*something*" is and how it acted when you began being naughty!! Oh! sweetheart, many, many nights when I lay in bed and think about my darling girl *it* acts the very same way, and longs for your warm body to crawl upon me, take *it* in your soft, smooth hands, and then work *it* up very slowly between your opened legs!!!! God! Alice can you imagine me reading your tempting notes in bed last night; and the way I must have felt and how that "*something*" which belongs to me acted!! . . . Baby love, do you remember when we were in bed together and how I used to ask you, dear, for you to do it, because I couldn't manage *it* myself? You always were able to make both of us happy, weren't you, darling? Yes, honeybunch, I just loved for you to crawl upon me and do it all yourself, because you never failed and you knew how, didn't you Alice? Sweetheart, am I tempting you and does it bring back memories of past days?

Oh! Alice, love, be good, dear child, because I want you in the days to come and remember to keep our *secret* locked safely in your heart.[66]

Once he finished, Davis asked whether Leonard loved Alice when he wrote the letter. Leonard admitted that he did but that he did not design the letter to tempt Alice with thoughts about sex. "You didn't think that it might tempt this girl—writing about that 'something' acting the way it did when she was nearby?" Leonard replied that he did not.[67]

Then Leonard and Davis entered into a dialogue that focused on what Leonard referred to in the letter as his "something." Davis asked whether Leonard wrote the next letter to entertain or to provide "pleasant sensations" for himself. Leonard responded, "My being true to Alice—I being true to Alice, I had no other outlet to relieve my emotions except by my letters, and in them I put my very heart and soul. At least, I have a clear conscience that I gave my word of honor to Alice of being true." Although Leonard tried to defend himself, in response to Davis's question he accepted the attorney's description of his letter as "smut."[68]

Leonard's letter, Exhibit S, conformed to Davis's narrative to the extent it served as an instance of Leonard reminding Alice of their sexual pleasures at the hotel. Such a letter did not go far enough, however, to illustrate Leonard's upper-class self-indulgence. Moreover, Leonard's letter mentioned Alice's sexual expertise, which could reinforce Mills's contention that Alice's greater experience with sex bewitched and blinded Leonard.

To ensure the jury would find Leonard's actions repellant, Davis turned to the second mystery letter, Defendant's Exhibit M-1, dated 6 June 1922. Davis read:

> It makes me feel so happy, darling, when I hear from you and especially when you write about how you used to caress me and make me feel as though I were in heaven. Oh! Alice, dear, you certainly did tempt me when you told me the way you used to crawl upon me and lay upon my stomach. Do you ever think, when you are lying in bed at night, how I used to love to make you passionate with my warm lips and the way I did it? . . . Do you ever long for my lips? Yes, love, my warm lips and tongue, which have often made you very, very happy. You said you liked my ways, didn't you, dear? Well, sweetheart, I just love your little ways too. They are all so gentle and have a manner all their own. Do you remember, honeybunch, how I used to put my head between you legs and how I used to caress you with my lips and tongue? You loved to have me do that, didn't you, old scout? Can't you feel me, darling, as I am talking to you, trying to recall past days when we were in bed together? Oh! I often think when I used to lift up your nightgown and crawl down to the foot of the bed, so as I could be right under you. "Please, dear, come." Do you recall how I asked you to do that. Oh! blessed child, when my lips and tongue were making you so happy you used to say to me, "Oh, Len, Oh! Len." You were in heaven, dear, because your old faithful, true boy was with you . . . love one, you asked me to write an interesting letter like you sent me, so I have tried my best. Have I tempted you, sweetheart, and have I made you imagine I am right next to you?[69]

After Davis finished with Exhibit M-1, which he hoped would establish Leonard's indulgence in "unnatural" sexual practices, Leonard admitted that he loved Alice when he wrote this letter. Yet he still only had "visions" of marrying her.[70] In contrast to his testimony about his 11 July letter, Leonard agreed that he had hoped to tempt Alice with this note, but only because she asked for it. Immediately, Davis asked whether Alice's letters used "any language like this." Leonard conceded that he had no such letter and agreed with Davis that his contained "the vilest kind of smut."[71]

One reason Leonard's letter was so "vile" according to Davis was because

Leonard described "unnatural" acts. Davis used his questions about this letter to buttress his construction of Leonard as an upper-class seducer but with an added element of sexual degeneracy or perversion. To do this, Davis asked whether Leonard meant and did the "things" he wrote about in June 1922. Leonard replied with a yes to both questions. Davis, however, wanted to make it clear to the jury that Leonard engaged in forbidden acts. He asked, "You knew better than that, didn't you? Withdrawn. Do you remember telling this jury that your conduct with this girl was natural?" Leonard admitted that he did. Davis probed further, "You had no suspicion inside of you that to put your head between her legs was an unnatural thing?" Leonard again responded that he did not.[72]

In comments on Leonard's letter and on newspaper accounts of the trial, the *New Yorker* opined that Davis had hit his mark when he labeled Leonard's sexual behaviors perverse. "Even the pink-sheeted early editions," the magazine asserted, "could not muster sufficient courage to print the famous letter, which, at some future date, may be incorporated in the American parallel of Krafft-Ebing's works." Nevertheless, copies of the letter had hit the streets. According to the magazine, "hucksters" on the streets of New York sold them only to men as they called out " 'Th' Rhinelander letter, dollar a copy. Th' real thing, mister—not a woid left out.' " The *New Yorker* was referring to Richard von Krafft-Ebing, author of the well-known 1888 work *Psychopathia sexualis*, that dealt with sexuality and degeneracy and pointed to the "homosexual" as "the prime violator of 'natural drives.' " The magazine was apparently intimating that Leonard's actions violated "natural drives."[73]

In the courtroom, Davis emphasized the perverted and unnatural nature of Leonard's sexual acts with Alice. Davis seemed disturbed that Leonard did not find his own actions abhorrent and pursued this point:

> [Davis:] You were bringing some kind of sex delight to this girl without the use of your own natural organs?
> [Leonard:] Yes.
> [Davis:] Using your tongue?
> [Leonard:] Yes.
> [Davis:] You hadn't the slightest suspicion, in doing that in the Marie Antoinette, that that was an unnatural thing?
> [Leonard:] I did not; no.
> [Davis:] Have you any suspicion about it now?
> [Leonard:] No.

[Davis:] You still tell this jury that you think that is a natural thing to do? Is that it?

[Leonard:] As far as I know.

[Davis:] As far as you know now. You don't know any better now?

[Leonard:] No.

[Davis:] And you haven't heard since that it was an unnatural thing?

[Leonard:] No.[74]

Americans had long viewed oral sex as unnatural. In the post-Revolutionary period, according to John D'Emilio and Estelle Freedman, Americans categorized oral sex, along with anal sex and other "nonprocreative sexual acts," as sodomy and prohibited these acts in statutes that criminalized "crimes against nature." Even the free-love movement in the 1870s opposed oral sex as unnatural. By the end of the nineteenth century, America's medical establishment had labeled sodomy a disease.[75]

Despite the sexual transformations of the early twentieth century, and the growing separation of sex from procreation, oral sex still occupied a liminal position. New York's code of criminal law contained an entire section on "Crime Against Nature." New York law provided for up to twenty years in prison for a conviction for sodomy, an act defined as "a person who carnally knows in any manner any animal or bird; or carnally knows any male or female person by the annus [sic] or by or with the mouth; or voluntarily submits to such carnal knowledge." Other states also criminalized so-called crimes against nature. It is difficult to gauge whether such practices were widespread despite the legal prohibition. Kevin White suggests that oral sex may have been one aspect of petting in the 1920s based on the results of sex researcher Alfred Kinsey's later sex survey of women and a few articles from the 1930s.[76] While some unmarried couples likely engaged in oral sex in the twenties, these actions were probably perceived by many as unnatural or perverse.

Labeling oral sex as unnatural gave Davis the room to suggest that Leonard's failure to distinguish between "natural" and "unnatural" sex acts mirrored his failure to make a similar and obvious distinction in regard to race—and thereby marry Alice. Leonard's failure to recognize either divisions of race or the difference between "natural" and "unnatural" sexual practices merely reflected the state of his degeneracy.[77]

During much of Lee Parsons Davis's cross-examination of Leonard, the press attributed Leonard's courtship behavior with Alice to the actions of a man acting within the bounds of a modern ideology of white masculinity that valued male sexual aggression. This ideology, however, did not value "perversion" or "degeneracy," labels that were particularly loaded in the 1920s and that Davis applied to Leonard's actions. The press did not respond to Leonard's letter, Exhibit M, in the same positive way it had to his other letters and testimony about his relationship with Alice when they portrayed Leonard as a modern lover. Instead, the press endorsed Davis's version of Leonard as a sexually debased aristocrat. The *Daily Mirror* compared Leonard to Harry Thaw, one of the stars of an earlier New York upper-class sex scandal who had shot and killed the architect Stanford White for his affair with Thaw's wife, the actress Evelyn Nesbit. The *Daily Mirror* went so far as to assert that Leonard's behaviors were worse than Thaw's act of murder, saying that Thaw, "in his wildest days, was never guilty of the vile things Rhinelander gloats over." On the same day, the *Mirror*'s editorial referred to Leonard as "Kip the Beast" and proclaimed that he deserved public degradation.[78]

The public also weighed in on Leonard's behavior. A writer to the *Daily News* rejoiced that the Rhinelander trial was one where money did not "hush up a blueblood's sins." Another letter writer called Leonard's thoughts and actions "filthy" and wondered about the rest of New York's elite. Moreover, some New Yorkers who either heard the letters in the courtroom, read about them in the papers, or found bootlegged copies on the street were so appalled that they reported Leonard to the postal authorities for violating laws that prohibited the mailing of indecent literature.[79] By the time Davis finished reading Leonard's letters, he conveyed a new image of Leonard to the jury and those interested in the trial. Leonard now appeared the very image of a degenerate blueblood.

Despite Davis's efforts to taint Leonard with the charge of degeneracy, Leonard still refused to agree that Alice did not lie to him about her race. When Davis challenged Leonard and asked, "You were willing to marry the girl that did these things with you in the Hotel Marie Antoinette, who had confessed her impurity to you, but you were unwilling to marry one who had the slightest taint of colored blood?," Leonard retorted, "As to the color, I drew the line."[80]

SEVEN :

"Poor Little Cupid" and the Marriage Contract

Poor Little Cupid has grown very careless of late and some of the results of his thoughtlessness are swelling court blotters, throwing the mantle of gloom around the firesides of the great white world, and otherwise disturbing the social strata of numerous fortune-makers, to say nothing of subtracting from the family safe certain alimony bonuses and counsel fees. And this is all because Poor Little Cupid has become so careless that first one Nordic and then another persists in crossing the racial line and allying his matrimonial self with an African blonde or brunette.—"Poor Little Cupid," *New York Amsterdam News*, 11 February 1925

The grounds upon which an annulment of a marriage for fraud may be obtained in this state differ in some degree from those required in most other jurisdictions. . . . The fraud must be such that had it not been practiced the marriage would not have been entered into.—*Carmody's New York Practice* (1924)

IN THE 1920S, race mattered. African ancestry could limit people's livelihoods. It could determine where they lived. African ancestry could also be a matter of life and death. Although most lynchings took place in the South, the riots in the summer of 1919 in Chicago and Washington, D.C., showed that not only white southerners engaged in violence against African Americans. Northern bloodshed continued through the 1920s as many whites battled to keep blacks out of their neighborhoods in cities like Detroit and New York.[1]

In the 1920s, marriage, like race, mattered too. According to many historians, the institution of marriage came under greater scrutiny in the 1920s. Americans feared rising divorce rates (one out of every seven marriages that decade ended in divorce) and the attractions of companionate marriage or so-called trial marriages.[2] In 1925, noted psychoanalyst Dr. Beatrice M. Hinkle contributed an essay to *Harper's Magazine* in which she lamented the "chaos of modern marriage." According to Hinkle, many younger Americans had experienced "a complete change in attitude, often in the form of a violent revolt against the former ideals and customs affecting the marriage relation." Consequently, "the general uncertainty and instability in the relation is probably more marked [here] than in any other country." Given these uncertainties, Hinkle declared, "People all over the land are aroused by the disturbed conditions and they are arguing, writing, and preaching about it from all angles, in an effort to stem the tide of disaffection and disruption which is making such inroads upon this ancient institution."[3]

Hinkle attributed marital chaos to changes in American social and economic life and the impact of those changes on women's lives. Women had gained the right to vote nationwide only five years before Hinkle penned her essay. Hinkle also pointed a finger at the "pursuit of personal happiness, which has so largely supplanted the conception of duty and responsibility to others as the dominant force in the marriage relation." The pursuit of personal happiness sometimes led directly to divorce court. When Elaine Tyler May compared divorce records from the 1920s with those from the 1880s, she found that spouses who wanted a divorce in the 1920s focused on problems with their husband or wife's "personal appearance" or lack of "youthfulness."[4]

The search for individual happiness in marriage subverted some of the traditional objectives of marriage, at least according to those who opposed divorce. Joseph Morschauser, the presiding *Rhinelander* judge, strongly disapproved of absolute divorce and legal separations. Instead, he supported what he perceived as the traditional attributes of marriage. In a 1923 lawsuit for a separation he denied alimony to a woman on the grounds that she had failed to fulfill her marital responsibilities. "She must stop dancing with other men," he asserted. "She should stay home and take care of it." During the same year, Justice Morschauser received national attention when he referred to divorce as "a cancer in the vitals of American life" and proposed its abolition to preserve "the sacredness of marriage" and "protect the home."[5]

When it came time to choose a marriage partner in the 1920s, concerns over race and concerns about marriage often converged. By 1927, twenty-nine states (primarily southern and western) outlawed marriages between different races. But race mattered for marriage even in northern states like New York, where no laws forbade interracial marriages. Many New Yorkers believed, as the editors of the *Daily News* put it, that the "curse of race prejudice in this country does not permit love to laugh at its laws and its locksmiths" even if such a love would not violate "the laws of God or man." Marriage should only unite a man and a woman from the same racial category.[6]

Since both race and marriage mattered in the 1920s, their combination might prove volatile and even a matter of life and death. In late August 1922, for example, the "curse of race prejudice" drove a young nurse, Margaret Van Cleaf of Rochester, New York, to end her life in the waters of the Genessee River. Only twenty-one, Margaret committed suicide after she rejected a marriage proposal from "a young man, said to be from one of the most prominent of Rochester's families," even though she loved him. Why would a young, pretty, and intelligent nurse kill herself instead of marrying the man she loved? Margaret drowned rather than tell her white suitor she possessed "Negro blood" that she inherited from her father, the son of a "Scotchman" and a "colored woman." Her mother, a white woman, made Margaret promise never to marry because of her African ancestry.[7] In Margaret's eyes and those of her mother, the "Negro strain" in her "blood" prevented her from marrying a white man and having children.

Even though the "laws of God or man" did not prohibit their union, race mattered enough that Margaret must have felt she needed to tell her beau about her "Negro ancestry" before marriage. On the brink of entering into the marriage contract, she may have believed she could not keep such a secret. Perhaps Margaret felt it would be a lie to conceal her ancestry because she recognized that race made a difference for marriage. Since she intentionally kept her African ancestry hidden while she trained and worked as a nurse, Margaret knew that ignoring it, whether by acts of commission or omission, violated America's racial ideology. According to American notions of race, Margaret passed as white so long as she kept her father's background secret.

If Margaret had identified herself openly as colored, however, she might not have been able to continue to work as a nurse. She might have had to return to the world of domestic service to which she belonged before she moved to Rochester to pursue nursing. If African ancestry could so deeply affect her job prospects, it would probably limit her marital options. Once her sweetheart knew the "truth," she faced the possibility of rejection. Even though Margaret would be the same person after her disclosure, even though she would look the same, smile the same, think the same, and love the same, she might find that in his eyes she had changed. Perhaps unable to face her suitor's new perspective and to keep her promise to her mother, Margaret left her secret with her lifeless body in the river.[8]

A *New York Amsterdam News* editorial about Margaret Van Cleaf published a few months later expressed the hope that her story would serve as a useful morality tale. The newspaper disapproved of passing and noted approvingly that Van Cleaf refused to marry while passing for white. Instead, her "honesty and devotion" to her sweetheart became "too much to allow her to deceive him, so she ended her life, rather than to be his wife, a colored white woman. Her course, while it is to be deplored, ought to show every woman engaged the folly of deception."[9] The *Amsterdam News* accepted the idea that passing constituted a deception with serious consequences for marriage. Not everyone, however, believed racial identity needed to be revealed before marriage.

In the same year that Margaret Van Cleaf committed suicide, John Stovall, a Bronx insurance agent, asked the courts to annul his marriage because his twenty-one-year-old bride, Gene, lied about her ancestry before they married. Mrs. Stovall, unlike Margaret Van Cleaf, did not think ancestry mattered for marriage. She declared that since "nobody had ever questioned her as to her race ties, she had felt no obligation to boast of her possession of the blood of the Pharaohs." She also flippantly remarked that she never inquired into her husband's ancestry before they wed. Perhaps Mrs. Stovall meant to imply that she recognized that only an African background negatively affected marriage unless one's spouse had African ancestry too.[10]

When Leonard Rhinelander filed for his annulment from Alice in 1924, almost no one questioned the underlying assumptions of Leonard's lawsuit—that deception about race constituted an adequate legal basis to dissolve a marriage in New York. Arthur Brisbane, a nationally syndicated writer for William Randolph Hearst's newspapers, raised a few questions that hinted at the unspoken ideas about race and marriage inherent in Leonard's lawsuit. In the pages of the *New York American* Brisbane wondered how a lawsuit based on racial deception could be brought in the courts of New York State. But he also noted that the Rhinelander marriage united Leonard, "whose people for several generations have not worked for a living and are, therefore, called 'aristocrats,'" and Alice, a "woman with negro blood" whose "people have always worked hard; therefore she is no aristocrat."[11] Brisbane presumed this marriage between a white "aristocrat" and a "Negro" worker dealt a "terrible blow" to the "aristocratic New York family."[12]

Leonard's request for an annulment on the basis of Alice's lies about "colored blood" struck Brisbane as curious. Brisbane accurately described the current state of New York law when he remarked, "A man in New York could not get a divorce on the ground that his wife had deceived him about a British or Celtic strain of blood."[13] Well-aware that New York did not forbid marriage between those considered white and those considered black, and did not distinguish between "British blood," "Celtic blood," or "African blood," Brisbane opined that a "court's decision as to an African strain in a State where miscegenation is not illegal will be enlightening."[14] Would deception about only one kind of ancestry (African) matter for marriage in New York?

If New York did not forbid interracial marriage, why did Leonard's lawyers use claims about Alice's ancestry to justify their lawsuit? Indeed, when Leonard's lawyer Leon Jacobs requested that New York's courts hear Leonard's annulment trial quickly, he characterized the Rhinelander marriage as a public threat. Jacobs's argument in favor of a speedy trial alluded to the problems posed by miscegenation. Consequently, Jacobs, declared, "this case is notorious and famous. The great American public, the state and society are vitally interested in the final outcome thereof. That both the plaintiff and the defendant should know as speedily as possible whether they are husband and wife or not."[15] Speed was required because the public needed to know if such a marriage could continue and serve as a visible challenge to normative concepts of marriage.

The reliance by Leonard's lawyer on fears of miscegenation tapped into a powerful undercurrent of racial thought in the North. In the early twentieth century, Americans in northern states like New York feared that interracial relationships posed a threat to marriage—an institution described by New York's highest court in the 1920s as "the foundation upon which must rest the perpetuation of society and civilization." As one well-regarded treatise writer on domestic relations law remarked, "Marriage is a relation divinely instituted for the mutual comfort, well-being, and happiness of both men and women, for the proper nurture and maintenance of offspring, and for the education in turn of the whole human race."[16] Given the weighty functions assigned to marriage, any challenge to normative conceptions of the institution jeopardized society itself. Although marriage in the 1920s appeared to be an institution in "chaos," the conventional model of marriage still centered on a heterosexual couple entering into a relationship with certain rights, duties, and obligations to legally procreate. Such a couple would preferably belong to the same racial group, as would their children—a preference enforced by the law in most states.

Many white Americans worried that the Great Migration would lead to greater numbers of interracial marriages. The *Daily News* noted the problems created by such marriages: "There is neither rhyme nor reason to the colored man or colored woman who marries across the line. . . . All unnecessary discussion and agitation of this question cannot but tend toward increased friction and strained relations between the races." Part of the friction was attributable to the fact that those "colored men and women" who married across the line sought to achieve social equality with whites.[17]

As early as 1910 and 1913, New York legislators, dismayed by the famous African American prizefighter Jack Johnson's marriages to white women, introduced bills into the legislature to prohibit interracial marriage. Although the proposals never passed, the timing of their introduction may reflect the first stirring of anxiety over interracial marriage as the northern flow of black migrants began. Other northern states also attempted to pass similar laws in the teens and twenties. The April 1913 issue of the *Crisis* reported on the NAACP's efforts to oppose antimiscegenation bills introduced into the legislatures of Illinois, Wisconsin, New York, Ohio, Michigan, and Iowa. By the mid-1920s a number of northern states had proposed legislation to bar miscegenation. Throughout the decade, the *Crisis* charted all northern attempts to enact "anti-intermarriage" laws and the NAACP's efforts to defeat them.[18]

Despite the failure to prohibit intermarriage in New York and most northern states, strong public disapproval of mixed marriages manifested itself in other ways. Issuers of marriage licenses in northern states sometimes took it into their own hands to deny licenses to couples they identified as mixed race. In 1914, a Michigan county clerk tried to keep a white man from marrying a "young lady of color." In fact, Michigan county clerks seemed to make a habit of trying to deny marriage licenses to black-white couples.[19] In 1923, a Pennsylvania court clerk also refused to issue a marriage license to a black man and a white woman. Not only the bureaucrats who issued marriage licenses attempted to prevent intermarriage. In Ohio, for example, the Youngstown police arrested a teenage white girl who tried to obtain a marriage license to marry a young black man. After the police tried unsuccessfully to persuade the girl to give up her fiancé, they placed the couple on a train heading back to Cleveland, where they had come from.[20]

Public opinion and parental disapproval could also discourage interracial marriages. In early November 1925, the *New York Daily Mirror* wrote about the weeping parents of a New Jersey white woman who had returned to her home with a New York City marriage license that identified her prospective groom as a Negro. The bride's mother announced that she and her husband had not known their daughter's fiancé, a Columbia University graduate, was colored. "I often remarked to Helen that he was dark complected for a white man," the mother stated. "I always thought he was Spanish. Oh God, don't let my little girl marry him."[21] The *Daily Mirror*, as well as other New York papers, reported that the husband-to-be had passed for white but that his fiancée knew his background. The *Daily Mirror* observed that white and black residents of Montclair, New Jersey, where the couple planned to live, "declared they would have nothing to do with the couple. Police paraded the streets to prevent race disturbances." Ultimately, given the combination of parental and community censure, the young woman decided to halt the wedding. Whites and blacks in Montclair breathed a sigh of relief at the news. When the *Daily Mirror* later published a letter to the editor from a white woman who asked why the marriage was a problem so long as the parties loved each other, the newspaper replied that both blacks and whites disapproved and that "only unhappiness can come of such marriages."[22]

The Ku Klux Klan in the 1920s also expressed their hatred and fear of black-white marriages in the North. A female leader of the Klan from Oklahoma even advocated the death penalty for any white person "convicted of degrading the blood of the white race by mixing it with any of the inferior races." She justified her call for such a law with her claim that more than eight thousand Negro men had married white women in Chicago. In 1926, the *Daily News* reported on the Klan's attempt to prevent the marriage of a seventeen-year-old girl who had a "mulatto" mother and a white father to a "prosperous young white farmer" from Putnam County, New York.[23]

Even the fictional portrayal of interracial marriage in the North generated negative public response. In 1924 the staging of Eugene O'Neill's play *All God's Chillun Got Wings* in a Manhattan theater led to a hysterical outcry in the press. When the director cast a black man (Paul Robeson) and a white woman as a married couple, the white press criticized the play for dramatizing miscegenation. Many feared that violence would greet the play's opening night.[24]

Some Americans blamed an increase in intermarriage on white fascination with African American culture in the 1920s, especially the growing popularity of jazz. H. L. Mencken suspected the "vogue" of black culture in cities like New York led to interracial marriages.[25] In a discussion of black and tan cabarets, Chandler Owens agreed that whites sought out "the Negro, that is [in] the social equality equation, the Negro is the sought, rather than the seeking factor." While there was a great deal of anxiety expressed about race mixing in the 1920s, no one knew how much took place. George Schuyler claimed that few mixed marriages took place in New York, but he intimated,

"There is considerable racial inter-mixture under cover," adding, "or should one use the plural?"[26]

Even if some white Americans sought relationships across the color line, they were met with disapproval by many white and black northerners in an era obsessed with racial purity.[27] The 1920s were *the* height of the drive for racial purity and the high point of eugenics in the United States. Advocates of pure races who promoted eugenics fixated on miscegenation as a critical problem. As a critic of eugenics put it in the *Journal of Negro History*, the "race inequalitarian is obsessed with the idea of the menacing nature of miscegenation. He believes that race mixing spells disaster."[28] Given these beliefs, many eugenicists supported legal restrictions on interracial marriage.

Well-known racial polemicist Madison Grant provided one reason for regulating interracial marriage. He predicted that "when it becomes thoroughly understood that the children of mixed marriages . . . belong to the lower type, the importance of transmitting in unimpaired purity the blood inheritance of ages will be appreciated . . . and to bring half-breeds into the world will be regarded as a social and racial crime of the first magnitude." Such "half-breeds" also threatened the stability of race and potentially could cross the color line and pass as white.[29]

Passing would necessarily result in additional interracial marriages, especially in an era when large numbers of people left the communities where they (and their ancestors) were known.[30] As early as 1902, *The Colored American Magazine* proclaimed, "Thousands of persons of mixed blood have immigrated to the North, where they have intermarried with Caucasians, and are known as such." Five years later, African American clubwoman Fannie Barrier Williams suggested that passing and the "dangers of mistaken identity" were on the rise in the North, which meant that potential spouses needed to carefully investigate each other before marriage. In the 1920s, W. A. Plecker of the Virginia State Registrar's Office became convinced that some of his state's "near-whites" left Virginia, moved North, and married whites.[31] An inadvertent interracial marriage could prove disastrous to the maintenance of racial purity. In 1930, a former social worker discussed her efforts to remove a woman who passed as white from a life of prostitution because "she was a real danger to the white race. She might sometime marry a white man. For the sake of the white race I felt she must return to her people."[32]

By 1922, the *Amsterdam News* linked John Stovall's annulment case to the perception that more African Americans passed as white and married white. According to the *Amsterdam News*, "speculation is rife as to whether the courts could stand the burden if every wifie and every hubby with the least drop of Negro blood in their veins were sued for separation. It is said that thousands of light[-]colored people are at present 'passing' and that somewhere between one and two million apparently white people have colored blood in their veins, themselves apparently unaware of the fact." The paper pointed to the growing potential for havoc in the marriage market if passing continued and many future spouses turned out to be ignorant of their own or their future mate's African ancestry. A later commentator on passing declared that many "unacknowledged Negroes" married "white folks." The very idea that "unacknowledged Negroes" might marry "unsuspecting" whites threatened common social understandings of marriage as a union between persons of the same race.[33]

What happened if some "white folks" suspected their spouse passed as white? In the South or the West, antimiscegenation laws would govern such marriages. Twenty-six out of the twenty-nine states that prohibited interracial marriage declared these marriages "void," without any legal effect. White spouses in those states who identified the person they married as black could go to court to obtain a judicial declaration that the marriage never existed in the eyes of the law. According to Charles Mangum, "There seems to be little doubt that most courts would hold that fraudulent concealment of the fact that a person has Negro blood would be grounds for an annulment of marriage."[34]

Courts might not always agree with the facts offered by the spouse who brought the lawsuit, however. In 1910, for example, a North Carolina court refused to grant a divorce to Frank Ferrall, who contended he did not know his wife, Susie, was "of negro descent within the third generation" when they wed. Frank never claimed that Susie lied to him before they wed. The North Carolina courts found that Ferrall did not prove that Susie fit into the statutory category of Negro in North Carolina.[35]

Other courts dissolved similar marriages when the evidence showed they were interracial. In 1922 the Arizona Supreme Court agreed with a lower appellate court's decision to annul the marriage of Joe and Mayellen Kirby. Joe Kirby asserted that he possessed "Caucasian blood" and produced his mother to support his claim, while his evidence (based again on his mother's words as well as his own) demonstrated Mayellen was "of negro blood." Kirby never raised the question of whether his wife lied to him.[36] Some cases brought under antimiscegenation law were complaints that one spouse had deceived the other.

In a study of California annulment law from 1890 to 1910, two legal historians uncovered a case in which a husband sued for an annulment on the grounds of fraud and racial identity. California prohibited interracial marriage, but in this case, the court didn't annul the marriage because the husband changed his mind, perhaps because he believed his wife was really half Samoan.[37] Historian Willard Gatewood also recounts the story of Francis Dwyer, who went to the Nebraska courts to annul his marriage to his wife, Clara, because she "had negro blood in her veins." Francis claimed Clara deceived him. Although Nebraska banned interracial marriage, the court did not annul the marriage because Dwyer could not prove Clara was not white. Despite the Nebraska court's decision to uphold the Dwyer marriage, the *Chicago Defender* criticized Nebraska's antimiscegenation law and argued the Dwyer case would never have reached court except for "the unwisdom of such legislation." To the extent the husband used Nebraska law as a tool to break up his marriage, the *Chicago Defender* found the existence of this law particularly appalling in a northern state.[38]

In states that did not have similar laws, some spouses attempted to use the legal system to end a marriage they determined inadvertently interracial. As early as 1915, Arthur Little, a druggist from Detroit, sought a divorce from his wife, Alma, because he claimed she concealed "Negro blood in her veins." Alma Little, described as a "pronounced blond" with "strictly Caucasian features," reportedly planned to ask the anthropologist Franz Boas to analyze her racial background. Given the uncertainties of scientific determinations of race, the African American press expressed doubts that Boas or any other scientist could prove anything about Mrs. Little's ancestry, saying, "If this golden-haired blond really has Negro blood in her veins, not a husband in the world can feel assured that his wife is not a Negress." Boas never appeared in court, though, to weigh in on Mrs. Little's ancestry. Instead, the Little's divorce action ended after Mrs. Little agreed to a divorce based on the grounds of cruelty.[39]

In New York, spouses (of any ancestry) could not end their marriage unless they met the requirements of New York's laws on divorce and annulment—the only available legal tools. Strict rules governed marriage in New York, which reflected the state's public policy to preserve marriage as a permanent status. As one New York court described state policy, "Marriage is a contract under our law, but it results in the establishment of a relation which the state will not dissolve without strong grounds." Throughout the nineteenth century and most of the twentieth, New York's divorce law allowed husbands and wives to divorce only if adultery were involved.[40] Given the restrictive nature of New York's divorce law, and given that in the thirty-seven days Leonard and Alice lived together as husband and wife there was little chance for, much less any evidence of, adultery, Leonard and his lawyers turned to the only other available tool: annulment.[41]

Although successful divorce and annulment actions lead to the same conclusion—the end of a marriage—important structural differences separate the two. A successful divorce action dissolves a marriage that no longer works. A successful annulment proceeding, however, invalidates a marriage as of the moment the marriage took place. In this way, a court creates a legal fiction: the annulled marriage *never* existed. The roots of annulment law in the United States date back to church regulation of marriage in England. Christianity intended marriage as a life-long sacrament, and canon law provided for its dissolution only through an annulment under limited circumstances. In the American context, annulment law continued to be applied on narrow grounds. At the end of the nineteenth century, Franklin G. Fessenden, a legal scholar writing in the *Harvard Law Review*, explained why annulment law only applied in limited circumstances. He pointed out that it constituted a powerful tool given its ability to retroactively dissolve a marriage. Since the retroactive dissolution of a marriage constituted a more drastic termination of a relationship than the sundering of a valid marriage in a divorce, Fessenden suggested that annulment proceedings should be reserved for only those circumstances when a divorce would "not give a sufficient remedy for the wrong done. These cases demand a more radical treatment. The injury is such as to require an annulment, that is an entire destruction of the marriage *ab initio*."[42]

The substantial implications of an annulment must have been attractive to Leonard Rhinelander's family. Indeed, as one treatise writer in the 1920s noted, the "effect of such a judgment is to restore the parties to the marriage to their original status before the marriage took place. The marriage status is not merely put to an end, but wiped out altogether for all purposes." Only forty years earlier Leonard's grandparents had hoped to have his uncle William's "inappropriate" marriage annulled. In the case of Leonard's marriage to Alice, an annulment would expunge Leonard's interracial marriage from the public record, return Leonard and Alice to their status as single, and thereby separate the races.[43]

Given the symbolic meaning of annulment, the Rhinelanders may have hoped a successful annulment suit would erase the "taint" of color Leonard brought to the family, and thus "re-whiten" the family name. Since the marriage would never have existed, Alice Jones would never have been Mrs. Rhinelander, with the change in status and the potential shift in racial categorization implied in the Rhinelander name. Alice Jones Rhinelander would be stripped of her marital name and denied any of the protections and benefits of marriage. The status quo would be maintained—a colored girl could only be colored and lower class.[44]

A judicial declaration of annulment also possessed other significant material advantages for the Rhinelanders. At this time in New York, as soon as a woman married she acquired a dower right in her husband's real estate. Although the term "dower right" is a peculiar piece of legal jargon derived from the law of property, it had a very real economic impact: A one-third interest in all of a husband's lands went to his wife upon his death. Although the interest lasted only until the wife's death, it meant that the properties affected could not be sold in whole until the wife either consented to the sale or died.[45]

Since the Rhinelanders owned valuable Manhattan real estate, they must have been particularly sensitive to any claims on land. Marriage was significant to the family because it is *the* institution where property passes down through the generations. A link between the marriage relation and property rights had long been recognized in American law. A late-nineteenth-century treatise on the "law of husband and wife" described marriage law and property law as "very closely blended." The patriarchs of the Rhinelander family may have harbored dynastic pretensions. When the *New York Times* wrote about William Christopher Rhinelander's 1878 will, it observed that a large portion of his assets would be tied up in a trust. The *Times* suggested that the paterfamilias had "inherited a strong bias toward the English method of keeping family estates together and regarding them as almost sacredly indivisible."[46] This "bias" allowed the threat of disinheritance (being cut off from the family property) for inappropriate marriage choices to be deployed by the family. Any family member who disobeyed the family rules could not inherit the family property that supported the family's social standing. Leonard, as one of Philip Rhinelander's two living sons, would be due to inherit a sizable portion of the family assets. His marriage to a woman well outside the family's social set would be extremely disturbing.

The Rhinelanders may not have liked the idea of a woman of color and lower status with a valid legal stake in their wealth (the source of their claim to elite status). As legal scholar Adrienne Davis observes in her examination of antebellum sexuality, race, and property, "property relationships are a key way of establishing and maintaining social and political power." Davis's study of black-white sexual relationships and inheritance before the Civil War points to the strong disposition against transfers of wealth from whites to blacks. If Leonard and Alice had a child, their son or daughter would possess African ancestry and could inherit Rhinelander property. Even sixty years after the end of the Civil War, by allying his family with a woman deemed inferior, Leonard threatened the status of his family, which belonged to a social group that defined itself by its exclusionary nature as well as its wealth.[47]

But a successful annulment case would dissolve the Rhinelander marriage and destroy any legal rights Alice might possess in Rhinelander properties, since no dower rights survived an annulment. The wealth of the Rhinelander family would not fall into the hands of a potentially colored woman and any of her progeny. An annulment would also mean that Alice would receive no alimony, and would have no right to any of Leonard's other property at his death.[48]

Although an annulment might provide numerous economic and psychological benefits to Leonard and his family, the mere filing of legal papers did not guarantee the dissolution of a marriage. New York law allowed courts to annul marriages only for specific reasons. The existence of a few narrow, statutory bases for annulment underscored the state's interest in preserving marriage. No provision of New York's annulment law referenced race or ancestry. Instead, the law deemed certain incestuous or bigamous marriages void. Such marriages did not even require a judicial declaration to render them nonbinding. In contrast, four other kinds of marriages were deemed "voidable" by a court, which meant that a spouse needed to go into court and request that a judge void the marriage. Only if the court agreed with the complaining spouse would the marriage be annulled. The first three types of voidable marriages were if a party to the marriage was underage, physically incapable, or not able to consent to marriage because of "a want of understanding." In addition, a marriage might be voidable if a husband or wife consented to marry because of force, fraud, or duress.[49]

To meet the threshold to file for an annulment, Leonard's attorneys had to identify the exact provision of law applicable to Leonard and Alice's marriage. Neither Leonard nor Alice was underage at the time of their wedding. They did not show any signs of being physically incapable of consummating their marriage—in fact, quite the opposite. Although Isaac Mills spent a large part of his opening statement to the jury and his questions to the first witnesses on

Leonard's "mental backwardness," and the press characterized Leonard's testimony with words like "stuttering," "stammering," "halting," or "jerky," Leonard's lawyers did not claim Leonard was mentally incapable of consenting to marriage. If Leonard was truly mentally incapable of marrying, New York law provided that his father could have filed for an annulment on Leonard's behalf. Yet this option was not chosen, probably because legal precedent in New York required that a mentally incapable spouse be either an "idiot" or a "lunatic."[50] Identifying Leonard as an "idiot" or "lunatic" for these purposes may have been too drastic a response to Leonard's marriage for the Rhinelanders and their lawyers. Especially in an era when most Americans regarded these afflictions as hereditary and a trait of families like the Kallikaks or the Jukes, who appeared in well-known contemporary studies of degenerate families, the Rhinelanders may not have wanted to associate their name with such conditions.[51]

Instead, Leonard and his lawyers argued that Leonard's consent to his marriage was induced by fraud. By this, they meant that Alice deceived Leonard into marriage; he did not agree to marry across the color line. Although such a claim fell under a broad reading of New York law, it would not necessarily lead to an annulment. Not all frauds or misrepresentations before marriage could lead to an annulment. As one historian of marriage law points out, the "realities of courtship" were such that individuals could misrepresent their social status or character in some way before they married.[52] Courts could not wipe out every marriage where one spouse claimed the other lied about something before they wed. If they could courthouses would be overflowing with disgruntled spouses who expected to have their marriages dissolved.

Given New York's commitment to preserving marriage, New York courts made it very difficult for spouses to obtain annulments for fraud in the early twentieth century. Nevertheless, Leonard and his attorneys contended that the gravity of his claims should outweigh the judiciary's predisposition to uphold marriage. Particularly in an era of rising concerns over marriage, passing, interracial marriage, and eugenics, a claim that someone disguised her identity as a colored person or Negro before marriage was alarming. Leonard's lawyers must have calculated that the courts would agree with them and grant Leonard his annulment.[53]

Leonard and his lawyers had good reasons for believing a court would find a lie about race sufficient fraud to annul his marriage. Over the course of the nineteenth century and into the twentieth, states exercised greater legal control over marriage to protect normative conceptions of the institution. Historian Michael Grossberg's study of nineteenth-century domestic relations law charts a shift away from a "free marriage market" to increased state control over marriage. The new marriage rules that resulted "reveal particular moral, religious, social and physiological traits considered fundamentally threatening to domestic life and social order."[54] These new marital regulations acted to shore up the boundaries of normal marriage.

In the late nineteenth and early twentieth centuries, as eugenics reached its popular heights in the United States, many marital proscriptions revolved around race and other "physiological" characteristics.[55] By the 1920s, one study of marriage and the state promoted state interventions in marriage. The authors contended,

> Marriage . . . is a contract apart from all other contracts in that, for individual welfare and public welfare, it must be surrounded by the state with conditions not required in other contracts. These conditions fix degrees of consanguinity and affinity; they protect immaturity by establishing a minimum age for marriage; they strive to prevent fraud in marriage, to safeguard marital unions against communicable disease and defect, as also against compulsion and duress. These are all things that could not be done effectively by the individual citizen or by a more informal organization than that of the state.

Marriage needed rigorous protection because it functioned as a "procreative institution" to reproduce fit citizens.[56] Therefore, the state had to look closely at marriages that deviated from the norm.

Interracial marriages were clearly perceived as transgressive. Not only Leonard and his lawyers believed that New York courts might look seriously at a case alleging racial fraud. In the teens and twenties, other husbands and wives sought to annul their marriages in New York alleging that the person they married deceived them about their race before they wed. The trickle of racial fraud cases into New York's judicial system attests to growing concerns over interracial marriage and racial passing in the North. In each of the approximately thirteen cases filed in New York courts between 1916 and 1925, the individual who sought the annulment claimed his or her spouse passed as white but was really black.[57]

Since New York's annulment statute did not enumerate which fraudulent acts justified ending a marriage, courts had to determine on a case-by-case basis the deceptions during courtship that would justify annulling a marriage.

As Franklin Fessenden observed in 1899, "to define the kind of fraud which will lead the courts to relieve the innocent party is a matter of some difficulty." In finding only certain claims of deception significant enough to end a marriage, however, courts shed light on those acts considered a threat to marriage. Fessenden suggested that court decisions on marital fraud tended to reflect public policy, or, as one modern legal analyst suggests, they helped "flesh out our understanding of marriage" as courts determined what constituted a fraudulent deception.[58]

In order to parse the significance of Justice Morschauser's decision to allow the Rhinelander annulment trial to be heard in front of a jury, the general rules of marital annulment law in the United States need examination. New York's rules concerning annulment of marriages for fraud differed significantly in some respects from the national rule, and that difference both affected the Rhinelander trial and affects our understanding of the underlying meanings of this case. Most states defined marital fraud narrowly, and granted annulments only when an individual's fraudulent acts affected his or her ability to cohabit or procreate—acts deemed "at the essence of marriage." In Minnesota, where there was no law against interracial marriage, a trial judge ruled in January 1925 that race did not constitute valid grounds for an annulment based on fraud. Judge R. D. O'Brien of St. Paul denied an annulment to Otis Ostmann, who claimed his wife was not white and had deceived him about her race. Ostmann's attorney argued that his client's case could be brought if it could be proved the wife used fraud and deception. The lawyer for Mrs. Ostmann, however, argued race did not constitute sufficient grounds for an annulment. Moreover, since the husband knew his wife's relatives before their marriage and knew they were not white, no fraud could have taken place.[59]

Since this case never appeared in any published legal reporter, it is difficult to know why Judge O'Brien determined race did not provide a legal basis for an annulment. The Minnesota Supreme Court's decision in an annulment case involving an alleged lie about sanity six months later, however, provides insight into the St. Paul decision. In *Robertson v. Roth*, the supreme court held that "concealment or deception by one of the parties as to the defects of character, morality, chastity, habits and temper is not ground for annulment. These are accidental qualities which do not constitute the basis for the marriage relation." Accordingly, "mistakes and disappointments in personal qualities or character cannot be made the basis of a dissolution of the marriage relation. The individual desire must yield to the public welfare." Consequently, a wife's failure to disclose past episodes of insanity could not lead to an annulment.[60]

In reaching this decision, Minnesota's highest court declared that "concealment in order to annul a marriage *must go to the very essence of the contract*." The court described the types of cases where fraud or concealment affected the "essence" of the marriage contract. The frauds listed included deception related to syphilis, tuberculosis, or leprosy. These deceptions would be grounds for annulment because they "destroy the consent which blots out all semblance of contract—or . . . impose at the time of marriage upon the one wronged, burdens and obstacles wholly unexpected and of such character that they tend to the destruction of domestic happiness and promoting humiliation disclosing a situation intolerable to society and detrimental to the marriage relation."[61] Applying similar reasoning, Judge O'Brien might well have concluded that Mrs. Ostmann's ancestry resembled other "defects of character, morality, chastity, habits and temper" and therefore constituted an "accidental" quality that did not affect the "essence" of the marital contract.

When the Minnesota Supreme Court held that the type of concealment or fraud had to affect the "essence" of the marriage contract, it cited approvingly the leading nineteenth-century annulment case *Reynolds v. Reynolds*. This 1862 Massachusetts decision played a "pivotal role" in American marriage law because it loosened earlier rules that made it almost impossible for spouses to obtain an annulment for fraud.[62]

In the early nineteenth century, American courts had grappled with the question of whether to apply the rules of fraud related to general contracts to lawsuits involving marriage. Some judges feared that applying commercial contract law to marriage would make it easier to dissolve marriages and thereby undermine the judiciary's commitment to uphold the institution. Most American courts decided the marriage contract differed from other contracts, therefore the rules imposed in cases of marital fraud were even more stringent than those of general contract law, and only a few kinds of fraud could lead to an annulment.[63]

This limited definition of marital fraud, however, sometimes led to results that undercut normative conceptions of marriage. The judges in *Reynolds v. Reynolds* recognized this dilemma and provided a narrow modification designed to produce better outcomes. In the *Reynolds* case, a thirty-year-old woman, Bridget Reynolds, told her husband, Michael, a seventeen-year-old, that she was a virgin. Bridget turned out to be pregnant by another man at the time she married Michael. When the groom learned of Bridget's pregnancy, he left her and went to court to end their marriage. The Massachusetts court held that fraudulent acts that "go directly to the essentials of the marriage contract" could result in an annulment. Bridget Reynolds's pregnancy by another man at the time of her marriage meant she could not immediately bear Michael Reynolds's child. Since Bridget's deceptions affected her ability to fulfill her part of the marriage contract, that is, bear her husband's child, her fraudulent acts went to the essence of that contract.[64]

When the court granted Michael Reynolds his annulment, its decision produced a more "flexible" rule for annulments based on fraud while it also upheld American courts' desire to preserve marriage. Without this change, Michael Reynolds would have been legally bound to stay married to Bridget and raise a child not his own—a scenario that undermined traditional expectations of marriage and the family. As the *Reynolds* decision noted, the "great object of marriage in a civilized and Christian community is to secure the existence and permanence of the family relation, and to insure the legitimacy of offspring." With *Reynolds*, the court established a new rule on fraud and marriage, which soon was adopted by other states.[65]

Franklin Fessenden believed the principles enunciated in *Reynolds*, the so-called American rule, while difficult to apply, had the benefit of providing relief (the dissolution of the marriage) in "cases of extreme hardship." By the end of the nineteenth century, legal treatise writer James Schouler affirmed the significance of the *Reynolds* rule when he summed up the state of annulment law, making it clear that the "marriage relation is not to be disturbed for trifles, nor can the cumbrous machinery of the courts be brought to bear upon impalpable things.... Fraudulent misrepresentations of one party as to birth, social position, fortune, good health, and temperament, cannot therefore vitiate the contract. *Caveat emptor* is the harsh but necessary maxim of the law."[66] Husbands and wives took each other for better and for worse unless an act of fraud affected the essence of marriage.

Most American states followed the *Reynolds* "essence of the contract" rule into the twentieth century. The highest court in Massachusetts reaffirmed the *Reynolds* rule in 1921 when it denied an annulment on the grounds of fraud for a "manifestly wicked deception." In this case, a wife filed for an annulment after her husband lied to her about his name, occupation, and relatives and deserted her two weeks after the wedding. While the Massachusetts court agreed that the husband's acts were deceptive, the written opinion observed, "Not every error or mistake into which an innocent party to a marriage may fall, even though induced by disingenuous or false statements, silences or practices, [which] affords grounds for its annulment." Although the wife "was deluded as to his name and place of residence, that did not affect his personality. His representations as to relatives in another part of the country merely concerned his social standing."[67] In other words, the husband's lies did not affect the essence of his marital contract.

At this point in the opinion, the judges suggested that though the facts did not entitle the wife to an annulment, she could have broken her agreement to marry, without worrying about a breach of promise to marry lawsuit, if she had determined the truth before the marriage. The court pointed to an 1894 Massachusetts case *Van Houten v. Morse* as precedent. *Van Houten* revolved around the question of whether a man's fiancée misrepresented her racial identity.[68] The *Van Houten* opinion showed that the discovery of such a misrepresentation *before* marriage could justify a refusal to enter into the marriage contract but not an annulment because, "after the ceremony of marriage and the subsequent cohabitation, brief though it was, a change of status took place affecting both the parties and the community."[69] These deceptions did not affect the essence of the marriage contract; marriages based on lies about identity—even racial identity—could not be annulled under the "essence of the marriage" rule. Under this legal standard, annulment cases based on racial fraud seemed unlikely to succeed in court.

Beginning at the turn of the twentieth century, however, New York judges began to turn away from the *Reynolds* "essence of the marriage" test when, in 1903, the New York Court of Appeals laid out a new interpretation of the law of annulment and fraud in a major decision. In *DiLorenzo v. DiLorenzo*, New York's highest court addressed whether judges could grant an annulment where a wife pretended that she had given birth to her husband's child before they married. Johanna DiLorenzo, however, never gave birth. Instead, she located a baby and presented it to Gregorio DiLorenzo as his own.[70] Since *DiLorenzo* involved a baby that did not belong to the husband, the facts resembled those in *Reynolds*, except Johanna DiLorenzo was not pregnant when she married. Under the *Reynolds* "essence of the marriage" test, Gregorio DiLorenzo could not obtain an annulment since Johanna could physically bear his child at the time of their marriage.

The New York Court of Appeals, however, rejected the *Reynolds* test. Judge Gray, writing for a unanimous court, held that a "material" fraud, which he defined as an act that "had it not been practiced, the party would not have consented to the marriage," entitled a spouse to an annulment. Gray acknowledged the uniqueness of the marriage contract—"public policy is concerned with the regulation of the family relation"—but, he added, in New York, unlike other jurisdictions, "our law considers marriage in no light other than as a civil contract." Both spouses needed to freely and fully consent to enter into the marriage contract, just like any party to an ordinary commercial contract, in order for the contract to be valid and binding. Given this emphasis on consent, the court of appeals annulled the DiLorenzo's marriage since Johanna's lies were "such as to deceive a reasonably prudent person and to appeal to his sense of honor and of duty." Therefore, she practiced a "gross fraud." Gregorio would never have agreed to marry if he had known the truth about the child.[71]

After making its decision, the court proceeded to set the rule for when a New York court could annul a marriage for fraud: "If the plaintiff proved to the satisfaction of the court that, through misrepresentation of some fact, which was an essential element in the giving of his consent to the contract of marriage and which was of such a nature as to deceive an ordinarily prudent person, he has been victimized, the court is empowered to annul the marriage." Thus the *DiLorenzo* opinion and the test of "material fraud" went beyond *Reynolds*, expanding the boundaries of the types of actions that might lead to an annulment. One legal commentator in the 1920s characterized the court's decision as a "complete reversal of position" from the *Reynolds* rule.[72]

The *DiLorenzo* decision moved New York courts closer to treating fraud in marriage the same way courts dealt with fraud in the commercial arena, which contradicted almost one hundred years of judges distinguishing between fraud in marriage contracts and fraud in commercial contracts. The earlier refusals to treat the marriage contract as equivalent to a commercial agreement were intended to uphold the institution of marriage. Even the U.S. Supreme Court believed that marriage was no ordinary contract. In its 1888 decision in *Maynard v. Hill*, the Supreme Court wrote, "Whilst marriage is often termed by text writers and in decisions of courts a civil contract—generally to indicate that it must be founded upon the agreement of the parties, and does not require any religious ceremony for its solemnization—it is something more than a mere contract." The justices noted that like any contract, both parties to the marital pact needed to consent. "Other contracts may be modified, restricted, or enlarged, or entirely released upon the consent of the parties," they added. "Not so with marriage. The relation once formed, the law steps in and holds the parties to various obligations and liabilities." Marriage, the justices concluded, "is an institution, in the maintenance of which in its purity the public is deeply interested, for it is the foundation of the family and society, without which there would be neither civilization nor progress."[73] The courts of New York in *DiLorenzo* and later cases never explained why New York treated marriage contracts like commercial agreements in cases of fraud and thereby potentially undermined the permanence of marriage.

Legal commentators as well as judges in other states attributed New York's new rule to the state's narrow divorce laws. The Wisconsin Supreme Court thought that the types of annulment cases that appeared in New York might present marital stories of "extreme hardship" that could not be resolved under New York divorce law, therefore judges lowered the bar for access to annulment.[74] At the time Leonard brought suit to annul his marriage to Alice, no published law or judicial precedent stated that knowledge of a potential partner's race constituted an essential element of a person's consent to marriage. Because New York did not prohibit interracial marriage, it was not at all clear that the law of marital fraud extended to such cases. A judge in Justice Morschauser's position would need to decide whether knowledge of someone's ancestry counted as a "material" fact that would, as a matter of law, affect a decision to marry. Under the *DiLorenzo* rule, if a person with African ancestry described himself as white before marriage, the question that would need to be answered in court would be whether his spouse would have refused to marry him if she had known the truth. To modern thinking, this question might not seem to have an obvious answer.

Even during the era of Alice and Leonard's marriage, an observer might wonder how to resolve that issue. When a judge on New York's high court in the early 1930s summed up the state of the law, he indicated, "Surely every misrepresentation leading up to marriage cannot be material,—the fact that a brunette turned to a blond overnight, or that the beautiful teeth were discovered to be false . . . would lead no court to annul the marriage for fraud." Indeed, in the teens and twenties New York judges threw cases out of court before trial when spouses claimed that their husbands or wives deceived them about loving them before marriage or when a husband told his wife he was twenty-one though he was only twenty.[75]

In fact, the reported decisions on marital fraud from this era demonstrate that New York courts generally required a pretty serious misrepresentation before granting annulments on the grounds of fraud. In typical cases, courts allowed annulments to take place where a wife had been another man's mistress before their marriage, or a husband concealed a venereal disease, or a wife hid the presence of insanity in the family, or a husband denied his addiction to cocaine and heroin. In the case of a concealed addiction to drugs in the early 1920s, a court ruled it would be "a cruel injustice" to keep a deceived spouse "bound by ties of marriage to a dopefiend."[76] In a time of mounting fears over interracial marriage and passing in New York, the question of whether deception about racial identity before marriage would have been equally threatening provides insight about the intensity and extent of those fears.

Leonard Rhinelander's attorneys claimed that Alice's false representations about race mattered for Leonard's decision to marry. In Isaac Mills's opening statement, he argued that "any material misrepresentation or concealment of a material fact—material to the matrimonial relationship, such that if known to the other party it would naturally have prevented the marriage—is sufficient ground for such an action of annulment."[77] Mills and Leon Jacobs pointed to *DiLorenzo* and later New York cases for the proposition that a material fact would be one in which if the misled party had known the true facts, he or she would not have wed: "It cannot be doubted that, at least in this country, the fact that one party to the marriage . . . was of negro blood in substantial part, whereas the other was of pure white blood" would be a material fact. Leonard's lawyers went on to support their argument of materiality when they noted that "the feeling against such a marriage is very strong among American white people."[78]

Mills and Jacobs acknowledged that New York did not proscribe interracial marriage but suggested that the "great and public interest" in the *Rhinelander* trial stood as evidence of the "general feeling" against interracial marriage. In their view, Leonard needed to know Alice Rhinelander's ancestry before marriage because knowledge about race constituted an essential element in consenting to marry, since the "general feeling" opposed such marriages. Moreover, Isaac Mills declared to the jury that while Leonard "was ready to accept her inferior social position, her less wealth, her poverty, her inferior social position, he knew these things, he was ready to take them; but this ancient and proud lineage, he would not inflict upon it the undying disgrace of an alliance with colored blood. That is where he drew the line."[79] In Mills's presentation, Leonard did not want to be tied involuntarily in the "cruel" bonds of an interracial marriage.

The assignment of Leonard's case to Justice Joseph Morschauser in the supreme court of Westchester County proved lucky for Leonard, although more than mere luck might have been involved. Leonard's lawyers may have chosen to file the annulment suit in Westchester to gain access to Morschauser, who adhered to a very liberal interpretation of New York's rules on annulment and fraud.[80] Four years before Leonard tried to end his marriage to Alice, Morschauser annulled another marriage on the grounds of racial deception. In 1919, Sybil Neale claimed her husband passed as white when she noticed that "her mother-in-law was wearing a wig over kinky hair. She went immediately to her lawyer and asked him to make a secret investigation." After the investigation Sybil filed for an annulment and claimed she would not have married Theodore Neale if she had known he was a Negro.[81] Morschauser agreed and granted the annulment

One year later, Justice Morschauser put in writing his thoughts on annulment for fraud when he decided a case that did not involve racial deception. Justice Morschauser observed in *Sheridan v. Sheridan* that the question of what kind of fraud should result in an annulment "has led to a great amount of discussion and difference of opinion." In Morschauser's mind, "if upon the whole case there is fraud, there is no reason why a party defrauded should not be relieved. Indiscreet and unsuitable marriages frequently are contracted, for 'love is blind,' and perhaps always will be." Following this analysis, the presence of fraud should trigger an annulment no matter the type of deception.[82]

After philosophizing on the blindness of love, Morschauser suggested that when most people chose a marriage partner, they decide based on appearances and used their best judgment. But, he added, "if the individual is deceived by the acts and falsehoods of an unscrupulous, scheming person, there should be no reason to refuse to render relief to the person deceived, when this can be done without injury to anyone, except the person who practiced the fraud. If the pretense is capable of deceiving, it is sufficient. The important question of fact is how far the representation affected the mind of the person defrauded." In *Sheridan*, a wife complained that her husband misrepresented himself as honest (the couple never lived together and the husband never intended to consummate the marriage). Since, according to Morschauser, Mrs. Sheridan would never have married Mr. Sheridan had she known he only wanted to marry her for her money, she deserved an annulment. In another case from 1921, Judge Morschauser annulled a marriage when a wife alleged that her husband, a "socialist preacher," concealed two criminal convictions and his "economic and social views." After Morschauser granted the annulment (perhaps not coincidentally right in the midst of the postwar Red Scare), the wife suggested that her former husband "should have married a strong Russian woman with socialistic beliefs."[83]

Although not every judge in New York during this period extended the reach of New York law as far as Morschauser by annulling a marriage based on a husband's dishonesty, he was not the only judge faced with annulment cases based on racial deception. In 1922, the *Chicago Defender* reported that a Bronx Supreme Court justice annulled Marie and Arthur Price's marriage after Mrs. Price claimed that her spouse possessed "Ethiopian blood." She did not learn this secret until after the wedding when the husband's cousin visited and informed her that Arthur's father came from "Ethiopian stock."[84]

One of the most striking facts about the *Rhinelander* case and its surrounding hoopla (and similar lawsuits, like the Prices') is that the lawyers, the judge, and commentators in the press, with a few notable exceptions, accepted the idea that the racial identity of one's spouse was a material fact that needed to be known before marriage. They all assumed that as a matter of law, passing was a racial fraud that justified the annulment of a marriage. In the *Rhinelander* case, neither set of attorneys disagreed with the theory behind Leonard's fraud claim, though they debated the existence of whether the facts *proved* that fraud had occurred. Both sides, and the judge, all tacitly agreed that such a marriage constituted a material fraud even though New York law did not ban interracial marriages.[85]

While New York law did not preclude marriage across the color line, the state's courts readily admitted that one public policy behind marriage was "the purpose of begetting offspring."[86] In cases involving racial deception, courts may have assumed that part of their role was to uphold normative conceptions of marriage, which included monitoring the reproduction of new citizens of the state. If normative ideals of marriage revolved around same-race partners, then a lie about racial identity could lead to the inadvertent production of children who fell outside the norm. In that view, such a lie would be something that mattered more than other, lesser deceptions.[87]

Davis's apparent acquiescence to this position stands out. As Alice's lawyer, his responsibility was to represent her to the best of his ability. As an experienced litigator, he would have known that part of his responsibility was to advance every argument, to take any step legally allowable, to help her win her case. Litigators often challenge by way of pretrial motions any suspect or weak claims made by their opponents. In this case, Davis never challenged the unspoken assumption made by Mills and Justice Morschauser that if Alice had lied about her race, that lie provided Leonard with a valid reason for annulling their marriage.[88]

Davis's failure to challenge the validity of Leonard's claim particularly stands out after considering the lengths to which Davis went to try to win

Alice's case. Requiring Alice to expose herself in the jury room in front of white men was a remarkable tactic, which must have cost Alice a great deal. Davis was willing to engage in that behavior but did nothing to challenge the underlying validity of Leonard's claim of material fraud. It was as though Davis just could not grasp that racial deception, if it had occurred, might not be serious enough to warrant annulling an otherwise happy marriage.

Davis's apparent inability to believe that race did not matter enough to authorize an annulment of a marriage reflected the realities of the day. Society at large and the courts accepted without argument the notion that passing, if proven, automatically constituted grounds for ending a marriage.[89] Without a statute blocking interracial marriage, and without even any reported court decisions explicitly stating that racial deception was material enough to authorize annulment, New York's legal establishment seems to have formulated and adhered to an unwritten rule that racial deception mattered. In my research I have been unable to find record of any case in which that position was challenged. Every lawsuit that I found was decided solely on the facts of the case in question; that is, whether the person charged with fraud really lied about his or her race, and whether the spouse really believed the lies.[90]

New York judges in the 1910s and 1920s, in the process of resolving disputes about marriages, revealed that their understanding of marriage relied upon a racialized view of the institution despite New York's lack of an antimiscegenation statute. They presumed that if a white husband or white wife had known that his or her spouse lied about racial identity, they would *never* have married them. Marriage was meant to be a union between two members of the same race, or if they were of different races, that had to be known to each up front. Lying about love did not disturb New York's judges; lying about race did.

Since the annulment case of *Rhinelander v. Rhinelander* made it into a New York courtroom on the grounds that Alice had fraudulently induced Leonard to marry across the color line, in order to win his case and end Leonard's marriage "for the sake of the white race" Isaac Mills's argument had to focus on Leonard and Alice's courtship. Mills needed to demonstrate the steps by which Alice deceived Leonard into marriage. To illustrate the problems of miscegenation, Mills presented to the jury a particular picture of Alice Jones Rhinelander and thereby attempted to convince the jury to free Leonard from his marriage. Mills linked Alice's sexual behavior to her racial identity and portrayed Alice Jones as a sexually loose colored woman.

Mills's reading of Alice's letters did not necessarily produce the results he sought, at least in the eyes of the press. At the end of the first week of the Rhinelander trial, the *New York Times* reported on the courtroom laughter in response to the many letters that Mills read in which Alice warned Leonard about the other men after her. On the same day in the *Daily Mirror*, George Buchanan observed that "Alice's repeated reference to White Way celebrities brought amused smiles to the faces of the listeners, to whom it was obvious that the girl had been merely indulging in dream romances to evoke jealousy in the heart of her absent lover." On the other hand, Grace Robinson claimed in the *Daily News* that Alice's letters "revealed . . . a reincarnated Cleopatra with up-to-date gold-digging instincts." In reviewing the testimony and evidence from the previous week, the *New York Herald Tribune* recognized that Alice's letters could be interpreted in different ways: "Were they written by an ambitious 'vampire' or were they the result of the befuddled gropings of an illiterate girl who expressed a genuine love?"[91]

Even if New York's newspapers did not know if Alice was Cleopatra, a "vampire," or just a girl in love, they voiced their disapproval of interracial marriages. By the end of November, the *Daily News* specifically discussed "miscegenation" and the press's handling of the trial. In an editorial, the *Daily News* argued that the Rhinelander annulment trial presented a tragedy that some newspapers treated as "only a smutty comedy, a subject for ribald jests or sub rosa comment." The paper contended that the Rhinelander trial was not "offensive" and deserved serious attention because it concerned a key issue of the twentieth century, the desire to maintain racial purity.[92] "Miscegenation," according to the *Daily News*, "is frowned upon by decent persons but not roundly denounced" in circumstances when a couple does not marry or "where the actors in the drama occupy extremely minor places in our social structure." Thus, the editors argued that the behavior that deserved denunciation was Leonard's marriage to Alice. Indeed, the editors suggested that if Leonard "had gone no further than to place the battered crown of illicit love upon the brow of Alice Jones," there would be no news story. "Instead of being regarded as an indiscreet bachelor by the few who might have known, he and the girl he married are viewed today by the millions as degraded violators of an age-old human law."[93]

After explaining why the Rhinelander annulment trial deserved serious press coverage, the editors of the *Daily News* reminded their readers why interracial marriage merited a harsher response than did mere "illicit connection": "First, marriage is an open defiance, a rebellion against the code which forbids miscegenation; and second, marriage is more likely to produce children and mix the races forever." Thus, the Rhinelander annulment trial presented the "most tremendous central theme of which we have knowledge."[94] The *Daily News* agreed with Isaac Mills and the eugenicists that interracial marriages violated society's rules and disrupted normative conceptions of marriage and the family even if such marriages did not violate New York's laws. In their view, a lie that convinced a spouse to enter into a marriage without knowing the other spouse's racial identity would be a serious transgression.

EIGHT :

Blind Love and the Visibility of Race

A French friend sent us this extract from Paris, France, *Quotidien*: Monsieur Rhinelander who is an American millionaire married one day Miss Alice Jones who is the daughter of a taxi-cab driver. Free Americans have no prejudices. But a month after the marriage Mr. Rhinelander suddenly perceived that he had married a Negress. Then he asked for a divorce. Free Americans have strange prejudices. Mr. Rhinelander's discovery may well seem astonishing because of its delay. For a husband might put some time into discovering that his wife's father was a taxi-cab driver; but he would need to be astonishingly short-sighted, myopic or distracted not to be able to see at once that he was having dealings with a Negress.—"A French View of the Rhinelanders," *Crisis*, December 1926

THROUGHOUT LEE PARSON DAVIS'S cross-examination of Leonard he barraged the hapless husband with questions about his perception of the Jones family before his marriage. Focusing on George Jones, the now-acknowledged source of the Jones daughters' African ancestry, Davis asked repeatedly whether Leonard could see Jones's color. At one point, Leonard admitted the lights were turned on in Alice's house the day he met her father; yet George Jones's skin color did not surprise him. When Davis asked Leonard to characterize George Jones's complexion in court, Leonard replied, "It is rather dark. He is rather dark." Davis asked, "Just verging off white?" Leonard disagreed. He insisted Jones looked darker to him in the courtroom than he did when they first met. Leonard's admission that George Jones now appeared darker suggests Leonard learned to "see" color and race in a new light during the trial. Color may not have mattered as much to Leonard when he met, courted, and wed Alice Jones, but in the glare of the courtroom it mattered.[1]

When the *Evening Journal*'s Margery Rex commented on this portion of Leonard's testimony, she did not find surprising his observation that Jones seemed darker in court. Instead, Rex compared Leonard to other men blinded by love who only over time see clearly. "Of course George Jones looks darker now. Love's young dream with coloratura accompaniment is a different shade now, not so rosy." A few days later, Rex returned to the same topic, asking, "How could Kip keep from suspecting that his Alice had colored blood?" She could only suggest that the blinders of "love" kept Leonard from seeing Alice. "Kip in love shut his aristocratic eyes to the complexion of his beloved half black girl. . . . Now family pride has constituted a powerful eye-opener."[2] Davis's job in defending his client would be to prove that Leonard's eyes had always been open.

Yet at this point in the trial, Davis might still fall short of establishing to the jury's satisfaction that Leonard knew Alice's color before they wed. During Leonard's cross-examination, Leonard offered contradictory and confusing statements about what and when he knew about Alice's ancestry. The jury could still decide Alice had deceived Leonard. Davis needed to cement the obviousness of Alice's skin color in the minds of the jury. When they finally sat down to deliberate, Davis wanted the twelve men to have no doubts about the transparency of her ancestry.

To settle the question of Alice's skin color and racial ancestry, Davis shaped his case to tap into certain ideas about race. During the 1920s popular notions about how one could determine racial ancestry began to shift away from an explanatory language based on blood to a system that understood race based on vision.[3] The greater use of vision to ascertain race reflected the growing fears of the white population during an era in which distinctions between the black and white races began to decline. Moreover, in an increasingly urbanized North, shifting populations of African American migrants and foreign immigrants made it difficult to apply a "one-drop" rule of race. The one-drop rule, based on notions of blood as race, required societal knowledge of African ancestry, no matter how inexact. In "mongrel" New York such information might be hard to come by.[4]

In the year between 1924, when the initial stories of the Rhinelander marriage hit the front pages, and 1925, when the trial began, the press and the lawyers advanced a variety of answers to the question of how to determine race. Nationality, geographic origin, occupational and social status, legal documents, reputation, self-description, and legal definitions had all been offered to establish racial identity. All had been found wanting. During the trial Davis even turned to slang as a way to pinpoint racial identity. To do so, Davis read aloud in court a letter from Leonard to Alice in which Leonard wrote the phrase "strutting parties," a variant of the word "struts" and a synonym for Harlem "rent parties" in the 1920s. Davis adopted a southern accent to pronounce those words, which the press interpreted as "his best negro dialect." Although Leonard agreed that Alice used the phrase "strutting parties," he denied it alerted him to her racial background.[5]

Davis's question about this "typically negro expression" and his use of an accent reflected his understanding of the changes wrought in the North by the Great Migration. Davis calculated that his use of Harlem slang combined with a southern accent would signal to the jury that Leonard could not have mistaken Alice's identity. Yet Davis may not have reckoned with the fact that African American slang, like other aspects of African American culture, became part of the larger white American culture in the 1920s. In fact, when Davis asked Leonard whether someone with "clear white skin might use this term 'strutting party' without exciting any suspicion as to her color," Leonard replied that she could certainly do so.[6]

The varying strategies adopted to determine Alice's skin color and ancestry speak to the uncertainties about both the source and the meaning of race in this era. This uncertainty reflected a shift in the ideology of race. The decade of the twenties saw biological notions of race come under siege from newer explanations of race based on culture promoted by anthropologists like Franz Boas. Neither Davis nor Mills drew on concepts of race as culture in making their case. Instead, both lawyers stayed on the biology side of the biology-versus-culture debate.[7]

From the very outset of the case, Leon Jacobs and Isaac Mills maintained that Alice had told Leonard that she and her family were white, he believed her, and he married her. During the trial, Mills contended that Alice fooled Leonard by claiming Spanish ancestry and telling him she was white. Mills never argued explicitly that her appearance deceived Leonard. Yet his arguments assumed the Joneses (except for Elizabeth) passed as white. Therefore, their bodies did not reveal their race; instead, their bodies concealed their blood.

Particularly in Mills's opening address he stressed Alice's "substantial strain of black blood," drawing on the one-drop rule. Mills's use of the adjective "substantial," however, suggests that he believed Alice possessed more than one drop and that this blood came to Alice from her father. His reliance on heredity to explain Alice's black blood accounts for his surprise during the trial that Alice's attorneys never spent any time or money to research George Jones's ancestry to prove he was not colored. Mills's use of the language of blood indicated his belief that racial identity did not rest on visible signs. Instead, race, as an inherited trait, circulated through and permeated the entire body. For Mills, race could be revealed by character, by behavior, and, above all, by blood.[8] Mills demonstrated this belief in inherited racial characteristics when he returned again and again to Alice's sexual behavior. Mills's questions alluded constantly to stereotypes of African American women's sexual depravity.

Not only Isaac Mills linked race to blood in the twenties. This connection remained popular in the early twentieth century when many Americans chattered about "bad blood," "tainted blood," "blue blood," and "colored blood." Not surprisingly, Madison Grant drew on the language of blood to discuss pure races, race mixing, and the superiority of "Nordic blood." Even more liberal thinkers on race relied on blood-based ideas about race. In 1925 anthropologist Melville Herskovits described as "nonsense" blood-based discussions of race. Yet in the very same article, when Herskovits discussed popular attitudes toward race mixing, he suggested that passing for white led to "Negro blood in small quantities liberally distributed throughout the white population of this country." Even though Herskovits recognized the absurdity of equating race with blood, he could not get away from the pervasive language of blood.[9]

When Lee Davis conceded on the second day of the trial that Alice possessed "some colored blood," the defense accepted the terms set by Isaac Mills. Like Mills, Davis acknowledged the one-drop rule, but he built his defense on a different conception of race, albeit one still based on biology and the body. In his opening statement, Davis invoked visual differences of race. He pointed out that everyone could look at Elizabeth Jones's face and know she was "pure English." With this gesture, Davis tried to shift the logic of the case away from blood as the test to vision.[10] Davis mocked Mills's contention that Alice deceived Leonard and repeatedly offered to the jury a vivid comparison that resonated with early-twentieth-century white Americans: how could anyone believe that a "Chinaman" was "American," let alone that a black woman was white?

Davis's choice of this comparison reflected extant beliefs about the physical distinctiveness of race. In fact, only one month before the Rhinelander trial

Alice Jones Rhinelander and her sisters, Grace Miller (left) and Emily Brooks (right) seated in the courtroom. © Bettmann/Corbis.

Melville Herskovits wrote that the term "White Negroes" was as strange as a "Caucasian Chinaman." Herskovits's comment points out that just as many white Americans believed in strong differences between whites and blacks, so too did they believe that the differences between Asians and whites were unbridgeable. Only two years earlier the U.S. Supreme Court supported this conclusion when it found East Asians and others excluded from citizenship so racially different from white Americans that they could not assimilate into American society.[11]

Pursuing the theme of visible difference, Davis played up the visual aspects of race. Over and over again he asked Alice and her sisters (although not their parents) to stand up. Alice, Grace, and Emily took off their hats, waved their arms, and held up their hands in front of the jury at Davis's request. Davis did not need Elizabeth or George Jones to rise since the public (and presumably the jury) already identified them as white and black, and thus their identity did not remain open to question. Even though Leonard had testified that

George Jones had told him he was white, Davis's questions made that claim seem absurd.

After Leonard agreed that George Jones had told him he was English, Davis inquired whether Leonard had ever met any Englishmen, perhaps in his wealthy father's home. Leonard conceded that he knew what the English looked like. Davis then pounced: "And when Mr. Jones told you he was an Englishman you believed that he was pure English?" Again Leonard agreed. Then Leonard admitted he believed George Jones was an Englishman with jaundice. Davis asked, "Didn't it strike you that he had had that attack of jaundice for some time?" Of course, the subtext of all of Davis's questions was that a person could not be both English and colored, just as a person could not be both Chinese and American.[12]

The Jones daughters, as products of an interracial marriage, however, might have been more difficult to categorize than their father. Davis wanted to accustom the jury to seeing the Jones sisters as colored to remove any doubt that Leonard knew Alice's background. In this way, Davis reduced race to skin color (physical appearance) and conditioned the jury and others present in the courtroom to see the entire Jones family, except for Elizabeth Jones, as colored.[13]

Davis's deployment of visual difference to code racial identity seemed, in part, a reaction to the uncertainties offered by blood as a racial test. In Davis's opening statement, he remarked that "lineage" and "ancestry" might be indeterminable and consequently an insufficient basis to determine race. His use of race as a visible trait to defend Alice from Leonard's charges also found support in contemporary scientific theories about race. Many of the scientists who studied "mixed races" stressed physical features as a significant marker of racial difference.[14]

In 1925, Melville Herskovits argued that when scientists studied racial mixture, "the most outstanding trait to be studied is that of skin color." Only the previous year, Herskovits informed readers of *Opportunity* that although culture mattered in studying race, "when we discuss race, there is the physical basis that underlies all the other considerations." When Herskovits concluded his study of the "American Negro," he argued that skin color constituted a major difference between the American Negro and white Americans.[15] Herskovits also found that though the American Negro was of mixed race, the category was remarkably homogeneous. This homogeneity could be deduced from anthropometric measurements of physical features. Thus, he argued, the American Negro possessed a new physical form derived from the original features of Negroes, Indians, and whites. This new physical type differentiated all American Negroes from white Americans.[16]

Not only Herskovits focused on the relationship between race and physical appearance. In a December 1925 speech, renowned Harvard scientist E. A. Hooton elaborated the methods of racial analysis based on physical attributes. He observed that the term "race" possessed loose popular meanings expressed in phrases such as the "Jewish race" or the "Irish race." Hooton criticized these common understandings, declaring, "All anthropologists agree that the criteria of race are physical characters. The tests of racial distinction are the morphological and metrical variations of such bodily characters as hair, skin, nose, eyes, stature—differences in shape and proportion of the head, the trunk and the limbs."[17] Thus, differences in race could be seen and measured, and, implicitly, these purely visual markers served to define race.

Hooton's dismissal of popular racial categories like the "Irish race" or the "Jewish race" as imprecise accords with historian Matthew Jacobson's study of the "reconsolidation" of whiteness that began in the 1920s. By the twenties, according to Jacobson, the differences attributed to "ethnic whites" were no longer perceived visually as they had been in the past. Instead, ethnic difference became marked and perceived by differences in culture. All "whites" became gradually subsumed under the term "Caucasian." Consequently, visible markers of race began to differentiate only between the black and white races.[18] Thus, by 1931, even the *Journal of the American Medical Association* could give an answer suggesting clear-cut visual differences between black and white in response to a physician's request for advice on how to distinguish between a "white" child and an "apparently . . . Negro" child born to a white woman. The journal told the inquiring doctor that "skin color is the only reliable guide."[19]

During the trial, Davis played up every aspect of Leonard's actions before his marriage that revealed Leonard's opportunities to observe Alice's physical features. In particular, Davis made much of the fact that Leonard photographed Alice during their 1922 hotel stay. Leonard's possession of these pictures during his years apart from Alice seemed to Davis significant evidence that Leonard knew Alice's race before they wed. Davis's excessive interest in these particular photographs suggests that he believed the pictures exposed Alice's ancestry to any observer's eye.[20]

The belief that racial difference could be recorded in photographs found support in scientific studies that relied on photography to map out the boundary lines of race. In the mid-nineteenth century, Harvard scientist Louis

Agassiz asked a photographer to take daguerreotypes of slaves to examine racial difference. Later in the century, the British founder of eugenics, Francis Galton, created composite photographic portraits of racial types that he believed, as visual culture scholar Shawn Michelle Smith concludes, demonstrated "visual evidence of '*biological* essence.'"[21] Smith's study of photography and "visual culture" in the nineteenth century analyzes how scientific photographs, family portraits, and baby books helped to form racial identities. Americans used photography and other visual media to explore what different genders, races, and classes "look[ed] like," and their explorations shaped the ways that Americans read facial types. For many white middle-class Americans, images of the "others" in American society reflected the supremacy of white Americans in the country's racial hierarchy.[22]

In the late nineteenth and early twentieth centuries, white Americans often used photography to create demeaning stereotypes of African Americans, such as postcards depicting African American men as watermelon-carrying chicken thieves. Yet the creation of images denigrating African Americans did not pass without comment by African Americans. Indeed, such images were contested by those who, like W. E. B. DuBois, constructed photographic "counter-archives" to challenge prevailing views about race and "a long-standing tradition of scientific race photography." At the turn of the twentieth century, DuBois curated a photographic exhibit of African Americans for the 1900 Paris Exhibition that depicted an African American middle class in the South. DuBois's collection included a section titled "Types of American Negroes" that portrayed the wide variety of physical traits among those considered African American; it "highlight[ed] the paradoxes of racial classification in Jim Crow America."[23] Thus, well before the 1920s, photography had already served an important function in studies of race, in attempts both to fix rigid racial boundaries and to question them.

At least two studies of mixed-race persons undertaken in the 1920s used photographs to discuss visual aspects of race. Well-known eugenicist Charles B. Davenport and Caroline Bond Day, a Radcliffe College graduate who studied with E. A. Hooton, created separate "scientific archives" to explore racial mixture. Davenport wanted to study race mixing to demonstrate the resulting disharmonies. In contrast, Day's study of "Negro-White families" hoped to provide a positive portrayal of mixed-race persons, much like DuBois hoped to do with his 1900 exhibit.[24]

In 1926, when Charles Davenport and his associate, Morris Steggerda, received a grant to examined racial "crossing" in Jamaica, they assumed physical differences between races would be visible: "Certainly races of mankind differ in physical proportions, just as dogs do; and just as dogs differ in their instincts and capacity to take advantage of special training, so it would not be strange if humans differ in these respects."[25] To determine the racial identity of their Jamaican subjects, Davenport and Steggerda asked questions about genealogy, took physical measurements, and "gathered opinions of reliable persons concerning the color of the measured persons." In 1928, Steggerda described how he and Davenport divided their subjects into the categories of "Blacks," "Browns," and "Whites" based on observations and the opinions of teachers (a number of their subjects were children). Davenport and Steggerda also relied on photographs and focused on "physical evidence" to ascertain ancestry and determine that the disharmonies of racial crossing revealed themselves on the body. Their final report published in 1929 contained photographs so their readers could see for themselves.[26]

Like Davenport and Steggerda's report, Day's study of "Negro-White" families assumed that physical characteristics of race could be read on the body by most people. In much of her work published by the Division of Anthropology of Harvard University, Day emphasized a visual language to classify race. At the same time, however, Day's study also resonated with the racial language of blood. In the research Day undertook in the 1920s under the supervision of E. A. Hooton, she categorized her human subjects on the basis of quantities of "Negro," "Indian," and "white" blood to the degree of eighths and sixteenths. At times, Day yoked together the concepts of vision and blood to ascertain racial ancestry. In one discussion of her subjects, Day observed that people's skin color changed along with their hair "as [they] approach the European type. There are also certain group types which are recognizable as standard, namely mulattoes, quadroons, and octoroons." Nevertheless, in one chapter of Day's study, E. A. Hooton questioned the value of blood in thinking about race. Referring to the percentage of Day's subjects who considered themselves "pure Negroes," Hooton commented, "actually no one can know his exact racial composition, no matter how assiduously he may inquire into his pedigree. Sooner or later (and often sooner than later) one turns up an ancestor whose racial antecedents are dubious."[27] Such an argument echoed Lee Davis's claims about the fallibility of genealogy expressed in his opening statement to the jury.

After Day completed her preliminary discussion of race, she analyzed a series of photographic plates that depicted members of "Negro-White" families. The plates consisted of photographs arranged in the form of family trees with the oldest generation at the top of the page and the newest at the bottom. When Day discussed the plates, she interpreted the individual photographs and faces to find evidence of physical aspects of black, white, and Indian origins. In examining one photograph of a woman, Day contended that her subject, "unless scrutinized closely, has no appearance of Negro or Indian blood." Day's statement implied that her subject appeared white but that under "close scrutiny" her "Negro blood" might be perceived.[28]

Although Day evinced a great deal of certainty when she interpreted the photographs and assigned the subjects to racial categories, she acknowledged some doubts about the transparency of race in photography. In referring to a picture of one female subject, Day observed, "Beatrice has the most negroid nose of the five sisters figured, *if the photographs are to be trusted*." Despite her skepticism, Day's study presumed physical characteristics of race could be read on the face. At one point in her discussion, Day remarked that one subject possessed "Italian" features, although she neglected to describe them. Day assumed her readers would know what she meant. Notwithstanding Day's acceptance that physical markers of race could be seen in photographs, her study also suggested that at some point these markers disappeared. Day contended that in the case of octoroons, "I have been able so far to see no traces whatever of Negro admixture."[29]

Like the photographic archives created by Caroline Day and Charles Davenport for the scientific study of mixed race, newspaper photographs and other visual material produced during the Rhinelander trial helped to shape, and were shaped by, the visual language of race. Many of the tabloids lavishly illustrated their reports on Leonard and Alice Rhinelander with photographs of the participants and the crowds. One critic of the tabloids argued that their success depended on their use of pictures: "Because pictures don't lie. Or at least the boob doesn't think they lie. He no longer believes anything he *reads* in the newspapers, but he believes everything he *sees*." Yet what people saw was already shaped by earlier photographs and other visual representations of African Americans and race. In 1924, the *Messenger* criticized the newspapers and tabloids for depicting African Americans in photographs as "buffoons, clowns, criminals." DuBois had also criticized white photographers for not knowing how to properly photograph colored skin.[30]

Throughout the Rhinelander trial, the *Daily News*, "New York's Picture Newspaper," printed small portraits of the lawyers, witnesses, and other participants. Even the *New York Times* published pictures of the Rhinelanders in their rotogravure section. These photographs gave those readers who could not attend the Westchester trial a way to visualize the trial's cast of characters.[31] Their vision, however, might be shaped by the accompanying text.

As early as 14 November 1924, the day news of the Rhinelander wedding first reached the front pages of the New York City press, the first photographic image of Alice Jones Rhinelander helped define the story of the marriage. In its late afternoon edition, the *Daily News* pulled off a journalistic coup by offering their readers a full, front-page portrait of Alice Jones Rhinelander. The photograph emphasized Alice's face; she appeared to look straight at the reader. New Yorkers would see this picture immediately when they came across this edition of the paper on newspaper stands. The positioning of the picture invited readers to look closely at Alice. But the *Daily News* left nothing to the imagination with the headline "HIS COLORED BRIDE."[32]

Despite the explicit front-page characterization of Alice as colored the text in the *Daily News* provided inconsistent and contradictory descriptions of Alice. Earlier that day, before the publication of the photograph, the paper claimed Alice had a "light complexion." The edition that featured the photograph described Alice as "extremely dark." Yet one year later, the same reporter who had characterized Alice as "extremely dark," Grace Robinson, described Alice as "white-skinned." Other newspapers had similar difficulties trying to fix racial identity through visual markers and photographs: a day before the trial began in 1925, the *Evening Journal* published a photograph of Alice's father and asked the reader whether George Jones was white or black.[33]

During the trial, questions of how to tell black from white surfaced constantly in press accounts. Reporters often wrote about the physical appearance of Alice and her family. On the first day of the trial, the *New York Herald Tribune* presented to its readers a detailed account of Alice's appearance: Alice wore "a dark satin hat pulled down close about her dusky face, a maroon coat trimmed with what the fashion experts described as either imitation fox or imitation wolf; sand-colored stockings and black shoes. . . . Around her throat was a circlet of pearls which the fashion experts avowed were imitation also." The use of the word "dusky" to describe Alice's skin color hinted at the ambiguities of Alice's identity, while the attribution of the term "imitation" to describe her fur trim and pearls alluded the sense that Alice was trying to be something she was not.[34]

While some newspapers' photographs hinted at the uncertainties of race and class, others seemed to signal a serious interest in demarcating sharp boundary lines between racial categories. Some papers published photographic series resembling photographic archives generated for scientific research. Only two days into the trial, the *Evening Journal* printed on its front page a photomontage composed of three portraits of Alice next to three portraits of Leonard. Tightly focused on the faces of the wedded couple, the photographs invited readers to examine and compare Alice and Leonard's physical features. Yet, like its competitor the *Daily News*, the *Evening Journal* did not leave its readers without cues to inform their analysis: Alice was the "Colored Wife," while Leonard was the "Rich Youth," obviously white.[35]

Although photography offered the promise that it could reflect ancestry and thus race truthfully, at least one incident during the trial suggested pictures might be untrustworthy. During the trial, the *Daily Mirror* reported the rumor that the Jones home contained a portrait of George Jones as a white man. In reference to this picture, Isaac Mills informed the press that his investigators determined that "for many years the Jones family pretended to be whites. I was not at all surprised to learn that such a photograph was on exhibition in their parlor. It was there for the obvious purpose of deceiving persons who visited that house." Since the *Mirror* believed this photograph might prove important, it re-created it for their readers. The *Mirror* published two side-by-side pictures of George Jones: one labeled a "regular photo" of Jones and the other described as a "retouched photo showing him as he would look if white."[36]

Although Lee Parsons Davis introduced a number of photographs into evidence, he did not remain content to rely solely on pictures to prove his contention of the visibility of race. Instead, on the afternoon of Monday, 23 November, three days before Thanksgiving, Davis returned to the subject of Alice's skin color, Leonard's claim that Alice had passed, and Leonard's eyesight. After asking Leonard about all three, Davis surprised the courtroom when he announced, "I desire to have Mrs. Rhinelander brought in here, and I am going to request that this courtroom be further cleared, because I am going to ask this witness to identify the color of her skin." With this declaration, Lee Davis brought to the fore his major line of defense for Alice. Day after day Davis's cross-examination of Leonard had repeatedly hammered one point: Leonard could not have been misled about Alice's ancestry; her face and body revealed it to anyone who looked. Now Davis wanted Leonard to look at Alice at the same time the jury did and then answer the critical question: what color is she? At that moment, the twelve men on the jury with their own eyes would know whether Alice deceived Leonard.[37]

While Davis based his defense of Alice on the visibility of race, at times he entertained some unease about the absolute persuasiveness of vision to determine race. If, as Davis implied, race marked the body's surface, on faces, hands, and arms, which everyone in the courtroom had already seen, what else could Alice reveal to the jury? Perhaps the jury thought Alice used makeup or powder to lighten her complexion. The marriage bureau clerk in October 1924 thought she was white. Yet Davis's request indicated that even if Leonard somehow missed the elements of race on Alice's face and arms, or even if they were disguised, he could not have missed them on the parts of her body covered in public.[38]

Given the vogue for tanning sweeping white America in the twenties, the unveiling of parts of the body unexposed to sunlight could prove necessary to make sure the differences between a tanned white skin and colored skin could be distinguished. During the trial, Davis even asked Leonard whether he thought Grace Jones was a tanned white woman when they first met. Scientific studies of mixed-race groups that focused on skin color as a marker of race often cited examinations of particular areas of skin on the human body unexposed to sunlight. Scientists claimed these portions of the skin would reveal the true nature of the skin's color and thus racial identity.[39]

Immediately after Davis proposed that Leonard and the jury view the defendant in private, Isaac Mills jumped to his feet and objected. "There is no warrant for that whatever. He has had this Jones family—I don't mean to use any disrespectful term—he has had them stand up a dozen times in court and had the jury look at them, and had the witness look at them and answer. Now, the proposition to exhibit the naked body of this girl to this jury is not competent." Justice Morschauser told Mills that Davis could not display Alice completely naked to the jury but agreed to let the jury take a closer look at her. In agreeing to Davis's proposal, Justice Morschauser indicated he felt the question of Alice's racial identity and whether Leonard knew it before they married remained open. Morschauser took into account that Alice's body was covered in the courtroom and that the purpose of Davis's proceeding would be to determine "whether [Leonard] ought to have known that she was of colored blood and was justified in believing that when he saw her body." Morschauser added, "I don't know what her body is going to be." Alice's body would show the judge and jury whether Leonard had any reason to believe she was white.[40]

After Morschauser ruled Davis could exhibit Alice's body to the jury, he and the attorneys argued over how to proceed. Davis recommended they relocate to the judge's chambers. Justice Morschauser agreed that Alice should be displayed outside the courtroom, since the proceeding "may be embarrassing to the young lady," and he proposed to move into the jury room (an all-male and all-white space). Morschauser suggested that the court stenographer, Mills, and Davis accompany the jury. Davis reminded the judge Leonard needed to go along too.[41]

Once it became clear that Davis's proposal would go ahead, Mills sputtered, "You go through the farce of exposing her body and asking him if she is the girl. What a ridiculous thing that is! Is there any possible question about it? He has been asked to look at her a dozen times in Court." He declared, "It is an indecent proceeding your Honor." Morschauser replied, "I doubt that it is an indecent proceeding to let them look at her back." Quickly Davis expanded the list of body parts and added, "I am only going to let them look at her upper body and lower limbs." In vain, Mills continued to argue that, of course, Leonard could identify Alice as Alice; he already admitted he saw her naked at the hotel.[42] But whether Leonard could identify Alice was not the point; instead, the question was, what would the jury see on Alice in private that they could not see in open court?

Davis's request clearly startled Leonard's lawyers. It also proved unusual because it tampered with regular courtroom procedure. During a jury trial, a lawyer's ability to tell his client's story is constrained by the rules of procedure applicable in the courtroom. When Davis asked the judge to halt the trial to exhibit Alice to the jury, he was in the middle of his cross-examination of Leonard. Mills had not finished presenting Leonard's case to the jury. He still had additional witnesses he planned to call to support Leonard's case. At this point in the trial, the rules of procedure prevented the defense from offering its own witnesses. Davis could not call Alice yet to testify as a witness in her own behalf.[43]

During the cross-examination of a witness, however, a lawyer can offer letters, documents, or other physical evidence, i.e., "real evidence," to contradict or discredit the witness on the stand. Davis planned to use Alice as "real evidence." Early-twentieth-century legal scholars defined such evidence as that "acquired directly by the court or jury themselves, through the medium of their own senses, by an inspection of the subject-matter itself." One legal treatise described real evidence as "the tribunal's own view of a thing shown to it." Under the laws of evidence, real evidence could be introduced by lawyers in both civil and criminal cases. Examples of real evidence introduced in civil cases included real estate or the injured portions of a person's body in a personal injury lawsuit. In criminal cases, the female victim of a rape case might be presented as real evidence if a question existed about whether she was under the age of consent. Presiding judges had the discretion to decide whether or not to allow a jury to see real evidence. Since real evidence was believed to constitute "the most natural and most efficient" kind of evidence, judges often allowed a visual inspection to proceed.[44] During this exhibition, Alice would not be permitted to testify. Instead she would stand as silent evidence to be inspected by the jury.

In calling for Alice to be displayed before the jury, Davis continued the process he had already begun, of transforming her, at least partly, from a married woman into an inanimate object, a "thing" to be "shown" (Davis had already had her display parts of herself while in open court). This status was confirmed by Justice Morschauser's reference to Alice's body as "it" several times during the lawyers' argument over whether to allow the display. By reducing his client to the status of an object to be viewed by the jury, Davis offered Alice herself as the "most natural and efficient" and primary evidence to contradict Leonard's testimony that he never realized she was colored. As an astute attorney, Davis must have known that most experts on evidence believed real evidence was "entitled to the greatest weight" when the decider of facts (in this case, the jury) assessed the value of the evidence introduced at trial.[45]

Davis calculated that the jury would agree with him that Alice's race revealed itself on her body. The jurors' use of their own senses would outweigh the other forms of evidence brought in during the annulment trial. Although a risky tactic, and one that seemed to betray his client's best interest, Davis's move made sense. The *Evening Journal* agreed that the "negro features and pigmented skin of Mrs. Rhinelander's colored relatives, will provide mute corroboration of their testimony that only a blind man could have failed to know Alice came of a family of negroes."[46] Davis arranged this "mute corroboration" to win over the jury because the evidentiary proof so far introduced during the trial appeared inconclusive on the question of whether Alice deceived Leonard. Davis chose this point in the trial to escalate his reliance on the visibility of race to win Alice's case.

This moment proved crucial: the contest between blood and vision reached its peak. Mills's repeated objections underscored the competing ideologies of race embedded in the lawyers' legal strategies. Since Mills argued that race equaled blood, which could be revealed through character, he could not agree to Davis's strategy to let the jurors categorize Alice by race through the use of their own eyes. When Justice Morschauser again confirmed his decision to allow Davis to continue and observed, "There is no evidence of what her condition is to the eye—whether it is dark or light. And for that limited purpose it may be received," he suggested the still uncertain answer to the question of how to ascertain race.[47]

Other courts had grappled with this question before, though few in the North. During the era of slavery, some slaves challenged their status as chattel in southern courtrooms by claiming they were white. Southern antebellum courts relied on three possible avenues to determine racial ancestry: they might explore a person's "personal history," apply the standards of racial science, or evaluate a person's "performance" of whiteness. The ability to "perform whiteness" required "doing the things a white man or woman did." Someone who claimed to be white might also be exhibited to the jury.[48]

Even after slavery ended, southern courts still found themselves in the business of making racial determinations. Prosecutors in miscegenation cases might offer to "make profert of the person" to support their claims. At the end of the nineteenth and in the early twentieth centuries, the Alabama Supreme Court agreed prosecutors might "make profert of the person" to determine identity in cases of interracial adultery when the race of one defendant seemed too indeterminate for conviction. In 1890, an Alabama jury inspected a man to determine whether he was a Negro. In a similar case eighteen years later in which a female defendant had been accused of being a prostitute, the prosecution needed to determine whether she was white. The convictions for miscegenation in both cases indicate that juries felt they could see race when they examined the defendants. Even in the 1920s, Alabama courts confirmed that making profert of a person to determine his or her race was appropriate.[49]

Only a few years before the Rhinelanders battled over their marriage, the U.S. Supreme Court issued major decisions on naturalization where a unanimous Court offered a test to prove racial ancestry. Federal law provided that only "free white persons" and "aliens of African nativity" or "persons of African descent" could become naturalized citizens. Few immigrants claimed African ancestors or African nativity, so most immigrants claimed the status of "free white persons" to achieve citizenship. Federal courts, therefore, needed to determine who counted as a white person for these purposes and drew on two strands of thought: scientific theories of race and "common knowledge."[50] Until the early twentieth century, courts would reach similar decisions regardless of which idea guided their reasoning. By the 1910s, however, the developing science of race began to contradict common knowledge. Therefore, determinations of whether different people from the same country or ancestral group were white might differ, depending on the federal court hearing the case and which test applied.[51]

These contradictions came to a head in the 1920s, when the Supreme Court issued two important rulings on whiteness and citizenship. In the 1922 case of *Ozawa v. United States*, the Supreme Court had to decide the eligibility for citizenship of Takao Ozawa, a person of the "Japanese race" born in Japan. According to the Supreme Court, federal naturalization law intended to "confer the privilege of citizenship upon that class of persons whom the [Founding] fathers knew as white, and to deny it to all who could not be so classified." To determine who fell into this category of "white," the Supreme Court sifted through a number of tests and rejected one after another. Finally, they turned to science and common knowledge for help. The Court held that "white persons" were members of "what is popularly known as the Caucasian race," so it determined that Ozawa did not fall under the rubric of "white person." The Japanese could not be "Caucasians," a finding supported by science; therefore, they were not white persons entitled to American citizenship.[52]

In determining that a Japanese person could not be Caucasian, the Supreme Court rejected the test of color to determine Ozawa's whiteness. Ozawa had argued that his white complexion made him white. The Court argued that skin color alone could not determine race because color might vary too greatly even among members of the same race. Indeed, the Supreme Court observed there might be a great deal of variation in skin color "even among Anglo-Saxons, ranging from imperceptible gradations from the fairer blond to the swarthy brunette, the latter being darker than many of the lighter hued persons of the brown or yellow races." Consequently, the justices suggested the test of color would "result in a confused overlapping of races and a gradual merging of one into the other, with out any practical line of separation." In an era when sociologists like Edward Reuter suggested that American whites had started to darken, leading to blurred lines between black and white, and white supremacists like Madison Grant feared mongrelization, the Supreme Court's reasons for why the skin color test would not work were troublesome.[53]

Despite the Supreme Court's attempt in *Ozawa* to establish a definitive rule for determining naturalization cases, only three months later it found itself presented with a case in which science seemed the problem instead of the solution. In *United States v. Thind*, Bhagat Singh Thind, a "high caste Indian of full Indian blood," claimed he was "Aryan" and thus "Caucasian." Consequently, Thind argued he could become an American citizen. In the face of a brown-skinned Hindu claiming to belong to the scientific category of "Caucasian" and therefore white, the Supreme Court balked and abandoned scientific tests. The Court hastily maintained that scientific definitions of "Caucasian" were much too broad and included too many groups (the "Polynesians," the "Hamites of Africa") who would not be popularly considered "Caucasian." "We venture to think that the average well informed white American would learn with some degree of astonishment that the race to which he belongs is made up of such heterogeneous elements." Therefore, the Court offered a new test to determine who could be a "white person."[54]

The Supreme Court's new test for whiteness proposed that "the words 'free white persons' are words of common speech, to be interpreted in accordance with the understandings of the common man." The Supreme Court dismissed the "speculations of the ethnologists" and went so far as to argue that "it is a matter of *familiar observation and knowledge* that the physical group characteristics of the Hindus render them readily distinguishable from the various groups of persons in this country commonly recognized as white."[55] Since Hindus do not "look" white and their physical being demonstrates their "racial difference," Bhagat Singh Thind could not be a "white person." Thus by 1924, the Supreme Court offered the test of common knowledge about race and "physical group characteristics" to determine the content of whiteness for naturalization.[56]

By displaying Alice to the jury, Davis relied on a similar "common sense" concept of race, assuming the jury would draw on "familiar observation and knowledge" to confirm both Alice's ancestry and that Leonard must have known of that ancestry. The standards to determine racial ancestry in antebellum cases and in the South no longer seemed applicable. Examining Alice's "personal history" did not seem conclusive in an era and location where family history might get lost. After all, New York wasn't Virginia, where the state registrars could review records dating back to slavery to ascertain ancestry. Applying the current standards of science might not work either, according to the Supreme Court, or it might just point to visible markers as the determinant of difference. Looking to see whether someone could "perform" whiteness might not work in an era when the "mongrelization" of American culture meant that so-called white women danced to jazz, displayed tanned, brown skin, or used Harlem slang just as much as African American women did.

Justice Morschauser suggested Alice's mother accompany her into the jury room so there would be another woman present. Davis agreed to hold his questions for Leonard until they returned to the courtroom. The court stenographer reported what happened next:

> The Court, Mr. Mills, Mr. Davis, Mr. Swinburne, the jury, the plaintiff, the defendant, her mother, Mrs. George Jones, and the stenographer left the courtroom and entered the jury room. The defendant and Mrs. Jones then withdrew to the lavatory adjoining the jury room and, after a short time, again entered the jury room. The defendant, who was weeping, had on her underwear and a long coat. At Mr. Davis [sic] direction she let down the coat, so that the upper portion of her body, as far down as the breast was exposed. She then, again at Mr. Davis' direction, covered the upper part of her body and showed to the jury her bare legs, up as far as the knees.

When Davis finished, Justice Morschauser, the attorneys, the stenographer, the jury, and Leonard returned to the courtroom. Alice and her mother did not do so.[57]

Once back in court, Davis began to ask Leonard whether he had just seen his wife's upper body. Before Leonard could answer, Mills interrupted to demand the trial record properly reflect the proceedings in the jury room. Mills requested that the record indicate Alice's "back, breast and legs to just above the knee" had been exhibited in the jury room. Once the court stenographer adjusted the record, Davis asked Leonard whether he had seen those parts of Alice's body in the jury room. Leonard responded that he saw only Alice's back and chest, not her legs. Then Davis asked the critical question he had been leading up to throughout the trial, the question that pitted Leonard's vision of Alice against the perception of the jurors: "Your wife's body is the same shade as it was when you saw her in the Marie Antoinette with all of her clothing removed?" Without any hesitation, Leonard agreed, and on that point Davis ended his cross-examination.[58]

New York's press greeted the news of Davis's exhibition of Alice's body with an outburst of comments on its significance. The *Daily Mirror* characterized the display as a "coup" because Davis showed the jury that Alice's "color precludes the possibility of Kip's contention that when he married Alice Jones he thought her white." Grace Robinson assured her readers, "The examination, horrible as it was, was vital to the presentation of her case. For the Alice that the jurors saw was dark—so dark that even the most unscientific observer must have said she was undoubtedly colored." Since Justice Morschauser did not allow reporters into the jury room, Robinson's claim that Alice's body revealed she was "undoubtedly colored" must have been shaped by Davis's strategy (as well as the previous reports and photographs in the press) to make sure everyone saw Alice as "dark."[59]

Earlier historical understandings of race, especially superstitions that race left particular signs on even a passing body (a half moon on the nails or spots on the back), were also echoed in Robinson's report. Indeed the *Evening Journal* understood that Alice "partly disrobed" to "further the contention of her counsel that Leonard Kip Rhinelander could not have been deceived as to her negro blood."[60] So convinced that Davis had exposed Alice's true racial ancestry, Grace Robinson informed her readers that not only Alice's skin color but her body parts told the tale. "Her back, especially, was a near ebony, being several shades darker than her face, which rouged and powdered, at times presented a latin aspect." Robinson asserted that Davis correctly thought some people believed Alice used enough makeup on her face to effectively hide her racial origins. The *Evening Journal* made a similar point when it suggested that "darker than the girl's face is her body and limbs, for her countenance has been made paler by years of continuous bleaching with acidulous lotions." But Grace Robinson also pointed to other portions of Alice's body as racial markers: "The breasts, indisputable evidence of negro origin, were obviously those of a colored woman." Although Robinson identified Alice's breasts as definitely those of a "colored woman," she did not let her readers know what about Alice's breasts gave that away. As far as Robinson was concerned, even though she did not see Alice in the jury room, Alice's back and breasts betrayed her as colored.[61]

Not everyone agreed that Davis had changed the course of the trial. At least one reporter from the *Evening Journal* sniffed that the procedure did not reveal anything beyond what could be seen every day in court. The reporter could not understand the fuss since Alice's "long thin arms and hands, which are every day revealed by her short-sleeved gown could scarcely be considered as characteristic of even a well-tanned Caucasian."[62] Yet displaying Alice's flesh to the jurors might have succeeded in finally pinning down Alice's racial ancestry, even for the larger public, which may have still entertained some questions.

It took the work of New York's most sensational tabloid to reveal inadvertently both the effectiveness and the absurdity of Davis's method of determining race. The editors of the outrageous tabloid the *New York Evening Graphic*, realized that since no newspaper could photograph the display of Alice's body, any New Yorkers hungry for physical evidence of Alice's identity had nothing to look at on the front pages of the *Daily News* and other papers. Consequently, the *Graphic*'s art department reconstructed the scene by creating a composite photograph based on previously taken pictures of the trial's participants. The *Graphic*'s so-called composograph featured a half-nude Alice Rhinelander in front of her husband, the lawyers, the judge, and her mother with the caption, "Alice Disrobes in Court to Keep Her Husband." Not surprisingly for the *Graphic* (referred to by its critics as the *Pornographic*), the paper sexualized the scene when it showed Alice in a scanty slip instead of the lowered coat described by the court stenographer.[63]

The very term "composograph" evoked eugenics' founder Francis Galton's composite photographs of racial types and linked the function of Galton's photos to demarcate the visual markers of race with the racial shaping of the *Graphic*'s composite photograph. Although the art department used previously taken photos of people like Isaac Mills and Elizabeth Jones, the *Graphic* hired a white "showgirl" as a body double for Alice. Then the *Graphic* tinted the showgirl's photo to "give the effect of a light-colored girl." This tinting so effectively created the illusion of race that, according to one source, the showgirl sued the *Graphic* because she feared her appearance in the photograph might taint her as colored.[64]

After the dramatic unveiling of Alice's body to the jury and in the press, Isaac Mills attempted to repair the damage inflicted by Davis on Leonard's case. Mills tried to reorient the discussion to his ideas about blood as race. When Mills conducted his redirect examination of Leonard, he brought in additional evidence to buttress his conception of blood as race. He even brought in additional witnesses to corroborate Leonard's claim that Alice passed as white. Mills returned Leonard to the stand and drew Leonard's attention back to the last letter read by Davis into evidence, the infamous Exhibit M. Mills asked Leonard why he did "that thing." Leonard told Mills he acted at Alice's request and in this way portrayed Alice as the initiator of perverse sexual activities.[65]

Mills followed up with other questions all designed to focus on Alice as the expert on sexuality and the seducer of the more innocent Leonard. Mills's questions emphasized Alice's knowledge of contraceptives and abortions. Mills even tried to get Leonard to testify about Alice's sister Grace's sexual life. Mills wanted Leonard to tell the jury his married friend Carl had told him he had sex with Grace the day they met in 1921. Mills hoped this information would confirm his argument that the Jones girls were sexually

New York Evening Graphic's composite photograph "Alice Disrobes in Court to Keep Her Husband," published 25 November 1925.

loose and promiscuous colored girls on the make for white men. Davis, however, objected to such testimony as hearsay, and Justice Morschauser refused to allow Mills to pursue the subject. Davis complained out loud about Mills trying to "drag" Grace through the "mire" as he had Alice and declared, "There was never any necessity for all this filth." Mills, however, replied, "Oh yes, it is absolutely competent." In his mind, the Jones daughters' behavior reflected their racial ancestry.[66]

After Mills tried unsuccessfully to get additional evidence about Alice's character as a reflection of her ancestry into the testimony, he presented two witnesses who described how Alice lied to them about her race. Joseph and Miriam Rich, a couple from the town of Mount Vernon, had become friendly with Leonard and Alice after Leonard returned to New York from Arizona. Joseph, a furniture salesman, first met Leonard and Alice in the summer of 1924 when Leonard bought bedroom furniture. A few months later, Joseph and his wife invited the now-married Rhinelanders to their home for dinner. The two couples even ventured into Manhattan to catch the Marx Brothers show "I'll Say She Is" and eat dinner. Both Riches told the court that Alice claimed Spanish ancestry to explain away her complexion when Miriam questioned Alice about why she wore a long-sleeved dress while Mrs. Rich showed up in an evening dress. Clearly, Mrs. Rich had expected that spending time with the Rhinelanders meant a sophisticated society evening, though the foursome ended up at an inexpensive "chop suey" restaurant.[67]

Mills questioned both Mr. and Mrs. Rich about Alice's stay at their home in November 1924 after Leon Jacobs had taken Leonard away from the Joneses. The Riches testified that they had spoken to Alice about the reports in the press about her color. Joseph Rich recalled that Alice told them she would spend "every dollar that her father had" to sue the papers for calling her colored. Joseph and Miriam Rich also testified that Alice claimed to be English "of Spanish descent." Rich said Alice let them know that she had told Leonard she was white. He remembered Alice recalling how Leonard would "rather marry an Indian than a negress." Alice also told the Riches that Leonard let her know he "would stick to her" if she could prove her whiteness.[68]

When Davis stood up to cross-examine Joseph Rich he needed to discredit him, and, as he had done with Leonard throughout the trial, Davis focused his questions on how the Riches could have been deceived by Alice since her race was so obvious. In response to Davis's queries, Joseph Rich admitted his eyesight was fine. When Davis asked about the evening with the Rhinelanders in a Chinese restaurant he inquired about Joseph Rich's ability to see Alice. Rich agreed with Davis he could see Alice was "dark" in the restaurant. Rich added, however, "She is darker today than she was then." At this pronouncement, the spectators in the courtroom burst into laughter. An angry Justice Morschauser declared, "I will have to clear the room unless you stop your giggling. If you do not do it you will have to leave the court room. If this happens once more, fair warning to you, out you go." After this reproving statement from the judge, Davis asked Alice, who had returned to the courtroom, to stand up and take off her hat. Then Davis asked Rich whether he could see Alice "clearly" and whether she looked darker now. Rich maintained that she did so. Davis next asked whether the lights had been on in the "chop suey" restaurant; Rich could not remember. Rich then piped up that one reason Alice might be darker in court was because she felt nervous, "just the same as I am." He thought Alice had worn powder on her face though none on her hands when they first met. Rich kept insisting that Alice really appeared darker in court than when she stayed in his home, although he could not quantify how much darker.[69]

By this point, Rich may have been embarrassed that he and his wife, who had aspirations to boost their social status by associating with the Rhinelanders, had hurt their standing by hosting a colored woman in their home. The Riches had hoped to pursue a close friendship with Leonard and Alice. Even after Leonard left Alice, the Riches attended a dinner at the Joneses' home in December 1924 and claimed to have eaten with twenty white people, including Alice's father. Miriam Rich testified that she thought George Jones was either English or perhaps Spanish because he spoke with an English accent and dropped his "h's." Indeed, when Davis cross-examined Miriam Rich, she claimed she felt humiliated because others laughed at her for believing Alice was white. Her husband claimed George Jones, like his daughter Alice, appeared darker in court.[70]

The Riches turned out to be Leonard's last witnesses. Now attention turned to the defense. With the eyes of the courtroom spectators upon him, Davis stood up and opened his defense of Alice Jones Rhinelander. Many in the courtroom, as well as frustrated seekers of seats left outside to wait, expected Davis to call Alice as the first witness. Davis, however, disappointed the crowd when he informed Justice Morschauser his client had suffered a breakdown in the aftermath of the events of the preceding day and needed a break. Davis announced that he was prepared to continue without her. Although Davis had scored points with his display of Alice's body, he planned to present a few witnesses to bolster his argument that no one could believe Alice was a white woman.

Reflecting the critical role the press had played so far in the Rhinelander's married life, Davis chose as his first witness Barbara Reynolds, a Westchester reporter. Reynolds told the jury about her interview with Leonard the day the story of his marriage broke when he revealed he knew he had married the daughter of a colored man. Unable to contradict Reynolds's damaging testimony or to destroy her credibility, Isaac Mills was reduced to asking her whether she was a married woman and her husband's name.[71]

Davis then chose to call a hostile witness to the stand: Leonard's attorney, Leon Jacobs. Under Davis's grilling, Jacobs admitted he worked as a lawyer in an office surrounded by offices for different Rhinelander family interests. On cross-examination by Mills, Jacobs described himself as the manager of properties in different Rhinelander family corporations. In response to Mills's friendly questioning, Jacobs denied acting as Philip Rhinelander's personal attorney, though he started to work for Leonard in the spring 1924. Although Davis could not conclusively demonstrate that Jacobs, as Philip Rhinelander's agent, had initiated Leonard's annulment lawsuit, Jacobs's testimony revealed a very close relationship between the lawyer and the Rhinelander family's valuable property holdings.[72]

After Jacobs stepped down from the witness chair, Davis called the first member of the Jones family to the stand: Emily Jones's husband, Robert Brooks, the so-called colored butler. Davis began his questioning by asking whether Brooks "was of colored blood." Brooks said yes. In response to Davis's inquiries about his relationship with Leonard Rhinelander, Brooks recalled meeting Leonard in 1921. Over time, Leonard began to call him "Bob" and Robert Brooks called him "Leonard." He could not remember a time when Leonard objected to his "color." Indeed, Robert described Leonard and Alice dining with the Brookses and playing with Roberta, Alice's young niece. Leonard even played poker with Brooks and his friends. Brooks also declared, "All of my friends are colored."[73]

After Davis finished with Brooks, it became evident that the attorney would not continue that day since Alice could not or would not testify. When Morschauser began to adjourn court until the next morning, Mills chose this point in the trial to change his tactics. He stood up and made a motion to amend Leonard's pleadings with a new charge against Alice. Leonard's existing complaint alleged Alice had deceived Leonard when she called herself white. Now Mills asked Justice Morschauser to add in a new assertion that Alice "concealed" her "colored blood" from Leonard. Mills argued Alice had a *duty* to tell Leonard because he had no other way to know her blood. Mills's new claim implied that Alice's racial identity could not be seen. Such a claim flew in the face of the assumptions that supported Davis's unveiling of his client's body the day before, which suggested that nothing had been concealed. Mills's efforts at this late date in the trial may have reflected a sense of desperation on the part of Leonard's lawyers, who most likely worried that the previous day's exhibition might lead to their loss of the case. In addition, Mills's argument that Alice had a duty to tell Leonard before they wed underscored Mills's argument that race should be considered a material fact to know before marriage.[74]

Not surprisingly, Davis opposed Mills's motion. He spluttered, "First they said she said too much and now she didn't say enough." Mills retorted that the jury could determine whether Alice had deceived Leonard by maintaining silence about her color. Justice Morschauser allowed Mills to amend Leonard's complaint. Mills may not have cleared this change with Leonard. When

Davis later recalled Leonard to the stand to question him about his new claim that Alice kept silent, Leonard still maintained she told him she was white.[75]

Despite Mills's success in adding in a new charge against Alice, Davis doggedly pursued his strategy to mark Alice's ancestry as visible to the eye. On Wednesday morning, he called to the stand the physician who treated Alice for the flu in 1922. During his testimony, Dr. Caesar McClendon recalled that he frequently saw a white man—Leonard Rhinelander—in the Joneses home. Davis then asked, "Now, for the purpose of the record, it is necessary for me to ask you, are you a colored man?" McClendon assented to that description. At that point, Justice Morschauser interjected, "Following that up, don't you think the record ought to show how he appears? He can describe himself." Davis commented that no one in the room could doubt Dr. McClendon was a colored man, adding, "I suppose Judge Mills will concede that clearly in appearance he is a colored man." Mills agreed. When Davis observed that McClendon was "of dark face," Mills interjected, "Of dark face. Darker than Mr. Jones." Once the judge, Mills, and Davis had settled on Dr. McClendon's color, Davis asked the doctor to give his opinion about Alice's body. Dr. McClendon informed Davis and the court that Alice's body had a "dark complexion," almost as dark as his.[76]

After Dr. McClendon stepped down from the witness chair, Emily Brooks, Alice's oldest sister, was sworn in. Under Davis's questioning, Emily recalled meeting Leonard well before he wed Alice. She told Davis about the times Leonard joined the Brookses for dinner in their living quarters above a garage next to the home of the family that employed her husband as their butler. In response to a question about her ancestry, Emily told the jury that she was aware of her "colored blood." On cross-examination, Mills tried to raise doubts about the Joneses' openness about their ancestry. He asked Emily a number of questions about her daughter Roberta and learned Roberta had auburn hair and attended a white Sunday school. Although Emily Brooks readily agreed with the depiction of herself as a colored woman, Justice Morschauser interrupted Mills's cross: "I would like to have the record show, if you want to, as to her color. That is, if you want to. We haven't anything on the record. We can get something on. Perhaps we can describe it better than she can." Justice Morschauser's comments revealed he accepted the "common sense" view that color and racial ancestry could be seen. Yet some uncertainty must have lingered in Morschauser's mind if he believed Dr. McClendon could describe himself accurately but Emily Brooks might not. Perhaps like her sister, Emily was only able to stand silently and let others assess her color.⁷⁷

Davis tried to describe Emily's color. Yet after asking Emily to remove her hat, Davis admitted he could not. Despite his action the previous day to show his client's body to the jury to stress the obviousness of color, in the face of trying to find words to describe Emily Brooks, Davis came up wanting. At this point, Mills suggested the jury could see her themselves and Davis pointed out that Emily's photograph had already been introduced as evidence.⁷⁸

Once Emily Brooks finished, Davis called her youngest sister, Grace Jones Miller, to the stand. Immediately, Davis asked her to remove her hat and then asked whether she knew she had colored blood. Grace acknowledged she knew about her colored blood and, in response to Davis's questions, gave her version of how she met Leonard back in 1921. On cross-examination, Mills aimed to show that Grace schemed to marry a white man. He also asked her how she ended up described as "white" on her marriage license. Like Alice, Grace was designated "white" by a county clerk who perceived her as such because she was accompanied by a white fiancé. Mills also insinuated that Grace had undergone an abortion after Carl Kreitler, Leonard's electrician friend, impregnated her. Grace denied it.⁷⁹

After Grace left the stand, Davis continued calling members of the Jones family and requested that Alice's mother testify about her husband's ancestry and Alice's color. Speaking with an English accent, Elizabeth Jones affirmed that her great-grandparents and grandparents were "pure white English stock." When Davis questioned her about her marriage to George Jones, Elizabeth told Davis she knew George Jones was colored when they wed. According to her, George Jones did not mind the label "colored" but did not want to be referred to as a "negro." It is difficult to know what exactly Elizabeth's husband meant when he accepted the terminology of "colored" but rejected "Negro." In Great Britain, the term "coloured" encompassed people with African, West Indian, South Asian, or Arab ancestry.⁸⁰

Elizabeth Jones's matter-of-fact discussion of her marriage to a colored man suggests that at the time of her wedding to George Jones in Yorkshire, the (non-colored) English did not perceive such marriages to be as threatening as white Americans believed interracial marriages were in the 1920s. Unlike the many states in the United States that enacted antimiscegenation laws, Great Britain never outlawed interracial marriage. By the time Elizabeth and George wed in 1890, persons of African descent had made a home in England for at least three centuries, though never in large numbers. In the nineteenth century, blacks in Great Britain lived in urban areas but also in more rural areas, as did George Jones, who met his wife when they both worked as servants on the same country estate. Consequently, although the England of George and Elizabeth Jones in no way resembled an egalitarian Eden, ideas about race and racism did not operate in the same way as in the United States.[81]

At times speaking in a voice so quiet that the judge urged her to speak up, Elizabeth Jones defended her daughter from Leonard's claim that she passed as white. She contradicted Leonard's testimony that he questioned Alice about color in her presence. Mrs. Jones also testified that she never heard Alice tell Leonard she was white. Nor did she ever hear George Jones tell Leonard he had Spanish ancestry. Moreover, when the newspapers broke the story of Leonard's marriage, Leonard told his new mother-in-law that "he had married the girl he wanted and he did not care for anybody."[82]

On cross, Mills attempted to undermine the grandmotherly witness's testimony. First, he tried to show how Elizabeth Jones failed to guard her daughters' virginity. Mills also wanted the jury to see her as a scheming woman who hoped to marry her half-breed daughters to white men. Mills's aggressive attack on Mrs. Jones may have done Leonard's case more harm than good. Accounts in the press pointed to a growing public sympathy for Mrs. Jones. By the time Davis conducted a redirect examination, Elizabeth Jones further damaged Leonard's case when she recalled for the jury the many times Leonard visited their home and ate meals with the entire family before he married Alice.[83]

By this point in the trial, the newspaper coverage resonated with the language of the visibility of race and color. The *Times* contrasted Emily Brooks's and Grace Miller's "dusky" color with their English mother's "pale face." Grace Robinson called the two Jones sisters "handsome quadroon girls, of more striking appearance than Alice." Robinson also asserted that the defense witnesses had shown Leonard could not have been unaware of Alice's color. The African American witnesses had become "specters—dark shadows down the path of the last of the Huguenots."[84]

Once Elizabeth Jones finished on the stand, Davis called his final witness for the day. He began with a witness whose presence surprised Leonard's lawyers: Ross Chidester, the Rhinelander family chauffeur in 1921 and 1922. Chidester had tried to contact Leonard's lawyer, Leon Jacobs, during the trial, but Jacobs never followed up. Davis had tracked Chidester down working as a driver and salesman for a local bakery. Chidester testified about his work for

Philip Rhinelander and recalled having a friendly relationship with Philip's son, Leonard; the two had discussed the stock market, cars, and sports. He also remembered the first time he saw Alice Jones. Davis asked whether Chidester had seen Alice's face; he admitted he did.[85]

Davis then asked Chidester about the day in December 1921 when he drove Leonard and Alice to the Hotel Marie-Antoinette. Chidester first picked Leonard up at The Orchards in Connecticut and waited while Leonard completed his packing. While Leonard finished up, he showed Chidester a clock he had purchased as a Christmas present for Alice. Chidester then testified that he blurted out, "Do you mean to tell me you bought her a Christmas present?" When Leonard said yes, Chidester asked him, "Don't you know her father is a colored man?" Chidester explained he had seen George Jones through the front window of the Joneses' home on another occasion when he had driven Leonard and Alice around. According to Chidester, Leonard swiftly replied, "I don't give a damn if she is." At that, Chidester told the courtroom, "I had a notion to take him out in front of the school and kick the shit out of him." Quickly Justice Morschauser interrupted to ask what Leonard said next. Chidester admitted Leonard did not respond and merely finished packing.[86]

Once Leonard had fastened his bag, Chidester drove him to Westchester to pick up Alice. When Leonard left the car to check in at the Hotel Marie-Antoinette, Alice handed Chidester a Christmas present of a five dollar bill, which he accepted despite his discomfort with her color. On cross-examination, Mills tried to shake Chidester's credibility, but Chidester stuck to his testimony. Mills was reduced to asking Chidester about every job he had had since 1910.[87]

At the end of the day on Wednesday, Justice Morschauser adjourned the trial until after the Thanksgiving holiday and weekend. On Thursday, Leonard ate dinner in a hotel with a few of his lawyers while Alice sat down to turkey surrounded by family. On the following Monday, November 30, the trial resumed. Davis recalled Elizabeth Jones as a witness, and she testified that Alice's body color had remained the same from birth. After these final questions to Alice's mother about her daughter's complexion, Davis announced that he had no further witnesses to call. Audible gasps filled the courtroom. To the consternation of the opposing lawyers and the surprise of Justice Morschauser, the courtroom spectators, and the press, Davis rested his case. He never called either Alice Jones Rhinelander or George Jones as witnesses for the defense. Perhaps Alice's body had already said it all.[88]

NINE :

The Trial Ends

Not since the mountaineers of Tennessee sought to strike the anthropoids from their line of ancestry have the newspapers given us such a gaudy story as that now current, detailing the efforts of a laboriously civilized youth to forfend the probability of Negroid progeny. In the years to come, the Dayton affair may be revived more frequently by theologians and crossroad deacons and co-educational classes in journalism. But the herd at large will hark back to the Rhinelander story as the classic example of what may be done with a real, juicy scandal.
—MORRIS MARKEY, "The Current Press," *New Yorker*, December 1925

AS THE RHINELANDER annulment trial drew to a close, Margery Rex of the *Evening Journal* asked a few questions that struck at the heart of one meaning of the trial in the 1920s. Rex observed that one topic lingered in everyone's mind, "If Alice wins, or Kip wins—regardless of outcome—will the two attempt ever again to live together?" Rex continued, "As far as Alice and Kip are concerned, no one but possibly Philip Rhinelander, the youth's father, cares whether or not they do live together. If Kip wants a colored wife, you hear on all sides, who should worry if he has one?" Indeed, Rex suggested, "Is it not Kip's own affair, if his own sense of inferiority leads him to find pleasure only in the company of those beneath him socially?"[1]

Nevertheless, as Rex seemed well aware, a marriage between someone considered white and someone considered colored troubled many New Yorkers in the 1920s. Consequently, Rex agreed with Leonard's lawyers and many commentators on the annulment trial when she declared that Leonard and Alice's marriage possessed a social significance beyond the two people involved. Rex proclaimed that Leonard's marriage was not his own affair, "NOT WHEN THESE ASSOCIATIONS MAY POSSIBLY REPEAT THE SAME SOCIAL PROBLEM THROUGH THE CHILDREN THAT RESULT." Leonard's "association" with Alice and the possibility that they might produce children (who, like the ambiguous Alice might have the ability to pass) would make more difficult the task of drawing racial boundary lines.[2]

Rex reminded her readers that "public opinion is always against marriage between colored and white" because such marriages lead to the "burdening of the future race with unnecessary drawbacks." In an era in which the desire for racial purity reached a fevered pitch, the reproduction of children might be, as Rex bemoaned, a living and breathing threat to those who believed in the purity of either the white or black race. Moreover, Rex asked, "DID HE [LEONARD] INTEND TO CONTINUE THE LINE OF HALF WHITES UNDER THE RHINELANDER NAME?" In other words, did Leonard intend to devalue the exclusivity of the white elite.[3]

Other commentators also understood that the verdict would speak to the deep concerns about race, class, and marriage that epitomized the era. Indeed, the December editorial in the *Messenger* wondered how an all-white jury would decide the case given the strong emphasis on racial purity in the twenties. The *Messenger* worried that Alice "must overcome the vicious dogma and fiction of the alleged superiority of Lothrop Stoddard's and Madison Grant's pet Nordic breed. This, to say the least, is no easy task. It is deeply entrenched in the warp and woof of American life." The *Messenger* editors also suspected the odds favored Leonard because he was white and wealthy.[4]

Under the rules of civil procedure governing the trial, the side with the burden of proving the case speaks last to the jury, giving Lee Parsons Davis as counsel for the defense the first chance to address the jurors.[5] Right after lunch on the Monday after Thanksgiving, Davis stood up and began, "May it please the Court and gentlemen, I do not know whether you can realize the feelings that are coursing through my body at this moment. Upon my shoulders rests a tremendous responsibility. I stand between this young girl, practically in the beginning of womanhood, I am the only one to stand between her and absolute ruin."[6]

Davis then proceeded to savagely attack Leonard's legal team: "They have torn from her ruthlessly every scrap of respectability that a woman loves most." Davis then pointed to the jurors and declared, "There is not any other thing they can do to this girl except one. And that is for you twelve men to come into this courtroom and add the last straw, for you, sir, and you, and each one of you to walk in here and add the last straw and say 'Alice Rhinelander, you go out into this world a fraud.'" "So you see, gentlemen," he continued, "it is a terrible responsibility to stand between this girl and such a verdict at your hands."[7]

Expecting that Mills would appeal to prejudice to support his client's case, Davis reminded the jury that when the lawyers examined them before the trial, he had only asked if they could be fair. "If there is any man in this jury box that has any feeling of race hatred in his veins, applicable to this case," Davis added, "you cannot be fair unless you cast it aside." In a remark that alluded to the high level of public anxiety over the trial, Davis touched on "the echoes from the street" that led him to worry about the effects of "race hatred or prejudice or passion." The press had reported that all the participants in the trial (including the jurors) had received a high volume of mail on the subject of the trial—most of it negative.[8]

Before addressing the main arguments in defense of his client, Davis took some time to address a few preliminary issues and at the same time impugn his adversary's case. As he had throughout the trial, Davis called attention to Leon Jacobs's role as the "brains" behind the trial and implied that Leonard's father, not Leonard, instigated the annulment action. He characterized Isaac Mills's opening statement to the jury and his description of Leonard's mental state as cruel. "He painted this boy, now in manhood, as being some sort of a boob, brain-tied." Davis asserted that the evidence showed Leonard was not brain-tied, only "tongue tied." He blamed his opponent for placing unnecessary "filth" on the trial record.[9] Davis used this complaint to justify his decision to keep Alice off the witness stand, saying he wanted to prevent Mills from further destroying Alice's reputation.

As evidence of Mills's treachery, Davis excoriated him for revealing the existence of Elizabeth Jones's first child born out of wedlock. Davis then took up another strand of his argument that he hoped would win the case when he explained why he did not call George Jones as a witness. Davis told the jury,

"You have a right to use your powers of observation in this court room. Mr. Jones is a mulatto! That is no disgrace and it is not his fault." By invoking the jury's power of observation, Davis reminded the jurors of his position that race was a visible trait.[10]

Davis also summed up the ways in which Leonard's contradictory testimony belied his lawyer's case. Davis asserted that Leonard's testimony disproved Mills's claims that Alice seduced and enticed Leonard into marriage. Leonard's own words proved he had met Alice's brother-in-law, Robert Brooks, well before 1924. Therefore, the existence of the "colored brother-in-law" should have alerted him to his wife's ancestry. To Mills's claim that Alice tried to make Leonard jealous, Davis responded that he and Mills came from a different generation and that Alice's conduct was not unusual for young women in the 1920s.[11]

Then Davis addressed what some saw as *the* major obstacle for Alice's case. He took up the lingering question of whether Leonard and Alice would resume their relationship if the jury's verdict favored Alice. Davis observed, "In this great state of New York there is no law against a negro marrying a white," but he insisted that while "I have my views that blacks have just as much right to live as whites. . . . I don't know that I believe in mixing the blood."[12] Davis returned repeatedly to this issue during his statement to the jury, at one point, mentioning that both he and his opponent had received a great deal of mail on this subject. "It may be that there might be some feeling in the minds of some one of you and possibly properly," he said: " 'Why, here, we are not going by our verdict to compel Leonard Rhinelander to live with Alice Rhinelander.' Well, now, gentlemen, you are not called upon to do any such thing. You are only called here to decide whether at this juncture these two shall be separated on the ground of fraud. It must be apparent to each and every one of you that these two young people can never live together." Later in his summation, Davis circled back yet again to this subject and insisted, in a voice raised to a shout, that Leonard and Alice would never live together again. "Don't go out to your jury room and say 'Here. We won't tie this young man up with one with colored blood.' " He told the jury to remember that the events in court "destroyed" any chance that the couple would live together again. At this pronouncement, Alice wept while her mother tried to comfort her.[13]

Davis's repeated assurances that Leonard and Alice would never live together again spoke to the high level of anxiety over miscegenation and marriage that permeated the trial. The press recognized that Davis needed to make these statements, because white jurors might be reluctant to render a decision in Alice's favor if they thought the couple would resume their marriage. Grace Robinson pointed out that Davis had to "remove from the minds of the jury the consideration which has threatened to defeat Alice."[14] In addition to assuring the jury that Leonard and Alice would not revive their relationship as husband and wife if Alice won, Davis defended Alice from the charges of fraud and deceit. Davis remarked that the first real issue was whether Alice had colored blood. Davis submitted, "We have . . . conceded that she has some colored blood. We haven't made any concession that she is a negress." While Davis denied that Alice was a "Negress," he reasoned that the exact amount of Alice's colored blood remained unknown and, because of this uncertainty, her ancestry might not keep her from marrying a white man in a state that prohibited marriages between black and white.[15]

Davis's references to lingering questions about the exact quantity of Alice's colored blood highlighted the uncertainties of using blood to determine racial identity in the 1920s. Indeed, Davis contributed to greater confusion when he drew on the language of blood as race to indicate that "in determining who a negro is, probably it depends upon the amount of blood." Mistakenly, Davis asserted that some states prohibited marriages between the races through "a thirty-second" test (presumably the percentage of colored blood that made one a Negro), which they used to ascertain who fell within the bounds of their statutes. Mills, however, interjected that the percentage of blood varied by state.[16]

Once Davis reminded the jurors that the defense had conceded Alice possessed some colored blood, he argued that they needed only to decide whether Alice told Leonard before the marriage that she was white and Leonard believed it. Since Leonard bore the evidentiary burden of proof, Mills would have to prove this claim by a preponderance of the evidence. Anticipating that Mills would consider particular incidents as evidence that Alice passed as white, Davis retold the defense's narrative to preempt Mill's version. Davis discussed Alice's response to Leonard's amended complaint back in January 1925, when she refuted Leonard's claim that she possessed colored blood. Davis resorted to legal technicalities to explain why Alice denied her colored blood. He insisted that Alice's denial did not establish that she passed. Instead, it served as a legal tactic designed to force Leonard and his lawyers to prove her color. Davis also countered allegations that Alice and her family passed as white and pointed to legal documents such as the Jones sisters' birth certificates to confirm that the family did not deny their color. Tellingly, Davis never referred to the early press coverage of his client in the fall of 1924, at which time Alice had disavowed any colored ancestry.[17]

Instead, for the second time during the trial, Davis challenged Mills's proposition that Alice deceived Leonard with the question of whether someone would believe "a person [who] says 'I am a pure white American citizen' and you see a pigtail hanging down his back and eyes like this (indicating)." Davis's caricature of Chinese immigrants directed the jury to physical difference as the basis for racial difference. Davis's comparison suggested that to believe Alice could pass would be equally ridiculous: "If a girl has clearly colored blood in her family and she says to a man 'I am pure white' if he is not colorblind he will say 'That is foolish,' that he didn't believe it." Therefore, when the jurors determined whether Alice represented herself to Leonard as white and Leonard relied on that representation, they should remember that "law that is not founded on common sense is not good law."[18] Davis's turn to "common sense" and visual differences of race offered the promise that racial identity could be ascertained without resorting to messy formulations of blood, which he argued was inadequate to the task.

After a brief discussion of the absurdity of Leonard's new charge that Alice committed fraud by silence, a tired Davis asked to end his statement for the day. Justice Morschauser adjourned court until the next morning. On Tuesday morning, Davis began by warning the jurors again about Mills's rhetorical tricks: "The Judge, undoubtedly, will go back to the early history of the Huguenots." But, he continued, "I do not criticize any family's good name but I say this, that no man or boy living has a right to hide behind a smokescreen of a long family name." Davis pointedly emphasized Alice and Leonard's "difference in opportunities" due to their contrasting social stations: "Why this boy is beyond his years. His face shows it. This young woman, the evidence shows it had to work at an early age and the proof of that is the fact that she did not have the opportunity to educate herself as you and I have had the opportunity."[19]

Davis then lashed out at Leonard for allowing his lawyers to use Alice's love letters and for "cold-bloodedly" identifying them as hers. "I can't conceive of a man, to accomplish any end, that would sit in the witness chair, especially a man brought up surrounded by everything that is refined, and calmly let his lawyers put those rotten letters in."[20] He criticized Leonard's father and argued that Philip Rhinelander knew Alice's color since he sent his own lawyer to separate them at the Hotel Marie-Antoinette in January 1922. "Do you think for a minute gentlemen, that he would be spending all of that money . . .

to break up the match between Alice and Leonard Rhinelander . . . and not inquire who he was going with and what she was? That is why Mr. Philip Rhinelander is not in court. He knows."[21]

At times perching on the wooden rail of the jury box, Davis continued to attack Leonard's case by accusing Leonard of acting the aggressor in pursuing a relationship with Alice. He excused his own decision to have the jury inspect Alice's body. "A boy of twelve would have known that colored blood was coursing through her veins. You saw it in a good light." Davis expressed surprise that even though Leonard had engaged in degenerate sexual practices with Alice, he still maintained he did not know her color. Moreover, Davis scoffed at Leonard's claim that Alice told him she was white and argued that since Alice revealed to Leonard her intimate secret—she was not a virgin when they met—she would not lie about her race.[22]

Davis then returned to his point that Leonard knew Alice's color. He drew on "common sense" to help the jurors decide whether Alice had passed and deceived Leonard. Davis reminded the jury that if Leonard knew *before* he married Alice that she was of colored blood, he was not entitled to an annulment. Consequently, Davis asked the jurors to put themselves in Leonard's shoes and see what he should have seen. "Now gentlemen, this is not said to hurt you Alice, but you saw her with her hat off. You saw her in the jury room, or a portion of her body. . . . Who could be fooled by her?" Under Davis's formulation, the jurors would have to be "fools" to accept Leonard's contention that he did not see Alice's color.[23]

When Davis pointed to every member of Alice's family, except her mother, and maintained no one could be fooled by them, Davis insisted that knowledge of Alice's color was obvious and readily available for those who had eyes to see. Suggesting the utter absurdity of the notion that Alice's African ancestry might not be visible, Davis ridiculed Leonard's case: "I expected an amendment to the complaint almost any minute, alleging that Leonard Kip Rhinelander was color blind or totally blind. But they haven't gone that far. Maybe they didn't think of it in time. He isn't blind." Turning his attention back to the twelve jurors, Davis told them, "go into your jury room, and, in the face of what you saw here, come back into this court room and say that he believed that he was marrying into a family that was pure white."[24]

Davis's focus on making sure the jury saw Alice's color became even more evident when he intimated that any jury member who could not do so must be mentally deficient—a particularly stinging accusation in the eugenics-soaked atmosphere of the 1920s. "You are not inmates of Bloomingdale," he said.

"Come into the jury room with a verdict in favor of this plaintiff and tell men just that—that with this before you he didn't know it." Everyone in the courtroom understood Davis's reference to "Bloomingdale"—the Bloomingdale Insane Asylum, New York State's first mental hospital, which opened in New York City in 1821 but relocated to White Plains in 1894.[25]

Despite Davis's allusion to insanity, he had to be careful that the jury did not interpret Leonard's behavior with Alice as a sign of mental weakness and thereby accept Mills's argument that Leonard was gullible. Instead, Davis tapped back into his earlier theme that Leonard, the aristocratic seducer, pursued Alice, the colored maid from a "humble home": "Ah, he knew [that Alice was colored] and he liked it until the family name intervened, gentlemen. I repeat again, he knew it and he liked it until some unforeseen power, to protect the family name, got back of him, and here he is, and he must go through with it."[26]

At the end of the day, a now husky-voiced Davis criticized the Rhinelander family's actions in defending the family's exclusivity. Indeed, Davis claimed that the Rhinelanders "wrecked everybody in sight. They have thrown this girl into the sewer and the slime, and she has only one thing left—one—to be saved from the charge of being a defrauder." Davis appealed to the jurors' sense of responsibility, remarking that if Alice is found guilty, she "will walk out of this courtroom shunned by those of the colored race. That poor girl will walk out of this courtroom shunned by the white race. God, what a life! And the Rhinelanders have brought it about." Finally, with his hands raised, voice lowered, tears in his eyes, Davis asked, "Now, are you, on this evidence, going to take away the only thing she has? Are you? Or are you, at least, going to say to this bunch 'You have ruined the whole outfit, but we will give her something. We will turn her out loose, whether she is black, white or colored, and say that this is a damnable outrage for this man to ever charge her with fraud.'"[27] Although in the heat of the moment Davis suggested that the jury did not need to consider Alice's race, this was clearly a rhetorical flourish since the whole thrust of his argument centered on the jurors' certain "knowledge" that she was colored. Davis finished by thanking the jury, and Justice Morschauser adjourned the trial for the day.

When court opened on Wednesday morning, yet another dismal, cold, and rainy day, spectators filled the room awaiting the appearance of Isaac Mills and his final presentation of Leonard's case. Wearing his black skullcap, Mills began his closing remarks to the twelve jurors with the observation that he had the "privilege" of "talking to you as man to man." Mills asserted a common link between himself and the jurymen as men, a link that Mills intended to draw on during his closing argument. In particular, Mills wanted to appeal to the twelve men in their patriarchal roles as white fathers and citizens.[28]

Mills told the jury that Leonard's annulment trial was a case of "very great importance." He compared his role as Leonard's attorney to death penalty defense work: "I consider this case of equal importance. I look upon it as a case of life and death. You might as well, gentlemen of this jury, bury that young man six feet deep in the soil of the old churchyard where his early American ancestors sleep, as to consign him to be forever chained to that woman." Grace Robinson picked up on Mills's dire language, reporting that Mills "called on the jury to decide, once and for all, whether the tragedies of miscegenation should be authorized in this state." By taking this approach, Mills suggested to the jury that its primary role would be to break up a miscegenous marriage.[29]

As a member of the legal profession, Isaac Mills knew that only the state legislature could enact a law to prohibit interracial marriage. Nevertheless, he contended that an annulment trial constituted an appropriate forum to dissolve such a marriage. To elide the differences between a statute that prohibited marriages between the races and an annulment action, Mills argued that because matrimonial actions involved public policy issues, the "People of the State of New York" became the third party to Leonard's lawsuit. Mills insisted that New York's public policy opposed miscegenation and thus the only verdict satisfactory to the trial's "third party" would be to end Leonard's marriage.[30]

Mills, speaking slowly and dramatically, implored the jurors in their paternal roles as protectors of the white race to annul the Rhinelander marriage. Indeed, Mills proclaimed, "Why, gentlemen, stop and think. There isn't a father among you—and you remember I sought to get fathers—there isn't a father among you who would not rather see his son in his casket than to see him wedded to a mulatto woman." Mills suggested to the jury that their decision could be based on their feelings against marriages between the races and their desire to maintain racial purity through regulating the reproductive choices of their children.[31]

Despite his repeated references to the negative effects of race mixing, Mills made an effort to show he did not needlessly invoke prejudice as the basis for a decision in the case. Instead, Mills claimed that the desire for racial purity transcended racial lines. He declared, "This feeling of race does not belong to the whites alone. Decent blacks have the same feeling." Although Mills suggested that African Americans felt equally unhappy about interracial marriage, his arguments against such marriages revealed the exaggerated nature of his concern. He did not mean to imply any equality between the races. Indeed, Mills suggested a troubling vision of the results of race mixture when he remarked, "Happily, gentlemen, there are no children, and there can be none, but you may consider, perhaps, what would be the condition if there were. You have only to look at this Jones family. You need not look into history. You need not look into fiction. You need not look anywhere but at this Jones family. What a pitiable spectacle it is." Moreover, Mills emphasized the taint conveyed by marriage with African Americans when he pondered, "What has life for [Leonard] if he is to remain chained to that woman?"[32]

Like his opponent, Mills criticized his adversary's handling of the case. Mills blasted Davis for resting his case without putting Alice or her father on the stand. He also countered Davis's criticism that Mills never called Philip Rhinelander as a witness. Raising his voice to a shout, Mills blamed Philip for his failure to supervise his son and prevent Leonard from marrying Alice. "They have no just complaint that Philip Rhinelander is not here, but I make complaint that he is not here." In Mills's view, Philip had failed to ensure that his son did not marry beneath him and damage the family's whiteness. The press described Mills's rhetorical style as one that relied heavily on biblical and other classical stories to illuminate his points. Mills even resorted to the story of the prodigal son when he discussed the Rhinelanders' father-son relationship.[33]

As he had during the rest of the trial, Mills linked race to character to describe Alice. When Mills forecast Alice's future in the event of a verdict for Leonard, he commented, "She has all that buoyant temperament which belongs to her race. This trial past, these newspapers bent on other scandals, her name out of the prints, she will soon rally." At that point, according to Mills, Alice's true essence would assert itself and determine her future. Mills assured the jury that a verdict that ended the marriage would benefit Alice, too. Indeed, Mills suggested, "she will gain a husband in her own race and life will have happiness for her again, as it has proved to have for her older sister, Emily, who did not assume such vaulting ambition but accepted, at nineteen years of age, the honest proposition of a colored man, Brooks." By marrying someone of her own race, Alice would be made happy because the natural order would be maintained. Alice would and should, he argued, live a life contained by the particular race- and class-based limits of her birth.[34]

Since Mills contended that miscegenation was monstrous and threatened the natural order, he dealt with the question of how Leonard engaged in such an act by facing the issue of Leonard's mental abilities. Contrary to his earlier assertions of Leonard as feebleminded, he now denied that he had characterized Leonard as a "fool." Davis had undercut much of this description when he cross-examined Leonard. Yet, Mills did not completely cede the point about Leonard's mental abilities. Instead, he observed, "It is a problem, I admit, how much intelligence he does possess." Now Mills claimed that at the time the eighteen-year-old Leonard met Alice he suffered with a "physical infirmity" coupled with some "mental backwardness." This combination caused Leonard to have the intelligence of a fourteen- or fifteen-year-old.[35]

In contrast to Leonard's immaturity, Mills argued, Alice was older and "mind you, women of her race mature earlier." Indeed, Mills declared, "women of that race mature earlier, gain such beauty as they may have, earlier; such power of charm and attraction for the opposite sex, and in turn, they fade sooner." Mills frequently pointed out the age difference between Alice and Leonard, and by the end of his summation, Alice, in his telling, was almost twice as old as Leonard. Mills also added that Leonard did not think either Grace or Alice Jones were "pure" girls.[36] As Mills portrayed the couple's relationship, Alice, as Jezebel used her sexual lures to trap the younger Leonard into a miscegenous relationship.

To emphasize his characterization of Alice as Jezebel, Mills repeated his earlier argument that Alice had made Leonard her love slave and so Leonard could not tell black from white. As evidence, Mills pointed to the Exhibits S and M, the two letters that Davis had introduced to depict Leonard as a degenerate aristocrat. Mills reversed Davis's reading of Leonard's correspondence. He insisted to the jurors that the letters "show that that boy, by her ministrations had been reduced to the utter depths of degradation. Do you remember it plainly? The thing was done for her pleasure. . . . What challenge that was to the womanhood of this country." Mills placed the blame for the sexual acts described in Leonard's letters on Alice and explained them as typical of her race: "That was not a white man's act. That was an act of the black-and-tan. . . . That shows beyond all argument, all question, that he was her slave, that he was reduced to the very depths of the most bottomless degradation of which you can conceive." Mills even compared Leonard to "great men" like Admiral Horatio Nelson and Alexander Hamilton, who could not resist the charms of an evil woman. In these words, Mills invoked both the Jezebel and the "vamp" who reduced her prey to degraded shells of their former selves.[37]

Mills's focus on the evils of miscegenation and his insistence that Alice passed as white presented a precarious strategy at a time when racial indeterminacy produced great anxiety. Instead of resolving racial ambiguity, Mills's strategy underscored the very existence of this unsettling possibility. Yet Mills called attention to numerous incidents in which Alice and the rest of her family passed as white. He accused the Jones family of starting to pass "only after Emily married, it was only in these later years, that the mother and the daughters, too, became carried away with this passion to associate with the whites." He also pointed out that Alice was accepted as white at the Hotel Marie-Antoinette and at other hotels on the couple's premarital trip to New England. In addition, Mills made much of the fact that the county clerk designated both Alice and her sister Grace as white on their marriage licenses even though, according to Mills, Grace, unlike Alice, appeared "to have more of the conformation and features of the mulatto." In a provocative challenge to the defense lawyers, Mills even suggested that Alice and her family passed as white to Judge Swinburne and Lee Davis and that this explained why Davis waited until the second day of the trial to admit Alice had colored blood. Mills also offered Miriam Rich's social ambitions as proof that Alice passed: "You do not think that Mrs. Rich with her idea of society would have mingled with those people if she thought they were of colored blood. Of course not."[38]

In addition to recounting the times that Alice and her family passed as white, Mills stressed the Jones family's appearance and Alice's ability to pass. First, Mills remarked that Leonard did not see Alice "amid the turmoil and tumult of this trial, where a hundred fingers were pointing at her, where a hundred tongues were proclaiming her colored blood." Mills thus suggested that perceptions of race depended on context. Mills also called attention to Alice's representations of herself as white when reporters first descended on the couple in November 1924. Moreover, Mills reminded the jury that Leonard had been to Havana and seen "white people there with dark skins, just as dark as Mr. Jones."[39] Leonard's knowledge of dark-skinned yet white Cubans could explain how he could be deceived by Alice and also reinforce Mills's argument that she passed.

To persuade the jury that Leonard deserved an annulment, Mills struck directly at his opponent's case and asked the jury to look closely at George Jones. Mills hammered away at Davis's linking of race with physical appearance. Mills insisted that "every feature of his face is distinctly caucasian except the color. I say if by some miracle you could change the color of his skin as he sits there he would pass anywhere for a white man."[40] Ironically, by conceding that Jones's skin was colored, Mills reinforced Davis's connection between race and appearance. Yet Mills also contended at one point that a person could be dark, but not white, like Cubans. The confusion evident at times in Mills's rhetoric, however, pointed to the instability of race and the weakness of his strategy at a moment when New Yorkers, along with the rest of the country, sought more certainty about race.

Mills returned again to Alice's appearance to demonstrate her ability to pass. He compared her features to her father's and maintained that Alice also exhibited a Caucasian physiognomy: an aquiline nose and thin lips. As Davis had done earlier, Mills cast himself in the role of Alice's protector when he recalled for the jury that he had protested against her "indecent exposure": "It was utterly unnecessary that you should see her body. I do not care what the negro doctor said. Every one of you knows that the portions of the body which are covered up of a person who is light at all are lighter than the portions that are exposed to the sun and to the elements."[41]

Mills's criticism of the exhibition of Alice also, perhaps inadvertently, underscored the constructed nature of race and Davis's efforts to naturalize race through vision. Mills claimed that the only reason he went in to the jury room was because he "was afraid there might be some staining, or something of that sort." In other words, Mills suspected that the defense might attempt to darken Alice's body with makeup to make her "look" colored. Mills, however, observed that "her appearance by herself would not condemn her anywhere as being of colored blood. Not at all."[42] For Mills to win the case, Alice needed to look white and race had to be blood that could be hidden from view.

When Mills came to the end of his closing statement after almost twelve hours, he once again invoked the evils of miscegenation. In a soft voice, Mills told the jury,

> Gentlemen, I am at the end. God knows that I have given to the case of this young man the best that is in me, the utmost of my strength and vigor. The responsibility will now pass from my shoulders upon yours. Your verdict, gentlemen, shall answer once more that ancient question put in Holy Writ: "Can the Ethiopian change his skin?" This mother, in her love for her girls, from her ambition—I am not going to abuse her—entered upon that problem. It cannot be done. Your answer, gentlemen, to that ancient question, by your verdict, must be in the negative—"No, it cannot be done."

After drawing on this Old Testament text from Jeremiah, which could be understood as a reference to passing, Mills observed that this case had been a "hard task" but "I have performed it, it seems to me, so that you can have no hesitation whatever in giving to this young man, as I ask you to do, a chance to live, a chance to redeem himself and to redeem the name which, by his folly, he has besmirched under the bedevilment of the defendant."[43]

Finally, Mills beseeched the jurors to free Leonard "from this horrid, unnatural, absurd, terrible union." The *Times* labeled Mills's closing statement "a frank appeal against miscegenation, on the theory that mixing the races is bad for society." The *Daily News* remarked, "It is generally conceded in White Plains that if the jury finds a verdict favorable to Rhinelander, it will be with the idea of granting him deliverance from the girl who, his attorney claims, enslaved him body and soul when he was an 18-year-old boy and had never known a woman."[44]

Once the attorneys wound up their closing remarks, Justice Morschauser began his charge to the jury, laying out the legal framework for the jurors' deliberations. A judge's charge to the jury gives the judge an opportunity to discuss the issues of fact that the jury must decide. During the charge, a judge might choose to review the trial evidence as it relates to the disputed issues of fact, but a judge needs to ensure his discussion of the facts do not sway the jury.[45] Although Justice Morschauser most likely met the standards set by law, his discussion of the law and evidence clearly accepted Davis's arguments about the visibility of race. For example, when Morschauser briefly reviewed the trial testimony, he recalled that Alice's brother-in-law, Robert Brooks, had testified that he was colored. Somewhat gratuitously, Morschauser added, "Well, it was apparent to all of us that he had colored blood in him. We did not have to have him tell us that."[46]

A more significant sign that Davis's conception of race had gained ground in the trial occurred when Morschauser turned to the legal meaning of the defense's decision to dispense with Alice and her father as witnesses. The language that Morschauser used with the jury implied that Alice and her father's testimony might be superfluous because the jury had seen them seated in the courtroom every day. When Morschauser told the jury that the absence of a potential defense witness did not result automatically in any presumptions in favor of Leonard's case, he remarked that they could draw an inference from Davis's decision not to call them as witnesses. The jury could find that Alice misrepresented herself based on the proof offered by Mills, yet they still needed to consider the facts shown by the defense, which, as listed by Morschauser, revolved primarily around visual evidence.[47]

Morschauser offered the jury a series of images that they could take into account: "You may consider that [Leonard] saw the colored father and brother-in-law; that he saw and knew the surroundings of the defendant; that he slept at her father's house; that he saw the white mother and the defendant's sisters; that he was on very friendly terms with them all; that he saw the defendant's body and all of it; the upper part of her shoulders, her back and her waist, and the small part above her knees that was exhibited to you . . . ; that he saw her arms as well. He says they were of the same color as when he saw them on previous occasions." Given all of these visual cues, Morschauser asked, "did he not realize that she was of colored blood and that she was not a full white woman?" If Leonard had the means to learn the truth of Alice's color, "by ordinary intelligence," Morschauser instructed the jury, then he was required to do so and could not claim fraud.[48]

While Justice Morschauser instructed the jury on the facts and the applicable law, he also affirmed Isaac Mills's contention (never challenged by the defense) that race mattered for marriage in New York. Morschauser informed the jurors that when a man married a woman of colored blood without knowledge of her blood, but she knew it and married him after lying to him about her color, the marriage could be annulled. Moreover, if the woman knew the husband would not have married her if he had known she had fraudulently concealed her race, then an annulment could be granted. After this reminder that race was deeply implicated in the annulment trial, Justice Morschauser nevertheless added, "In the final determination of this case . . . if you allow yourselves to be influenced by your sympathy or prejudice, you do the parties an injustice."[49]

At this point, after an hour and twenty minutes of the judge charging the jury, the attorneys had the right to request that the judge explain anything that the lawyers felt he had left out. Mills asked Morschauser to charge the jury that the term "colored blood" meant the same thing in the seven questions the jury would need to answer to decide the case. Morschauser then told the jury that " 'colored blood' really means, when you get to it, that her skin is colored." In this courtroom, colored blood now equaled colored skin.[50]

After the charges, the jury foreman led the other jurors to the jury room to begin their deliberations. Leonard and his lawyers and Alice, her lawyers, and family went to separate anterooms in the courthouse to await the verdict.

Davis smoked a number of cigarettes. Given the heated nature of the trial and fears that the verdict might provoke violence, the Westchester County sheriff ordered 150 deputies on duty at the courthouse while the spectators hoped for a swift verdict. Unfortunately for all, other than the deputies presumably paid for their time, no quick verdict was forthcoming.[51]

Instead, the jurors went out to eat and then returned to consider the case. Leonard lunched with Leon Jacobs. After the meal, Leonard did not return to the courtroom. Alice and her family removed themselves to Lee Davis's offices across the street from the courthouse to continue to wait. At around four o'clock, the jury returned to the courtroom with a few questions about the testimony of the reporter Barbara Reynolds. Both Davis and Mills agreed that Leonard never denied that he told Reynolds on 13 November 1924 that he knew he had married the daughter of a colored man.[52]

Later in the afternoon, the jury dined, and by six returned to continue their discussions. Despite the hour, a large number of spectators remained in the heavily guarded courthouse and continued to await some word from the jury. Rumors circulated that the jurors were "wrangling" in the jury room with loud voices. Finally, at 11:25 P.M., a court attendant entered the now mostly deserted courtroom. Only twenty reporters and a few spectators remained. The attendant announced to those waiting that the jurors had reached a verdict. The twelve men had gone home to bed. Following Justice Morschauser's instructions, the verdict would be announced the next day, Saturday, in open court at ten in the morning.[53]

When court opened on a dark and gloomy Saturday morning, 5 December, Alice sat between her parents and her lawyer. Leonard either refused to attend or his lawyers kept him away. Given the intense interest the annulment trial had aroused, eager members of the public jammed the brightly lit courtroom. The jurors handed the sealed envelope with the verdict to the court clerk. The clerk opened it and handed the contents to Justice Morschauser. As the newspaper photographers' cameras clicked, Morschauser read:

> The first question is this: "At the time of the marriage of the parties, was the defendant colored and of colored blood?" Your answer to that is "Yes."
>
> The second question is: "Did the defendant before the marriage by silence conceal from the plaintiff the fact that she was of colored blood?" Your answer to that is "No."
>
> The third question: "Did the defendant before the marriage represent to the plaintiff that she was not of colored blood?" Your answer is "No."

The fourth question is this: "Did the defendant practice said concealment or make said representation with the intent thereby to induce the plaintiff to marry her?" You have answered that "No."

The fifth question: "Was the plaintiff by said concealment or by said representation, or by both, induced to marry the defendant?" You answer that "No."

The sixth question is this: "If the plaintiff had known that defendant was of colored blood, would he have married her?" Your answer to that is "Yes."

The seventh question is unanswered.

After the verdict that favored Alice on every count, Mills requested that each member of the jury be polled on his answers. Each confirmed his agreement with the verdict. Mills then rose to his feet, congratulated his adversary for his win, and immediately made a motion to have the verdict set aside. He requested a new trial on the grounds that the verdict contradicted the evidence, the trial had been unfairly conducted, and the judge's charge to the jury prejudiced Leonard's case.[54]

Although Mills appealed Leonard's annulment trial through New York's judicial system for the next two years, the jury's verdict and the judge's subsequent decision to deny Leonard an annulment showed that the display of Alice's flesh confirmed her racial identity to the jury's satisfaction.[55] No fraud took place; Alice did not pass as white. In an era of shifting ideas about race, "common sense" notions prevailed because they best met the needs of a white North uneasy over the uncertainties of race and desirous of preserving the benefits and value of whiteness. The decision in the Rhinelander trial exposed northern society in the process of "inventing race" in response to the pressures of its particular historical moment.[56] The boundary between black and white appeared stable even in a state that did not define race.

Media response to the verdict varied; most of the papers endorsed the "common sense" interpretation of race that prevailed. The *Herald Tribune* thought the verdict meant that although the jurors sympathized with Leonard's predicament (being married to a woman of color), the weight of the evidence, including their own eyesight, precluded them from finding that Alice deceived him. The *Herald Tribune* quoted one juror who said that "if we had voted according to our hearts the verdict would have been different." On the Sunday morning after the verdict, the *Daily News* published a full-page portrait of a smiling Alice Jones flanked by her parents. The caption affirmed

Alice Rhinelander seated between her mother, Elizabeth Jones, and father, George Jones, after winning the annulment trial. Alice is still wearing her wedding ring on her left hand. Photograph taken in Lee Parsons Davis's law office. © Bettmann/Corbis.

the power of Davis's arguments about race, as it told the reader to "note the strong facial resemblance of father and daughter. A study of the Caucasian mother's face and her daughter's shows little or no likeness."[57]

In the aftermath of the verdict, Alice Rhinelander agreed to an interview in Lee Davis's office across from the White Plains courthouse. During the interview, reporters asked Alice whether she would return to Leonard. In a low voice, she responded, "I can't say that," and then perhaps mindful of her attorney's strenuous arguments that she and Leonard would never resume their relationship quickly added, "No." Grace Robinson's report on Alice's interview reveals how thoroughly Davis succeeded in fashioning a counter-narrative of the case. Indeed, Robinson claimed that, to her eyes, Alice looked like a child. "It seemed incredible that she was the vampire, the lustful woman that Judge Mills had painted in court." Robinson also pointed out that Alice answered questions "in the respectful manner of a well-trained youngster or a maid servant."[58]

Although "common sense" visual explanations of race trumped Mills's language of "blood," inconsistent responses to the verdict revealed the continued existence of multiple understandings of race. Indeed, when Grace Robinson commented on Alice's physical appearance after the verdict, she inadvertently undermined the link between physical appearance and racial identity affirmed by her own newspaper's front page. Robinson thought that "Alice looked extremely Caucasian as to skin. There was a deftly applied tint to her dusky cheeks and, she had made generous but not vulgar use of powder." During the trial, according to Robinson, Alice appeared rarely in makeup. Consequently, "the dark color of her face was more apparent."[59]

Once the trial concluded, however, Robinson remarked that "those who saw her yesterday could understand readily that Alice with a background of beauty and luxury, in a setting different from the crowded little home . . . might pass for a tropical beauty of pure Aryan ancestry." Although the image of an "Aryan tropical beauty" seemed self-contradictory (but perhaps a representation of the image white women hoped to project by tanning), Robinson's description of Alice raised again the subject of passing. At the same time, the term "Aryan" did not necessarily imply "white," since the Supreme Court had decided two years earlier that "Aryans" from India were not white.[60]

Most commentators favored the jury's finding and agreed that Leonard knew Alice's color. When reporters from the *New York World* canvassed New Yorkers in City Hall Park, a few of those interviewed declared that while they agreed with the verdict, they still felt the marriage should be ended. George

Alice Rhinelander standing alone in her lawyer's office still clutching her handkerchief after the verdict. © Bettmann/Corbis.

Jordan, a Manhattan printer, declared, "I don't believe they should have married, but the jury was right." D. J. Feeney, a Brooklyn accountant, offered, "My verdict would be to give her $50,000 and annul the marriage." In contrast, a married woman from Staten Island told the *World*'s reporter, "I'm glad she won. I pity her. He's wealthy, and these wealthy men—." Some African Americans only reluctantly answered reporters' questions. A carpenter argued that if Alice knew she was colored she should not have married Leonard. "I think she thought she was too good for fellows like us."[61]

Much of the commentary on the verdict suggested that the outcome of the Rhinelander trial benefited African Americans and demonstrated that white northerners were not prejudiced. The *Amsterdam News* reported the invasion of Harlem by reporters from the city's dailies who sought out its residents' response to the verdict. The paper declared that most residents "unanimously" favored the verdict. It also made it clear, however, that "Harlem was for Alice without caring anything personally for Alice." It proudly proclaimed that Harlem supported Alice as a symbol of "Negro womanhood" throughout the world. "The price she paid was a high one, but . . . the victory was worth it."[62] After the *Daily News* sent its inquiring photographer to Harlem, "that important colored community," it claimed that the general reaction was that the verdict made Leonard pay for the pain he had caused Alice. One respondent, a male educator, felt that the verdict reflected justice for colored people, although the only place a couple like Leonard and Alice could live together would be "Timbuctoo [sic]."[63]

In the *Amsterdam News*'s editorial pages, Edgar Grey addressed the meaning of the Rhinelander trial, arguing that the decision made a difference because it dealt with the legal status of African American women in New York. Grey contended that the underlying premise of Leonard's case was to "emphasize a long social practice and to establish an ancient legal opinion . . . established in other sections of the country; to wit: that a white man may at any time indulge in [a] sexual relationship with a Negro woman and seek the protection of the law against her social and legal claims growing out of this relationship." Indeed, many African Americans opposed the enactment of antimiscegenation laws in the North on just those grounds: that such laws made African American women especially vulnerable to sexual harassment.[64]

Grey argued that the Rhinelander jury's decision constituted a victory for black women. The verdict to deny Leonard an annulment showed that New York law, unlike the laws in southern states, protected African American women. Nevertheless, Grey chastised African Americans, and especially women, for entering into intimate relationships with white Americans. Similarly, the Philadelphia *Christian Recorder* suggested that "every Negro girl over sixteen" should read the trial testimony to learn how white men pursue black women. Indeed, the *Recorder* pointed out that the verdict should not encourage such relationships; instead, it "merely says that a marriage between the races cannot be annulled at the will of the white party merely because he wants it annulled." Since the Rhinelanders may very well have sought an annulment for Leonard on the grounds that it would serve to erase a marriage from the public record, their failure to achieve that goal stood as a symbol that such erasure was not a given in New York.[65]

In addition to applauding the Rhinelander verdict for its fairness to African American women, many interpreted the jury's decision as a sign that prejudice was not as strong in the North as in the South. Both the *New York Times* and the *Amsterdam News* noted approvingly that the jurors indicated there had been no debate over race prejudice or miscegenation in the jury room. The *Nation* applauded the verdict and lauded the jury for holding "out against the seductions of all these forms of prejudice." In the *Nation*'s opinion, the verdict "paid no respect to wealth or social standing or even a white skin." The *Amsterdam News* concluded that Isaac Mills's appeal to race prejudice, which the paper asserted "could not have been more stinging if it had come from the lips of the Imperial Wizard of the Ku Klux Klan," did not work. In W. E. B. DuBois's editorial on the trial in the *Crisis*, he, too, was pleased that "race prejudice" did not influence the verdict.[66]

Similar comments favorable to the Rhinelander decision appeared in the pages of *Opportunity*, which commended the "fair-mindedness of judge and jury." The *New York Age* felt that the verdict demonstrated the jurors remained "unaffected by any appeal to color prejudice," which explained "why New York deserves the position it holds as the Empire State."[67] The *Christian Recorder* also considered the location of the trial in New York significant. It praised the results of the case and declared, "The Rhinelander case is a decided step for justice. It means progress." The *New York World* hailed the verdict, too: "The result of the Rhinelander case gives cause for new faith in American institutions. . . . It is refreshing . . . to see a new North—a North weaned away from those ante-bellum sentiments on race which in recent years it has been too readily learning."[68]

Even though most analysts of the Rhinelander verdict interpreted it as a victory for Alice and for African Americans and a sign of northern reason, that was not completely the case. In many ways, the verdict constituted a Pyrrhic victory for Alice. Her private letters had been read aloud in court and reprinted in the papers for everyone to read. Her sexual life had been discussed by strangers. Her own lawyer had her undress in a roomful of strangers. If she had at times in the past passed as white, the notoriety she had gained over the past year precluded that happening again. The existence of her mother's illegitimate child had been disclosed to the public at large. Her life and her family's lives had been made fodder for the tabloids and the rest of the press.

In addition, the post-trial emphasis on the lack of obvious race prejudice obscured the race-based hierarchies embedded in the Rhinelander trial. Although the judge and jury did not annul Leonard and Alice's marriage (Alice remained Mrs. Rhinelander), Lee Davis had made it clear that they would not live together even if she won. Thus, the verdict did not endorse interracial marriage or social equality in New York. Moreover, the underlying premise of Leonard's lawsuit, that race was intimately connected to marriage—even in New York—was not negated by the verdict. As an editorial in *Opportunity* observed, one "important angle of the Rhinelander annulment suit which no amount of clever editorial skirting, or summary disgust, or pity for the self-inflicted smirch upon the blazing escutcheon of a proud old family can overshadow" was the underlying premise of the trial that marriage with Negroes constituted a "complete and defiling impurity."[69] W. E. B. DuBois contended that one "shame" of the trial was "the awful truth that if Rhinelander had used this girl as concubine or prostitute, white America would have raised no word of protest; white periodicals would have printed no headlines, white ministers would have said no single word. It is when he legally and decently marries the girl that Hell breaks loose and literally tears the pair apart." A report in the *New Statesman*, a British weekly journal, observed that the *Rhinelander* case did not necessarily make sense but "the average American citizen [held] the orthodox view as to the evil and horror of miscegenation." "To millions of Americans," the paper went on, "it will seem natural and proper that the Rhinelander family, when confronted in their own household by the apparition they abominate more deeply than anything in the world of experience, should employ any available means of escape and be ready, if necessary, to pour out their accumulated wealth."[70]

Although Leonard had failed to prove Alice lied to him by a preponderance of the evidence, the Rhinelander verdict did nothing to reduce the apparent position of New York's courts: knowledge about African ancestry constituted an essential qualification for marriage (a point explicitly confirmed in Justice Morschauser's charge to the jury). Indeed, a little-noticed annulment case in the Bronx Supreme Court decided in November of the same year dissolved a marriage on similar grounds. Therefore, the verdict in favor of Alice could still stand for the proposition that a *proven* misrepresentation about African ancestry during courtship would lead to an annulment.[71]

The publicity generated by the Rhinelander annulment trial may also have spurred an increase in the number of proposals to prohibit interracial marriage introduced into legislatures over the next few years. Rumors swirled in the African American press that Klan-influenced legislation had been sent to the New York Senate in 1926. In the same year, Coleman Blease, a U.S. senator from South Carolina, planned to introduce a bill to create a national ban on interracial marriage. Senator Blease believed his bill would prevent marriages like the Rhinelanders in states outside of the South: "I want to wipe out such disgraceful unions as the Rhinelander marriage." One year later, Connecticut, Maine, Massachusetts, Rhode Island, New Jersey, and Pennsylvania all introduced antimiscegenation legislation. One African American newspaper joked that the Connecticut state lawmaker who proposed such a bill must have been related to Leonard Rhinelander.[72]

Continued controversies over interracial marriage also surfaced in the North after the Rhinelander verdict. In 1926, the *Crisis* recounted the persistent focus of reporters "hot on the trail of Negro blood" and currently investigating three possible interracial marriages in New York and New Jersey. The *Afro-American* reported in the summer of 1926 that a young white woman had been committed to a state institution for the feebleminded when she sought to marry a "colored Cuban." A former New York City police detective's article in a 1926 issue of *True Confessions* magazine declared that "the social problem offered by mixed marriages is one that cannot be regulated entirely by law. The law will be flouted if love overreaches the dictates of training and custom." The detective also observed that the intense national fascination with the Rhinelander trial spoke to "the vital importance attached to miscegenation in the United States."[73]

The conduct of the Rhinelander trial and its verdict also signaled that racial identity needed to be clearly defined. For in a decade characterized by the migration of African Americans to the North, the peak years of the Ku Klux Klan, and stiff restrictions on immigration, passing presented a threat to the belief that racial purity could be maintained. An essay in the *Messenger* by Thomas Kirksey, a Chicago lawyer, made clear the meaning of the verdict for racial purity: "Make no mistake about it, we, as colored people, find ourselves in the midst of a people in whom the pride of race is stronger than religion, a people, who, apparently, would decline existence even if they could not be Nordic." Kirksey also suggested the impossibility of maintaining racial purity: "When the attorney for the plaintiff in the Rhinelander proceedings talks about a 'horrible, unnatural, and absurd marriage' the social scientist smiles. He is reminded of the person who tried to sweep the ocean back with a broom." In response to this threat, whiteness needed to be differentiated from blackness, and Alice Jones Rhinelander could only be nonwhite. Indeed W. E. B. DuBois argued, "Why could the press persecute, ridicule and strip naked, soul and body, this defenseless girl? Because so many white Americans have black blood which might come to light, they pounce and worry like wolves to prove their spotless family." One method to uphold racial purity and deny racial ambiguity was to make sure that Alice Rhinelander was firmly identified as colored and not white.[74]

Not only race purity seemed at stake in the Rhinelander annulment trial; class exclusivity—especially the rarified status of the white upper class—came under attack. Both W. E. B. DuBois and Margery Rex identified one of the significant but mostly unspoken facets of the case in the courtroom. DuBois observed after the trial, "IF ANYTHING MORE HUMILIATING to the prestige of white America than the Rhinelander case has occurred recently it has escaped our attention." *The Negro World* chimed in: Leonard Rhinelander "offended in two ways. He married outside his social class and he married outside his race group."[75] Leonard's request for an annulment, most likely at the demand of his family, was designed to protect the Rhinelander family's property, not only the real estate and securities owned by the family but also the family's acknowledged status as white and upper class.

Ironically, the trial and the lawyers' arguments over Leonard and his abilities and intentions, no matter which argument the jury and public believed, acted to reduce the Rhinelander family's status. Either Leonard was a feebleminded nitwit capable of being fooled by a maid, demonstrating a precipitous decline in the potency of the family bloodline, or he was a man who wanted to marry across the color line and as such struck down the exclusivity of the family name. Some members of Leonard's family felt tainted by the notoriety surrounding the case. Leonard's older sister Adelaide fled to France with her husband in 1926 to escape the publicity.[76]

Since Alice won the annulment trial, her legal ties to Leonard continued to symbolize the problems posed by a cross-class and interracial marriage. Not surprisingly, Leonard renewed his legal efforts to dissolve his marriage. By the spring of 1927, however, Leonard's legal options in New York ran out when the New York Court of Appeals (the state's highest court) refused to overturn the lower court's verdict that upheld his marriage. In the aftermath of the court of appeal's decision, Leonard stopped paying alimony to Alice. Then he disappeared.[77]

Conclusion

It is indeed a mad nation. . . . At times when I think of the Rhinelander case, for instance, I have to ask myself, whether it is not I who am the fool for imagining that such things shouldn't be.—J. A. ROGERS, *Messenger*, January 1926

Property. The word is also commonly used to denote everything which is the subject of ownership, corporeal or incorporeal, tangible or intangible, visible or invisible, real or personal; everything that has an exchangeable value or which goes to make up wealth or estate.—*Black's Law Dictionary*

AS LEGAL HISTORIAN Michael Grossberg reminds us, "For reasons intrinsic to each case *and* its moment in time, some trials produce arresting social dramas."[1] In 1925, the Rhinelander annulment trial became a "social drama" because it emerged at a moment when the meaning of race in the American North seemed unclear in light of the convergence of historically specific circumstances, including the high rate of foreign immigration and, most important, the northward migration of African Americans. The movement of African Americans to the North and the region's economic, social, and political opportunities produced a series of heated conflicts over access to these resources.[2] At the same time, the Great Migration made it difficult to apply existing rules of racial classification, such as the one-drop rule, which relied on knowledge of ancestry. In the shifting populations of the North in the 1920s, a shared record of ancestry would be one of the first things lost in the journey.

The dangers of passing, a phenomenon that many speculated increased in the wake of the Great Migration, rested in an attempt by the passing person to receive the advantages granted to white people at a time when many northern whites felt called on to defend their exclusive access to these benefits. Thus the heated response to passing pointed out the deep need of whites to maintain control over their threatened property: their whiteness.[3] Passing, understood as fraud, meant that someone was taking something valuable (membership in a superior racial category) that did not belong to him or her. The belief that passing could take place required believing in the existence of "black" and "white" as both real and different. Yet fears that the rate of passing were on the rise emphasized the lack of any definitive way to distinguish between black and white. Since the Rhinelander trial had to end with a verdict that would determine whether or not Alice deceived Leonard about her race (did Alice pass?) the judge and jury's decision might provide guidance to others about who was black and who was white. The Rhinelander trial had the potential to provide some definition and clarity to the issue.

In many ways, Alice Jones Rhinelander as depicted by the newspapers, the lawyers, and the judge embodied the problem of race mixture and the shape of things to come in the North if white Americans did not police the boundaries of race. Alice's racial ambiguity emerged in the varied labels others used to describe her, ranging from colored, to mulatto, to quadroon, from "white skinned" to "chocolate brown." As the effects of the African American northward migration and foreign immigration continued to shape New York, many northerners, like Madison Grant, who valued their identity as white, predicted that New York would become too ethnically and racially mixed and thus a more difficult place to draw fixed lines of race. Leonard and Alice's high-profile marriage symbolized this uncertainty and raised questions about the links between marriage, class, and race.[4]

By ultimately consigning Alice to the category of colored and upholding the idea that knowledge about race before marriage mattered, the Rhinelander trial reinforced northern racism. Racism places people into an inferior category that shapes "their social, economic, civic, and human standing," and the Rhinelander trial can be read as one narrative of early-twentieth-century racism. Alice, now firmly categorized as a colored woman and a maid, had been exposed as a woman who overreached her racial and class constraints by dating and then marrying Leonard.⁵

W. E. B. DuBois recognized the connection between Alice's aspirations and the conduct of the annulment trial: "Here is a woman 'accused' of Negro blood. Accused because out of slavery and house service, ignorance and poverty she has raised herself." Conflicts over race in the twenties often revolved around issues of consumption, so Alice's efforts to enjoy an automobile, nice furniture, and a decorated apartment through her liaison with Leonard became problematic. As the perceptive *Evening Journal* reporter Margery Rex put it, how could Alice, "the humble daughter of a colored cabman," win the love of "a young man of birth, position and general elegance?" How could "Alice have the nerve," especially when "ALICE KNEW SHE WAS NOT WHITE." Only whites could have the right to fully enjoy the fruits of mass production, and the Rhinelander trial stood as a warning of what might await someone trying to move beyond their socially defined status.⁶

The British journal the *New Statesman* grasped the structural implications of the Rhinelander annulment trial and verdict at the time, perhaps more clearly than American observers: "It is obvious ... that the Rhinelander case is of great social significance in America for several reasons, some of which are related to the swiftly changing status of the Negro in the American nation." The Great Migration had set off what the *New Statesman* understood as a "racial revolution" that would upset established expectations of the links between ascribed racial identity and access to opportunity. Significantly, the migration to the North produced a "transformation of the economic map." Perhaps most unsettling to northern whites, the *New Statesman* observed, was that "of the twelve million Negroes in the country a great part are earning the wages of white men." With those wages, African Americans were "buying land and property in every city. Negroes are advancing rapidly in commerce. They are making good in the professions."⁷

According to the *New Statesman*, these changes in the status of African Americans posed challenges for white northerners: "In the great cities of the North and Middle West the Negro community has become a social and political unit which has to be seriously reckoned with by the civic and State parties and authorities—in, for example, Chicago, Detroit and New York." The potential of the migration to economically, politically, and socially transform the North provoked "an intensified racial consciousness." Consequently, remarked the *New Statesman*, "it is in relation to that consciousness, of social position and racial inferiority, that the Rhinelander case would seem to possess an historic importance."[8]

Not surprisingly, given the potential of the Great Migration to challenge understandings of the appropriate relationship between "social position and racial inferiority," the themes of consumption and property appear repeatedly in the story of Alice and Leonard. Given the rise of the mass consumer culture in the 1920s, Leonard and Alice's relationship was shot through with patterns of consumption. Alice's dreams of ten dollar bills raining on her head, Leonard's complaints about how "horrible" it was to shop for his sister's wedding when he was so "prominent," and Leonard's ownership of a new car, which he let Alice drive in exchange for physical intimacies, all reflect that reality. Yet it is also noteworthy that one of the driving forces, if not *the* driving force, behind the decision to file suit on Leonard's behalf, whether that decision was made by Leonard, his father, or a family retainer, was the protection of property. And the protection, of course, was not only of the Rhinelander real estate, the source of the family's fortune, from any claims of dower that could be made by Alice but also of the propertylike privileges to which the Rhinelander family felt entitled, both as members of the ruling class in New York and as white people. As W. E. B. DuBois pointed out after the trial, the "prestige of white America" had been tarnished by Leonard's marriage and the annulment trial.[9]

The *Rhinelander* case was not the only legal action related to a perceived transgression of racial boundaries in the arena of consumption and property that garnered national attention in 1925. As reporter Margery Rex had indicated, one major question in the Rhinelander trial was whether Leonard and Alice would live together. This issue of the races living together surfaced regularly during the era of the Great Migration as residential segregation increased in the North. The Sweet murder trial in Detroit, which began only a few weeks before the Rhinelander trial, for example, garnered a prominent position in the *Amsterdam News* because, as the paper explained, it was a clear-cut case of African Americans defending their rights to own property—a home.[10]

In 1927, Kelly Miller, a professor at Howard University, linked residential segregation and interracial marriage to explain why both were regulated by those who demanded white purity. Miller compared white Americans' desire to residentially separate themselves from blacks with their fear of miscegenation. "Intermarriageability [sic] is the acid test of good neighborhood. Whenever two easily distinguishable groups are forbidden to intermarry by law or custom, they will both find themselves uncomfortable in close residential proximity."[11] Strong opposition to interracial marriages in the North mirrored negative reactions to integration of neighborhoods, particularly as evidenced by the *Sweet* case. But, the success of efforts to keep people from different races from marrying and living next to each other depended on knowing who belonged to what race. Despite the absurdities of race exposed in the *Rhinelander* case, many Americans remained convinced that making racial distinctions was doable, desirable, and absolutely necessary.

For example, in New York State, only a little over ten years after the *Rhinelander* decision, yet another court case raised the question of how to determine racial identity in a state still lacking a legal definition of race. This time the issue arose in litigation over a restrictive covenant in a Westchester County deed that precluded the sale of property to a Negro. In February 1937, a white homeowner filed suit in Westchester to eject her neighbors, Pauline and Joshua Cockburn, from their property on the grounds that their purchase violated a restrictive covenant. The covenant prohibited the sale or lease of land to "negroes or any person or persons of the negro race or blood, except that colored servants may be maintained on the premises." The Cockburns denied that they were Negro under the terms of the covenant. Arthur Garfield Hays, a lawyer affiliated with the American Civil Liberties Union who worked with Clarence Darrow on the Sweet trial, represented the Cockburns with the support of the NAACP.[12]

Hays defended the Cockburns on the grounds that restrictive covenants violated New York public policy, as well as the Thirteenth and Fourteenth Amendments to the U.S. Constitution. According to an internal NAACP memorandum, Hays also planned to argue that "it is impossible under the laws of the State of New York and it is also impossible for experts to determine what is a Negro. For example, would very white-skinned people with a small amount of Negro blood be Negroes? . . . Mrs. Cockburn, herself [the actual property owner], is half Italian and approximately one-sixteenth colored blood. On the other hand, Mr. Cockburn is very dark."[13]

Hays suggested in a letter to the NAACP's Walter White, "I do not quite understand why the question was never raised before, but it is about time that someone raised the point that there are practically no Negroes in the United States." Hays contended that it was impossible to determine who was a Negro in the same way that no one could tell "what a Jew is, and I'd like to be helpful in getting the courts to do away with artificial distinctions among people of the human race." Hays added, "only Nazis know what pure races are."[14]

One month before the Cockburn trial commenced in White Plains, Roy Wilkins, the assistant secretary of the NAACP, wrote to a few New Yorkers to ask if they would act as "exhibits" during the trial. Wilkins explained that Hays "would like to have in the court room a few 'white Negroes' and a few 'dark white people.'"[15] During the trial, Joshua Cockburn testified that he had been called a "man of color" as well as "Negro." According to the *New York Times*, anthropologist Otto Klineberg, who later contributed to Gunnar Myrdal's 1944 race-relations opus, *The American Dilemma*, testified about the meaning of the term "Negro." Klineberg reasoned that most Negroes were not really "true Negroes." In addition, Klineberg argued that "skin color and other physical features are not conclusive evidence." Consequently, he concluded that Joshua Cockburn was not necessarily a Negro and that Pauline Cockburn, the legal owner of the house, was definitely not.[16]

Unfortunately for Hays, Otto Klineberg, and the Cockburns, the case of *Ridgway v. Cockburn* came before a judge who already possessed ideas about who or what counted as Negro or colored. The justice assigned to the case was none other than Lee Parsons Davis. Davis had just been elevated to the bench in 1937. In his written decision in *Ridgway v. Cockburn*, Justice Davis ruled that restrictive covenants did not violate New York's public policy, and since the U.S. Supreme Court had upheld a restrictive covenant in 1926, the Westchester covenant did not violate the U.S. Constitution.[17]

After Davis dismissed the constitutional challenges, he faced the question of Pauline and Joshua Cockburn's identities. Although New York State law and the restrictive covenant did not define "Negro," Davis concluded that Pauline Cockburn was "partly 'colored'" and her husband "in every outward appearance [was] what would be called, in common speech, a Negro." Davis disagreed with the defense and the defense's expert that "Negro" referred only to those of "unmixed African blood." Instead, Davis held that the covenant language had to be given "its natural and ordinary meaning," in other words, "common sense," equated with visual perception, should apply.[18]

Unlike lawyer Davis's arguments for Alice Rhinelander in 1925 that though she was colored that did not necessarily mean she was a Negress, Justice Davis found that "Negroes" meant "colored persons" and that therefore the defendant and her husband were "Negroes." By 1937 intermediate racial categories held no meaning. The category of mulatto had already disappeared from the U.S. Census, never to return. Davis also dismissed the defense's efforts to void the restrictive covenant because its language about race was too indefinite. Arthur Garfield Hays had suggested that the racial terminology in the restrictive covenant was vague and a court could not determine what sorts of people fell within its bounds. As someone who had participated in the processes that made certain ideas about race "real" despite their absurdity in the 1920s, Justice Davis found that *he* could easily make such a determination and protect the white homeowner's property, because "common sense" still worked.[19] Thus, once Davis identified the Cockburns as Negroes they could only live in this Westchester neighborhood as servants, not as owners of property.

The vexing links between property, race, and class highlighted in *Ridgway v. Cockburn* continued to bedevil Leonard and Alice Rhinelander well into the 1940s. When Leonard disappeared from New York in 1927, still Alice's lawful husband, he remained obligated under common law to financially support his wife. He did not. By December, Alice filed a lawsuit in Westchester County that asked for a judgment "separating the parties from bed and board" and requested support payments. Alice charged Leonard with abandonment and cruel and inhuman treatment. Process servers hired by Alice's lawyers, however, could not find Leonard. Rumors circulated in the press that the Rhinelanders had offered Alice $60,000 if she would end her legal action against Leonard and allow him to seek an out-of-state divorce. Alice's lawsuit apparently ended because no one could properly serve Leonard with legal papers.[20]

In the spring of 1929, Alice filed yet another lawsuit in New York—this time against Leonard's father for alienation of affection. She sought $500,000 (the equivalent of over six million dollars today) in damages from Philip Rhinelander for his role in separating her from Leonard. During the same year, Leonard moved to Nevada, a notorious divorce mill in the twentieth century, especially for New Yorkers burdened by New York's restrictive divorce statute. Leonard established residency in Nevada, and then began a divorce action against Alice. In December 1929, the Nevada courts gave Leonard his divorce, but the Nevada divorce decree made no provision for Alice's financial support. Moreover, under New York law, an out-of-state divorce was invalid unless both spouses appeared in court in the other state.[21]

Since Leonard and Alice remained married in the eyes of New York law, Alice filed still another legal proceeding in New York for a separation in February of 1930. Although Leonard now lived in Nevada, New York law allowed Alice to sue Leonard for a separation because the couple had married in New York and Alice still resided there. As part of Alice's action to legally separate from Leonard, she asked for financial support. During the course of this legal contest, the Westchester County Supreme Court ordered Leonard to support Alice until the court made its final decision. Leonard apparently still refused to make any payments to Alice. Consequently, the supreme court sequestered Leonard's personal property and any rents and profits from his real property. In other words, the court authorized the seizure of Leonard's assets and appointed a receiver to pay support to Alice. Any appointed receiver would be required to preserve Leonard's holdings, allocate any rents and profits as the court saw fit, and prevent Leonard from selling off his New York assets to keep them out of Alice's reach.[22]

Not surprisingly, Alice's actions to sequester Leonard's properties and other assets finally brought the Rhinelander family to the negotiating table. Sometime between the date that Alice's attorneys served Leonard with separation papers and the summer of 1930, the Rhinelanders decided to come to terms with Alice once and for all. If the New York courts granted Alice a separation and required Leonard to support her, the couple would still be legally married. Without any change in their then-current legal status, Alice would still be entitled to her dower rights in Leonard's property, and if Leonard died before she did, she would be entitled to a share of his ownership interests in the Rhinelander family properties and companies. In other words, Alice would remain Mrs. Rhinelander with access to the sources of the Rhinelander family's status and wealth. Moreover, if Alice won her alienation of affections lawsuit against Philip, she would gain an additional half-million dollars. The hearing in New York of a separation lawsuit and a trial for alienation of affections would also revive the press's interest in the story of Leonard and Alice Rhinelander. An alienation of affections trial might well bring out previously undisclosed details about Philip Rhinelander's orchestration of Leonard's annulment trial. Given these legal realities, it is no surprise that the Rhinelanders decided to cut a deal.[23]

In the summer of 1930, Alice and Leonard signed an agreement to provide Alice with monetary support, but only under certain conditions. According to the terms of a contract drafted by Philip Rhinelander's attorney (still Spotswood Bowers), Alice and Leonard agreed that they had separated and "all marital relations between them ceased" in 1924 "for existing causes which were insurmountable." In these words, the agreement recognized that the reasons behind their separation (Leonard's family's and society's disapproval of his potentially interracial marriage) could not be overcome. Even more significantly, the very first full recital paragraph of the contract baldly stated its underlying motivation: "it being mutually desirous of the benefits thereby resulting to each to definitely settle for all time their respective interests in all *property or claims to property whether present or prospective, contingent or vested, now or hereinafter acquired by either or both.*" Since Alice most likely owned little or no property, she still lived at home with her parents, and the Great Depression had already begun, the party most interested in eliminating Alice's rights in Rhinelander properties, and in protecting the property interests threatened by Alice's various lawsuits, was the Rhinelander family.[24]

In the rest of the contract, Leonard agreed to provide Alice with some "future support," but he wanted to make sure that Alice would not go after his assets in other states if he left Nevada. Consequently, Leonard agreed that Alice could re-open the Nevada divorce case, make a legal appearance in the Nevada courts, and either ask the court to provide for her financial support from Leonard or enter a defense to Leonard's divorce claims. If the Nevada court found Alice's defense valid and denied Leonard his divorce, Leonard agreed to pay Alice $31,500 in three payments and $3,800 a year payable in quarterly installments so long as she remained his wife. In the event the Nevada court revised the divorce decree to include a provision for Alice's support, Leonard agreed he would pay her $31,500 in one check and $3,600 a year in quarterly payments for her "natural life."[25]

As her part of the bargain, Alice would end her separation action against Leonard in New York and cancel the New York court's appointment of a receiver to hold Leonard's properties. In addition, she consented to stop her alienation of affections case against Philip Rhinelander. Both Leonard and Alice agreed that they would live apart and leave each other alone. More significantly, Alice consented to extinguish "all rights or claims of dower, inheritance and descent, and all rights or claims to a distributive share of his [Leonard's] personal estate, and all other rights and interests or claims in any manner arising or accruing out of the marriage relation." Leonard made a similar agreement, although Alice's waiver of her rights mattered more and directly promoted the Rhinelander family's interests, since Leonard would more likely than Alice die in possession of a substantial estate. And if Leonard died without a will and before his father, once Alice gave up her dower rights, Philip would inherit Leonard's estate. If Philip died before Leonard, Leonard's estate would pass upon Leonard's death to his sister, Adelaide. Either way, Leonard's property would remain in the hands of his family.[26]

In addition to Alice ceding rights of inheritance, Leonard and Alice both agreed that they had the right to do whatever they wanted with their own property, even if they died without a will, "as if the parties . . . *had never been married*." Moreover, Alice renounced her right to use the Rhinelander name and agreed that "she will not in any way use or make reference to the name of

Rhinelander in connection with any appearance upon the stage or in connection with any writing or lecture." Thus, by 1930, the ultimate goal of the 1925 annulment trial to ensure a permanent separation and leave the couple as if they had never married would be achieved. Alice would also renounce the family name and be plain Alice Jones once again.[27] Although the agreement did not directly state its underlying function, in essence it served as a method for Alice to accept and be bound by the terms of Leonard's Nevada divorce, as modified by this 1930 contract, in exchange for Leonard's commitment to pay support. As an addendum to Leonard and Alice's agreement, Philip Rhinelander agreed to act as a guarantor for Leonard's payments to Alice. If Leonard stopped payments to Alice, his father and his father's "heirs, executors and administrators" would be required to continue them. Pursuant to these agreements signed by Philip, Leonard, and Alice in July 1930, Alice petitioned the Nevada courts to reconsider Leonard's divorce decree and include new provisions for her support. By doing so, Alice rendered that divorce decree enforceable against her under New York law. Faced with an agreement by both parties, the Nevada court modified its decree to include the terms of Leonard and Alice's new agreement.[28]

By the end of 1930, almost ten years after Leonard and Alice first met, their marriage no longer existed. Leonard returned to New York and took up the position of auditor at the Rhinelander Real Estate Company. Alice relinquished any residual claims to elite whiteness conferred by her continued use of the Rhinelander name, as well as her claim to dower or inheritance rights in Rhinelander property. In exchange, Alice received a lump sum payment of $31,500, only $1,500 of which went to her; the rest went to her lawyers. She began to receive her yearly sum of $3,600 directly from Philip Rhinelander; Leonard never sent her a check. Today, $31,500 would be the equivalent of over $380,000 and the annual payments to Alice would be the equivalent of over $45,000.[29] Despite the significance of the dollar amount of the Rhinelanders' payments to Alice, they constituted a pittance compared to the value of the Rhinelander family's assets.

Only six years after Leonard and Alice signed their agreement, the now thirty-three-year-old Leonard succumbed to pneumonia. Pictures of Leonard published in the 1930s press depict a heavy and bloated figure. After Leonard's early death, his father, following the advice of Spotswood Bowers, continued to pay Alice. Four years later, in March 1940, Philip Rhinelander died at the age of seventy-four. His will written in 1939 described his estate as one which "consists largely of interests in real estate." According to Philip's will, his only surviving child, Adelaide, would receive his personal effects and the rest of his estate would be divided between Adelaide and her two nieces (daughters of Leonard's oldest brother, Philip Kip). Nothing in Philip's will referred to his payments to Alice Jones or his guaranty of his son's obligation to Alice.[30]

Two months before Philip died, Alice received her usual remittance from the Rhinelanders. But the next quarterly check, due April 1940, never came. Philip Rhinelander's yearly disbursements to Alice equaled only 0.004 of his gross estate, but his heirs, including Adelaide, opposed these payments as "an onerous demand for life support." In fact, apparently anticipating Philip's death, only a few months before he died Adelaide had asked her attorneys to provide an opinion on the legality of her father's guaranty of Leonard's payments. Adelaide's lawyers gave their assessment that the 1930 contract signed by Alice, Leonard, and Philip would not be enforceable, saying that the agreement violated public policy in New York because it promoted divorce. Based on that opinion, Adelaide instructed her father's executors to stop paying Alice Jones.[31]

Adelaide's efforts to prevent her father's estate from making payments to Alice led to yet another legal battle between Alice Jones and the Rhinelanders. In May 1940, Alice filed a claim against Philip's estate. During that same month, Philip's executors scrambled to find a legal justification to deny her claim. First, their attorneys requested a legal opinion from a Nevada judge about the validity of Leonard and Alice's 1930 agreement. In their letter, the executors' law firm of Alexander & Keenan enclosed a copy of the opinion that Adelaide received from her law firm. They also informed the Nevada judge that "Alice Jones Rhinelander was a Negress. Leonard Kip Rhinelander was white." Therefore, they argued, "we take the liberty of suggesting the possibility that occurred to us that, under the provisions . . . of the Statutes of Nevada [the Nevada antimiscegenation law], and the public policy therein declared, it might be that your State would refuse to recognize the marriage . . . even though it was valid where made, and, if so, it might further be possible that under the laws of your State the contract based on such marriage might be either illegal or unenforceable." The judge found Leonard, Alice, and Philip's 1930 agreement valid under Nevada law. Although miscegenation constituted a "gross misdemeanor" in Nevada, it didn't matter because Leonard and Alice had married in New York.[32]

After failing to procure a favorable Nevada legal opinion, the executors and their attorneys solicited high-powered legal advice from the retired chief judge of New York's highest state court. In Alexander & Keenan's December

1940 letter to Judge Frederick E. Crane, they requested yet another opinion about Alice's claims. Like the Nevada judge, Judge Crane concluded that "there [was] no escaping the meaning" of the 1930 agreement that bound Leonard and Philip Rhinelander, and their estates, to make annual payments until Alice's death. By March 1941, Philip's executors concluded that they had to allow Alice's claim against his estate.[33]

Adelaide, however, still disagreed. In September of 1941, in the Nassau County Surrogate's Court, where Philip's will had been filed, Surrogate Howell took testimony from witnesses to determine whether or not to allow Alice's claims. Alice may have felt a sense of urgency by this point, since, according to the press, Philip's executors had already begun to liquidate his estate. Almost two weeks before the hearing began, at least six properties from Philip's estate had been sold.[34]

During the hearing in Nassau County, the bulk of the evidence revolved around determining the validity of Alice's claim on Philip's estate (Adelaide's lawyers argued that since Leonard and Alice's marriage violated Nevada antimiscegenation law, their Nevada agreement on the divorce had to be illegal, too). Most of the testimony consisted of Alice's and Leonard's lawyers describing the rounds of negotiations that led up to the 1930 contract between Leonard and Alice. Leon Jacobs had actually brought the checks payable to Alice out to Nevada by train in 1930. Jacobs testified that he knew at the time he would give the money to Alice's lawyers only if she agreed to ask the Nevada court to modify the divorce decree. Alice would have received nothing if she contested the divorce. Despite the sometimes confusing testimony over whether the 1930 agreement purchased Alice's consent to Leonard's divorce, the Nassau County Surrogate ruled in November 1941 that Philip's guaranty required his estate to pay Alice $3,600 every year for the rest of her life.[35]

This lawsuit, like Leonard's earlier one, wound its way through two levels of appellate courts. After Adelaide appealed the surrogate court's decision, an intermediate appellate court agreed with the Rhinelander family and invalidated the underlying contract because it violated New York's public policy against divorce. Alice Jones, however, sought to overturn this decision. One year later, the New York Court of Appeals reversed the intermediate court and ruled that Philip Rhinelander's heirs and his estate remained obligated to pay Alice. Alice had waived and released any right to use the Rhinelander name; as her lawyer pointed out during the appeal, she had given up something that both sides considered of value. Alice remained entitled to be paid for severing her connections with the family and Philip Rhinelander's estate continued to pay her $3,600 a year for more than forty years until her death.[36]

When Alice died in a Westchester hospital on 13 September 1989, she had never remarried. At her death, almost exactly sixty-eight years after Alice met Leonard, her bank account contained $25,000; she owned a one-third interest in the Jones family home on Pelham Road, worth about $70,000. The death certificate filed in Westchester County identified her as "Alice Jones" and indicated she spent almost a year in the hospital before she died. Significantly, the death certificate also maintained that Alice Jones had *never* been married.[37]

All of the legal maneuvering and negotiation, temporary resolution, and subsequent conflict between Alice and the various Rhinelanders following the end of the 1925 annulment trial only serves to confirm the centrality of property to Leonard and Alice's story and the deep connections between property and race. If Leonard's family weren't wealthy landowners, the couple would have never met, since Leonard never would have been sent to The Orchards to be treated for his supposed deficiencies. And if by some chance they had met under different circumstances, their courtship would have been markedly different, and his family would not have gone to such extraordinary lengths to destroy their marriage. As it was, property (both in its tangible form of valuable New York land and in the form of a highly valued status as white) constituted a lurking presence throughout Leonard and Alice's courtship, marriage, and the subsequent annulment trial.

The Rhinelander family's response to Leonard and Alice's marriage and separation demonstrates that the family viewed property (in all its aspects) with a nigh-on religious fervor. The final contract between Leonard and Alice, guaranteed as it was by Philip, merely served to confirm in writing, to *document*, that by the time it was prepared and signed the most important aspects of their relationship centered on the property rights created by their 1924 marriage. Using property and race as an analytical tool to approach the story of Alice and Leonard gives us an opportunity to better understand the hidden depths of what might otherwise be misunderstood as either (or both) a tawdry tale of reciprocal cynical manipulations or a simple love story.[38]

Of course, more than just concerns about property, wealth, and race circulated through the bundled narratives that comprised Alice and Leonard's tale. Shifting conceptions of sexuality and gender, cultural change and confusion, personal ambivalence and media frenzy, to name just a few, were all bound up in the story. But through the sometimes moving, contradictory, confusing, and ultimately poignant story of Leonard and Alice and the time and place in which they lived, we can more clearly glimpse how ideas about race, class, and marriage shaped their lives and the lives of others. Indeed, the narrative of the Rhinelander annulment trial must be properly understood as one part of a larger story: the expansion of a system of racial hierarchy in the American North that took off after the Great Migration gave rise to "an intensified racial consciousness," particularly in locations like New York. Although ultimately some of the Rhinelander family wealth ended up with Alice Jones, her final agreement with Leonard maintained the unequal distribution of assets that characterized one critical difference between those considered white and those designated black in the twentieth century. Moreover, the links between race and property evident in the strenuous efforts undertaken by the Rhinelanders to dissolve the marriage between Leonard and Alice anticipated the continued expansion of the connections between race and property that would structure race relations in the North throughout the rest of the twentieth century.[39]

The story of the Rhinelander annulment trial makes it clear that race mattered for marriage—even in a northern state that did not prohibit marriages across racial lines—and that it mattered more than any question about a couple's love for each other. And echoes of this privileging of particular races in matters of marriage continue today. Recent statistics on interracial marriage suggest that race still matters for marriage to Americans—more than forty years after the U.S. Supreme Court decided *Loving v. Virginia*.[40] Understanding *Rhinelander v. Rhinelander* in all its complexities may help us grasp why Americans still make race matter.

Notes

ABBREVIATIONS

AJ	Alice Jones
CPMR	*Cases and Points: Records and Briefs in the Matter of Rhinelander*
CPRR	*Cases and Points: Records and Briefs in the Case of Rhinelander v. Rhinelander*
LKR	Leonard Kip Rhinelander
NYA	*New York American*
NYAN	*New York Amsterdam News*
NYDM	*New York Daily Mirror*
NYDN	*New York Daily News*
NYEJ	*New York Evening Journal*
NYEP	*New York Evening Post*
NYHT	*New York Herald Tribune*
NYT	*New York Times*
PNAACP	Papers of the National Association for the Advancement of Colored People, Library of Congress, Washington, D.C. (microfilm edition at Alexander Library, Rutgers University, New Brunswick, N.J.)

RG 29   Bureau of the Census Records, Record Group 29, National Archives, College Park, Md.

TNCF   Tuskegee Institute News Clippings File, Tuskegee, Alabama (microfilm edition at Princeton University Library, Princeton, N.J., and Kent State University Library, Kent, Ohio)

INTRODUCTION

1 The description of the day's weather for 9 November 1925, comes from a report published the next day. See *NYDM*, 10 November 1925, 1, final edition. A copy of Leonard's summons and complaint and Alice's answer can be found in the two-volume record of the Rhinelander annulment trial prepared for an appeal to New York's highest court, the Court of Appeals. See *CPRR*. The two volumes include the transcript from the almost-two-week trial, copies of the legal pleadings, copies of most of the evidence introduced during the trial, and the appellate briefs. I located copies of the *Cases and Points* for the *Rhinelander* case in the New York State Supreme Court Library in Buffalo, New York, and the Law Library at Cornell University in Ithaca, New York.

2 In recent years, historians have written a number of histories of trials. The ones that have influenced me the most include Goodman, *Stories of Scottsboro*; Boyle, *Arc of Justice*; Berenson, *Trial of Madame Caillaux*; Grossberg, *Judgment for Solomon*; Fox, *Trials of Intimacy*; Linda Gordon, *Great Arizona Orphan Abduction*; and Edward Larson, *Summer for the Gods*. I have also found the following articles useful: Goodman, "For the Love of Stories"; Thomas, "Michael Grossberg's Telling Tale"; Allan Megill, "Recounting the Past"; and Carlo Ginzburg, "Checking the Evidence."

3 Two examples of contemporary accounts of the Rhinelander trial that recognized its larger significance appear in "Black and White in New York" and Editorial, "Greek Tragedy—Not Bedroom Farce," *NYDN*, 21 November 1925, 13, pink edition. See also Merz, "What Makes a First-Page Story?," 156. Merz's article concluded that in 1925 the top news items all involved a "story of a personal fight between well identified antagonists which involves the element of suspense" (158). Another example of a scandal over the demise of the marriage of a wealthy New Yorker involved the divorce trial of James Stillman, an executive at National City Bank. The owner of the *Daily News* called for heavy press coverage of this society scandal. See McGivena, *News*, 88. See also "Sell the Papers!" 6. Two years later, the New York papers fell over themselves to cover the scandalous marriage and separation of "Peaches" and "Daddy" Browning, a wealthy real estate owner in New York. See Stevens, *Sensationalism*

and the New York Press, 109. For a recent history of the Scopes trial, where a Tennessee schoolteacher was prosecuted for violating a state law that prohibited teaching evolution, see Edward Larson, *Summer for the Gods*.

4   Charles Merz ("What Makes a First-Page Story?" 156) includes the story of Gerald Chapman in his top ten stories of 1925. In 1927, journalist Silas Bent discussed Gerald Chapman and how the press made the "gunman and murderer" into a hero. See his "Invasion of Privacy," 836.

5   According to historian Peter Wallenstein, the Dutch colony of New Amsterdam prohibited interracial sex. See his *Tell the Court I Love My Wife*, 253. See also *Loving v. Virginia*, 388 U.S. 1 (1967).

6   New York's divorce laws are discussed in Friedman, *History of American Law*; Hartog, *Man and Wife in America*; Basch, *Framing American Divorce*; and Paul H. Jacobson, *American Marriage and Divorce*. For an in-depth discussion of New York's annulment statute, see chapter 7.

7   A previously published account of the Rhinelander trial was written without the benefit of the trial transcript (a major source for my book). Instead, historians Earl Lewis and Heidi Ardizzone relied mainly on the newspaper reports. Although their book was written with a great deal of narrative brio, their failure to locate the transcript until after their publication date, along with their lack of legal background, led them to several errors, and to misunderstand several critical concepts. For example, Lewis and Ardizzone did not recognize, or at least did not discuss, the legal significance and symbolic connotations of Leonard's annulment action, which sought to create the legal fiction that his marriage never existed. Similarly, they mistakenly referred to New York's highest court, to which two separate appeals were addressed during the legal aftermath of Leonard's marriage to Alice, as the New York Supreme Court, when in fact it was, and still is, the New York Court of Appeals. In addition, given that Leonard Rhinelander came from a New York family whose wealth rested on its ownership of valuable Manhattan properties, Lewis and Ardizzone never discussed how a husband's annulment action could lead to the severance of a wife's dower rights—that is, a married woman's right to inherit an interest in her husband's land. The term "dower rights" only appears when Lewis and Ardizzone include an excerpt from the *Chicago Defender*. See Lewis and Ardizzone, *Love on Trial*, 209 (dower rights), 243, 251 (incorrect court names).

8   *Schaeffer v. Schaeffer*, 160 A.D. 48 (App. Div. 1913) ("I think we have not yet arrived at a legal stage which requires an annulment of a marriage because one party or both parties were untruthful to each other in their mutual protestations of all-consuming and undying love. Marriage is yet a status on which depends the idea of a family, and on which in turn has arisen the structure of civilization as we know it.") See also May, *Great Expectations*, 61–62, and

Dumenil, *Modern Temper*, 130–31. Legal historian Michael Grossberg (*Governing the Hearth*, 38) suggests an even earlier connection between romantic love and marriage dating back to the early nineteenth century.
9 A detailed discussion of Leonard's lawyers' arguments appears in chapter 7.
10 Brisbane, "Today," *NYA*, 28 November 1924, 1. Brisbane began his "Today" column for the Hearst papers in 1917; it appeared in 200 daily papers and 1,200 weekly papers nationwide. See Staudacher, "Arthur Brisbane." This unspoken link between race and marriage even in a state without an antimiscegenation statute contributes to the persistence of the "taboo" against black-white marriages. Thus I disagree with historians like Renee Romano, who optimistically concludes her study of post–World War II black-white marriage. See Romano, *Race Mixing*, 2, 250. A recent analysis of data on black-white marriages reported that in 2002, only 0.7 percent of all American marriages included couples in which one party was identified as white and the other as black. See Doyle, "Progress of Love," 33. Renee Romano (*Race Mixing*, 3) uses the term "taboo."
11 Indeed, one outcome of a successful annulment lawsuit brought by a husband would be the end of a wife's dower rights in her husband's property.
12 In her treatise on property law legal scholar Laura Underkuffler points out that conceptions of property can include the notion that property is "an assertion of self" (*Idea of Property*, 1).
13 DuBois, "Souls of White Folk"; Cheryl Harris, "Whiteness as Property."
14 The idea that race is socially constructed has become a truism in modern scholarship. Recently philosophers and so-called race theorists have been discussing what exactly this entails. See, for example, Haslanger, "Gender and Race"; Mallon, "'Race'"; Mallon, "Passing, Traveling and Reality"; Fields, "Whiteness, Racism, and Identity," 48; Fields, "Of Rogues and Geldings," 1400–1401; and Holt, *Problem of Race*, 22. See also Eduardo Bonilla-Silva ("Rethinking Racism," 469), who discusses "racialized social systems." Thomas Holt (*Problem of Race*, 20) contends that certain stereotypes or images related to race tend to reoccur because "a new historical construct is never entirely new and the old is never entirely supplanted by the new." In a sense, the term "race" in America can be seen as a type of palimpsest, in which the definitions and glosses pertinent to the term in one period are partially erased, overwritten, and obscured by the understandings of the term that are held by later generations, that may have evolved from the earlier ones, and that are then overwritten and obscured by even later meanings and arguments.
15 Jordan, *White Over Black*; Edmund Morgan, *American Slavery, American Freedom*; Berlin, *Many Thousands Gone*; Walter Johnson, *Soul by Soul*, 82; Holt, *Problem of Race*; Fields, "Of Rogues and Geldings."
16 As many historians of the 1920s observe, significant changes in class relations, gender relations, and industrial production marked this era. Thomas Holt sug-

gests that early-twentieth-century meanings of race and racism can be linked to the rise of mass consumption in modern America, when "items of consumption" became one method "by which people constitute[d] *who* they were" (*Problem of Race*, 74). Consequently, Holt points to conflicts over consumption as the new location where Americans reshaped the meaning of race and the contents of racism. See also Holt, "Marking Race, Race-Making, and the Writing of History," 7.

17 Examples of recent scholarship on race in the North include Leslie Harris, *In the Shadow of Slavery*; Foote, *Black and White Manhattan*; Sacks, *Before Harlem*; Boyle, *Arc of Justice*; Biondi, *To Stand and Fight*; and Theoharis and Woodard, eds., *Freedom North*. See also Gilmore, *Defying Dixie*, for study of the "long civil rights movement."

18 Race continues to matter for love and property in the early twenty-first century. Recent *New York Times* articles have addressed discrimination and homeownership. See Anahad O'Connor, "Firm Steered Home Buyers, Group Says," *NYT*, 24 March 2006, NY Region (fair housing group accuses Westchester real estate company of steering white home buyers away from neighborhoods perceived as African American or Hispanic); Bob Tedeschi, "All's Fair in Love, War and Lending?" *NYT*, 16 July 2006, real estate (Center for Responsible Lending study shows that African Americans offered a higher interest rate on fixed rate loans than white Americans with similar credit histories.); Janny Scott, "Report Alleges Bias by a Real Estate Giant," *NYT*, 11 October 2006, section B, 6, late edition (Brooklyn real estate company accused of steering white home buyers away from African American neighborhoods and not giving African American home buyers the same kinds of information as white home buyers); and Marcelle S. Fischler, "Civil Rights; Pushing the Fight Against Racial Segregation," *NYT*, 25 March 2007, section 14LI, 6, late edition (new fair housing laws in Nassau and Suffolk counties enacted to reduce high rate of segregated suburbs on Long Island). The rate of black-white marriage rose during the last half of the twentieth century, but the data indicates such marriages still take place at a relatively low rate. See Gullickson, "Black/White Interracial Marriage Trends," 299; Census Bureau, "Married-Couple and Unmarried Partner Households"; and Doyle, "Progress of Love."

19 Bessie, *Jazz Journalism*; Nasaw, *Chief*, 322; Herskovits, "Negro's Americanism," 354.

20 As Laura Hanft Korobkin ("Maintenance of Mutual Confidence," 10) reminds us, "all litigation is essentially conducted by constructing, presenting, and interpreting narrative versions of past events."

21 A court stenographer reproduced Alice's and Leonard's letters that appear in the trial transcript. The letters may contain mistakes in language or other errors that did not appear in the originals. Where I use quotations from the letters I leave in

any errors that appeared in the original trial transcript. I only had access to the courtship letters reproduced in the transcript that were chosen by Leonard's and Alice's lawyers to use as evidence during the annulment proceeding.

22 AJ to LKR, 1 June 1923, Exh. 108; AJ to LKR, 21 August 1922, Exh. 64, *CPRR*.

23 Dumenil, *Modern Temper*, 76–78; Steven Ross, *Working-Class Hollywood*, 200–201.

24 AJ to LKR, 16 January 1922, Exh. 56; AJ to LKR, 22 January 1922, Exh. 89; AJ to LKR, 18 June 1922, Exh. 68; AJ to LKR, 22 July 1922, Exh. 73; AJ to LKR, 7 August 1922, Exh. 61; AJ to LKR, 8 November 1922, Exh. 110, all in *CPRR*.

CHAPTER ONE

1 A photograph of the Westchester County Courthouse appears in Griffin, *Westchester County and Its People*, 81. Descriptions of the day's events in court are in *CPRR*, 696; "Kip's Mystery Notes Read," *NYEJ*, 23 November 1925, 1, final night extra; Grace Robinson, "Alice Bares Her Dark Body," *NYDN*, 24 November 1925, 3, pink edition; George Buchanan, "Mrs. Rhinelander Disrobes to Prove Color," *NYDM*, 24 November 1925, 3, final edition; and "Rhinelander's Wife Cries Under Ordeal," *NYT*, 24 November 1925, 3.

2 Leonard's complaint and his first amended complaint in *CPRR*, 7–8, 9–11.

3 The description "extraordinary" comes from "Kip's Mystery Notes Read: Women Are Ejected From Court," *NYEJ*, 23 November 1925, 1, final night extra; an "ordeal" and "Gethsemane" are from Robinson, "Mistrial Near as Lawyers Clash Before Mystery Letter Is Read," *NYDN*, 24 November 1925, 3, pink edition.

4 Descriptions of Leonard with Valentino hair in "Kip Was Colored Girl's Slave, Lawyer Charges," *NYDM*, 10 November 1925, 3, final edition. Photograph of Leonard with spats smoking a cigarette was on the front page of *NYDN*, 11 November 1925, 1, pink edition; and "Flappers Agog as Rhinelander Plays the Stoic," *NYDN*, 11 November 1925, 2, pink edition.

5 Somewhat conflicting information about the Rhinelander family can be found in Hassell, *Rhinelander Family in America*; Rhinelander, *One Branch of the Rhinelanders* (according to this book, the original ancestor landed in Philadelphia in 1727 but died in New Rochelle by 1737; it also draws on Hassell for some information); Reynolds, *Genealogical and Family History of Southern New York*, 1:317–19; Norbury, *Colonial Families of the United States*, 431–33; and "The Rhinelander Family," *NYT*, 23 June 1878, 2. As early as the antebellum era, the Rhinelander family was considered one of New York's wealthiest. See Pessen, "Political Democracy," 36.

6 Henry James, *Washington Square*. The Rhinelander family home was located at 14 Washington Square North. See "Miss Rhinelander's Will," *NYT*, 27 June 1914, 6; and Editorial, "Old Mansions Give Way to Apartment," *NYT*, 30 April 1922,

35. Information on the value of William Rhinelander's estate in "The Rhinelander Estate," *NYT*, 25 June 1878, 5; and Gray, "Family That Sought To Set an Architectural Example," *NYT*, 10 October 1999, Real Estate, 7.

7 Burrows and Wallace, *Gotham*, 1074; Rhinelander, *One Branch of the Rhinelanders*, 26–27; Reynolds, *Genealogical and Family History of Southern New York*, 1:317–19; Hassell, *Rhinelander Family in America*; "Rhinelander Real Estate Partition Suit," *NYT*, 17 November 1901, 12. Some of the properties owned by the Rhinelanders included 130 Broadway at Cedar Street, 171–185 6th Avenue at 12th Street, 109–113 West 12th Street, 161–169 6th Avenue at 12th Street, 1627–1633 2nd Avenue, 240 East 86th Street, and 1660 2nd Avenue at 86th Street. See "In the Field of Real Estate," *NYT*, 3 December 1902, 14.

8 Information on the Kip family in Hamm, *Famous Families of New York*, 1:217–26, and Reynolds, *Genealogical and Family History of Southern New York*, 1:319. See also "Ex-Mayor William V. Brady," *NYT*, 1 April 1870, 5; and "Reports on Kip Estate," *NYT*, 1 September 1922, 12. Details on Adelaide Kip Rhinelander's death can be found in "Mrs. P. Rhinelander Is Burned to Death," *NYT*, 12 September 1915, 1. Leonard Rhinelander also testified about his mother's death; see *CPRR*, 384–85.

9 Information on the Rhinelanders and their war service in Rhinelander, *One Branch of the Rhinelanders*, 27 n. 57. The World War I Memorial in Harvard University's Memorial Church lists Thomas Jackson Oakley Rhinelander as a deceased member of the Class of 1920. See <www.memorialchurch.harvard.edu/history/ww1.shtml> (14 May 2008).

10 "Miss Alexander Is Lieutenant's Bride," *NYT*, 19 June 1918, 11; "Miss Rhinelander to Wed a Banker," *NYT*, 14 September 1921, 16; "Miss Rhinelander Weds J. S. Shackno," *NYT*, 10 November 1921, 19.

11 Information on the Knickerbocker Greys in Kisseloff, *You Must Remember This*, 117–88. Leonard's brothers are listed on the roster for the still existing Knickerbocker Greys at <www.knickerbockergreys.org/oldroster.htm> (14 May 2008). The Knickerbocker Greys were founded in 1881. See Shapiro, "Celebrating 125 with the Knickerbocker Greys," *New York Sun*, 17 April 2006, <www.nysun.com/article/31070> (14 May 2008); and Eric Konigsberg, "Manhattan's Littlest Soldiers," *NYT*, 11 March 2007, 19.

12 J. Provost Stout, a former tutor for the Rhinelander family, testified that Leonard found it hard to learn when he was about six years old. See *CPRR*, 133–34. Information on Leonard's stuttering comes from the testimony of four witnesses: Julie Despres, Leonard's sister's former governess; Sidney Ussher, an Episcopalian clergyman in charge of Leonard's Sunday school; J. Provost Stout; and L. Pierce Clark, the director of The Orchards. According to his obituary, L. Pierce Clark was a well-known neurologist and a former head of a number of societies involved in "mental hygiene." See "Dr. L. Pierce Clark, Psychiatrist

Dies," *NYT*, 4 December 1933, 21. During the trial, the press reported that Leonard stuttered. For one example, see Robinson, "Girl Agreed Reluctantly to His Plan, He Admits in Stammering Recital of Romance," *NYDN*, 12 November 1925, 3, pink edition. Clark diagnosis in *CPRR*, 50. See also Orchards Records, Exh. 17, *CPRR*, 51, 53, and 56.

13 Records from The Orchards introduced into evidence show that LKR arrived with his father on 14 February 1921. An employee of The Orchards testified that Philip never visited again. See Orchards Records, Exh. 17, *CPRR*, 51; and testimony of Thomas Uniker, *CPRR*, 77.

14 See chapter 2 for discussion of late-nineteenth-century and early-twentieth-century European immigration. Information on the Jones family comes from birth certificates and the ship manifests introduced into evidence. The ship manifest indicates the Joneses held British citizenship and sailed from Liverpool to America. It lists George as a thirty-eight-year-old laborer, traveling with his thirty-year-old wife, Elizabeth, and a six-year-old child, Ethel. They brought only three pieces of luggage to the United States. See *CPRR*, 24–27, 45; and *Passengers List, District of the City of New York, Port of New York, S.S. Majestic*, 18 March 1891, <www.ancestry.com> (22 September 2006). Elizabeth Jones testified that she met George in Bradford, England, located in West Yorkshire. See testimony of Elizabeth Jones, *CPRR*, 889, 904–6.

15 Physical descriptions of Alice Jones Rhinelander in Robinson, "I'm Not Colored Cries the Bride of Rhinelander," *NYDN*, 14 November 1924, 3, afternoon edition; and "Rhinelander Absent as Jury Is Chosen in Annulment Suit," *NYEP*, 9 November 1925, 1. Information on Alice's work as a domestic in testimony of Leonard Rhinelander, Elizabeth Jones, and Grace Miller, *CPRR*, 475–76, 885, and 914. Working as a laundress was hard work, yet some women chose this form of labor instead of working inside an employer's home. See Sacks, *Before Harlem*, 118.

16 The story of how Leonard and Alice met has been pieced together from the sometimes conflicting testimony of Leonard Rhinelander, *CPRR*, 135–45, 499–500, 600–615; Grace Jones Miller, *CPRR*, 878–88; and Elizabeth Jones, *CPRR*, 890, 914, 927–29. I also draw on the portions of Leonard and Alice's correspondence introduced as evidence. Orchards records also discuss some of Leonard's activities in 1921 and early 1922; see *CPRR*, 61–65.

17 Information about Leonard's car comes from his testimony, *CPRR*, 601. Orchards records also indicate he purchased a new car in September of 1921; see *CPRR*, 61. See also testimony of Leonard Rhinelander, *CPRR*, 600, 698–99.

18 Westchester County, "a favorite home and playground for the city," was not a homogeneous community. The county was divided into wealthy and middle-class suburbs as well as a few small cities such as New Rochelle (the family home of Alice Jones) and White Plains (the location of the annulment trial).

See Lundberg, Komarovsky, and McInerny, *Leisure*, 27–28. As of 1926, New Rochelle's Chamber of Commerce described the roads between New Rochelle and New York City as paved with macadam and concrete. It also provided a figure of 40,000 people for New Rochelle's population. See New Rochelle Chamber of Commerce, *New Rochelle*. Kenneth Jackson discusses the beginnings of Westchester County in his *Crabgrass Frontier*, 166.

19 Testimony of Leonard Rhinelander, *CPRR*, 135–38, 601–5; testimony of Grace Miller, *CPRR*, 878–80. Carl Kreitler never appeared as a witness.

20 Testimony of Grace Miller, *CPRR*, 880–82; testimony of Leonard Rhinelander, *CPRR*, 138, 140, 499, 609. Going to the movies became popular entertainment for Americans of all classes in the 1920s. See Steven Ross, *Working Class Hollywood*, 175; and Kyvig, *Daily Life in the United States*, 78–80. For the description of the location of Jones home, see testimony of Thomas Uniker, *CPRR*, 80, and testimony of Leonard Rhinelander, *CPRR*, 617–18.

21 Testimony of Leonard Rhinelander, *CPRR*, 499–500; testimony of Grace Miller, *CPRR*, 882–83; testimony of Elizabeth Jones, *CPRR*, 927–28.

22 Testimony of Leonard Rhinelander, *CPRR*, 150. Sometimes Carl drove him, after Leonard lost his license temporarily when he hit a policeman. See LKR to AJ, 28 September 1921, Exh. F, *CPRR*; and testimony of Grace Miller, *CPRR*, 887–88.

23 Reynolds, *Genealogical and Family History of Southern New York*, 1:317; French, ed. *History of Westchester County*, 1:756; and New Rochelle Chamber of Commerce, *New Rochelle*, n.p. The Chamber of Commerce described New Rochelle's train station as only sixteen miles from Grand Central Station.

24 New Rochelle Chamber of Commerce, *New Rochelle*, n.p. A description of the Jones home in "Society Youth Weds Cabman's Daughter," *NYT*, 14 November 1924, 1. Photograph of their house in *NYDN*, 15 November 1924, 3, final edition.

25 Information on the early days of Leonard and Alice's courtship comes from testimony of Leonard Rhinelander and letters between the two dated from 1921 to 1924 introduced as evidence during the trial. See AJ to LKR, 6 December 1921, Exh. 24; AJ to LKR, 9 December 1921, Exh. 25; and LKR to AJ, 16 January 1922, Exh. R, all in *CPRR*. See also Kyvig, *Daily Life*, 81; "Charlie Chaplin," *Who's Who in the Twentieth Century*; and James Weldon Johnson, *Black Manhattan*, 186–89.

26 Testimony of Leonard Rhinelander, *CPRR*, 444–45; testimony of Robert Brooks, *CPRR*, 851; testimony of Emily Brooks, *CPRR*, 871–72; testimony of Elizabeth Jones, *CPRR*, 929; testimony of Leonard Rhinelander, *CPRR*, 150, 847. As of 1921 only 35 percent of Americans had a telephone in their home. See *Historical Statistics of the United States*, Series R1–12, 783.

27 Bailey, *From Front Porch to Back Seat*, 80; Fass, *Damned and the Beautiful*, 218. An increase in sexual encounters among the young took place as parents could

no longer closely control their children's dating activity. See Clement, *Love for Sale*, 222; and LKR to AJ, 7 October 1921, Exh. J, *CPRR*.

28 LKR to AJ, 25 October 1921, Exh. L; AJ to LKR, 27 October 1921, Exh. 19; LKR to AJ, 28 October 1921, Exh. K, all in *CPRR*; Irwin, *Highlights of Manhattan*, 213. See also "Miss Rhinelander Weds J. S. Shackno," *NYT*, 10 November 1921, 19.

29 LKR to AJ, 29 October 1921, Exh. M; AJ to LKR, 17 November 1921, Exh. 21, both in *CPRR*.

30 AJ to LKR, 4 November 1921, Exh. 20; AJ to LKR, 6 December 1921, Exh. 24, both in *CPRR*.

31 LKR to AJ, 2 December 1921, Exh. Q; LKR to AJ, 9 December 1921, Exh. P; AJ to LKR, 6 December 1921, Exh. 24, all in *CPRR*. Examples of affectionate expressions in letters: "dearest" in LKR to AJ, 28 October 1921, Exh. K; "sweet heart" in AJ to LKR, 17 November 1921, Exh. 21; "Honeybunch" in LKR to AJ, 9 December 1921, Exh. P, all in *CPRR*.

32 Testimony of Leonard Rhinelander, *CPRR*, 586–89; testimony of Ross Chidester, *CPRR*, 937.

33 Information on hotel stay comes from Leonard's testimony and letters. See testimony of Leonard Rhinelander, *CPRR*, 154–57, 591–94; and testimony of Hotel Marie-Antoinette clerk Henry Mousees, *CPRR*, 204–5. See also Irwin, *Highlights of Manhattan*, 325.

34 AJ to LKR, 2 January 1922, Exh. K; AJ to LKR, 6 January 1922, Exh. 48, both in *CPRR*. It is unclear whether Alice had another suitor. The man she told Leonard about, New Rochelle firefighter Eddie Holland, testified that they never had a relationship. See testimony of Edward Holland, *CPRR*, 302–3. He did admit that he had known her for about fifteen years. It's possible that they had some kind of relationship that Holland did not want to discuss because Alice had already been identified by her lawyer as colored. The press emphasized that Holland was white. See photograph of Holland in "Suitors Rhinelander Bride Alleged Were Pursuing Her," *NYEJ*, 16 November 1925, 3, final news edition.

35 AJ to LKR, 6 January 1922, Exh. 48 ("feeling sickly . . . worried about what to do"); AJ to LKR, 14 January 1922, Exh. 110; AJ to LKR, [undated] January 1922, Exh. 89, all in *CPRR*. Leonard testified that he received Exhibit 89 toward the end of January; see testimony of Leonard Rhinelander, *CPRR*, 346. Conversion of money into 2007 dollars comes from the CPI Inflation Calculator available from the United States Department of Labor, Bureau of Labor Statistics, <www.bls.gov/cpi> (1 June 2007).

36 AJ to LKR, 16 January 1922, Exh. 56, *CPRR*. The first laboratory test for pregnancy did not exist until 1926. See Tone, *Devices and Desires*, 70. I also thank Dr. Mary D. Pryor for discussing this point with me.

37 LKR to AJ, 16 January 1922, Exh. R, *CPRR*; testimony of Leonard Rhinelander, *CPRR*, 157–58, 638–42; testimony of clerk, Henry Mousees, *CPRR*, 205–6. The

failure rate of condoms in the 1920s approached 50 percent. See Tone, *Devices and Desires*, 70.

38 Testimony of Leonard Rhinelander, *CPRR*, 158–62; LKR to AJ, 27 February 1922, Exh. V; AJ to LKR, 28 February 1922, Exh. 95; AJ to LKR, 1 March 1922, Exh. 96, all in *CPRR*. The firm of Bower & Sands served as attorneys in an 1895 lawsuit involving the Rhinelander estate, and Spotswood Bowers served as Philip Rhinelander's attorney until at least the 1930s. See *Stewart v. Keating*, 15 Misc. 44 (Supreme Court, New York County, 1895), and testimony of Frank M. Gagliardi, *CPMR*, 49.

39 AJ to LKR, 24 March 1922, Exh. 66; AJ to LKR, 19 May 1922, Exh. 28; AJ to LKR, 24 March 1922, Exh. 99 (polo coat), all in *CPRR*.

40 Telegram from LKR to AJ, 22 May 1922, Exh. 58, *CPRR*. During the trial, however, Leonard admitted that he knew Alice worked as an "upstairs girl" who made beds for a wage; see testimony of Leonard Rhinelander, *CPRR*, 475.

41 AJ to LKR, 23 May 1922, Exh. 57, *CPRR*.

42 AJ to LKR, 31 May 1922, Exh. 69, *CPRR*.

43 Ibid., 22 July 1922, Exh. 73.

44 Ibid., 29 June 1922, Exh. 100; ibid., 21 August 1922, Exh. 54; ibid., 31 May 1922, Exh. 69.

45 AJ to LKR, 12 September 1922, Exh. 76, *CPRR*.

46 Ibid., Exh. 84.

47 LKR to AJ, 19 September 1922, Exh. E-1, *CPRR*.

48 Testimony of Leonard Rhinelander, *CPRR*, 166–67; Bingmann, "Prep School Cowboys"; Cole, *Private Secondary Education for Boys*, 37; AJ to LKR, 4 November 1922, Exh. 77; AJ to LKR, 13 November 1922, Exh. 93, both in *CPRR*.

49 Leonard testified that he had written approximately 300 letters to Alice before they wed; see testimony of Leonard Rhinelander, *CPRR*, 465–66. Examples of such letters include AJ to LKR, 31 May 1922, Exh. 30; AJ to LKR, 18 January 1923, Exh. 83, both in *CPRR*. See also AJ to LKR, 20 April 1923, Exh. 94, *CPRR*.

50 AJ to LKR, 16 February 1924, Exh. 44, *CPRR*.

51 Ibid., 12 March 1924, Exh. 46.

52 Information on Leonard returning East comes from his testimony, *CPRR*, 168, 713–16. Elizabeth Jones testified about Leonard's stay in the Joneses' home; see *CPRR*, 891–92. See also LKR to Elizabeth Jones and George Jones, 16 August 1924, Exh. W; and postcards from LKR to Alice's parents, undated, Exhs. X, Y, Z, A-1, B-1, C-1, and D-1, all in *CPRR*.

53 "Takes Over His Estate," *NYT*, 22 August 1924, 13; testimony of furniture salesman Joseph Rich, *CPRR*, 719; Leonard K. Rhinelander and Alice B. Jones marriage license, Exh. 7, *CPRR*, 28–29; testimony of Leonard Rhinelander, *CPRR*, 548–49, 705; conversion of Leonard's 1924 inheritance into 2007 dollars from CPI Inflation Calculator, <www.bls.gov/cpi> (1 June 2007).

54 Testimony of Joseph Rich, *CPRR*, 720; testimony of Leonard Rhinelander, *CPRR*, 170–72, 549; testimony of Elizabeth Jones, *CPRR*, 894; *Standard Star of New Rochelle*, 13 November 1924.

55 The phrase "jazz journalism" comes from a late-1930s history of the tabloids. See Bessie, *Jazz Journalism*. One reporter testified about the intense press interest in the Rhinelanders; see testimony of William Lawby, *CPRR*, 289. Historians of journalism argue that the creation of the tabloids in the late teens and twenties did not decrease the circulation of the established papers. See Covert, "View of the Press," 93; and Brazil, "Murder Trials," 164. Newspapers elsewhere in the country, like William Allen White's *Emporia Gazette*, published in Kansas City, also carried news of the Rhinelanders. See Griffith, "Mass Media Come to the Small Town," 150. See also "Kip Rhinelander Has Negro Bride Records Disclose," *Atlanta Constitution*, 16 November 1924, TNCF, reel 20, frame 18.

56 Stevens, *Sensationalism and the New York Press*, 120–21; Bessie, *Jazz Journalism*, 82. Newspapers were increasingly devoted to the "sale of news, opinion and entertainment" in this era when the changed economic structure of the newspaper industry promoted bold changes in style and format. See Covert, "View of the Press," 67. Data on 1924 circulation of the *New York Daily News* comes from Emery and Emery (*Press and America*, 389), who assert the newspaper had the largest circulation of any American paper.

57 According to William Randolph Hearst's recent biographer, Hearst first tried to pay the owners of the *New York Daily News* to shut it down. They refused the offer. Hearst decided to publish his own tabloid. See Nasaw, *Chief*, 322. Bernarr McFadden also published physical culture and confessional magazines like *True Story* and *True Romance*. See Stevens, "Media and Morality," 28. In 1938, Simon Michael Bessie (*Jazz Journalism*, 205) claimed that the style of papers like the *Evening Graphic* led its competitors to make their stories more sensational.

58 "Society Dazed at Rhinelander Nuptial News," *NYDN*, 14 November 1924, 3, pink edition. See also McGivena, *News*, 137. McGivena's history of the *New York Daily News* notes that by 1925 the pink edition was a big part of the paper's total circulation. Moreover, the " 'Pink' led to a curious custom. In residential neighborhoods when the weather was good, men would go out to take a walk, or air the dog, or pick up a beer; and then assemble near a newsstand to await the arrival of the Pink. By the time the paper was delivered, groups as large as 50 would be waiting for it" (McGivena, *News*, 137). See also Bessie, *Jazz Journalism*, 99–100.

59 "Society Dazed at Rhinelander Nuptial News," *NYDN*, 14 November 1924, 3, pink edition.

60 Watkins-Owens, *Blood Relations*, 1–4. According to Watkins-Owens, the rate of West Indian immigration went down after 1924 after the imposition of quotas. She concludes that about 40,000 West Indians ended up in New York from

1900 to 1930. See also David Levering Lewis, *W. E. B. DuBois: The Fight for Equality*, 83.
61 "Society Dazed at Rhinelander Nuptial News," *NYDN*, 14 November 1924, 3, pink edition.
62 Ibid.
63 Ibid.
64 "Society Youth Weds Cabman's Daughter," *NYT*, 14 November 1924, 1.
65 The *Times* also observed that the groom "said he was white" (ibid.).
66 Ibid. Clifton Hood's analysis of the ways elite New Yorkers at the end of the nineteenth and the beginning of the twentieth centuries tried to control New York history to bolster their sense of superiority and class identity helps explain why the *Times* exalted the historic links of the Rhinelanders to New York and the country. See Hood, "Journeying to 'Old New York.'"
67 Improved technology and faster distribution of newspapers in the 1920s created a large readership, which led to "multiple daily editions" to keep up with fast-changing events. Consequently, "threats of looming deadlines insured high sales but frequently undermined concern for news accuracy and balance in the interests of 'getting it on the streets'" (Covert, "View of the Press in the Twenties," 92).
68 "Blueblood Weds Colored Girl," *NYDN*, 14 November 1925, 3, home edition; Katzman, *Seven Days a Week*, 44. Katzman defines domestic service as work performed by "general servants (maid-of-all work), chambermaids, child nurses, cooks, waitresses in families, day workers, laundresses, and other similar workers in private households." At the end of the nineteenth and the beginning of the twentieth centuries, domestic service tended to be done by immigrants and African Americans. See also Dumenil, *Modern Temper*, 117; Palmer, *Domesticity and Dirt*; and Clark-Lewis, *Living In, Living Out*, 12. No evidence seems to exist to show that Alice ever worked as a babysitter.
69 "Blueblood Weds Colored Girl," *NYDN*, 14 November 1925, 3, home edition; Mumford, *Interzones*, xviii–xix; Cott, *Public Vows*, 163–64. The shifting descriptions of Alice exemplify the process by which, as Barbara Fields observes, "the truth that physical description follows race, not the other way around" ("Slavery, Race, and Ideology," 118).
70 "Blueblood Weds Colored Girl," *NYDN*, 14 November 1925, 3, home edition. For a detailed discussion of Philip Rhinelander's brother, see chapter 5.
71 Ibid.
72 Information about Barbara Reynold's interview of Leonard Rhinelander appears in the trial transcript: *CPRR*, 822–37.
73 "Blueblood Weds Colored Girl," 14 November 1925, 3, home edition. Emphasis is in the original.
74 Ibid.

75 "His Colored Bride," *NYDN*, 14 November 1924, 1, afternoon edition. For an additional discussion of this photograph, see chapter 8.
76 "Social Registerites Stunned at Mixed Marriage," *NYDN*, 14 November 1924, 3, afternoon edition.
77 Information on Grace Robinson comes from Ishbel Ross's 1936 history of women in journalism. According to Ross (*Ladies of the Press*, 7, 279), "Robinson starred so often in the role of front-page girl that she has no competitor in the number of big stories she has covered within a given period of time. She did the Halls-Mills and the Snyder-Gray trials for the *New York Daily News*, and scores of other assignments that any man might envy." The Rhinelander annulment trial was Robinson's first big trial. See Chapman, *Tell It to Sweeney*, 219; and McGivena, *News*, 281–82.
78 Robinson, "I'm Not Colored Cries the Bride of Rhinelander," *NYDN*, 14 November 1924, 3, afternoon edition. According to Charles Mangum, such libel suits were not uncommon in the South. Mangum cited a number of cases from the late teens and twenties in the South and West; see his *Legal Status of the Negro*, 18. Such cases seemed to appear only rarely in the North. Historian Matthew Guterl (*Color of Race*, 134) describes an unusual example from the 1920s in which Cyril Briggs, a member of the African Blood Brotherhood, successfully sued Marcus Garvey for libel after Garvey called him white.
79 Robinson, "I'm Not Colored Cries the Bride of Rhinelander," *NYDN*, 14 November 1924, 3, afternoon edition. For a discussion of claims of Spanish ancestry and passing, see chapter 4.
80 "Young Rhinelander's Bride Denies Taint," *NYEJ*, 14 November 1924, 1, final news edition.
81 "Taint Story Denied by Bride," *NYEJ*, 14 November 1924, 1, final news edition.
82 Discussion of the *Standard Star*'s report on the Rhinelander wedding and the swift reaction of New York City reporters to that account can be found in the testimony of William Lawby, a New York City reporter, CPRR, 284–99.
83 "Rhinelander and Wife Vanish on Honeymoon," *NYHT*, 15 November 1924, 3.
84 "Rhinelander and Bride Vanish," *NYDN*, 15 November 1924, 3, home edition; testimony of Elizabeth Jones, CPRR, 897; "Annulment of Rhinelander Match Seen," *NYEJ*, 22 November 1924, 1, final news edition.
85 "Bride of Rhinelander Once Called Mulatto," *NYDN*, 15 November 1924, 3, pink edition.
86 Robinson, "Rhinelander Triangle Bared," *NYDN*, 15 November 1924, 3, final edition; Robinson, "Rhinelander Love Nest Found," *NYDN*, 16 November 1924, 3, home edition. Eugene Kinkle Jones of the Urban League estimated that Westchester County had about "thirty-eight established colored churches" for "a total Negro population of 11,066" ("Negro Migration in New York State," 11). Moreover, if George Jones were of West Indian descent, that might explain the

family's attendance at an Episcopal church. Many New Yorkers who came from the British Caribbean worshiped at Episcopal churches. See Sacks, *Before Harlem*, 180.

87 "Bride of Rhinelander Once Called Mulatto," *NYDN*, 15 November 1924, 3, pink edition.

88 "Bride of Rhinelander Once Called Mulatto," *NYDN*, 15 November 1924, 3, pink edition.

89 Robinson, "Rhinelander Triangle Bared," *NYDN*, 15 November 1924, 3, final edition.

90 "Rhinelanders Flee Glare of Publicity," *NYT*, 15 November 1924, 6.

91 "Rhinelander Match Probed by Lawyers," *NYEJ*, 15 November 1924, 3, final news edition. As of 1920, 30 percent of all African American women who worked did so as laundresses. See Katzman, *Seven Days A Week*, 74. Thus race and class combined to position Alice as a colored servant. See also Higginbotham, "African-American Women's History," 258–62; Katzman, *Seven Days a Week*, 75–76; and Lynch-Brennan, "Ubiquitous Bridget," 334.

92 "Rhinelander Match Probed by Lawyers," *NYEJ*, 15 November 1924, 3, final news edition. Like the *Daily News* and the *Times*, the *Evening Journal* reported the story about Alice being identified as a mulatto.

93 The *Emporia Gazette* is discussed in Sally Griffith's "Mass Media Come to the Small Town," 150. See also "Kip Rhinelander Has Negro Bride Records Disclose," *Atlanta Constitution*, 16 November 1924, TNCF, reel 20, frame 18; and "A Mixed Marriage in High Life," *Negro World*, 22 November 1924, TNCF, reel 20, frame 19. Mia Bay's study of African American ideas about whites (*White Image in the Black Mind*, 189) notes that Marcus Garvey and his supporters espoused an essentialist view of race. Garvey's rhetoric emphasized racial purity and condemned race mixing. He also seemed to have a dim view of those considered "mulatto." See Garvey, "An Exposé of the Caste System," 56. See also Robinson, "Rhinelander Triangle Bared," *NYDN*, 15 November 1924, 5, final edition.

94 "Rhinelanders Drop from Public Sight," *NYT*, 16 November 1924, 13; Robinson, "Rhinelander Love Nest Found," *NYDN*, 16 November 1924, 3, home edition; "Servants Hide Rhinelanders," *NYA*, 16 November 1924, 2-L; testimony of Leonard Rhinelander, *CPRR*, 388.

95 Testimony of Leon Jacobs, *CPRR*, 843; testimony of Leonard Rhinelander, *CPRR*, 174–75.

96 Testimony of Joseph Strong, *CPRR*, 87, 100–101, 103–4, 110; testimony of Leonard Rhinelander, *CPRR*, 175. Some confusion existed about the value of the mortgages signed over by Rhinelander to Jacobs; estimates ranged from $50,000 to $200,000. See testimony of Leonard Rhinelander, *CPRR*, 462–64. Those mortgages today would be worth between half a million and two million

dollars. Leonard apparently signed over these assets to his lawyer solely because Jacob told him to, without any question as to the wisdom of the assignment or whether he would receive anything in return.

97 Testimony of Leonard Rhinelander, *CPRR*, 174, 388; testimony of Leon Jacobs, *CPRR*, 843; testimony of Miriam Rich, *CPRR*, 813.
98 Testimony of Leonard Rhinelander, *CPRR*, 388–95; testimony of Joseph Strong, *CPRR*, 105.
99 Testimony of Joseph Strong, *CPRR*, 94–95; testimony of Elizabeth Jones, *CPRR*, 897–99. Strong denied Jacobs made the comment about the Ku Klux Klan in Strong testimony, *CPRR*, 111. Leonard's trial lawyer later conceded Jacobs had done so; see *CPRR*, 1360.
100 Testimony of Joseph Strong, *CPRR*, 114, 118–19.
101 Summons and Complaint, *CPRR*, 6–8; Carmody, *Treatise on Pleading and Practice*, 253.
102 "Rhinelander Sues to Annul Marriage; Alleges Race Deceit," *NYT*, 27 November 1924, 1.
103 "Rhinelander Files Annulment Suit," *NYA*, 27 November 1924, 1.
104 "Bride to Fight Rhinelander Suit," *NYEJ*, 28 November 1924, 3, final news edition. On the same day, the *Times* reported on Alice's lawyer and how Alice "suffer[ed] from extreme nervousness and weeps a great deal" ("Rhinelander's Bride Said to Be Grieving," *NYT*, 28 November 1924, 13).
105 "Bride to Fight Rhinelander Suit," *NYEJ*, 28 November 1924, 3, final news edition; *United States v. Thind*, 261 U.S. 204 (1923). See also Haney Lopez, *White by Law*. For further discussion of *Thind*, see chapter 8.
106 "Rhinelander's Wife Denies She Is Negro," *NYT*, 29 November 1924, 15.
107 Ibid; "Mrs. Rhinelander Files Answer to Annulment Suit," *NYAN*, 3 December 1924, TNCF, reel 20, frame 13. A similar article appeared in the *New York Evening Journal*: "Bride Plans to Sue Father of Rhinelander," *NYEJ*, 29 November 1924, 3.
108 On the absence of New York law defining race, see Mangum, *Legal Status of the Negro*, 4; and Stephenson, *Race Distinctions in American Law*, chap. 2.
109 "Rhinelander's Wife Denies She Is Negro," *NYT*, 29 November 1924, 15; "Bride Accuses Kip's Father," *NYA*, 29 November 1924, 3. The *American* also reported that Swinburne "pointed out that Rhinelander based his action not on the color of his bride, but upon the allegation of fraud." The paper quoted Swinburne: "'I am not prepared to admit that the father of my client is a colored man.'"
110 "Rhinelander Bride Fears He Is Captive," *NYT*, 30 November 1924, 14.
111 "Defeat Is Wish of Rhinelander," *NYA*, 30 November 1924, L-3. On Monday, 1 December, the *American* claimed that the City Clerk of New Rochelle helped keep the Rhinelander marriage a secret at Leonard Rhinelander's insistence. See "Rhinelander's Bride May Sue," *NYA*, 1 December 1924, 3.

112 "Help Rhinelander's Bride," *NYT*, 2 December 1924, 5; "Rhinelander Takes Auto He Gave Bride," *NYA*, 2 December 1924, 1.
113 "Mrs. Rhinelander Has Answer Ready," *NYT*, 5 December 1924, 23.
114 Defendant's Answer, *CPRR*, 9; "Rhinelander's Bride Replies to His Suit with Complete Denial of Deceit Charges," *NYT*, 9 December 1924, 1; "Rhinelander's Wife Retorts," *NYA*, 9 December 1924, 17.
115 Plaintiff's Amended Complaint, *CPRR*, 9–11. Since a plaintiff needs to make statements of fact to support a request for an annulment, the phrase "on information and belief" allows a plaintiff to allege facts that he or she *believes* exist but does not have direct knowledge of at the time. See Carmody, *Treatise on Pleading and Practice*, 155.
116 Plaintiff's Amended Complaint, *CPRR*, 9–11.
117 Plaintiff's Bill of Particulars, *CPRR*, 14–15; Defendant's Answer to Amended Complaint, *CPRR*, 11. While the legal papers flew back and forth, the press reported rumors that the Rhinelander family wanted to pay Alice to accept an annulment. See "Mrs. Rhinelander to Fight Bride's Attorney Says She Will Not Settle Husband's Annulment Suit," *NYT*, 3 December 1924, 11; "Rhinelander Case Rumors," *NYT*, 4 December 1924, 23; "Rhinelander's Cash Spurned," *NYA*, 17 December 1924, second edition, 4.

CHAPTER TWO

1 Irwin, *Highlights of Manhattan*, 4, 30. My description of New York City also draws on Erenberg, *Steppin' Out*; Douglas, *Terrible Honesty*; and David Levering Lewis, *When Harlem Was in Vogue*.
2 Irwin, *Highlights of Manhattan*, 325; Douglas, *Terrible Honesty*, 14–15. The front pages of the papers indicated their price.
3 Douglas, *Terrible Honesty*, 5; Cobb, *New York*, 35, 36.
4 Kevles, *In the Name of Eugenics*, 75; Grant, *Passing of the Great Race*, 91–92. See also Gossett, *Race*, 353; Guterl, *Color of Race*, 32–35; and Barkan, *Retreat of Scientific Racism*, 69.
5 Recently, historians have debated the value of the concept of "whiteness" in studying the past. See special issue of the *International Labor and Working-Class History* journal from October 2001 devoted to examining whiteness studies. Peter Kolchin ("Whiteness Studies") suggests that most historians overuse the term without defining it or historically contextualizing it and that paying "greater attention to historical and geographical context" in analyzing whiteness may produce better histories of race in America. In his study of race in contemporary Detroit, anthropologist John Hartigan also criticizes scholars' use of the term but suggests that the term can be salvaged by making sure to pay attention to the "local settings" in which ideas about whiteness develop. Conse-

quently, I find Hartigan's definition of whiteness, "a web of assumptions of normativity maintaining the social privileges and powers linked to white skin," useful. Hartigan makes it clear that in analyzing whiteness one needs to examine class and race together. See Hartigan, *Racial Situations*, 6. I have no problems using the word "whiteness" in discussing the 1920s, given W. E. B. DuBois's use of the term in *The Souls of White Folk*.

6   Stoddard, "II—The Impasse at the Color-Line," 510. Stoddard's significance is discussed in Guterl, *Color of Race*, 51–55. Many historians have noted the proliferation of these aspects of white American society in the 1920s. Stanley Coben (*Rebellion Against Victorianism*, 74–75) interprets the adoption of African American music and dances by whites as a challenge to the formerly dominant ethos of Victorianism. See also Douglas, *Terrible Honesty*.

7   For a discussion of immigration in New York City, see Binder and Reimers, *All the Nations Under Heaven*; Lenkevich, *New York City: A Short History*; Higham, *Strangers in the Land*; and Rosenwaike, *Population History of New York City*, 55–130. Passengers List, District of the City of New York, Port of New York, S.S. Majestic, 18 March 1891, <www.ancestry.com> (22 September 2006).

8   Burrows and Wallace, *Gotham*, chap. 63; Rosenwaike, *Population History of New York City*, 92–93, Tables 36, 37, 39, and Table B-1; David J. Goldberg, *Discontented America*, 140–42. In 1891, 560,319 immigrants came to the United States. Of this number, 546,085 came from Europe, and 66,605 of that number came from the United Kingdom. In contrast, 76,055 Italian immigrants arrived that year. See *Historical Statistics of the United States*, Series C 89–119, 107; and *Fourteenth Census of the United States, State Compendium, New York*, Table 9, Composition and Characteristics of the Population, for Counties: 1920.

9   Rosenwaike, *Population History of New York City*, 116–17, 141, Table 69; Osofsky, *Harlem*, 128–29; Eugene Kinkle Jones, "Negro Migration in New York State," 8; *Fourteenth Census of the United States, State Compendium, New York*, Table 9, Composition and Characteristics of the Population, for Counties: 1920. The 1920 census statistics from New York show a total population in Westchester as of 1920 as 344,436. This number had increased by 21.7 percent since 1910. See *Fourteenth Census of the United States, State Compendium, New York*, Table 1, Population—New York Area and Population of Counties: 1850–1920. See also Charles S. Johnson, "New Frontage on American Life," 284. Although Johnson considered migrants from the West Indies to be "Negro New Yorkers," they may not have always self-identified as such. See Fields, "Whiteness, Racism, and Identity," 51; and Winston James, *Holding Aloft the Banner of Ethiopia*.

10 For discussions of the Great Migration, see Marks, *Farewell—We're Good and Gone*; Henri, *Black Migration*; and Trotter, *Great Migration in Historical Perspective*.

11 Rosenwaike, *Population History of New York City*, 116–17, 141, Table 69; Eugene

Kinkle Jones, "Negro Migration in New York State," 8. The largest number of immigrants from the West Indies came between 1911 and 1924. See Watkins-Owens, *Blood Relations*, 4; and Sacks, *Before Harlem*, 18–19.

12 DuBois, "Brothers, Come North," 105. Violence against African Americans in the South also helped propel the migration. See Tolnay and Beck, "Rethinking the Role of Racial Violence."

13 Recent studies of the Great Migration's impact on Detroit are Wolcott, *Remaking Respectability*, and Boyle, *Arc of Justice*. For a discussion of the migration to Cleveland, see Kusmer, *Ghetto Takes Shape*. See also Eugene Kinkle Jones, "Negro Migration in New York State," 8–9.

14 Eugene Kinkle Jones, "Negro Migration in New York State," 9.

15 Stoddard, *Rising Tide of Color*, 165.

16 Gerstle, *American Crucible*, 114–15; Stoddard, "II—Impasse at the Color-Line."

17 Jackson, *Ku Klux Klan in the City*, 175–79 (A Klan defector claimed twenty-one "klaverns" existed in New York City.) Blee, *Women of the Klan*, 17; David J. Goldberg, *Discontented America*, 119, 139, 60–61; Dumenil, *Modern Temper*, 201; "'Ell's Cross' Seen in B'klyn," *NYAN*, 13 December 1922, 1; Editorial, "Klan Burns Cross on Columbia Campus," 137; Editorial, "Caps, Gowns and Fiery Crosses," 131–32; "Memorandum of O. D. Williams to Mr. Johnson," 26 July 1924, PNAACP, Part 5, reel 2; "Immediate Release," 9 September 1925, PNAACP, Part 5, reel 2.

18 Bagnall, "Spirit of the Ku Klux Klan," 265, 267.

19 Boas, "This Nordic Nonsense," 502, 503. Boas's article responded to Madison Grant's earlier essay, "America for the Americans." George Frederickson (*Black Image in the White Mind*, 330) describes Boasian thoughts on race as "liberal environmentalism." See also Miller, "Separate Communities for Negroes," 829.

20 Wiggam, *New Decalogue of Science*, 109; Haller, *Eugenics*, 6, 58; Selden, *Inheriting Shame*, 1. Growing consciousness about race was not restricted to white Americans. See Sampson, "Race Consciousness and Race Relations," and Work, "Taking Stock of the Race Problem."

21 Selden, *Inheriting Shame*, 23, 33, 69. Kevles, *In the Name of Eugenics*, 61–62; Lee D. Baker, *From Savage to Negro*, 92.

22 Wiggam, "Rising Tide of Degeneracy," 25. According to Daniel Kevles (*In the Name of Eugenics*, 59), Wiggam popularized eugenics through magazine articles and Chautauqua lectures.

23 Grant, "America for the Americans," 350–51, 348; White, "Paradox of Color," 363. Martha Biondi (*To Stand and Fight*, 39) points out that New Yorkers elected the first African American to the state legislature in 1917. According to Gilbert Osofsky (*Harlem*, 171), five additional African Americans from New York City took seats in the state legislature in the 1920s. See also Eugene Kinkle Jones, "Negro Migration in New York State," 11.

24 Reilly, *Surgical Solution*, 72; Hoffman, "Problem of Negro-White Intermixture and Intermarriage," 188.
25 Grant, *Passing of the Great Race*, xxix–xxx; Hasian, *Rhetoric of Eugenics*, 55; Kevles, *In the Name of Eugenics*, 92–93; Edward J. Larson, *Sex, Race, and Science*, 1.
26 Degler, *In Search of Human Nature*, 49–51; Kevles, *In the Name of Eugenics*, 82–83. A contemporary discussion of intelligence testing is in Charles S. Johnson, "Mental Measurements of Negro Groups." Not all African Americans opposed eugenics. An article in the 1924 *Crisis* proposed that eugenics was "interested in breeding for tomorrow a better Negro" (Beckham, "Applied Eugenics," 177). One year later E. Franklin Frazier criticized the article in "Eugenics and the Race Problem."
27 Grant, *Passing of the Great Race*, 167; Fitzgerald, *Great Gatsby*, 12. Matthew Guterl discusses the postwar vogue for Nordicism in *Color of Race*, 41–43. For critiques of Nordicism, see Boas, "This Nordic Nonsense," 502–11; and Bond, "Intelligence Testing and Propaganda," 61.
28 Grant, *Passing of the Great Race*, 19–21, 32–33, 167, 191, and 228. According to Matthew Guterl (*Color of Race*, 35) out, Grant believed the Great War constituted "race suicide" for the white races.
29 Grant, *Passing of the Great Race*, 263, 90.
30 Matthew Frye Jacobson, *Whiteness of a Different Color*, 80–84; Wiggam, *Fruit of the Family Tree*, 188; Gerstle, *American Crucible*, 103–15; Dumenil, *Modern Temper*, 207; Ngai, *Impossible Subjects*, 20–26, 37; Ngai, "Architecture of Race," 72. See also Higham, *Strangers in the Land*, 327.
31 Dumenil, *Modern Temper*, 207; Watkins-Owens, *Blood Relations*, 3, 27; Domingo, "Restricted West Indian Immigration," 299; "West Indian Immigration." See also Rogers, "West Indies and the Quota." Ngai (*Impossible Subjects*, 24–25) argues that the quota system in the 1924 law created "a hierarchy of desirability" among Europeans while at the same time it created a distinct opposition between whites and those considered "not white," who were completely excluded. See also Matthew Frye Jacobson, *Whiteness of a Different Color*, 83; Grant, "American for the Americans," 355; and Stoddard, "Permanent Menace from Europe," 226.
32 "The Negro's Northward Exodus," 4; Marks, *Farewell—We're Good and Gone*; Henri, *Black Migration*; Trotter, *Great Migration in Historical Perspective*. Florette Henri (*Black Migration*, 81–91) also discusses the effects of the migration on northern cities. See also David Levering Lewis, "Parallels and Divergences," 550; Osofsky, *Harlem*, 40–43; Kusmer, *Ghetto Takes Shape*, 161–63; and Sacks, *Before Harlem*, 38.
33 "Race Hatred North and South," 358; James Weldon Johnson, *Black Manhattan*,

126–28; Sacks, *Before Harlem*, 39–42; Osofsky, *Harlem*, 46–49; David Levering Lewis, *W. E. B. Du Bois: Biography of a Race*, 387–407; Dumenil, *Modern Temper*, 287–88; Tuttle, *Race Riot*.

34 Eleazer, "Trends in Race Relations in 1926," 17; Barbeau and Henri, *Unknown Soldiers*, 175–89; Nikki Brown, *Private Politics and Public Voices*; "A Transformed Race," 179.

35 New York Civil Rights Law, Chapter 7, Article 4, Sections 40 and 41, as cited in Cahill, ed., *Cahill's Consolidated Laws*, 160; Douglas, *Terrible Honesty*, 314; Osofsky, *Harlem*, 42; Friss, "Blacks, Jews, and Civil Rights," 79–80.

36 Holt, *Problem of Race*, 60. Robinson v. Zappas, 277 A.D. 208 (App. Div. 1929) (waitress and ice cream); Johnson v. Auburn and Syracuse Electric Railroad Co., 222 N.Y. 443 (N.Y. 1918) (dancing pavilion); Norman v. City Island Beach Co., 126 Misc. 335 (Sup. Ct. 1926) (bathing beach); Joyner v. Moore-Wiggins Co., 152 A.D. 266 (App. Div. 1912) (orchestra seats). The plaintiffs won in the *Johnson* and *Joyner* cases.

37 Friss, "Blacks, Jews, and Civil Rights," 80, 91–93. New York's African American newspapers reported that white residents in New York City were unhappy about African Americans on the beaches. See, for example, "Rockaway Would Bar Negroes," *NYAN*, 5 August 1925, 8. Both the African American press and the white papers covered the New York City beauty pageant. See "Negress in 3rd Place, Beauty Contest Is Off, Flushing Festival Officials Refuse to Admit Color Line, but Cancel Election," *NYT*, 5 April 1924, 18; Editorial, "Beauty Contest Called Off," 137; and "When Is a Contest Not a Contest?" 80. Ann Douglas discusses the growing difficulties faced by African Americans in public places in *Terrible Honesty*, 314. African Americans knew that the Great Migration had serious ramifications. See, for example, "Jim-Crowing," 282. The *Messenger* forecast in 1923 that the "hegira of Negroes North" would "produce new social and economic problems which the Negroes will be compelled to grapple with in the North" (Editorial, "Aftermath of the Exodus," 858–59).

38 Meyer, *As Long As They Don't Move Next Door*, 6, 20, 24–27; Buchanan v. Warley, 245 U.S. 60 (1917).

39 Grant, *Passing of the Great Race*, 88; "Segregation Fight Spreads North," *NYAN*, 30 September 1925, 12 (Johnstown mayor ordered any "Negroes and Mexicans" who had not lived there for at least seven years to leave); "High Handed?" *Time*, 24 September 1923; "'A Just Rebuke,'" *Time*, 1 October 1923; "Deportations from Pennsylvania Town," *NYAN*, 19 September 1923, 1; "Cauffill Defeated: Pennsylvania Governor Acts Promptly in Johnstown Deportation of Negroes," *NYAN*, 26 September 1923, 1; "Johnstown," *Opportunity*, November 1923, 349; Meyer, *As Long As They Don't Move Next Door*, 27; David Levering Lewis, "Parallels and Divergences," 553.

40 Meyer, *As Long As They Don't Move Next Door*, 31. *Corrigan v. Buckley*, 271 U.S. 323 (1926); *Shelley v. Kraemer*, 344 U.S. 1 (1948). For a historically informed discussion of *Corrigan* and *Shelley* by a legal scholar, see Klarman, *From Jim Crow to Civil Rights*, 212–17.

41 An excellent treatment of the *Sweet* case appears in Boyle, *Arc of Justice*. Stephen Meyer's *As Long As They Don't Move Next Door* (38–45) discusses the incident. See also Walter White, "Negro Segregation Comes North," *Nation* (October 21, 1925): 458–60; and Eleazer, "Trends in Race Relations in 1926," 17. Eleazer called the rise in white attacks on black property in northern and Midwestern cities the "most disquieting interracial trend of the year." The use of violence to protect the whiteness of particular neighborhoods persisted well beyond the 1920s. I remember as a child in the early 1970s hearing about a West Indian family whose house in a predominantly white neighborhood in Staten Island, New York, was burned down. See Paul L. Montgomery, "Fire at Black's House Stirs Fear and Rumor in S. I. Block," *NYT*, 25 April 1972, 85. For a discussion of conflicts over housing in the North during and after World War II, see Sugrue, *Origins of the Urban Crisis*, and Freund, *Colored Property*.

42 Lilienthal, "Trial of Two Races." Information on *Outlook* magazine in Tebbel, *American Magazine*, 206; and Marzolf, "Americanizing the Melting Pot," 114.

43 Editorial, "South's Triumph!," 386; DuBois, "Tragedy of 'Jim Crow,'" 169; Editorial, "Aftermath of the Exodus," 858; Sacks, *Before Harlem*, 109–12, 124; Eugene Kinkle Jones, "Negro Migration in New York State," 10; "Race Barriers Slowly Crumbling," 34. The article in the *Literary Digest* suggested that although more lynchings took place in the South in 1926 than in 1925, "better relations" existed between blacks and whites. See also Duncan, "Changing Race Relationship," 3, 17; and Gilmore, *Defying Dixie*, 15–17. A. Philip Randolph and Chandler Owens worked as editors of the *Messenger* in 1922. One historian describes Owen as "a brilliant writer and analyst" (see Kornweibel, *No Crystal Stair*, 27, 49–51).

44 David Levering Lewis, *When Harlem Was in Vogue*, 162; Huggins, *Harlem Renaissance*, 89; James Weldon Johnson, *Black Manhattan*, 160. See also Erenberg, *Steppin' Out*, 255–58.

45 Pickens, "Color and Camouflage," 773, 774. See also Erenberg, *Steppin' Out*, 258.

46 Proctor, "La Femme Silhouette," 93; Sylvester Russell, *Amalgamation of America*, n.p.; Hoysradt, "Enigma," 268. In 1924, a *Messenger* editor claimed that white women passed as colored to make it into colored chorus lines. See Owen, "Good Looks Supremacy," 82.

47 Proctor, "La Femme Silhouette," 93. David Roediger (*Colored White*, 139) describes Italians as "inbetween" people in the early twentieth century. See also Matthew Frye Jacobson, *Whiteness of a Different Color*, 57–62. Arnold Hirsch ("E Pluribus Duo?," 8) suggests that some European immigrant groups were

"temporarily" suspended between blackness and whiteness until the 1920s. A lively scholarly debate over the racial status of Italians in the early twentieth century exists. For a perspective that differs from Roediger and Jacobson, see Thomas Guglielmo, *White on Arrival*, 10, 28. Roediger's recent response is in his *Working Toward Whiteness*. For additional discussions of whiteness and Italians, see Guglielmo and Salerno, eds. *Are Italians White?*

48 "'Up North,' by a Mulatto," 224.
49 Mencken, "Editorial," 159, 160, 161.
50 Ibid., 160, 161.
51 Mumford, *Interzones*, 161; Stoddard, *Rising Tide of Color*, 166; Grant, *Passing of the Great Race*, 91–92. A more in-depth discussion of marriage and miscegenation in the 1920s appears in chapter 7.
52 Bureau of the Census, *200 Years of U.S. Census Taking*, 55.
53 Ibid.; "Instructions to Enumerators—Census of 1890," in Wright, *History and Growth of the United States Census*, 187.
54 W. O. Brown, "Racial Inequality," 48; Mencke, *Mulattoes and Race Mixture*, 101; Williamson, *New People*, 62; Gatewood, *Aristocrats of Color*, 154; Davenport and Steggerda, *Race Crossing in Jamaica*, 471–72; "Dangers of Race Mixture," 403; Reuter, "Hybrid as a Sociological Type," 62. Funding for *Race Crossing in Jamaica* came from Wickliffe Preston Draper, resident of New York City and wealthy heir of textile manufacturers. See Tucker, *Funding of Scientific Racism*, 20–22, 30–32.
55 Williamson, *New People*, 117; Mencke, *Mulattoes and Race Mixture*, 101. Much of the historical work done on mulattoes seems interested in why white Americans fail to distinguish mulattoes and blacks from each other. Both John Mencke and Joel Williamson ask this question in setting out the purposes of their historical studies. It seems to me that this question is seriously flawed, since the very asking assumes that categories called black, white, and mulatto really exist. See also Reuter, *Mulatto in the United States*, 103–4; and Sollors, *Neither Black nor White yet Both*, 132.
56 "Dangers of Race Mixture," 403. See also "Shall We All Be Mulattoes," 23; W. A. Plecker, "Racial Improvement," 3, *Virginia Medical Monthly* (November 1925) in Box E-2-4:9, Racial Betterment, Kentucky Academy of Science, Harry H. Laughlin Papers, Pickler Memorial Library, Special Collections, Truman State University, Kirksville, Mo. (Many thanks to Kent State University doctoral candidate Rachel Oley for sharing with me the sources she found in the Harry Laughlin Papers.); Grant, *Passing of the Great Race*, 82; and Gregg, "Mulatto," 1069.
57 For one discussion of the "Jezebel" image, see K. Sue Jewell, *From Mammy to Miss America*, 46–47. Deborah Gray White (*Ar'n't I A Woman*, 29) historicizes the Jezebel figure, who was "governed almost entirely by her libido," in the

antebellum South. See also Guy-Sheftall, "Body Politic," 23. My discussion of the "Jezebel" image in the story of the Rhinelanders appears in chapter 3. See also Proctor, "La Femme Silhouette," 93; and Caleb Johnson, "Crossing the Color Line," 527.

58 Gregg, "Mulatto," 1066–67; Walter White, "Paradox of Color," 366–67. Walter White's light complexion made him useful to the NAACP, especially to investigate lynchings. See Janken, *White*. David Lewis (*W. E. B. Du Bois: The Fight for Equality*, 82–83) discusses Garvey's complaints about light-skinned African Americans. See also Gregg, "Mulatto," 1068.

59 A 1926 study of "mongrel Virginians" asserted a "growing interest in the subject of racial mixtures particularly in the South." See Estabrook and McDougle, *Mongrel Virginians*, 7. Peggy Pascoe also comments on this increased interest in her "Miscegenation Law," 58–59; see also Mumford, *Interzones*, 161. This scientific interest in mixed race still exists. In 2005, the *New York Times* published an essay by geneticist Armand Marie Leroi in which he argues in favor of the continued significance of "race" and suggests the usefulness of studying "people of mixed race ancestry" ("A Family Tree in Every Gene," *NYT*, 14 March 2005, 21). This revival of interest has sparked opposition. A good introduction to the debates over genetics and race appears in a series of essays commissioned by the Social Science Research Council to respond to Leroi's *Times* op-ed: "Is Race 'Real'?"

60 According to Herskovits ("Color Line," 206–7), "various attempts have been made to distinguish between persons of different degrees of mixture, and the term mulatto, meaning a half-Negro half-white person, is still in general use; other similar terms, such as quadroon, octoroon, or zambo, are also employed. But this method is clumsy, to say the least." Herskovits completed the manuscript by 1927, but his study wasn't published until 1930. Zora Neale Hurston assisted Herskovits in many of the studies he undertook in New York. See Herskovits, *Anthropometry of the American Negro*.

61 Herskovits, "Preliminary Observations," 69. Herskovits argued in 1925 that "what we have in America is not the Negro at all, but a some-part-Negro" ("Color Line," 204). For a lengthier discussion of race as "blood," see chapter 8.

62 Herskovits, "Correlation of Length and Breadth of Head," 87, 95; Herskovits, "American Negro Evolving," 900; Herskovits, "Critical Discussion," 396. The scientist T. Todd Wingate agreed with Herskovits's views. See his "Entrenched Negro Physical Features," 57. Wingate studied the skin color of cadavers. See also Herskovits, "American Negro Evolving," 899.

63 In this article, Herskovits concluded that the "American Negro" was an "actual physical fact"; few of his subjects had a white parent. See Herskovits, "American Negro Evolving," 900, 902. Given Herskovits's interest in studying race through

looking at race mixture, it seems significant that he never proposes to study the "American White." Herskovits, "Critical Discussion," 402.

64 Kathy Peiss (*Hope in a Jar*, 150–51) discusses the mid-twenties "craze" for suntanning among white women. One advertising slogan for a tanning product, "Tre-jur," proclaimed that a "lily white complexion is 'passé.'" Peiss suggests that white women felt comfortable darkening their skin because they believed the dividing line between black and white held firm. See also George Schuyler, "Keeping the Negro in His Place," 474.

CHAPTER THREE

1 My discussion of trial practice is informed by works on trial tactics written for the use of lawyers during the first half of the twentieth century. See Cutler, *Successful Trial Tactics*; Wellman, *Art of Cross-Examination*; Carmody, *Treatise on Pleading and Practice*; and Clevenger, *Clevenger's Supreme Court Practice*. Between the time Alice Rhinelander answered Leonard's amended complaint in January 1925 and the opening of the trial in November, a few events took place. In January, Leonard's attorneys requested a jury trial. Under New York law, the parties to an annulment suit had the right to a jury. The press reported in the same month that Alice's attorneys had sent an agent to England to investigate Alice's paternal ancestry. By April, rumors published in the press speculated that Leonard might seek a Nevada divorce. During the same month, Leonard's lawyers denied that he had been disinherited. By early May, Leonard's lawyers filed a number of motions to frame the issues of the case and ask the court for a trial preference to have the case heard early. See "Rhinelander Asks Jury," *NYT*, 23 January 1925, 23; "Joins Rhinelander Case," *NYT*, 12 February 1925, 5; "More in Rhinelander Suit," *NYT*, 19 February 1925, 7; "Delay in Rhinelander Suit," *NYT*, 3 March 1925, 25; "Denies Rhinelander Row," *NYT*, 26 April 1925, 24; "Rhinelander Kin May Help His Wife," *NYT*, 7 May 1925, 21; "Rhinelander Trial in Fall," *NYT*, 21 May 1925, 28; and "Rhinelander Case Decision Reserved," *NYAN*, 20 May 1925, 3. See also *Order Settling Issues*, 18 May 1925, *CPRR*, 12–13. Information on New York's court system and annulment trials comes from Carmody, *Treatise on Pleading and Practice*, 20–22, 937, and Bergan, *History of the New York Court of Appeals*.

2 This description of the courtroom and spectators comes from press accounts. Every newspaper commented on the crowds in the courtroom. For a description that one-third of the court consisted of people of color, see "Kip Rhinelander Is 'Brain-Tied,' Counsel Pleads," *NYHT*, 10 November 1925, 14; Robinson, "Colored Girls' Wiles Blinded Kip, Says Mills," *NYDN*, 10 November 1925, 3, pink edition; and Rex, "Color Line Stressed in Rhinelander Case," *NYEJ*, 10

November 1925, 2, special extra edition. The same edition of the *New York Evening Journal* featured a front-page photograph of the disappointed spectators outside the courtroom. See "Crowds of Colored, White Persons Pack Courtroom as Rhinelander Fights for Annulment of Marriage," *NYEJ*, 10 November 1925, 1, special extra edition. The need for deputy sheriffs appears in "Rhinelander Absent As Jury Is Chosen in Annulment Suit," *NYEP*, 9 November 1925, 1. Chambermaids and porters at the trial appear in "Kip Was Colored Girl's Slave, Lawyer Charges," *NYDM*, 10 November 1925, 3, final edition. See also "Calls Rhinelander Dupe of Girl He Wed," *NYT*, 10 November 1925, 1.

3 "Lionel Barrymore Divorced in 14 Days; Name of Correspondent Is Not Disclosed," *NYT*, 22 December 1922, 1. During the course of Morschauser's career as a Westchester judge he was known as "not a stickler for decorum." On hot summer days, he gave male jurors permission to take off their coats and vests. See "Justice Morschauser, Jurist, Dies at 84," *NYT*, 4 November 1947. The date Morschauser was elected supreme court justice is in French, ed., *History of Westchester County*, 2:920.

4 The names of the legal teams appear in *CPRR*, 19.

5 Biographical information on Isaac Mills in *Biographical History of Westchester County*, 1:44–45; Griffin, *Westchester County and Its People*, 2:81, 86. Lawyers in New York City formed the first modern bar association in 1870. See Friedman, *American Law in the Twentieth Century*, 282; and French, ed., *History of Westchester County*, 2:920–21.

6 Character actor David Warfield originally appeared in vaudeville and comedy in New York City in the 1890s. He became well known for playing stereotyped Jewish characters. At the turn of the twentieth century, theatrical impresario David Belasco hired Warfield to act in serious productions, where Warfield garnered good reviews. "Warfield, David," *The Oxford Companion to American Theatre*, 3rd ed., ed. Gerald Bordman and Thomas Hischak, <www.oxfordreference.com> (10 October 2007). On who exactly was footing the legal bills, see *CPRR*, 168, 464–65.

7 Biographical information on Lee Parsons Davis in "Lee Parsons Davis Dies at 79; Lawyer Was a Retired Justice," *NYT*, 24 November 1961, 31; information on the years Davis served as district attorney comes from Griffin, *Westchester County and Its People*, 2:87. Information on Coudert Brothers comes from *Encyclopedia of New York*, 288.

8 Mills, Davis, and Morschauser all knew each other. One local history of Westchester County (see Henry Townsend Smith, *Westchester County in History*, 152) claimed Isaac Mills served as one of the three examiners who admitted Morschauser to the bar. In addition, when Isaac Mills sat as a judge, Judge Morschauser's brother appeared in Mills's courtroom as the attorney for a

former "telephone girl" seeking a legal separation from her wealthy husband. See "Ex-Telephone Girl Sues Rich Husband," *NYT*, 5 January 1908, 8. In 1922, Davis appeared as an attorney in a case before Justice Morschauser. See "Seek Ward Secret from Mrs. Curtis," *NYT*, 14 July 1922, 6. Both Mills and Davis made references during the trial that implied their previous acquaintance.

9 Description of Alice's attire comes from *NYT*, 10 November 1925, 1; Robinson, *NYDN*, 10 November 1925, pink edition, 3; and *NYEJ*, 10 November 1925, special extra, 1. Description of Jones family on the first day comes from "Calls Rhinelander Dupe of Girl He Wed," *NYT*, 10 November 1925, 1; *NYDN*, 10 November 1925, final, 4 (photograph); and *NYEJ*, 9 November 1925, final night extra, 3. Description of George Jones as Spanish in "Flappers Agog as Rhinelander Plays the Stoic," *NYDN*, 11 November 1925, pink edition, 2. A photograph of Madison Grant in 1925 appears in Guterl, *Color of Race*, 29. I doubt Grant would have been amused by the comparison.

10 "Calls Rhinelander Dupe of Girl He Wed," *NYT*, 10 November 1925, 1; "Rhinelander Trial On," *NYEJ*, 9 November 1925, 1, final night extra edition. See Kerber, "A Constitutional Right to Be Treated Like American Ladies," 30; and Ritter, "Jury Service and Women's Citizenship."

11 List of jurors' hometowns and occupations in "Calls Rhinelander Dupe of Girl He Wed," *NYT*, 10 November 1925, 1. Reporters noted Leonard's absence from the morning session. Lee Davis mentioned it a number of times during the trial. For one example, see *CPRR*, 1140–41.

12 Leonard's entrance with a bodyguard in *NYDN*, 10 November 1925, final, 3; and *NYHT*, 10 November 1925, 14. One example of a newspaper's account that Leonard did not look at Alice appears in "Brides 426 Love Notes Lured Him, Says Rhinelander," *NYEJ*, 10 November 1925, 1, final news edition. Francis Carmody's contemporaneous treatise on New York practice for lawyers discussed the purpose of a lawyer's opening statement and described its function as to "make clear to the jury the general nature of the questions in issue. The usual way for the party to open is to state the nature of the issues and what he expects to prove" (*Treatise on Pleading and Practice*, 405).

13 *CPRR*, 1081.

14 Ibid., 1082. Cheryl Harris ("Whiteness as Property," 1741) notes that false claims to whiteness "diminish its value and destroy the underlying presumption of exclusivity." Thus it was important to be careful about who was recognized as white.

15 *CPRR*, 1084–85.

16 Ibid., 1085. The term "pure white stock" echoed the language used in the new immigration laws, which referred to "native stock" in determining quotas. See Ngai, *Impossible Subjects*, 26. Even the existence of a law defining "white" did

not necessarily mean the end of confusion. See discussion of Virginia racial purity laws and the attempts to pin down definitions of black and white in chapter 4.

17 CPRR, 1085–86.
18 Ibid., 1087–88.
19 Ibid. 1089–91.
20 Ibid., 1088–92.
21 Ibid., 1092. Mills's reference to Leonard's brother and World War I might have been an effective method of raising sympathy for Leonard and his family. It was only seven years after the end of the war, and Armistice Day was only two days away.
22 CPRR, 1094. Rafter, *White Trash*; Haller, *Eugenics*, 95–110.
23 Wiggam, "Rising Tide of Degeneracy," 31. In Daniel Kevles's study of eugenics (*In the Name of Eugenics*, 131) he observed that the wealthy were often not included in statistics on feeblemindedness because they kept their family members out of public institutions and sent them to private institutions.
24 CPRR, 1094.
25 Ibid., 1095–96.
26 Ibid., 1099.
27 Dijkstra, *Evil Sisters*, 12, 20. "Rhinelander Love Notes Bared," *NYEJ*, 10 November 1925, 1, special extra edition; CPRR, 1100. Joanne Meyerowitz points out that one of the original meanings of the "vamp" was a woman whose "sexual powers drained male energy." Meyerowitz (*Women Adrift*, 128) also discusses another twentieth-century image of womanhood, the "gold-digger," a woman who is after men for their money. The "gold-digger" image was also woven into Mills's strategy to depict Alice in such a way that a male jury would grant Leonard his annulment. Mills read aloud to the jury a letter that Alice wrote in June of 1923, two months after they were engaged, where she dreamed of being kissed by Leonard and showered with ten-dollar bills. See CPRR, 380–81.
28 CPRR, 1099–1102.
29 Ibid., 1102.
30 Ibid., 1104.
31 Ibid., 1105–6. Only a few months earlier, Morschauser expressed his support of the right of the press to report on divorce cases when he was asked to respond to a British proposal to restrict press coverage. Morschauser even suggested that newspaper reporting performed the valuable service of helping to prevent collusion between the parties in some divorce cases. See "Curb on Divorce News Not Found for U.S.," *NYT*, 2 August 1925, special features, 8.
32 "Kip Rhinelander Is 'Brain-Tied,' Counsel Pleads," *NYHT*, 10 November 1925, 14. Although the press began to call Leonard "Kip," Alice did not do so. She occasionally called him "Len." The *Herald Tribune*'s description of Leonard also

seems reminiscent of the ways in which Ellin Mackay described some of the men from her own social set in her article in the *New Yorker* on cabarets. She complained that many society men were uninteresting, pale-faced young men. See Mackay, "Why We Go to Cabarets," 7–8. Stephen J. Gould (*Mismeasure of Man*, 168) discusses Henry Goddard's study of the Kallikak family and the belief that mental deficiencies could be visible. See also Robinson, "Colored Girl's Wiles Blinded Kip, Mills Says," *NYDN*, 10 November 1925, 2, final edition.

33 Rex, "Color Line Stressed in Rhinelander Case," *NYEJ*, 10 November 1925, 3, final news edition. "Margery Rex" was the pseudonym for Julia McCarthy. According to Ishbel Ross (*Ladies of the Press*, 198), Rex was a "busy girl who did news, features, dramatic criticism and, in the beginning, illustrated her own work." Rex reported for the *Evening Journal* from 1918 through 1928. She covered a number of big stories, including major divorces and trials.

34 "White Mother Quietly Soothes Alice at Trial," *NYDM*, 10 November 1925, 4, final edition. The *Daily Mirror* also published a photograph of Leonard on the front page and described him as "much more serious and mature than popularly thought" ("First Photo of Kip," *NYDM*, 10 November 1925, 1, final edition). See also Rex, "Color Line Stressed in Rhinelander Case," *NYEJ*, 10 November 1925, 3, final news edition.

35 "Flappers Agog as Rhinelander Plays the Stoic," *NYDN*, 11 November 1925, 2, pink edition; "Rhinelander's Wife Admits Colored Blood," *NYT*, 11 November 1925, 1.

36 *CPRR*, 1106–7; Robinson, "As a Suitor He Lost Stammer Records Show," *NYDN*, 11 November 1925, 2, pink edition; "Rhinelander's Bride Admits Negro Blood," *NYHT*, 11 November 1925, 10; "Deceived by Jones Girl His Plea," *NYEJ*, 11 November 1925, 1–2, 2, special extra.

37 *CPRR*, 1107. Although Davis claimed that he admitted Alice's color only for the purposes of this trial, he had to have known that this identification would not be limited to the confines of the courtroom. See "Corned Beef 'N Cabbage—Ice Cream—Kip's Bride Hungry," *NYDN*, 20 November 1925, 3, pink edition.

38 *CPRR*, 1109–10.

39 Ibid., 1111. The term "un-American" was widely used during World War I and its aftermath. Davis may have applied it to the Rhinelanders to help counter Mills's attempts to drum up sympathy for Leonard's brother, who had been killed in the war. Frederick Lewis Allen discusses white Protestant fears of anything deemed alien or "un-American" in his *Only Yesterday*, 52.

40 *CPRR*, 1111–13.

41 Ibid., 1115. Although this information had nothing to do with the issues and facts on trial, Mills introduced it in part to emphasize the "character" and behavior of the Jones family. He also introduced this evidence in order to physically compare the half-sister to her other sisters. The newspapers tried to

uncover more information about this half-sister and speculated that she was the illegitimate daughter of the then-unmarried servant Elizabeth Jones and her British aristocratic employer. Some reporters wondered how similar her daughter's experiences were to hers and whether Leonard was also an aristocrat who took advantage of a servant. See Rex, "Like Mother, Like Alice in Rhinelander Case," *NYEJ*, 27 November 1925, 3, final news edition.

42 *CPRR*, 1116–17. Definition of hearsay in *Black's Law Dictionary*, 852.
43 *CPRR*, 1117–18. The treatment of America's black troops in Europe is briefly discussed in David Levering Lewis, *W. E. B. Du Bois: Biography of a Race*, 571–72, and Nikki Brown, *Private Politics and Public Voices*, 96–97. A discussion of the shifting views of the British about race can be found in Lorimer, *Colour, Class, and the Victorians*; Gerzina, *Black Victorians/Black Victoriana*; and Tabili, "We Ask for British Justice."
44 *CPRR*, 1118–19.
45 Ibid., 1119–20.
46 *CPRR*, 1120. In the 1920s, 20 percent of all employed women worked as domestic servants or in laundries; that rate, however, was much higher for African American women, with about 75 percent working as farm laborers, servants, and laundresses. See Kessler-Harris, *Out to Work*, 236–37. See also Katzman, *Seven Days a Week*, 74. In terms of the inappropriateness of a Rhinelander marrying a "maid," Davis may have been referring to the fact that an uncle of Leonard's had been disinherited at the end of the nineteenth century for marrying an Irish maid. For more on Leonard's uncle, see chapter 5.
47 *CPRR*, 1120, 1122–23.
48 Ibid., 1128.
49 Ibid., 1131.
50 "Yes, She's Colored," *NYDN*, 11 November 1925, 1, pink edition; "Rhinelander's Bride Admits Negro Blood," *NYHT*, 11 November 1925, 10.
51 *NYHT*, 13 November 1925, 17.
52 *CPRR*, 30–37.
53 Dr. L. Pierce Clark was a fifty-five-year-old New York neurologist at the time of his testimony. He received a medical degree from New York University in 1892 and acted as a consulting neurologist for the Manhattan State Hospital and the Craig Colony for Epileptics. He was also a visiting neurologist for the Randalls Island Hospital and the School for Mental Defectives. Clark acted as a trustee for the Letchworth Village for Mental Defectives in New York. He had served as the president of the National Association for the Study of Epilepsy, the New York Neurological Society, and the American Psychopathological Association. According to his obituary, Clark was known for his analyses of famous dead men. See "Dr. L. Pierce Clark, Psychiatrist Dies," *NYT*, 4 December 1933, 21.
54 *CPRR*, 50, 74. When Davis cross-examined Dr. Clark, he focused on Leonard's

improvements at The Orchards and his newfound ability to take the lead in social events. Davis connected Leonard's improving condition with the start of his courtship of Alice Jones in September of 1921.
55 CPRR, 51, 52–53, 61, 62.
56 Ibid., 122, 128–29, 134. A description of the former Rhinelander governess in a black veil appears in "Kip Stammers, Alice Shrinks," NYDN, 12 November 1925, 4, pink edition.
57 CPRR, 127–29.
58 Ibid., 135.
59 "Rhinelander an Alert Witness, Brisk in Replies," New York World, 12 November 1925, 1; NYT, 12 November 1925; "Kip Stammers, Alice Shrinks—So It's Big Day for Spectators," NYDN, 12 November 1925, 3, pink edition. The newspapers frequently described Leonard on the stand stuttering or otherwise having serious speech difficulties.
60 CPRR, 135.
61 Mills found it telling that Grace Jones, like her older sister, Alice, married a white man. He made it a point to bring it up when he questioned Grace and her mother. See CPRR, 883–84, 928; and CPRR, 136–37. Isaac Mills frequently used leading questions in his direct examination of Leonard. These kinds of questions are generally inappropriate on direct examination and can only be used on cross-examination. See Cutler, *Successful Trial Tactics*, 102. At one point during the trial, Davis objected to Mills's reliance on leading questions to query Leonard about a topic related to race. Justice Morschauser let Mills proceed and remarked that "under the circumstances, he must have great latitude here, with the witness' impediment" (CPRR, 171).
62 Meyerowitz, *Women Adrift*, 102, 145 n. 3; Clement, *Love for Sale*, 45 (Clement suggests that working-class African American women might engage in treating with white men, believing they had money to spend); Ruth M. Alexander, "Girl Problem," 18, 50–52. There was also a belief in the 1920s that working-class women commodified their sexuality and consequently engaged in sexual behavior without love. By doing so, their sexuality was not seen as legitimate. See Haag, "In Search of 'The Real Thing,'" 566–67.
63 A few places where Justice Morschauser approves of Mills's leading questions. See, for example, CPRR, 140, 171.
64 CPRR, 141–42.
65 Nell Irvin Painter discusses the image of the "oversexed-black-Jezebel" in her "Hill, Thomas, and the Uses of Racial Stereotype," 207–10. Painter argues that "in American iconography the sexually promiscuous black girl—or more precisely, the yellow girl—represents the mirror image of the white woman on the pedestal" (207). See also Guy-Sheftall, "Body Politic," 15. White working-class women were also often depicted as overly sexual. See Haag, "In Search of the

'Real Thing,'" 566–67. Painter argues that representations of black women's sexuality differ from those of white working-class women because black women were perceived as the instigators of sexual acts. See her "Hill, Thomas, and the Uses of Racial Stereotype," 210.

66 For one discussion of the Jezebel image during slavery, see White, *A'r'nt I a Woman*. Deborah Gray White's recent work on black clubwomen, *Too Heavy a Load*, describes the ways they challenged the overly sexualized image of black women in the early decades of the twentieth century. For other discussions of the responses of black women to these stereotypes, see Higginbotham, *Righteous Discontent*; and Wolcott, *Remaking Respectability*. Evelyn Brooks Higginbotham argues that the "metalanguage of race signifies, too, the imbrication of race within the representation of sexuality" ("African-American Women's History," 262).

67 Carby, "Policing the Black Woman's Body in an Urban Context," 73. Sharon Ullman (*Sex Seen*, 6) argues that both the Great Migration and increased foreign immigration sparked moral panics about sexuality in northern cities; see also DuCille, "Blue Notes on Black Sexuality," 203. Eulalia Proctor discusses the appeal of chorus girls in "La Femme Silhouette," 93. Caleb Johnson ("Crossing the Color Line," 526) suggested that octoroons possessed a "potent" sex appeal for white men. Kevin Mumford's analysis of the impact of the Great Migration on the North (*Interzones*, 93–117) includes a discussion of the numbers of black women who worked as prostitutes.

68 Rex, "Color Line Stressed in Rhinelander Case," *NYEJ*, 10 November 1925, 3, final news edition; Hinkle, "Chaos of Modern Marriage," 7.

69 *CPRR*, 149, 163, 164, and 476.

70 Ibid., 141–42, 408, 1194.

71 "Rhinelander Tells Story of Courtship," *NYT*, 12 November 1925, 1; Morris Markay, "A Day in the Country," *New Yorker*, 28 November 1925, 9.

72 *CPRR*, 148.

73 Bailey, *From Front Porch to Back Seat*, 17. Bailey's study of dating focuses primarily on white middle-class Americans. Elizabeth Clement's more recent study of relationships in the first half of the twentieth century and the emergence of dating focuses on working-class youth from different ethnic and racial backgrounds in New York City. See Clement, *Love for Sale*, 218–22. See also Fass, *Damned and the Beautiful*, 22.

74 *CPRR*, 163–65. Some white middle-class youth engaged in premarital sex as long as it led to marriage. Moreover, precursor activities like "petting" would be engaged in, but again with an eye to marriage. See Fass, *Damned and the Beautiful*, 262, 268. Elizabeth Clement (*Love for Sale*, 1) discusses "treating" and sexual behavior during the same period. In the twentieth century, according to Clement, the premarital intercourse rate among the working class rose.

75 *CPRR*, 153–54; Robinson, "Colored Suitor to Aid Kip," *NYDN*, 16 November 1925, 3, pink edition.
76 *CPRR*, 154–55. Leonard's version of this story, where he persuades Alice to let him stay with her in the hotel, contradicts Mills's opening statement.
77 *CPRR*, 344–45. The press did not really discuss this letter since they could not talk about abortion in print. In her study on the sex lives of working-class women between 1880 and 1930, Joanne Meyerowitz (*Women Adrift*, 106) discusses the dangers of unintended pregnancies and notes that the more "sophisticated" knew to turn to contraception or abortion. See also Clement, *Love for Sale*, 226. By the end of the nineteenth century abortion was illegal in the United States. See Mohr, *Abortion in America*; and Tone, *Devices and Desires*, 16.
78 *CPRR*, 167.
79 "Rhinelander Insists Wife Posed as White," *NYHT*, 13 November 1925, 17; *CPRR*, 185–86. Davis restored these excerpts to their entire context. Alice also wrote that she missed Leonard and enjoyed reading his letters. Davis made sure that the jurors knew that in the same letter Alice told Leonard that she was worried he was ill: "[M]y poor Broken heart as worried for you every night since your departing." She also told him that both her mother and father would be happy to see him and described her father's recent birthday party. See *CPRR*, 188–89.
80 *CPRR*, 186. Alice's letter hinted that Leonard's side of their correspondence might be just as sensational as her letters. See *CPRR*, 189. In a letter from June of 1922, Alice also wrote an explicit letter about how Leonard used to hold and touch her. She seemed to justify their activity to him and herself by stating, "but never mind, dearest its all if life, Especially when each one loves, one another like we do" (*CPRR*, 368–70). Thus, Alice's narrative of love justified their sexual activity. For a discussion of the way women needed to have a love story to legitimate their claim to being sexual persons, see Haag, "In Search of the 'Real Thing,'" 567–68. Davis's remark is in *CPRR*, 190.
81 *CPRR*, 217–19. Davis made sure to read the opening paragraph of this letter in which Alice thanked Leonard for sending cards and letters when she was sick. Alice also told him, "I am just as soon, as I am well, I am going to look, for a new position. Because I am happier, when I am working."
82 *CPRR*, 326; *CPRR*, 243.
83 "Negro Bride's Counsel Says Vamping Is New," *NYEJ*, 12 November 1923, 3, special extra.
84 *CPRR*, 225, 226 (emphasis in original).
85 Robinson, "Rhinelander's Suitor Role," *NYDN*, 12 November 1925, 3, pink edition; Robinson, "Rhinelander's Love Secrets," *NYDN*, 13 November 1925, 2, pink edition; "Kip Without Sin Till He Met Colored Bride, He Swears," *NYDM*, 12 November 1925, final edition, 1; Buchanan, "Alice Faithful to Kip After 'Trial Marriage,'" *NYDM*, 13 November 1925, 3, final edition.

86 "Loved Rhinelander, Wife's Letters Say," *NYT*, 13 November 1925, 1.
87 Rex, "Love Put 'Dimmers' on Rhinelander's Eyes," *NYEJ*, 25 November 1925, 1, latest afternoon edition.

CHAPTER FOUR

1 "White but Black," 498. *Century Magazine* was widely read in the 1920s. See Tebbel, *American Magazine*, 128. Some contemporary commentators, such as Louis Fremont Baldwin (*From Negro to Caucasian*, 2), claimed that many whites did not know about passing. But, as this chapter will demonstrate, the existence of a wide variety of early-twentieth-century discussions of passing suggests that New Yorkers (black and white) seemed well aware of it.

2 The use of formal state documents reflects the role of the state as a "powerful 'identifier,' not because it can create 'identities' . . . but because it has the material and symbolic resources to impose the categories, classificatory schemes, and modes of social counting and accounting with which bureaucrats, judges, teachers, and doctors must work and to which non-state actors must refer" (Brubaker and Cooper, "Beyond 'Identity,'" 16).

3 *CPRR*, 1109. Thomas Holt (*Problem of Race*, 18) argues that historians need to do more than merely analyze how race is a constructed category. For an insightful review of Holt's book, see Kevin Gaines, "Race at the End of the 'American Century,'" 209–10. A discussion of race as ideology can be found in Fields, "Slavery, Race, and Ideology."

4 Defining passing leads to difficulties, especially when the definition relies on the phenomenon it tries to explain. For examples of such definitions, see Williamson, *New People*, 100; Teresa Kay Williams, "Race-Ing and Being Races," 166; and Ron Mallon, "Passing, Traveling and Reality," 646. Legal scholar Randall Kennedy (*Interracial Intimacies*, 283, 285) defines passing as "a deception that enables a person to adopt specific roles or identities from which he or she would otherwise be barred by pervading social standards." In his view, passing constitutes a "deception" or a conscious "concealment."(Kennedy's definition raises the question of what he means by deception—deception from whose perspective?) For an earlier definition, see Conyers and Kennedy, "Negro Passing," 215.

5 In thinking about passing as a process I am indebted to Rogers Brubaker and Frederick Cooper, who, in their essay "Beyond 'Identity'" (14–17), point out the necessity of thinking about what scholars mean when they use the language of "identity." They observe that we need to recognize that neither identity nor race necessarily has an exact definition. In terms of identity, they propose using the language of "identification" to explain the process wherein someone actively identifies or categorizes others. Similarly, Barbara Fields's essays differen-

tiating between concepts of "race" and "racism" point out that over-relying on the concept of "race" instead of analyzing "racism" makes "the act of a subject into an attribute of the object" (see "Whiteness, Racism, and Identity," 48; and "Of Rogues and Geldings," 1398).

6. George Schuyler, "Who Is 'Negro'? Who Is 'White'?" 53, 56. Schuyler attributed the existence of the "celebrated Rhinelander case in New York" to superstitious beliefs in race. See p. 55. See also Fields, "Of Rogues and Geldings," 1400, 1405; and Fields, "Whiteness, Racism, and Identity," 48.

7. The notion that the "essence" of race is not necessarily visible but is instead based on interior difference is reflected in the belief that people "pass." See Sollors, *Neither Black nor White yet Both*, 248. Eva Saks ("Representing Miscegenation Law," 57) contends that the "notion that race could be forged or hidden or the concept of 'invisible blackness,' . . . produced the phenomenon of 'passing': blacks who passed as white." See also Michaels, *Our America*, 132.

8. Holt, *Problem of Race*; Fields, "Slavery, Race, and Ideology," 101.

9. Holt, *Problem of Race*, 20.

10. Jordan, *White Over Black*, 171; Berlin, *Many Thousands Gone*, 140, 323. Slaves not only tried to "pass as white" and, thereby, free; they also tried to pass as free people of color. See Franklin and Schweninger, *Runaway Slaves*, 131–33. Clearly, achieving the status of "free," as opposed to being "white," mattered to slaves.

11. In 1852, Harriet Beecher Stowe's *Uncle Tom's Cabin* included a slave who passed as Spanish and free. Weinauer, "'Most Respectable Looking Gentleman'"; Stern, "Spanish Masquerade"; Gross, *Double Character*, 67; Walter Johnson, *Soul by Soul*, 156. See also Hodes, *White Women, Black Men*, 118.

12. Walter Johnson, "Slave Trader"; Gross, "Litigating Whiteness"; Holt, *Problem of Race*, 37.

13. Baldwin, *From Negro to Caucasian*, 6–7. In the 1920s, Melville Herskovits ("Color Line," 206) suggested that passing became more of an issue after emancipation.

14. Cheryl Harris, "Whiteness as Property"; Saks, "Representing Miscegenation Law," 47; Cheryl Harris, "Review Essay: *Whitewashing Race*." For another discussion of "property rights" in "whiteness," see Bell, "Property Rights in Whiteness," 75–83. For a discussions of passing in the 1920s that included comments on its benefits, see "Detecting Color," *Chicago Defender*, 10 December 1921, TNCF, reel 11, frame 904 (article discusses how passing allows one to "climb the ladder of fame and fortune in a land where prejudice outweighs ability." The *Defender* claimed that "in one of our largest department stores in Chicago can be found many 'passers.'"). See also Pickens, "Migrating to a Fuller Life."

15. Pickens, "Racial Segregation," 365.

16. Cheryl Harris, "Whiteness as Property," 1745; Saks, *Before Harlem*, 109–12.

17 Cheryl Harris, "Whiteness as Property"; Saks, "Representing Miscegenation Law"; Ray Stannard Baker, *Following the Color Line*, 158.
18 CPRR, 1102, 1442.
19 Dominguez, *White by Definition*, 23; Stephenson, *Race Distinctions in American Law*, chap. 2; Mangum, *Legal Status of the Negro*, 1–17. Ian Haney Lopez (*White by Law*, 9) argues that law is "one of the most powerful mechanisms by which any society creates, defines, and regulates itself."
20 Hale, *Making Whiteness*; Pascoe, "Race, Gender, and the Privileges of Property," 102–3; Bardaglio, *Reconstructing the Household*, 180–81; Grossberg, *Governing the Hearth*, 138–40; Pascoe, "Race, Gender, and Intercultural Relations," 6; Wallenstein, *Tell the Court I Love My Wife*, chap. 11.
21 Williamson, *New People*, 103; Gatewood, *Aristocrats of Color*, 151.
22 "Intermarriage With Negroes," 862 n. 16.
23 Young, *Colonial Desire*, 105, 125; DuBois, "Negro Problem," 242–43.
24 Saks ("Representing Miscegenation Law," 40, 48) notes that these fictions "transformed race into an intrinsic, natural, and changeless entity: blood essentialized race." See also Jordan, *White Over Black*, 165–66. In 1925, the *New York Amsterdam News* reported that a Russian scientist claimed to have developed "a new method of clinical analysis" to identify "Negro blood" ("Can Identify Negro Blood," NYAN, 29 July 1925, 12). One week later, an *Amsterdam News* editorial joked about this new test and wondered what the Russian scientist would discover after he tested "mulatto blood" (Editorial, NYAN, 5 August 1925, editorial and feature page).
25 Mangum, *Legal Status of the Negro*, 1–2, 9–10. Mangum describes North Carolina as such a state.
26 *Plessy v. Ferguson*, 163 U.S. 537, 552 (1896). For a recent discussion of the *Plessy* decision that analyzes the case as a narrative of passing, see Mark Golub, "*Plessy* as 'Passing.'"
27 Chestnutt, *House Behind the Cedars*, 114–15. African American filmmaker Oscar Micheaux filmed *The House Behind the Cedars* in 1923 and two years later promoted it by connecting it to the *Rhinelander* trial. See Regester, "Headline to Headlights"; and Ray Stannard Baker, *Following the Color Line*, 151.
28 Ray Stannard Baker, *Following the Color Line*, 151. Legal scholar Gilbert Stephenson (*Race Distinctions in American Law*, 12) referred to Baker's question in his discussion of the legal definitions of "Negro." Fourteen years after *Following the Color Line* was published, a professor of economics and sociology echoed Baker's language about the curious question, "What is a Negro?" He concluded, "The law must draw the line somewhere to avoid endless confusion" (Duncan, "Changing Race Relationship," 93–94). Almost twenty years after Baker, other authors still pointed out the absurdity of the question. Melville Herskovits even

exclaimed, "White Negroes! It seems almost as curious as it would be to speak of a Caucasian Chinaman or of an amorphous form" ("Color Line," 204).

29 Baker, *Following the Color Line*, 164, 151.

30 Ibid., 161, 164.

31 Juda Bennett's discussion of literary representations of passing (*Passing Figure*, 22–23) contends that the period between the two world wars saw the appearance of numerous stories on passing. See also Gosselin, "Racial Etiquette," 48. Discussion of the rumors about Warren Harding appears in Williamson, *New People*, 106; DuBois, "Family Tree," 55; and Frances Russell, *Shadow of Blooming Grove*, 413.

32 "Enlist as White," *Freeman* (Evansville, Ind.), 31 August 1918, TNCF, reel 7, frame 640; "Visits Parents Here and Stops at White Hotel," *Afro-American*, 31 October 1919, TNCF, reel 9, frame 424; Gustavus Adolphus Steward, "White," *The Nation*, 17 October 1923, TNCF, reel 17, frame 151; Green, *Secret City*, 207. See also Adele Logan Alexander, *Homelands and Waterways*, 455. For a contemporary discussion of passing in Washington, see William H. Jones, *Recreation and Amusement Among Negroes*, 147. See also Kreizenbeck, "Garland Anderson's *Appearances*," 38.

33 Ulm, "Our Diminishing Tide of Color," 609; Editorial, "The Vanishing Mulatto," 291; "Mulattoes, Merging with Whites, Termed 'Vanishing Race' by Editor," *Star* (St. Louis, Mo.), 31 March 1927, TNCF, reel 27, frame 467. Louis Fremont Baldwin also discusses census statistics in *From Negro to Caucasian*, 34. Melville Herskovits criticized the 1920 census for an undercount of mulattoes in his "American Negro Evolving a New Physical Type," 901.

34 Florette Henri (*Black Migration*, 71–72, 190) argues that "mulattoes" migrating from the South chose to identify as "white" in the North, though she does not really provide any evidence.

35 Adams, "Some Interesting Facts," 226. Fannie Barrier Williams ("Perils of the White Negro," 423) suggested that passing and "the dangers of mistaken identity" were on the rise in the North. As anthropologist John Hartigan reminds us, "We need to pay attention to the local settings in which racial identities are actually articulated, reproduced, and contested, resisting the urge to draw abstract conclusions about blackness and whiteness" (*Racial Situations*, 4). See also Hodes, "Mercurial Nature and Abiding Power of Race," 85; Peter Kolchin, in "Whiteness Studies," 172, suggests that historians should pay "greater attention to historical and geographic context."

36 Pickens, "Passing for White Is Subject Discussed by a Noted Orator and Scholar of the Race," *Birmingham Reporter*, ? June 1921, TNCF, reel 12, frame 899. See also Sylvester Russell, *Amalgamation of America*. Russell's pamphlet is not paginated.

37 Carter, "*Crossing Over*," 376. See also Pickens, "Migrating to a Fuller Life."
38 "South's Social Equality Idea Is Under Fire," *New York World*, reprinted in the *Afro-American* (Baltimore), 19 May 1922, TNCF, reel 15, frame 209; Caleb Johnson, "Crossing the Color Line," 528. Johnson, however, suspected that more passing took place in Chicago and Philadelphia than in New York. See "Crossing the Color Line," 526.
39 Reuter, *American Race Problem*, 59. For another discussion of the ways in which relocating made it easier to pass, see Herskovits, "Color Line," 206. Herskovits mentioned that "light Negro" males could "pass" as white, move to a new community, and marry white and thereby introduce "Negro blood" into white America. In 1944 two social scientists suggested that the rise of cities and greater mobility led to passing. See Wirth and Goldhamer, "Hybrid and the Problem of Miscegenation," 307.
40 Sacks, *Before Harlem*, 112; "Employment of Colored Women in Chicago," *Crisis*, January 1911, 24–25, 25; Gustavus Adolphus Steward, "White," *The Nation*, 17 October 1923, TNCF, reel 17, frame 151. See also "Here and There by the Observer," *Half-Century* 16 (March–April 1924): 19. More recently, Cheryl Harris ("Whiteness as Property," 1710–11) describes her grandmother passing as white to take a job in a store to support her family.
41 Baldwin, *From Negro to Caucasian*, title page, preface. See also Pickens, "Migrating to a Fuller Life." Although it is impossible to determine whether passing was truly "in vogue" in the twenties, many commentators wrote about passing as if it were. For other reports on passing, see "Is World's Champion Hurdler White?" *Afro-American*, 30 May 1924, TNCF, reel 20, frame 28; and "Trying to Get Away From Their Race," *Houston Informer*, 1 March 1924, TNCF, reel 20, frame 33 (claimed that about 300,000 to 400,000 people passed for white).
42 Editorial, "Crossing Over," 3–4; Owens, "Good Looks Supremacy," 82, 90. Joel Williamson (*New People*, 102–3) argues that the rate of passing rose in the South along with the rate of oppression. Owens suggested that passing rose for similar reasons in the North. See also Editorial, "Melange," 356, which claimed that since blacks could not tell if they would be treated well or badly by whites they might resort to passing as white; see Pickens, "Racial Segregation," 365.
43 Walton, "'Pride of Race' Powerful Play," *New York Age*, 20 January 1916, TNCF, reel 4, frame 1025; Ashby, *Redder Blood*; Caleb Johnson, "Crossing the Color Line."
44 "White but Black," 498. Walter White made very similar comments in his contribution to *The New Negro* ("Paradox of Color," 364–65). Some in the 1920s suspected that White wrote the *Century* article; see "No Hard Job to Pass for White Man," *Afro-American*, 7 February 1925, TNCF, reel 22, frame 287. Gibson, "Concerning Color," 418; and Reuter, *Race Mixture*, 71. See also a 1922 dissertation on African American migration, which claimed that some "mulattoes"

have "'gone over to the whites'" because they could "change their name and say they are Mexican, Armenian, Italian, Brazilian, etc." (Duncan, "Changing Race Relationship," 96–97). See also testimony of Leonard Rhinelander, *CPRR*, 622–24.

45 Reuter, "American Mulatto," 41–42.
46 Ibid., 42.
47 Fauset, "Sleeper Wakes"; Fauset, *Plum Bun*; Grayson, "Over the Line," 4; Scott, "Color Line," 5. See also Rudolph Fisher's two-part story, "'High Yaller.'"
48 Thadious Davis, *Nella Larsen*, 5, 141; Larsen, *Passing*; Walter White, *Flight*; Ashby, *Redder Blood*.
49 Van Vechten, *Nigger Heaven*; Ferber, *Show Boat*; Shapiro, "Edna Ferber," 58–60. Information on *Black Boy* in James Weldon Johnson, *Black Manhattan*, 206. In *Our America*, a literary study of modern American identity in the 1920s, Walter Benn Michaels (*Our America*, 25) argues that the character of Gatsby is perceived by some in the novel as not quite "white." See also Barbara Will, "*The Great Gatsby* and the Obscene Word," 132–33.
50 One historian of the eugenics movement in the South argues it focused on "protecting and purifying the Caucasian race" (Edward J. Larson, *Sex, Race, and Science*, 1). See also Sherman, "'Last Stand,'" 71.
51 Sherman, "'Last Stand,'" 77; J. Douglas Smith, *Managing White Supremacy*, 81; "Virginia Has 20,000 Who Are White or Colored at Will," *Afro-American*, 21 March 1924, TNCF, reel 20, frame 4.
52 Sherman, "'Last Stand,'" 77; J. Douglas Smith, *Managing White Supremacy*, 87–89; Plecker, "Correspondence: A Protest from Virginia," *The Nation*, 20 April 1924, TNCF, reel 20, frame 3. Plecker was responding to an earlier editorial, "Fellow-Caucasians!," *The Nation*, 9 April 1924, 388 (The editorial argued the absurdity of the law and asked "fellow-Caucasians," "Are you willing to admit that all the blood of your race cannot absorb and dissolve and obliterate a single drop from another racial stock?"). See also "Shall We All Be Mulattoes," 23.
53 Sherman, "'Last Stand,'" 77–78. The Racial Integrity Act also prohibited whites from marrying nonwhites, although Virginia law already did so. See J. Douglas Smith, *Managing White Supremacy*, 80 (fear of passing as impetus for bill). In 1928, Walter Plecker lobbied for a federal law to require the federal census bureau to publish a list of heads of families from each census as far back as 1800. Plecker felt this information would help track racial identity and reduce passing. See Reilly, *Surgical Solution*, 73.
54 Sherman, "'Last Stand,'" 79, 88.
55 W. A. Plecker, "Race Mixture and the Next Census," reprinted from *Eugenics* 2 (March 1929), Box D-4-3:12 Racial Integrity; and W. A. Plecker to Pal S. Beverly, 12 October 1929, Box D-4-3:12 Racial Integrity, both in Harry H. Laughlin Papers, Pickler Memorial Library, Special Collections, Truman State University,

Kirksville, Mo. In Plecker's letter he informs Beverly about what appears in various government records about Beverly's racial ancestry. See also J. Douglas Smith, *Managing White Supremacy*, 223–28; and Sherman, "'Last Stand,'" 89–90.

56 Pickens, "'Mulattoes' and 'Anglo-Saxon Clubs,'" *NYAN*, 20 May 1925, editorial and feature page. In 1925 W. E. B. DuBois ("Anglo-Saxon at Bay," 10) also mocked the idea of race purity, citing the number of southern mulattoes and those who "knowing and unknowingly" pass.

57 One exception in the definition of white was for someone who possessed "less than one sixty-fourth of the blood of an American Indian," so long as the rest of his or her racial makeup was Caucasian. See J. Douglas Smith, *Managing White Supremacy*, 85, 88.

58 Nobles, *Shades of Citizenship*, xi–xii. In political scientist Melissa Nobles's comparative study of the census in the United States and Brazil, she argues that the census at times mirrors contemporary ideas about race while at others it helps create notions of race. She posits the years 1850–1930 as an era where the census helped create Americans' ideas about race. See ibid., 25–26. See also U.S. Bureau of the Census, *200 Years of U.S. Census Taking*, 22–63.

59 *Congressional Record*, 50th Cong., 2d sess., 2246. Wright, *History and Growth of the United States Census*, 187.

60 See discussion of 1890 Census in U.S. Bureau of the Census, *Negro Population 1790–1915*, 207; U.S. Bureau of the Census, *200 Years of U.S. Census Taking*, 41, 50, 58, 60; Records of the Office of the Director, Office Records of William M. Steuart, 1922-1932, "Fifteenth Decennial Census," RG 29, Entry 141, Box 1; and Williamson, *New People*, 114.

61 U.S. Bureau of the Census, *Negro Population 1790–1915*, 207.

62 As early as 1921, the Census Advisory Committee noted the drop in the count of mulattoes. In November 1921, the committee passed a resolution that declared, "The marked increase in the proportion of mulattoes in 1910, as compared with the returns for preceding censuses, may have been due to employment of a large number of colored enumerators in 1910." They suggested comparing the 1920 and 1910 census results and looking to see where more "colored enumerators had been employed" (Census Advisory Committee, "Advisory Committee November 1921 Resolutions," RG 29, Entry 148, Box 71). The Census Advisory Committee's resolution seemed to suggest that perhaps only certain enumerators could tell if someone was a mulatto.

63 Census Advisory Committee, "Resolutions Adopted by the Advisory Committee, December 14-15, 1928," RG 29, Entry 148, Box 72.

64 Census Advisory Committee, "J.A. Hill, author, 'Population Classified by Race and Nativity,'" RG 29, Entry 148, Box 72.

65 Ibid.

66 U.S. Decennial Censuses, 1900, 1910, 1920, 1930. The 1930 census is the last one open to public view. See <www.ancestry.com> (12 May 2008).

67 DuBois, "Browsing Reader," 234, 248–50. DuBois's idea that the fear of finding a "black strain in the family" underlay "the desperate efforts of the Caucasians to 'preserve the integrity of the white race' " can also be found in L. L. Davis, "Clinging to Straws," 6.

68 *CPRR*, 170.

69 Ibid., 171.

70 Ibid., 173.

71 Ibid., 174.

72 Ibid., 176.

73 Ibid., 176–77.

74 Ibid., 281–86. Davis objected to Lawby's testimony because any statements Alice made about her race during the interview took place *after* her marriage to Leonard. Lawby's testimony could not serve as evidence that Alice deceived Leonard *before* they wed. Justice Morschauser, however, disagreed. See ibid., 287–99.

75 Ibid., 287–99; ibid., 624–25.

CHAPTER FIVE

1 Curtis, *Closing Argument*, 27–32; "The Man Who Shot Drake; A Weak-Minded Member of a Wealthy Family," *NYT*, 21 June 1884, 1.

2 William Rhinelander's lawyer feared his client's family's "wealth and indifference, if not bitterness," would lead to William's lifelong confinement in an asylum. See "Is Rhinelander Insane," *NYT*, 25 July 1884, 5; and Curtis, *Closing Argument*, 25–26. New York's statutory authorization for annulments can be found in New York Domestic Relations Law, Chapter 14, Article 2, Section 7, in Cahill, ed., *Cahill's Consolidated Laws*. For a discussion of annulment law, see chapter 7. Such an effort was not unique to the Rhinelanders. Sven Beckert (*Monied Metropolis*, 34) describes how one wealthy father hoped to have his daughter declared a lunatic after she wed the family coachman.

3 "The Man Who Shot Drake; A Weak-Minded Member of a Wealthy Family," *NYT*, 21 June 1884, 1; "Rhinelander's Oddities," *NYT*, 20 August 1884, 8. A later article mentions that Margueretta had worked as a maid for the Rhinelanders. See "Rhinelander Sued by Waitress Wife," *NYT*, 14 November 1910, 6. Lynch-Brennan, "Ubiquitous Bridget"; Diner, *Erin's Daughters in America*, 80–94. She does not appear as a member of the Rhinelander household in the 1870 census; see Ninth Census of the United States, <www.ancestry.com> (12 May 2008).

4 "The Man Who Shot Drake; A Weak-Minded Member of a Wealthy Family," *NYT*, 21 June 1884, 1. The name of William's wife appears with different spell-

ings in the press and in William's lawyer's closing argument. I use the variant of her name found in William's lawyer's materials under the assumption that it is most likely the correct spelling. See Curtis, *Closing Argument*, 25.

5 Hassell, *Rhinelander Family in America*; "Rhinelander Indicted," *NYT*, 19 July 1884, 2.

6 Matilda Rhinelander quotation in "Talking About His Life," *NYT*, 28 August 1884, 8. See also Curtis, *Closing Argument*, 29. Julia Rhinelander's will is discussed in *Stewart v. Keating*, 15 Misc. 44 (Supreme Court, New York County, 1895). Julia's sister Serena also cut William out of her will. See "Miss Rhinelander's Will," *NYT*, 27 June 1914, 6.

7 Testimony of reporter Barbara Reynolds, *CPRR*, 823; report on Leonard's disinheritance in "Rhinelander Disinherited," *NYAN*, 29 April 1925, 1; and "Family Disinherits L. K. Rhinelander," *NYT*, 28 October 1925, 27.

8 Wharton, *Backward Glance*, 10. For more on Edith Wharton, see Kassanoff, *Edith Wharton and the Politics of Race*. William Rhinelander quotation in "Talking About His Life," *NYT*, 28 August 1884, 8. Wharton uses the same phrase in *Backward Glance*, 79.

9 As Sven Beckert (*Monied Metropolis*, 3) points out, "unlocking the history of upper-class Americans" opens a window into "the dynamics of economic, social, and political change" and deserves historians' attention. Recently, some historians have begun to turn their attention to the history of the white upper class. See works by Maureen Montgomery, Sven Beckert, Clifton Hood, and Thomas Kessner listed in bibliography.

10 Burrows and Wallace, *Gotham*, 1003–8; Binder and Reimers, *All the Nations Under Heaven*, 49; Kenny, "Race, Violence, and Anti-Irish Sentiment."

11 Wiebe, *Search for Order*; Sklar, *Corporate Reconstruction of American Capitalism*; Livingston, *Origins of the Federal Reserve System*; Beckert, *Monied Metropolis*; Kessner, *Capital City*; Kyvig, *Daily Life in the United States*, 7; Dumenil, *Modern Temper*.

12 Painter, *Standing at Armageddon*, 4; Beckert, *Monied Metropolis*, 207, 211.

13 Beckert, *Monied Metropolis*, 4–6. Drawing on class formation theory, Beckert uses the term "bourgeoisie" instead of "aristocracy" or "upper class" to describe elite New Yorkers. Beckert argues that the term "bourgeosie" fits elite New Yorkers because it "refers to a particular kind of elite whose power, in its most fundamental sense, derived from the ownership of capital rather than birthright, status, or kinship" (6).

14 Beckert describes the Knickerbocker group of New Yorkers as the city's "mercantile elite." He also examines the growth of New York's industry in *Monied Metropolis*, 20–21, 46; see also Wecter, *Saga of American Society*, 103; Wharton, *Backward Glance*, 56; and Hermione Lee, *Edith Wharton*, 20. Wharton's mother

came from a branch of the Rhinelanders not quite as wealthy as that of William Rhinelander's.

15 Bernstein, *New York City Draft Riots*; Beckert, *Monied Metropolis*, 141; Kenny, "Race, Violence, and Anti-Irish Sentiment," 372.
16 Painter, *Standing at Armageddon*, 40–50. Built in 1879 at East 66th Street and Park Avenue, the Seventh Regiment Armory looks like a fortress. Its interiors were designed by Stanford White and Louis Comfort Tiffany. See Burrows and Wallace, *Gotham*, 1037, 1077. Information on the Rhinelander's contributions are in Hunting, "Seventh Regiment Armory in New York City."
17 Painter, *Standing at Armageddon*, xxviii; Burrows and Wallace, *Gotham*, 1012–13; Beckert, *Monied Metropolis*, 192–95.
18 Kessner, *Capital City*, 161, 193, 196–97; Burrows and Wallace, *Gotham*, 1028–29, 1032–33; Beckert, *Monied Metropolis*, 215, 220–24.
19 Beckert, *Monied Metropolis*, 151; Kessner, *Capital City*, 34–37; Wharton, *Backward Glance*, 5; Burrows and Wallace, *Gotham*, 1074; Homberger, *Mrs. Astor's New York*, 230–31; Jaher, "Nineteenth-Century Elites," 64–65. Contra to Beckert, Jaher argues that the Knickerbockers lost both social and economic power after the Civil War. Leonard's grandfather William Rhinelander was William Christopher Rhinelander's only son. See "The Rhinelander Family," *NYT*, 23 June 1878, 2. By 1883, five years after William Christopher's death, the younger William controlled the family's real estate properties.
20 Beckert, *Monied Metropolis*, 256. See also Burrows and Wallace, *Gotham*, 1072–75.
21 Cable, *Top Drawer*, 20. Another historian of New York's upper class argues that Mrs. Astor's role of social arbiter countered "the destabilizing effects of demographic growth, urban expansion, and social mobility" (Montgomery, "Female Rituals," 49). See also Erenberg, *Steppin' Out*, 12; and Homberger, *Mrs. Astor's New York*.
22 Maureen Montgomery ("Female Rituals," 48) argues that "in the 1870s, Mrs. Astor combined traditional rituals of access and exclusion with conspicuous public display to demarcate the boundaries of New York's social elite." Richard Brodhead ("Regionalism and the Upper Class," 157) describes this display as the "articulation of a new-style 'high' social class." At the end of the nineteenth century, the white middle and upper classes worried about the "unruly" working classes in the cities. See Lears, *No Place of Grace*, 28–30.
23 Montgomery, "Female Rituals," 49. Frederic Jaher ("Style and Status," 263) described how New York's elite in the late nineteenth century set itself apart by spending lots of money. See also Van de Water, "Jazz and Gin," 205; Homberger, *Mrs. Astor's New York*, 120; Veblen, *Theory of the Leisure Class*, 120–22; and "Boudoir Gossip" (October 1899), 9.

24 Burrows and Wallace, *Gotham*, 1083; "Notes and Queries," 4; "Personal," *Harper's Bazaar*, 6 January 1894, 7; "Mrs. WM. Rhinelander Dies," *NYT*, 14 February 1914, 11. Wealthy New Yorkers used history to bolster their status. See Hood, "Journeying to 'Old New York.'" According to T. J. Oakley Rhinelander's obituary ("T. J. O. Rhinelander Dies in Home at 88," *NYT*, 26 July 1946, 21), he belonged to the Union Club, Badminton Club, St. Nicholas Club, the St. Nicholas Society, Huguenot Society, the Society of the War of 1812, the Sons of the Revolution, the Military Order of Foreign Wars, and the Society of Colonial Wars.

25 Baltzell, *Protestant Establishment*, 113; Wecter, *Saga of American Society*, 233; Burrows and Wallace, *Gotham*, 1073; Beckert, *Monied Metropolis*, 265. The *Social Register* reached its peak for authoritativeness in 1925, when it covered twenty-one cities. See Amory, *Who Killed Society?*, 125; and Baltzell, *Protestant Establishment Revisited*, 8.

26 Hassell, *Rhinelander Family in America*; "American Country Home on the Rhine"; Beckert, *Monied Metropolis*, 270. Jackson Lears contends that the upper-class fascination with genealogy and medieval coats of arms linked concerns over class and race and "provided an upper class under stress with valuable emblems of unity and exclusiveness" (*No Place of Grace*, 188).

27 Burrows and Wallace, *Gotham*, 1087–88. Wealthy Jewish men had belonged to New York's exclusive men's clubs until the end of the nineteenth century, when white society began to define itself by a certain kind of exclusive whiteness. See Beckert, *Monied Metropolis*, 265–66; and Hammack, *Power and Society*, 65–67.

28 Maureen Montgomery describes upper-class marriages as "the social counterpart to corporate mergers in the business world" because marriage "contributed to the consolidation of networks of economic and social power" ("Female Rituals," 49). See also Beckert, *Monied Metropolis*, 259–60; and Montgomery, "Gilded Prostitution." Marital mergers might only work in one direction. A participant-observer of New York society, May King Van Rensselaer (*Social Ladder*, 17) argued that "women of social standing may elevate obscure husbands to their own level but men who marry beneath them usually sink to the standards of their wives." This may help explain some of the reactions to Leonard Rhinelander's marriage to Alice Jones, which was perceived to lower Leonard to her family's status.

29 Montgomery, "'Fruit that Hangs Highest.'"

30 Jaher, "Style and Status," 281. For another discussion of marriage between American heiresses and titled foreigners, see Wecter, *Saga of American Society*, 386–427; Montgomery, *Displaying Women*; and Beckert, *Monied Metropolis*, 259–60. Beckert suggests that such marriages displayed the self-confidence of late-nineteenth-century upper-class New Yorkers. Although these alliances spoke to the wealth of New York's upper class, they also suggest a certain anxiety

about American social status. For a recent account of the late-nineteenth-century marriage of an American heiress to a European aristocrat, see Stuart, *Consuelo and Alva Vanderbilt*. See also "An American Princess," *NYT*, 11 July 1909, magazine, 10; and "Miss Stewart Weds To-Day," *NYT*, 15 September 1909, 1.

31 "The Man Who Shot Drake; A Weak-Minded Member of a Wealthy Family," *NYT*, 21 June 1884, 1. The "demimonde" and upper-class white males are discussed in Erenberg, *Steppin' Out*, 53; Burrows and Wallace, *Gotham*, 955–59; and Dunlop, *Gilded City*.

32 "Misalliances," *NYT*, 11 September 1884, 4.

33 Wharton, *Backward Glance*, 23.

34 See "Rhinelander Declared Sane," 5; "He Would Not Shoot Again," *NYT*, 24 June 1884, 5; "Mr. Rhinelander's Visitors," *NYT*, 26 June 1884, 8; and "Rhinelander in the Tombs," *NYT*, 23 June 1884, 8.

35 "Rhinelander in the Tombs," *NYT*, 23 June 1884, 8. William's lawyer argued in court in an attempt to have his client freed on a writ of habeas corpus that "Rhinelander belonged to one of the oldest families of this city, whose other members he had offended by marrying an Irish lady, whom he esteems as a loyal and noble wife" ("Rhinelander Seeking Freedom," *NYT*, 4 July 1884, 8). See also Matthew Frye Jacobson, *Whiteness of a Different Color*, 48–52; Thomas Nast, "The Ignorant Voter," *Harper's Weekly*, 9 December 1876, 985, <http://elections.harpweek.com/1876/cartoons—1876-list.asp?year=1876> (21 September 2008); and "Fashion's Votaries," *Puck*, 10 July 1878, 6.

36 "Is Rhinelander Insane?" *NYT*, 25 July 1884, 5.

37 "Rhinelander's Mental Balance," *NYT*, 14 August 1884, 8.

38 "Mr. Rhinelander's Mind," *NYT*, 22 August 1884, 8; "Rhinelander's Own Story," *NYT*, 27 August 1884, 8.

39 Curtis, *Closing Argument*, 5, 55. "Rhinelander Not Insane," *NYT*, 31 October 1884, 8; "Rhinelander Declared Sane"; "Lawyer Drake Dead," *NYT*, 29 March 1885, 7.

40 "Rhinelander Sued by Waitress Wife," *NYT*, 14 November 1910, 6; "Rhinelander Admits Bigamy," *NYT*, 15 November 1910, 1; "Rhinelander Set Free," *NYT*, 15 December 1910, 1; "W. C. Rhinelander Cut Off by Mother," *NYT*, 28 February 1914, 1. Curiously, the family genealogist (or someone else) who left William off the family tree included a copy of an undated and untitled newspaper clipping about William's decision to not contest his father's will with the materials located in the New York Public Library. See Hassell, *Rhinelander Family in America*.

41 "Many Pretty Weddings," *NYT*, 12 April 1888, 8.

42 "Wedding of Miss Edith C. Sands," *NYT*, 7 June 1894, 4. See "Boudoir Gossip" (October 1899), 13 (Mr. and Mrs. T. J. Oakley Rhinelander returned from Europe with clothes from Paris); "Town and Country Life," *Town & Country*,

20 September 1902, 20 (Philip and Adelaide Rhinelander in the White Mountains of New Hampshire with her parents); "Town & Country Calendar," *Town & Country*, 31 January 1903, 3 (Mr. and Mrs. T. J. Oakley hosted a dinner); "Town and Country Life," *Town & Country*, 19 December 1903, 20 (Adelaide and Philip Rhinelander in resort town of Lakewood, New Jersey); and "Lakewood Nites," *NYT*, 15 November 1903, 8; and "Social and Travel Notes," *Town & Country*, 25 June 1904, 3 (Philip and Adelaide left Manhattan for the White Mountains).

43 Muccigrosso, "New York Has a Ball"; Beckert, *Monied Metropolis*, 1–2, 334; M. C. Schuyler, "Social Growth of New York," 123; Dunlop, *Gilded City*, 21–36. The *Times* provided a list of the guests and costumes ("The Bradley Martin Ball," *NYT*, 7 February 1897, 10).

44 "Town and Country Life," *Town & Country*, 20 July 1907, 18.

45 Kisseloff, *You Must Remember This*, 117–18; "Miss Alexander Is Lieutenant's Bride," *NYT*, 19 June 1918, 11; "Social Notes," *NYT*, 11 February 1920, 11; "Miss Rhinelander Weds J. S. Shackno," *NYT*, 10 November 1921, 19.

46 Language of "invasion" in Van de Water, "Jazz and Gin," 218.

47 Van Rensselaer and Van de Water, *Social Ladder*, 164. Mrs. John King Van Rensselaer self-identified as a Knickerbocker.

48 Painter, *Standing at Armageddon*, 346–59, 368–70; Dumenil, *Modern Temper*, 35–36, 62–63; David J. Goldberg, *Discontented America*, 50, 66, 76; Kyvig, *Daily Life in the United States*, 9, 12.

49 Painter, *Standing at Armageddon*, 362–65; James Weldon Johnson, *Black Manhattan*, 246; David Levering Lewis, *When Harlem Was in Vogue*, 17–21; David Levering Lewis, *W. E. B. Du Bois: The Fight for Equality*, 1, 7–8, 70–71.

50 Lynch-Brennan, "Ubiquitous Bridget."

51 In November 1924, the *Daily News* reported on a divorce complaint filed by a "wealthy New York clubman" against his wife, an "ex-Follies dancer" ("Dancer Keeps Mum on Divorce Charge," *NYDN*, 16 November 1924, 3, home edition). The next week, the *New York American* printed a story about a "scion of [a] Prominent New York family" who admitted and then denied marrying a "Fifth Avenue Modiste." A few weeks later, the *New York American* publicized a rumor that a wealthy New Yorker planned to marry a "working girl." See "Maxwell Wed! 'Oh No, I'm Not,'" *New York American*, 24 November 1924, 1; and "Drexel to Wed Working Girl?," *New York American*, 14 December 1924, 4-L. The paper claimed that the bride-to-be worked in advertising and was not in the *Social Register* but had been gradually introduced into and accepted by New York society.

52 Or paternal approval—see "Milwaukee Girl Weds Her Riding Instructor," *NYT*, 12 February 1925, 5. This article reported on the elopement of a rich lumber-

man's daughter who her father felt married beneath her. The father threatened to seek an annulment.

53   Cartoon, "Marriage and the Color Line," *Chicago Defender*, 6 December 1924, TNCF, reel 20, frame 31.
54   For a discussion of the process by which distinctions among different white races began to disappear after 1924, see Matthew Frye Jacobson, *Whiteness of a Different Color*, 98. The phrase "dusky Cinderella" appears in "Rhinelander Protested Use of Love Notes," *NYHT*, 17 November 1925, 19.
55   Rogers, "Critic," 34.
56   "Mrs. L. Kip Rhinelander in Social Register, Despite Race Assertions in Husband's Suit," *NYT*, 11 March 1925, 1 (emphasis mine).
57   The phrase "unadulterated, exclusive and rare" comes from Cheryl Harris, "Whiteness as Property," 1737.
58   As the historian Tessie Liu reminds us, "Understanding race as an element of social organization directs our attention to forms of stratification. The centrality of reproduction, especially in the transmission of common substance through heterosexual relations and ultimately through birth ... allows us to see the gendered dimensions of the concept of race" ("Teaching the Differences Among Women," 577). Werner Sollors (*Neither Black nor White yet Both*, 4) points out that "the hackneyed notion of 'pure blood' always rests on the possibility and the reality of 'mixed blood.'"
59   Rogers, "Critic," 34.
60   "To Drop Mrs. Rhinelander," *NYT*, 16 March 1925, 19; Wecter, *Saga of American Society*, 235–36.
61   Wecter, *Saga of American Society*, 235–36.
62   Ibid.; "Half-Breed Guide Named by Stillman in Divorce Suit," *NYT*, 12 March 1921, 1 (the Stillman divorce came before Justice Morschauser too).
63   Wecter, *Saga of American Society*, 235–36; "Kip Dropped by Social Register," *NYEJ*, 25 November 1925, 1, city edition.
64   "Mrs. Rhinelander Scares 400," *NYAN*, 18 March 1925, 2.
65   After World War I, "society figures, reversing the previous course of relations, began to pursue athletes and entertainers[,] and the search for sensation replaced that continuity of tradition which held the old guard together" (Jaher, "Style and Status," 274). Edith Wharton (*Backward Glance*, 6) also pointed to the war as a turning point for New York's upper class. See also Amory, *Who Killed Society?*, 108; and Cable, *Top Drawer*, 204. The decline in the practice of chaperoning helped mark this shift. See Montgomery, "'Fruit that Hangs Highest,'" 187; and Cable, *Top Drawer*, 204.
66   William Leach's discussion of the culture of consumption from the late nineteenth century through the twenties observes that even by the 1890s women

who did not belong to society could buy imitation jewels and fake furs to emulate wealthy women. See Leach, "Transformations in a Culture of Consumption."

67 Mackay, "Why We Go to Cabarets," 7. In his editorial in *American Mercury* on the Africanization of American culture H. L. Mencken makes clear the threat posed by the cabaret for some white Americans, the very threat that probably occasioned the criticism of white society youth for going to such places. Mencken described cabarets as "places essentially African in character, there to dance African dances to music by African musicians." According to Mencken, these Africanisms even reached into private parties in white homes. And in a comment that spoke to a sense of the world turned topsy-turvy, Mencken declared that "the dark brother has triumphed. The proud Nordic blond, pushing always, has pushed at last into colored society."

68 Mackay, "Why We Go to Cabarets," 7–8. I read this article very differently than Ann Douglas. Douglas (*Terrible Honesty*, 373) interprets Mackay's article as a criticism of the dullness of society parties. Mackay and her friends enjoyed cabarets as exciting places where they could mingle with strangers and friends. Although this reading fits well with Douglas's arguments about "mongrel" Manhattan in the 1920s, it does not seem sustained by Mackay's actual words. Mackay claimed that she preferred to go to cabarets with her carefully chosen upper-class friends and that they maintained their own insulated social bubble by ignoring the other people around them. Douglas also described Mackay's article as "flippantly impassioned about the right to make casual choices," a claim that seems to me the opposite of what Mackay said she was interested in doing.

69 Mackay, "Why We Go to Cabarets," 7–8. Ellin Mackay's status in New York society in the 1920s embodied a change in society. Although her wealthy father owned a telegraph company, his father, John Mackay, came to New York as a Catholic immigrant from Ireland in the 1840s. John Mackay made a fortune in silver mines in Nevada. His wife, Ellin's grandmother, wanted a life in high society and moved to Paris and London in the 1880s, not New York. Clarence Mackay moved to New York and married a woman from a Knickerbocker family (and an Episcopalian). They lived in a mansion on Long Island. By the 1920s, Clarence Mackay's social standing was secure enough that he hosted a party for the Prince of Wales at the Mackay's Long Island estate. Ellin danced with the prince. See Bergren, *As Thousands Cheer*, 216–17, 225–27, 229–39; and "C. H. Mackay Host of Prince of Wales," *NYT*, 7 September 1924, 19. The *Times* lists Leonard's older brother, Philip Kip, and his wife as guests, along with the Astors and the Vanderbilts.

70 Caleb Johnson, "Crossing the Color Line," 528. One anecdote of passing from the *Half-Century* described the surreptitious visit of a passing woman to her mother, who could not pass. When the daughter leaves her mother's house, she

steps into a limousine to return to her wealthy white husband. See "Here and There by the Observer," 6.

71 Mencken, "Editorial," 160.

72 Rogers, "Critic," 34. The play Rogers referred to was the 1924 production of Eugene O'Neill's *All God's Chillun Got Wings*, which generated a great deal of controversy. See Mumford, "On Stage: The Social Response to 'All God's Chillun Got Wings,'" in *Interzones*, and Douglas, *Terrible Honesty*, 102. Even the Vanderbilts criticized Leonard Rhinelander. The *New York American* reported that when "prominent society man" Reginald C. Vanderbilt returned from summer vacation in Europe and was informed of the Rhinelander marriage, he replied, "'I think I know the young man. It's all too bad isn't it'" ("R. C. Vanderbilt and Wife Return," *NYA*, 16 November 1924, 2-L).

73 On the same day that Rogers mentioned the Rhinelanders in his column, "The Critic" (p. 34), he also discussed white Americans' desire for a tan. Rogers claimed that in Asbury Park, New Jersey, white "life-guards, burnt so dark, that they were eligible for the jim-crow car, were the envy, particularly of the women." At the same time, Rogers observed, whites segregated African Americans on the same beach.

74 News of Leonard Rhinelander's disinheritance was not confirmed until October 1925 when his lawyers responded to Alice Rhinelander's motion for increased counsel fees. Rumors that he would be disinherited had circulated for months. See "Rhinelander Disinherited," *NYAN*, 29 April 1925, 1; "Family Disinherits L. K. Rhinelander," *NYT*, 28 October 1925, 27.

75 "Mrs. Rhinelander Scares 400," *NYAN*, 18 March 1925, 2. Later testimony and evidence revealed that Leonard enjoyed the family pleasures available at the Jones's home. In one letter Leonard told Alice how much he disliked society girls. See *CPRR*, 544–45. According to the *Amsterdam News*, Alice also said that Leonard knew that she was colored before they married, claiming, "It didn't make any difference to him then. And I don't think it does now."

76 Lears, *No Place of Grace*, 28–32. See also the classic discussion of conspicuous consumption, Veblen, *Theory of the Leisure Class*.

77 Jaher, "Style and Status," 282; "Many Pretty Weddings," *NYT*, 12 April 1888, 8; Bederman, *Manliness and Civilization*, 192–93.

78 Haller, *Eugenics*, 80.

79 Read, *Abolition of Inheritance*, 61–62, 129; Wiggam, "Rising Tide of Degeneracy," 27. See also Chester, *Inheritance, Wealth, and Society*; Aldrich, *Old Money*, 112; Hasian, *Rhetoric of Eugenics*, 22. In a discussion of Madison Grant's book, *The Passing of the Great Race*, in 1917, the *Crisis* referred to Franz Boas's review, which argued that no evidence existed to prove the superiority of any race. Moreover, the magazine added, if the principles of eugenics were strictly followed, "many of the scions of North-European nobility who do conform with

Mr. Grant's racial requirements would have to be removed from our society, on account of their degeneracy" ("Looking Glass," 76).

CHAPTER SIX

1 *CPRR*, 1114, 1121.
2 Katzman, *Seven Days a Week*, 216–18; Buchanan, "Rhinelander in Trap, Refuses to Quit Trial," *NYDM*, 18 November 1925, 3, final edition. Perhaps Leonard pursued Alice *because* she was a maid. In a discussion of interracial sexuality in the South, Nell Irvin Painter ("Of *Lily*, Linda Brent, and Freud," 248) discusses Freud's suggestion that middle- and upper-class men might be impotent with the women of their own class. Leonore Davidoff ("Class and Gender in Victorian England," 96) discusses middle- or upper-class male sexual fascination with servants in Victorian England. Citing Davidoff, Painter sees a parallel between European elites and slaveholders in the South. This assertion of white men's sexual privilege increased the numbers of African American women who moved North during the Great Migration. See also Hine, "Black Migration to the Urban Midwest," 130.
3 *CPRR*, 475; Jacqueline Jones, *Labor of Love*, 164. Davis also asked whether Leonard knew Alice lacked an education. Leonard admitted he did. See *CPRR*, 475–76. The press described Leonard's letters as well written, a fact that served as evidence of his upper-class upbringing as well as a negation of the claim that he was feebleminded. See "Kip Rhinelander Admits Ardent Pursuit of Wife," *NYHT*, 18 November 1925, 21.
4 *CPRR*, 476.
5 Bederman, *Manliness and Civilization*, 7, 11–12, 18–19, 48. See also Hoganson, *Fighting for American Manhood*.
6 Bederman, *Manliness and Civilization*, 19. Kevin White (*First Sexual Revolution*, 2, 10, 146) sees a move between a nineteenth-century ideal of "character" for men embodied in the "Masculine Achiever" or the "Christian Gentleman" to a new style of masculinity in the early twentieth century. By the 1920s "primitive" masculinity was more valued than gentlemanly behavior. For a recent discussion of similar changes that looks at African Americans, see Summers, *Manliness and its Discontents*.
7 Bederman, *Manliness and Civilization*, 12–15, 19; Kevin White, *First Sexual Revolution*, 2.
8 Mash notes in "Rhinelander Jury Deliberating; Verdict Expected Before Night," *New York Sun*, 4 December 1925, 1. Margery Rex ("Was Rhinelander's Love a Fraud," *NYEJ*, 19 November 1925, final news edition, 3) also argued that Leonard was a "man" because he married Alice despite opposition. During

World War I, American soldiers exhibited different kinds of masculinity, including "aggressive and highly sexual" forms of masculinity. See Clement, *Love for Sale*, 155.

9 *CPRR*, 600–602. Davis also pointed out that Leonard drank alcohol and knew how to play poker. See *CPRR*, 441–42, 448.
10 Ibid., 604–5.
11 Ibid., 608–12.
12 Ibid., 879–81. Grace testified that on her first car ride with Leonard and his friends, they stopped when Carl left the car to get a haircut.
13 Ibid., 445–46; Rex, "Kip's Mind Befuddled by His Blind Love," *NYEJ*, 20 November 1925, 3, final news edition.
14 *CPRR*, 450–51.
15 Kevin White, *First Sexual Revolution*, 19, 158; Lynd and Lynd, *Middletown*, 266. Leonard and Alice's letters indicate that they went to the movies together and separately.
16 *CPRR*, 477. Leonard also interjected that Alice was not a virgin and that he "wasn't the first one" (*CPRR*, 478).
17 Kevin White, *First Sexual Revolution*, 155–56. White takes the phrase "rapid sentiment formation" from a 1930s sociological study of dating by Willard Waller, "The Rating and Dating Complex." Waller's definition of courtship excluded "Negro and white" relationships on the presumption that they never led to marriage. Waller discussed the use of a "line" to encourage an attachment. See Waller, "Rating and Dating Complex," 727, 733. For more on dating, see Bailey, *From Front Porch to Back Seat*. Another historian of American courtship argues that there was a "wide gulf" between courtship practices for couples who courted in 1900 and those in the 1920s. See Rothman, *Hands and Hearts*, 289. See also Clement, *Love for Sale*. "Kip's Litany of Love," *NYDM*, 20 November 1925, 4.
18 This discussion draws on Jane Larson's and Michael Grossberg's analysis of these two types of lawsuits. See Larson, "'Women Understand So Little,'" 382–400; and Grossberg, "Broken Promises," 33–63. The *Evening Journal* even compared the Rhinelander trial to breach of promise actions. See "Five Women Whose Court Actions Reveal Sour 'Notes' in Letters Inadvertently Written on 'Love's Sweet Song,'" *NYEJ*, 21 November 1925, 2, final news edition. The *New Yorker* also observed in a discussion of the Rhinelander trial that the "first thing presented in any divorce action . . . or, as the papers have it 'heart balm suit,' will be the letters that passed between the principals when their hearts were credulous. But never before have we had such quantity, such fervor, nor, indeed, such a tincture of humor-providing that you get your fun out of erroneous spelling and faulty syntax" (Markey, "Current Press," 11).

19 Larson, "'Women Understand So Little,'" 383–89.
20 Legislatures repealed seduction statutes because they "represent[ed] an outdated sexual puritanism" (Larson, "'Women Understand So Little,'" 379).
21 Simmons, "Modern Sexuality," 157–60. See also D'Emilio and Freedman, *Intimate Matters*, 223, 241; and Tone, *Devices and Desires*. Elizabeth Clement's study of the working class in New York City (*Love for Sale*, 17) shows a rise in premarital sex at the end of the nineteenth and beginning of the twentieth centuries. See also Bailey, *From Front Porch to Back Seat*, 80.
22 These changes in sexuality presented both men and women in "a world in flux" (Ullman, *Sex Seen*, 18–19).
23 Kevin White, *First Sexual Revolution*, 147. Larson, "'Women Understand So Little,'" 393–98; Grossberg, *Governing the Hearth*, 63.
24 In a postscript, Leonard wrote, "I know you are taking good care of my ring and my pin. I am glad you have them, no matter how much I miss them" (*CPRR*, 456–57). As with Alice's letters, I retain the exact spelling and punctuation as they appear in the excerpts from Leonard's letters transcribed into the court record.
25 *CPRR*, 459. The *Daily Mirror* and other papers printed Leonard's letters. In one edition, excerpts appeared under the title "Kip's Litany of Love" with sections headed "YEARNING," "JEALOUSY" AND "LOVE VOWS" (*NYDM*, 20 November 1925, 4, final edition). Despite Davis's narrative, the papers still relied on the theme of love to describe the Rhinelander marriage.
26 *CPRR*, 466–68. The automobile was acknowledged in the 1920s as a new place for sexual activity away from the eyes of parents. See Bailey, *From Front Porch to Back Seat*, 19.
27 *CPRR*, 469–72. Later testimony suggests that Alice may have been in New York on the day of Adelaide Rhinelander's wedding. See *CPRR*, 935. By the 1890s, society weddings in New York City had become media spectacles. See Montgomery, "Female Rituals," 47–67. See also Stuart, *Consuelo and Alva Vanderbilt*.
28 Robinson, "Kip on Conquest, He Admits," *NYDN*, 18 November 1925, 3, pink edition; "Kip Rhinelander Admits Ardent Pursuit of Wife," *NYHT*, 18 November, 1925, 21. The *Herald Tribune* characterized Leonard's letters as more literate than Alice's. The reporter also noted that Leonard's testimony contradicted his lawyers' arguments about who pursued whom.
29 *CPRR*, 452.
30 Ibid., 453.
31 By the twenties, Americans were acknowledging that women had sexual desires and were not merely passionless creatures, although not all agreed on how and when women should act on them. See D'Emilio and Freedman, *Intimate Matters*, 233; and Dumenil, *Modern Temper*, 131–34. According to Sharon Ullman (*Sex Seen*, 19), films released in the period between 1896 and 1910 "demonstrated a surprising recognition of female desire and sexual availability."

32 CPRR, 453–54. Davis also read a letter in which Leonard asked Alice to find an apartment in Manhattan. "You know, love, you said you would do anything for your boy, and I will do anything for you, dear girl," Leonard wrote. "Supposing, Alice, we take a trip to New York on Friday and see what we can find?" (CPRR, 495).
33 CPRR, 511.
34 Ibid., 512. "Rhinelander Wilts; Gets Adjournment," NYT, 19 November 1925, 6; "Expect Father to Testify for Kip," NYEJ, 19 November 1925, 2, final news edition; "Rhinelander Near Collapse in 'Net of Lies,'" NYHT, 19 November 1925, 21.
35 CPRR, 590.
36 Ibid., 512–13. Leonard did admit that he saw part of her legs and some of her breasts through her nightgown. See ibid., 648.
37 Ibid., 594. Davis was alluding to the informal segregation policies adopted by many places of public accommodation in New York.
38 CPRR, 594–95. The condom was the second most popular form of birth control in the 1920s and 1930s. Rubber condoms had existed since the 1840s, but, according to Andrea Tone, they were not widely used in the United States until the 1860s. The popularity of the condom as a contraceptive in the 1920s and 1930s reflected its greater use during World War I by American soldiers. See Gordon, *Woman's Body, Woman's Right*, 203; and Tone, *Devices and Desires*, 69, 136.
39 CPRR, 650.
40 Ibid., 651.
41 Ibid., 501–2.
42 Ibid., 574.
43 Ibid., 575–78.
44 Ibid., 579.
45 "Poison Letters Sent to Rhinelander Jury," NYDM, 2 December 1925, 2, news edition. The article reported that lawyers for both sides had been receiving "threatening letters inspired by race prejudice" and that letter writers were now targeting the jury.
46 D'Emilio and Freedman, *Intimate Matters*, 186.
47 "Anti-Intermarriage Bill in Michigan," 66. A few years later, DuBois argued that "prohibition of such legal marriage is a direct bid for bastards and prostitutes and removes all civilized protection from colored girls and women" (DuBois, "Opinion of W. E. B. DuBois," 128–29). Many African Americans followed the Rhinelander trial because they felt it could be a backdoor way to accomplish the same result as antimiscegenation legislation.
48 CPRR, 548–49.
49 Ibid., 550–55.

50 Robinson, "Court Halts Grill as Kip Wilts," *NYDN*, 19 November 1925, 3, final edition. A discussion of changes in sexual behavior during courtship appears in Clement, *Love for Sale*.
51 Robinson, "Court Halts Grill as Kip Wilts," *NYDN*, 19 November 1925, 3.
52 *CPRR*, 559–71. Returning often to his understanding of what it meant to be a man, Davis asked, "And you knew at the time that you were doing an unmanly and indecent thing, didn't you?" At the same time, Davis also tried to get Leonard to admit that his actions were based on the fact that Alice was of "lowly station." Leonard refused to agree and conceded he would do the same with a girl from his own class, so long as the girl suggested the deception. Davis also asked, "If a woman deceives you, in order to get a jury to say that, you would be willing to drag the woman in the gutter, after you have used her body? Is that your idea of manhood?" Leonard replied that he was following his counsel's orders and that he was justified since Alice had deceived him. See ibid., 564–65.
53 Ibid., 619. Continuing with his argument that Leonard had to have known the Jones family's color, Davis asked when Leonard first stayed the night in the Jones home. After Leonard replied that it was only after his return from school in Arizona in 1924, Davis made Leonard describe the cramped interior of the Jones's home. Davis hoped to show that when Leonard stayed with the Joneses, Mr. Jones vacated his room and moved to a smaller bedroom. Regarding the nights when "Mr. Jones had to get out of his bed . . . and go into this smaller room," Davis asked whether Leonard ever entertained questions about Jones's color. Leonard allowed that he never gave it any thought. See ibid., 619–20.
54 "Rhinelander Suit Suddenly Halted," *NYT*, 20 November 1925, 9; "Rhinelander Begs for Time; Case Goes off Until Monday," *NYEJ*, 20 November 1925, 1–2, final news edition.
55 "Rhinelander Suit to Go On, Says Mills," *NYT*, 21 November 1925, 1. Justice Morschauser granted the request but then launched into a reminder to the jury—yet again—to stay away from newspapers. Morschauser told the jury not to draw any conclusions from the different adjournments granted during the trial. The judge emphasized why he felt his warnings were so necessary: "Everybody is on edge in a case of this kind, and I want to keep my jury as well as myself free from any outside influences and any inferences" (*CPRR*, 654–55).
56 "Rhinelander Suit to Go On, Says Mills," *NYT*, 21 November 1925, 1; "Kip's Counsel Split Over Annulment Suit," *NYDM*, 21 November 1925, 3, final edition.
57 "Kip's Counsel Split Over Annulment Suit," *NYDM*, 21 November 1925, 3; Grace B. Robinson, "Kip Suit in Father's Hands," *NYDN*, 21 November 1925, 3, pink edition.
58 "Kip's Counsel Split Over Annulment Suit," *NYDM*, 21 November 1925, 3. The *Evening Journal* also reported rumors of a split in Leonard's legal team over whether or not to continue the case. A new rumor surfaced that Davis hoped to

subpoena Leonard's father to testify. The *Evening Journal* also reported that Leonard, the "young aristocrat, who normally looks twice his twenty-two years, left court pale and shaking, looking like a man of sixty" and appeared close to a physical and mental collapse. See "Father of 'Kip' Is Sought," *NYEJ*, 21 November 1925, 1, final news edition. On its editorial page, the *Journal* printed a cartoon titled "How to Cook a Kippered Rhinelander" (*NYEJ*, 21 November 1925, 16, final news edition) that depicted Lee Parsons Davis, as a chef, roasting Leonard, the fish, on a hot witness stand.

59 "Rhinelander's Mystery Notes Defiantly Read," *NYHT*, 24 November 1925, 23.
60 *CPRR*, 656.
61 Ibid., 658–59. Descriptions of Davis jumping to his feet are in "Rhinelander's Wife Cries Under Ordeal," *NYT*, 24 November 1925, 3; and Robinson, "Mistrial Near As Lawyers Clash Before Mystery Letter Is Read," *NYDN*, 24 November 1925, 3, pink edition.
62 *CPRR*, 660–61. Description of Mills in "Rhinelander's Wife Cries Under Ordeal," *NYT*, 24 November 1925, 3. In response to Mills, Davis sputtered that they should just wait and see if the case would proceed. He objected to Mills's "stump speech" and asked for a short recess to consult with his colleagues on whether to request a mistrial. Morschauser told Davis it was unlikely that he would grant such a motion, but he allowed for the break. After a break, Davis made a motion for a mistrial due to the "prejudicial comments of the senior counsel for the plaintiff" (*CPRR*, 662). Justice Morschauser denied the motion.
63 *CPRR*, 663.
64 Ibid., 664–65. At this point in the trial transcript, the court reporter noted that "some women leave court room."
65 *CPRR*, 676–79. Crowded hallways in "Rhinelander's Mystery Notes Defiantly Read," *NYHT*, 24 November 1925, 23. The *Daily Mirror* (24 November 1925, 4, second final edition) also published a photo titled "Women Barred from Court at Kip's Trial," where the caption described the guards. Alice and her parents' absence from court at this point in "Kip's Mystery Notes Read; Women Are Ejected from Court," *NYEJ*, 23 November 1925, 1, final night extra; and Robinson, "Alice Bares Her Dark Body," *NYDN*, 24 November 1925, 3, pink edition. However, only Alice and her mother leave in Buchanan, "Crowds Battle for Transcript of Kip's Letters," *NYDM*, 24 November 1925, 3, second final edition.
66 *CPRR*, 1073–76. Even the transcript signals that these letters were considered different from the other courtship letters. In general, the other letters were reproduced alongside the transcription of the surrounding testimony. This letter and the next were separated from the other trial testimony.
67 *CPRR*, 680. The *Herald Tribune* reported that two female reporters were allowed to remain in the courtroom while Leonard's letters were read. See "Rhinelander's Mystery Notes Defiantly Read," *NYHT*, 24 November 1925, 23. Grace

Robinson reported that she was one of three women who remained. See Robinson, "Vile Pen in Blueblood's Hand Pitiable, Says Woman Writer," *NYDN*, 24 November 1925, 6, final edition.

68 *CPRR*, 682.
69 The letter is called M-1 in the transcript, *CPRR*, 685, but appears as N-1 in the exhibits section, *CPRR*, 1076.
70 Ibid., 685.
71 Ibid., 686–87.
72 Ibid., 688; Foucault, *History of Sexuality*, 39–49. The degeneracy attributed to Leonard by Davis was different from that attributed to him by Isaac Mills.
73 "Talk of the Town," *New Yorker*, 5 December 1925, 4. The *Daily News* reported that peddlers sold Leonard's letters on Chicago streets for twenty-five dollars. See "Leonard's Letters Bring $25 in Chicago Sale," *NYDN*, 28 November 1925, 4, third final edition. See also Gilman, *Difference and Pathology*, 198.
74 *CPRR*, 688–89.
75 D'Emilio and Freedman, *Intimate Matters*, 122, 164.
76 New York Penal Law, Chapter 41, Article 66, Section 690, in Cahill, ed., *Cahill's Consolidated Laws*; Ullman, *Sex Seen*, 154 n. 87; Kevin White, *First Sexual Revolution*, 150; D'Emilio and Freedman, *Intimate Matters*, 336. A 1930 marriage manual promoted "genital kisses" for married couples. See Melody and Peterson, *Teaching America About Sex*, 100.
77 *CPRR*, 688–89. Interracial sex could also be categorized as "unnatural."
78 "Text of Rhinelander's Scarlet Letters Read to Jury," *NYDM*, 24 November 1925, 3, final edition; Editorial, "The Dirty Rhinelander," *NYDM*, 24 November 1925, 17, final edition. Grace Robinson declared that Leonard's shocking letters "made the reflective hearer question the value of the elaborate system of education with which the rich surround their children" ("Vile Pen in Blueblood's Hand Pitiable, Says Woman Writer," *NYDN*, 24 November 1925, 3, final edition). See also Dunlop, *Gilded City*.
79 Letter to the editor from "Office Worker," *NYDN*, 19 December 1925, 15, pink edition; letter to the editor from "A Flake from the Lower Crust," *NYDN*, 22 December 1925, 23, pink edition; "Surprise Is Planned by Kip," *NYEJ*, 28 November 1925, 1, final news edition.
80 *CPRR*, 692.

CHAPTER SEVEN

1 Eleazer, "Trends in Race Relations in 1926," *Opportunity*, January 1927, 16–17; James Weldon Johnson, *Black Manhattan*, 246; David Levering Lewis, *When Harlem Was in Vogue*, 17–21; Boyle, *Arc of Justice*.
2 Dumenil, *Modern Temper*, 130; Cott, *Grounding of Modern Feminism*; Ullman,

Sex Seen, 124; Kevin White, *First Sexual Revolution*, 172; Rebecca L. Davis, " 'Not Marriage at All.' "

3. Hinkle, "Chaos of Modern Marriage," 1. A 1929 publication on "modern" marriage used the word "chaotic" to describe it. See Wile and Winn, *Marriage in the Modern Manner*, viii.
4. Hinkle, "Chaos of Modern Marriage," 10; Elaine Tyler May, *Great Expectations*, 77.
5. "Preferred Cabarets to Home, So Judge Denies Her Alimony," *NYT*, 17 November 1923, 15; "Should End Divorce, Morschauser Says," *NYT*, 26 March 1923, 1; "No Divorce, Ever," *Time*, 31 March 1923. Morschauser's obituary described him as a "foe of easy divorce" ("J. Morschauser, Jurist, Dies at 84," *NYT*, 4 November 1947, 25).
6. Editorial, "Inter-Marriage," *NYDN*, 16 September 1922, TNCF, reel 15, frame 205. A growing body of scholarship that explores the links between race and marriage exists. Most historians who study antimiscegenation legislation would agree with Nancy Cott that such laws constitute the "most striking" state regulation of marriage. Cott argues that antimiscegenation laws constitute "powerful evidences of public authority using marriage policy to create a social order of racial separation and hierarchy" (Cott, "Giving Character to Our Whole Civil Polity," 118, 119). For a small sample of the existing literature, see Cott, *Public Vows*, and Wallenstein, *Tell the Court I Love My Wife*. Peter Bardaglio (*Reconstructing the Household*, 49) notes that southern antimiscegenation laws did not reduce interracial sex. The goal was to prohibit sex between black men and white women, not to prevent white men from gaining sexual access to black women.
7. "Friends Shocked by Suicide of Pretty Nurse Who Killed Self Because of Negro Blood," *Rochester Herald*, 2 September 1922, TNCF, reel 15, frame 204; "Negro Strain in Blood Sends Girl to Suicide," *Southwestern New York Post Express*, 30 August 1922, TNCF, reel 15, frame 204.
8. "Friends Shocked By Suicide of Pretty Nurse Who Killed Self Because of Negro Blood," *Rochester Herald*, 2 September 1922, TNCF, reel 15, frame 204; "Negro Strain In Blood Sends Girl to Suicide," *Southwestern New York Post Express*, 30 August 1922, TNCF, reel 15, frame 204. A 1925 national survey of nursing school admissions showed that out of 1,696 accredited schools, 1,588 barred African Americans. See Burnette, "Looking Back."
9. Editorial, "Can One Drop of Blood Change You?" *NYAN*, 1 November 1922, TNCF, reel 15, frame 202.
10. "Wife Is Colored, He Says in Suit," *NYAN*, 6 December 1922, 1. There was no follow-up article, so I do not know who won or lost. The records of New York annulment cases and other matrimonial proceedings are not open to anyone other than the involved parties for one hundred years without a court order. See

New York's Domestic Relations Law, Article 13, Section 235, in Consolidated Laws of New York, <http://public.leginfo.state.NY.US/menugetf.cgi> (10 October 2008), and *New York Opinion of the Attorney General (Informal)*, 1978, no. 264. My telephone conversations with Mark Nussbaum of the Office of the County Clerk, Bronx County, in August of 2005 confirmed that such information would not be made available.

11 Brisbane, "Today Little Countries Stand Back. Enough for One Century. Coolidge Lives in This Era. Her African Blood," *NYA*, 28 November 1924, 1.

12 Brisbane suggested that a significant legal precedent might come out of Leonard's lawsuit if he won—so long as the disparity in wealth between the Rhinelanders and the Joneses did not prevent Alice from contesting it: "New York State legalizes marriages between Africans and whites. The young woman is nearly white. What will the [United States] Supreme Court say about a few drops of colored blood?" Brisbane wondered if those "few drops" meant that Alice was a "Negro" and therefore made the Rhinelander marriage interracial. See Brisbane, "Today Little Countries Stand Back. Enough for One Century. Coolidge Lives in This Era. Her African Blood," *NYA*, 28 November 1924, 1. But even if the Rhinelander marriage was interracial, if Leonard was, as everyone assumed, white, and Alice was deemed legally colored, New York law did not directly provide a remedy.

13 Brisbane, "Today Little Countries Stand Back. Enough for One Century. Coolidge Lives in This Era. Her African Blood," *NYA*, 28 November 1924. Arthur Brisbane referred incorrectly to Leonard's lawsuit as a divorce action. Leonard filed for an annulment. As we shall see, these two kinds of lawsuits had different legal and symbolic ramifications.

14 As Brisbane made clear, only interracial marriages between certain races were considered legally troubling. Matthew Jacobson argues that during the twenties differences between certain white races such as the Celtic, Anglo-Saxon, or Slavic started to diminish as white Americans consolidated into a larger group of Caucasians, who were differentiated from Negroes. See Matthew Frye Jacobson, *Whiteness of a Different Color*, 8, 111. See also Guterl, *Color of Race*. In 1941, however, the supreme court, New York County, granted an annulment on the grounds of fraud when a wife complained that her husband, a German, deceived her about his status as a naturalized American citizen. Before the marriage, she told her future husband she could not marry an alien and disliked Nazis. The court observed that since the Nazis were terrible and American citizenship wonderful, the wife was entitled to her annulment. See *Laage v. Laage*, 176 Misc. 190 (Supreme Court, New York County, 1941). Five years later, the supreme court in Cayuga County refused to annul a marriage when a wife claimed that her husband told her he was German when he was in fact Polish. When the judge asked whether her husband was still the same person she

married no matter his "race," the wife said no. See *Pawlowski v. Pawlowski*, 65 N.Y.S. 2d 413 (Supreme Court, Cayuga County, 1946). Prohibiting marriage across the color line denied interracial relationships the legal imprimatur of marriage and prevented the birth of legitimate racially mixed children. Legal regulation of interracial marriage dates back to America's colonial era. New York did not have such a statute in the colonial era under the English. As a Dutch colony, however, it prohibited interracial sex. Of the northeastern colonies, only Massachusetts and Pennsylvania passed legislation prohibiting interracial marriage. See Fowler, *Northern Attitudes Towards Interracial Marriage*, 63; and Wallenstein, *Tell the Court I Love My Wife*, 253. These types of statutes became particularly popular in the South and West after the Civil War. See Grossberg, *Governing the Hearth*, 138. In a legal treatise on the law and the "Negro," which appeared in 1940, its author noted that such laws appeared in twenty-eight states, mainly in the South and the West. See also Mangum, *Legal Status of the Negro*, 238.

15 "Rhinelander Kin May Help His Wife," *NYT*, 7 May 1925, 21; "Rhinelander Rumors Fly Thick and Fast," *NYAN*, 13 May 1925, 12.

16 *Mirizio v. Mirizio*, 242 N.Y. 74, 81 (1926); Schouler, *Treatise on the Law of Domestic Relations*, 13. A 1929 book on marriage argued that "the chief interest that society has in any union is whether or not it produces a family that will hold together" (Wile and Winn, *Marriage in the Modern Manner*, xix). The normative heterosexual model of marriage plays a key role in current debates over legalizing marriages between people of the same sex. Recently, New York's Court of Appeals ruled that the state constitution did not require the state to recognize same-sex marriages. The decision in *Hernandez v. Robles* (7 N.Y. 3d 338 [2006]) observed that when New York adopted its Domestic Relations Law in 1909, the "universal understanding" of marriage was that it was between a husband (man) and a wife (woman). Recent debates over the nature of marriage have led scholars from a variety of disciplines, not just history, to closely examine the institution. See Stein, "Symposium: Abolishing Civil Marriage."

17 Editorial, "Inter-Marriage," *NYDN*, 16 November 1922, TNCF, reel 15, frame 205; Mumford, *Interzones*, 161. Aaron Gullickson's recent research on trends in interracial marriage ("Black/White Interracial Marriage Trends," 303, 309) suggests that during the Great Migration the "white outmarriage ratio" should have increased as more African Americans (available as spouses) moved North. Instead, his statistical study of census data indicates that the outmarriage ratio for whites declined. Between 1880 and 1930, the "odds of interracial marriage" noticeably fell.

18 Fowler, *Northern Attitudes Towards Interracial Marriage*, 299–311; Cott, *Public Vows*, 163–64. Kevin Mumford (*Interzones*, 7) also discusses the white backlash against Johnson and sees it as a "prelude" to white response to the Great

Migration. See also "Intermarriage," 296–97; "Anti-Intermarriage Bill in Michigan," 66; "Anti-Intermarriage Bills," 232; and "Concubinage," 50.

19 "Intermarriages," *Chicago Defender*, 14 November 1914, TNCF, reel 2, frame 569; "William Lee Finally Marries White Girl," *Chicago Defender*, 9 December 1916, TNCF, reel 4, frame 1034 (couple applied in Michigan first and refused a license, then married in Wisconsin); "Negro Refused Permit to Wed," *Menominee Michigan Leader*, 29 June 1917, TNCF, reel 6, frame 51.

20 "Mixed Marriage Is Barred in Chester," *The Advocate*, 28 August 1923, TNCF, reel 17, frame 169; "White Girl Tried to Marry a Negro," *Youngstown Vindicator*, 29 July 1918, TNCF, reel 7, frame 648.

21 "College Man Reveals Color on Wedding Eve," *NYDM*, 7 November 1925, 3, final edition. Kevin Mumford discusses what appears to be the same incident in *Interzones*, 215 n. 43.

22 "College Man Reveals Color on Wedding Eve," *NYDM*, 7 November 1925, 3, final edition; "Girl Sacrifices Love for Colored Man for Parents," *NYDM*, 9 November 1925, 3, final edition. See also "Girl Refuses to Wed Colored College Man," *NYDN*, 8 November 1925, 2, home edition; "Favors Mixed Marriages," *NYDM*, 9 November 1925, 15, final edition. For an earlier example of public disapproval of intermarriage in the North, see "The Ghetto" (220–21), an article about a New Jersey marriage.

23 "Marrying of Whites and Negroes Is 'Worse than Murder!' Says Klan Woman," *Pittsburgh Courier*, 7 February 1925, TNCF, reel 22, frame 262; "Colored Bride Hides from Klan," *NYDN*, 26 April 1926; "Colored Bride and Mate Still Hide from Klan," *NYDN*, 28 April 1926; In the same year, the *Crisis* observed that newspaper reporters were "hot on the trail" of stories involving the "intermarriage of persons 'suspected' of Negro blood with whites" ("That Drop of Blood," 90).

24 For a discussion of controversy over O'Neill's play, see Mumford, "On Stage: The Social Response to *All God's Chillun Got Wings*," in *Interzones*, and James Weldon Johnson, *Black Manhattan*, 192–95.

25 Mencken, "Editorial."

26 Owens, "Black and Tan Cabaret"; see also Mumford, *Interzones*, 30–33; George Schuyler, "These 'Colored' United States," 348. Schuyler claimed that more white women than white men were involved in miscegenation in New York, which made such relationships particularly troubling. He may have been correct when he posited that few black-white marriages took place. See Gullickson, "Black/White Interracial Marriage Trends," 303. Nell Painter (" 'Social Equality,' " 49) notes that the phrase "social equality" is usually "sexually charged."

27 Some African Americans disapproved of marriages between blacks and whites. The *Daily Mirror* recorded the opinion of some African American New Yorkers on the Rhinelander marriage. One woman stated, " 'We consider Leonard Rhine-

lander with the "white trash!" I wouldn't wipe my feet on him!' " She added, " 'If I had a daughter I'd rather see her dead than the wife of a white man!' " See "Kip Faces Court Grilling as Trial Resumes Today," *NYDM*, 16 November 1925, 2, final edition.

28 Hasian, *Rhetoric of Eugenics*, 55; W. O. Brown, "Racial Inequality?" 47, 54.
29 Grant, *Passing of the Great Race*, 60. See also Gregg, "Mulatto."
30 By the mid-1940s, St. Clair Drake and Horace R. Cayton argued that fear of interracial marriage was "closely associated" with fears of passing. Like the fear of interracial marriage, anxiety over passing was also linked to the Great Migration. Indeed, the social scientists Melville Herskovits and Edward Reuter claimed that some blacks moved to new communities, disappeared into whiteness, and married whites. See Drake and Cayton, *Black Metropolis*, 159; Herskovits, "Color Line," 206; Reuter, *American Race Problem*, 59; and Reuter, "American Mulatto," 42.
31 Adams, "Some Interesting Facts," 226; Fannie Barrier Williams, "Perils of the White Negro," 423; Carter, "Crossing Over," 376. W. A. Plecker to H. H. Laughlin, 24 November 1928; and W. A. Plecker to H. H. Laughlin, 17 November 1930, in Box D-4-3:12 Racial Integrity, in Harry Laughlin Papers, Pickler Memorial Library, Special Collections, Truman State University, Kirksville, Mo. An editorial in a Houston paper in 1924 suggested that over 300,000 African Americans passed throughout the country. See "Trying to Get Away from Their Race," *Houston Informer*, 1 March 1924, TNCF, reel 20, frame 33.
32 Forrester, "Is 'The Negro Problem' White or Black?" 333. For more on deception and passing, see Sollors, *Neither Black nor White yet Both*, 249; and Kennedy, *Interracial Intimacies*, 283–85.
33 "Wife Is Colored, He Says in Suit," *NYAN*, 6 December 1922, 1; Caleb Johnson, "Crossing the Color Line," 526.
34 "Intermarriage with Negroes—A Survey of State Statutes," 859, 863. Peter Wallenstein describes the variety of American antimiscegenation laws as an "antimiscegenation regime," which he defines as "the complex of power and policies that long supported legal restrictions on what marital partners people with various racial identities were allowed to choose from and what groups were forbidden" (Wallenstein, *Tell the Court I Love My Wife*, 7). Mangum, *Legal Status of the Negro*, 254.
35 *Ferrall v. Ferrall*, 153 N.C. 174 (1910). Randall Kennedy discusses the *Ferrall* case in *Interracial Intimacies*, 238–41. An earlier commentator on *Ferrall* interpreted it as a form of "marital revenge" (Sickels, *Race, Marriage, and the Law*, 142).
36 *Kirby v. Kirby*, 24 Ariz. 9 (1922). Peggy Pascoe discusses *Kirby* in "Miscegenation Law," 44–52. For additional annulment cases in which the state already prohibited miscegenation, see *Neuberger v. Gueldner*, 139 La. 758 (1916) (No annulment granted where white husband claimed wife really colored but trial judge

found her to be white); and *Sunseri v. Cassagne*, 191 La. 209 (1938) (White husband received annulment on grounds wife was a "person of color." The Louisiana Supreme Court remanded the case to lower court to allow wife to show evidence of her whiteness). See Brattain, "Miscegenation and Competing Definitions of Race."

37 Grossman and Guthrie, "Road Less Taken," 320. For a lawsuit with a similar result in Missouri, see "Vagaries of Prejudice," 144, and "Along the Color Line," 232.

38 Gatewood, "Perils of Passing." "Racial Intermarriages," *Chicago Defender*, 9 August 1919, TNCF, reel 9, frame 433. See also *Theophanis v. Theophanis*, 244 Ky. 689 (1932) (Court found no fraud and refused to annul marriage where husband claimed wife deceived him about being a mulatto).

39 "Can't Tell Wives from Negro Women," *Topeka Plain Dealer*, 12 February, 1915, TNCF, reel 3, frame 714. The same story appears in "Cannot Tell," *Richmond Planet*, 6 March 1915, TNCF, reel 3, frame 716. The article in the *Richmond Planet* attributes the story to the *New York American*. Later articles reported that Mr. Little worked to dig up information about his wife's childhood to show she was African American. See "Little Says His Wife Went to Negro School," *Free Press* (Detroit, Mich.), 14 April 1915, TNCF, reel 3, frame 725. The *Crisis* also reported on the Little divorce action in "Along the Color Line," 167. See also "Is She a Negress? Court Not to Say," *Leavenworth Kansas Times*, 3 June 1915, TNCF, reel 3, frame 731. A later case in Michigan apparently led to an annulment. See "White Girl–Negro Marriage Annulled," *Detroit Michigan Times*, 30 June 1919, TNCF, reel 9, frame 441. In 1921, the *Evening World* reported that a Connecticut judge had annulled an unconsummated marriage in which the "Negro" husband allegedly lied about his racial classification to obtain a marriage license. See "Negro Blood in Husband Suspected, Marriage Is Annulled," *NYC Evening World*, 19 December 1921, TNCF, reel 12, frame 887.

40 *Libman v. Libman*, 169 N.Y.S. 900 (Supreme Court, New York County, 1918); see also *Lapides v. Lapides*, 254 N.Y. 73 (N.Y. 1930) ("Mere non-disclosure as to birth, social position, fortune, good health and temperament cannot vitiate the marriage contract."); Hartog, "Marital Exits and Marital Expectations," 116–17; Friedman, *American Law in the Twentieth Century*, 436; Nelson, *Legalist Reformation*, 49–50; and Paul H. Jacobson, *American Marriage and Divorce*, 113.

41 Lawrence Friedman (*History of American Law*, 502) suggests that New York's rigid divorce statute led to more annulment suits in that state than in other jurisdictions. This was so, Friedman argues, because annulments "were a loophole in the divorce laws, less distasteful, though less certain, than trumped-up adultery." William Nelson (*Legalist Reformation*, 50) suggests that New York spouses had a third route to end their marriage: head to another state to divorce and hope that New York would recognize it.

42 Fessenden, "Nullity of Marriage," 112. Joanna Grossman and Chris Guthrie's small study of annulment cases filed in one California county from 1890 through 1910 ("Road Less Taken," 323–28, 330) point to five reasons why California spouses sought annulments at the turn of the twentieth century: no provision of the divorce law fit their situation; a successful annulment suit meant the marriage never existed; a particular religion prohibited divorce; it was often easier to remarry after an annulment; and there were no financial obligations (such as alimony) in the wake of a successful case. Some of these reasons may have appealed to Leonard and his attorneys as they searched for a legal escape from his marriage.

43 Carmody, *Treatise on Pleading and Practice*, 940.

44 Ironically, Leonard's annulment suit and the ensuing publicity only strengthened the link between Leonard and Alice in the public's mind. Obituaries of Leonard's relatives and other notables involved in the trial that appeared in the *New York Times* even a number of years later usually mentioned Leonard and Alice. See "P. K. Rhinelander Dies Here at 42," *NYT*, 22 May 1939, 17 (Leonard's older brother who never attended the trial); "Lee Parsons Davis Dies at 79," *NYT*, 24 November 1961, 31; and "Samuel Swinburne, Retired Jurist, 70," *NYT*, 16 May 1938, 17.

45 See Shamas, Salmon, and Dahlin, *Inheritance in America*, 86. New York's dower law in the 1920s is in New York Real Property Law, Chapter 51, Article 6, Section 190, in Cahill, ed., *Cahill's Consolidated Laws*. Additional legal provisions on distribution of property to widows can be found in New York Decedent Estate Law, Chapter 13, Article 3, Section 98, in Cahill, ed., *Cahill's Consolidated Laws*. Peggy Pascoe discusses the links between miscegenation law, property rights, and marriage in her "Race, Gender, and Intercultural Relations."

46 Schouler, *Treatise on the Law of Husband and Wife*, 2; "The Rhinelander Estate," *NYT*, 25 June 1878, 5.

47 Adrienne Davis, "Private Law of Race and Sex," 268.

48 Carmody, *Treatise on Pleading and Practice*, 940. See Conclusion for a discussion of the continued importance of property-related claims to the Rhinelanders.

49 New York Domestic Relations Law, Chapter 14, Article 2, Sections 5 and 7, in Cahill, ed., *Cahill's Consolidated Laws*; Grossman and Guthrie, "Road Less Taken," 325; Geoffrey May, *Marriage Laws and Decisions*, n. 2, 7–8 (*void ab initio*); Schouler, *Treatise on the Law of Domestic Relations*, 19 (*void ab initio*).

50 Leonard is described as "stuttering" in Buchanan, "Rhinelander in Trap, Refuses to Quit Trial," *NYDM*, 18 November 1925, 3, final edition. The word "stammering" appears in the headline "Rhinelander's Suitor Role—Girl Agreed Reluctantly to His Plan, He Admits in Stammering Recital of Romance," *NYDN*, 12 November 1925, 3, pink edition. See also Carmody, *Treatise on Pleading and Practice*, 926–27.

51 The Kallikaks and the Jukes were described as degenerate family clans in well-known studies of the era. See Rafter, *White Trash*.

52 Grossberg, *Governing the Hearth*, 116. A fraud claim could counter one narrative about the Rhinelander marriage that had started to emerge in the pretrial coverage and undermined the exclusivity of upper-class whiteness. This story line portrayed Leonard and Alice's relationship as contented, albeit interracial.

53 Nelson, *Legalist Reformation*, 50–54. In 1959, Paul Jacobson (*American Marriage and Divorce*, 113) remarked that both New York and California had relatively high rates of annulments compared to other states. Jacobson's data, however, comes from 1940–56, after the Rhinelander trial took place.

54 The phrase "free marriage market" comes from Michael Grossberg, "Guarding the Altar," 201. See also Grossberg, *Governing the Hearth*, 103.

55 Grossberg, "Guarding the Altar," 199.

56 Richmond and Hall, *Marriage and the State*, 335. Marriage is discussed as a "procreative institution" in Lindsay, "Reproducing a Fit Citizenry," 541.

57 These kinds of cases prove difficult to track since New York public policy prohibits the release of information on these kinds of marital actions. Only two race fraud cases appear in New York's reported decisions: *Taylor v. Taylor*, 181 N.Y.S. 894 (Supreme Court, Bronx County, 1920), and *Rhinelander v. Rhinelander*. I found other cases through newspaper accounts in the *New York Times*, the *Amsterdam News*, and the Tuskegee Institute News Clippings File. These annulment suits include *Rouget v. Rouget* (1916), *Neale v. Neale* (1919), *Lehr v. Lehr* (1920), *Jones v. Walsh* (1920), *Price v. Price* (1922), *Bornn v. Bornn* (1922), *Harris v. Harris* (1924), *Stovall v. Stovall* (1922), *Williams v. Williams* (1923), *Malillo v. Malillo* (1924), and *Rosell v. Rosell* (1925). I have in my possession the certificates of dissolution from two of the above cases from the Bronx Supreme Court: *Price v. Price* (Supreme Court, Bronx County), index no. 596-22, and *Rosell v. Rosell* (Supreme Court, Bronx County), index no. 4339–25. The 1924 case of *Harris v. Harris* may have involved a number of different kinds of deception, including social status, parentage, and morality. At some point during the trial a claim was raised that the defendant-wife was the daughter of a "Memphis quintaroon." The husband was a former vice president of National City Bank. See "Mrs. Harris Hears Story of Her Past," *NYT*, 28 February 1924, 7; "'Lie' Whispers Wife As Harris Testifies," *NYT*, 29 February 1924; "Harris Was Misled by Wife, Jury Finds," *NYT*, 5 March 1924, 19; and "Love Child May Be Daughter of Negro Mistress," *Pittsburgh Courier*, 5 April 1924, TNCF, reel 20, frame 16.

58 Fessenden, "Nullity of Marriage," 113; Borton, "Sex, Procreation," 1096; Hartog, *Man and Wife in America*, 1. See also Cott, *Public Vows*, 52.

59 "Refuses to Annul Marriage for Color," *NYAN*, 11 February 1925, 14. This case does not seem to have produced a published reported decision or to have been

covered by the *New York Times*. See also "Racial Intermarrying," *East Tennessee News*, 5 February 1925, TNCF, reel 22, frame 304; "Race of Bride Ruled Out Divorce Court," *Chicago Defender*, 31 January 1925, TNCF, reel 22, frame 319; and "Judge Upholds Mixed Marriages in the West," *Pittsburgh Courier*, 7 February 1925, TNCF, reel 22, frame 319. The *Afro-American*'s report claims that the judge denied the annulment because the husband knew his wife was "colored" before they wed. See "Court Refuses White Husband Freedom," *Afro-American*, 7 February 1925, TNCF, reel 22, frame 319.

60 *Robertson v. Roth*, 163 Minn. 501, 504 (Minn. 1925).
61 Ibid. (emphasis mine).
62 Grossberg, *Governing the Hearth*, 116–18.
63 Ibid.; "Nature of Fraud Required to Annul a Marriage."
64 *Reynolds v. Reynolds*, 85 Mass. 605 (Mass. 1862).
65 Grossberg, *Governing the Hearth*, 118–19; *Reynolds v. Reynolds*, 85 Mass. 605 (Mass. 1862).
66 Fessenden, "Nullity of Marriage," 123; Schouler, *Treatise on the Law of Husband and Wife*, 42.
67 Vanneman, "Annulment of Marriage for Fraud," 497; *Chipman v. Johnston*, 237 Mass. 502 (Mass. 1921).
68 *Van Houten v. Morse*, 162 Mass. 414 (Mass. 1894). See also Kennedy, *Interracial Intimacies*, 281–83.
69 *Chipman v. Johnston*, 237 Mass. 502 (Mass. 1921). The decision in *Chipman* may not have deterred Massachusetts spouses from trying to get an annulment on the grounds of race fraud. The *Afro-American* reported that a white baseball player sued his wife for an annulment on these grounds. As far as I can tell, this case, supposedly filed in Suffolk Superior Court, never resulted in a reported decision, and I did not find a follow-up article. See "Lives With Wife 4 Years, Finds She's Colored," *Afro-American*, 4 May 1923, TNCF, reel 17, frame 142.
70 One of the last New York cases to follow *Reynolds* is *Fisk v. Fisk*, 39 N.Y.S. 537 (App. Div. 1896). *DiLorenzo v. DiLorenzo*, 174 N.Y. 467 (N.Y. 1903).
71 *DiLorenzo v. DiLorenzo*, 174 N.Y. 467 (N.Y. 1903). New York law describes marriage in this way: "Marriage, so far as its validity in law is concerned, continues to be a civil contract, to which the consent of parties capable in law of making a contract is essential" (New York Domestic Relations Law, Chapter 14, Article 3, Section 10, in Cahill, ed., *Cahill's Consolidated Laws*).
72 *DiLorenzo v. DiLorenzo*, 174 N.Y. 467 (N.Y. 1903); Vanneman, "Annulment of Marriage for Fraud," 509.
73 *Maynard v. Hill*, 125 U.S. 190, 210–11 (1888).
74 *Wells v. Talham*, 180 Wis. 654 (Wis. 1923). In the 1920s a number of case notes published in reputable law reviews described New York's law on annulment and fraud as a "liberal rule." See "Marriage and Divorce-Annulment for Fraud–

Breach of Promise," 209; "Nature of Fraud Required to Annul a Marriage," 663 n. 6 (New York had a "somewhat broader policy"); and "Marriage-Annulment-Fraud," 708. See also Borton, "Sex Procreation," 1076 n. 33. Vanneman ("Annulment of Marriage for Fraud"), however, disagreed with this analysis. At times New York's courts appeared confused about which rule applied. This confusion stemmed, in part, from a 1904 decision issued by the court of appeals that seemed to return to the principles of the *Reynolds* rule. See *Svenson v. Svenson*, 178 N.Y. 54 (N.Y. 1904). By 1910, however, courts appeared to subscribe to the standards set out in *DiLorenzo*. See *Domschke v. Domschke*, 138 A.D. 454 (App. Div. 1910). A *Harvard Law Review* note on the *Domschke* decision opined that the New York court had gone too far and "on grounds of public policy the wisdom of the doctrine of the principal case may well be questioned" ("Marriage. Nullification," 157).

75 Judge Crane in dissenting opinion in *Shonfeld v. Shonfeld*, 260 N.Y. 477, 488 (N.Y. 1933). For cases that addressed whether a spouse lied about love before marriage, see *Schaeffer v. Schaeffer*, 144 N.Y.S. 774 (App. Div. 1913); *Griffin v. Griffin*, 204 N.Y.S. 131 (Supreme Court, Kings County, 1924), aff'd, 209 A.D. 883 (App. Div. 1924) (no opinion); and *Williams v. Williams*, 130 N.Y.S. 875 (Supreme Court, Oneida County, 1911).

76 *Domschke v. Domschke*, 138 A.D. 454 (mistress); *Smith v. Smith*, 112 Misc. 371 (Supreme Court, Kings County, 1920) (insanity); *O'Connell v. O'Connell*, 201 A.D. 338 (App. Div. 1922) (drug addiction).

77 "Opening for Plaintiff," CPRR, 1081.

78 *Brief of Appellant* (New York Court of Appeals), 18–19, in CPRR.

79 "Opening for Plaintiff," CPRR, 1102. In contrast to Leonard's lawyers' claims, Davis presented evidence from Ross Chidester, the Rhinelander's chauffeur, that Leonard "didn't give a damn" that Alice's father was colored (CPRR, 936).

80 Under the rules of New York civil practice, Leonard's lawyers could file in any county in which Leonard maintained residence. Since Leonard had lived for years in Manhattan and moved there once again after separating from Alice, he presumably would have had the right to file in the Manhattan courts as well. This suggests that Leonard's lawyers "forum-shopped" for a judge sympathetic to Leonard's claim. With only seven judges sitting in Westchester, and with Morschauser receiving a great many marital cases in that jurisdiction, Morschauser would likely handle the case. Morschauser was well known in the legal community for his work in a variety of divorce cases, and he had also written and commented on various aspects of matrimonial law. See "Morschauser, Jurist, Dies at 84," NYT, 4 November 1947, 25. For a contemporary discussion of venue in New York courts, see Clevenger, *Clevenger's Supreme Court Practice*, 116.

81 The *Neale* case was never reported in the official legal reporters. My informa-

tion on it comes from " 'Indian' Husband Was Mulatto: Is Divorced," *New York City Journal*, 6 January 1920, TNCF, reel 11, frame 240.

82 *Sheridan v. Sheridan*, 186 N.Y.S. 470 (Supreme Court, Westchester County, 1921).

83 Ibid.; "Mrs. Bouck White Wins Annulment," *NYT*, 20 July 1921, 13. In 1924, a Brooklyn judge criticized some judges for making it too easy to get an annulment following the *DiLorenzo* decision. See "Court Denounces 'Trial Marriages,'" *NYT*, 5 December 1924, 23.

84 "'Indian' Husband Was Mulatto; Is Divorced," *New York City Journal*, 6 January 1920, TNCF, reel 11, frame 240; "White Woman Finds She Wedded a Negro," *Pittsburgh Dispatch*, 2 November 1919, TNCF, reel 9, frame 428; "Ethiopian Blood Leads Wife to Ask Divorce," *Chicago Defender*, 18 March 1922, TNCF, reel 15, frame 208; *Price v. Price*, index no. 596-22, Certificate of Dissolution. This certificate indicates that Marie Price won an annulment action against her husband, Arthur Price, in the Supreme Court of Bronx County, New York. The judgment of annulment was entered on 21 June 1922. I also have a copy of the minutes or entries of the case (dates of filings of pleadings, etc.) since they are a public record. According to the entries, Marie Price began the case in February of 1922. By March, the judge had granted the annulment in a nonjury trial. Thanks to Mark Nussbaum of the Office of the Bronx County Clerk, Bronx Supreme Court, for his help in determining which records could be viewed. See also report of annulment action between Joseph Alonso Rouget and Emma Rouget, in which the wife claimed that the husband was not white but Haitian ("Dislikes Haitian Hubby," *Chicago Defender*, 2 December 1916, TNCF, reel 4, frame 1037). In New York, only one reported decision in addition to *Rhinelander v. Rhinelander* touched on the question of the relationship between marriage, fraud, and race. In the 1920 case of *Taylor v. Taylor*, a wife filed to annul her marriage on the grounds that her husband induced her to marry when he represented that he was "white" although he had "Negro blood." Unfortunately, no decision was ever issued that addressed the validity of the wife's claim. The husband had the case dismissed because he had already obtained a divorce from his wife in the District of Columbia for adultery. See *Taylor v. Taylor*, 181 N.Y.S. 894 (Supreme Court, Bronx County, 1920).

85 Leonard Rhinelander's appellate brief written after the trial by his lawyers argues that race was material, though they cited no supporting case law. Instead, they pointed to miscegenation laws in other states and general attitudes against such marriages as evidence that race is material. See *Brief of Appellant* (New York Court of Appeals), 18–19, in CPRR. The argument that passing constitutes race fraud, deception, or concealment suggests that such an act is designed to get someone else to give up something valuable or to inflict an injury on someone. In the instance of passing, the "something" valuable that is

taken is the claim to whiteness, and the injury inflicted is being married to a person of the wrong color.

86 *Mirizio v. Mirizio*, 242 N.Y. 74 (N.Y. 1926). In a legal brief submitted to the court of appeals in the 2006 landmark case *Hernandez v. Robles* involving same-sex marriage, advocates of same-sex marriage argued that reproduction was never "an essential element of marriage" in New York. Citing the language in *Mirizio* about marriage and "begetting offspring," the brief argued that such language merely constituted *dicta* and not the court's ruling. For the purposes of attorneys advocating a particular position in court, the distinction between *dicta* and the ruling matters. For my purposes, the fact that New York's highest court in the 1920s alluded to reproduction as essential to marriage is relevant. Indeed, the lawyers in *Hernandez v. Robles* conceded that economic interdependency is central to ideas about marriage and that since economic connections are passed down through the generations, some form of reproduction is required. See Suzanne Goldberg, "Sexuality and Marriage," 265.

87 *Sheridan v. Sheridan*, 186 N.Y.S. 470 (Supreme Court, Westchester County, 1921).

88 Cutler, *Successful Trial Tactics*, 47. Justice Morschauser made this assumption explicit in his charge to the jury at the end of the trial. See chapter 9.

89 A few years earlier, a Manhattan woman lost a similar lawsuit because the judge found no evidence that she had been deceived by her husband. See "Born a White Man, His Marriage Stands," *NYT*, 2 May 1922, TNCF, reel 15, frame 192; and "Chicago Daily Editor Born in Danish West Indies Wins out against Wife's Annulment Plea," *NYDN*, 6 May 1922, TNCF, reel 15, frame 192.

90 In August 1923, the *Amsterdam News* published a report about a Manhattan woman, Millicent Gwendolyn Williams, who sought to annul her marriage to a man from Barbados. Williams claimed that her husband deserted her a day after their wedding in October 1921. One year later, the husband sent a letter to inform her that he had concealed that he was a "West Indian Negro." See "Married Negro; White Girl Seeks Annulment," *NYAN*, 22 August 1923, 1. In 1924, Michael Malillo from Queens, New York, filed suit to annul his marriage to his wife, Rita, claiming he discovered she was of "Negro parentage" when he met her parents a few weeks after the wedding. See "Asks Court to Annul Marriage," *NYAN*, 21 May 1924, TNCF, reel 20, frame 14. One year later, a Bronx woman filed suit against her husband alleging that he was "colored" and had claimed to be a "prince." See "Sues Husband 'Prince' for Annulment of Vow," *NYAN*, 14 October 1925, sec. 2, p. 9. The wife, Elizabeth Rosell, won her case. I have a copy of the certificate of dissolution from the Bronx Supreme Court that indicates that a judgment of annulment was entered on 10 February 1926 (see *Rosell v. Rosell* [Supreme Court, Bronx County], index no. 4339-25). It appears from the entries in the public record for the *Rosell* case that it took place almost simultaneously with the *Rhinelander* trial. The wife's summons and

complaint were filed with the court in October of 1925, and the judge made his decision on 14 November 1925. Obviously the *Rosell* case did not receive the same level of publicity as *Rhinelander v. Rhinelander*, since it did not feature a protagonist from a wealthy and well-known New York family.

91 "Told Rhinelander He Had Many Rivals," *NYT*, 14 November 1925, 1; George V. Buchanan, "Alice Tries Jealousy to Win Kip's Return," *NYDM*, 14 November 1925, 3, news edition; Grace B. Robinson, "Alice's Crude Notes Baited Wealthy Scion," *NYDN*, 14 November 1925, 3, pink edition. "Rhinelander to Face Ordeal on Stand This Week," *NYHT*, 15 November 1925, 11.

92 Editorial, "Greek Tragedy—Not Bedroom Farce," *NYDN*, 21 November 1925, 13, pink edition.

93 Ibid.

94 Editorial, "Greek Tragedy—Not Bedroom Farce," *NYDN*, 21 November 1925, 13, pink edition. Aaron Gullickson's study of black-white marriage trends and his conclusion that the "white outmarriage ratio" dropped during the era of the Great Migration suggests that the *Daily News* correctly spotted a taboo against interracial marriages. See Gullickson, "Black/White Interracial Marriage Trends," 303.

CHAPTER EIGHT

1 *CPRR*, 614–15.

2 Rex, "Kip's Mind Befuddled by His Blind Love," *NYEJ*, 20 November 1925, 3, final news edition; Rex, "Love Put 'Dimmers' on Rhinelander's Eyes," *NYEJ*, 25 November 1925, 1, latest afternoon edition.

3 This reliance on vision still shapes American understandings. Lionel McPherson and Tommie Shelby ("Blackness and Blood," 178–79) note that most Americans possess "a vague, shared sense that race is somehow related to visible, inherited physical characteristics (e.g., skin color, hair type, physique) and continental origins (i.e., Europe, the Americas, Africa, and Asia)."

4 F. James Davis (*Who Is Black?*, 5) observes that the "one-drop rule" can be described in different ways. It can apply to someone with "*any* known African black ancestry"; it can be called a "one black ancestor rule," the "traceable amount rule," or the "hypo-descent rule." Both Davis and Joel Williamson (*New People*, 1–2) argue that the one-drop rule applied in both the South and the North by the early twentieth century. McPherson and Shelby ("Blackness and Blood," 181–86) suggest that African Americans no longer accept the one-drop rule. They don't venture an opinion on whether Americans who currently perceive themselves as white still accept it.

5 *CPRR*, 486–87. A vivid description of rent parties or "struts" appears in David Levering Lewis, *When Harlem Was in Vogue*, 107–8; and Summers, *Manliness*

    and Its Discontents, 177–78. See also "Rhinelander Says He Pursued Girl," *NYT*, 18 November 1925, 4.

6 *CPRR*, 486–89; "Rhinelander Says He Pursued Girl," *NYT*, 18 November 1925, 4; Irving Lewis Allen, *City in Slang*, 75.

7 Fields, "Ideology and Race in American History," 146; Omi and Winant, *Racial Formation in the United States*, 11. Peggy Pascoe charts a long-term shift in racial ideologies over the course of the twentieth century from an ideology of race based on biology through a "modernist racial ideology" ("Miscegenation Law," 61). See also Gossett, *Race*, 416–18; Bay, *White Image in the Black Mind*, 8–9; and Baker, *From Savage to Negro*, 107.

8 Sollors, *Neither White nor Black yet Both*, 248; Saks, "Representing Miscegenation Law," 48–49. For a contemporary short story that assumes behavior reflects hidden blood, see Anita Scott Coleman, "The Brat," the story of "Old Jennie," who talks about her son who passes as white yet "sings like only one of my race can sing" (106).

9 Grant, *Passing of the Great Race*, 82; Herskovits, "Color Line," 205, 206.

10 Recently Susan Courtney pointed to Hollywood's role in "contribut[ing] to the ascension of the visual as a dominant location and guarantee of racial meaning in the twentieth century." In her analysis of twentieth-century film and race, Courtney discusses the 1959 production of *Night of the Quarter Moon*, which appears to have drawn heavily from the details of the Rhinelander trial (although Courtney does not mention this). The film includes an annulment trial involving a race fraud suit brought by a wealthy white husband who is a Korean War veteran. During the climactic trial scene, the wife's lawyer tears her clothes to display her body to the jury. The film ends with the couple happily staying together. See Courtney, *Hollywood Fantasies of Miscegenation*, 113, 217–24. See also Omi and Winant, *Racial Formation in the United States*, 59–61.

11 Herskovits, "Color Line," 204; *United States v. Thind*, 261 U.S. 204 (1923).

12 *CPRR*, 625–26.

13 Examples of Davis asking Emily, Alice, and Grace to stand, take off their hats, or display their hands are in *CPRR*, 300 (Alice), 427 (Emily), 433 (Grace), 511 (Alice), 741 (Alice), 877 (Emily).

14 In 1925, Melville Herskovits ("Preliminary Observations," 69) commented that the "study of race, and racial differences, has become, in the past few years, of increasing importance in the practical problems of the day." See also Barnes, "Inheritance of Pigmentation"; Davenport and Steggerda, *Race Crossing in Jamaica*; Dunn, "Biological View of Race Mixture"; Wingate and Van Gerder, "Quantitative Determination of Black Pigmentation"; and Wingate, "Entrenched Negro Physical Features."

15 Herskovits, "Preliminary Observations," 69. See also Herskovits, "Racial Hysteria," 167; and Herskovits, *The Anthropometry of the American Negro*, 3, 178.

16 Herskovits, "Correlation of Length and Breadth of Head in American Negroes," 95; Herskovits, "American Negro Evolving a New Physical Type," 899–900. According to Herskovits, hair would not serve as a useful trait to study because it could be changed by hair products. See Herskovits, *Anthropometry of the American Negro*, 3. Herskovits hedged a bit about the efficacy of skin color as a guide to race in "Color Line," 205–6. Other scientists believed skin color was useful to study as an attribute of race. For one example, see Barnes, "The Inheritance of Pigmentation." The study of the links between skin color and race or ancestry continues into the twenty-first century. See, for example, Parra, Kittles, and Shriver, "Implications of Correlations between Skin Color and Genetic Ancestry."

17 Hooton, "Methods of Racial Analysis," 75. Hooton belonged to the Galton Society and was "the most influential physical anthropologist in the country during the interwar years" (Barkan, *Retreat of Scientific Racism*, 68, 101). Hooton believed that skin color alone would not establish racial identity: "Racial classification must be made upon the basis of a sum total of significant morphological and metrical features" ("Methods of Racial Analysis," 77). Other scientists agreed that race was based on recognizable physical differences. For one example, see Castle, "Biological and Social Consequences of Race-Crossing," 145. In the article, Castle, also from Harvard, referred to Hooton's January 1926 article and agreed that, for biologists, "racial distinctions" were based on "easily recognizable and measurable differences perpetuated by heredity irrespective of the environment" ("Biological and Social Consequences of Race-Crossing," 145).

18 Matthew Frye Jacobson, *Whiteness of a Different Color*, 95–96. In the 1920s, William Rhinelander's Irish wife would no longer be perceived as racially different. See Guterl, *Color of Race*, 98–99.

19 "Queries and Minor Notes," 1822. This reply to a Tennessee doctor observed that hair and head shape were unreliable. In addition, "laboratory tests will not be of much assistance when nothing is known regarding paternity" (ibid., 1822). This 1931 medical advice diverges from an account of a physician and racial determination almost twenty years earlier. In 1911 the *Crisis* discussed the story of an eleven-year-old girl who sought release from a "Negro institution" on the grounds she was white. A physician examined her and "confessed that it is impossible to declare positively just which race the girl belongs to" ("Along the Color Line," 6).

20 In an essay on photography and the "real," critic A. D. Coleman points out that since courts accept photographs as evidence, this demonstrates our "blind faith" that "what we see in a photograph is 'real'" (Coleman, "Lies Like Truth," 46). See also Trachtenberg, *Reading American Photographs*, 6.

21 Wallis, "Black Bodies, White Science," 102; Shawn Michelle Smith, *American*

Archives, 92; Shawn Michelle Smith, *Photography on the Color Line*, 46–47. See also Sekula, "Body and the Archive," 18–19, 51.

22 Shawn Michelle Smith, *American Archives*, 3–5, 225.

23 A copy of this photographic postcard appears as plate 3 in Lemons, "Black Stereotypes as Reflected in Popular Culture," 112. Willis, *Picturing Us*, 15–17; Shawn Michelle Smith, *Photography on the Color Line*, 62; Lewis and Willis, *Small Nation of People*; Sekula, "Body and the Archive," 56.

24 Day, *Study of Some Negro-White Families*. Day's book contains an introduction and a chapter written by E. A. Hooton, which is based on Day's research. See also Davenport and Steggerda, *Race Crossing in Jamaica*.

25 Davenport and Steggerda, *Race Crossing in Jamaica*, 5, 468. Charles Davenport often analogized the study of humans with that of canines. In an article published the same year as this book, Davenport opined that "in their morphological differences, then, the different races of mankind have all the different characteristics of different races of dogs" (Davenport, "Do Races Differ in Mental Capacity?," 70). Not surprisingly, Davenport answered the question he posed in the essay's title with a resounding yes. He even remarked that his research showed that "negroes" had a "better sense of rhythm" while whites showed a superior ability to "exercise common sense" (Davenport, "Do Races Differ in Mental Capacity?" 78, 89).

26 Davenport and Steggerda, *Race Crossing in Jamaica*, 22; Steggerda, "Physical Development of Negro-White Hybrids," 121. In 1930 W. E. Castle lambasted Davenport and Steggerda's study, arguing that the "inharmonious" results of race crossing that they claimed to have found were not obvious from the pictures included in the book. See Castle, "Race Mixture and Physical Disharmonies," 605.

27 Day, *A Study of Some Negro-White Families*, 9; Hooton, "Anthropometry of Some Small Samples," 43. Day's interest in race went beyond her anthropological studies. In 1926, she published a short story ("The Pink Hat") about a mulatto teacher who, when she wears her pink hat, passes. By the end of the story, the teacher stops passing.

28 Day, *Study of Some Negro-White Families*, 35. Day's comment may reflect the belief that only someone like herself could discern the less visible marks of race. See Robinson, "It Takes One to Know One," 715. Robinson examines the ways in which members of an "in group," the group people pass out of, claim to be "privy to the visual codes that evade the duped spectators of the pass." In the teens and twenties, many believed African Americans could spot a passer. In Washington, D.C., movie theaters hired African Americans to expose passers who tried to enter segregated theaters. See Constance McLaughlin Green, *Secret City*, 207. See also Adele Logan Alexander, *Home-*

lands and Waterways, 455; and William H. Jones, Recreation and Amusement Among Negroes, 147.

29 Day, *Study of Some Negro-White Families*, 26, 10 (emphasis added). The comments about Beatrice and her sisters resemble those about Alice and her sisters in the New York press.
30 Nathan, "Clinical Notes," 363. Shawn Michelle Smith (*Photography on the Color Line*, 10) argues that people do not look at photographs in a vacuum: "each photograph enters a visual terrain that has been mapped and codified by other photographs, in the service of competing discourses. One recognizes a photograph and deciphers its various means by posing it (consciously or not) in relation to other photographs." In the *Messenger*, the editors announced their decision to print pictures of accomplished and beautiful black women because the mainstream press did not. See Editorial, "Exalting Negro Womanhood," *Messenger*, January 1924, 7; and DuBois, "Photography," *Crisis*, October 1923, 249–50.
31 Allan Sekula ("Body and the Archive," 58) has argued that the existence of photographic archives created for scientific purposes helped to legitimate the presence of photographs in the mass media. Miles Orvell (*Real Thing*, 198) also notes that photographs help people make sense of the world. He argues that in the twentieth century photojournalism began to take over this role from print journalism.
32 "His Colored Bride," *NYDN*, 14 November 1924, 1, afternoon edition. Terry Barrett (*Criticizing Photographs*, 92) comments that photographic meaning is easily changed "especially if text is added to it. Photographs are relatively indeterminate in their meaning; their meaning can be easily altered by how they are situated, how they are presented."
33 Alice described with a "light complexion" in "Society Dazed at Rhinelander Nuptial News," *NYDN*, 14 November 1924, 3, pink edition. The phrase "extremely dark" in Robinson, "I'm Not Colored Cries the Bride of Rhinelander," *NYDN*, 14 November 1924, 3, afternoon edition. Alice described as "white-skinned" in "426 Rhinelander Love Letters," *NYDN*, 10 November 1925, 3, final edition. See also "George Jones," *NYEJ*, 9 November 1925, 3, city edition.
34 "Kip Rhinelander Is 'Brain-Tied,' Counsel Pleads," *NYHT*, 10 November 1925, 14.
35 "Kip Rhinelander Drowses, Colored Wife Smiles, as Rich Youth's 'Inferiority Complex' Is Told of in Court," *NYEJ*, 11 November 1925, 1, final news edition.
36 O'Sullivan, "Jones Posed as White in Photo, Kip Charges," *NYDM*, 30 November 1925, 3, final edition. O'Sullivan also reported that the defense wanted to know the extent to which Leonard needed glasses.
37 *CPRR*, 693. Davis assumed people see "race directly, rather than through the distorting lens of socially contingent ideas" (Haney Lopez, *White by Law*, 100).

38 During the trial, witnesses were asked whether Alice used powder to lighten her complexion. See testimony of Joseph Rich, *CPRR*, 741. For a discussion of makeup and race, see Peiss, *Hope in a Jar*, chap. 7.

39 *CPRR*, 612. Herskovits, a proponent of skin color as a marker of racial difference, nevertheless observed that the "measurement of pigmentation is a matter of judgment, and the subjective element will vary largely with the different individuals who do the measuring." See Herskovits, "Age Changes in Pigmentation," 323. Even modern studies of skin color focus only on certain parts of the body, such as the inner side of the upper part of the arm. See Parra, Kittles, and Shriver, "Implications of Correlations," S55.

40 *CPRR*, 693–94; "Rhinelander's Wife Cries Under Ordeal," *NYT*, 24 November 1925, 3; *CPRR*, 694.

41 *CPRR*, 694–95.

42 Ibid., 695.

43 Carmody, *Carmody's New York Practice*, 409, 410, 419.

44 Hughes, *Illustrated Treatise on the Law of Evidence*, 2; Wigmore, *Treatise on the Anglo-American System of Evidence*, 214 (emphasis added).

45 Hughes, *Illustrated Treatise on the Law of Evidence*, 178.

46 "Kip Dropped by Social Register," *NYEJ*, 25 November 1925, 1, city edition.

47 *CPRR*, 695.

48 Ariela Gross ("Litigating Whiteness," 112–13) and Walter Johnson ("Slave Trader) discuss incidents in which people's bodies were displayed to determine their color and status. Michael Elliott ("Telling the Difference") discusses an 1866 Michigan racial-determination case that relied on notions of blood.

49 *Linton v. State*, 88 Ala. 216 (Ala. 1890), and *Jones v. State*, 156 Ala. 175 (Ala. 1908); *Weaver v. State*, 22 Ala. App. 469 (Ct. App. 1928). It is hard to tell from these decisions to what extent the defendants had to expose their bodies.

50 The best study of the naturalization cases can be found in Haney Lopez, *White by Law*, 1–6.

51 Ibid., 63–77.

52 *Ozawa v. United States*, 260 U.S. 178, 195 (1922). See also Haney Lopez, *White by Law*, 79–86; and Ngai, *Impossible Subjects*, 45–46.

53 *Ozawa v. United States*, 260 U.S. 178, 197 (1922); Reuter, "American Mulatto," 41–42; Grant, *Passing of the Great Race*.

54 *United States v. Thind*, 261 U.S. 204, 211 (1923). See also Haney Lopez, *White by Law*, 90–91; and Ngai, *Impossible Subjects*, 49.

55 *United States v. Thind*, 261 U.S. 204 (1923) (emphasis added).

56 As Haney Lopez remarks in *White by Law*, 91, with the *Thind* decision many Indians lost their previously granted citizenship.

57 Or perhaps they did. The trial transcript doesn't specifically mention whether Alice and her mother returned. Even when a jury inspection is objected to on

the grounds of indecency, judges still usually allow real evidence to be introduced but limit who gets to see it. See Hughes, *Illustrated Treatise on the Law of Evidence*; *CPRR*, 696; Dolan, "Alice Tears Her Pride to Shreds to Hold Her Man," *NYDN*, 24 November 1925, 3, pink edition; and "Two 'Mystery' Notes Read," *NYEP*, 23 November 1925, 1.

58 *CPRR*, 696–97.

59 Buchanan, "Mrs. Rhinelander Disrobes to Prove Color," *NYDM*, 24 November 1925, 3, final edition; Robinson, "Alice Bares Her Dark Body," *NYDN*, 24 November 1925, 3, pink edition; "Kip's Mystery Notes Read; Women Are Ejected from Court," *NYEJ*, 23 November 1925, 1, final night extra.

60 "Kip's Mystery Notes Read; Women Are Ejected from Court," *NYEJ*, 23 November 1925, 1, final night extra. A discussion of the physical signs believed to reveal the true race of a person passing as white can be found in Elmer Carter, "Crossing Over," 376–78 ("a smudge near the spinal column, a nigrescent spot at the base of the finger nails, a fuliginous cast to the eye"); and Sollors, *Neither Black nor White yet Both*, 151. Nella Larsen mentions these superstitions in *Passing*.

61 Robinson, "Alice Bares Her Dark Body," *NYDN*, 24 November 1925, 3, pink edition; "Kip's Mystery Notes Read; Women Are Ejected from Court," *NYEJ*, 23 November 1925, 1, final night extra. The *Herald Tribune* also reported that "it was said that her body is perceptibly darker than her face" ("Rhinelander's Mystery Notes' [sic] Defiantly Read," *NYHT*, 24 November 1925, 23). For a discussion of the focus on black women and their bodies and breasts see Jennifer Morgan, "'Some Could Suckle Over Their Shoulder'"; Guy-Sheftall, "Body Politic"; and Carla Williams, "Naked, Neutered, or Noble."

62 "Kip Bared His Soul, Alice, Her Body," *NYEJ*, 24 November 1925, 1, latest afternoon edition.

63 My discussion of the *New York Evening Graphic* draws on Lester Cohen, *New York Evening Graphic*, 95–101; Stevens, *Sensationalism and the New York Press*, 139; and Mallen, *Sauce for the Gander*, 28–29. This picture drew a great deal of criticism. Even two years later, Oswald Garrison Villard ("Are Tabloid Newspapers a Menace?") cited this composograph when he complained that the tabloids constituted a menace to society.

64 Lester Cohen, *New York Evening Graphic*, 101; Mallen, *Sauce for the Gander*, 29.

65 *CPRR*, 698.

66 Ibid., 701–11.

67 Ibid., 720–24, 739–40, 760. In befriending the Riches, Leonard again showed his ability to build relationships outside of his family's social set. Not only was Mr. Rich a furniture salesman, but the couple was apparently Jewish. At one point during the trial, Mrs. Rich complained that Alice's sister Emily scorned her in court because she was Jewish. See ibid., 763–64.

68 Ibid., 725, 762.

69 Ibid., 740–42.
70 Ibid., 742–43, 790.
71 Ibid., 822–37.
72 Ibid., 837–44.
73 Ibid., 847–53.
74 Ibid., 858–62.
75 Ibid., 858–62, 931.
76 Ibid., 868–69.
77 Ibid., 871–77.
78 Ibid., 877.
79 Ibid., 878–88.
80 Ibid., 888–95; Tabili, "We Ask for British Justice," 42; Bland, "White Women and Men of Colour," 30.
81 Tabili, "We Ask for British Justice," 5, 15. Tabili points to the 1920s and 1930s in Britain as an era in which race mattered. See also Green, "Re-Examining the Early Years," 47; Killingray, "Tracing Peoples of African Origin," 51–52; Haynes, "Teaching Twentieth-Century Black Britain," 140; Bland, "White Women and Men of Colour," 31. Thanks to my former colleague Alison Fletcher for pointing me in the right direction for literature on the history of Great Britain and race.
82 CPRR, 888–96.
83 Ibid., 907–8, 929.
84 "Says Rhinelander Knew of Girl's Race," NYT, 26 November 1925, 3; Robinson, "Swears Kip Knew as Suitor," NYDN, 26 November 1925, 3, pink edition.
85 CPRR, 933–35.
86 Ibid.
87 Ibid., 937–38, 942–61. On redirect examination, Davis tried to get Chidester to testify about whether he told his employer, Leonard's father, about Leonard's relationship with Alice. Mills objected, and Justice Morschauser would not let Davis continue with this line of inquiry, but it seems likely that Chidester did tell Leonard's father. This might explain how a Rhinelander family lawyer found Leonard and Alice at the Hotel Marie-Antoinette in January 1922. See ibid., 961–63.
88 Ibid., 966, 969; O'Sullivan, "Kip Rhinelander to Get More Surprises," NYDM, 27 November 1925, 3, final edition.

CHAPTER NINE

1 Rex, "Problem of Offspring Averted for Kip," NYEJ, 2 December 1925, 3, final news edition.
2 Ibid. Quotations are capitalized in the original.
3 Ibid. Quotations are capitalized in the original.

4   Editorial, "The Rhinelander Case," 388.
5   Before the attorneys' closing statements, Davis made three legal motions. First, he called to strike the "Spanish Kid," or "Harvard," letter as evidence that Alice passed. Then, he moved to take away from the jury the question of whether Alice committed fraud by concealment on the grounds that Mills had not introduced any evidence to support this claim. Finally, Davis tried to have the entire case dismissed. Morschauser denied all three motions and sent the case and all the evidence to the jury. See *CPRR*, 1004. Davis never made a motion to dismiss the case on the grounds that racial deception was not grounds for an annulment.
6   Both lawyers' closing statements take up over three hundred pages in the trial transcript. According to the *Times*, Davis spoke for more than seven hours. The *Mirror* estimated that Mills spoke for nearly twelve hours. See "Rhinelander Jury Warned by Defense," *NYT*, 2 December 1925, 3; Buchanan, "Rhinelander's Fate in Jury's Hands Today," *NYDM*, 4 December 1925, 3, news edition; and *CPRR*, 1131–32.
7   *CPRR*, 1131–32.
8   Ibid., 1134; "Poison Letters Sent to Rhinelander Jury," *NYDM*, 2 December 1925, 2, news edition; "Kip's Negress Bride Attacked by Mills," *NYEJ*, 2 December 1925, 3, final news edition (judge, jurors, and other parties involved in the case all received "scurrilous letters").
9   *CPRR*, 1138, 1144–48. Davis blamed Mills for requesting a jury trial and thus corrupting America's youth who read newspaper accounts of the trial.
10 Ibid., 1159. By the time the Rhinelander trial went up on appeal, Alice's lawyers argued that "the law is based upon common sense . . . there is no duty resting upon one party to divulge a condition that is open, obvious and known to the other party" (*Respondent's Brief* [Court of Appeals], 11 in *CPRR*).
11 *CPRR*, 1177.
12 Ibid., 1181–82.
13 Ibid., 1191, 1268.
14 Robinson, "Trial Filth Made Bride an Outcast, Her Lawyer Cries," *NYDN*, 2 December 1925, 3, second final edition. See also "Rhinelander Jury Warned by Defense," *NYT*, 2 December 1925, 3.
15 *CPRR*, 1181–82.
16 Ibid., 1182–83.
17 Ibid., 1154–67.
18 Ibid., 1184. The parenthetical "indicating" was put into the trial transcript most likely by the court stenographer to refer to Davis's physical movement.
19 Ibid., 1192.
20 Ibid., 1222.
21 Ibid., 1229.

22 Ibid., 1242, 1247.
23 Ibid., 1252. Davis's point mirrors Sylvester Russell's discussion of the migration of passing to the North. Russell described the actions of those he called "lily white colored girls" in "fooling" white men into believing that they were white. Russell connected this "fooling" to the "fooling" of African American women by white men during slavery. See Russell, *Amalgamation of America*.
24 CPRR, 1253.
25 Ibid., 1253; Grob, "Bloomingdale Insane Asylum," 119.
26 Ibid., 1253.
27 Davis's suggestion that the jurors should turn Alice "out loose" could also have been interpreted as another effort on Davis's part to reassure the jurors that Alice's connection to Leonard would end. See ibid., 1274.
28 Ibid., 1275.
29 Ibid., 1277; Robinson, "Flames of Race Prejudice Fanned by Lawyer in Plea for Scion," *NYDN*, 3 December 1925, 3, pink edition. Lee Davis suspected that Mills would appeal to the jurors' sense of themselves as male citizens and had called on them to resist Mills's appeals to patriotism and loyalty to Westchester County and New York State. See CPRR, 1270–71.
30 CPRR, 1287.
31 Ibid., 1277, 1289, 1287. The *Daily News* published a front-page photograph of Isaac Mills gesticulating to the jury, captioned, "How Could He Love This Mulatto?" *NYDN*, 3 December 1925, 1, news edition.
32 CPRR, 1289. Mills correctly observed that some African Americans also wanted to preserve the purity of their race. Marcus Garvey is perhaps the best-known proponent of similar views on miscegenation. See Marcus Garvey, "An Exposé of the Caste System."
33 CPRR, 1315–16, 1319; Robinson, "Alice Can't Change Her Color," *NYDN*, 4 December 1925, 3, final edition.
34 CPRR, 1289. Unlike Davis, who discussed the "amount" of Alice's "colored blood" (CPRR, 1182) but still seemed unsure about how best to define her, Mills repeatedly described Alice as a member of "her race" or "her own race." His use of this language seems to reflect the hardening of racial lines in the 1920s.
35 Ibid., 1299.
36 Ibid., 1299.
37 Ibid., 1349–50. According to the *Daily News*, when Mills began to discuss these letters, spectators who had started to leave their seats returned. See Robinson, "Flames of Race Prejudice Fanned by Mills in Asking Jury's Verdict," *NYDN*, 3 December 1925, 3, final news edition. Mills's reference to a "black and tan" act invoked the image of the so-called black and tan cabarets. See Owens, "Black and Tan Cabaret," 97. See also Mumford, *Interzones*, and Mumford, "Homosex Changes," 400, 406.

38 *CPRR*, 1321, 1433.
39 Ibid., 1355, 1428.
40 Ibid., 1429.
41 Ibid., 1431.
42 Ibid., 1431–32. Given Mills's stated fear that the defense lawyers might "stain" Alice's body before they showed her to the jury, it's curious that Mills offered Al Jolson as a witness during the trial. Al Jolson, the well-known black-faced comedian and singer testified that he was not in the Adirondack Mountains on a date that Alice Jones claimed he was in a 1922 letter to Leonard. Perhaps Mills realized, through Jolson, that "black-face" or the appearance of being black might be merely a theatrical device. See Jolson's testimony in ibid., 434.
43 Ibid., 1442; Jer. 13:23. Louis Fremont Baldwin's pamphlet on passing was titled, *From Negro to Caucasian; or, How the Ethiopian Is Changing His Skin*. Elmer Carter's essay on passing ("Crossing Over") mentions "whitewashed Ethiopians."
44 *CPRR*, 1442; "Lay Son's Plight to Rhinelander Sr.," *NYT*, 3 December 1925, 3; "Speedy Verdict Expected to Fix Alice's Status," *NYDN*, 4 December 1925, 3, pink edition.
45 Carmody, *Treatise on Pleading and Practice*, 430–31.
46 *CPRR*, 1030.
47 Ibid., 1039–41. The question of whether any presumption arose from the failure of one party to the lawsuit to call a witness became the major legal issue in the appeals after the verdict in this trial. See *Rhinelander v. Rhinelander*, 245 N.Y. 510 (N.Y. 1927), *aff'g*, 219 A.D. 189 (App. Div. 1927).
48 *CPRR*, 1041–43.
49 Ibid., 1043–47.
50 Ibid., 1049. Morschauser's equation of blood with color confirms the conception of race that Davis emphasized throughout the trial. It also confirms the larger societal turn to color as a way to determine race. See also Guterl, *Color of Race*, 155.
51 O'Sullivan, "Police Prepared to Halt Rioting as Jury Debates," *NYDM*, 4 December 1925, 3, news edition.
52 *CPRR*, 1055–57; O'Sullivan, "Police Prepared to Halt Rioting as Jury Debates," *NYDM*, 4 December 1925, 3, news edition.
53 "Rhinelander Jury Reaches a Decision After Twelve Hours," *NYT*, 5 December 1925, 1. The *Daily Mirror* reported on the sounds of arguments and laughter in the jury room ("Rhinelander Jury Struggles for Decision," *NYDM*, 5 December 1925, 3, news edition). See also Robinson, "Justice to Open Jury's Decision in Court Today," *NYDN*, 5 December 1925, 3, third final edition.
54 *CPRR*, 1058–59. The seventh question was whether Leonard cohabited with Alice after he learned of her race. The jury did not answer this question because

they had already agreed that he knew about her race all along. See also Appellant's Brief (Court of Appeals), 4 in CPRR.

55 See Carmody, *Treatise on Pleading and Practice*, 938–39; and *Rhinelander v. Rhinelander*, 245 N.Y. 510 (1927), aff'g, 219 A.D. 189 (App. Div. 1927).

56 See Fields, "Slavery, Race, and Ideology," 107.

57 "Rhinelander Loses; Wife Will Ask Separation," *NYHT*, 6 December 1925, 14. A slightly different version of the juror's statement appeared in the *Times*. According to the *Times*, the juror had said the verdict "might," not "would," have been different. See "Rhinelander Loses; No Fraud Is Found; Wife Will Sue Now," *NYT*, 6 December 1925, 1; and photograph in the *Daily News* titled, "Alice Victor, Now to Sue Leonard," *NYDN*, 6 December 1925, 1, home edition.

58 Robinson, "Leonard Absent as Verdict Against Him Is Read," *NYDN*, 6 December 1925, 3, home edition; "Rhinelander Loses, Wife Will Ask Separation," *NYHT*, 6 December 1925, 14; "Rhinelander Loses; No Fraud Is Found," *NYT*, 6 December 1925, 1. The reporters also asked whether she still loved him. She answered that she did and she didn't. When they remarked that Alice and Leonard had been very much in love, she replied with a remark that every paper commented on because of her grammar: "Yes, we was."

59 Robinson, "Leonard Absent as Verdict Against Him Is Read," *NYDN*, 6 December 1925, 3, home edition.

60 Ibid., 3.; *United States v. Thind*, 261 U.S. 204 (1923).

61 "Public for Rhinelander Verdict; Southerner Sore, Criticises [sic] Jury," *New York World*, 6 December 1925, TNCF, reel 22, frame 289.

62 Whitmark, "Rhinelander Verdict Meets Harlem's Approval," *NYAN*, 9 December 1925, 1.

63 "Kip Paying Piper, General Opinion of Colored Folk," *NYDN*, 6 December 1925, 4, home edition. The *Daily News* also spoke to "a colored author of some note" who suggested that the verdict showed that the races could not live together without miscegenation taking place. Indeed, he commented that the United States was a "melting pot" and that the "trend in America is definitely toward racial homogeneity." In contrast, Zora Hurston suggested to the *Daily News* reporter that both parties practiced some deception, adding, "I do not think Kip is as stupid as he pretended. Society should not allow them to live together again. I do not believe that they would be happy."

64 Grey, "What the Rhinelander Case Means to Negroes," *NYAN*, 9 December 1925, editorial and feature page. Although Edgar Grey remarked that New York's judiciary had never decided what constituted a Negro, he assumed that Alice was one and applauded the *Rhinelander* decision on these grounds.

65 Ibid.; "The Rhinelander Case," *Christian Recorder* (Philadelphia), 10 December 1925, TNCF, reel 22, frame 286.

66 "Rhinelander Loses; No Fraud Is Found; Wife Will Sue Now," *NYT*, 6 December 1925, 1; Whitmark, "Rhinelander Verdict Meets Harlem's Approval," *NYAN*, 9 December 1925, 1. Whitmark suggested one explanation for why Mills's theme of the horrors of miscegenation did not work: "Crackers don't thrive on Westchester air." As we shall see in the Conclusion to this book, although "crackers" might not have existed in the leafy enclaves of Westchester, white Americans who wanted to differentiate themselves from African Americans did. See "Editorial Paragraphs," 691; and DuBois, "Rhinelander," 112–13.

67 Editorial, "Rhinelander's Suit," 4. See also a later editorial in *Opportunity* that compared the decision to responses to O'Neill's play *All God's Chillun Got Wings* and found New York a state "liberal enough to give Alice Rhinelander an intermarriage decision against her rich husband, Kip" (Editorial, "Race Versus Color," 207). See also Editorial, "The Rhinelander Verdict," *New York Age*, 12 December 1925, TNCF, reel 22, frame 282.

68 "The Rhinelander Case," *Christian Recorder* (Philadelphia), 10 December 1925, TNCF, reel 22, frame 286; *New York World*, 8 December 1925, TNCF, reel 22, frame 289. J. A. Rogers reported on French impressions of the trial, which they characterized as "one of those freak cases possible only in America" (Rogers, "The Critic: Do They Tell the Truth," 12).

69 Editorial, "Rhinelander's Suit," 4. The *St. Louis Argus* observed that "the fundamental principle in the Rhinelander case, is that of intermarriage" ("The Rhinelanders and Intermarriage," *St. Louis Argus*, 4 December 1925, TNCF, reel 22, frame 302).

70 DuBois, "Rhinelander," 113; "Black and White in New York," *New Statesman*, 5 December 1925, 230–32.

71 *Rosell v. Rosell* (Supreme Court, Bronx County), index no. 4339–25. The scanty press clippings on this case (including a short piece in the *New York Amsterdam News*) suggest that the wife brought suit for an annulment on the grounds her husband had misrepresented himself as a colored Inca prince. Three years before the *Rosell* case, the same court annulled a marriage when the wife claimed her husband had deceived her and he was really a West Indian. See *Price v. Price* (Supreme Court, Bronx County), index no. 596-22.

72 Information on proposed legislation in Fowler, *Northern Attitudes Towards Interracial Marriage*, 318–19. See also "Bill to Prohibit Inter-Marriages," *Burlington (North Carolina) News*, 5 February 1926, TNCF, reel 25, frame 79; "Bars Mixed Marriage," *Chicago Defender*, 27 February 1926, TNCF, reel 25, frame 80; "The Looking Glass," *Crisis*, June 1926, 90–91, 90; "Connecticut's Anti-Marriage Bill," *St. Louis Argus*, 28 January 1927, TNCF, reel 27, frame 462; "Intermarriage with Negroes: A Survey of State Statutes," 858–59; and "Miscegenation Bills," *New York Age*, 12 March 1927, TNCF, reel 27, frame 473. The *New York Age*

reported that a state senator from Poughkeepsie had introduced an antimiscegenation bill into the legislature in 1926; it never became law. See "N.A.A.C.P. Battle Front," 118.

73 "That Drop of Blood," 90; "White Woman Seeks to Wed Cuban—Crazy?" *Afro-American*, 17 July 1926, TNCF, reel 25, frame 89; "Loves Negro; Family Says She's Crazy," *Chicago Bee*, 17 July 1926, TNCF, reel 25, frame 89. See also "Suitor Jilted Her Because of Colored Blood, Girl States," *Pittsburgh Courier*, 7 August 1926, TNCF, reel 25, frame 102; and "Mixed Marriages Probed by Noted Detective Chief," *Chicago Defender*, 22 May 1926, TNCF, reel 25, frame 77. Renee Romano (*Race Mixing*) examines post–World War II responses to black-white marriages in the North.

74 Kirksey, "Reflections Upon Race," 381. The *Afro-American* pointed out that the jury found Alice "colored" but not a "Negro," suggesting that intermediate racial categories between black and white still existed. See "Mrs. Kip No Negro, Colored Says the Jury," *Afro-American* (Baltimore, Md.), 12 December 1925, TNCF, reel 22, frame 286. See also DuBois, "Rhinelander," 112–13.

75 Rex, "Problem of Offspring Averted for Kip," *NYEJ*, 2 December 1925, 3, final news edition; DuBois, "Rhinelander," 112; Editorial, "Those Who Would Marry Outside," *Negro World*, 21 November 1925, TNCF, reel 22, frame 295.

76 DuBois suggested that the "high Nordic stream which produced super-men is here represented by a poor decadent descended from the best blood of white America" ("Rhinelander," 112). The story of Adelaide's removal to Paris and her subsequent return is in "J. St. Chaqueneau and Wife Separate," *NYT*, 10 January 1928, 2. The *New York Times* reported that Adelaide and her husband had moved to Paris in 1926 and Adelaide's husband changed the spelling of his last name from "Shackno" to "Chaqueneau." By 1928, the Chaqueneaus had divorced after Adelaide filed an action in Reno. See "Rhinelander Heiress Gets Divorced at Reno," *NYT*, 6 May 1928, 28.

77 *Rhinelander v. Rhinelander*, 245 N.Y. 510 (N.Y. 1927), aff'g, 219 A.D. 189 (App. Div. 1927); "Still Seek Rhinelander," *NYT*, 26 January 1928, 11.

CONCLUSION

1 Grossberg, *Judgment for Solomon*, 91.
2 Conflicts over the new opportunities available in the North emerged during the riots of the Red Summer of 1919. Clashes over access to housing in white neighborhoods, unsegregated schools, and good jobs continued through the 1920s.
3 Cheryl Harris, "Whiteness as Property," 1745. In 1919, the *Crisis* warned its readers to be "on the alert" for attempts by whites to curtail their rights even though African Americans could vote in northern and western states. See "Jim

Crowing," 282. White northerners maintained the privileges of whiteness through efforts such as one Ivy League college's attempts to restrict its African American students from full access to the college experience. See Raymond Pace Alexander, "Voices from Harvard's Own Negroes," 29–31.

4   This explains why H. L. Mencken referred to the Rhinelander marriage when he discussed the Africanization of American culture in an editorial in *American Mercury*, 161. See also Mumford, *Interzones*, xviii–xix.
5   Fields, "Whiteness, Racism, and Identity," 48.
6   DuBois, "Rhinelander," 112. On race and consumption in the 1920s, see Holt, *Problem of Race*, 74; Weems, *Desegregating the Dollar*, chap. 1; and Rex, "Humble Alice Won Kip, Aristocrat, on Nerve," *NYEJ*, 1 December 1925, 3, final news edition. Since the trial was conducted in such a way as to destroy Alice's character as well as literally stripping her, it might serve as a warning of what could happen to someone else who acted in the same way. In this manner, the trial arguably resembled other intimidations such as the attempts to vandalize or destroy homes purchased by African Americans in "white" neighborhoods.
7   "Black and White in New York," 230–32.
8   Ibid.
9   DuBois, "Rhinelander," 112–13.
10 In his autobiography, Walter White describes the 1920s as a decade in which "from Los Angeles, California, to Westchester County, New York, there were threats, burning of Ku Klux Klan fiery crosses, and mob violence when Negroes sought to escape the ghetto and move into 'white' neighborhoods" (*Man Called White*, 73). My reading of the *Amsterdam News* for much of 1925 reveals that the paper featured the *Sweet* case more than the Rhinelander trial. Kevin Boyle discusses the African American press and the Sweets in *Arc of Justice*, 245.
11 Miller, "Separate Communities for Negroes," 827–31. Northern whites also pointed to the close connection between residential segregation and interracial marriage. In 1918, a Chicago neighborhood newsletter for white property owners equated the two: "The effrontery and impudence that nurses a desire on the part of the Negro to choose a white as a marriage mate will not result in making the Negro a desirable neighbor" (quoted in Tuttle, *Race Riot*, 173–74 n. 28).
12 *Ridgway v. Cockburn*, 163 Misc. 511 (Supreme Court, Westchester County, 1937). Although the *New York Times* and the NAACP papers identify Joshua Cockburn as a ship captain, neither mentions that he was likely the same Captain Cockburn affiliated with Marcus Garvey and his Black Star Line. See Tony Martin, *Race First*, 153. Hays assisting Clarence Darrow in Boyle, *Arc of Justice*, 254–55. After the Rhinelander trial, the *Chicago Bee* compared Lee Parsons Davis's "patriotic work" for Alice with Darrow's in the *Sweet* case. See Editorial, "The New Faith," *Chicago Bee*, 12 December 1925, TNCF, reel 22, frame 279.
13 "Memorandum on the Cockburn Case," 3 February 1937, PNAACP, "NAACP

Administrative File—Segregation—Residential—White Plains, N.Y., December 7, 1930–June 15, 1937," part 5, reel 2, frame 222. The NAACP's memoranda show the continued use of language that closely associated blood with color. The *New York Post* reported that Hays also argued that "the Cockburns are superior to their neighbors in intelligence, background and social graces" ("Race Issue Raised in Ejection Suit," *New York Post*, 1 February 1927, PNAACP, "NAACP Administrative File—Segregation—Residential—White Plains, N.Y., December 7, 1930–June 18, 1937," part 5, reel 2, frame 219).

14 Arthur Garfield Hays to Walter White, dated 19 February 1937, PNAACP, "NAACP Administrative File—Segregation—Residential—White Plains, N.Y., December 7, 1930–June 15, 1937," part 5, reel 2, frame 232.

15 Roy Wilkins to Dr. Myra Logan, 16 March 1937, PNAACP, "NAACP Administrative File—Segregation—Residential—White Plains, N.Y., December 7, 1930–June 15, 1937," part 5, reel 2, frame 242. Most likely Wilkins considered Dr. Logan a "white Negro." A photograph of Dr. Logan appears in Day, *Study of Some Negro-White Families*, plate 38. A brief description of Dr. Logan, a daughter of Adella Hunt Logan, appears in Adele Logan Alexander, "Myra Adele Logan," 731.

16 "Negro Ouster Suit on in Westchester," *NYT*, 23 March 1937, 2.

17 "Lee Parsons Davis Inducted," *NYT*, 5 January 1937, 15. Davis had continued to practice law after successfully defending Alice. Five years after the Rhinelander trial, Davis appeared again in an annulment lawsuit before Justice Morschauser. This time, Davis represented Natalie Guggenheim, the wealthy spouse of the "son of a baggage master." Miss Guggenheim received her annulment. See "Guggenheim Bridal Annulled by Court," *NYT*, 25 January 1930, 17; and *Ridgway v. Cockburn*, 163 Misc. 511 (Supreme Court, Westchester County, 1937), citing *Corrigan v. Buckley*, 271 U.S. 323 (1926).

18 *Ridgway v. Cockburn*, 163 Misc. 511; "Negro Ban Upheld in Edgemont," *NYT*, 8 June 1937, 27.

19 *Ridgway v. Cockburn*, 163 Misc. 511. Lee Davis remained on the bench until he retired in 1952. See "Justice Davis at 70 Retires This Week," *NYT*, 28 December 1952, 24. Davis's opinion accords with molecular anthropologist Jonathan Marks's discussion of changing understandings of race in the twentieth century. Marks argues that by the 1930s, Americans understood race as "simple facts of ancestry and appearance." Consequently, Marks suggests that the phenomenon of passing no longer posed the same set of concerns as it had when Americans believed in race as internal essence. See Jonathan Marks, "The Realities of Race," Social Science Research Council, "Is Race Real," <http://raceandgenomics.ssrc.org> (14 May 2008).

20 Suzanne Goldberg, "Sexuality and Marriage," 263; "Still Seek Rhinelander," *NYT*, 26 January 1928, 11; "Sheriffs Fail to Find Rhinelander for Suit," *NYT*,

18 February 1928, 18; "No Order Is Signed in Rhinelander Suit," *NYT*, 4 October 1928, 16.
21 "L. Kip Rhinelander Dead of Pneumonia," *NYT*, 21 February 1936, 17; Friedman, *American Law in the Twentieth Century*, 436. As of 1927, Nevada had a three-month residency requirement for divorce. See Paul H. Jacobson, *American Marriage and Divorce*, 103; and Paine, "As We See It in Reno," 720. CPI Inflation Calculator, <www.bls.gov/cpi> (1 June 2007).
22 Appellant's Brief, *CPMR*, 3–4; Respondent's Brief, *CPMR*, 4. In the 1940s, Alice's lawyer claimed she started the 1930 separation suit after she ran out of money. See Appellant's Reply Memorandum, *CPMR*, 4.
23 Information from the 1940s lawsuits over Philip Rhinelander's estate hints strongly at Philip's role in Leonard's annulment action. See Appellant's Brief, *CPMR*, 21. Alice's lawyer in the 1940s suggested that the Rhinelanders in 1930 had wanted "to stop all litigation that would involve the Rhinelander name with a colored person" (Appellant's Reply Memorandum, *CPMR*, 4).
24 A copy of the agreement is filed with Philip Rhinelander's estate in the Nassau County Surrogate's Court under Estate File # 34455 and in *CPMR*, Objectants Exh. 1, 110–21. Recital paragraphs (sometimes referred to as "Whereas clauses") are a standard legal drafting technique used by lawyers to contextualize agreements. They document the factual background behind the agreement in addition to the understanding of the parties as to their intent and reasons for entering into the agreement. Although they can contain errors or outright misrepresentations, they demonstrate at the very least what the parties want other people to think their agreement is about. I thank Richard Edward Pryor II for sharing his expertise on drafting legal documents. Information that Alice still lived with her parents comes from the *Fifteenth Census of the United States, 1930*, <www.ancestry.com> (10 May 2008).
25 Leonard and Alice's 1930 agreement, Nassau County Surrogate's Court, Estate File # 34455 and in Objectant's Exh. 1, *CPMR*.
26 Ibid.
27 In the 1940s, Alice's attorneys argued that when she signed the 1930 agreement, "there was a lucrative field open to Alice Jones to write magazine articles or appear in vaudeville to exploit the Rhinelander family history, all of which would have brought shame and disrepute on the Rhinelander family." See Appellant's Brief, *CPMR*, 22 (emphasis added).
28 Additional information about the agreement between Leonard, Philip, and Alice can be found in *In the Matter of Rhinelander*, 264 A.D. 607 (App. Div. 1942); *In the Matter of Rhinelander*, 290 N.Y. 31 (N.Y. 1943).
29 "L. Kip Rhinelander Dead of Pneumonia," *NYT*, 21 February 1936, 17; Appellant's Brief, *CPMR*, 5, 14.
30 "L. Kip Rhinelander Dead of Pneumonia," *NYT*, 21 February 1936, 17. After

Leonard's death, the *New York Times* reported that he left everything to his father. Leonard left an estate with less than $5,000 in real estate and under $5,000 of personal property. See "Rhinelander Will Filed," *NYT*, 28 February 1936, 4; "Maj. Rhinelander Dies in Long Beach," *NYT*, 19 March 1940, 25; "Rhinelander Left Estate to Family," *NYT*, 27 March 1940, 13; and Last Will and Testament of Philip Rhinelander, *CPMR*, 20–28.

31 Brief of Adelaide Thomas in *CPMR*; William Friedman to Mrs. John L. Thomas, 24 February 1940, Objectant's Exh. A, *CPMR*, 139–41. Adelaide also tried to keep the estate from paying small annuities to people who most likely were longtime servants of Philip Rhinelander.

32 Alice filed her claim against Philip Rhinelander's estate under the name of Alice Jones (since she had given up the Rhinelander surname). See AJ *Affidavit of Claim* (9 May 1940), Surrogate's Court Nassau County; Alexander & Keenan to Honorable George A. Bartlett, 20 May 1940, Objectant's Exh. B, *CPMR*, 142–44; and L. E. Blaisdell, "Opinion Rhinelander v. Rhinelander," Objectant's Exh. C, *CPMR*, 144–46. Judge Bartlett had asked L. E. Blaisdell, a Reno attorney, to write an opinion responding to Alexander & Keenan. See L. E. Blaisdell to George A. Bartlett, 18 June 1940, Objectant's Exh. E, *CPMR*, 149–51.

33 Alexander & Keenan to Hon. Frederick E. Crane, 16 December 1940, Objectant's Exh. D, *CPMR*, 147–49; Frederick E. Crane Opinion (undated), Objectant's Exh. F, *CPMR*, 151–56; "Intermediate Account of Proceedings to and Including March 31, 1941," *CPMR*, 29–33. Schedule H of the Intermediate Account states that the executors would allow Alice's claim despite Adelaide's protests.

34 "Dwelling Is Sold by Rhinelanders," *NYT*, 12 September 1941, 38; "Heirs Sell Vacant Lot," *NYT*, 15 September 1941, C29. During the testimony taken before the surrogate court, Alice's lawyer expressed concerns about making sure that enough of Philip's assets remained intact to continue to pay Alice her $3,600 for the rest of her life. He worried that Philip's executors would collude with Adelaide to make sure nothing was left for Alice. See Testimony of 24 November 1941, *CPMR*, 79–82.

35 *CPMR*, 34–109, 157–82.

36 *In the Matter of Rhinelander*, 264 A.D. 607 (App. Div. 1942), rev'd 290 N.Y. 31 (N.Y. 1943). A February 1990 letter from Chemical Bank written after Alice's 1989 death confirms that the trust department at the bank had been sending her the yearly payments from Philip's estate. See *In the Matter of the Estate of Alice B. Jones*, Surrogate Court, Westchester County, file no. 2932/1989.

37 When Alice appealed the appellate court's decision, her lawyer argued that Leonard and Philip, as well as Philip's estate, had benefited from the 1930 agreement, Appellant's Brief, *CPMR*, 14. See *In the Matter of Rhinelander*, 290 N.Y. 31 (N.Y. 1943); and *In the Matter of the Estate of Alice B. Jones*, Surrogate

Court, Westchester County, file no. 2932/1989. See also Lewis and Ardizzone, *Love on Trial*, 259–60. The authors of *Love on Trial* find it significant that Alice's gravestone identifies her as "Alice Rhinelander." Although someone in Alice's family must have chosen the surname for the stone, Alice remained legally a Jones. Even her family recognized her legal name. In the papers filed to settle Alice's estate after her death, the forms identify the decedent as "Alice B. Jones." At the time of Alice's death, her survivors included her sister Grace, her niece, Roberta (Emily's daughter), and Roberta's son, the administrator of Alice's estate. Information from the Social Security Administration on Alice's death also identifies her as "Alice B. Jones." See Social Security Death Index (Alice B. Jones), <www.ancestry.com> (9 May 2007).

38 Appellant's Brief, *CPMR*, 3–4, 14. Alice's lawyer argued that Alice's concessions in the 1930 agreement had even "enriched" Leonard's father. Adelaide's attorneys did not contest that argument. See Respondent's Brief, *CPMR*, 14–15. Whatever surname Alice used by the end of her life, by that point the value of the name to the Rhinelander family may have lessened. Those most concerned about the impact of Leonard's marriage on the family name were long dead by the 1980s. Leonard's oldest brother, Philip Kip, died in 1939, followed by their father in 1941. Their uncle, T. J. Oakley, died in 1946. Leonard's sister, Adelaide Thomas, died in 1976. See "P. K. Rhinelander Dies Here at 42," *NYT*, 22 May 1939, 17; "T. J. O. Rhinelander Dies at Home at 88," *NYT*, 26 July 1946, 21; and "Deaths," *NYT*, 14 June 1976, 34. Even before Adelaide died, the Rhinelander's had sold off their real estate holdings, which they had hung on to through the Depression and World War II. In 1961, the *New York Times* reported that the Rhinelander Real Estate Company had sold its still-valuable land holdings to a group of investors including Harry Helmsley. See "Big Sale Is Slated by Rhinelander," *NYT*, 13 July 1961, Business & Financial, 49; and "Buyer of Rhinelander Parcels Asks 8.7 Million for the 14 Units," *NYT*, 15 July 1961, Business & Financial, 31.

39 "Black and White in New York," *New Statesman*, 230–32. In his study of post-1945 suburban segregation, David M. P. Freund argues that "whites' ideas about race and their preoccupation with property were relational and mutually constitutive" (Freund, *Colored Property*, 38). Freund's work suggests that the postwar growth of homeownership among white northerners propelled a new way of thinking about the links between race and property. Since the Rhinelanders owned a great deal of property well before World War II, they may have recognized those links before most northern whites had.

40 As of 2002, only 0.7 percent of all American marriages were black-white. See Doyle, "The Progress of Love," 33. *Loving v. Virginia*, 388 U.S. 1 (1967). The continued low rates of such marriages after the *Loving* decision suggest that the taboo against interracial marriage between those considered white and those

considered black retains some of its power. Recently, the *New York Times* wedding pages described the marriage of two Harvard graduates: a doctor (the wife) and a lawyer (husband). The groom's father (identified as white) refused to attend the wedding of his son to an African American pediatrician ("the fourth generation of college-educated women in her family"). See Devon Sipher, "Vows," *NYT*, 21 October 2007, style section, 15.

Bibliography

MANUSCRIPTS

Albany, New York
    New York State Library
        Cases and Points: Records and Briefs in the Matter of Rhinelander
            (New York Court of Appeals, 1943).
Buffalo, New York
    State Supreme Court Library
        Cases and Points: Records and Briefs in Rhinelander v.
        Rhinelander (New York Court of Appeals, 1927).
College Park, Maryland
    National Archives
        U.S. Bureau of the Census Records, Record Group 29
Kirksville, Missouri
    Truman State University, Pickler Memorial Library, Special Collections
        Harry H. Laughlin Collection
Tuskegee, Alabama
    Tuskegee Institute Department of Records and Research
        Tuskegee Institute News Clippings File, Microfilm edition (Microfilm edition
            at Firestone Library, Princeton University, Princeton, N.J., and Kent State
            University Library, Kent, Ohio)
Washington, D.C.
    Library of Congress, Manuscript Division
        Papers of the National Association for the Advancement of Colored People

(Microfilm edition at Alexander Library, Rutgers University, New Brunswick, N.J.)

COURT CASES

Buchanan v. Warley. 245 U.S. 60 (1917).
Chipman v. Johnston. 237 Mass. 502 (Mass. 1921).
Corrigan v. Buckley. 271 U.S. 323 (1926).
DiLorenzo v. DiLorenzo. 174 N.Y. 467 (N.Y. 1903).
Domshke v. Domshke. 138 A.D. 454 (App. Div. 1910).
Ferrall v. Ferrall. 153 N.C. 174 (N.C. 1910).
Fisk v. Fisk. 39 N.Y.S. 537 (App. Div. 1896).
Griffin v. Griffin. 204 N.Y.S. 131 (Supreme Court, Kings County, 1924), aff'd, 209 A.D. 883 (App. Div. 1924).
Hernandez v. Robles. 7 N.Y. 3d 338 (N.Y. 2006).
Johnson v. Auburn and Syracuse Electric Railroad Co. 222 N.Y. 443 (N.Y. 1918).
Jones v. State. 156 Ala. 175 (Ala. 1908).
Joyner v. Moore-Wiggins Co. 152 A.D. 266, (App. Div. 1912).
Kirby v. Kirby. 24 Ariz. 9 (Ariz. 1922).
Laage v. Laage. 176 Misc. 190 (Supreme Court, New York County, 1941).
Lapides v. Lapides. 254 N.Y. 73 (N.Y. 1930).
Libman v. Libman. 169 N.Y.S. 900 (Supreme Court, New York County, 1918).
Linton v. State. 88 Ala. 216 (Ala. 1890).
Loving v. Virginia. 388 U.S. 1 (1967).
Maynard v. Hill. 125 U.S. 190 (1888).
Mirizio v. Mirizio. 242 N.Y. 74 (N.Y. 1926).
Neuberger v. Gueldner. 139 La. 758 (La. 1916).
Norman v. City Island Beach Co. 126 Misc. 335 (Supreme Court, New York County, 1926).
O'Connell v. O'Connell. 201 A.D. 338 (App. Div. 1922).
Ozawa v. United States. 260 U.S. 178 (1922).
Pawlowski v. Pawlowski. 65 N.Y.S. 2d 413 (Supreme Court, Cayuga County, 1946).
Plessy v. Ferguson. 163 U.S. 537 (1896).
Reynolds v. Reynolds. 85 Mass. 605 (Mass. 1862).
In the Matter of Rhinelander. 290 N.Y. 31 (N.Y. 1943).
In the Matter of Rhinelander. 264 A.D. 607 (App. Div. 1942).
Rhinelander v. Rhinelander. 245 N.Y. 510 (N.Y. 1927), aff'g, 219 A.D. 189 (App. Div. 1927).
Ridgway v. Cockburn. 163 Misc. 511 (Supreme Court, Westchester County, 1937).
Robertson v. Roth. 163 Minn. 501 (Minn. 1925).

Robinson v. Zappas. 277 A.D. 208 (App. Div. 1929).
Schaeffer v. Schaeffer. 160 A.D. 48 (App. Div. 1913).
Shelley v. Kraemer. 344 U.S. 1 (1948).
Sheridan v. Sheridan. 186 N.Y.S. 470 (Supreme Court, Westchester County, 1921).
Shonfeld v. Shonfeld. 260 N.Y. 477 (N.Y. 1933).
Smith v. Smith. 112 Misc. 371 (Supreme Court, Kings County, 1920).
Stewart v. Keating. 15 Misc. 44 (Supreme Court, New York County, 1895).
Sunseri v. Cassagne. 191 La. 209 (La. 1938).
Svenson v. Svenson. 178 N.Y. 54 (N.Y. 1904).
Taylor v. Taylor. 181 N.Y.S. 894 (Supreme Court, Bronx County, 1920).
Theophanis v. Theophanis. 244 Ky. 689 (Ky. 1932).
United States v. Thind. 261 U.S. 204 (1923).
Van Houten v. Morse. 162 Mass. 414 (Mass. 1894).
Weaver v. State. 22 Ala. App. 469 (Ct. App. 1928).
Wells v. Talham. 180 Wis. 654 (Wis. 1923).
Williams v. Williams. 130 N.Y.S. 875 (Supreme Court, Oneida County, 1911)

GOVERNMENT RECORDS

Congressional Record. Washington, D.C., 1888–89.
Nassau County Surrogate's Court. "In the Matter of the Appraisal of the Estate of Philip Rhinelander, Deceased." File No. 34455.
———. "In the Matter of the Estate of Philip Rhinelander." File No. 34555.
New York Office of the Attorney General. "Opinion of the Attorney General (Informal) no. 264." 1978.
U.S. Bureau of the Census. *Fourteenth Census of the United States. State Compendium. New York.* <http://www.census.gov/prod/www/abs/decennial/1920.htm>. 23 September 2008.
———. *Historical Statistics of the United States: Colonial Times to 1970.* Washington, D.C.: Government Printing Office, 1976.
———. "Married-Couple and Unmarried Partner Households: 2000." 2003, <http://www.census.gov/prod/2003pubs/censr-5.pdf>. 22 September 2008.
———. *Negro Population 1790–1915.* 1918. Reprint, New York: Arno Press and the New York Times, 1968.
———. *200 Years of U.S. Census Taking: Population and Housing Questions, 1790–1990.* Washington, D.C.: Government Printing Office, 1989.
Westchester County Surrogate's Court. "In the Matter of the Estate of Alice B. Jones." File No. 2932/1989.

NEWSPAPERS AND MAGAZINES

New York American
New York Amsterdam News
New York Daily Mirror
New York Daily News
New York Evening Journal

New York Evening Post
New York Herald Tribune
New York Times
Time

ARTICLES

Abrams, Kathryn. "Hearing the Call of Stories." *California Law Review* 79 (July 1991): 971–1052.
Adams, Cyrus Field. "Some Interesting Facts." *Colored American Magazine*, July 1902, 226.
Alexander, Adele Logan. "Myra Adele Logan." In *Black Women in America: An Historical Encyclopedia*, edited by Darlene Clark Hine, Elsa Barkley Brown, and Rosalyn Terborg-Penn, 731. Bloomington: Indiana University Press, 1993.
Alexander, Raymond Pace. "Voices from Harvard's Own Negroes." *Opportunity*, March 1923, 29–31.
"Along the Color Line." *Crisis*, April 1911, 6.
"An American Country Home on the Rhine Which Is Now Owned by Mr. T. J. Oakley Rhinelander and Mr. Philip Rhinelander of New York." *Town and Country*, 13 May 1911, 39, <http://www.proquest.com/>. 14 May 2008.
"Anti-Intermarriage Bill in Michigan." *Crisis*, June 1921, 66.
"Anti-Intermarriage Bills." *Crisis*, March 1926, 232.
Bagnall, Robert W. "The Spirit of the Ku Klux Klan." *Opportunity*, September 1923, 265–67.
Barnes, Irene. "The Inheritance of Pigmentation in the American Negro." *Human Biology* 1 (September 1929): 321–81.
Beckham, Albert Sidney. "Applied Eugenics." *Crisis*, August 1924, 177–78.
Bell, Derrick. "Property Rights in Whiteness—Their Legal Legacy, Their Economic Costs." In *Critical Race Theory: The Cutting Edge*, edited by Richard Delgado, 75–83. Philadelphia, Pa.: Temple University Press, 1995.
Bent, Silas. "The Invasion of Privacy." *The North American Review*, 1 September 1927, 399, <http://www.proquest.com/>. 14 May 2008.
"Black and White in New York." *The New Statesman*, 5 December 1925, 230–32.
Bland, Lucy. "White Women and Men of Colour: Miscegenation Fears in Britain after the Great War." *Gender and History* 17 (April 2005): 29–61.
Boas, Franz. "This Nordic Nonsense." *Forum*, October 1925, 502–11.
Bond, Horace Mann. "Intelligence Testing and Propaganda." *Crisis*, June 1924, 61–64.

Bonilla-Silva, Eduardo. "Rethinking Racism: Toward a Structural Interpretation." *American Sociological Review* 62 (June 1997): 465–80.

Borton, Laurence Drew. "Sex, Procreation, and the State Interest in Marriage." *Columbia Law Review* 102 (May 2002): 1089–1128.

"Boudoir Gossip." *Pictorial Review*, 15 October 1899, 13, <http://www.proquest.com/>. 14 May 2008.

"Boudoir Gossip." *Pictorial Review*, 15 November 1899, 9, <http://www.proquest.com/>. 14 May 2008.

Brattain, Michelle. "Miscegenation and Competing Definitions of Race in Twentieth Century Louisiana." *Journal of Southern History* 71 (August 2005): 621–50.

Brazil, John R. "Murder Trials, Murder, and Twenties America." *American Quarterly* 33 (Summer 1981): 163–84.

Brodhead, Richard. "Regionalism and the Upper Class." In *Rethinking Class: Literary Studies and Social Formations*, edited by Wai Chee Dimock and Michael T. Gilmore, 150–74. New York: Columbia University Press, 1994.

Brown, W. O. "Racial Inequality: Fact or Myth?" *Journal of Negro History* 16 (1931): 43–60.

Brubaker, Rogers, and Frederick Cooper. "Beyond 'Identity.'" *Theory and Society* 29 (2000): 1–47.

Burnette, Georgia. "Looking Back: Black Nurses Struggle for Admission to Professional Schools." *Afro-Americans in New York Life and History* 28 (July 2004): 85–99.

Carby, Hazel V. "'It Jus Be's Dat Way Sometime': The Sexual Politics of Women's Blues." *Radical America* 20 (1986): 9–22.

———. "Policing the Black Women's Body in an Urban Context." *Critical Inquiry* 18 (Summer 1992): 738–55.

Carlson, A. Cheree. "'You Know It When You See It': The Rhetorical Hierarchy of Race and Gender in Rhinelander v. Rhinelander." *Quarterly Journal of Speech* 85 (May 1999): 111–28.

Carter, Elmer A. "Crossing Over." *Opportunity*, December 1926, 376–78.

Castle, W. E. "Biological and Social Consequences of Race-Crossing." *American Journal of Physical Anthropology* 9 (April–June 1926): 145–56.

———. "Race Mixture and Physical Disharmonies." *Science*, n.s., 71 (13 June 1930): 603–6.

Cohen, Lizabeth. "The Class Experience of Mass Consumption: Workers as Consumers in Interwar America." In *The Power of Culture: Critical Essays in American History*, edited by Richard Wightman Fox and T. J. Jackson Lears, 135–60. Chicago: University of Chicago Press, 1993.

Coleman, A. D. "Lies Like Truth: Photographs as Evidence." In *The Digital Evolution: Visual Communication in the Electronic Age: Essays, Lectures and Interviews, 1967–1998*, 46–52. Tucson, Ariz.: Nazraeli Press, 1998.

Coleman, Anita Scott. "The Brat." *Messenger*, April 1926, 105.

"Concubinage." *Crisis*, February 1928, 50.

Conyers, James E., and T. H. Kennedy. "Negro Passing: To Pass or Not to Pass." *Phylon*, Fall 1963, 215–23.

Cott, Nancy. "Giving Character to Our Whole Civil Polity: Marriage and the Public Order in the Late Nineteenth Century." In *U.S. History as Women's History: New Feminist Essays*, edited by Linda K. Kerber, Alice Kessler-Harris, and Kathryn Kish Sklar, 107–21. Chapel Hill: University of North Carolina Press, 1995.

———. "Marriage and Women's Citizenship in the United States, 1830–1934." *American Historical Review* 103 (December 1998): 1440–74.

"Coudert Brothers." In *The Encyclopedia of New York City*, edited by Kenneth T. Jackson, 288. New Haven: Yale University Press, 1995.

Covert, Cathy. "A View of the Press in the Twenties." *Journalism History* 2 (Autumn 1975): 66–96.

"Dangers of Race Mixture." *Current History*, December 1927, 403.

Davenport, Charles B. "Do Races Differ in Mental Capacity?" *Human Biology* 1 (January 1929): 70–89.

Davidoff, Leonore. "Class and Gender in Victorian England: The Diaries of Arthur J. Munby and Hannah Cullwick." *Feminist Studies* 5 (Spring 1979): 87–141.

Davis, Adrienne D. "The Private Law of Race and Sex: An Antebellum Perspective." *Stanford Law Review* 51 (January 1999): 221–88.

Davis, L. L. "Clinging to Straws." *Half-Century Magazine*, May–June 1924, 6.

Davis, Rebecca L. " 'Not Marriage at All, But Simply Harlotry': The Companionate Marriage Controversy." *Journal of American History* 94 (March 2008): 1137–63.

Day, Caroline Bond. "The Pink Hat." *Opportunity*, December 1926, 379–80.

———. "Race-Crossing in the United States." *Crisis*, March 1930, 81.

deRochemont, Richard G. "The Tabloids." *American Mercury*, October 1926, 187–92.

Domingo, W. A. "Restricted West Indian Immigration and the American Negro." *Opportunity*, October 1924, 298–99.

———. "What Are We, Negroes or Colored People?" *Messenger*, May–June 1919, 23–25.

Doyle, Roger. "The Progress of Love." *Scientific American* 289 (October 2003): 33.

DuBois, W. E. B. "The Anglo-Saxon at Bay." *Crisis*, May 1925, 7–11.

———. "Brothers, Come North." *Crisis*, January 1920, 105–6.

———. "The Browsing Reader." *Crisis*, July 1929, 234.

———. "The Family Tree." *Crisis*, December 1920, 55.

———. "The Negro Problem." Chapter 12 in *The Negro*. New York: Henry Holt, 1915. Reprint, Philadelphia. University of Pennsylvania Press, 2001.

———. "Opinion of W. E. B. DuBois." *Crisis*, January 1927, 128–29.

———. "Rhinelander." *Crisis*, January 1926, 112–13.

———. "The Souls of White Folk." Chap. 2 in *Darkwater: Voices from within the Veil*. New York: Harcourt, Brace and Howe, 1920.

———. "The Tragedy of 'Jim Crow'." *Crisis*, August 1923, 169–72.
DuCille, Ann. "Blue Notes on Black Sexuality: Sex and the Texts of Jessie Fauset and Nella Larsen." In *Sex, Gender, and Race Since the Civil War*, edited by John C. Fout and Maura Shaw Tantillo, 193–219. Chicago: University of Chicago Press, 1993.
Dunn, L. C. "A Biological View of Race Mixture." *American Sociological Society* 19 (1925): 47–56.
Editorial, "Aftermath of the Exodus." *Messenger*, November 1923, 858–59.
Editorial, "Beauty Contest Called Off." *Messenger*, May 1924, 137.
Editorial, "Caps, Gowns and Fiery Crosses." *Opportunity*, May 1924, 131–32.
Editorial, "Crossing Over." *Opportunity*, May 1923, 3–4.
Editorial, "Exalting Negro Womanhood." *Messenger*, January 1924, 7.
Editorial, "Faces." *Opportunity*, January 1928, 3–4.
Editorial, "Fellow-Caucasians." *Nation*, 9 April 1924, 388.
Editorial, "Klan Burns Cross on Columbia Campus." *Messenger*, May 1924, 137.
Editorial, "Melange." *Opportunity*, December 1925, 356.
Editorial, "Race Versus Color." *Messenger*, June 1927, 207.
Editorial, "The Rhinelander Case." *Messenger*, December 1925, 388.
Editorial, "Rhinelander's Suit." *Opportunity*, January 1926, 4.
Editorial, "The South's Triumph!" *Messenger*, April 1922, 386.
Editorial, "The Vanishing Mulatto." *Opportunity*, October 1925, 291.
"Editorial Paragraphs." *Nation*, 16 December 1925, 691.
Eleazer, Robert B. "Trends in Race Relations in 1926." *Opportunity*, January 1927, 16–17.
Elliott, Michael. "Telling the Difference: Nineteenth-Century Legal Narratives of Racial Taxonomy." *Law and Social Inquiry* 24 (Summer 1999): 611–36.
"Employment of Colored Women in Chicago." *Crisis*, January 1911, 24–25.
Fauset, Jessie. "The Sleeper Wakes: A Novelette in Three Installments." *Crisis*, August 1920, 168–73; September 1920, 226–29; October 1920, 267–74.
Fessenden, Franklin G. "Nullity of Marriage." *Harvard Law Review* 13 (June 1899): 110–23.
Fields, Barbara J. "Ideology and Race in American History." In *Region, Race, and Reconstruction*, edited by J. Morgan Kousser and James M. McPherson, 143–77. New York: Oxford University Press, 1982.
———. "Of Rogues and Geldings." *American Historical Review* 108 (December 2003): 1397–1405.
———. "Slavery, Race, and Ideology in the United States of America." *New Left Review* 181 (1990): 95–118.
———. "Whiteness, Racism, and Identity." *International Journal of Labor and Working-Class History* 60 (Fall 2001): 48–56.
Fisher, Rudolph. " 'High Yaller': A Story." *Crisis*, October 1925, 281–86, and November 1925, 33–38.

Forrester, Julia Mansfield. "Is 'The Negro Problem' White or Black?" *Crisis*, October 1930, 333–35.

Frazier, E. Franklin. "Eugenics and the Race Problem." *Crisis*, December 1925, 91–92.

———. "Social Equality and the Negro." *Opportunity*, June 1925, 165–68.

Friss, Evan. "Blacks, Jews, and Civil Rights in New York, 1895–1913." *Journal of American Ethnic History* 24 (Summer 2005): 70–99.

Gaines, Kevin. "Race at the End of the 'American Century.'" *Radical History Review* 87 (Fall 2003): 207–25.

Garvey, Marcus. "An Exposé of the Caste System." In *Philosophy and Opinions of Marcus Garvey*, vol. 2, edited by Amy Jacques-Garvey. 1923. Reprint, New York: Atheneum, 1992.

Gatewood, Willard B. "The Perils of Passing: The McCarys of Omaha." *Nebraska History* 2 (Summer 1990): 64–70.

"The Ghetto." *Crisis*, September 1913, 220–21.

Gibson, Charles F. "Concerning Color." *Psychoanalytic Review* 18 (1931): 413–25.

Gilman, Sander. "Black Bodies, White Bodies: Toward an Iconography of Female Sexuality in Late Nineteenth-Century Art, Medicine, and Literature." *Critical Inquiry* 12 (Autumn 1985): 204–42.

Ginzburg, Carlo. "Checking the Evidence: The Judge and the Historian." *Critical Inquiry* 18 (Autumn 1991): 79–92.

Goldberg, Suzanne. "Sexuality and Marriage: A Historic Guide to the Future of Marriage for Same-Sex Couples." *Columbia Journal of Gender and Law* 15 (2006): 249–72.

Golub, Mark. "*Plessy* as 'Passing': Judicial Responses to Ambiguously Raced Bodies in *Plessy v. Ferguson*." *Law & Society Review* 39 (2005): 563–600.

Goodman, James. "For the Love of Stories." *Reviews in American History* 26 (1998): 255–74.

Gosselin, Adrienne. "Racial Etiquette and the (White) Plot of Passing: (Re) Inscribing 'Place' in John Stahl's *Imitation of Life*." *Canadian Review of American Studies* 28, no. 3 (1998): 46–67.

Grant, Madison. "America for the Americans." *Forum*, September 1925, 346–55.

Grayson, Jay. "Over the Line." *Half-Century Magazine*, January–February 1925, 4.

Green, Jeffrey. "Re-Examining the Early Years of Samuel Coleridge-Taylor, Composer." In *Black Victorians/Black Victoriana*, edited by Gretchen Holbrook Gerzina, 39–50. New Brunswick, N.J.: Rutgers University Press, 2003.

Gregg, William W. "The Mulatto: Crux of the Negro Problem." *Current History*, March 1924, 1065–70.

Griffith, Sally F. "Mass Media Come to the Small Town: The *Emporia Gazette* in the 1920s." In *Mass Media Between the Wars: Perception of Cultural Tension, 1918–1941*, edited by Catherine L. Covert and John D. Stevens, 141–55. Syracuse, N.Y.: Syracuse University Press, 1984.

Grob, Gerald N. "Bloomingdale Insane Asylum." In *The Encyclopedia of New York City*, edited by Kenneth T. Jackson, 119. New Haven: Yale University Press, 1995.

Gross, Ariela. "Litigating Whiteness: Trials of Racial Determination in the Nineteenth-Century South." *Yale Law Journal* 108 (October 1998): 109–88.

Grossberg, Michael. "Broken Promises: Judges and the Law of Courtship." Chap. 2 in *Governing the Hearth: Law and Family in Nineteenth-Century America*. Chapel Hill: University of North Carolina Press, 1985.

———. "Guarding the Altar: Physiological Restrictions and the Rise of State Intervention in Matrimony." *American Journal of Legal History* 26 (July 1982): 197–226.

Grossman, Joanna, and Chris Guthrie. "The Road Less Taken: Annulment at the Turn of the Century." *American Journal of Legal History* 40 (July 1996): 307–30.

Gullickson, Aaron. "Black/White Interracial Marriage Trends, 1850–2000." *Journal of Family History* 31 (July 2006): 289–312.

Guy-Sheftall, Beverly. "The Body Politic: Black Female Sexuality and the Nineteenth-Century Euro-American Imagination." In *Skin Deep, Spirit Strong: The Black Female Body in American Culture*, edited by Kimberly Wallace-Sanders, 13–36. Ann Arbor: University of Michigan Press, 2002.

Haag, Pamela. "In Search of 'The Real Thing': Ideologies of Love, Modern Romance, and Women's Sexual Subjectivity in the United States, 1920–1940." *Journal of the History of Sexuality* 2 (1992): 547–77.

Harris, Cheryl. "Review Essay: *Whitewashing Race*: Scapegoating Culture." *California Law Review* 94 (2006): 907–43.

———. "Whiteness as Property." *Harvard Law Review* 106 (1993): 1707–91.

Hartog, Hendrik. "Marital Exits and Marital Expectations in Nineteenth Century America." *Georgetown Law Journal* 80 (October 1991): 95–129.

Haslanger, Sally. "Gender and Race: (What) Are They? (What) Do We Want Them to Be?" *Nous* 34 (March 2000): 31–55.

Haynes, Douglas M. "Teaching Twentieth-Century Black Britain." *Radical History Review* 87 (Fall 2003): 139–45.

"Here and There by the Observer." *Half-Century Magazine*, January–February 1925, 6.

Herskovits, Melville J. "Age Changes in Pigmentation of American Negroes." *American Journal of Physical Anthropology* 9 (1926): 321–27.

———. "The American Negro Evolving a New Physical Type." *Current History*, September 1926, 898–903.

———. "The Color Line." *American Mercury*, October 1925, 204–8.

———. "Correlation of Length and Breadth of Head in American Negroes." *American Journal of Physical Anthropology* 9 (1926): 87–97.

———. "A Critical Discussion of the 'Mulatto Hypothesis.'" *Journal of Negro Education* 3 (July 1934): 389–402.

———. "The Negro's Americanism." In *The New Negro*, ed. by Alain Locke, 353–60. New York: Albert & Charles Boni, 1925. Reprint, New York: Atheneum, 1983.

———. "Preliminary Observations in a Study of Negro-White Crossing." *Opportunity*, March 1925, 69–74.

———. "The Racial Hysteria." *Opportunity*, June 1924, 166–68.

Higginbotham, Evelyn Brooks. "African-American Women's History and the Metalanguage of Race." *Signs* 17 (winter 1992): 251–74.

Hine, Darlene Clark. "Black Migration to the Urban Midwest: The Gender Dimension, 1914–1945." In *The Great Migration in Historical Perspective: New Dimensions of Race, Class, and Gender*, edited by Joe William Trotter Jr., 127–46. Bloomington: Indiana University Press, 1991.

Hinkle, Beatrice M., M.D. "The Chaos of Modern Marriage." *Harper's Magazine*, December 1925, 1–13.

Hirsch, Arnold R. "E Pluribus Duo? Thoughts on 'Whiteness' and Chicago's 'New' Immigration as a Transient Third Tier." *Journal of American Ethnic History* 23 (Summer 2004): 7–44.

Hodes, Martha. "The Mercurial Nature and Abiding Power of Race: A Transnational Family Story." *American Historical Review* 108 (2003): 84–118.

Hoffman, Frederick L. "Problem of Negro-White Intermixture and Intermarriage." In *Eugenics in Race and State, vol. II: Scientific Papers of the Second International Congress of Eugenics (1921)*, 175–88. Baltimore: Williams and Wilkins, 1923.

Holt, Thomas. "Marking Race, Race-Making, and the Writing of History." *American Historical Review* (February 1995): 1–20.

Hood, Clifton. "Journeying to 'Old New York' Elite New Yorkers and Their Invention of an Idealized City History in the Late Nineteenth and Early Twentieth Centuries." *Journal of Urban History* 28 (September 2002): 699–719.

———. "An Unusable Past: Urban Elites, New York City's Evacuation Day, and the Transformations of Memory Culture." *Journal of Social History* 37 (2004): 883–913.

Hooton, Earnest A. "The Anthropometry of Some Small Samples of American Negroes and Negroids." In Caroline Bond Day, *A Study of Some Negro-White Families in the United States*, 42–107. Cambridge: Peabody Museum of Harvard University, 1932.

———. "Foreword." In Day, *A Study of Some Negro-White Families in the United States*.

———. "Methods of Racial Analysis." *Science*, n.s., 63 (January 22, 1926): 75–81.

Hoysradt, Eleanor. "Enigma." *Crisis*, August 1929, 268.

Hunting, Mary Anne. "The Seventh Regiment Armory in New York City." *Magazine Antiques*, January 1999, 158–67, <http://findarticles.com>. 14 May 2008.

"Intermarriage." *Crisis*, April 1913, 296–97.

"Intermarriage With Negroes—A Survey of State Statutes." *Yale Law Journal* 36 (1927): 858–66.

"Is Race 'Real'? Social Science Research Council Web Forum," <http://raceandgenomics.ssrc.org>. 14 May 2008.

Jaher, Frederic Cople. "Nineteenth-Century Elites in Boston and New York." *Journal of Social History* 5 (Fall 1972): 32–77.

———. "Style and Status: High Society in Late Nineteenth-Century New York." In *The Rich, the Well-Born and the Powerful: Elites and Upper Classes in History*, edited by Frederic Cople Jaher, 258–84. Urbana: University of Illinois Press, 1973.

"Jim Crowing." *Crisis*, April 1919, 282.

Johnson, Caleb. "Crossing the Color Line." *Outlook and Independent*, 26 August 1931, 526–28, 542–43.

Johnson, Charles S. "Mental Measurements of Negro Groups." *Opportunity*, February 1923, 21–25.

———. "The New Frontage on American Life." In *The New Negro*, edited by Alain Locke, 278–98. New York: Albert and Charles Boni, 1925. Reprint, New York: Atheneum, 1983.

Johnson, Walter. "The Slave Trader, the White Slave, and the Politics of Racial Determination in the 1850s." *Journal of American History* 87 (June 2000): 13–38.

"Johnstown." *Opportunity*, November 1923, 349.

Jones, Eugene Kinkle. "Negro Migration in New York State." *Opportunity*, January 1926, 7–11.

Kenny, Kevin. "Race, Violence, and Anti-Irish Sentiment in the Nineteenth Century." In *Making the Irish American: History and Heritage of the Irish in the United States*, edited by J. J. Lee and Marion R. Casey, 364–80. New York: New York University Press, 2006.

Kerber, Linda. "A Constitutional Right to Be Treated Like American Ladies: Women and the Obligations of Citizenship." In *U.S. History as Women's History: New Feminist Essays*, edited by Linda K. Kerber, Alice Kessler-Harris, and Kathryn Kish Sklar, 17–35. Chapel Hill: University of North Carolina Press, 1995.

Killingray, David. "Tracing Peoples of African Origin and Descent in Victorian Kent." In *Black Victorians/Black Victoriana*, edited by Gretchen Holbrook Gerzina, 51–67. New Brunswick, N.J.: Rutgers University Press, 2003.

Kirksey, Thomas. "Reflections Upon Race." *Messenger*, December 1926, 363.

Kolchin, Peter. "Whiteness Studies: The New History of Race in America." *Journal of American History* 89 (June 2002): 154–73.

Korobkin, Laura Hanft. "The Maintenance of Mutual Confidence: Sentimental Strategies at the Adultery Trial of Henry Ward Beecher." *Yale Journal of Law and the Humanities* 7 (1995): 1–48.

Kreizenbeck, Alan. "Garland Anderson's *Appearances*: The Playwright and His Play." *Journal of American Drama and Theatre* 6 (Spring/Summer 1994): 28–48.

Larson, Jane. " 'Women Understand So Little, They Call My Good Nature "Deceit" ': A Feminist Rethinking of Seduction." *Columbia Law Review* 93 (March 1993): 374–471.

Leach, William R. "Transformations in a Culture of Consumption: Women and Department Stores, 1890–1925." *Journal of American History* 71 (1984): 319–42.

Lemons, J. Stanley. "Black Stereotypes as Reflected in Popular Culture, 1880–1920. *American Quarterly* 29 (Spring 1977): 102–16.

Lewis, David Levering. "Parallels and Divergences: Assimilationist Strategies of Afro-American and Jewish Elites from 1910 to the Early 1930s." *Journal of American History* 71 (1984): 543–64.

Lewis, Earl, and Heidi Ardizzone. "A Modern Cinderella: Race, Sexuality, and Social Class in the Rhinelander Case." *International Journal of Labor and Working-Class History* 51 (Spring 1997): 129–47.

Lilienthal, David E. "A Trial of Two Races." *Outlook*, 23 December 1925, 629–30.

Lindsay, Matthew J. "Reproducing a Fit Citizenry: Dependency, Eugenics, and the Law of Marriage in the United States, 1860–1920." *Law and Social Inquiry* 23 (Summer 1998): 541–85.

Liu, Tessie. "Teaching the Differences Among Women from a Historical Perspective: Rethinking Race and Gender as Social Categories." In *Unequal Sisters: A Multicultural Reader in U.S. Women's History*, 2d ed., edited by Vicki L. Ruiz and Ellen Carol DuBois, 571–83. New York: Routledge, 1994.

"The Looking Glass." *Crisis*, June 1926, 90–91.

"The Looking Glass." *Crisis*, June 1917, 75–76.

Lynch-Brennan, Margaret. "Ubiquitous Bridget: Irish Immigrant Women in Domestic Service in America, 1840–1930." In *Making the Irish American: History and Heritage of the Irish in the United States*, edited by J. J. Lee and Marion R. Casey, 332–53. New York: New York University Press, 2006.

Mackay, Ellin. "Why We Go to Cabarets: A Post-Debutante Explains." *New Yorker*, 28 November 1925, 7.

Markey, Morris. "The Current Press." *New Yorker*, 5 December 1925, 11.

———. "A Day in the Country." *New Yorker*, 28 November 1925, 9.

Madigan, Mark. "Miscegenation and the 'Dicta of Race and Class': The *Rhinelander* Case and Nella Larsen's *Passing*." *Modern Fiction Studies* 36 (Winter 1990): 523–29.

Mallon, Ron. "Passing, Traveling and Reality: Social Constructionism and the Metaphysics of Race." *Nous* 38 (December 2004): 644–73.

———. "'Race': Normative, Not Metaphysical or Semantic." *Ethics* 116 (April 2006): 525–51.

"Marriage and Divorce-Annulment for Fraud–Breach of Promise to Have Second Ceremony in Catholic Church." *Yale Law Journal* 33 (December 1923): 209–10.

"Marriage-Annulment-Fraud." *Columbia Law Review* 20 (June 1920): 708.

"Marriage. Nullification. Misrepresentations as to Prior Chastity." *Harvard Law Review* 24 (December 1910): 157.

Marzolf, Marion. "Americanizing the Melting Pot: The Media as a Megaphone for the Restrictionists." In *Mass Media Between the Wars*, edited by Catherine L.

Covert and John D. Stevens, 107–25. Syracuse, N.Y.: Syracuse University Press, 1984.

McPherson, Lionel K., and Tommie Shelby. "Blackness and Blood: Interpreting African American Identity." *Philosophy and Public Affairs* 32 (2004): 171–92.

Megill, Allan. "Recounting the Past: 'Description,' Explanation, and Narrative in Historiography." *American Historical Review* 94 (June 1989): 627–53.

Mencken, H. L. "Editorial." *American Mercury*, October 1927, 159–61.

Merz, Charles. "What Makes a First-Page Story? A Theory Based on the Ten Big News Stories of 1925." *New Republic*, 30 December 1925, 156.

Miller, Kelly. "Separate Communities for Negroes. Two Points of View, I. The Causes of Segregation." *Current History*, March 1927, 827–31.

Montgomery, Maureen. "Female Rituals and the Politics of the New York Marriage Market in the Late Nineteenth Century." *Journal of Family History* 23 (January 1998): 47–67.

———. "'The Fruit that Hangs Highest': Courtship and Chaperonage in New York High Society, 1880–1920." *Journal of Family History* 21 (April 1996): 172–91.

Morgan, Jennifer. "'Some Could Suckle Over Their Shoulder': Male Travelers, Female Bodies, and the Gendering of Racial Ideology, 1500–1770." *William and Mary Quarterly*, 3rd ser., 54 (January 1997): 167–92.

Muccigrosso, Robert. "New York Has a Ball: The Bradley Martin Extravaganza." *New York History* 75 (April 1994): 297–320.

Mumford, Kevin. "Homosex Changes: Race, Cultural Geography, and the Emergence of the Gay." *American Quarterly* 48 (September 1996): 395–414.

Nathan, George Jean. "Clinical Notes." *American Mercury*, March 1926, 363–66.

"The Nature of Fraud Required to Annul a Marriage." *Columbia Law Review* 22 (November 1922): 662–65.

"The N.A.A.C.P. Battle Front." *Crisis*, April 1928, 118.

"The Negro's Northward Exodus." *The Literary Digest*, 29 August 1931, 4.

Ngai, Mae M. "The Architecture of Race in American Immigration Law: A Reexamination of the Immigration Act of 1924." *Journal of American History* 86 (June 1999): 67–92.

"Notes and Queries." *New York Genealogical and Biographical Record Devoted to the Interests of American Genealogy and Biography*, 1 April 1891, 104, <http://www.proquest.com/>. 14 May 2008.

Ottley, Roi. "5 Million U.S. White Negroes." *Ebony*, May 1948, 25–28.

Owens, Chandler. "The Black and Tan Cabaret—America's Most Democratic Institution." *Messenger*, February 1925, 97.

———. "Good Looks Supremacy: A Perspicacious Perusal of the Potencies of Pulchritude by a Noted Authority." *Messenger*, March 1924, 80–82, 90.

Paine, Swift. "As We See It in Reno." *North American Review*, 1 June 1930, 720, <http://www.proquest.com/>. 14 May 2008.

Painter, Nell Irvin. "Hill, Thomas, and the Uses of Racial Stereotype." In *Race-Ing Justice, En-Gendering Power: Essays on Anita Hill, Clarence Thomas, and the Construction of Social Reality*, edited by Toni Morrison, 207–10. New York: Pantheon Books, 1992.

———. "Of *Lily*, Linda Brent, and Freud: A Non-Exceptionalist Approach to Race, Class, and Gender in the Slave South." *Georgia Historical Quarterly* 76 (Summer 1992): 241–59.

———. "'Social Equality,' Miscegenation, Labor and Power." In *The Evolution of Southern Culture*, edited by Numan V. Bartley, 46–67. Athens: University of Georgia Press, 1988.

Parra, E. J., R. A. Kittles, and M. D. Shriver. "Implications of Correlations Between Skin Color and Genetic Ancestry for Biomedical Research." *Nature Genetics Supplement* 36 (November 2004): 554–60.

Pascoe, Peggy. "Miscegenation Law, Court Cases, and Ideologies of 'Race' in Twentieth-Century America." *Journal of American History* 83 (June 1996): 44–69.

———. "Race, Gender, and Intercultural Relations: The Case of Interracial Marriage." *Frontiers* 12, no. 1 (1991): 5–18.

———. "Race, Gender, and the Privileges of Property: On the Significance of Miscegenation Law in the U.S. West." In *Over the Edge: Remapping the American West*, edited by Valerie J. Matsumoto and Blake Allmendinger, 215–30. Berkeley: University of California Press, 1999.

"Personal." *Harper's Bazaar*, 6 January 1894, 7, <http://www.proquest.com/>. 14 May 2008.

Pessen, Edward. "Political Democracy and the Distribution of Power in Antebellum New York City." In *Essays in the History of New York: A Memorial to Sidney Pomerantz*, edited by Irwin Yellowitz, 21–42. Port Washington, N.Y.: Kennikat Press, 1978.

Pickens, William. "Color and Camouflage: A Psychoanalysis." *Messenger*, July 1923, 773–74.

———. "Migrating to a Fuller Life." *Forum*, 1 November 1924, 600, <http://www.proquest.com/>. 14 May 2008.

———. "'Mulattoes' and Anglo-Saxon Clubs." *New York Amsterdam News*, 20 May 1925, editorial and feature page.

———. "Racial Segregation." *Opportunity*, December 1927, 364–67.

Proctor, Eulalia. "La Femme Silhouette: The Bronze Age." *Messenger*, February 1925, 93.

"Queries and Minor Notes." *Journal of the American Medical Association* 97 (12 December 1931): 1822.

"Race Barriers Slowly Crumbling." *The Literary Digest*, 12 February 1927, 34.

"Race Hatred North and South." *The Colored American Magazine*, December 1906, 358–59.

"Race versus Color." *Messenger*, June 1927, 207.

Regester, Charlene. "Headline to Headlights: Oscar Micheaux's Exploitation of the Rhinelander Case." *Case Western Journal of Black Studies* 22 (Fall 1998): 195–204.

Reuter, Edward Byron. "The American Mulatto." In *Annals of the American Academy of Political and Social Science*, Vol. 140, The American Negro (November 1928): 36–43. <http://www.jstor.org/stable/1016830>. 25 September 2008.

———. "The Hybrid as a Sociological Type." *Papers and Proceedings of the American Sociological Society*, Vol. 19 (29–31 December 1924): 59–68.

"Rhinelander Declared Sane." *The National Police Gazette* 22 (November 1884), <http://www.proquest.com/>. 14 May 2008.

Ritter, Gretchen. "Jury Service and Women's Citizenship before and after the Nineteenth Amendment." *Law and History Review* 20 (Autumn 2002): 479–515.

Robinson, Amy. "It Takes One to Know One: Passing and Communities of Common Interest." *Critical Inquiry* 20 (Summer 1994): 715–36.

Roediger, David. "The Pursuit of Whiteness: Property, Terror, and Expansion, 1790–1860." *Journal of the Early Republic* 19 (1999): 579–600.

Rogers, J. A. "The Critic." *Messenger*, January 1925, 34–35.

———. "The Critic: Do They Tell the Truth." *Messenger*, January 1926, 12.

———. "Critical Excursions and Reflections." *Messenger*, February 1924, 49.

———. "The West Indies and the Quota." *Messenger*, September 1924, 295.

Saks, Eva. "Representing Miscegenation Law." *Raritan* 8 (Fall 1988): 39–69.

Sampson, J. Milton. "Race Consciousness and Race Relations." *Opportunity*, May 1923, 15–19.

"Scholarly Controversy: Whiteness and the Historians' Imagination." *International Journal of Labor and Working-Class History* 60 (October 2001): 1–92.

Schuyler, George. "Keeping the Negro in His Place." *American Mercury*, August 1929, 469–76.

———. "These 'Colored' United States." *Messenger*, October–November 1925, 344–49.

———. "Who Is 'Negro'? Who Is 'White?'" *Common Ground*, Autumn 1940, 53–56.

Schuyler, M. C. "The Social Growth of New York: Costume Balls." *Arthur's Home Magazine*, 1 March 1897, 123, <http://www.proquest.com/>. 14 May 2008.

Scott, William H. "The Color Line." *Half-Century Magazine*, June 1918, 5.

Sekula, Allan. "The Body and the Archive." *October* 39 (1986): 3–64.

"Sell the Papers! The Melody of American Journalism." *Harper's*, June 1925, 1–9.

"Shall We All Be Mulattoes?" *Literary Digest*, 7 March 1925, 23–24.

Shapiro, Gary. "Celebrating 125 with the Knickerbocker Greys." *New York Sun*, 17 April 2006, <www.nysun.com/article/31070>. 17 November 2006.

Shapiro, Ann R. "Edna Ferber, Jewish American Feminist." *Shofar: An Interdisciplinary Journal of Jewish Studies* 20 (Winter 2002): 52–60.

Sheridan, Clare. "Contested Citizenship: National Identity and the Mexican Immi-

gration Debates of the 1920s." *Journal of American Ethnic History* 21 (Spring 2002): 3–36.
Sherman, Richard B. " 'The Last Stand': The Fight for Racial Integrity in Virginia in the 1920s." *Journal of Southern History* 54 (February 1988): 69–92.
Simmons, Christina. "Modern Sexuality and the Myth of Victorian Repression." In *Passion and Power: Sexuality in History*, edited by Kathy Peiss and Christina Simmons, 157–60. Philadelphia: Temple University Press, 1989.
Smith, Valerie. "Reading the Intersection of Race and Gender in Narratives of Passing." *Diacritics* 24 (Summer–Fall 1994): 43–57.
"Social and Travel Notes." *Town and Country*, 25 June 1904, 3, <http://www.proquest.com/>. 14 May 2008.
Stanton, Lucia. " 'Those Who Labor for My Happiness': Thomas Jefferson and His Slaves." In *Jeffersonian Legacies*, edited by Peter S. Onuf, 147–80. Charlottesville: University of Virginia Press, 1993.
Staudacher, Lucas G. "Arthur Brisbane." In *Dictionary of Literary Biography* (1984).
Steggerda, Morris. "Physical Development of Negro-White Hybrids in Jamaica, British West Indies." *American Journal of Physical Anthropology* 12 (July–September 1928): 121–38.
Stein, Edward. "Symposium: Abolishing Civil Marriage: An Introduction." *Cardozo Law Review* 27 (January 2006): 1155.
Stern, Julia. "Spanish Masquerade and the Drama of Racial Identity in *Uncle Tom's Cabin*." In Ginsberg, ed., *Passing and the Fictions of Identity*, 103–30.
Stevens, John D. "Media and Morality in the Twenties." *History Today* 39, no. 11 (November 1989): 25–29.
Stoddard, Lothrop. "II—The Impasse at the Color-Line." *Forum*, 1 October 1927, 510, <http://www.proquest.com/>. 14 May 2008.
———. "The Permanent Menace from Europe." In *The Alien in Our Midst; or, "Selling Our Birthright for a Mess of Pottage"; The Written Views of a Number of Americans (present and former) on Immigration and Its Results*, edited by Madison Grant and Chas. Stewart Davison. New York: The Galton Publishing Co., 1930.
"Talk of the Town." *New Yorker*, 5 December 1925, 4.
"That Drop of Blood." *Crisis*, June 1926, 90.
Thomas, Brook. "Michael Grossberg's Telling Tale: The Social Drama of an Antebellum Custody Case." *Law and Social Inquiry* 23 (spring 1998): 431–58.
Tolnay, Stewart E. and E. M. Beck. "Rethinking the Role of Racial Violence in the Great Migration." In *Black Exodus: The Great Migration from the American South*, edited by Alferdteen Harrison, 120–35. Jackson: University of Mississippi Press, 1991.
"Town & Country Calendar." *Town & Country*, 31 January 1903, 3, <http://www.proquest.com/>. 14 May 2008.
"Town & Country Life." *Town & Country Life*, 20 September 1902, 20, <http://www.proquest.com/>. 14 May 2008.

"Town & Country Life." *Town & Country*, 19 December 1903, 20, <http://www.proquest.com/>. 14 May 2008.

"Town & Country Life." *Town & Country*, 20 July 1907, 18, <http://www.proquest.com/>. 14 May 2008.

"A Transformed Race." *Crisis*, August 1918, 178–79.

Ulm, Aaron Henry. "Our Diminishing Tide of Color." *Current Opinion*, May 1922, 605–9.

"'Up North' by a Mulatto." *Crisis*, September 1925, 223–24.

"Vagaries of Prejudice." *Crisis*, August 1911, 144.

Van de Water, Frederic. "Jazz and Gin." In *The Social Ladder*, by May King Van Rensselaer and Frederic Van de Water. New York: Henry Holt, 1924.

Vanneman, Henry W. "Annulment of Marriage for Fraud." *Minnesota Law Review* 9 (May 1925): 497–517.

Villard, Oswald Garrison. "Are Tabloid Newspapers a Menace?" *Forum*, 1 April 1927, 485, <http://www.proquest.com/>. 14 May 2008.

Waller, Willard. "The Rating and Dating Complex." *American Sociological Review* 2 (1937): 727–34.

Wallis, Brian. "Black Bodies, White Science: The Slave Daguerreotypes of Louis Agassiz." *Journal of Blacks in Higher Education* 12 (Summer 1996): 102–6.

Weinauer, Ellen M. "'A Most Respectable Looking Gentleman': Passing, Possession, and Transgression in *Running a Thousand Miles for Freedom*." In *Passing and the Fictions of Identity*, edited by Elaine K. Ginsberg, 37–56. Durham, N.C.: Duke University Press, 1996.

"West Indian Immigration." *Crisis*, December 1924, 57.

"When Is a Contest Not a Contest?" *Crisis*, June 1924, 80.

White, Walter. "The Paradox of Color." In *The New Negro*, edited by Alain Locke, 361–68. New York: Albert & Charles Boni, 1925. Reprint, New York: Atheneum, 1983.

"White but Black: A Document on the Race Problem." *Century Magazine*, November 1924–April 1925, 492–99.

Wiggam, Albert E. "The Rising Tide of Degeneracy: What Everybody Ought to Know About Eugenics." *World's Work*, November 1926, 25–33.

Will, Barbara. "*The Great Gatsby* and the Obscene Word." *College Literature* 32 (Fall 2005): 125–44.

Williams, Carla. "The Erotic Image Is Naked and Dark." In *Picturing Us: African American Identity in Photography*, edited by Deborah Willis, 129–34. New York: New Press, 1994.

———. "Naked, Neutered, or Noble: The Black Female Body in America and the Problem of Photographic History." In *Skin Deep, Spirit Strong: The Black Female Body in American Culture*, edited by Kimberly Wallace-Sanders, 182–200. Ann Arbor: University of Michigan Press, 2002.

Williams, Fannie Barrier. "Perils of the White Negro." *Colored American Magazine*, December 1907, 421–23.

Williams, Teresa Kay. "Race-Ing and Being Races: The Critical Interrogation of Passing." In *"Mixed Race" Studies: A Reader*, edited by Jayne O. Ifekwunigwe, 166–70. London: Routledge, 2004.

Wingate, T. Todd. "Entrenched Negro Physical Features." *Human Biology* 1 (January 1929): 57–69.

Wingate, T. Todd, and Leona van Gerder. "The Quantitative Determination of Black Pigmentation in the Skin of the American Negro." *American Journal of Physical Anthropology* 4 (1921): 239–60.

Wirth, Louis, and Herbert Goldhamer. "The Hybrid and the Problem of Miscegenation." In *Characteristics of the American Negro*, edited by Otto Klineberg. New York: Harper & Brothers, 1944.

Wolfe, Patrick. "Land, Labor and Difference: Elementary Structures of Race." *American Historical Review* 106 (June 2001): 866–905.

Work, Monroe N. "Taking Stock of the Race Problem: A Statistical Review in Interpretation of the Facts at the End of the Year 1923." *Opportunity*, February 1924, 41–47.

BOOKS

Aldrich, Nelson W., Jr. *Old Money: The Mythology of America's Upper Class*. New York: Alfred A. Knopf, 1988.

Alexander, Adele Logan. *Homelands and Waterways: The American Journey of the Bond Family, 1846–1926*. New York: Vintage Books, 2000.

Alexander, Ruth M. *The "Girl Problem": Female Sexual Delinquency in New York, 1900–1930*. Ithaca, N.Y.: Cornell University Press, 1995.

Allen, Frederick Lewis. *Only Yesterday: An Informal History of the Nineteen-Twenties*. New York: Harper & Row, 1931. Reprint, New York: Harper & Row, 1957.

Allen, Irving Lewis. *The City in Slang: New York Life and Popular Speech*. New York: Oxford University Press, 1993.

Amory, Cleveland. *Who Killed Society?* New York: Harper & Brothers, 1960.

Anderson, Margo. *The American Census: A Social History*. New Haven: Yale University Press, 1988.

Ashby, William M. *Redder Blood: A Novel*. New York: Cosmopolitan Press, 1915. Reprint, New York: AMS Press, 1975.

Bailey, Beth L. *From Front Porch to Back Seat: Courtship in Twentieth Century America*. Baltimore: Johns Hopkins University Press, 1988.

Baker, Lee D. *From Savage to Negro: Anthropology and the Construction of Race, 1896–1954*. Berkeley: University of California Press, 1998.

Baker, Ray Stannard. *Following the Color Line: American Negro Citizenship in the Pro-

gressive Era. New York: Doubleday, Page & Co., 1908. Reprint, New York: Harper Torchbooks, 1964.

Baldwin, Louis Fremont. *From Negro to Caucasian; or, How the Ethiopian Is Changing His Skin.* San Francisco: Pilot Publishing Co., 1929.

Baltzell, E. Digby. *The Protestant Establishment: Aristocracy and Caste in America.* New York: Random House, 1963.

———. *The Protestant Establishment Revisited: The Collected Papers of E. Digby Baltzell.* Edited by Howard G. Schneiderman. New Brunswick, N.J.: Transaction Publishers, 1991.

Banton, Michael. *Racial Theories.* Cambridge: Cambridge University Press, 1987.

Barbeau, Arthur E., and Florette Henri. *The Unknown Soldiers: African-American Troops in World War I.* Philadelphia: University of Pennsylvania Press, 1974. Reprint. New York: Da Capo Press, 1996.

Bardaglio, Peter W. *Reconstructing the Household: Families, Sex, and the Law in the Nineteenth-Century South.* Chapel Hill: University of North Carolina Press, 1998.

Barkan, Elazar. *The Retreat of Scientific Racism: Changing Concepts of Race in Britain and the United States Between the World Wars.* Cambridge: Cambridge University Press, 1992.

Barrett, Terry. *Criticizing Photographs: An Introduction to Understanding Images.* 2d ed. Mountain View, Calif.: Mayfield Publishing Co., 1996.

Basch, Norma. *Framing American Divorce: From the Revolutionary Generation to the Victorians.* Berkeley: University of California Press, 1999.

Bay, Mia. *The White Image in the Black Mind: African American Ideas About White People, 1830–1925.* New York: Oxford University Press, 2000.

Beckert, Sven. *The Monied Metropolis: New York City and the Consolidation of the American Bourgeoisie, 1850–1896.* Cambridge: Cambridge University Press, 2001.

Bederman, Gail. *Manliness and Civilization: A Cultural History of Gender and Race in the United States, 1880–1917.* Chicago: University of Chicago Press, 1995.

Bennett, Juda. *The Passing Figure: Racial Confusion in Modern American Literature.* New York: Peter Lang Publishing, 1996.

Berenson, Edward. *The Trial of Madame Caillaux.* Berkeley: University of California Press, 1992.

Bergan, Francis. *The History of the New York Court of Appeals.* New York: Columbia University Press for the William Nelson Cromwell Foundation, 1985.

Bergren, Lawrence. *As Thousands Cheer: The Life of Irving Berlin.* New York: Viking, 1990.

Berlin, Ira. *Many Thousands Gone: The First Two Centuries of Slavery in North America.* Cambridge: Harvard University Press, 1998.

Bernstein, Iver. *The New York City Draft Riots: Their Significance for American Society and Politics in the Age of the Civil War.* New York: Oxford University Press, 1990.

Bessie, Simon Michael. *Jazz Journalism: The Story of the Tabloid Newspapers.* New York: E. P. Dutton & Co., 1938.
Binder, Frederick M., and David M. Reimers. *All the Nations Under Heaven: An Ethnic and Racial History of New York City.* New York: Columbia University Press, 1995.
Biographical History of Westchester County, N.Y. Illustrated. Vol. 1. Chicago: The Lewis Publishing Co., 1899.
Biondi, Martha. *To Stand and Fight: The Struggle for Civil Rights in Postwar New York City.* Cambridge: Harvard University Press, 2003.
Black's Law Dictionary. Rev. 4th ed. St. Paul, Minn.: West Publishing, 1968.
Blee, Kathleen M. *Women of the Klan: Racism and Gender in the 1920s.* Berkeley: University of California Press, 1991.
Boyle, Kevin. *Arc of Justice: A Saga of Race, Civil Rights, and Murder in the Jazz Age.* New York: Henry Holt, 2004.
Brown, Nikki. *Private Politics and Public Voices: Black Women's Activism from World War I to the New Deal.* Bloomington: Indiana University Press, 2006.
Burke, Peter, ed. *New Perspectives on Historical Writing.* University Park: Penn State University Press, 1992.
Burrows, Edwin G., and Mike Wallace. *Gotham: A History of New York City to 1898.* New York: Oxford University Press, 1999.
Cable, Mary. *Top Drawer: American High Society from the Gilded Age to the Roaring Twenties.* New York: Atheneum, 1984.
Cahill, James C., ed. *Cahill's Consolidated Laws of New York.* Chicago: Callaghan and Company, 1923.
Carmody, Francis X. *A Treatise on Pleading and Practice in New York Including Particular Actions and Special Proceedings with Forms.* New York: Clark Boardman, 1924.
Chapman, *Tell It to Sweeney: The Informal History of the New York Daily News.* New York: Doubleday and Company, 1961.
Chester, Ronald. *Inheritance, Wealth, and Society.* Bloomington: Indiana University Press, 1982.
Chestnutt, Charles W. *The House Behind the Cedars.* Boston: Houghton Mifflin, 1900. Reprint, New York: Penguin Books, 1993.
Clark-Lewis, Elizabeth. *Living in, Living out: African American Domestics and the Great Migration.* New York: Kodansha International, 1996.
Clement, Elizabeth Alice. *Love for Sale: Courting, Treating, and Prostitution in New York City, 1900–1945.* Chapel Hill: University of North Carolina Press, 2006.
Clevenger, Joseph R. *Clevenger's Supreme Court Practice.* New York: Joseph R. Clevenger, 1921.
Cobb, Irwin S. *New York.* New York: George H. Doran Co., 1924.
Coben, Stanley. *Rebellion Against Victorianism: The Impetus for Cultural Change in 1920s America.* New York: Oxford University Press, 1991.

Cohen, Lester. *The New York Evening Graphic: The World's Zaniest Newspaper*. Philadelphia: Chilton Books, 1964.

Cole, Robert Danforth. *Private Secondary Education for Boys in the United States*. Philadelphia: Westbrook Publishing Co., 1928.

Coleman, A. D. *The Digital Evolution: Visual Communication in the Electronic Age: Essays, Lectures and Interviews, 1967–1998*. Tucson, Ariz.: Nazraeli Press, 1998.

Cott, Nancy. *The Grounding of Modern Feminism*. New Haven: Yale University Press, 1987.

———. *Public Vows: A History of Marriage and the Nation*. Cambridge: Harvard University Press, 2000.

Courtney, Susan. *Hollywood Fantasies of Miscegenation: Spectacular Narratives of Gender and Race, 1903–1967*. Princeton, N.J.: Princeton University Press, 2005.

Curtis, George M. *Closing Argument of Hon. George M. Curtis, Counsel for Respondent, In the Matter of the Inquiry into the Sanity of William C. Rhinelander*. 2 September 1884. N.p., 1884.

Cutler, A. S. *Successful Trial Tactics*. New York: Prentice-Hall, 1949.

D'Emilio, John, and Estelle B. Freedman. *Intimate Matters: A History of Sexuality in America*. New York: Harper & Row, 1988.

Davenport, Charles B., and Morris Steggerda. *Race Crossing in Jamaica*. Washington, D.C.: Carnegie Institution of Washington, 1929. Reprint, Westport, Conn.: Negro Universities Press, 1970.

Davis, F. James. *Who Is Black? One Nation's Definition*. University Park: Penn State University Press, 1991.

Davis, Thadious. *Nella Larsen, Novelist of the Harlem Renaissance: A Woman's Life Unveiled*. Baton Rouge: Louisiana State University Press, 1994.

Day, Caroline Bond. *A Study of Some Negro-White Families in the United States*. Cambridge: Peabody Museum of Harvard University, 1932.

Delgado, Richard, ed. *Critical Race Theory: The Cutting Edge*. Philadelphia, Pa.: Temple University Press, 1995.

Dijkstra, Bram. *Evil Sisters: The Threat of Female Sexuality and the Cult of Manhood*. New York: Alfred A. Knopf, 1996.

Diner, Hasia R. *Erin's Daughters in America: Irish Immigrant Women in the Nineteenth Century*. Baltimore: Johns Hopkins University Press, 1983.

Dominguez, Virginia R. *White by Definition: Social Classification in Creole Louisiana*. New Brunswick, N.J.: Rutgers University Press, 1986.

Douglas, Ann. *Terrible Honesty: Mongrel Manhattan in the 1920s*. New York: Farrar, Straus & Giroux, 1995.

Drake, St. Clair, and Horace R. Cayton, *Black Metropolis: A Study of Negro Life in a Northern City*. New York: Harcourt, Brace, 1945.

DuBois, W. E. B. *Darkwater: Voices from within the Veil*. New York: Harcourt, Brace and Howe, 1920.

Dumenil, Lynn. *Modern Temper: American Culture and Society in the 1920s.* New York: Hill & Wang, 1995.

Dunlop, M. H. *The Gilded City: Scandal and Sensations in Turn-of-the-Century New York.* New York: William Morrow, 2000.

Emery, Edwin, and Michael Emery. *The Press and America: An Interpretive History of the Mass Media.* 5th ed. Englewood Cliffs, N.J.: Prentice-Hall, 1984.

Erenberg, Lewis A. *Steppin' Out: New York Nightlife and the Transformation of American Culture, 1890–1930.* Westport, Conn.: Greenwood Press, 1981.

Estabrook, Arthur H., and Ivan E. McDougle. *Mongrel Virginians: The Win Tribe.* Baltimore: Williams and Wilkins, 1926.

Fass, Paula S. *The Damned and the Beautiful: American Youth in the 1920s.* New York: Oxford University Press, 1977.

Fauset, Jessie Redmon. *Plum Bun: A Novel Without a Moral.* New York: Frederick A. Stokes Co., 1928. Reprint, Boston: Beacon Press, 1990.

Ferber, Edna. *Show Boat: A Novel.* Garden City, N.Y.: Doubleday, Page and Co., 1926.

Fett, Sharla M. *Working Cures: Healing, Health, and Power on Southern Slave Plantations.* Chapel Hill: University of North Carolina Press, 2002.

Fitzgerald, F. Scott. *The Great Gatsby.* In *Three Novels of F. Scott Fitzgerald.* New York: Charles Scribner's Sons, 1925. Reprint, New York: Charles Scribner's Sons, 1953.

Foote, Thelma Wills. *Black and White Manhattan: The History of Racial Formation in Colonial New York City.* New York: Oxford University Press, 2004.

Foucault, Michel. *The History of Sexuality.* Vol. 1, *An Introduction.* Translated by Robert Hurley. New York: Vintage Books, 1990.

Fowler, David H. *Northern Attitudes Towards Interracial Marriage: Legislation and Public Opinion in the Middle Atlantic and the States of the Old Northwest, 1780–1930.* New York: Garland Publishing, 1987.

Fox, Richard Wightman. *Trials of Intimacy: Love and Loss in the Beecher-Tilton Scandal.* Chicago: University of Chicago Press, 1999.

Franklin, John Hope, and Loren Schweninger. *Runaway Slaves: Rebels on the Plantation.* New York: Oxford University Press, 2000.

Frederickson, George M. *The Black Image in the White Mind: The Debate on Afro-American Character and Destiny, 1817–1914.* New York: Harper & Row, 1971.

French, Alvah P., ed. *History of Westchester County, New York.* Vols. 1 and 2. New York: Lewis Historical Publishing Co., 1925.

Freund, David M. P. *Colored Property: State Policy and White Racial Politics in Suburban America.* Chicago: University of Chicago Press, 2007.

Friedman, Lawrence M. *American Law in the Twentieth Century.* New Haven: Yale University Press, 2002.

———. *A History of American Law.* 2nd ed. New York: Simon and Schuster, 1985.

Gatewood, Willard. *Aristocrats of Color: The Black Elite, 1880–1920.* Bloomington: Indiana University Press, 1990.

Gerstle, Gary. *American Crucible: Race and Nation in the Twentieth Century*. Princeton, N.J.: Princeton University Press, 2001.

Gerzina, Gretchen Holbrook, ed. *Black Victorians/Black Victoriana*. New Brunswick, N.J.: Rutgers University Press, 2003.

Gilman, Sander. *Difference and Pathology: Stereotypes of Sexuality, Race, and Madness*. Ithaca, N.Y.: Cornell University Press, 1985.

Gilmore, Glenda Elizabeth. *Defying Dixie: The Radical Roots of Civil Rights, 1919–1950*. New York: W. W. Norton, 2008.

Ginsberg, Elaine K., ed. *Passing and the Fictions of Identity*. Durham, N.C.: Duke University Press, 1996.

Goddard, Henry H. *The Kallikak Family: A Study in the Heredity of Feeble-Mindedness*. New York: MacMillan, 1912. Reprint, New York: Arno Press, 1973.

Goldberg, David J. *Discontented America: The United States in the 1920s*. Baltimore: Johns Hopkins University Press, 1999.

Goldberg, David Theo. *Racial Subjects: Writing on Race in America*. New York: Routledge, 1997.

Goodman, James. *Stories of Scottsboro*. New York: Pantheon Books, 1994.

Gordon, Linda. *The Great Arizona Orphan Abduction*. Cambridge: Harvard University Press, 1999.

———. *Woman's Body, Woman's Right: Birth Control in America*. Rev. and updated. New York: Penguin Books, 1990.

Gossett, Thomas F. *Race: The History of an Idea in America*. Dallas, Tex.: Southern Methodist University Press, 1963.

Gould, Stephen J. *The Mismeasure of Man*. New York: W. W. Norton, 1981.

Grant, Madison. *The Passing of the Great Race; or, The Racial Basis of European History*. New and rev. ed. New York: Charles Scribner's Sons, 1918. Reprint, New York: Arno Press and the New York Times, 1970.

Grant, Madison, and Chas. Stewart Davison, eds. *The Alien in Our Midst; or, "Selling Our Birthright for a Mess of Pottage"; The Written Views of a Number of Americans (present and former) on Immigration and Its Results*. New York: The Galton Publishing Co., 1930.

Green, Constance McLaughlin. *The Secret City: A History of Race Relations in the Nation's Capital*. Princeton, N.J.: Princeton University Press, 1967.

Griffin, Ernest F. *Westchester County and Its People*. Vols. 1 and 2. New York: Lewis Historical Publishing Co., 1946.

Gross, Ariela J. *Double Character: Slavery and Mastery in the Southern Courtroom*. Princeton, N.J.: Princeton University Press, 2000.

Grossberg, Michael. *Governing the Hearth: Law and Family in Nineteenth-Century America*. Chapel Hill: University of North Carolina Press, 1985.

———. *A Judgment for Solomon: The D'Hauteville Case and Legal Experience in Antebellum America*. Cambridge: Cambridge University Press, 1996.

Guglielmo, Jennifer, and Salvatore Salerno, eds. *Are Italians White? How Race Is Made in America*. New York: Routledge, 2003.

Guglielmo, Thomas. *White on Arrival: Italians, Race, Color, and Power in Chicago, 1890–1945*. New York: Oxford University Press, 2003.

Guterl, Matthew Pratt. *The Color of Race in America, 1900–1940*. Cambridge: Harvard University Press, 2001.

Haizlip, Shirlee Taylor. *The Sweeter the Juice: A Family Memoir in Black and White*. New York: Simon and Schuster, 1994.

Hale, Grace Elizabeth. *Making Whiteness: The Culture of Segregation in the South, 1890–1940*. New York: Pantheon Books, 1998.

Haller, Mark H. *Eugenics: Hereditarian Attitudes in American Thought*. New Brunswick, N.J.: Rutgers University Press, 1963.

Hamm, Margherita Arlina. *Famous Families of New York: Historical and Biographical Sketches of Families Which In Successive Generations Have Been Identified with the Development of the Nation*. Vol. 1. New York: G. P. Putnam's Sons, 1902.

Hammack, David C. *Power and Society: Greater New York at the Turn of the Century*. New York: Columbia University Press, 1987.

Haney Lopez, Ian F. *White by Law: The Legal Construction of Race*. New York: New York University Press, 1996.

Harris, Leslie M. *In the Shadow of Slavery: African Americans in New York City, 1626–1863*. Chicago: University of Chicago Press, 2003.

Harrison, Alferdteen, ed. *Black Exodus: The Great Migration from the American South*. Jackson: University of Mississippi Press, 1991.

Hartigan, John. *Racial Situations: Class Predicaments of Whiteness in Detroit*. Princeton, N.J.: Princeton University Press, 1999.

Hartog, Hendrik. *Man and Wife in America: A History*. Cambridge: Harvard University Press, 2000.

Hasian, Marouf Arif, Jr. *The Rhetoric of Eugenics in Anglo-American Thought*. Athens: University of Georgia Press, 1996.

Hassell, B. D. *The Rhinelander Family in America*. New York: Privately printed, 1896.

Henri, Florette. *Black Migration: Movement North, 1900–1920*. New York: Anchor Press/Doubleday, 1975. Reprint, New York: Anchor Books, 1976.

Herskovits, Melville J. *The Anthropometry of the American Negro*. New York: Columbia University Press, 1930.

Higginbotham, Evelyn Brooks. *Righteous Discontent: The Women's Movement in the Black Baptist Church, 1880–1920*. Cambridge: Harvard University Press, 1993.

Higham, John. *Strangers in the Land: Patterns of American Nativism, 1860–1925*. 2d ed. New Brunswick, N.J.: Rutgers University Press, 1988.

Hodes, Martha. *White Women, Black Men: Illicit Sex in the Nineteenth-Century South*. New Haven: Yale University Press, 1997.

Hoganson, Kristine. *Fighting for American Manhood: How Gender Politics Provoked the*

Spanish-American and Philippine-American Wars. New Haven: Yale University Press, 1998.

Holt, Thomas C. *The Problem of Race in the Twenty-First Century*. Cambridge: Harvard University Press, 2000.

Homberger, Eric. *Mrs. Astor's New York: Money and Social Power in a Gilded Age*. New Haven: Yale University Press, 2002.

Huggins, Nathan Irvin. *Harlem Renaissance*. New York: Oxford University Press, 1971.

Hughes, T. W. *An Illustrated Treatise on the Law of Evidence*. Chicago, Ill.: Callaghan & Co. 1906.

Irwin, Will. *Highlights of Manhattan*. New York: The Century Co., 1927.

Jackson, Kenneth T. *Crabgrass Frontier: The Suburbanization of the United States*. New York: Oxford University Press, 1985.

———. *The Ku Klux Klan in the City, 1915–1930*. New York: Oxford University Press, 1967.

Jacobson, Matthew Frye. *Whiteness of a Different Color: European Immigrants and the Alchemy of Race*. Cambridge: Harvard University Press, 1998.

Jacobson, Paul H. In collaboration with Pauline F. Jacobson. *American Marriage and Divorce*. New York: Rinehart, 1959.

James, Henry. *Washington Square*. New York: Harper & Brothers, 1880.

James, Winston. *Holding Aloft the Banner of Ethiopia: Caribbean Radicalism in Early Twentieth-Century America*. London: Verso, 1998.

Janken, Kenneth R. *White: The Biography of Walter White, Mr. NAACP*. New York: New Press, 2003.

Jewell, K. Sue. *From Mammy to Miss America and Beyond: Cultural Images and the Shaping of U.S. Social Policy*. New York: Routledge, 1993.

Johnson, James Weldon. *Black Manhattan*. New York: Alfred A. Knopf, 1930. Reprint, New York: Da Capo Press, 1991.

Johnson, Walter. *Soul by Soul: Life Inside the Antebellum Slave Market*. Cambridge: Harvard University Press, 1999.

Jones, Jacqueline. *Labor of Love, Labor of Sorrow: Black Women, Work, and the Family from Slavery to the Present*. New York: Basic Books, 1985.

Jones, William H. *Recreation and Amusement Among Negroes in Washington, D.C.: A Sociological Analysis of the Negro in an American Environment*. 1927. Reprint, Westport, Conn.: Negro Universities Press, 1970.

Jordan, Winthrop. *White Over Black: American Attitudes Toward the Negro, 1550–1812*. Chapel Hill: University of North Carolina Press, 1968. Reprint, New York: W. W. Norton, 1977.

Kassanoff, Jennie A. *Edith Wharton and the Politics of Race*. Cambridge: Cambridge University Press, 2004.

Katzman, David M. *Seven Days a Week: Women and Domestic Service in Industrializing America*. New York: Oxford University Press, 1978.

Kennedy, Randall. *Interracial Intimacies: Sex, Marriage, Identity, and Adoption.* New York. Pantheon Books, 2003.

Kessler-Harris, Alice. *Out to Work: A History of Wage-Earning Women in the United States.* New York: Oxford University Press, 1982.

Kessner, Thomas. *Capital City: New York City and the Men Behind America's Rise to Economic Dominance, 1860–1900.* New York: Simon and Schuster, 2003.

Kevles, Daniel J. *In the Name of Eugenics: Genetics and the Uses of Human Heredity.* New York: Alfred A. Knopf, 1985. Reprint, Cambridge: Harvard University Press, 1995.

Kisseloff, Jeff. *You Must Remember This: An Oral History of Manhattan from the 1890s to World War II.* New York: Harcourt, Brace, 1989.

Klarman, Michael J. *From Jim Crow to Civil Rights: The Supreme Court and the Struggle for Racial Equality.* Cambridge: Harvard University Press, 2004.

Kornweibel, Theodore. *No Crystal Stair: Black Life and the Messenger, 1917–1928.* Westport, Conn.: Greenwood Press, 1975.

Kusmer, Kenneth L. *A Ghetto Takes Shape: Black Cleveland, 1870–1930.* Urbana: University of Illinois Press, 1978.

Kyvig, David E. *Daily Life in the United States, 1920–1940: How Americans Lived Through the "Roaring Twenties" and the Great Depression.* Chicago: Ivan R. Dee, 2004.

Larsen, Nella. *Passing.* In *An Intimation of Things Distant: The Collected Fiction of Nella Larsen,* edited by Charles L. Larson. New York: Anchor Books, 1992.

Larson, Edward J. *Sex, Race, and Science: Eugenics in the Deep South.* Baltimore: Johns Hopkins University Press, 1995.

——. *Summer for the Gods: The Scopes Trial and America's Continuing Debate Over Science and Religion.* New York: Basic Books, 1997.

Latham, Angela J. *Posing a Threat: Flappers, Chorus Girls, and Other Brazen Performers of the American 1920s.* Hanover, N.H.: University Press of New England for Wesleyan University Press, 2000.

Lears, Jackson. *No Place of Grace: Antimodernism and the Transformation of American Culture, 1880–1920.* New York: Pantheon Books, 1981.

Lee, Hermione. *Edith Wharton.* New York: Alfred A. Knopf, 2007.

Lee, J. J., and Marion R. Casey, eds. *Making the Irish American: History and Heritage of the Irish in the United States.* New York: New York University Press, 2006.

Lenkevich, George. *New York City: A Short History.* New York: New York University Press, 2002.

Lewis, David Levering. *W. E. B. DuBois: The Fight For Equality and the American Century, 1919–1963.* New York: Henry Holt, 2000.

——. *W. E. B. DuBois: Biography of a Race.* New York: Henry Holt, 1993.

——. *When Harlem Was in Vogue.* New York: Alfred A. Knopf, 1981. Reprint, New York: Oxford University Press, 1989.

Lewis, David Levering, and Deborah Willis. *A Small Nation of People: W. E. B. Du Bois and African American Portraits of Progress*. New York: Amistad, 2003.

Lewis, Earl, and Heidi Ardizzone. *Love on Trial*. New York: W. W. Norton, 2001.

Livingston, James. *Origins of the Federal Reserve System: Money, Class, and Corporate Capitalism, 1890–1913*. Ithaca, N.Y.: Cornell University Press, 1986.

Locke, Alain, ed. *The New Negro*. New York: Albert and Charles Boni, 1925. Reprint, New York: Atheneum, 1983.

Lorimer, Douglas A. *Colour, Class, and the Victorians: English Attitudes to the Negro in the Mid-Nineteenth Century*. New York: Holmes & Meier, 1978.

Lundberg, George A., Mirra Komarovsky, and Mary Alice McInerny. *Leisure: A Suburban Study*. New York: Columbia University Press, 1934.

Lynd, Robert S., and Helen Merrell Lynd. *Middletown: A Study in Contemporary Culture*. New York: Harcourt, Brace and Co., 1929.

Mackenzie, George Norbury, ed. *Colonial Families of the United States of America, in Which Is Given the History, Genealogy and Armorial Bearings of Colonial Families Who Settled in the American Colonies*. New York: The Grafton Press, 1907.

Mallen, Frank. *Sauce for the Gander*. White Plains, N.Y.: Baldwin Books, 1954.

Mangum, Charles S., Jr. *The Legal Status of the Negro*. Chapel Hill: University of North Carolina Press, 1940. Reprint, New York: Johnson Reprint, 1970.

Marks, Carole. *Farewell—We're Good and Gone: The Great Black Migration*. Bloomington: Indiana University Press, 1989.

Martin, Tony. *Race First: The Ideological and Organizational Struggles of Marcus Garvey and the Universal Negro Improvement Association*. Dover, Mass.: Majority Press, 1976.

May, Elaine Tyler. *Great Expectations: Marriage and Divorce in Post-Victorian America*. Chicago: University of Chicago Press, 1980.

May, Geoffrey. *Marriage Laws and Decisions in the United States: A Manual*. New York: Russell Sage Foundation, 1929.

McGivena, Leo E. *The News: The First Fifty Years of New York's Picture Newspaper*. New York: News Syndicate Co., 1969.

Melody, M. E., and Linda M. Peterson. *Teaching America About Sex: Marriage Guides and Sex Manuals from the Late Victorians to Dr. Ruth*. New York: New York University Press, 1999.

Mencke, John G. *Mulattoes and Race Mixture: American Attitudes and Images, 1865–1918*. Ann Arbor, Mich.: UMI Research Press, 1979.

Meyer, Stephen Grant. *As Long As They Don't Move Next Door: Segregation and Racial Conflict in American Neighborhoods*. Lanham, Md.: Rowman and Littlefield, 2000.

Meyerowitz, Joanne. *Women Adrift: Independent Wage Earners in Chicago, 1880–1930*. Chicago: University of Chicago Press, 1988.

Michaels, Walter Benn. *Our America: Nativism, Modernism, and Pluralism*. Durham, N.C.: Duke University Press, 1995.

Mohr, James C. *Abortion in America: The Origins and Evolution of National Policy*. New York: Oxford University Press, 1978.

Montgomery, Maureen. *Displaying Women: Spectacles of Leisure in Edith Wharton's New York*. New York: Routledge, 1998.

———. *"Gilded Prostitution": Status, Money, and Transatlantic Marriages, 1870–1914*. London: Routledge, 1989.

Morgan, Edmund. *American Slavery, American Freedom: The Ordeal of Colonial Virginia*. New York: W. W. Norton, 1975.

Mumford, Kevin J. *Interzones: Black/White Sex Districts in Chicago and New York in the Early Twentieth Century*. New York: Columbia University Press, 1997.

Myrdal, Gunnar. *An American Dilemma: The Negro Problem and Modern Democracy*. New York: Harper & Brothers, 1944.

Nasaw, David. *The Chief: The Life of William Randolph Hearst*. Boston: Houghton Mifflin, 2000.

———. *Going Out: The Rise and Fall of Public Amusements*. New York: Basic Books, 1993.

Nelson, William E. *The Legalist Reformation: Law, Politics, and Ideology in New York, 1920–1980*. Chapel Hill: University of North Carolina Press, 2001.

Ngai, Mae M. *Impossible Subjects: Illegal Aliens and the Making of Modern America*. Princeton, N.J.: Princeton University Press, 2004.

New Rochelle Chamber of Commerce. *New Rochelle: The City of the Huguenots*. New Rochelle, N.Y.: The Knickerbocker Press, 1926.

Nobles, Melissa. *Shades of Citizenship: Race and the Census in Modern Politics*. Palo Alto, Calif.: Stanford University Press, 2000.

Omi, Michael, and Howard Winant. *Racial Formation in the United States: From the 1960s to the 1980s*. New York: Routledge, 1986.

Orvell, Miles. *The Real Thing: Imitation and Authenticity in American Culture, 1880–1940*. Chapel Hill: University of North Carolina Press, 1989.

Osofsky, Gilbert. *Harlem, The Making of a Ghetto: Negro New York, 1890–1930*. 2d ed. New York: Harper & Row, 1968. Reprint, New York: Harper Torchbooks, 1971.

Painter, Nell Irvin. *Standing at Armageddon: The United States, 1877–1919*. New York: W. W. Norton, 1987.

Palmer, Phyllis. *Domesticity and Dirt: Housewives and Domestic Servants in the United States, 1920–1945*. Philadelphia: Temple University Press, 1989.

Peiss, Kathy. *Hope in a Jar: The Making of America's Beauty Culture*. New York: Henry Holt, 1998.

Rafter, Nicole Hahn, ed. *White Trash: The Eugenic Family Studies, 1877–1919*. Boston: Northeastern University Press, 1988.

Read, Harlan. *The Abolition of Inheritance*. New York: MacMillan, 1919.

Reilly, Philip R. *The Surgical Solution: A History of Involuntary Sterilization in the United States*. Baltimore: Johns Hopkins University Press, 1991.

Reuter, Edward B. *The American Race Problem: A Study of the Negro*. Rev. ed. New York: Thomas Y. Crowell, 1927. Reprint, New York: Thomas Y. Crowell, 1970.

———. *The Mulatto in the United States: Including a Study of the Role of the Mixed-Blood Races Throughout the World*. 1918. Reprint, New York: Johnson Reprint Co., 1970.

———. *Race Mixture: Studies in Intermarriage and Miscegenation*. New York: McGraw-Hill, 1931.

Reynolds, Cuyler. *Genealogical and Family History of Southern New York and the Hudson River Valley*. Vol. 1. New York: Lewis Historical Publishing Company, 1914.

Rhinelander, John B. *One Branch of the Rhinelanders in the USA: From 18th Century German Rotgerbers to 19th Century Old New Yorkers to 20th Century Dispersed Americans*. N.p., 2000.

Richmond, Mary E., and Fred S. Hall. *Marriage and the State: Based Upon Field Studies of the Present Day Administration of Marriage Laws in the United States*. New York: Russell Sage Foundation, 1929.

Roediger, David. *Colored White: Transcending the Racial Past*. Berkeley: University of California Press, 2002.

———. *The Wages of Whiteness: Race and the Making of the American Working Class*. London: Verso, 1991.

———. *Working Toward Whiteness: How America's Immigrants Became White*. New York: Basic Books, 2005.

Romano, Renee. *Race Mixing: Black-White Intermarriage in Postwar America*. Cambridge: Harvard University Press, 2003.

Rosenwaike, Ira. *Population History of New York City*. Syracuse, N.Y.: Syracuse University Press, 1972.

Ross, Ishbel. *Ladies of the Press: The Story of Women in Journalism by an Insider*. New York: Harper & Brothers, 1936.

Ross, Steven. *Working-Class Hollywood: Silent Film and the Shaping of Class in America*. Princeton, N.J.: Princeton University Press, 1998.

Roth, Philip. *The Human Stain*. Boston: Houghton Mifflin, 2000.

Rothman, Ellen K. *Hands and Hearts: A History of Courtship in America*. New York: Basic Books, 1984.

Russell, Frances. *The Shadow of Blooming Grove: Warren G. Harding in His Times*. New York: McGraw-Hill, 1968.

Russell, Sylvester. *The Amalgamation of America: Normal Solution of the Color and Inter-Marriage Problem*. Chicago: Sylvester Russell Book Concern, 1920.

Sacks, Marcy. *Before Harlem: The Black Experience in New York City Before World War I*. Philadelphia: University of Pennsylvania Press, 2006.

Scanlon, Jennifer. *Inarticulate Longings: The Ladies' Home Journal, Gender, and the Promises of Consumer Culture*. New York: Routledge, 1995.

Schouler, James. *A Treatise on the Law of Domestic Relations*, 6th ed., students edition. Edited by Arthur W. Blakemore. Albany, N.Y.: Matthew Bender and Co., 1921.

———. *A Treatise on the Law of Husband and Wife*. Boston: Little, Brown, 1882.

Schudson, Michael. *The Power of News*. Cambridge: Harvard University Press, 1995.

Selden, Steven. *Inheriting Shame: The Story of Eugenics and Racism in America*. New York: Teachers College Press, 1999.

Shamas, Carole, Marylynn Salmon, and Michel Dahlin. *Inheritance in America from Colonial Times to the Present*. New Brunswick, N.J.: Rutgers University Press, 1987.

Sickels, Robert J. *Race, Marriage, and the Law*. Albuquerque: University of New Mexico Press, 1972.

Sklar, Martin J. *The Corporate Reconstruction of American Capitalism, 1890–1916: The Market, the Law, and Politics*. New York: Cambridge University Press, 1988.

Smith, Henry Townsend. *Westchester County in History*. White Plains, N.Y.: H. T. Smith, 1912.

Smith, J. Douglas. *Managing White Supremacy: Race, Politics, and Citizenship in Jim Crow Virginia*. Chapel Hill: University of North Carolina Press, 2002.

Smith, Shawn Michelle. *American Archives: Gender, Race, and Class in Visual Culture*. Princeton, N.J.: Princeton University Press, 1999.

———. *Photography on the Color Line: W. E. B. Du Bois, Race, and Visual Culture*. Durham, N.C.: Duke University Press, 2004.

Sollors, Werner. *Neither Black nor White yet Both: Thematic Explorations of Interracial Literature*. New York: Oxford University Press, 1997.

St. Clair, Drake, and Horace R. Cayton. *Black Metropolis: A Study of Negro Life in a Northern City*. New York: Harcourt, Brace, 1945.

Stephenson, Gilbert. *Race Distinctions in American Law*. New York: D. Appleton and Company, 1910.

Stevens, John D. *Sensationalism and the New York Press*. New York: Columbia University Press, 1991.

Stoddard, Lothrop. *The Rising Tide of Color Against White-World Supremacy*. New York: Charles Scribner's Sons, 1920.

Stuart, Amanda Mackenzie. *Consuelo and Alva Vanderbilt: The Story of a Daughter and a Mother in the Gilded Age*. New York: Harper Collins, 2006.

Sugrue, Thomas J. *The Origins of the Urban Crisis: Race and Inequality in Postwar Detroit*. Princeton, N.J.: Princeton University Press, 1996.

Summers, Martin. *Manliness and Its Discontents: The Black Middle Class and the Transformations of Masculinity, 1900–1930*. Chapel Hill: University of North Carolina Press, 2004.

Tabili, Laura, *"We Ask for British Justice": Workers and Racial Difference in Late Imperial Britain*. Ithaca, N.Y.: Cornell University Press, 1994.

Tebbel, John. *The American Magazine: A Compact History*. New York: Hawthorn Books, 1969.

Theoharis, Jeanne, and Komozi Woodard, eds. *Freedom North: Black Freedom Struggles Outside the South, 1940–1980*. New York: Palgrave Macmillan, 2003.

Tone, Andrea. *Devices and Desires: A History of Contraceptives in America*. New York: Hill and Wang, 2001.

Trachtenberg, Alan. *Reading American Photographs: Images as History from Matthew Brady to Walker Evans*. New York: Hill and Wang, 1989.

Trotter, Joe William, Jr., ed. *The Great Migration in Historical Perspective: New Dimensions of Race, Class, and Gender*. Bloomington: Indiana University Press, 1991.

Tucker, William H. *The Funding of Scientific Racism: Wickliffe Draper and the Pioneer Fund*. Urbana: University of Illinois Press, 2002.

Tuttle, William M., Jr. *Race Riot: Chicago in the Red Summer of 1919*. New York: Atheneum, 1970.

Ullman, Sharon R. *Sex Seen: The Emergence of Modern Sexuality in America*. Berkeley: University of California Press, 1997.

Underkuffler, Laura. *The Idea of Property: Its Meaning and Power*. New York: Oxford University Press, 2003.

Van Rensselaer, May King, and Frederic Van de Water. *The Social Ladder*. New York: Henry Holt, 1924.

Van Vechten, Carl. *Nigger Heaven*. New York: Alfred A. Knopf, 1926. Reprint, New York: Harper Colophon, 1971.

Veblen, Thorstein. *The Theory of the Leisure Class*. 1899. Reprint, Boston: Houghton Mifflin, 1973.

Wallace-Sanders, Kimberly, ed. *Skin Deep, Spirit Strong: The Black Female Body in American Culture*. Ann Arbor: University of Michigan Press, 2002.

Wallenstein, Peter. *Tell the Court I Love My Wife: Race, Marriage, and Law: An American History*. New York: Palgrave MacMillan, 2002.

Watkins-Owens, Irma. *Blood Relations: Caribbean Immigrants and the Harlem Community, 1900–1930*. Bloomington: Indiana University Press, 1996.

Wecter, Dixon. *The Saga of American Society: A Record of Social Aspiration, 1607–1637*. New York: Charles Scribner's Sons, 1937.

Weems, Robert E., Jr. *Desegregating the Dollar: African American Consumerism in the Twentieth Century*. New York: New York University Press, 1998.

Wellman, Francis L. *The Art of Cross-Examination*. New York: Macmillan, 1924.

Wharton, Edith. *A Backward Glance*. New York: Charles Scribner's Sons, 1933. Reprint, 1962.

White, Deborah Gray. *Ar'n't I a Woman?: Female Slaves in the Plantation South*. New York: W. W. Norton, 1985.

———. *Too Heavy a Load: Black Women in Defense of Themselves, 1894–1994*. New York: W. W. Norton, 1999.

White, Kevin. *The First Sexual Revolution: The Emergence of Male Heterosexuality in Modern America*. New York: New York University Press, 1993.

White, Walter. *Flight.* New York: Alfred A. Knopf, 1926.

———. *A Man Called White: The Autobiography of Walter White.* New York: Viking Press, 1948.

Wiebe, Robert H. *The Search for Order, 1877–1920.* New York: Hill and Wang, 1967.

Wiegman, Robyn. *American Anatomies: Theorizing Race and Gender.* Durham, N.C.: Duke University Press, 1995.

Wiggam, Albert E. *The Fruit of the Family Tree.* Indianapolis, Ind.: Bobbs-Merrill, 1924.

———. *The New Decalogue of Science.* Garden City, N.Y.: Garden City Publishing Co., 1923.

Wigmore, John Henry. *A Treatise on the Anglo-American System of Evidence in Trials at Common Law: Including the Statutes and Judicial Decisions of all Jurisdictions of the United States and Canada.* 2nd ed. Boston: Little, Brown, 1923.

Wile, Ira S., and Mary Day Winn. *Marriage in the Modern Manner.* New York: Century Co., 1929.

Williams, Gregory. *Life on the Color Line: The True Story of a White Boy Who Discovered He Was Black.* New York: Dutton, 1995.

Williamson, Joel. *New People: Miscegenation and Mulattoes in the United States.* New York: Free Press, 1980. Reprint, Baton Rouge: Louisiana State University Press, 1995.

Willis, Deborah, ed. *Picturing Us: African American Identity in Photography.* New York: New Press, 1994.

Wolcott, Victoria W. *Remaking Respectability: African American Women in Interwar Detroit.* Chapel Hill: University of North Carolina Press, 2001.

Wright, Carroll D. *The History and Growth of the United States Census, Prepared for the Senate Committee on the Census.* Washington, D.C.: Government Printing Office, 1900. Reprint, New York: Johnson Reprint Corporation, 1966.

Young, Robert J. C. *Colonial Desire: Hybridity in Theory, Culture and Race.* London: Routledge, 1995.

DISSERTATIONS AND THESES

Bingmann, Melissa. "Prep School Cowboys: The Education of the Elite at Western Ranch Schools." Ph.D. diss., Arizona State University, 2003.

Duncan, Gerald Hannibal. "The Changing Race Relationship in the Border and Northern States." Ph.D. diss., University of Pennsylvania, 1922.

Index

Page numbers in italics indicate illustrations.

Abortion, 10, 19, 85, 204, 210
Adams, Cyrus Fields, 98
African Americans: census coding of, 54; changing status of, 241; civil rights suits brought by, 49–50; cultural vogue of, 42, 52–53, 58, 84, 163, 186, 201, 300 (n. 67), 335 (n. 4); definitions of, 94–97, 105; demeaning stereotypes of, 80–82, 121, 142, 181, 191, 193, 204–5, 223; as domestic servants, 33, 75, 125, 134, 245; as immigrants from Caribbean, 25, 42, 43, 48; inheritance rights and, 169; limited options for, 93, 100, 157; migration to North of (*see* Great Migration); in New York, 25, 42–46, 48, 49, 52, 100, 241; "one-drop" rule and, 95, 105, 185, 186, 187, 217, 239–40, 321 (n. 4); photographic images of, 191, 193; physical typology and, 189–90, 203; racial identification of, 56, 199, 243–45; race mixing and, 1, 2, 42, 55–56, 57, 159; racial line blurring and, 90, 102–3, 200; as racist target, 44, 48–52; Rhinelander trial verdict and, 233–34; violence against, 48, 50, 51, 116, 157, 335 (n. 10); women's sexual vulnerability and, 146, 233–34. *See also* Passing

Afro-American (newspaper), 236
Agassiz, Louis, 190–91
Alabama, 105, 199
All God's Chillun Got Wings (O'Neill), 163, 333 (n. 67)
Amalgamation of America, The (Russell), 98–99
American Civil Liberties Union, 243
American Dilemma, The (Myrdal), 244
American Mercury, 53, 130, 300 (n. 67)
American Museum of Natural History, 46
"American Negro" (Herskovits), 189

American Race Problem, The (Reuter), 100
Amsterdam News, 7–8, 105, 157, 160, 164–65, 233–34; on Rhinelander marriage, 131, 139; on *Sweet* case, 242
Anglo-Saxon Clubs of America, 104–5
Annulment: divorce differentiated from, 167; "essence of marriage" rule and, 175; fraud grounds for, 4–6, 12, 35–38, 58, 63, 80, 157, 160–61, 165, 166, 169, 170–75, 177–80, 227; insanity grounds for, 113–14, 122; limited application of, 167; major nineteenth-century case of, 173–75; New York State and, 4–5, 113, 160, 169–72, 175–80, 235–36, 314 (n. 41), 316 (n. 53), 317 (nn. 70, 71, 72); property rights and, 168, 237, 242, 248, 252; state laws for, 166, 172–73. *See also* Rhinelander trial
Anthropometric measurements, 189, 190
Antimiscegenation laws, 4, 104, 146–47, 158–59, 164–66, 165, 178, 181, 210; African American opponents of, 233; New York and, 162, 221, 236; race determinations and, 95–96, 199, 217
Appearance (play), 98
Ardizzone, Heidi, 255 (n. 7)
Arizona, 21–22, 68, 165
Aryan race, 36, 188, 200–201, 231
Astor family, 117–18

"Bad blood" concept, 187
Bagnall, Robert, 44
Baker, Ray Stannard, 89, 93, 96–97
Baldwin, Louis Fremont, 100–101, 286 (n. 1)
Bara, Theda, 68
Beckert, Sven, 117, 294 (nn. 9, 14)
Berlin, Irving, 54, 130

"Beyond Identity" (Brubaker and Cooper), 286 (n. 5)
Biology vs. culture debate, 186–87
Birth certificates, 65, 77, 90, 105, 110, 217–18
Birth control. *See* Contraception
Black and tan cabarets, 163, 223, 330 (n. 37)
Black Boy (play), 104
"Black-face" performers, 331 (n. 42)
Black's Law Dictionary, 239
Blake, Eubie, 17
Blease, Coleman, 236
"Blood as race" metaphor. *See* Blood-based racial identity
Blood-based racial identity, 117, 130–31, 185–87, 189, 192, 198, 204, 208–9, 217, 225, 227, 231, 239–40, 243, 321 (n. 4); state laws and, 95–96, 104–5
Bloomingdale Insane Asylum, 219–20
"Blue blood" concept, 127, 187
Boas, Franz, 44–45, 56, 166, 186, 301–2 (n. 79)
Bowers, Spotswood, 20, 31, 246, 248
Bradley Martin Ball (1897), 123
Breach of promise suits, 138, 140
Brisbane, Arthur, 5, 160–61
"Bronze Age" (1920s), 52, 55
Brooks, Emily Jones (Alice's sister), 14, 15, 17, 25, 26, 28, 39, 60, 62, 68, 76, 188, 222, 224, 327 (n. 67); birth certificate of, 65, 217–18; "colored" identification of, 31, 34, 73, 189, 209–10, 211, 216, 226; marriage of, 108, 110
Brooks, Robert (Alice's brother-in-law), 17, 26, 28, 60, 62, 76, 124, 209, 222; "colored" identification of, 31–32, 34, 68, 73, 108, 110, 208, 227
Brooks, Roberta (Alice's niece), 208, 209, 339 (n. 37)
Broun, Heywood, 99

374 : INDEX

"Brown beauty" chorus line, 52, 55
Brubaker, Rogers, 286 (n. 5)
Buchanan, George, 182
Buchanan v. Warley (1917), 50

Cabarets, 81, 83, 84, 129, 130, 163, 281 (n. 32)
Café Society, 129
California, 20, 21; annulment in, 166, 315 (n. 42), 316 (n. 53)
Capitalism, 115, 134–35
Carby, Hazel, 82
Caribbean area. *See* West Indies
Carmody's New York Practice, 157
Carter, Elmer A., 99
Catholics, 44, 114, 115, 119
Caucasians, 47, 102, 125, 190, 200–201, 224, 225, 231
Census (N.Y.S.), 33, 90
Census (U.S.): passing and, 98, 104, 106; racial categories and, 54, 105–8, 244; urbanization and, 45
Century Magazine, 89–90, 101
Chaperones, 119
Chapman, Gerald, 3
Chesnutt, Charles W., 96
Chicago, 48, 52, 100, 103, 241; race riot (1919), 157
Chicago Defender, 43, 125, 166, 180
Chidester, Ross, 211–12
Chinese physical appearance, 71, 187, 188, 189, 218
Chipman v. Johnston (Mass., 1921), 317 (n. 69)
Citizenship. *See* Naturalization
Civil rights, 7, 49–51, 146
Civil War, 6, 54, 116
Clark, L. Pierce, 14, 78, 259–60 (n. 12)
Class. *See* Elite; Social class
Class conflict, 3, 115–17, 121, 124
Clubs and societies, 118

Cockburn, Joshua and Pauline, 243–45
Colored American Magazine, 98, 164
Color line. *See* Passing
Columbia College School of Law, 61
Columbia University, 13, 44, 162
Commercial contracts, 173, 177
"Common knowledge" racial theory, 199–201
"Common sense" notions, 71–72, 229, 231, 244, 245
Companionate marriage, 157–58
Competitive capitalism, 115
Composograph, 204, 205
Condoms, 144, 204
Consumer culture, 3, 9, 115, 118, 129, 131, 241, 242
Contraception, 140, 144, 204
Contract law, 173, 174–77
Cooper, Frederick, 286 (n. 5)
Corporate capitalism, 115, 135
Corrigan v. Buckley (1926), 51
Courtney, Susan, 322 (n. 10)
Court of Appeals, New York, 175–77, 238, 250, 255 (n. 7), 311 (n. 16)
Craft, Ellen, 91–92
Crane, Frederick E., 250
"Crimes against nature," 155
Crisis (journal), 50, 53, 103, 112, 146, 162, 184, 234, 236
"Crossing the Color Line" (Johnson), 89
Cubans, 224, 225
Culture, race and, 186–90
Current History, 55, 56–57
Current Opinion, 98
Curtis, George M., 122

Dancing, 42, 53, 81, 84
Darrow, Clarence, 51, 243
Dating practices, 83–84, 138, 140
Davenport, Charles, 47, 55, 56, 191–92, 193

Davis, Adrienne, 168–69
Davis, Lee Parsons, 60–63, 67, 74, 77–79, 81, 224, 228; Alice's baring of body and, 181, 195–99, 201–4, 208, 219, 235; background and style of, 61–62; basic argument of, 38–39, 65, 192, 195–99, 226; closing statement of, 214–20; cross-examination of Leonard by, 111, 135–48, 155–56, 184, 185, 195, 203, 204, 223; defense strategy of, 70–71, 132, 133–34, 142, 150–54, 187–88, 209, 231; defense witnesses and, 207–12; generation gap and, 77, 83–84, 134, 138, 140, 216; jury selection and, 62–63; mystery letters and, 145, 149, 150–56, 204, 223; opening statement of, 70–77, 90, 133, 192; plaintiff's case and, 65, 66, 77, 79, 82–83, 85, 110–11, 205–7; real evidence and, 197–98; restrictive covenant ruling by, 244–45; three pre-closing motions of, 329 (n. 5); trial persona of, 77; visibility of race focus of, 71–72, 180–81, 185–89, 192, 195–99, 209, 216, 218–20, 224–27, 231, 244, 245; witnesses of, 207–12, 215, 222, 226
Day, Caroline Bond, 191–93
Deception, 2, 147, 148, 217, 219, 229; marital, 40, 173, 174, 175, 177–78, 208; about sexual intent vs. color, 138, 140. *See also* Fraud; Passing
Degeneracy, 67, 68, 79, 132, 151–56, 223
D'Emilio, John, 155
Depression, economic, 116, 123
Despres, Julie, 79, 259 (n. 12)
Detroit, 241, 242; race violence (1925), 51, 157
Dijkstra, Bram, 68
DiLorenzo, Johanna and Gregorio, 175, 176, 177

DiLorenzo v. DiLorenzo (N.Y., 1903), 175–76, 177, 178, 317 (nn. 71, 72)
Divorce, 128; annulment vs., 167; in Nevada, 245, 247, 248, 249–50, 277 (n. 1); New York's narrow grounds for, 4, 160–61, 166–67, 177, 238, 314 (n. 41); rising rate of, 157, 158
Domestic service: African Americans as, 33, 90, 125, 134, 159; Irish immigrants as, 113, 114, 121, 125; sexual exploitation of, 133–34, 141, 220
Domingo, W. A., 48
Dominguez, Virginia, 94
Double standard, 140
Douglas, Ann, 41, 300 (n. 68)
Dower right, 168, 242, 246, 247, 248, 255 (n. 7), 256 (n. 11)
Draft Riot of 1863 (N.Y.C.), 116
Drake, John, 122
DuBois, W. E. B., 6, 10, 43, 51, 191, 193; "blood as race" and, 95; on passing, 108; on Rhinelander trial, 112, 142, 234, 235, 237, 241, 242
Dwyer, Francis and Clara, 166

Eastern European immigrants, 57, 102, 125
Economic opportunity, 41–42, 100–101, 159, 240, 241, 242
Elite, 114–32; degeneracy and, 132, 151–52, 156, 223; exclusivity of, 119–24, 127–28, 132, 214, 237; internal distinctions among, 116, 117, 131; property rights of, 168, 241, 248; seduction of servants by, 133–34, 137, 141, 142, 144, 146, 220; social change and, 115, 124, 129–30; unsuitable marriages and, 111, 112–16, 119, 123–25, 127, 128, 132, 282 (n. 46); whiteness as intrinsic to, 123, 127, 214, 237; women's role and, 118, 119–20

England, 15, 26, 32, 42, 65–66, 68, 90, 189, 206; annulment law and, 167; racial views in, 73, 210–11, 235
Episcopal Church, 18, 32, 114
"Essence of marriage" rule, 175
"Ethnic whites," 102, 125, 190
Etiquette (Post), 128
Eugenics, 41, 45–48, 50, 51, 54–56, 58, 62, 170, 171, 182, 183, 219–20; antimiscegenation laws and, 164; Boas rebuttal to, 301–2 (n. 79); composograph and, 204; fears of, 67, 132; on mulatto inferiority, 56; photographic documentation and, 191; physical appearance theories of, 69; "blood as race" belief of, 95; race mixture studies of, 191–93; racial definition laws and, 104; U.S. high point of, 164. *See also* Racial purity
Eugenics Research Association, 47
European nobility, 119–20
Evidence, laws of, 197–98

Fauset, Jessie, 103
Feeblemindedness, 67, 79, 132, 223, 236, 280 (n. 23)
Feeney, D. J., 233
Ferber, Edna, 103
Ferrall, Frank, 165
Fessenden, Franklin G., 167, 172, 174
Fields, Barbara, 286–87 (n. 5)
Fisk v. Fisk (N.Y.S., 1896), 317 (n. 70)
Fitzgerald, F. Scott, 46, 104
Flaming Youth (film), 137
Flight (White), 103
Following the Color Line (Baker), 89, 96–97
Fool There Was, A (film), 68
Four Hundred, 117–18, 119–20, 125, 129, 131, 131–32
Fourteenth Amendment, 243
Fraud: as annulment grounds (*see under* Annulment); definitions of marital, 172–73, 177–78; male seduction tactics and, 138; racial misrepresentation as, 12, 35, 36, 39, 68, 70, 160–61, 165, 166, 170–71, 175, 177, 178, 180–81, 227, 240; test of "material," 176
Freedman, Estelle, 155
Free-love movement, 155
"French View of the Rhinelanders, The" (article), 184
From Negro to Caucasian (Baldwin), 100–101
Front-page girls, 29

Galton, Francis, 204
Garvey, Marcus, 25, 33, 43, 56, 330 (n. 32), 335 (n. 12)
Gatewood, Willard, 95, 166
Genealogy, 73, 95, 113, 118–19, 192, 321 (n. 4)
Generation gap, 77, 81, 83–84, 134, 138, 140, 216
Gobineau, Count de, 44
Goddard, Henry, 281 (n. 32)
Gold-digger image, 280 (n. 27)
Gould, Jay, 117, 130
Grant, Madison: antimiscegenation laws and, 164; George Jones's resemblance to, 62; immigration restriction and, 47, 48; pure blood belief of, 55, 104, 187, 200, 214; race mixing fears of, 41, 44, 45, 50, 54, 57, 103, 240, 301–2 (n. 79); racial classifications of, 46–47
Great Britain. *See* England
Great Gatsby, The (Fitzgerald), 46, 104
Great Migration, 1, 3, 7, 42, 43, 48, 49, 51, 52; effects in North of, 82, 185–86, 236, 240–42; interracial marriage fears and, 161, 162; passing and, 98, 99, 100, 101; social implications of, 99, 239–42, 252

Grey, Edgar, 233–34
Gross, Ariela, 92
Grossberg, Michael, 171, 239
Guggenheim, Natalie, 336 (n. 17)

Hair (as racial indicator), 193
Half-Century Magazine, 103
Hammerstein, Oscar, 103–4
Harding, Warren G., 97, 124
Harlem, 50, 52, 233–34
Harlem Renaissance, 52, 103
Harlem slang, 186, 201
Harper's Magazine, 82, 158
Harper's Weekly, 121
Harris, Cheryl, 256 (n. 13), 287 (n. 14), 290 (n. 40)
Hartigan, John, 269–70 (n. 5)
Harvard Law Review, 167
Harvard University, 14, 101, 123; race studies, 190–91, 192
Hassell, B. D., 119
Hays, Arthur Garfield, 243, 244–45
Hearst, William Randolph, 5, 24, 31, 160
Heredity, 45, 67, 95, 132, 170, 187. *See also* Blood-based racial identity
Hernandez v. Robles (N.Y., 2006), 311 (n. 16), 320 (n. 86)
Herskovits, Melville, 56–57, 187, 188, 189–90, 313 (n. 30), 322–23 (nn. 14, 15, 16)
Hill, Joseph, 107
Hinkle, Beatrice M., 82, 158
Holland, Eddie, 262 (n. 34)
Hooton, E. A., 189, 191, 192
Hotel Marie-Antoinette, 18–19, 20, 23, 34, 41, 67, 84–85, 86, 143, 150–51, 152, 156, 190, 202, 212, 218, 224
House Behind the Cedars, The (Chesnutt), 96
Howard University, 102, 242
Huguenots, 13, 16, 65, 69, 72, 218

Hurst, Fannie, 104
Hurston, Zora, 332 (n. 63)

Imitation of Life (film), 104
Immigration, 3, 14, 52, 67, 113–16, 124, 125, 135, 240; naturalization and, 188, 199, 200; race and, 25, 26, 29, 31, 33, 41–48, 102–4, 185, 239; restrictions on, 5, 42, 47–48, 53, 57, 71, 236
India, 36, 43, 188, 200–201, 231
Insanity, 113–14, 116, 121–22, 132, 172
Intelligence tests, 46
Interracial marriage, 54, 157; African American views of, 233–34, 312–13 (n. 27), 330 (n. 32); annulment to remove taint of, 167; blood as race theory and, 117; British acceptance of, 210–11; consensual, 127, 146–47; deception and, 160, 170, 175; fears about, 46, 93–94, 111, 125, 128, 140, 161–64, 170, 171, 178, 182–83, 214, 216–17, 221–23, 224, 226, 242–43; message of Rhinelander trial and, 147, 151, 221, 222–23, 226, 227, 234, 235–36, 242, 252; New York law and, 4, 5, 29, 146, 160–61, 177, 178, 180, 227, 236; numbers of, 164, 339–40 (n. 40); offspring of, 93–94, 164, 180, 183, 189, 214, 221; passing and, 98, 164–65; proposed national ban on, 236; public opinion against, 77, 162–63, 214, 231, 233; social barrier erosion and, 130; U.S. Supreme Court legalization of, 252. *See also* Antimiscegenation laws
Irish immigrants, 113, 114, 115, 116, 119, 121, 125
Italian immigrants, 42, 53, 57, 102, 125

Jackson, William, 49
Jacobs, Leon, 34, 35, 60, 61, 63, 64, 83,

178, 206, 209, 211, 218, 228; Alice's racial identity and, 109–10; as "brains" behind trial, 215; as defense hostile witness, 207–8; Rhinelander divorce decree and, 250
Jacobson, Matthew, 190
James, Henry, 13
Japanese physical appearance, 200
Jazz, 42, 53, 84, 163, 201
"Jazz journalism," 24
Jews, 44, 50, 54, 130, 243, 327 (n. 67)
Jezebel image, 55, 80, 81, 85, 223, 275–76 (n. 57)
Jim Crow, 43, 49, 51, 191
Johnson, Albert, 47
Johnson, Caleb, 89, 100, 101
Johnson, Carroll, 49
Johnson, Charles, 42, 98
Johnson, Jack, 162
Johnson, James Weldon, 52
Johnson, Walter, 92
Johnson-Reed Act (1924), 47–48, 57
Johnstown (Pa.) race riot, 50
Jolson, Al, 331 (n. 42)
Jones, Alice Beatrice (Alice Rhinelander), 2, 30, 188, 230, 232; alimony award to, 238, 245–46, 248; background of, 9–10, 14–15, 42, 75, 90; baring of body in court by, 2, 11–12, 181, 195–99, 201–4, 205, 207, 208, 219, 225, 227, 235; birth certificate of, 65, 110, 217–18; birth of, 14–15; charge of concealment of "colored blood" against, 108–11, 208–9; death and burial of, 251; domestic service jobs of, 9, 15, 20–21, 25, 28, 33, 75, 90, 125, 134; fraud complaint served to, 35; fraud exoneration of, 229; investigative reporters and, 32–33; jealousy ploys of, 21, 22–23, 85–86, 145, 182, 216; later life of, 251; lawsuits against Rhinelanders of, 245–46, 249; letters of (*see* Letters); makeup use and, 203, 231; physical appearance of, 15, 26, 27–28, 31, 36, 70, 90, 207, 219, 225, 231; post-trial interview of, 231; press contradictory descriptions of, 194; Pyrrhic victory for, 235; racial ambiguity of, 70–71, 77, 240; racial categorization of, 240–41; racial issues and, 1, 6, 11, 26–28, 32–34, 38, 39, 41, 54, 57, 58, 62, 65, 66, 70, 71, 75, 76, 79, 81, 107–11, 125, 186–90, 208, 217, 219, 220, 237, 248; renunciation of Rhinelander name by, 247–48, 250–51; Rhinelander settlement with, 246–51, 252; seductress depiction of, 67–68, 69, 71, 72, 80–82, 85–86, 88, 133, 137, 142, 181–82, 204, 216, 223; separation suit filed by, 245; sexual expertise of, 153; skin color of, 12, 26, 29, 36, 143, 194, 195–96, 202–4, 206, 207, 212, 226; *Social Register* and, 127–28; survivors of, 339 (n. 37); "white" self-identification of, 12, 26, 29, 31, 32, 35, 36, 39, 58, 63–64, 65, 66, 68, 71, 88, 89, 109, 140, 156, 178, 186, 195, 204, 205–7, 209, 217–19, 224. *See also* Rhinelander, Leonard and Alice; Rhinelander trial
Jones, Elizabeth (mother), 15, 16, 17, 35, 36, 60, 62, 108, 224, 230; Alice's baring of body and, 201–2, 204, 212; background of, 14, 25, 26, 32, 42, 73, 210; as defense witness, 210–11, 212; Leonard's deception of, 147, 148; white identity of, 37, 54, 75, 107, 186, 187, 188, 189, 210, 211, 227; white oldest daughter of, 65, 73, 76, 215, 235
Jones, Emily (sister). *See* Brooks, Emily Jones

INDEX : 379

Jones, Eugene Kinkle, 43
Jones, George (father), 17, 60, 62, 230; Alice's facial resemblance to, 231; background of, 14, 26, 32, 36, 37, 42, 66, 73, 90, 111, 189, 207, 210, 211; census designation of, 107–8; "colored" identity of, 24–26, 28, 29, 31, 32, 34, 43, 54, 65, 66, 73, 75, 143, 144, 148, 184–85, 187, 188–89, 207, 210, 211, 212, 215–16, 224, 227; occupations of, 15, 25, 26, 124; physical appearance of, 62, 102, 184–85, 194, 207, 216, 224–25
Jones, Grace (sister). *See* Miller, Grace Jones
Jones, Lucretia Rhinelander, 116
Jones family, 32, 34, 35, 60, 62, 80, *188*; Alice's death and, 251; ancestry of, 15, 36, 68, 72, 73, 77, 90, 108, 109, 110–11, 206, 210–11; census racial classifications of, 33, 107–8; daughters' birth certificates, 65; as Episcopalians, 32, 114; house of, 17, 31–32, 34, 35, 75, 251; Leonard's awareness of color of, 75–76, 133, 135–36, 148–49, 184–85, 189, 207, 227; Leonard's first meetings with, 80–81, 135–36; Leonard's testimony about, 108–11; Leonard's visits with, 17, 70, 87; passing charge against, 67, 68, 88–90, 108–11, 194, 195, 217, 224; as race-mixing example, 222; racial and social status of, 2, 3, 26, 27, 31, 32, 33, 58, 72–73, 75; racial self-identification of, 36, 125, 186, 208, 217–18; trial lawyers' characterizations of, 77, 80; trial outcome and, 228, 235
Jordan, George, 231, 233
Jordan, Winthrop, 91
Journal of Negro History, 164
Joyner, Susan, 49

Kansas City Emporia Gazette, 33
Keough, Richard E., 61
Kern, Jerome, 103–4
Kinsey, Alfred, 155
Kip family, 13, 23, 25
Kips Bay (N.Y.C.), 13
Kirby, Joe and Mayellen, 165
Kirksey, Thomas, 236–37
Klineberg, Otto, 244
Knickerbocker Greys, 14, 123
Knickerbockers, 116, 117, 131
Krafft-Ebing, Richard von, 154
Kreitler, Carl, 9, 15, 16, 135, 204, 210
Ku Klux Klan, 5, 32, 34, 35, 41, 58, 234, 335 (n. 10); against interracial marriage, 163, 236; revival of, 44, 51, 236

Labor strikes, 115, 117, 124
Labor unions, 52
Lapides v. Lapides (N.Y., 1930), 314 (n. 40)
Larsen, Nella, 59, 103, 108, 327 (n. 60)
Lawby, William, 110–11
Leroi, Armand Marie, 276 (n. 58)
Letters (*Rhinelander* case), 2, 8, 234; of Alice, 19, 67–68, 82–88, 89, 182, 218; couple's separations and, 20, 22; as defense evidence, 37, 145, 149, 150–56, 204, 223; early courtship period and, 17–18, 180–81; of Leonard, 138, 140–42, 145–46, 186; as plaintiff's evidence, 67–68, 82–88, 89, 218; prurient details in, 84–85, 86, 149, 150–56, 204, 223; public reaction to, 10
Lewis, Earl, 255 (n. 7)
Libel, 31
Libman v. Libman (N.Y., 1918), 314 (n. 40)
Literary Digest, 48, 52
Literary works, 134, 163; on passing, 2, 59, 96–97, 103–4, 108
Little, Arthur and Alma, 166

Louisiana, 313–14 (n. 36), 324 (n. 36)
Love blindness, 185
"Love Will Find a Way" (song), 17
Loving v. Virginia (1967), 252
Lynching, 48, 116, 157, 276 (n. 58)
Lynd, Robert and Helen Merrell, 137

Mackay, Clarence, 129
Mackay, Ellin, 54, 129–30, 281 (n. 32), 300 (n. 69)
Mackay, John, 300 (n. 69)
Malillo, Michael and Rita, 320 (n. 90)
Mangum, Charles, 165, 266 (n. 78)
Manhood, 134–35, 140, 146, 147
Markey, Morris, 213
Marks, Jonathan, 336 (n. 19)
Marriage: annulment's retroactive dissolution of, 167; blurring of color and social lines and, 53–54, 125–27; contract law and, 173, 174–77; deception about race and, 140, 160, 170, 175, 208; eugenics movement and, 46, 171; fraud definition in, 172–73, 177–78; free consent and, 176; male deceivers and, 138, 140; New York legal system and, 4, 63, 160–61; normative ideals of, 161, 165, 180; personal happiness vs. traditional objectives of, 158; procreation and, 164, 172, 180, 311 (n. 16); property interlinked with, 168; same-sex, 311 (n. 16), 320 (n. 86); scrutiny in 1920s of, 3, 157–58, 161; significance of Rhinelander verdict to, 214, 240–41, 252; state laws and, 170–71; voidable types of, 169; white elite and, 112–17, 119–20, 122–23, 124, 128; women as pursuers of, 82, 86. *See also* Annulment; Divorce; Interracial marriage
"Marriage and the Color Line" (cartoon), 126

Marriage licenses, 65, 77, 90, 162, 210, 224; racial purity laws and, 104, 164
Martin, Bradley and Cornelia, 123
Masculinity, 123, 140; manliness vs., 134; popular image of, 53, 148, 155–56
Massachusetts, 236; annulment cases, 173–75, 318 (n. 74)
May, Elaine Tyler, 158
May Day riots (1919), 124
Maynard v. Hill (1888), 176–77
McClendon, Caesar, 209
McFadden, Bernarr, 24
McGuiness, Margueretta, 113, 115, 119, 120, 121, 122, 125, 134
Mellon, Andrew, 124
Mencken, H. L., 53–54, 130, 163, 300 (n. 67), 335 (n. 4)
Mental incapacity, 67, 169, 170, 177, 223, 236. *See also* Feeblemindedness; Insanity
Messenger (newspaper), 40, 51–52, 101, 125, 127, 130–31, 193, 214, 236–37, 239
Metropolitan Opera House, 13, 117
Miller, Albert, 108
Miller, Grace Jones (sister), 15–16, 33, 35, 38, 60, *188*, 339 (n. 37); birth certificate of, 65, 217–18; census designation of, 107, 108; "color" of, 75, 107, 108, 189, 210, 211, 224; Leonard's initial interest in, 67, 78, 80–81, 135–36, 140, 204, 210, 223; marriage of to white man, 283 (n. 61)
Miller, Kelly, 45, 242–43
Mills, Isaac N., 52, 60, 64, 70; adjournment request of, 149, 150; background and style of, 61, 62; baring of Alice's body and, 196, 197, 198, 202, 204, 225; central argument of, 67–68, 88–90, 94, 132, 170–71, 178, 181–82, 195, 204–7, 216, 217; changed charge of,

INDEX : 381

208–9, 217, 218; closing statement of, 94, 108–11, 220–26; conception of race of, 186–87, 198, 204, 231; cross-examinations by, 207, 209, 210, 211, 212; defense's rebuttal to, 71, 72, 73, 75; generation gap and, 77, 84; jury selection and, 62–63; leading questions of, 283 (n. 61); on miscegenation, 23, 94, 183, 221–23, 224, 226, 227; opening statement of, 64–69, 76–77, 94, 133, 136, 137, 142, 145, 169–70, 178, 186–87, 215–16, 220; rhetorical style of, 222; trial persona of, 76–77, 84; verdict appeal and, 229, 238; witnesses of, 77–86, 108–11, 331 (n. 42)

Mills, LeRoy, 60

Minnesota annulment case, 172–73

Mirizio v. Mirizio (N.Y., 1926), 311 (n. 16), 320 (n. 86)

Miscegenation. *See* Antimiscegenation laws; Interracial marriage

"Mongrelization," 5, 41–42, 45–47, 54, 55, 58, 200, 201, 276 (n. 59)

Montclair (N.J.), 163

Morschauser, Joseph, 65, 68, 70, 78, 79, 80, 85, 87, 149, 150, 177, 205, 206, 208, 209, 212, 218, 220, 283 (n. 61), 329 (n. 5); background of, 59–60, 61; baring of Alice's body and, 196–97, 198–99, 201–3; charge to jury of, 226–27, 236; disapproval of divorce of, 158; liberal interpretation of annulment and fraud of, 172, 178–79, 180; verdict reading by, 228–29

Movies, 9, 17, 53, 68, 81, 84, 104, 137; visibility of race and, 322 (n. 14)

Mulatto, 42; Alice seen as, 1, 2, 32, 33, 54, 66, 70, 71, 75, 81; allure of, 53, 82; definitions and images of, 54–57, 96–97, 223; disappearance as racial category of, 106–7, 244; incentives for passing by, 97, 98, 100, 101, 102–3, 105; physical features and, 97, 189–90, 191–93

Murders, 3, 51, 156

Myrdal, Gunnar, 244

NAACP, 43, 44, 45, 52, 93, 243, 244, 276 (n. 58); antimiscegenation bills and, 162; civil rights cases and, 50–51; founding of, 48

Nassau County Surrogate Court, 250

Nast, Thomas, 121

Nation, 97–98, 100, 104, 234

National Police Gazette, 121, 122

National Urban League, 42, 43, 98, 99

Naturalization, 188, 199, 200

Nazis, 243

Neale, Sybil and Theodore, 179

Negro. *See* African Americans

"Negro-White" families study (Day), 192–93

Negro World, 33, 237

Nesbit, Evelyn, 156

Neuberger v. Gueldner (La., 1916), 313–14 (n. 36)

Nevada divorce, 245, 247, 248, 249–50, 277 (n. 1)

"New cosmopolitanism," 53–54

New morality, 81, 138, 140, 216

New Negro, 99

Newport (R.I.), 25, 31

New Rochelle (N.Y.), 15–17, 26, 27, 33, 81; Jones family and, 17, 31–32, 34, 35, 75; Leonard and Alice's marriage in, 23–24, 83; Rhinelander ancestry and, 13, 16, 65, 72, 119

Newspapers. *See* Press

New Statesman, 235, 241–42

New York Age, 234

New York American, 34, 36, 38, 160–61

New York Athletic Club, 15, 25
New York City: African Americans in, 25, 42–44, 48, 49, 52, 53, 100, 164, 241; class conflict and, 115, 116; commuters to, 16, 24; dating and, 84; discrimination and, 50; elite society of, 114–32; heterogeneous population of, 40, 41–46, 52, 54, 57, 102, 115, 185, 240; "new cosmopolitanism" and, 53–54; newspaper diversity in, 7–8, 24, 41; passing and, 89–90, 101–2, 103, 164; racism and, 47, 48, 116, 157; Rhinelander prestige in, 13, 18, 125
New York City Railways Company, 61
New York Daily Mirror, 7, 25, 41, 87, 149, 156, 182, 195; on color of Jones family, 70; on display of Alice's body, 202; on interracial marriage, 162–63
New York Daily News, 7, 24–28, 41, 54, 69, 76, 80, 87, 133, 195; on Alice's letters, 85, 182; as first twentieth-century tabloid, 24–26; full-page portrait of Alice in, 29, 30, 194, 229, *230,* *231;* investigative reporting by, 32–33, 34; on Leonard's letters, 141; miscegenation concerns and, 158–59, 161, 182, 226; pink edition of, 264 (n. 58); trial portraits and, 193; trial verdict and, 233. *See also* Robinson, Grace
New Yorker, 83, 129–30, 154, 213, 281 (n. 32)
New York Evening Graphic, 24, 203–4, 205
New York Evening Journal, 31, 33, 36, 62, 68, 87–88, 213–14, 241; front-page photomontage in, 195; on plaintiff's case, 69–70; on skin color, 143, 185, 194, 198, 203; on women's pursuit of men, 86
New York Genealogical Society, 118
New York Herald Tribune, 7, 141–42; on Alice's letters, 182; on Alice's physical appearance, 194; on color of Alice's hands, 143; on defense's opening, 76; on Leonard's physical appearance, 69; on verdict, 229
New York National Guard, 115, 117
New York State: African American women's legal status in, 233–34; annulment law of (*see under* Annulment); birth certificate racial designations and, 65; census of, 33, 90; civil rights laws of, 49–50; "crimes against nature" and, 155; divorce law of, 4, 160–61, 166–67, 177, 238, 245, 250, 314 (n. 41); first mental hospital of, 220; high annulment rate in, 314 (n. 41), 316 (n. 53); interracial marriage and, 4, 5, 29, 146, 158–59, 160–62, 163–64, 180, 181, 183, 221, 227, 235–36; juries and, 62; marital property rights of, 168; marriage laws of, 4, 63, 175, 176, 177, 311 (n. 16), 320 (n. 86); "problem girls" and, 81; racial definitions and, 37, 90, 243, 252; racial fraud and, 181; restrictive covenants and, 243, 244–45
New York Times, 7, 13, 23, 34, 50, 113, 120, 121, 123, 244, 340 (n. 40); on Alice's letters, 83, 87; photographs of Rhinelanders and, 193–94; on Rhinelander annulment suit, 33, 35–36, 38–39, 54; on Rhinelander family trust, 168; on Rhinelanders' diverse backgrounds, 26–27; on Rhinelander trial, 62, 149, 182, 226, 234; on *Social Register,* 127–28; on visible color, 143, 211
New York World, 99, 231, 233, 234
Nigger Heaven (Van Vechten), 103
Night of the Quarter Moon (film), 322 (n. 10)

Nonprocreative sexual acts, 155, 311 (n. 16)
Nordicism, 41, 44, 46, 47, 53, 57, 187, 214
Norman, Conrad, 49
North Carolina, 165

O'Brien, R. D., 172, 173
Octoroons, 54–55, 82, 106, 192, 193
"One-drop" rule, 95, 105, 185, 186, 187, 217, 239–40, 321 (n. 4)
O'Neill, Eugene, 130, 163, 333 (n. 67)
Opportunity, 42, 48, 56, 189, 234, 235; on passing, 93, 94, 98, 99, 101
Oral sex, 153–55, 205
"Orange Riot" (N.Y.C.), 115
Orchards, The (Conn.), 9, 14, 15, 17, 19, 78, 212, 251
Ostmann, Otis, 172, 173
Outlook, 51, 99–100, 101
Owens, Chandler, 101, 163
Ozawa, Takao, 200
Ozawa v. United States (1922), 200

Paris Exhibition (1900), 191
Passing, 2, 26, 31, 39, 58, 59, 63–64, 89–111, 187; African American press on, 160, 164–65; alleged physical signs and, 327 (n. 60); anxiety over, 123, 140, 164, 178, 236–37, 240; blurring of color line and, 96–99, 102–3; children of interracial marriage and, 164, 180, 214; dangers of, 240; as deception, 88, 93–94, 138, 140, 156, 163, 179, 180, 186, 208, 236; definition of, 90–91; economic reasons for, 100–101, 159, 240; estimate of numbers, 98, 107; as fraud, 12, 35, 36, 39, 68, 70, 160–61, 165, 166, 170–71, 175, 177, 178, 180–81, 227, 240; heyday (1880s–1920s) of, 95; migration and,
98–101; physical appearance and, 96–97, 102; social class and, 101, 123, 129–30; whiteness concept and, 92–94
Passing (Larsen), 59, 104, 108, 327 (n. 60)
Passing of the Great Race, The (Grant), 41, 46–47, 301–2 (n. 79)
Pawlowski v. Pawlowski (N.Y.S., 1946), 310–11 (n. 14)
Pelham Manor (N.Y.), 32
Pennsylvania, 162, 236
Perversions, 154–56, 204, 219, 223
Philadelphia, 100
Photographs, 86, 150–51, 190, 229, 230, 231; to document race difference, 190–91, 192–93; newspaper trial reports with, 193–95, 203, 204; racial composite, 204, 205
Pickens, William, 52, 93, 98, 105
Plecker, W. A., 104, 105, 164
Plessy v. Ferguson (1896), 96
Plum Bun (Fauset), 103
Porter, Ellis, 97
Post, Emily, 128
Pregnancy, marital fraud and, 173–75
Premarital sex, 10, 18–20, 23, 67, 80, 84, 143–45, 146, 150–56; breach of promise suits and, 138; incidence of, 284 (n. 74)
Press: on Alice's baring of body, 202–4; on Alice's letters, 83, 85, 182; on first Rhinelander scandal, 121; on interracial marriages, 125–27, 182–83, 216–17, 221; on Leonard's courtship behavior, 87, 155–56; on Leonard's letters, 138, 141–42; on miscegenation laws, 5; New York diversity of, 7–8, 24, 41; racial identity focus of, 27–28, 32–34, 36, 38, 43, 54, 57–58, 70, 87–88, 89–90, 109, 110–11, 143, 194, 195,

211, 218; Rhinelander case coverage by, 1, 3, 9, 10, 35–37, 62, 68, 76–77, 135, 213, 222; on Rhinelander marriage, 24–32, 75, 110, 124–25, 130, 193–94, 207, 211; Rhinelander verdict and, 229, 231, 233–45; women reporters and, 29. *See also specific publications*

Presumption laws, 92

Price, Marie and Arthur, 180, 333 (n. 71)

"Pride of Race" (Walton), 101

"Problem of Race Mixture, The" (Baker), 96–97

Procreation, 172, 180, 183, 311 (n. 16); interracial marriage and, 93–94, 164, 180, 183, 189, 214, 221

Proctor, Eulalia, 52–53, 55

Profert of the person, 199

Progressive Era, 48, 93

Property: inheritance and, 114, 132, 168, 169, 248; legal definition of, 239; passing and, 240; race linked with, 5–6, 92–94, 242–45, 251; as Rhinelander case basic issue, 168, 237, 242, 245–51; social class and, 116, 168–69, 237, 241, 245, 248; whiteness as, 6, 92, 93–94. *See also* Real estate

Public accommodations, 6, 49–50

Quadroons, 54, 106, 192

Race violence, 31–32, 48–49, 50, 51, 116, 157, 335 (n. 10)

Racial identity, 1, 3, 7, 52–53, 56–58, 163; as annulment basis, 169, 175, 177, 178, 179, 180; anxieties about, 73, 90, 123, 131; blood vs. appearance as (*see* Blood-based racial identity; Visibility of race); British view of, 210–11; caricatured stereotypes of, 121; categories and, 47, 56, 244; character linked with, 222; classification confusions and, 107–8; "common knowledge" theory of, 199, 200, 201; "common sense" test of, 229, 231, 244, 245; definitions of, 36, 37, 54–57, 64, 104–5, 236–37; denial of (*see* Passing); determination of, 70, 91, 94–96, 185–86, 199–200, 240, 243–44; different images and, 56–57; dropping of intermediate categories of, 244; economic benefits and, 41–42, 100–101, 159, 240, 241, 242; erosion of, 41, 54, 57, 84, 90, 96–99, 102–3, 240; fraudulent misrepresentation of, 12, 35, 36, 39, 68, 70, 160–61, 165, 166, 170–71, 175, 177, 178, 180–81, 227, 240; hierarchies and, 235, 240, 252; historical view of, 91–92; ideological shift concerning, 186–87; ideologies of, 5, 41, 44 (*see also* Eugenics); "invisible blackness" and, 97–98; legal definitions of, 94–96; meaning of, 239–52; naturalization and, 188, 199, 200; official documents and, 65, 77, 90, 105, 162, 164, 210, 217–18, 224; photography and, 190–91, 192–93, 204; physical markers of, 166, 188–89, 192, 193; possibility of mistake in, 53, 57, 164; prevailing views (1920s) of, 5–6, 40–42, 44–46, 91, 157–59; property linked with, 5–6, 92–94, 242–45, 251; race-mixing fears and, 5, 41–42, 45–47, 54, 55, 58, 200, 201, 276 (n. 59); as Rhinelander trial core issue, 63–64, 65, 143–44, 180–83; significance of Rhinelander verdict to, 214; superstitions about, 203

Racial Integrity Act (1924, Va.), 104–5

Racial passing. *See* Passing

Racial purity, 45, 46, 47, 50, 51, 55, 57, 58, 104–5, 164, 182, 183, 187, 200;

African American view of, 330 (n. 32); "blood as race" metaphor and, 95–96, 187; fears about decline in, 185; impossibility of maintaining, 236–37; intermarriage as threat to, 214, 221–22, 242–43. *See also* Antimiscegenation laws; Eugenics

Racial scientists, 5, 41, 44–45, 56, 58; basis of race and, 186, 189, 199, 200, 201; photographic studies and, 190–91, 192; race mixing and, 56–57, 191–93, 196

Racism, 7, 44, 48–49, 214, 240–41

Read, Harlan, 132

Real estate: restrictive covenants and, 5, 50–51, 94, 242–45; Rhinelander holdings of, 13, 116, 168, 207, 208, 237, 242, 247–48, 248, 251; Rhinelander sales of, 339 (n. 38). *See also* Property

Real evidence, 197–98

Redder Blood (novel), 103

Red Scare, 124, 179

Red Summer (1919), 48, 334 (n. 2)

Rent parties, 186

Residential segregation, 50–51, 242–43

Restrictive covenants, 5, 50–51, 94, 242–45

Reuter, Edward, 55, 100, 102–3, 200, 313 (n. 30)

Rex, Margery, 146, 185, 213–14, 237, 241, 242; on interracial marriage, 87–88; skepticism of, 69–70, 82

Reynolds, Barbara, 28–29, 207, 228

Reynolds, Bridget and Michael, 173–75

Reynolds v. Reynolds (Mass., 1862), 173–75, 318 (n. 74)

Rhinelander, Adelaide (sister), 14, 141, 237, 247, 249, 250, 339 (n. 38); wedding of, 18, 123

Rhinelander, Adelaide Kip (mother), 8, 13–14, 25, 27, 66, 118, 122, 123

Rhinelander, Edith Sands (aunt), 118, 122–23

Rhinelander, Julia (great-aunt), 13, 114

Rhinelander, Leonard and Alice: background of, 8–9; continued legal ties of, 237–38; courtship period of, 8, 9–10, 16–20, 75, 78, 83–88, 136–37, 141–46, 181–82; first meeting of, 15, 80, 81; forced separation of, 20–22, 34–35; letters between (*see* Letters); marriage license of, 65; marriage of, 10, 23–24, 26, 31, 34–35, 53, 75, 83, 110, 114–15, 123–25, 130–31, 132, 194, 207, 211, 213–14, 241; post-trial status of, 245–52; premarital sex and, 10, 18–20, 23, 67, 80, 84, 86, 143–45, 150–51, 150–56, 190; publicity about, 1, 24–31, 34, 42, 43, 57–58; sexual initiative and, 137–38, 140, 141; social disparity between, 9–10, 13–15, 17–18, 20–21, 24, 25, 26, 27, 33, 37, 72, 75, 83, 124–25, 137, 141, 142, 160, 178, 218, 242. *See also* Jones, Alice Beatrice; Rhinelander, Leonard Kip

Rhinelander, Leonard Kip, 2, 64, 139; annulment lawsuit of, 5, 35–39, 66–68, 160–61, 169–70, 207–8, 215, 237, 246; annulment's attractiveness to, 169; automobile of, 15, 16, 17, 18, 78, 84, 242; background of, 8–9, 13–14, 17–18, 64–65, 251; death of, 248; degeneracy attributed to, 150–51, 204, 219, 223; degenerate blueblood characterization of, 154–56, 223; desire of to marry Alice, 146; disappearance of after trial, 238, 245; first journalist to interview, 28–29; inheritance potential of, 168; mental deficiency characterization of, 14, 66–67, 69–70, 71, 72, 75, 78, 79, 132, 170, 215, 220, 223, 237; New York society's

386 : INDEX

ejection of, 128–29, 130, 132; perception of Alice's color by, 38, 70, 71–72, 79, 109–10, 143, 144, 195–96, 197, 202, 207–9, 212, 219, 227, 231; perception of Jones family color by, 28, 75, 76, 102, 108–11, 133, 184–85, 190, 207, 210, 211, 212, 216, 227; physical appearance of, 9, 12–13, 69, 79; post-trial actions of, 238, 245–50, 277 (n. 1); public opinion on, 156; seducer characterization of, 133–34, 136–38, 140–45, 147–48, 219, 220; stutter of, 9, 14, 66, 67, 72, 75, 78, 80, 170, 215, 283 (n. 59); treatment files of, 78; trial's outcome and, 228; twenty-first birthday inheritance of, 23; whiteness of, 65; women trial spectators interest in, 135, 147. *See also* Rhinelander trial

Rhinelander, Matilda (grandmother), 112, 113–14, 118, 120, 122, 167

Rhinelander, Philip (father), 14, 15, 20–25, 68, 85, 212, 213; Alice's suit against, 245, 246, 247, 248, 250, 251; background of, 13, 26, 27, 119; brother's scandal and, 113, 122; death of, 248, 339 (n. 38); estate and will of, 168, 248–51; family life and, 123; Leonard's annulment case and, 72, 83, 149, 207–8, 215, 218–19, 222, 246; Leonard's marriage and, 24, 29, 31, 35, 68, 75, 114; New York society and, 118, 123; wedding of, 122

Rhinelander, Philip Kip (brother), 14, 123, 168, 247, 248, 315 (n. 45), 339 (n. 38)

Rhinelander, T. J. Oakley (brother), 14, 66, 79, 123

Rhinelander, T. J. Oakley (uncle), 113, 118, 119, 122–23, 339 (n. 38)

Rhinelander, William (grandfather), 13, 28, 112, 113, 114, 117, 118, 120, 167

Rhinelander, William Christopher (great-grandfather), 13, 168

Rhinelander, William Copeland (uncle), 112–16, 117, 119–22, 123, 124, 167, 282 (n. 46)

Rhinelander family, 5–6, 20, 80, 207–8, 220, 339 (n. 38); advantage of annulment for, 167–68, 169, 237, 242, 252; Alice's settlement with, 246–48; ancestry of, 8–9, 13–14, 16, 17–18, 64–65, 69, 72, 79, 118–19, 218, 251; annulment trial verdict's effect on, 237; chauffeur's trial testimony and, 211–12; class consolidation and, 116, 118, 122–24; disinheritance threat and, 168; inappropriate marriages and, 112–16, 119–22, 124, 167; as Knickerbockers, 116; property's importance to, 251; society weddings of, 118, 122–23; status and wealth of, 13–14, 16, 17–18, 26–28, 33, 64–65, 69, 72–73, 79, 116, 117, 125, 168–69, 207, 208, 218, 237, 242, 247–48, 251, 252

Rhinelander Real Estate Company, 13, 149, 248, 339 (n. 38)

Rhinelander trial, 59–88, 100, 133–83, 213–38; adjournments of, 149, 150; African American response to, 233–34; Alice's baring of body at, 2, 11–12, 181, 195–99, 201–4, 205, 207, 208, 219, 225, 227, 235; annulment case of, 2, 35–36, 160, 169–70, 172, 180–82, 237, 242, 248; annulment precedents and, 178–80; background of, 2–3, 11, 34–38; courtroom spectators and, 70, 79, 80, 87, 135, 147, 151, 228; defense exhibits S-1 and M-1 and, 145, 149, 150–55, 156, 204, 223; defense lawyers, 60–62 (*see* Davis, Lee Parsons; Swinburne, Samuel F.); effects of, 10,

234–38; incomplete transcripts of, 8; interracial marriage aspect of, 147, 161, 182–83, 213–14, 216–17, 221, 222–23, 226, 235–36, 242; Jones family members as witnesses in, 209–11; judge's summation/charge to jury and, 226–27, 236; jury selection and, 62–63; jury's reactions and, 66; as jury trial, 172; Leonard's testimony and, 66, 79–86, 108–11, 216; letters as evidence and (*see* Letters); multiple meanings of, 3–4, 6–7, 112, 172, 213–14, 236–37, 240–42, 251–52; newspaper coverage of (*see* Press); photography and, 29, 30, 41, *188*, 190, 193–94; plaintiff's lawyers and, 60, 61, 215–16 (*see also* Jacobs, Leon; Mills, Isaac N.); presiding judge of (*see* Morschauser, Joseph); pretrial publicity and, 24–34, 36, 38, 42, 43, 54, 57–58; public interest in, 42, 80, 149, 156; race as core issue of, 4, 5–6, 12, 63–64, 65, 108–11, 143–44, 180–83; scandalous material and, 142–43, 151–56, 215; skin color focus in, 184–86, 188–89; social significance of, 1, 5, 149, 214, 239–52; summation of, 214–26; theory behind fraud claim of, 180; verdict of, 228–29, 231, 233–37, 240, 241

Rhinelander v. Rhinelander (N.Y.S., 1925). *See* Rhinelander trial

Rich, Joseph and Miriam, 205–7, 224

Ridgway v. Cockburn (N.Y., 1937), 243–45

Rising Tide of Color Against White-World Supremacy, The (Stoddard), 44

"Rising Tide of Degeneracy, The" (Wiggam), 45

Robertson v. Roth (Minn., 1925), 172–73

Robeson, Paul, 104, 163

Robinson, Grace, 29, 31, 32–33, 217, 221, 231, 308 (nn. 67, 78); on Alice's letters, 87, 182; on Alice's skin color, 194, 202–3; on Jones sisters' skin color, 211; on Leonard as seducer, 141, 147; on Leonard's attraction to Alice, 87; on Leonard's lack of refinement, 133; on plaintiff's case, 69

Robinson, Harold, 49

Rogers, J. A., 125, 127, 130–31, 239

Roosevelt, Mr. and Mrs. Elliott, 122, 131

Roosevelt, Theodore, 122, 131–32

Rossell v. Rossell (Bronx, 1925), 320–21 (n. 90), 333 (n. 71)

Rouget, Alonso and Emma, 319 (n. 84)

Russell, Sylvester, 98–99

St. Thomas Episcopal Church, 18, 123

Saks, Eva, 93, 95

Same-sex marriage, 311 (n. 16), 320 (n. 86)

Sands, Edith Cruger, 122–23

Sanity. *See* Insanity

Saturday Evening Post, 9, 45

Schaeffer v. Schaeffer (N.Y.S., 1913), 255 (n. 8)

Schoenberg Castle, 119

Schouler, James, 174

Schuyler, George, 57, 91, 163–64

Science theories. *See* Racial scientists

Scopes "monkey trial," 3

Seduction, 68, 136–37; deception and, 138; female images of, 55, 68, 71, 80, 81, 85, 86, 223, 275–76 (n. 57); legal changes and, 140; master-servant, 133–34, 144, 146, 220

Segregation, 5, 41, 43, 48, 49–51, 57, 94–95, 96, 242–45; as motive for passing, 99, 101, 102

Separation (marital), 158, 245, 246

Seventh Regiment (N.Y.C.), 115, 117

Sexuality, 204–5, 251; male aggressiveness and, 156; movies and, 68, 137; new morality and, 138, 140; stereotype of African American women and, 80, 82, 142, 181, 204–5; "unnatural" acts and, 153, 154–56, 204, 219, 223. *See also* Premarital sex; Seduction

Shadd, A. E., 101

Sheik, The (film), 17, 53

Shelley v. Kraemer (1948), 51

Sheridan v. Sheridan (N.Y., 1920), 179

Show Boat (Ferber novel), 103

Show Boat (musical), 103–4

Shuffle Along (musical), 17, 52, 82

Sissle, Noble, 17

Skin color: mixed-race changes in, 193; passing and, 93–94; as racial identity guide, 190, 196, 200–201, 244; social class and, 27; Supreme Court racial identity ruling and, 200–201; tanning vogue, 42, 52–53, 57, 58, 196. *See also* Visibility of race; Whiteness

Slang, 186, 201

Slavery, 6, 81–82, 191, 199; passing and, 91–92

Sleeper Wakes, The (Fauset), 103

Smith, Shawn Michelle, 191

Social class, 5–6, 9, 112–32; blurring of color lines and, 53, 123, 130; class tensions and, 3, 115, 116–17, 121, 124; color equated with, 27; dating practices and, 84; eugenics theories and, 67; flux in boundaries of, 124, 129–30; inequality and, 235, 237; intermarriage and, 111; manliness vs. masculinity concepts and, 135; marital deception and, 174; misalliances and, 120, 128; passing and, 101, 123, 129–30; property rights and, 168–69, 237, 245; significance of Rhinelander verdict to, 214. *See also* Elite; Working class

Social Ladder, The (Van Rensselaer), 112

Social Register, 127–30

Sodomy, 155

Sollors, Werner, 91

"Souls of White Folk, The" (DuBois), 6, 11

Spanish ancestry claims, 31, 32, 57, 97, 102, 109, 186, 206, 207, 211

Standard Star, 24, 26, 28–29, 110

States: annulment laws of, 166, 169, 172–76; marriage control by, 170–71; racial definitions by, 96, 104–5; racial purity laws and, 104–5; seduction laws repeal by, 140; sodomy criminalization by, 155. *See also specific states*

Steggerda, Morris, 191–92

Sterilization, 46, 67

Stewart, Anita and William Rhinelander, 120

Stillman, Anne, 128

Stillman, James, 128, 254 (n. 2)

Stoddard, Lothrop, 41–42, 44, 45, 48, 57, 104, 214

Stout, J. Provost, 79, 259 (n. 12)

Stovall, John and Gene, 160, 164

Strong, Joseph, 35

Strutting parties, 186

Sunseri v. Cassagne (La., 1938), 324 (n. 36)

Suntans. *See* Tanning vogue

Supreme Court, Alabama, 199

Supreme Court, Arizona, 165

Supreme Court, Bronx, 180, 236, 320–21 (n. 90), 333 (n. 71)

Supreme Court, Louisiana, 324 (n. 36)

Supreme Court, Minnesota, 172, 173

Supreme Court, New York, 59–60, 61

Supreme Court, U.S.: Aryan racial ruling, 36, 188; interracial marriage ruling, 252; marital contract ruling, 176–77; naturalization rulings, 188, 199,

200–201, 231; racial determination ruling, 96; residential segregation laws and, 50–51
Supreme Court, Westchester County, 12, 245–46
Supreme Court, Wisconsin, 177
Sweet, Ossian and Gladys, 51, 242, 243
Swinburne, Samuel F., 36–39, 43, 61, 62, 70, 109, 202, 224

Tabloids, 7, 24–26, 36, 41, 203–4; Cinderella stories and, 125; trial photographs and, 193
"Tainted blood" concept, 187
Tanning vogue, 42, 52–53, 57, 58, 196, 201, 231
Taylor v. Taylor (N.Y.S., 1920), 319 (n. 84)
Thaw, Harry, 156
Thind, Bhagat Singh, 200–201
Thirteenth Amendment, 243
"Today" (Brisbane column), 5
"Treating," 81
Trial marriage, 158
True Confessions, 236

Underage marriage, 169
Union Club, 118
United States v. Thind (1923), 200–201
Universal Negro Improvement Association (UNIA), 25, 33–34, 43
"Unnatural" sexual acts, 153, 154–56, 204, 219, 223
Upper class. *See* Elite
Upper East Side (N.Y.C.), 13
Urbanization, 42, 45, 48, 241–42
Ussher, Sidney, 79, 259 (n. 12)

Valentino, Rudolph, 12, 17, 53, 137
Vampire ("vamp") image, 68, 71, 86
Van Cleaf, Margaret, 159–60
Van Houten v. Morse (Mass., 1891), 175

Van Rensselaer, May King, 112, 124
Van Vechten, Carl, 40, 57, 103
Veblen, Thorstein, 118
Victorian ideals, 134–35
Virginia Bureau of Vital Statistics, 105
Virginia racial purity law, 104–5
Virginia State Registrar's Office, 164
Visibility of race, 185–212, 216, 218–20, 231, 243, 244; color line and, 96–97; common sense argument of, 71–72; composite photographs and, 204; fixed essence theory vs., 91; mixed-race studies and, 191–93; press coverage and, 211; Rhinelander trial charge to jury and, 226–27; as Rhinelander trial defense, 71–72, 75, 216, 218, 219, 220, 224–25, 226; Rhinelander trial verdict confirming, 229
Voting rights, 62, 93, 158

Waldorf Hotel, 123
Wall Street, 13, 40, 115, 116
Walton, Lester, 101
Warfield, David, 278 (n. 6)
Washington, D.C., 44, 98; race riot (1919), 157
Washington, Freddie, 104
Washington Square (N.Y.C.), 13
Wecter, Dixon, 128
Wells v. Talham (Wis., 1923), 317 (n. 74)
Westchester County (N.Y.), 2, 12, 14, 15, 24, 26, 86; Alice's death in, 251; Alice's separation suit filed in, 245–46; foreign-born population of, 42; Leonard's departure from, 34–35; restrictive covenants and, 243–45; Rhinelander trial in, 61–63, 66, 79, 178–79, 228. *See also* New Rochelle; White Plains
Westchester County Bar Association, 61
West Indies, 25, 26, 29, 31, 33, 42, 43, 73,

90, 110, 320 (n. 90), 333 (n. 71); restricted immigration from, 47–48
Wharton, Edith, 114, 116, 120–21
White, Kevin, 140, 155
White, Stanford, 156
White, Walter, 45–46, 56, 101–2, 103, 243, 276 (n. 58), 290 (n. 44), 335 (n. 10)
Whiteness: Alice's appearance of, 12; altered physical characteristics of, 102–3; determination of, 105, 199–200, 201, 237; DuBois and, 269 (n. 5); elite's exclusivity and, 114–32, 123, 127, 214, 237; ethnic differences and, 125, 190; historians and, 269 (n. 5); as property right, 6, 92–94; as racial category, 56, 187, 191; racial purity belief and, 57, 104–5, 185, 187, 214; tanning vogue and, 42, 52–53, 57, 58, 196, 201, 231; U.S. Supreme Court ruling on, 200; value of, 41–42, 92–93, 240, 241, 242. *See also* Caucasians; Nordicism
White Plains (N.Y.), 2, 59, 244
White supremacy belief, 41–42, 44–47, 49, 62, 191, 200, 214
Wiggam, Albert E., 45, 47, 67, 132
Wilkins, Roy, 244
Williams, Fannie Barrier, 164
Williams, Millicent Gwendolyn, 320 (n. 90)
Williamson, Joel, 95
Wire services, 33
Wisconsin, 162, 177
"Women adrift" concept, 81
Women's suffrage, 62, 158
Working class, 114, 116–17, 125; masculinity concept and, 135; new sexual morality and, 81, 140
World War I, 8, 15, 43, 47, 73, 99, 115; African Americans and, 49; intelligence test results and, 46; postwar radicalism and, 124; Rhinelander brother death in, 14, 66, 79, 123
Wright, Carroll D., 106

www.ingramcontent.com/pod-product-compliance
Lightning Source LLC
Chambersburg PA
CBHW020637300426
44112CB00007B/138